# Resolving Family Conflicts

**The Family, Law & Society**
*Series Editor: Michael D Freeman*

**Titles in the Series:**

**Parents and Children**
*Andrew Bainham*

**Marriage and Cohabitation**
*Alison Diduck*

**The Multi-Cultural Family**
*Ann Laquer Estin*

**Domestic Violence**
*Michael Freeman*

**The Family, Law and Society**
*Michael Freeman*

**Resolving Family Conflicts**
*Jana B. Singer and Jane C. Murphy*

# Resolving Family Conflicts

*Edited by*

## Jana B. Singer
*University of Maryland, USA*

and

## Jane C. Murphy
*University of Baltimore, USA*

ASHGATE

Published by
Ashgate Publishing Limited
Gower House
Croft Road
Aldershot
Hampshire GU11 3HR
England

Ashgate Publishing Company
Suite 420
101 Cherry Street
Burlington, VT 05401-4405
USA

Ashgate website: http://www.ashgate.com

**British Library Cataloguing in Publication Data**
Resolving family conflicts
   1. Dispute resolution (Law) - United States 2. Domestic
   relations courts - United States 3. Family mediation -
   I. Singer, Jana B., 1955-  II. Murphy, Jane
   346.7'30173

**Library of Congress Cataloging-in-Publication Data**
Resolving family conflicts / edited by Jana Singer and Jane Murphy.
      p. cm. – (The Family, law & society ; 1)
  Includes bibliographical references and index.
  ISBN 978-0-7546-2659-6 (alk. paper)
  1. Dispute resolution (Law)–United States. 2. Domestic relations courts–United
States. 3. Family mediation–United States. 4. Child welfare–United States. I.
Singer, Jana B., 1955-  II. Murphy, Jane.

  KF505.5.R47 2008
  346.7301'50269–dc22

              2007031502

ISBN 978 0 7546 2659 6

Printed and bound in Great Britain by
TJ International Ltd, Padstow, Cornwall.

# Contents

*Acknowledgements*                                                                                                     *ix*
*Series Preface*                                                                                                       *xi*
*Introduction*                                                                                                         *xiii*

## PART I    THEORETICAL FOUNDATIONS

1   Gregory Firestone and Janet Weinstein (2004), 'In the Best Interests of Children:
    A Proposal to Transform the Adversarial System', *Family Court Review*, **42**,
    pp. 203–13.                                                                                                        3
2   Barbara A. Babb (1997), 'An Interdisciplinary Approach to Family Law
    Jurisprudence: Application of an Ecological and Therapeutic Perspective',
    *Indiana Law Journal*, **72**, pp. 775–7; 798–808.                                                                 19
3   Clare Huntington (2006), 'Rights Myopia in Child Welfare', *UCLA Law Review*,
    **53**, pp. 637–40; 656–72.                                                                                        33

## PART II    COURT PROCESSES AND STRUCTURE

### A    Historical Overview

4   Andrew Schepard (2000), 'The Evolving Judicial Role in Child Custody
    Disputes: From Fault Finder to Conflict Manager to Differential Case Management',
    *University of Arkansas Law Review*, **22**, pp. 395–412.                                                          55

### B    Problem-solving Courts

5   Greg Berman and John Feinblatt (2001), 'Problem-solving Courts:
    A Brief Primer', *Law and Policy*, **23**, pp. 125–6; 131–40.                                                      73
6   Robert Wolf (2000), 'Fixing Families: The Story of the Manhattan Family
    Treatment Court', *Journal of the Center for Families, Children and the Courts*,
    **2**, pp. 5–21.                                                                                                   83

### C    Unified Family Courts

7   Catherine J. Ross (1998), 'The Failure of Fragmentation: The Promise of a
    System of Unified Family Courts', *Family Law Quarterly*, **32**, pp. 3–5; 13–27; 30.                              103
8   Anne H. Geraghty and Wallace J. Mlyniec (2002), 'Unified Family Courts:
    Tempering Enthusiasm with Caution', *Family Court Review*, **40**, pp. 435–47.                                     119

## D   Family Mediation

### *1. Divorce and Child Access Mediation*

9   Robert E. Emery, David Sbarra and Tara Grover (2005), 'Divorce Mediation: Research and Reflections', *Family Court Review*, **43**, pp. 22–37. [Also published in the USA as 'Divorce Mediation', *International Family Law Journal*, **2005**, pp. 65–73]     143

10   Craig McEwen, Nancy Rogers and Richard Maiman (1995), 'Bring in the Lawyers: Challenging the Dominant Approaches to Ensuring Fairness in Divorce Mediation', *Minnesota Law Review*, **79**, pp. 1317–56; 1375–95.     159

11   Nancy Ver Steegh (2003), 'Yes, No, and Maybe: Informed Decision Making about Divorce Mediation in the Presence of Domestic Violence', *William & Mary Journal of Women and the Law*, **9**, pp. 147; 180–86; 195–8.     205

### *2. Child Welfare Mediation and Family Group Conferencing*

12   Clare Huntington (2006), 'Rights Myopia in Child Welfare: A Problem-solving Model: The Example of Family Group Conferencing', *UCLA Law Review*, **53**, pp. 672–95.     215

13   Amy Sinden (1999), 'Why Won't Mom Cooperate? A Critique of Informality in Child Welfare Proceedings', *Yale Journal of Law and Feminism*, **11**, pp. 339–58; 377–96.     237

## E   Managing High Conflict Cases

14   Christine Coates, Robin Deutsch, Hugh Starnes, Matthew Sullivan and BeaLisa Sydlik (2004), 'Parenting Coordination for High Conflict Families', *Family Court Review*, **42**, pp. 246–60.     277

15   Janet R. Johnston (2000), 'Building Multidisciplinary Professional Partnerships with the Court on Behalf of High-conflict Divorcing Families and their Children: Who Needs What Kind of Help?', *University of Arkansas Little Rock Law Review*, **22**, pp. 453–79.     297

## F   Pro Se Litigants

16   Russell Engler (1999), 'And Justice for All – Including the Unrepresented Poor: Revisiting the Roles of Judges, Mediators and Clerks', *Fordham Law Review*, **67**, pp. 1987–9; 2022–40; 2047–52; 2069–70.     319

17   Steven Berenson (2001), 'A Family Law Residency Program?: A Modest Proposal in Response to the Burdens Created by Self-Represented Litigants in Family Court', *Rutgers Law Journal*, **33**, pp. 107–17; 122–35.     345

# PART III  THE ROLE OF LAWYERS AND OTHER PROFESSIONALS

## A  Lawyers

18  Forrest S. Mosten (1995), 'Emerging Roles of the Family Lawyer: A Challenge
    for the Courts', *Family and Conciliation Court Review*, **33**, pp. 213–30.        371
19  Pauline Tesler (2004), 'Collaborative Family Law', *Pepperdine Dispute
    Resolution Law Journal*, **4**, pp. 317–32.                                         389
20  Barbara Glesner Fines (2008), 'Family Law in the Twenty-First Century: Note:
    Ethical Issues in Collaborative Lawyering', *Journal of the American Academy of
    Matrimonial Lawyers*, **21**, pp. 141–54.                                           403

## B  What Role for the Child's Voice?

21  Martin Guggenheim (2005), *What's Wrong with Children's Rights*, Cambridge, MA:
    Harvard University Press, pp. 153–67.                                               415
22  Nigel Lowe and Mervyn Murch (2001), 'Children's Participation in the Family
    Justice System – Translating Principles into Practice', *Child and Family Law
    Quarterly*, **13**, pp. 137–58.                                                     427
23  Barbara Ann Atwood (2005), 'Representing Children: The Ongoing Search
    for Clear and Workable Standards', *Journal of the American Academy of
    Matrimonial Lawyers*, **19**, pp. 183–99; 220–22.                                   447

## C  Mental Health Professionals And Interdisciplinary Collaboration

24  Mary Kay Kisthardt and Barbara Glesner Fines (2005), 'Making a Place at the
    Table: Reconceptualizing the Role of the Custody Evaluator in Child Custody
    Disputes', *Family Court Review*, **43**, pp. 229–32.                               463
25  Joan B. Kelly and Janet R. Johnston (2005), 'Commentary on Tippins and
    Wittmann's "Empirical and Ethical Problems with Custody Recommendations:
    A Call for Clinical Humility and Judicial Vigilance"', *Family Court Review*, **43**,
    pp. 233–8.                                                                          469

# PART IV  PREVENTIVE AND SUPPORTIVE STRATEGIES

26  Howard Fink and June Carbone (2003), 'Between Private Ordering and Public
    Fiat: A New Paradigm for Family Law Decision-making', *Journal of Law and
    Family Studies*, **5**, pp. 1–20; 25–38; 43–52.                                      481
27  Andrew Schepard (1998–99), 'Parental Conflict Prevention Programs and the
    Unified Family Court: A Public Health Perspective', *Family Law Quarterly*, **32**,
    pp. 95–7; 106–24.                                                                   525
28  Patrick Parkinson (2006), 'Keeping in Contact: The Role of Family Relationship
    Centres in Australia', *Child and Family Law Quarterly*, **18**, pp. 157–72.        543

*Name Index*                                                                           563

# Acknowledgements

The editors and publishers wish to thank the following for permission to use copyright material.

American Academy of Matrimonial Lawyers for the essay: Barbara Glesner Fines (2008), 'Family Law in the Twenty-First Century: Note: Ethical Issues in Collaborative Lawyering', *Journal of the American Academy of Matrimonial Lawyers*, **21**, pp. 141–54.

Blackwell Publishing for the essays: Gregory Firestone and Janet Weinstein (2004), 'In the Best Interests of Children: A Proposal to Transform the Adversarial System', *Family Court Review*, **42**, pp. 203–13. Copyright © 2004 by Association of Family and Conciliation Courts; Anne H. Geraghty and Wallace J. Mlyniec (2002), 'Unified Family Courts: Tempering Enthusiasm with Caution', *Family Court Review*, **40**, pp. 435–47. Copyright © 2002 by Association of Family and Conciliation Courts; Robert E. Emery, David Sbarra and Tara Grover (2005), 'Divorce Mediation: Research and Reflections', *Family Court Review*, **43**, pp. 22–37. [Also published in the USA as 'Divorce Mediation', *International Family Law Journal*, **65**, 2005]. Copyright © 2005 by Association of Family and Conciliation Courts; Nancy Ver Steegh (2003), 'Yes, No, and Maybe: Informed Decision Making about Divorce Mediation in the Presence of Domestic Violence', *William & Mary Journal of Women and the Law*, **9**, pp. 147; 180–86; 195–8; Christine Coates, Robin Deutsch, Hugh Starnes, Matthew Sullivan and BeaLisa Sydlik (2004), 'Parenting Coordination for High Conflict Families', *Family Court Review*, **42**, pp. 246–60. Copyright © 2004 by Association of Family and Conciliation Courts; Forrest S. Mosten (1995), 'Emerging Roles of the Family Lawyer: A Challenge for the Courts', *Family and Conciliation Court Review*, **33**, pp. 213–30; Mary Kay Kisthardt and Barbara Glesner Fines (2005), 'Making a Place at the Table: Reconceptualizing the Role of the Custody Evaluator in Child Custody Disputes', *Family Court Review*, **43**, pp. 229–32. Copyright © 2005 by Association of Family and Conciliation Courts; Joan B. Kelly and Janet R. Johnston (2005), 'Commentary on Tippins and Wittmann's "Empirical and Ethical Problems with Custody Recommendations: A Call for Clinical Humility and Judicial Vigilance"', *Family Court Review*, **43**, pp. 233–8. Copyright © 2005 by Association of Family and Conciliation Courts.

Copyright Clearance Center for the essays: Robert Wolf (2000), 'Fixing Families: The Story of the Manhattan Family Treatment Court', *Journal of the Center for Families, Children and the Courts*, **2**, pp. 5–21. Copyright © 2000 Journal of the Center for Children and the Courts; Catherine J. Ross (1998), 'The Failure of Fragmentation: The Promise of a System of Unified Family Courts', *Family Law Quarterly*, **32**, pp. 3–5; 13–27; 30. Copyright © 1998 by the American Bar Association; Craig McEwen, Nancy Rogers and Richard Maiman (1995), 'Bring in the Lawyers: Challenging the Dominant Approaches to Ensuring Fairness in Divorce Mediation', *Minnesota Law Review*, **79**, pp. 1317–56; 1375–95; Russell Engler (1999), 'And Justice for All – Including the Unrepresented Poor: Revisiting the Roles of Judges, Mediators

# Series Preface

The family is a central, even an iconic, institution of society. It is the quintessentially private space said, by Christopher Lasch, to be a 'haven in a heartless world'. The meanings of 'family' are not constant, but contingent and often ambiguous. The role of the law in relation to the family also shifts; there is increasing emphasis on alternative dispute-resolving mechanisms and on finding new ways of regulation. Shifts have been detected (by Simon Roberts among others) from 'command' to 'inducement', but it is not a one-way process and 'command' may once again be in the ascendancy as the state grapples with family recalcitrance on such issues as child support and contact (visitation) arrangements. Family law once meant little more than divorce and its (largely) economic consequences. The scope of the subject has now broadened to embrace a complex of relationships. The 'family of law' now extends to the gay, the transgendered, 'beyond conjugality', perhaps towards friendship. It meets new challenges with domestic violence and child abuse. It has had to respond to new demands – from women for more equal norms, from the gay community for the right to marry, from children (or their advocates) for rights unheard of when children were conveniently parcelled as items of property. The reproduction revolution has forced family law to confront the meaning of parentage; no longer can we cling to seeing 'mother' and 'father' in unproblematic terms. Nor is family law any longer a 'discrete entity'; it now interfaces with medical law, criminal law, housing law and so on.

This series, containing volumes on marriage and other relationships (and not just cohabitation), on the parent–child relationship, on domestic violence, on methods of resolving family conflict and on pluralism within family law, reflects these tensions, conflicts and interfaces.

Each volume in the series contains leading and more out-of-the-way essays culled from a variety of sources. It is my belief, as also of the editors of individual volumes, that an understanding of family law requires us to go beyond conventional, orthodox legal literature – not that it is not relevant – and use is made of it. But to understand the context and the issues, it is necessary to reach beyond to specialist journals and to literature found in sociology, social administration, politics, philosophy, economics, psychology, history and so on. The value of these volumes lies in their coverage as they offer access to materials in a convenient form which will not necessarily be available to students of family law.

They also offer learned and insightful introductions, essays of value in their own right and focused bibliographies to assist the pursuit of further study and research. Together they constitute a library of the best contemporary family law scholarship and an opportunity to explore the highways and byways of the subject. The volumes will be valuable to scholars (and students) of a range of disciplines, not just those who confront family law within a law curriculum, and it is hoped they will stimulate further family law scholarship.

MICHAEL D. FREEMAN
*University College London*

# Introduction

Over the past two decades, virtually all areas of family law have undergone major doctrinal and theoretical changes – from the definition of marriage, to the financial and parenting consequences of divorce, to the legal construction of parenthood. Family law scholars have analysed and critiqued these changes from a variety of perspectives. But scholars have paid less attention to another important set of family law developments: changes that signal a paradigm shift in the way that most family legal conflicts are resolved. These changes in family conflict resolution have transformed the practice of family law and fundamentally altered the way in which disputing families interact with the legal system. Moreover, the changes have important implications for the way that family law is understood and taught. Our objective in this volume is to examine the contours of this paradigm shift in family conflict resolution and explore its implications for family law practice and scholarship. In this Introduction, we describe the elements of the paradigm shift and sound some cautionary notes. We also highlight the major themes of the essays and excerpts that follow.

## I. Elements of the Paradigm Shift

### A. Rejection of Adversary Procedures

The paradigm shift explored in this volume encompasses a number of related components. The first component is a profound scepticism about the value of traditional adversary procedures. An overriding theme of recent family law reform efforts is that adversary processes are ill-suited to resolving disputes involving children. Similarly, social science research suggests that children's adjustment to divorce depends significantly on their parents' behaviour during and after the separation process: the higher the level of parental conflict to which children are exposed, the more negative the effects of family dissolution (Emery, 1994, p. 205; see also Chapter 9 herein). Armed with these social science findings, court reformers have argued that family courts should abandon the adversary paradigm, in favour of approaches that help parents manage their conflict and encourage them to develop positive post-divorce co-parenting relationships. Gregory Firestone and Janet Weinstein (Chapter 1) detail the aspects of the adversary model that disserve the interests of children and families. Adversary processes, they contend, 'legalize' complex family relationships and disempower parents and other participants. Divorce litigation is expensive and produces delays that conflict with a child's sense of time. The zealous advocacy demanded of lawyers unnecessarily exacerbates family conflict and improperly privileges individual rights over mutual interests and ongoing relationships.

Clare Huntington (Chapter 3) offers a similar critique of rights-based child welfare practice. Huntington argues that 'as currently implemented, the rights-based model of child welfare protects neither parent nor child in the typical case' (p. 33). In part, this is because rights create a win–lose mentality that fuels an adversarial relationship between parents and the state. In place of this adversarial process, Huntington proposes a problem-solving model designed to foster collaboration between the state and families involved in the child welfare system. Similarly, Firestone and Weinstein propose a comprehensive dispute resolution system for families in transition. This system would offer families an array of problem-solving mechanisms and supportive services and would accord traditional adversary procedures a sharply limited role in the overall resolution of family conflicts.

Family courts have embraced these insights and have adopted an array of non-adversary dispute resolution mechanisms designed to avoid adjudication of family cases. Divorce-related custody mediation is the best known and established of these procedures.[1] Robert E. Emery, David Sbarra and Tara Gover (Chapter 9) detail the reasons for the rapid spread of court-connected custody mediation and review the research on its effectiveness. The authors conclude that, while additional studies are needed, existing research strongly suggests that custody mediation increases settlement, reduces legal costs, enhances party satisfaction and improves long-term relationships between non-residential parents and children and between divorced parents.[2]

The appeal of non-adversary dispute resolution has moved beyond divorce-related custody cases to the more public realm of child welfare proceedings, where family group conferencing and other problem-solving approaches have begun to supplant more traditional adjudicative models (See, for example, Chandler and Giovannuci, 2004; Merkel-Holguin, 2004). Clare Huntington (Chapter 12) describes the theoretical underpinnings of family group conferencing and explores its potential for reforming the child welfare system. Similarly, Robert Wolf (Chapter 6) describes the creation and functioning of a family treatment court that handles child neglect cases involving substance-abusing parents. Drawing on a criminal drug court model, the Manhattan treatment court combines a problem-solving approach with extensive judicial monitoring, in order to rehabilitate drug-abusing parents and reunite them with children previously removed from their care. Greg Berman and John Feinblatt (Chapter 5) provide a broader context for these family court reforms by tracing the history of problem-solving courts and outlining their common goals and elements.

An increasing number of family lawyers have also rejected the adversary paradigm, in favour of a 'collaborative law' model. Pauline Tesler (Chapter 19) describes the basic elements of this collaborative model, under which lawyers and clients agree at the outset of the representation that the lawyers will withdraw if the matter proceeds to litigation.[3] Tesler argues that this withdrawal obligation gives collaborative lawyers a significant external incentive to remain at the negotiating table in the face of apparent impasse, since '[u]nlike litigation attorneys, collaborative lawyers share the risk of failure in collaboration with their clients' (p.

---

[1]    For a comprehensive examination of divorce-related custody mediation see Jay Folberg, Ann Milne and Peter Salem, 2004.

[2]    A recent survey of parents involved in custody and child support disputes indicates higher levels of satisfaction with mediation than with judges, attorneys or other court-connected services (Leite and Clark, 2007).

[3]    For a recent, comprehensive discussion of collaborative lawyering see Gary Voegele, Linda Wray and Ronald Ousky, 2007; see also Symposium, 2004. For a description of a team-based collaborative model, in which lawyers work closely with mental health professionals who serve as divorce coaches and child specialists see Susan Gamache, 2005.

396). Barbara Glesner Fines (Chapter 20) examines a number of ethical issues raised by the collaborative law model. These include concerns about lawyer competence and limited scope representation, as well as the possibility that a commitment not to litigate may compromise the lawyer's duty of zealous advocacy. Glesner Fines concludes that while collaborative lawyering presents an exciting variation on the growth of consensual, cooperative dispute resolution processes, family lawyers who adopt this model must be extremely diligent in their evaluation of clients, opposing counsel and their own skills and motivations in order to provide ethical representation.[4]

Forrest Mosten (Chapter 18) situates collaborative law in its larger social and professional context by examining a number of emerging roles for the family lawyer that stem from the shift to a less adversarial dispute resolution model. These emerging roles include dispute resolution manager, consultant during mediation, family advocate and preventive legal health care provider. The essays by Mosten, Glesner Fines and Tesler underscore the point made by two leading commentators that 'in the last quarter century, the process of resolving legal family disputes has, both literally and metaphorically moved from confrontation toward collaboration and from the courtroom to the conference room' (Schepard and Salem, 2006, p. 516).

### B. Recharacterizing Family Disputes as Social and Emotional Process

A second element of the paradigm shift is the assertion that most family disputes are not discrete legal events, but ongoing social and emotional processes. This re-characterization of family disputes began with the shift from fault-based to no-fault divorce; more recently, it has become one of the basic tenets of the movement for unified family courts. Barbara A. Babb (Chapter 2), a leading advocate of unified family courts, urges family law decision-makers to adopt an ecological approach that 'look[s] beyond the individual litigants involved in any family law matter, to holistically examine the larger social environments in which the participants live' (p. 23). Armed with this perspective, family court judges should fashion remedies that strengthen a family's supportive relations and that 'facilitate linkages for the litigants between and among as many systems in their lives as possible' (p. 23).

Thus re-characterized as social and emotional processes, family disputes require interventions that are not zealously legal, but rather collaborative, holistic and interdisciplinary. As Professor Babb explains, to positively affect family members' behaviour, 'family law remedies must reflect an integrated approach to family legal issues. This means that decision-makers must consider all of the parties' related family proceedings, as well as all of the institutions or organizations potentially affecting the behavior of families and children' (p. 23). In contrast to the narrow, issue-oriented focus of traditional adversary procedures, such an interdisciplinary focus invites judges to develop a holistic assessment of the family's legal and social needs and to devise more comprehensive legal remedies. Catherine Ross (Chapter 7) identifies both inter-disciplinary training and the provision of comprehensive family services as critical components of a unified family court system. Similarly, Patrick Parkinson (Chapter 28) describes recent efforts in Australia to establish a network of community-based family relationships centres

---

[4]    For additional discussion of these ethical issues see John Lande, 2003; see also Voegele, Wray and Ousky, 2007; Schwab, 2004).

that would help divorcing and separating parents avoid contested legal proceedings. An explicit goal of this initiative is to change cultural understandings so that decisions about post-separation parenting are no longer 'seen in the first place as a legal issue' (p. 548).

Understanding family conflict primarily as a social and emotional process, rather than a legal event, also reduces the primacy of lawyers and enhances the role of mental health professionals in the family court system. Janet Johnston (Chapter 15) describes how the traditional orientations of lawyers and therapists have fuelled divorce-related conflict; she then explains how lawyers and mental health professionals can work more collaboratively to meet the needs of high-conflict families. The 'delegalization' of family disputes also transforms the role of the judge. Unlike the solitary, detached jurist who presides over a courtroom isolated from the non-legal world, the modern family court judge functions as a 'team leader' who embraces interdisciplinary collaboration and coordinates a range of court-connected services (Boldt and Singer, 2006, p. 96).

## C. From Backward-Looking Adjudication to Forward-Looking Intervention

This new understanding of family disputes has also led to a reformulation of the goal of legal intervention in the family. Traditionally, legal intervention was a backward-looking process, designed primarily to assign blame and allocate rights; by contrast, under the new paradigm judges assume the forward-looking task of supervising a process of family reorganization. As Andrew Schepard (Chapter 4) explains, family court judges no longer function primarily as fault-finders or rights adjudicators, but as ongoing conflict managers. Indeed, Schepard analogizes the modern family court judge to a bankruptcy court judge overseeing the reorganization of a financially distressed business: 'The business is raising children and the parents – the managers of the business – are in conflict about how the task is to be accomplished. The court's aim is to get the managers to voluntarily agree on a parenting plan rather than impose one on them.' (p. 56) More generally, Greg Berman and John Feinblatt (Chapter 5) explain that problem-solving courts 'seek to broaden the focus of legal proceedings, from simply adjudicating past facts and legal issues to changing the future behaviour of litigants and ensuring the future well-being of communities' (p. 73).

The therapeutic jurisprudence movement incorporates this forward-looking perspective. As a number of scholars have noted, therapeutic jurisprudence provides the theoretical foundation for problem-solving courts, including unified family courts (Winick and Wexler, 2003; see Kuhn, 1998, pp. 67–8). From a therapeutic perspective, the goal of legal intervention is not merely to resolve disputes, but to improve the material and psychological well being of individuals and families in conflict. Family court judges embrace this therapeutic role by attempting to understand and address underlying family dynamics and by structuring interventions that 'aim to improve the participants underlying behaviour or situation' (Babb, Chapter 2, p. 20).

## D. Capacity Building to Empower Families and Promote Settlements

To achieve these therapeutic goals, family courts have adopted systems that de-emphasize third-party dispute resolution in favour of capacity-building processes that seek to empower families to resolve their own conflicts. Consistent with this philosophy, jurisdictions across the country have instituted mandatory divorce-related parenting education and other skill-building programmes. Andrew Schepard (Chapter 27) describes a number of these programmes and analyses their role in preventing and defusing family conflict. Similarly, the American Law Institute's *Principles of the Law of Family Dissolution* (2002) endorses individualized parenting plans as an alternative to judicial custody rulings and urges the adoption of court-based programmes that facilitate these voluntary agreements.[5] More recently, a number of family courts have added 'parenting coordinators' to their staff; these quasi-judicial officials assist high-conflict families to develop concrete parenting plans and to resolve ongoing parenting disputes that arise under these plans.[6] Christine Coates and her colleagues (Chapter 14) analyse the increased use of parenting coordination to manage high-conflict custody cases and explore the legal challenges that this practice has provoked. As Andrew Schepard (Chapter 4) explains, such capacity-building programs 'are the core of a newly created settlement culture, and trials are a last resort for particularly troublesome cases' (p. 56).

## E. Pre-Dispute Planning and Preventative Law

A fifth component of the paradigm shift is an increased emphasis on pre-dispute planning and preventive law. Familiar examples include the increased acceptance and enforceability of prenuptial and domestic partnership agreements (see, generally, Bix, 1998; Silbaugh, 1998). June Carbone and Harold Fink (Chapter 26) propose a more comprehensive planning approach to both pre-marital agreements and pre-birth determinations of parenthood. Their proposal combines private negotiation with mediation and up-front judicial approval to anticipate and resolve issues of parentage and post-separation obligation. By combining public and private processes, Fink and Carbone hope to capture the benefits of private ordering, while limiting the results of unequal bargaining power and providing a measure of protection for children. Proposals for mandatory or government-encouraged pre-marital education reflect a similar preventive theme. Over the past decade, the United States' government has invested substantial resources in public and private marriage education programmes aimed especially at low income partners (Dion, 2005). More generally, scholars and advocates of 'preventive law' have urged individuals to use legal mechanisms to anticipate and plan for family transitions (see, for example, Robbennolt and Johnson, 1999). This emphasis on publicly-supervised private ordering creates a hybrid model that expands the role of family lawyers and courts beyond their traditional dispute–resolution function. It also extends the time frame during which families interact with the legal system.

---

[5]  For additional discussion of parenting plans see Michael E. Lamb, 2002; Francis J. Catania, Jr., 2002. The American Academy of Matrimonial Lawyers has developed a model parenting plan. For a discussion of that model see Mary Kay Kisthardt, 2007.

[6]  In 2006, an interdisciplinary taskforce of the Association of Family and Conciliation Courts (AFCC) issued guidelines for parenting coordination that address the role, qualifications and ethical obligations of parenting coordinators. See AFCC Task Force on Parenting Coordination (2006), p. 164.

## F. International Perspectives

The paradigm shift that we describe is by no means unique to the United States. Indeed, in many ways, the transformation taking place in the United States today tracks developments that have been underway for several decades in a number of European and Commonwealth countries. For example, the Family Court of Australia, created in 1976, was an integral part of that nation's adoption of no-fault divorce. From the beginning, the Australian Family Court was envisioned as a new kind of legal institution – a pro-active and interdisciplinary enterprise that would blend law, counselling, social and dispute resolution services (Nicholson, 2002; see Parkinson, 2005). The New Zealand Family Court, created five years later, consciously followed the Australian example; both reflected what one New Zealand jurist later described as the enthusiasm of a 'more therapeutically optimistic time' (Elias, 2002, p. 297). Like their Australian counterparts, the New Zealand reformers 'recognized that the adversarial system was an inappropriate vehicle for the resolution of family disputes in the vast majority of cases, particularly where the continued parenting of children was an issue' (Nicholson, 2002, p. 287). Like current reformers in the United States, the architects of the Australian and New Zealand courts envisioned a collaborative and supportive forum in which the judge 'would be removed as a distinct power figure' and 'those involved in family conflicts [could] negotiate, settle and accept their own resolutions' (Elias, 2002, p. 297). Patrick Parkinson (Chapter 28) describes that nation's most recent family law reform efforts, which seek to redirect parenting disagreements away from the judicial system entirely and into community-based dispute-resolution centers.[7]

Scholars and court systems around the world are also struggling with a common set of dilemmas about how best to incorporate children's voices in divorce, custody and child protection proceedings.[8] Nigel Lowe and Mervyn Murch (Chapter 22) describe current debates in England over the appropriate extent and means of children's participation in the resolution of family legal disputes.[9] Excerpts from works by Martin Guggenheim (Chapter 21) and Barbara Ann Atwood (Chapter 23) present different American perspectives on this question. Professor Guggenheim criticizes advocates who seek to enhance children's participation in contested custody proceedings, particularly through legal representation. He notes that children ordinarily have no say in determining their living arrangements outside the context of divorce or parental separation, and he questions whether giving children a significant voice in disputed custody matters actually serves children's interests. Professor Atwood focuses more broadly on the legal representation of children in both abuse and neglect proceedings and private custody disputes. She notes that 'while many courts and commentators agree that children should have a "voice" in proceedings affecting their interests, the meaning of the child's voice is fraught with ambiguity' (p. 447). Despite the lack of clear guidance for children's representatives, Atwood emphasizes the value to children of having a lawyer

---

[7]    For a related proposal to remove divorce from the courts, based on the Danish system of administrative dissolution see Susan Zaidel, 2004.

[8]    For a comprehensive analysis of children's participation in child protection proceedings around the world see Jean Koh Peters, 2006.

[9]    For a thoughtful discussion of the challenges posed by a desire to incorporate children's views into the divorce process see Carol Smart, 2002.

advocate their wishes; she concludes that 'children can only benefit from the ongoing efforts to improve the performance of those who speak for them' (p. 455).

## G. The Promise of the New Paradigm

Taken together, these developments hold considerable promise for families. Most legal experts agree that adversary justice works best for antagonists with conflicting interests and no ongoing personal ties. Alternative dispute resolution procedures offer families a mode of conflict resolution that is both more enduring and less destructive of ongoing relationships than adversary litigation. Non-adversary processes are also more amenable to direct participation by family members – a particularly important feature, given the high percentage of family litigants who are not represented by counsel (see Berenson, Chapter 17). Similarly, judicial interventions that successfully build capacity and enhance problem solving skills should allow families to avoid the financial and emotional drain of future encounters with the legal system. On a more theoretical level, the paradigm shift that we describe appropriately rejects the mythology of the private family – a mythology that characterizes well-functioning families as fully autonomous and self-sufficient and that labels families that seek – or are subject to – state intervention as dysfunctional or inadequate.[10] The new paradigm recognizes instead that family and state governance are intertwined and that families need both private space and public support in order to function effectively.

## II.     Some Cautionary Notes

Despite the promise these developments hold for families in conflict, a number of cautionary comments are in order. Although these dramatic shifts in family dispute resolution have been underway for close to a decade, scholars and family policy makers have engaged in relatively little critical analysis of the risks and potential negative consequences of such change. This volume explores these concerns by examining: the limits of the institutional competence of courts, the surrender of fact-finding and decision-making to individuals without legal training, the loss of autonomy and privacy for family members subject to continuing court oversight, particularly low income families, and the disjunction between alternative dispute resolution and authoritative legal norms.

As with most discussions of relative strengths and weaknesses, many of the concerns raised here are really the 'flip-side' of a potential benefit. Giving courts the flexibility and informality to respond quickly to families in transition can lead to legitimate concerns about reduced accountability and fairness. Having the benefit of a variety of experts from a number of disciplines to address family conflict may result in confusion about roles and authority to act. Providing mechanisms to sustain co-operation and agreement achieved in court proceedings may threaten strongly valued norms of family privacy and autonomy. As with any reform, the value and impact of these developments must be evaluated in the context of available alternatives. And the potential risks posed by the new paradigm may well be worth taking given the demonstrated

---

[10]    For a thoughtful discussion of this mythology see Clare Huntington, 2007.

problems in the adversary system. But in order to begin a meaningful evaluation of these reforms it is critical to identify the potential problems and concerns.

## A. Questions about the Institutional Competence of Family Courts

Although families may benefit from the capacity-building and problem-solving approaches embraced in the new paradigm, it is unclear whether courts are competent to provide these services. As Anne Geraghty and Wallace Mlyniec (Chapter 8) explain, court-based procedures have historically been designed to determine facts and enforce norms. The unified family court movement has sought to expand these functions to address both the legal and non-legal problems of families who come to courts seeking resolution of their disputes. While the goals of the court system have expanded substantially, the structural changes contemplated in even the ideal family courts may not be sufficient to meet the reformers' ambitious agendas. Courts with their 'limited remedial imaginations', may not be the best institutional settings for resolving the non-legal issues proponents wish to place within their authority (Menkel-Meadow, 1996, pp. 5–7). As a result, the restructured family courts may be incapable of achieving the formidable task described by Geraghty and Mlyniec as 'provid[ing] coordinated holistic services ... to address the physical and mental needs of the family' (p. 121).

These institutional shortcomings may be particularly acute at a time when American trial courts' caseloads, particularly the family law cases, continue to grow and resources for these courts are on the decline in many states. Recruiting, training and retaining appropriate judicial and non-judicial staff for the multiple functions contemplated or, in some cases, statutorily mandated in these courts would challenge even a well-financed, broadly committed effort.

Geraghty and Mlyniec argue that asking a court system to take on these broader tasks may detract from its fundamental role as a forum for fair and authoritative dispute resolution. Scarce resources must be spread even more thinly and some courts may have difficulty meeting both basic dispute resolution functions and the broader and more ambitious goals of the new family courts. As several essays in this volume suggest, making good on the broad promise of reform for even a handful of parties may come at a substantial cost to long-held values of due process, family privacy and autonomy (Chapters 8 and 13; see also Hardcastle, 2003).

## B. The Surrender of Fact-Finding and Decision-Making to Non-lawyers

The new paradigm for family law decision-making contemplates substantial involvement and reliance on non-legal staff to 'manage' cases, provide court-connected services and assist fact-finders and decision-makers in achieving settlements or reaching decisions. Catherine Ross (Chapter 7) describes the perceived need for an expanded role for these new players in the system:

> Each court needs an intake team and a case manager for every family ... Courts should have well-trained resource personnel at all levels, including magistrate hearing-officers, special masters, media-tors, court clerks, social workers, and other service providers who can perform triage. ... Judges focus on complex cases by, among other things, delegating to others matters that can safely be handled by alternative forms of dispute resolution. If handled properly, many or most of these cases need never reach a judge (p. 108).

Non-legal and, in many instances, non-professional staff have always exercised enormous influence in child welfare proceedings where the state has intervened after allegations of child abuse or neglect.[11] But the new paradigm expands the role of such staff, particularly case managers and mediators, in both child protection and divorce and child access proceedings in the new model courts. Amy Sinden (Chapter 13) explores this expanded use of non-legal personnel in the context of child protection. She attributes the expanded role to the 'subtle dynamic' that 'arises on a day-to-day level in these cases, due in part to the prevalence of social work discourse and the tendency of the participants to view these cases in therapeutic rather than legalistic terms. This dynamic implicitly suppresses rights talk and discourages the participants from taking advantage of those procedural protections that do exist' (p. 240).

Although generally supportive of these developments, Clare Huntington (Chapter 3) notes the role of the family court movement in the expansion of informal, non-adversarial alternative dispute resolution mechanisms in child welfare cases. Under the new regime, social workers, 'coordinators,' and other non-legal actors play a central role in decisions about removal and placement of children where abuse or neglect is alleged. As Sinden explains, the danger for families, primarily poor, involved in these proceedings is that the disregard for statutory and constitutional norms will result in extensive state involvement in these families by non-judicial personnel prior to any judicial determination justifying such involvement. And decisions will be made in informal settings based upon the evaluations, however flawed, of staff with few standards for guiding these decisions and little or no opportunity for review.

The new paradigm has also expanded the role of such non-judicial personnel in family disputes involving divorce and child access in which the state is not a party. This expansion includes broader authority for professional staff drawn from mental health and social work backgrounds with relatively established roles, such as mediators and custody evaluators. It also includes non-legal personnel with new titles and somewhat less-established roles such as 'parenting coordinators' as described by Christine Coates et al. (Chapter 24). Other newly endowed non-judicial positions include early neutral evaluators (see, for example, Santeramo, 2004; Johnston, Chapter 15) and 'family law facilitators' (Chase, 2003).

These expanded roles are controversial. Two contributors to this volume respond to Timothy M. Tippins' and Jeffery Whittmann's (2005) critique of the growing reliance by judges on 'expert' opinions by non-legal personnel and call for an end to the practice of custody evaluators making recommendations to judges to resolve custody cases.[12] Mary Kay Kisthardt and Barbara Glesner Fines (Chapter 24) urge changes intended to reduce the role of custody evaluators in making the ultimate judgment about child placement in contested cases while preserving a role for these evaluators in a non-decisional capacity. In a companion piece, Joan B. Kelly and Janet R. Johnston (Chapter 25) accept much of the critique that custody evaluators have 'flimsy grounds (ethically, empirically, and legally) for making recommendations on the ultimate issue' of child placement (p. 474). They urge courts to limit the use of these non-legal players to conducting forensic custody evaluations in serious cases

---

[11]  See for example Murphy, 1998, p. 707, who concludes that child protective service workers who may have little or no experience or specialized education make most of the decisions in this arena.

[12]  As early as the 1980s, a few commentators recognized these shifts in both the rhetoric and decision-making in family disputes, particularly with regard to child access. Martha Fineman, in an early and much cited article, noted that the 'professional language of the social workers and mediators has progressed to become the public, then the political, then the dominant rhetoric' (Fineman, 1988).

of child abuse or neglect rather than routinely investigating and making recommendations in all contested custody cases.

## C. The Loss of Privacy and Autonomy for Families

A particularly troubling risk associated with the new paradigm in family dispute resolution is the increased loss of privacy that results from the expanded role of the family court. When family disputes are viewed as opportunities for therapeutic and holistic interventions in the family, increased state involvement in family life is inevitable. Of particular concern in the new model courts, however, is both the lack of clearly defined parameters for such intervention and the disparate impact expanded state intervention may have on poor families.

Increased reliance on informal procedures such as family group conferencing heightens the risk of unchecked state intervention and threats to due process in these cases. Amy Sinden describes these new informal procedures for resolving allegations of child abuse and neglect as a 'free ranging family therapy session' in which there is 'virtually no limit on the topics that can be discussed or on the people who may be invited to join' (Chapter 13, p. 258).

The new regime also raises similar concerns in divorce and child access proceedings. Both the enhanced goals of intervention and the expanded roles of court personnel increase the risk of due process violations and loss of privacy in family life. As noted by Catherine Ross (Chapter 7), one of the principle components of the new family court is that one judge will hear all matters involving a single family. Such an approach may result in both more informed and more efficient decision-making. But, as Geraghty and Mlyniec (Chapter 8) point out, it may also result in judges having access to information about a family that would be inadmissible in traditional adversarial proceedings. Judges may also reach decisions in one proceeding based upon conclusions reached in another. The risks of coercion and unwarranted interference increase as the judges' role in the new 'problem solving' family court shifts from mere dispute resolution to the less defined and potentially broader role of using their 'authority to motivate individuals to accept needed services and to monitor [the parties'] compliance and progress' (Boldt and Singer, 2006, p. 96: quoting Winick, 2003).

The threat to family privacy and autonomy is particularly high when families navigate the court system without lawyers. Stephen Berenson and Russell Engler have both contributed pieces to this volume that address the issue of the unrepresented litigant in family court. Berenson (Chapter 17) documents the broad scope of the problem and describes the burdens it creates for the unrepresented parties as well as for the court. He concludes that when family law disputes proceed through courts with no lawyers on one or both sides there is often 'a failure of legal justice for the parties to family law disputes' (p. 345).

The increase in unrepresented litigants may also require a rethinking of traditional assumptions about legal and judicial practice. Russell Engler (Chapter 16) begins by explaining that rules about who is authorized to give legal advice and requirements of judicial impartiality were developed with an assumption that parties appearing before courts would have full legal representation. Engler argues that these rules frustrate the goals of justice and fairness when applied to unrepresented litigants. The threat to justice and fairness includes unchecked state intrusion into the lives of poor families who lack access to legal representation. When the court orders mediation, represented parties may be able to bypass court sponsored programmes. Their attorneys can object to mediation, negotiate directly with opposing counsel or choose a private mediator. While courts have the authority to order services regardless of family income, parties whose attorneys have negotiated agreements can present those agreements at the first court proceeding and avoid referrals for services, thus remaining 'under the radar' of the court. For families without lawyers to navigate the system or without resources for outside experts or services, involvement in the web of interventions in the new family court is almost impossible to avoid.

## D. The Disjunction Between Alternative Dispute Resolution and Authoritative Legal Norms

In appropriate cases, mediation can empower parties, enhance their ability to work together in the future, and promote flexible and creative problem-solving. But participation in mediation also poses a serious risk that parties may waive important legal rights or enter into agreements that exacerbate conflict. This is particularly true when mediators are ill-equipped or poorly trained. Incompetent mediators can do great harm, especially to vulnerable parties for whom the 'empowering' promise of mediation can become, instead, an exercise in coercion and arm-twisting. This risk is particularly acute without appellate review, a public record, or established grievance procedures that, at least in theory, provide a check on a comparable risk of 'bad' judging.

The risks of mediation are heightened where parties are required to participate in mediation and lack information about legal norms.[13] Many mediation proponents argue that without complex rules of procedure and evidence and governing substantive law, parties can navigate the process of mediation themselves. Under this conception of family mediation lawyers have little or no role. Unless confronted with a court order for mediation, attorneys rarely mention mediation as an option for clients facing family breakup, either in divorce or through child welfare proceedings.[14] Mediators share the view that attorneys have little or no role to play in mediation. Some proponents of mediation actively discourage their participation.[15] But other commentators have recognized the critical role attorneys can play in preparing clients for mediation and in the mediation sessions themselves. Craig McEwen and his co-authors (Chapter 10) draw from findings of a study of the role of lawyers in court-mandated divorce mediation in Maine to argue that the presence of lawyers can help to ensure fairness in court-

---

[13]  The American Law Institute recognizes these risks in its *Principles of the Law of Family Dissolution [Principles]*. Although the *Principles* encourage courts to inform family disputants about the availability of mediation and other non-judicial procedures, they do not allow a court to mandate mediation. Moreover, the ALI Comments urge that parents 'be encouraged to confer with an attorney before deciding whether to engage in mediation, again during the process and before they reach a final agreement' (2000, §2.07).

[14]  In response to this concern, the American Bar Association (ABA) added language to its Comments to Model Rule 2.1 Scope of Advice suggesting that lawyers may be obligated to advise clients about the availability of alternative dispute resolution, noting that: 'when a matter is likely to involve litigation, it may be necessary ... to inform the client of forms of dispute resolution that might constitute reasonable alternatives to litigation' (ABA, 2004, R. 2.1 cmt. 5).

[15]  Mark Rutherford: 'For mediation to succeed as a profession and to reach its highest objectives, advocacy has no place in any part of the process. For outside counsel to advocate a client's interests contradicts the very essence of mediation and can produce inequitable results' (1986, p. 27).

mandated mediation. They conclude that lawyer participation can be a more effective way of making both the process and results of mediation fair than moving to voluntary mediation or creating a highly regulated approach to mediation.

But even if lawyers were accorded an increased role in mediation, there would be little benefit to low income litigants given the large numbers of parties who appear in family courts without lawyers.[16] Russell Engler (Chapter 16) examines the impact of lack of representation on parties in court-sponsored mediation, finding that the risk of loss of rights in that process is significantly greater for unrepresented parties. Even if the attorney does not attend the mediation, the represented party has far greater access to an expert source of information about judicial proceedings, each party's legal rights and remedies, and the parties' chances of success in court. No comparable source of information exists for the unrepresented party, given the current conception of the mediator's role as 'neutral.' Engler sees this as particularly dangerous when coupled with the pressure in court programmes to clear dockets through mediation. He concludes that mediators and other court personnel should rethink their roles in the light of the needs of unrepresented litigants.

The risks of mediation are also heightened in family disputes where one party is less powerful than the other.[17] Power imbalances may exist in cases where only one party is represented by an attorney or may result from race, gender, class, sexual orientation and cultural differences in mediation. The most disabling power imbalance in mediation may be in relationships where domestic violence has taken place. In these cases there has already been a severe abuse of power and the consequent power imbalance can make mediation impossible.[18] Nancy Ver Steegh's essay (Chapter 11) presents a particularly well-balanced and useful approach to resolving questions about the much debated issue of mediation and domestic violence. Recognizing the wide spectrum of quality in mediation options and the different circumstances facing abuse survivors, Ver Steegh argues against categorical answers to these issues. Instead, she urges an approach that permits domestic violence victims 'the opportunity to make an informed choice about which divorce process – mediated or adversarial – will best meet the needs of their families' (p. 205).

The risks posed by mediation in the face of a disabling power imbalance may also be present in 'family conferencing' in child welfare cases. While these cases may involve more attorneys than private family disputes, the attorney's role in family conferencing is almost as ill-defined and limited as in divorce and custody disputes (Kisthardt, 2006). And these cases are often marked by intimate partner violence and parties with limited education and resources

---

[16]   See Berenson (Chapter 17) where he describes a 1991–92 study of sixteen large urban areas nationwide finding that '72% of all domestic relations cases involved at least one unrepresented party' (p. 333); see also, Maryland Judiciary Administrative Office of the Courts Family Administration finding that 70 per cent of cases involving family disputes in Maryland involved at least one represented party (2007, pp. 29–30).

[17]   One of the earliest articulations of this position is the oft-cited article by Tina Grillo, 1991.

[18]   The Commentary to the ALI *Principles* (2000) notes that mediation poses an especially high risk of coercion and intimidation where domestic violence has occurred or is occurring (§2.07, Comment). The *Principles* therefore require that mediators screen for domestic violence and for other circumstances that may impede a party's capacity to participate in the mediation process. If there is credible evidence of such circumstances, then mediation should not occur unless reasonable steps are taken both to ensure the consent of each party to the process and to protect the safety of the victim (§2.07(2)).

(Murphy, 1998, p. 711). In addition to the power imbalance that may exist between family members, Amy Sinden notes that these cases also involve the 'substantial disparity of power' between parents, most often poor mothers, and the state which holds the 'palpable threat' of removing of their children (Chapter 13, p. 251). All of these circumstances create risks that the mother will suppress 'her point of view in order to achieve agreement' (p. 257) and not benefit from statutory or constitutional protections in place in the child welfare context.

Some existing research addresses these concerns (Emery, *et al.*, Chapter 9). But one of the difficulties in evaluating family mediation is the complexity of measuring 'success'. Given mediation's focus on 'needs' rather than 'rights,' measuring participant 'satisfaction' has been the dominant measure of success. Minorities and other traditionally less powerful groups may, however, have lower expectations about how well their needs can be met, thus rendering 'satisfaction' an inadequate measure of success for these individuals. This suggests that, in order to measure the 'success' of these new forms of dispute resolution, researchers must augment their focus on party satisfaction with more explicit consideration of 'fairness' in both process and outcome.

We hope readers of this volume will draw their own conclusions about the promise and risks of the paradigm shift we have described. Understanding and evaluating these changes should help prepare scholars and policy-makers for the challenging task of designing systems that serve the needs and protect the interests of families who seek both justice and conflict resolution.

## References

ABA (2004), *Model Rules of Professional Conduct*, American Bar Association.

American Law Institute (2002), *Principles of the Law of Family Dissolution: Analysis and Recommendations*, New York: Matthew Bender.

Association of Family and Conciliation Courts (AFCC) (2006), Task Force on Parenting Coordination, 'Guidelines For Parenting Coordination', *Family Court Review*, **44**, pp. 164–81.

Bix, Brian (1998), 'Bargaining in the Shadow of Love: The Enforcement of Premarital Agreements and How We Think about Marriage', *William and Mary Law Review*, **40**, pp. 145–207.

Boldt, Richard and Singer, Jana (2006), 'Juristocracy in the Trenches: Problem-Solving Judges and Therapeutic Jurisprudence in Drug Treatment Courts and Unified Family Courts', *Maryland Law Review*, **65**, pp. 82–99.

Catania, Francis J. Jr. (2002), 'Learning from the Process of Decision: The Parenting Plan', *Brigham Young University Law Review*, **2001**, pp. 857–89.

Chandler, S. and Giovannuci, M. (2004), 'Family Group Conferences: Transforming Traditional Child Welfare Policy and Practice', *Family Court Review*, **42**, pp. 216–31.

Chase, Deborah (2003), 'Pro Se Justice and Unified Family Courts', *Family Law Quarterly*, **37**, pp. 403–25.

Dion, M. Robin (2005), 'Healthy Marriage Programs: Learning What Works', *The Future of Children*, **15**, pp. 139–56.

Elias, Honorable Dame Sian (2002), 'Family Courts – 20 Years After Reform: The Family Court and Social Change', *Family Court Review*, **40**, pp. 297–305.

Emery, Robert E. (1994), *Renegotiating Family Relationships*: *Divorce, Child Custody and Mediation*, New York: Guilford Press.

Fineman, Martha (1988), 'Dominant Discourse, Professional Language, and Legal Change in Child Custody Decision Making', *Harvard Law Review*, **101**, pp. 727–74.

Folberg, Jay, Milne, Ann and Salem, Peter (eds) (2004), *Divorce and Family Mediation: Models, Techniques and Applications*, New York: Guilford Press.

Gamache, Susan (2005), 'Collaborative Practice: A New Opportunities to Address Children's Best Interest in Divorce', *Los Angeles Law Review*, **65**, pp. 1455–85.

Grillo, Tina (1991), 'The Mediation Alternative: Process Dangers for Women', *Yale Law Journal*, **100**, pp. 1545–610.

Hardcastle, Gerald (2003), 'Adversarialism and the Family Court: A Family Court Judges Perspective', *University of California Davis Journal of Juvenile Law and Policy*, **9**, pp. 57–125.

Huntington, Clare (2007), 'Mutual Dependency in Child Welfare', *Notre Dame Law Review*, **82**, pp. 1485–536.

Kisthardt, Mary Kay (2006), 'Working in the Best Interest of Children: Facilitating the Collaboration of Lawyers and Social Workers in Abuse and Neglect Cases', *Rutgers Law Record*, **30**, pp. 1–77.

Kisthardt, Mary Kay (2007), 'The AAML Model for a Parenting Plan', *Journal of the American Academy of Matrimonial Lawyers*, **10**, pp. 223–36.

Kuhn, Jeffrey A. (1998). 'A Seven Year-Lesson on Unified Family Courts: What We Have Learned Since the 1990 National Family Court Symposium', *Family Law Quarterly*, **32**, pp. 67–93.

Lamb, Michael E. (2002), 'Placing Children's Interests First: Developmentally Appropriate Parenting Plans', *Virginia Journal of Social Policy and the Law*, **10**, pp. 98–119.

Lande, John (2003), 'Possibilities for Collaborative Law: Ethics and Practice of Lawyer Disqualification and Process control in a New Model of Lawyering', *Ohio State Law Journal*, **64**, pp. 1315–384.

Leite, Randall W. and Kathleen Clark (2007), 'Participants' Evaluations of Aspects of the Legal Child Custody Process and Preferences for Court Services', *Family Court Review*, **45**, pp. 260–73.

Maryland Judiciary Administrative Office of the Courts Family Administration (2007), 2006 Annual Report of the Maryland Circuit Court Family Divisions and Family Services Programs, 29–30.

Menkel-Meadow, Carrie (1996), 'The Trouble with the Adversary System in a Postmodern, Multicultural World', *William. and Mary Law Review*, **38**, pp. 5–44.

Merkel-Holguin, Lisa (2004), 'Sharing Power with the People, Family Group Conferencing as a Democratic Experiment', *Journal of Sociology and Social Welfare*, **31**, pp. 155–73.

Murphy, Jane C., 'Legal Images of Motherhood: Conflicting Definitions from Welfare 'Reform,'Family and Criminal Law', *Cornell Law Review*, **83**, pp. 688–766.

Nicholson, Honorable Alastair (2002), 'Australian Family Law and the Family Court – A Perspective from the Bench', *Family Court Review*, **40**, pp. 279–96.

Parkinson, Patrick (2005), 'The Law of Post-Separation Parenting in Australia', *Family Law Quarterly*, **39**, pp. 507–25.

Peters, Jean Koh (2006), 'How Children Are Heard in Child Protective Proceedings in the United States and Around the World in 2005: Survey Findings, Initial Observations, and Areas for Further Study', *Nevada Law Journal*, **6**, pp. 966–1084.

Robbennolt, Jennifer K. and Johnson, Monica Kirkpatrick (1999), 'Legal Planning for Unmarried Committed Partners: Empirical Lessons for a Preventive and Therapeutic Approach', *Arizona Law Review*, **41**, pp. 417–57.

Rutherford, Mark (1986), 'Lawyers and Divorce Mediation: Designing The Role of "Outside Counsel"', *Mediation Quarterly*, **18**, pp. 27–36.

Santeramo, Jordan (2004), 'Early Neutral Evaluation in Divorce Cases', *Family Court Review*, **42**, pp. 321–35.

Schepard, Andrew and James Bozzomo (2003), 'Efficiency, Therapeutic Justice, Mediation and Evaluation: Reflections on a Survey of Unified Family Courts', *Family Law Quarterly*, **36**, pp. 333–59.

Schepard, Andrew and Peter Salem (2006), Foreword to the Special Issue on the Family Law Education Reform Project, *Family Court Review*, **44**, pp. 513–20.

Silbaugh, Katharine B. (1998), 'Marriage Contracts and the Family Economy', *Northwestern University Law Review*, **93**, pp. 65–143.

Smart, Carol (2002), 'From Children's Shoes to Children's Voices', *Family Court Review*, **40**, pp. 305–17.

Symposium (2004), 'Collaborative Family Law – the Big Picture', *Pepperdine Dispute Resolution Law Journal*, **4**, pp. 401–68.

Tippins, Timothy and Wittmann, Jeffrey (2005), 'Empirical and Ethical Problems with Custody Recommendations: A Call for Clinical Humility and Judicial Vigilance', *Family Court Review*, **43**, pp. 193–221.

Voegele, Gary, Wray, Linda and Ousky, Ronald (2007), 'Collaborative Law: A Useful Tool for the Family Law Practitioner to Promote Better Outcomes', *William Mitchell Law Review*, **33**, pp. 971–1027.

Winick, Bruce J. (2003), 'Therapeutic Jurisprudence and Problem-Solving Courts', *Fordham Urban Law Journal*, **30**, pp. 1055–90.

Winick, Bruce J. and Wexler, David B. (eds) (2003), *Judging in a Therapeutic Key: Therapeutic Jurisprudence and the Courts*, Durham: Carolina Academic Press.

Zaidel, Susan (2004), 'Taking Divorce out of the Context of Dispute Resolution', *Family Court Review*, **42**, pp. 678–80.

# Part I
# Theoretical Foundations

# [1]

# In the Best Interests of Children: A Proposal to Transform the Adversarial System

## Gregory Firestone and Janet Weinstein

*In the traditional family law and child protection litigation where the court is asked to make determinations based on the best interests of a minor, the adversarial, rights-based model often fails to serve the interests of children and families and may be more harmful than beneficial to children relative to other possible methods of dispute resolution. This article examines the shortcomings of such an adversarial, rights-based model; briefly highlights the literature on dispute resolution systems design; and then proposes a new approach to better serve the interests of children in family law and child protection cases.*

As many others have previously discussed, the adversary system is often unhealthy for children.[1] In the traditional family law litigation process and the child protection system where the court is asked to make determinations based on the best interests of a minor, the adversarial, rights-based model typically fails to serve the interests of children and families and may be more harmful than beneficial to children relative to other possible methods of dispute resolution.

## Shortcomings of the Adversary System

Our legal system generally relies on the notion that adversaries in a legal dispute will draw forth all information relevant to the contest in the process of putting forward their best positions, thereby allowing the decision maker to determine the "truth" and to make the best decision. Although the goal of an adversarial, rights-based model is to best serve the interests of children, the current system has a number of shortcomings that undermine the best intentions of the professionals involved.

*"Legalization" of human problems.* The best interests of children in divorce and child protection cases have become defined as primarily a legal problem; in reality, they are much more complex psychological, social, and legal problems that typically become intertwined

into other issues such as child support. Family relationships have become "legalized" in such a way that the system loses sight of the human problems in context and focuses only on addressing answers to the legal issues. The failure to better examine family problems contextually results in little recognition for the ecological perspective of family dynamics. Greater understanding of cultural mores, for example, has no place in a system bound by the act of fitting evidence into the fixed definitions of a statute. The law is not the appropriate forum for assisting dysfunctional families to function better. Resolution of the legal case often does little to improve or resolve the underlying family dynamics.

*Disempowerment and dehumanization of the participants.* Parents, accustomed to being the decision makers in matters pertaining to their children, typically become disempowered in litigation. In child protection cases where parents allegedly have failed to adequately care for or have abused or neglected their children, not enough effort is made to enable the parents to participate collaboratively with others in determining what services will be provided. In litigation, parents often become frustrated because rules of procedure and evidence may work to distort the facts on which the decision will be made. Parties may not be able to tell their stories, instead having to make the facts fit into the categorized requirements of the law. What seems to be actually relevant to the parties, what they need to say to feel heard, may not be presented to the court and may be seen as irrelevant to the proceeding.

Clearly this is also a dehumanizing experience. Although some attention has been paid to attempting to create a more humane and child-centered courtroom, the process of engaging in a battle with family members is rarely, if ever, a positive experience; certainly it is not for the children who are often placed in the middle of this warfare. Nor is it generally helpful to the parents or to the professionals who are trying to help them mend family relationships.

*Rights over interests.* Although the focus on the best interests of the child does create some pressure for parents' attorneys to couch their arguments in terms of what is best for the child, the court in child protection and custody disputes cannot ignore the rights of the parents. Concerns regarding gender equality have further[2] focused the discourse on parental rights; many believe the end product has been court orders that fail to honor family relationships.[3] This focus on the rights of the parents in custody and parenting disputes often occurs without a discussion of the responsibility adults owe to their children.

*Zealous advocacy.* The lawyer's ethical obligation to zealously represent his or her client is probably the cornerstone of the adversary system. The zealous advocate protects the rights of the client and cannot, according to principles of professional responsibility, do anything that would diminish the rights of the client. This kind of behavior is inappropriate for matters in which the court is required to determine the best interests of the child. Zealous advocacy of a client's rights may be counter to the best interests of the child, and such advocacy tends to further escalate existing conflict between the parties and cause greater harm to the child.[4]

*Destruction of ongoing relationships.* Preservation and healing of relationships between the contestants is not a consideration in this model, even though in cases involving the custody and welfare of a child, relationships are at the heart of the matter. Disputes involving the custody of children, particularly where abuse and/or neglect by one or both of the parents is alleged, tend to be among the most bitterly fought legal battles. It is critical to recognize that one of the most consistently reported findings of divorce research involves the toxic effect on children caught in the middle of ongoing conflict of their parents.[5] The adversary process makes enemies and exacerbates existing controversy. There is no healing element in the process to help to mend relationships that have been damaged or to promote future healthy interactions. The effects of these broken relationships on children and parents are devastating and long lasting.

*Delayed outcomes.* Litigation takes too long, especially considering a child's sense of time.[6] In fact, in a divorce, the custody issue may never be truly final until the children reach majority age. Until that time, the parents may engage in ongoing battles over the best interests of their children. There is little doubt that the consequences of uncertainty and instability can devastate a child and affect functioning and performance in all areas, particularly the ability to form satisfying relationships as an adult. Although it is important that the process not be steamrollered so as to result in injustice to the parents and child, delays that have no real positive role in the determination of the best outcome for a family and child are not justifiable.

*Expense of litigation.* The adversarial system is based on the idea that people will be represented by attorneys who will bring forth the best case. In family law cases, the vast majority of parties are unable to afford counsel.[7] In many jurisdictions, parents are unrepresented in child protection hearings, at least in the preliminary proceedings. Court time is also costly. Judges are paid for their expertise in the law and their skill in managing the trial process. Additionally, attorneys' fees for litigation involve preparation time and time spent in court waiting for cases to be called. Experts are expensive and, in most states, there are inadequate resources to pay for adequate forensic reports in child protection and family custody cases. The focus on the litigation process drains resources from where they are really needed, in the delivery of services to families who are experiencing transition and disruption. In child protection matters, the cost of attorneys' fees might be paid from the same budget that pays for services or social workers. In family court cases, parents might have to choose between having legal counsel and some other service, such as mental health or financial counseling.

*Limited information for decision making.* Special rules governing the relationship between attorney and client are an integral part of our adversary system. Client confidentiality and rules of evidentiary privilege mean that some information may come to the attention of the attorney but not be presented to the finder of fact, regardless of how relevant or material the information is to determining the appropriate outcome of the case. In proceedings where the judge is supposed to assess all the facts and make a determination as to the best interests of the child, barriers to full disclosure are barriers to accomplishing this end.

*Past oriented.* The adversary system is not dynamic and focuses largely on information about the past. Child protection and custody disputes are about the future welfare of the child. Although past acts may provide some help in thinking about the welfare of the child, they are not determinative. The family is a living entity, dynamic in nature, involving personalities and relationships that will change depending on how the family is reordered. Parenting may change after a divorce, so that an examination of parenting at the time of divorce is not necessarily the best indicator of what will occur later. The traditional legal approach requires a momentary snapshot judgment of the family structure, which does not serve the best interest of the child.

*Exclusion of others.* The adversary system typically involves a battle between the parties to the proceedings. Although others may participate as witnesses, third-party interests are not relevant to the outcome. Although the law may define the family as consisting of parents and children, others, including relatives, friends, counselors, and neighbors, can play substantial roles in the family. Particularly for cultures within our society in which extended family includes relatives as well as nonrelatives, the legal barriers that exclude these people from participating and contributing to the outcome restrict the ability to understand the family and its needs, and likely limit the number and quality of options for serving the best interests of children.

*Polarized role of experts.* The adversary system often pushes many helping professionals to become advocates for one position. Therapists, evaluators, teachers, physicians, and others often not trained to be advocates in the legal sense are usually more aware of the dynamic and contextual nature of the family and are uncomfortable taking such one-sided positions. For example, in child protection cases, social workers often become adversaries to the families they are supposed to serve. Similarly, mental health professionals who have testified frequently in best interest cases often adapt to the process with frightening success.[8] For example, mental health professionals who rely on the adversarial legal system as a source of income may be concerned with more than the threat of being embarrassed by skillful cross-examination. Where more than one mental health expert is involved, the fact that they may be testifying for opposing parties may also tend to draw them into the role of adversaries rather than neutral, objective witnesses and impede their interactions.[9] Opportunities for collaborative problem solving are foregone in allegiance to the adversarial process, which often only serves to confuse the issues with conflicting testimony.

*Compromised use of mental health services.* Parties who are in therapy may be more inclined to hide their own shortcomings for fear that any disclosures made in counseling may be later presented to the court. Mental health professionals often find that parties are less inclined to be open in counseling and that the expectation that a mental health professional may be called to testify can greatly impede mental health counseling.

*Error bias.* In the context of child protection and family custody proceedings, the first decision is often determinative of later decisions; thus, "an error at one stage is more likely to be maintained or exaggerated than reversed."[10] For example, in child protection cases, the first decision to remove a child might eventually result in the child's adoption, as the child-caretaker relationship grows and the parent is basically excluded from the child's life. If the risk to the child was not as great as initially feared, a family has been unnecessarily destroyed. Judges understandably are risk-aversive, and these tendencies may contribute to these initial errors.[11]

*Inadequate training of decision makers.* Our legal system has no special insight into the needs of children and families, nor do legal professionals typically have special training to deal with the complex and difficult issues that arise in these disputes. Judges and attorneys find themselves involved in the lives of families in an intimate way for which they never prepared in law school. The best interests standard, which has been criticized for being vague and for being an illusory determinant of the child's welfare,[12] exaggerates the training deficiencies because those who make the decisions are often forced to rely on their personal biases, experience, and intuition. Judges and attorneys frequently must rely on the word of other professionals, who have more specific training in issues relating to parent-child relationships, child development, and risk assessment, with little expertise to critically analyze such expert testimony.

*Role of children in litigation.* Although it is best to keep children out of the conflict arena where possible, in most cases children are well aware that their parents are involved in a dispute concerning them. In these situations, commentators disagree about the role of the child and about the role of children's attorneys. Children may come to court and be forced to take sides against one or both parents, or they may have their concerns expressed to the court by their attorney or guardian ad litem. The significance of what children say may not be understood, or the children's perspectives may not be presented to the court at all. Ultimately, proceedings that place children in the middle of an adversarial battle involving their parents are antithetical to the best interests of those children.[13]

## A Comprehensive Dispute Resolution System

We propose that a system that truly serves the needs of families in crisis should be based on an understanding of their needs. In addition, such a system should draw on the accumulated knowledge we have of private and freestanding dispute resolution systems. Below we summarize a few approaches to alternative dispute resolution (ADR) system design that include some principles we have incorporated into our proposal.

### Dispute Resolution Systems Design Theory

Ury, Brett, and Goldberg[14] outline six principles of dispute system design. They are (a) focus on interests, (b) loop-backs, (c) low costs rights and power backups, (d) consultation and feedback, (e) low- to high-cost sequence of procedures, and (f) provision of motivation, skills, and necessary resources. Although their book, *Getting Disputes Resolved*, was written to address organizational dispute resolution systems, we would suggest that these principles can also be applied to developing a comprehensive dispute resolution program that would better serve children and families, as discussed below.

Constantino and Merchant also offer complementary organizational dispute resolution principles that provide additional insights into the development of a comprehensive dispute resolution program. They are (a) develop guidelines for whether ADR is appropriate, (b) tailor the ADR process to the particular problem, (c) build in preventive methods of ADR, (d) make sure that disputants have the necessary knowledge and skill to choose and use ADR, (e) create ADR systems that are simple to use and easy to access, and (f) allow disputants to retain maximum control over choice of ADR method and selection of any third party whenever possible.[15]

Last, Rowe[16] offers additional considerations when developing organizational dispute resolution systems. Although addressing a different organizational system than family court, Rowe's suggested factors are also helpful here. According to Rowe, one should consider the following factors: (a) the values of the system, (b) the presence of many options, (c) multiple access points, (d) an organizational ombudsperson, (e) wide scope, and (f) continuous improvement.

## Proposal for a Comprehensive Dispute Resolution System for Families in Transition

We propose that it is time to consider developing a comprehensive dispute resolution program for families experiencing divorce or child protection problems that is built on the lessons learned about the inadequacies of the current approach and the contributions of the literature on dispute resolution system design. This proposed approach emphasizes a new thinking about family court services. It builds on the multidoor door courthouse concept[17] in a number of important ways. First, the program itself would be a private/public endeavor and, although intertwined with court programs, would be a free-standing operation that utilizes court services mostly for rights-based dispute resolution backups and for the filing of agreements and court documents. Public-private partnerships will likely become more necessary in the future as the volume of divorce and child protection cases continues to increase in many jurisdictions at a time when state budgets are increasingly limited in their ability to provide adequate funding for court operations. Although courts may still need to provide low cost or free services to indigent families, such services could be offered directly by the court or supported with court or community funding. Combining court services with private dispute resolution methods and other supportive services will also serve to create an independent, comprehensive dispute resolution system where litigation plays a very small role in the overall resolution of conflicts.

Second, rather than courthouse being the entry point, people would enter the system through consultation with a Dispute Resolution Coordinator (DRC). The DRC, unlike the "intake specialist" used in the multi-door courtroom concept, would be available for the family each time a new problem arises, allowing the family to "loop-back" through the system, accessing a variety of processes and services, depending upon the family's current needs. DRCs would be available in local communities, making them easily accessible to clients and not necessarily under the umbrella of the courthouse.

Third, the DRC's role would be different from the triage model of the multidoor courthouse. After proper screening for domestic violence, the DRC would empower the parties (when domestic violence and child protection concerns are not present) by offering them different methods of dispute resolution and enabling the parties, to choose their own preferred method. In cases involving domestic violence and/or child protection, the DRC would still seek to offer those dispute resolution options that were considered appropriate for the specific case. The DRC would not be involved in the resolution of substantive issues in the case. The role of the DRC would be to educate the parties concerning their dispute resolution options and assist them in choosing methods of dispute resolution. Thus, it would become an expectation that parties would seek resolution of disputes without having to come into the courthouse, which represents the adversarial system and a win/lose culture. Moving the major activities of dispute resolution out of the courthouse may be an essential step to changing the cultural expectations of how disputes are resolved. Fourth, we propose that the development of the comprehensive dispute resolution program be designed with initial and ongoing input from all stakeholders in the system, including families involved in divorce and child protection proceedings.

We believe it is time to consider implementing new dispute resolution systems that incorporate the values and ideas discussed below. What we present here is a basic outline; the specific mechanisms of any such system would vary depending upon community needs and resources.

*1. Availability of many dispute resolution options.* Families are unique, and the issues that families are dealing with in custody and child protection cases include financial concerns, parenting issues, mental health concerns, domestic violence, substance abuse, limited resources, third-party concerns, and so forth. A variety of problem-solving mechanisms should be available to families and should be affordable; services that cover a spectrum of economic resources should be available. Extended family members and other support persons should be encouraged to participate where their participation would assist in the resolution of the problem. The expectation in the system should be that parties will resolve their dispute, with the assistance of the system if necessary. Options for conflict resolution should include such ADR processes and services as mediation, parenting coordination, family group counseling, education, counseling, neutral evaluation (including custody evaluations), arbitration, litigation and more cost-effective rights-based options, and other methods that would provide the parties with what they need in their particular situations. In divorce cases, such options could be available for custody and noncustody issues, as ultimately it is in the best interests of children to have parents resolve all outstanding divorce issues in a timely and conflict-reducing manner. Dispute Resolution Counselors will need to be culturally competent to serve the needs of their communities, understanding that some problem-solving processes may be particularly suited for use with some groups and not others.

*2. Emphasis on interest-based approaches.* The best way to maximize the interests of children and families is to encourage interest-based problem solving. This problem-solving system will focus on the interests of the participants rather than on their legal rights. Although the system would include a mechanism for determining legal rights where necessary, the expectation on the part of all participants would be that they will focus on concerns related to family functioning, with a particular focus on the interests of the children. The dispute resolution program would encourage interest-based collaborative processes where the parties would be able to problem solve together and determine their own outcomes. Although knowledge of rights-based solutions would be encouraged to enable parties to make informed choices, the emphasis would be on building solutions that work best for the parties and their families. As such, the parties would be encouraged to find customized solutions that may not be an option in litigation where courts have a limited repertoire of remedies and typically do not have the time or resources to create individualized parenting plans for families.

Interest-based problem solving focuses on the needs of the individuals who are involved in the problem. Because it is tailored to deal with the specific issues of these particular people, it is more likely to maximize opportunity to address all needs. Parties are not restricted to discussing information that is determined to be legally relevant. People who are not parties to the legal action but who have an interest in the well-being of the family may be appropriate participants. Interest-based problem solving also fosters conflict reduction. The parties can experience that their concerns are being heard and addressed. In addition, the focus on interests, rather than winning, forces parties to find ways to solve their problems by working together. In turn, the parties learn skills that will allow them to avoid conflict in the future.[18]

*3. Focus on problem solving.* The system must reflect a cultural shift from a focus on winning to a focus on problem solving. The message received by participants from their initial entry into the system is that they are expected to resolve this dispute, with the help of the processes and services that will be made available to them, and that the interest of the system is the same as theirs-to protect the well-being of their children.

*4. Availability of affordable rights-based solutions.* Families need low-cost strategies to resolve their parenting and financial disputes. Similarly, states cannot afford the cost of litigating these matters if they are to use tax dollars wisely. As expensive dispute resolution strategies only drain families of essential resources at a critical time and limit a state's ability to provide necessary services, low-cost alternatives should be available. Therefore, when the parties fail to reach an interest-based solution or when interest-based strategies are not possible, there need to be multiple levels of options, including affordable rights-based resolution processes. The current family law and child protection system is complex and expensive, and even when alternatives such as special masters are used, the process tends to resemble litigation. Experts trained to determine these rights could more quickly and efficiently resolve many of the rights-based issues that are determined in family court, such as child and spousal support, and property interests. If the culture can be shifted so that expectations of the participants are not about winning or losing, but rather are about helping the family to make necessary changes, the parties could have these issues resolved by a third person, when they cannot reach agreement on their own, with less expense, paperwork, and formality. Although the determinations of these experts may be subject to court review, such review should be limited to procedural fairness-in other words, whether the decision maker considered all of the facts provided by the parties-and, if so, whether there was an abuse of discretion. Courts can create panels of professionals for determining these special issues, and the dispute resolution coordinator can offer the family a range of services.[19]

*5. The services of a DRC.* To be effective problem solvers, the parties must be provided with information about the dispute resolution process and the choices available to them. A DRC would serve as a consultant to the parties to advise them of their conflict resolution options and to empower them to choose the best options for themselves. When the parties are unable to agree upon a dispute resolution process, the DRC can mediate the process issue. In the event the parties do not agree on a particular method of dispute resolution, the parties could then be directed to proceed to a predetermined path of dispute resolution as set forth in the comprehensive dispute resolution program.[20] In child protection cases, the DRC would also ensure that the dispute resolution path was consistent with state-determined mandates for child protection judicial proceedings. This DRC would also help to ensure that the system of loop-backs works effectively, ensuring that families do not fall through the cracks but rather get assistance each time a problem arises. The DRC would also encourage parents to receive training in the skills they will need to succeed at solving their problems. In addition, this DRC would be able to track the success of the program and recommend improvements.

6. *Guidelines and screening.* Guidelines should be established to help in the determination of whether court intervention is required.[21] In some cases, interest-based and collaborative strategies would not be appropriate. For example, screening for domestic violence would need to be a part of an initial assessment to determine the appropriateness of ADR options for parties and, where appropriate, some services may not be offered to some families.[22] New programs to better address the special needs of domestic violence would need to be developed that better address concerns relating to safety, imbalances of power, and the special needs of children in these cases. Such programs would emphasize timely resolution in a manner that separates the victim and children from the batterer, provides specialized treatment as appropriate, and seeks to find ways to help children heal. Similarly, in child protection cases, appropriate screening would be necessary to ensure that children are not placed in danger in mediation. This screening could be provided by the child protection agencies and guardian ad litem or court-appointed special advocates already involved in such cases or other professionals as needed. Screening could also be designed to ensure that parties are competent to participate in mediation.

One might also consider appropriate screening to ensure that parties are not conducting themselves in a fraudulent manner. For example, parties could be asked to submit financial affidavits and, when necessary, a process of discovery could be implemented to ensure that all financial information is accurate.

7. *Support.* Families in times of stress need additional support. Divorce is difficult, as is participating in the child protection system. Even parents with the best intentions to minimize conflict are not always successful. A support system that helps people manage the changes in the family would include services such as job counseling and training, housing assistance, and respite care, as well as educational programs that could include topics such as collaborative methods for resolving divorce, conflict resolution skills for parents, the impact of divorce on children, and so forth.[23] The educational programs could be mandatory and required early, rather than late, in the divorce process.[24] To reduce costs, such programs could be available on videotape/DVD, through local court or university programs, or delivered via the Internet. Such programs would not only be helpful in resolving current disputes but may also enable parties to better resolve disputes in the future, therefore serving a preventive role as well. A team approach to providing services could help to ensure that the spectrum of support needed by parents and children would be available.

8. *Focus on future-oriented strategies.* Dispute resolution strategies must be future oriented. As discussed above, the past orientation of the legal system does not provide adequate

consideration of the future change and development of the family and the individuals who comprise it. Strategies for problem solving must include discussions of what will happen as the children mature and as the needs and parenting abilities of the parties change. Furthermore, there must be discussion of problem-solving mechanisms that will be in place as future concerns arise. Each new problem should not require, as they do now, filing of legal documents and an onerous process that stands in the way of getting the problems solved.

*9. Encouragement of professional collaboration.* Divorce and child protection matters are complex problems and that solutions require collaboration and the participation of many other professionals. All professionals involved need training in mental health, law, collaborative conflict resolution strategies, the dynamics of divorce, child development, the causes and consequences of child maltreatment, and the importance of interdisciplinary teams. Resources would also need to be committed to train court staff in more effective techniques for encouraging greater collaboration among professionals as well as among parties.[25]

*10. Empowerment of parents.* Parents need and more often will benefit from a process for resolving disputes more than they need or will benefit from outside decision-making services.[26] A process in which parents can fully participate and begin to take responsibility for the decisions that will reshape their lives does not occur when families must rely on judicial decision making. Although it may be true for child protection cases, divorce is not in and of itself a reason for the state to direct the lives of parents and children. Even in cases of child maltreatment, extended family members are often in a better position to participate in decision making, as shown by the successes of family group conferencing. Similarly, in child protection mediation, the families are often able to reach a consensus with child protection agencies, guardian ad litem, and others involved in the child protection case, and there is strong judicial support for such nonadversarial dispute resolution strategies such as mediation and family group conferencing.[27]

*11. Respect for families' privacy.* Given that the matters that come before a court in custody and visitation conflicts are very private in nature, they should be confidential rather than public. Unless good reason can be shown to open a family law proceeding, these hearings should be closed in a similar way that juvenile court cases are protected.

*12. Long-term thinking.* Prevention strategies can lessen the impact of these disputes on children and families. Families going through divorce require many of the same kinds of support that are needed by parents and children in the child protection system. Education about relationship maintenance, dealing with stress, communication skills, and budgeting is helpful to people who are changing the structure of their families. Furthermore, group, couple, and individual counseling can help people make the adjustments they need to the new family structure. Such services need to be available to families even before any legal action is taken.[28] Parents who receive services to help them cope with change will be able to minimize their conflict and, thus, minimize the damage to the children.

*13. Understandable process.* Families need an understandable process. The system must be simple, comprehensible, and easy to access, with multiple access points. The complexity and barriers to accessing the legal system are not appropriate to solving family problems. A dispute resolution coordinator might be the first point of access. There should be significantly less paperwork and procedure than what is now required in the legal process.[29] Record keeping would be solely for the purpose of tracking the family's needs and progress. To the extent they are still necessary, court forms, program intake forms, and other documents would need to be readily available, and helpful directions and assistance would be provided to aid parties in completing them.

*14. Ongoing evaluation.* The system must provide a mechanism for improving itself. It is particularly important for the participants to have the opportunity to give feedback regarding their experiences and suggestions as to how the system might be improved to better serve the needs of the parties. Similarly, the professionals involved in the system should have a process for commenting about their concerns and thoughts about how the system is working. Finally, there should be a procedure for tracking results to examine the efficacy of the system in terms of criteria such as decreases in litigation and better outcomes for children.

## Conclusion

A cultural shift in our expectations surrounding best-interest conflict resolution is essential. Rather than turning to the courts to make difficult relationship decisions, a comprehensive system needs to be in place that is based on an understanding of the psychological, social, and other dynamics that underlie these matters and encourages the development of collaborative, interest-based problem solving. The comprehensive dispute resolution program we offer here is based upon some of the principles of dispute resolution system design and built upon what we have learned in divorce and child protection cases. It attempts to fashion dispute resolution services to the needs of families going through difficult times rather than fit the families into a system that was never really intended to heal their problems. We believe that such a comprehensive system will not only best serve the interests of children and families, it will also offer families in transition a more humane and cost-effective method for resolving the difficult challenges that these families encounter.

We recognize that such a change will also permit families to resolve their disputes in ways that will be better attuned to the special cultural considerations of a given family. For example, permitting greater involvement of other family members in such methods as family group conferencing would enable families to better find solutions that build on family strengths in a manner that is more specific to their own culture, religion, and ethnicity. Similarly, in divorce, mediation would serve to encourage better communication between family members, and in child protection cases would serve to improve working relationships with caseworkers and others involved with the family. Such improved communication and problem solving could also serve to better enable the professionals to become more attuned to the cultural sensitivities and needs of the family.

Such a comprehensive dispute resolution system would also benefit from the recent emergence of collaborative and cooperative law practices where lawyers are committing themselves to working more collaboratively with couples and professionals and seeking resolution in a more interest-based and collaborative manner. Similarly, the emergence of unbundling of legal services also well lends itself to such a dispute resolution system where parties may benefit from specific and limited assistance from attorneys. Similarly, we would expect to see the emergence of other types of divorce coaches and consultants from other professions, including mental health and accounting.

To make this transformation, the current stakeholders in the system, including families and professionals, will need to be educated about the consequences of participating in the current adversary system and the possibilities of alternative processes. This would require local organization and the support of the family and juvenile courts. Attorneys would need to be trained to incorporate the values on which this proposal is made, beginning in law school. Interdisciplinary trainings and meetings would need to be conducted for all professionals working in the current system to develop new, collaborative ways of problem solving. The growing popularity and success of the collaborative law movement, particularly in the area of family law, is a good example of how this can occur.

Undertaking to transform the manner in which disputes are resolved in divorce and child protection proceedings would be a huge undertaking that must be carefully and thoughtfully developed. Such efforts might first begin with pilot programs or other methods of incremental development where changes can be deliberately and carefully analyzed in a systematic manner.

*Gregory Firestone, Ph.D., is Director of the University of South Florida Conflict Resolution Collaborative and Vice Chair of the Florida Supreme Court ADR Rules and Policy Committee.*

*Janet Weinstein, J.D., is Professor of Law and Director of the Clinical Internship Program at California Western School of Law in San Diego, California.*

**Notes**

[1]    *See*, e.g., Janet Weinstein, *And Never the Twain Shall Meet: The Adversary System and the Best Interests of Children*, 52 U. MIAMI L. REV. 79 (1997); Heather Crosby, *The Irretrievable Breakdown of the Child: Minnesota's Move Toward Parenting Plans*, 21 HAMLINE J. PUB. LAW & POLICY 489 (2000). For a discussion of the negative effects of parental conflict on children of divorce, *see generally* ANDREW SCHEPARD, CHILDREN, COURTS, AND CUSTODY: INTERDISCIPLINARY MODELS FOR DIVORCING FAMILIES 30 (2004) [hereinafter SCHEPARD, CHILDREN, COURTS AND CUSTODY].
[2]    ANDREA CHARLOW, AWARDING CUSTODY: THE BEST INTERESTS OF THE CHILD AND OTHER FICTIONS, IN CHILD, PARENT, AND STATE 3, 5-6 (S. Randall Humm et al. eds., 1994).
[3]    Francis J. Catania, Jr., *Accounting to Ourselves for Ourselves: An Analysis of Adjudication in the Resolution of Child Custody Disputes*, 71 NEB. L. REV. 1228, 1234-35 (1992).
[4]    For a discussion of the role of zealous versus competent advocacy by lawyers for parents in child custody disputes, see SCHEPARD, CHILDREN, COURTS AND CUSTODY, *supra* note 1, at 125-38. *See also*, Weinstein, *supra* note 1, at 163, for a discussion of the role of attorneys in a problem-solving system.

[5]    For example, *see, The Wingspread Conference Report in High Conflict Cases: Reforming the System for Children*, 39 FAM. CT. REV. 146 (2001).

[6]    JOSEPH GOLDSTEIN, ANNA FREUD, & ALBERT J. SOLNIT, BEYOND THE BEST INTERESTS OF THE CHILD (Free Press 1973).

[7]    *In re* Family Court Steering Committee, 794 So. 2d 518 (Fla. 2001) (stating that in 60% of new divorce cases filed in Florida, at least one party is pro se; in 80% of postjudgment matters at least one party is pro se). *See* SCHEPARD, *supra* note 1, at 40 for a discussion of the effect of pro se litigants on the child custody court's docket.

[8]    *See*, Richard A. Garner, M.D., *My Involvement in Child Custody Litigation*, 27 FAM. & CONCILIATION CTS. REV. 1 (1989).

[9]    *See* Weinstein, *supra* note 1, at 100; Garner, *id.*

[10]   Peggy Cooper Davis & Gautam Barua, *Custodial Choices for Children at Risk: Bias, Sequentiality, and the Law*, 2 U. CHI. L. SCH. ROUNDTABLEE 139 (1995).

[11]   *Id.*

[12]   *See, e.g.*, Annette R. Appell & Bruce A. Boyer, *Parental Rights vs. Best Interests of the Child: A False Dichotomy in the Context of Adoption*, 2 DUKE J. GENDER L. & POL'Y 63, 66 (1995) (arguing that the standard is vague and subject to arbitrary application and should not be used for decisions about whether to intervene); N. Dicon Reppucci and Catherine A. Crosby, *Law, Psychology, and Children: Overarching Issues*, 17 LAW & HUM. BEHAVV. 1 (1993) (regardless of how it is measured, the best interests of children are generally indeterminant, and largely a matter of values); Catherine A. Crosby-Currie, *Children's Involvement in Contested Custody Cases: Practices and Experiences of Legal and Mental Health Professionals*, 20 LAW & HUM. BEHAVV. 289 (1996) (the indeterminacy of the standard vests judges with a great deal of discretion and very little practical assistance).

[13]   *See* Weinstein, *supra* note 1, at 116.

[14]   WILLIAM URY, JEANNE BRETT, & STEPHEN GOLDBERG, GETTING DISPUTES RESOLVED, 42 (Jossey-Bass Publishers 1993).

[15]   CATHY CONSTANTINO & CHRISTINA S. MERCHANT, DESIGNING CONFLICT MANAGEMENT SYSTEMS: A GUIDE TO CREATING PRODUCTIVE AND HEALTH ORGANIZATIONS, 121 (Jossey-Bass Publishers 1996).

[16]   MARY ROWE, DISPUTE RESOLUTION IN THE NON-UNION ENVIRONMENT IN FRONTIERS IN DISPUTE RESOLUTION IN LABOR RELATIONS AND HUMAN RESOURCES (Sandra Gleason ed., Michigan State University Press 1997).

[17]   The concept of the multidoor courthouse was developed by Harvard Law Professor Frank E. A. Sander, who first presented it in 1976. Responding to growing public dissatisfaction with the justice system and serious overcrowding of court dockets, Sander conceived of a court that offered parties a variety of ways to solve their disputes. Rather than simply adding all cases to the litigation docket, multidoor courthouses direct disputants to "intake specialists" who assess the disputes and determine the optimal routes to resolution. Those routes may include assistance from community resource centers, early neutral evaluation, mediation, arbitration, minitrial, summary jury trial, or litigation, among others. The idea is to save time and money for both disputants and the court, while also improving satisfaction with the process by finding the most appropriate process for the situation. FRANK E. A. SANDER, VARIETIES OF DISPUTE PROCESSING, THE POUND CONFERENCE: PERSPECTIVES ON JUSTICE IN THE FUTURE (A. Leo Levin & Russell R. Wheeler eds., 1979). *See* SCHEPARD, *supra* note 1, at 50 for a discussion of the Pound Conference and the multidoor courthouse and the influence of both on how courts resolve child custody disputes.

[18]   Although we understand that court orders will still play a significant role in cases of domestic violence, child abuse, or neglect, as well as where child abduction is a concern, our goal is to change the culture so that expectations are focused on reaching resolution rather than warring. Similarly, legal authority may be required when parties fail to cooperate and cannot be persuaded to participate in

good faith in less adversarial processes. For example, parties who fail to disclose financial assets in a dissolution proceeding or who threaten to violate visitation orders may be more likely to do so under the threat of a court sanction. *See* Weinstein, *supra* note 1, at 159, discussing a collaborative problem-solving approach that uses teamwork and consensus building even in cases in which the courts must become involved and describing the narrow role of the court.

[19]   The complex legal system that currently processes family disputes is primarily a result of legislative, rather than constitutional, mandate. The regulation of family matters is an area traditionally left to the states under the 10th Amendment. A few particular issues have risen to the level of constitutional scrutiny, primarily those issues dealing with the child-parent relationship. The U.S. Supreme Court has determined that the rights of parents and children to family integrity and to maintain their relationships can only be disturbed when the court finds by clear and convincing evidence that the parent is unfit (Santosky v. Kramer, 455 U.S. 745 [1982]). Most of the decisions made by family and juvenile courts do not rise to this level because parental rights are not being terminated. In fact, the rights asserted in most family law cases are not considered significant enough to warrant the appointment of an attorney for an indigent party. *See* Weinstein, *supra* note 1, at 102 (discussing the right to be represented by counsel in these cases). The primary consideration should be whether due process is satisfied. Basically, that requirement is met if the party has "an opportunity to be heard in a meaningful manner." Mathews v. Eldridge, 96 S.Ct. 893 (1976). The constitution does not require a particular body to provide that opportunity, so as long as the process is fair and other appropriate mechanisms, similar to administrative law hearings, could be used. Of course, the intention of the proposed system is that the parties would be educated and counseled about alternative dispute resolution processes, rather than simply mandated to use them. Thus, if parties elect to use the services of private dispute resolution practitioners so that the parties themselves can eventually reach agreement, there is no issue of an inappropriate delegation of power to the private sector. In the end, we believe that parties who are empowered to participate in the resolution of their disputes will experience a more fair process and resolution than many now do by participating in the adversary system.

[20]   For some disputes, the parties may have a right to litigate at this point, depending on the nature of the underlying problem (i.e., those that give rise to constitutional concerns), but in most cases, the DRC could direct the parties to an appropriate process even without their agreement.

[21]   *See* SCHEPARD, *supra* note 1, at 118, for a discussion of screening of child custody disputes in the context of a judicial plan for Differential Case Management (DCM).

[22]   *See*, e.g., Nancy Ver Steegh, *Yes, No, and Maybe: Informed Decision Making About Divorce Mediation in the Presence of Domestic Violence*, 9 WM. & MARY J. WOMEN & L. 145, 186 (2003).

[23]   *See*, e.g., Alicia M. Homrich et al., *Program Profile: The Court Care Center for Divorcing Families*, 42 FAM. CT. REV. 141 (2004).

[24]   *See* SCHEPARD, *supra* note 1, at 68, for a discussion of the types of court-affiliated educational programs available for divorcing and separating parents and children and the research evaluating their effectiveness.

[25]   *See* Weinstein, *supra* note 1, at 157, suggesting interdisciplinary training including training in effective collaboration among disciplines.

[26]   Philip M. Stahl & Greg Firestone, *Guest Editors' Introduction*, 38 FAM. & CONCILIATION CTS. REV. 292, (2000).

[27]   *See, e.g.*, Greg Firestone, *Dependency Mediation: Where Do We Go From Here?* 35 FAM. & CONCILIATION CTS. REV. 222 (1997); NATIONAL COUNCIL OF JUVENILE AND FAMILY COURT JUDGES, RESOURCE GUIDELINES: IMPROVING COURT PRACTICE IN CHILD ABUSE & NEGLECT CASES (National Council of Juvenile and Family Court Judges 1995); Susan M. Chandler & Marilou Giovanucci, *Family Group Conferences: Transforming Traditional Child Welfare Policy and Practice*, 42 FAM. CT. REV. (forthcoming April 2004

[28]   *Supra* note 24.

[29]  *See*, D. A. Rollie Thompson, *The Evolution of Modern Canadian Family Law Procedure-The End of the Adversary System? Or Just The End of the Trial?* 41 FAM. CT. REV. 155, 173-75 (2003), for a discussion of the evolution of two tiers of family law procedure in Canadian, with one geared to self-represented litigants and simplified matters.

# [2]

# An Interdisciplinary Approach to Family Law Jurisprudence: Application of an Ecological and Therapeutic Perspective

Barbara A. Babb

## Introduction

The task of jurisprudence for legal realists is a practical aim to ensure that judicial decisionmaking promotes social welfare and increases the predictability of legal outcomes.[1] This focus on the functional effects of judicial decisionmaking requires sufficient knowledge of the social sciences to enable judges to understand social policy implications when fashioning legal remedies.[2] Legal realism has dominated judicial decisionmaking in most areas of the law.[3] Family law[4] jurisprudence, however, reflects the law's inconsistency with families real life experiences and with relevant social science research in child development and family relations.[5] Historically, judges have attempted to fashion morality in the determination of family legal issues rather than to devise legal remedies that accommodate how families live.[6] This approach to decisionmaking must change if family law jurisprudence is to effectuate the well-being of families and children. A new approach to family law jurisprudence can assist decisionmakers to account for the realities of families lives when determining family legal issues.

The lack of legal realism in family law is troublesome given the extent of court involvement in the lives of families and children. A recent Wall Street Journal article has revealed that family law cases constitute about thirty-five percent of the total number of civil cases handled by the majority of our nation's courts, a percentage which constitutes the largest and fastest growing part of the state civil caseload.[7] The focus of judicial decisionmaking in family law needs to become how the state intervenes in family life, rather than whether the state ought to intervene,[8] as court involvement itself constitutes state intervention.

Changes over the last few decades in the structure and function of the American family, as well as the relative complexity of contemporary family legal issues, challenge judges to adopt an appropriate jurisprudential philosophy that addresses these transformations. The tremendous volume and breadth of family law cases now before the courts, coupled with the critical role of the family in today's society to provide stable and nurturing environments for family members, require that judges understand relevant social science research about child development and family life. This informed perspective can assist decisionmakers to dispense justice aimed at strengthening and supporting families.[9]

This Article proposes an interdisciplinary approach to resolve family legal proceedings. The interdisciplinary perspective helps judges consider the many influences on human behavior and family life, thereby resulting in more pragmatic and helpful solutions to contemporary family legal issues. Part I of the Article begins with an overview of demographic information about the composition and function of the American family in today's society. It then reviews the scope of family law adjudication facing today's courts and justifies the need for decisionmakers to view family legal problems with an expansive focus. Part II argues for application of a behavioral sciences paradigm, or the ecology of human development,[10] to provide the social science basis for more effective and therapeutic jurisprudence[11] in family law. Demonstrating the relevance of this theoretical framework to fashion family legal outcomes, a novel application of social science within the law, makes clear the need to rely on social science theories and findings in family law adjudication. Part III of the Article explains how an ecological and therapeutic jurisprudential paradigm operates when applied to determine family legal matters, as well as how this interdisciplinary approach differs from traditional notions of adjudication.

*   *   *   *

## C. Adopting a Therapeutic Perspective

Family law adjudication by definition involves court intervention in the lives of families and children. In contrast to social science, law does not describe how people do behave, but rather prescribes how they should behave.[145] Thus, the following questions become pertinent: How deeply into the domestic realm can or should government go when it intervenes in the lives of families and children? Conversely, what is government's duty to families and children who are in legal and social distress? These political and philosophical questions still bedevil public officials in America today. Yet when society chooses to intervene, it must be done well and there must be accountability.[146]

The notion of intervention implies an ability to influence the underlying situation to make it more positive.[147] In family law adjudication, one function of court intervention ought to aim to improve the participants underlying behavior or situation.[148] Application of therapeutic jurisprudence[149] to family law can assist with this improvement effort. The concept of therapeutic jurisprudence emerges from the field of mental health law, where it is defined as follows:

> Therapeutic jurisprudence is the study of the role of the law as a therapeutic agent. It looks at the law as a social force that, like it or not, may produce therapeutic or anti-therapeutic consequences. Such consequences may flow from substantive rules, legal procedures, or from the behavior of legal actors (law yers or judges).

The task of therapeutic jurisprudence is to identify and ultimately to examine empirically relationships between legal arrangements and therapeutic outcomes. The research task is a cooperative and thoroughly interdisciplinary one . . . . Such research should then usefully inform policy determinations regarding law reform.[150]

The goal of therapeutic jurisprudence suggests a need to restructure the law and the legal process by applying behavioral science knowledge to accomplish therapeutic outcomes without interfering with traditional notions of justice.[151] The potential exists to apply therapeutic jurisprudence to family law.[152]

In the family law context, this concept of the law as a therapeutic agent is particularly relevant to situations where families experience intra- or inter-family crisis. Envisioning the court's role in these family crisis situations as that of facilitating more positive relationships or outcomes and of strengthening families functioning, or a prescriptive focus,[153] seems particularly appropriate.

Liberalized divorce laws[154] have encouraged a therapeutic focus by some professionals involved in these cases, thereby providing an example of the relevance of therapeutic jurisprudence to family law. As the legal focus in these divorce cases has shifted away from questions of fault surrounding marital breakup, the mental health profession's emphasis has centered on the effects of divorce on family members. [155] In turn, these professionals have advocate therapeutic intervention in the legal aspects of divorce in an attempt to transform the process to a more positive experience.[156]

This therapeutic focus in divorce served as the basis for many states to create conciliation courts with the advent of the liberalized divorce laws. These courts provided separated or divorcing couples with marital counseling.[157] States justified the creation of the courts by asserting their need to provide services to families to ease the families crises.[158] The role of the court system was therapeutic in that the system attempted to assist families to adjust more positively to the post-divorce context.[159] The therapeutic focus, however, stalled in the 1960s due to an inability to reconcile the focus with the advocacy process and to a concern about cost.[160]

Family law jurisprudence can adopt and expand this service-oriented and therapeutic focus. To accomplish this family law reform, a significant part of the task becomes creating a jurisprudential model that assists judges to fashion therapeutic interventions and outcomes for individuals and families.

To establish criteria designed to enhance the therapeutic nature of any reform, family law reformers can look to proponents of therapeutic jurisprudence in the field of mental health law. These reformers already have identified some of the issues to promote in constructing a therapeutic jurisprudential paradigm. Some of these issues include the ability of the reform to empower individuals by allowing them to learn self-determining behavior and acquire decisionmaking skills, as well as the ability of the reform to empower judges to exercise sufficient controls to minimize abuse of the therapeutic measures.[161] In the field of family law, therapeutic justice should strive to protect families and children from present and future harms, to reduce emotional turmoil, to promote family harmony or preservation, and to provide individualized and efficient, effective justice.[162]

Incorporating the notion of therapeutic jurisprudence, however, raises questions about whether proponents of the therapeutic model are neutral, or whether they have a bias toward procedures and results designed to ensure their continued involvement in the resolution process.[163] Applying therapeutic justice to family law also invites concerns about whether judges and lawyers should deviate from the traditional advocacy model of adjudication,[164] a system that can further splinter already fragmented family relationships due to the adversarial and protracted nature of many court proceedings. In resolving family law matters, where the parties have some degree of relationship to one another and likely need to continue their relationship to some extent, adjudication may not represent the most appropriate dispute resolution technique.[165] On the other hand, recognizing that adjudication is available as even a last resort can compel the parties in family law proceedings to adopt less extreme positions and to negotiate or mediate as dispute resolution techniques.[166] Mediation itself in related-party cases can prove a therapeutic process.[167]

The therapeutic jurisprudence perspective, or assessing the therapeutic impact of adjudication,[168] offers a useful philosophy around which to structure family law decisionmaking. Applying the notion of therapeutic jurisprudence does not mean that the law serves predominantly therapeutic ends, nor does it suggest that courts avoid other jurisprudential outcomes. An application of therapeutic jurisprudence to family law means that decisionmakers need to evaluate the therapeutic consequences of the application of substantive family law, as well as the therapeutic effects of court rules, practices, and procedures.[169] This concern about the therapeutic nature of family law decisionmaking, in combination with the application of the ecology of human development paradigm, underlies the interdisciplinary approach to family law jurisprudence proposed in this Article.

III. Expanding the Role of Social Science in the Law: An Ecological and Therapeutic Paradigm for Family Law Jurisprudence

The American macrosystem has evolved into one in which the judiciary is the arbitrator in most domains of family and community life.[170] Thus, perhaps unwittingly, family law decisionmakers, including judges and masters, play a critical role in shaping social policy.[171] Because the law compels parties involved in family legal matters to utilize the court system, the system has a corresponding responsibility to resolve these issues in a helpful way.[172] An approach to family law jurisprudence that structures decisionmaking by applying the ecology of human development paradigm, buttressed by notions of therapeutic jurisprudence, provides a functional family law jurisprudential model. This type of decisionmaking has the potential to facilitate problem-solving and to positively enhance the quality of parties daily lives, thereby rendering a more effective outcome for individuals and families.[173]

The ecological perspective conceptualizes individual and family development as a process that occurs as a result of the nurturance and feedback that individuals receive on a daily basis from their interpersonal relationships.[174] To be effective as a family law decisionmaking model, advocates, parties, and human services providers[175] must identify for decisionmakers the types and strengths of the microsystem relationships within which people function, or the relationships between and among family members. In addition, decisionmakers need to understand family members mesosystem relationships, or relationships between individuals and aspects of their immediate environment, such as neighborhoods, schools, and religious organizations. For example, in a custody proceeding, the judge needs to understand the degree of parental participation in their children's schooling.

According to the ecological perspective, development also occurs both directly and indirectly as a result of influences outside the family, or resulting from macrosystem influences, such as the parents employment setting.[176] As a consequence, advocates themselves must understand and elucidate for decisionmakers the effects of macrosystem influences on the family. In a custody proceeding, for example, the judge needs to know time demands of parental employment relative to time available for parents to engage in child-rearing activities.

Utilizing an ecological approach to family law jurisprudence implies that decisionmakers appreciate the importance of socially rich environments for family members, including environments that provide support to families and children through a mix of formal and informal relationships.[177] In addition, decisionmakers must recognize the interactions of individuals within a system and between systems over time and across the course of a lifetime, as each system participant continually adjusts to the other.[178] The responsibility of family law decisionmakers to foster supportive environments for individuals and families by adopting an ecological and therapeutic jurisprudential framework, then, challenges decisionmakers to look beyond the individual litigants involved in any family law matter, to holistically examine the larger social environments in which the participants live, and to fashion legal remedies that strengthen a family's supportive relationships. Decisionmakers must attempt to facilitate linkages for the litigants between and among as many systems in their lives as possible.

The adversarial nature of traditional methods of family law adjudication can further fragment the relationship between family law litigants. A court system that accommodates a range of dispute resolution techniques, including negotiation, mediation, and adjudication, is important to ecological and therapeutic family law jurisprudence. These methods enable judges to strike an appropriate balance between the parties own resolution of a family legal matter by their private ordering or agreement and full court trial of family law issues. Judges must have the ability to direct the parties to the most effective dispute resolution techniques for their particular situation.[179]

To positively affect family members behavior, thereby achieving a therapeutic outcome, family law remedies must reflect an integrated approach to family legal issues.[180] This means that decisionmakers must consider all of the parties related family legal proceedings,[181] as well as all of the institutions or organizations potentially affecting the behavior of families and children, including the community, peer groups, educational institutions, and religious organizations. Judges must know the neighborhoods of the families and children whose lives the courts influence in order to conduct this mesosystem and exosystem analysis.[182] This need for connection to the community also challenges the judiciary and the courts to become leaders in the community and to attempt to build procedures, dispositions, and structures that foster extended-family and community responsibility.[183]

In an effort to establish and nurture linkages between and among the microsystems, mesosystems, and exosystems within which family members participate, family law advocates, decisionmakers, and services providers must coordinate their efforts to assist individuals and families. This need for collaboration may result in shifting to social services[184] agencies external or adjunct to the court system some of the court's functions.[185] In the process of attempts at timely agency intervention to resolve families problems, however, [p]eople should not have to go to court to get help.[186] Society as a whole must begin to acknowledge that this type of intervention and support is therapeutic for families, rather than viewing the intervention as an indication that families have failed.[187] The fact that service agencies in our society generally are very highly specialized, with little integration among the various service agencies and with an emphasis on treatment of problems rather than on problem prevention,[188] complicates this facet of an ecological and therapeutic approach to family law decisionmaking.[189] On the other hand, the need for collaboration with other agencies does not mean that courts must relinquish their role as the last resort arbiter[190] of fundamental legal questions. To the contrary, courts must insist on maintaining this function, as this belongs uniquely to the adjudicative process. [191] An ecological and therapeutic approach to family law jurisprudence, however, does modify longstanding notions of adjudication.

Advocates and parties to disputes generally perceive adjudication as focused. They ask the judge to determine whether one party has a right or duty, rather than  request the judge to devise alternatives for the parties.[192] Adjudication of family legal proceedings in an ecological and therapeutic jurisprudential model, however, compels a judge to consider alternatives. The judge must attempt to establish as many linkages as possible between and among various systems within which family members participate.

In contrast to the resolution of disputes in a piecemeal process, where the judge's power to decide extends only to the issues presented,[193] application of the interdisciplinary family law jurisprudential model encourages judges to consider all of a family's legal proceedings and related issues. This type of problem identification enables judges to develop a holistic assessment of the family's legal and social needs and to devise more comprehensive legal remedies

Traditionally, judges conduct fact-finding at some distance from the social settings of the cases they decide.[194] This isolation can render judges' fact-finding misguided and uninformed. Pursuant to an ecological and therapeutic jurisprudential paradigm, judges' involvement with the community and its organizations enables the judges to understand the contextual basis for their fact-finding. This contextualized fact-finding allows judges to more realistically and effectively address litigants needs.

Finally, traditional notions of adjudication make no provisions for policy review, as judges base their decisions on precedent and behavior that predates the litigation.[195] Acknowledging that judges decisions in family legal proceedings constitute family intervention, the remedies judges fashion in an interdisciplinary jurisprudential paradigm need to reflect policies that support families.

Application of both the ecology of human development perspective and notions of therapeutic justice to the resolution of family legal proceedings provides a jurisprudential paradigm for family law decisionmaking that empowers the court. This jurisprudential framework offers a means for courts to approach family problems in a systematic manner and to more effectively resolve the many and complex family legal matters they face. The distinctiveness of the judicial process its expenditure of social resources on individual complaints, one at a time is what unfits the courts for much of the important work . . . . Retooling the judicial process to cope with the new responsibilities of the courts means enhancing their capacity to function more systematically in terms of general categories that transcend individual cases. Some . . . innovations are required.[196]

An interdisciplinary jurisprudential approach can refit the courts now, as well as adequately prepare the courts to effectively address the novel and complex family legal challenges of the future.

## Conclusion

This Article has proposed an interdisciplinary jurisprudential paradigm that provides a common analytic framework for the resolution of all family legal proceedings. The paradigm assists family law decisionmakers to account for the diversity among individuals, legal issues, social issues, and other related matters that constitute the cases before them and that create the plurality and richness of American society. The paradigm can operate within any decisionmaking structure or system for resolving family legal matters. As such, the ecological and therapeutic jurisprudential paradigm can enjoy broad and universal application.

Because parties seeking resolution of family legal matters entrust judges to make critical decisions affecting individuals and families daily lives, judges in these cases must be more than triers of fact. Family law decisionmakers must embrace as a goal of family law jurisprudence the need to strengthen individuals and families and to enhance their functioning. This objective challenges decisionmakers to examine the family holistically, identifying how family members interact with other aspects of the family ecology at the present time and over the course of time. Judges must know and understand the backgrounds and communities from which family law litigants and their legal issues emerge.

A novel and expanded role for social science in the law can assist with this task. Applying the ecology of human development paradigm to structure family law decisionmaking allows judges to identify the systems within which individuals and families function, as well as the organizations and human services agencies that can assist families in a therapeutic manner. In fashioning their legal remedies, judges must establish linkages between individuals and the various systems within which they operate. These remedies can strengthen families functioning by providing families with necessary support.

This Article has attempted to respond to calls for a change in legal perspective in family law decisionmaking,[197] as well as challenges to enhance cooperation between lawyers and social scientists concerned with family law and public policy.[198] Social science has contributed to the law in diverse ways since the beginning of this century. As society prepares to move into the next century, application of this interdisciplinary paradigm to resolve family legal proceedings represents an appropriate evolution in the collaboration between law and the social sciences. While the American family may face an uncertain future,[199] history assures us that some form of the family is certain to endure. An interdisciplinary paradigm for family law jurisprudence that applies the ecology of human development perspective and notions of therapeutic justice can ensure that family law decisionmakers and the courts are a source of strength and support for the continued and enhanced functioning of American families.

*Barbara A. Babb, J.D., is Associate Professor of Law and Director, Center for Families, Children and the Courts at the University of Baltimore School of Law.*

## Notes

[1]    THEODORE M. BENDITT, *Legal Realism, in* LAW AS A RULE AND PRINCIPLE 1-21 (1978), *reprinted in* DALE A. NANCE, LAW AND JUSTICE: CASES AND READINGS ON THE AMERICAN LEGAL SYSTEM 69 (1994)

[2]    *Id.* at 70.

[3]    Gary B. Melton & Brian L. Wilcox, *Changes in Family Law and Family Life: Challenges for Psychology*, 44 AM. PSYCHOLOGIST 1213, 1214 (1989)

[4]    Family law in this Article means a comprehensive approach to family law subject matter jurisdiction, including jurisdiction over cases involving divorce, separation, and annulment; property distribution; child custody and visitation; alimony and child support; paternity, adoption, and termination of parental rights; juvenile delinquency; child abuse and child neglect; domestic violence; criminal non-support; name change; guardianship of minors and disabled persons; withholding or withdrawal of life-sustaining medical procedures, involuntary admissions, and emergency evaluations. *See, e.g.*, DEL. CODE ANN. tit. 10 §§ 921-928 (1975 & Supp. 1994); HAW. REV. STAT. §§ 571-11 to 571-14 (1993); MD. CODE ANN., [FAM. LAW] § 1-201 (1991 & Supp. 1996); NEV. REV. STAT. ANN. § 3.223 (Michie Supp. 1995); N.J. REV. STAT. ANN. § 2A:434-8 (West 1987); S.C. CODE ANN. § 20-7-736 (Law Co-op. 1985 & Supp. 1996); VA. CODE ANN. § 16.1-241 (Michie Supp. 1996)

[5]    Melton & Wilcox, *supra* note 3, at 1214. Another scholar has critiqued the incoherence between the social reality of families and family law:

The current incoherence between family reality and the images of family in law expose the dominant ideology [of the traditional family model] and its role in policy formation. Refusing to address and to assess the continued viability of ideological assumptions, politicians and pundits resort to condemnation and to repressive policy suggestions. This pattern of reaction to changing family behavior should raise questions about the responsive capabilities of our law-making institutions.

Martha L.A. Fineman, *Masking Dependency: The Political Role of Family Rhetoric*, 81 VA. L. REV. 2181, 2186 (1995).

[6]    Melton & Wilcox, *supra* note 3, at 1214; *cf.* Anne C. Dailey, *Federalism and Families*, 143 U. PA. L. REV. 1787, 1790 (1995) (arguing that state legislatures and courts fashion laws and decisions in the domestic relations area by reflecting shared or community values about family life).

[7]    ST. JUSTICE INST., ST. CT. CASELOAD STAT. ANN. REP.. 1992 (Feb. 1994), *cited in* Amy Stevens, *The Busines of Law: Lawyers and Clients; More Than Just Torts*, WALL ST. J., July 1, 1994,

at B6; *see also* Gary B. Melton, *Children, Families, and the Courts in the Twenty-First Century*, 66 S. CAL. L. REV. 1993, 2006-07 (1993) (predicting that family law cases will increase and are likely to become more difficult).

⁸   SUSAN MOLLER OKIN, JUSTICE, GENDER, AND THE FAMILY 130 (1989).

⁹   *See* Frances E. Olsen, *The Myth of State Intervention in the Family*, 18 U. MICH. J.L. REF. 835, 854-55 (1985) (arguing that courts base their decisions in family law cases on policy considerations, which decisions thereafter affect the nature of family roles and relationships).

¹⁰   URIE BRONFENBRENNER, THE ECOLOGY OF HUMAN DEVELOPMENT (1979).

¹¹   David Wexler defines therapeutic jurisprudence as follows:

> Therapeutic jurisprudence is the study of the role of the law as a therapeutic agent. It looks at the law as a social force that, like it or not, may produce therapeutic or anti-therapeutic consequences. Such consequences may flow from substantive rules, legal procedures, or from the behavior of legal actors (lawyers or judges).

David B. Wexler, *Putting Mental Health into Mental Health Law: Therapeutic Jurisprudence*, *in* ESSAYS IN THERAPEUTIC JURISPRUDENCE 3, 8 (David B. Wexler & Bruce J. Winick eds., 1991)

¹⁴⁵   Monahan & Walker, *supra* note 107, at 489 (footnote omitted).

¹⁴⁶   Michael A. Town, The Unified Family Court: Therapeutic Justice for Families and Children 1 (Mar. 11, 1994) (transcript available in Chicago Bar Association Building).

¹⁴⁷   Irving E. Sigel, *The Ethics of Intervention*, *in* CHANGING FAMILIES 1, 8-9 (Irving E. Sigel & Luis M. Laosa eds., 1983).

¹⁴⁸   *See* Donald B. King, *Accentuate the Positive--Eliminate the Negative*, 31 FAM. & CONCILIATION CTS. REV. 9 (1993); *see also* Judith T. Younger, *Responsible Parents and Good Children*, 14 L. & INEQ. J.. 489, 501 (1996) (arguing that American families face an uncertain future, such that "[t] he need to strengthen and stabilize them seems obvious and calls for a change in legal perspective").

¹⁴⁹   Wexler, *supra* note 11, at 8; *see also* David B. Wexler & Bruce J. Winick, *Therapeutic Jurisprudence as a New Approach to Mental Health Law Policy Analysis and Research*, 45 U. MIAMI L. REV. 979, 989 (1991) ("The therapeutic jurisprudence perspective can provide a useful lens through which to view an existing body of literature in order to discover new value and applications."). A focus on the therapeutic aspects of jurisprudence calls for an expanded notion of jurisprudence:

> To speak of the therapeutic in a jurisprudential sense--to speak of it as a possible form of public discourse in any sense--may seem strange to many, because at first blush the very concept of the therapeutic would seem to be unremittingly private. After all, therapy is, or once was, based upon the concept of a wholly private space in which patient and therapist would explore, and perhaps remodulate, aspects of personality.

Kenneth Anderson, *A New Class of Lawyers: The Therapeutic as Rights Talk*, 96 COLUM. L. REV. 1062, 1081 (1996) (footnote omitted).

¹⁵⁰   Wexler, *supra* note 11, at 8 (footnote omitted).

¹⁵¹   David B. Wexler, *Therapeutic Jurisprudence and the Criminal Courts*, 35 WM. & MARY L. REV. 279, 280 (1993). A focus on therapeutic jurisprudence may assist with law reform efforts:

> When there is a substantial literature available, this type of research ... basically relates a body of relevant behavioral science to a body of law and explores the fit between the two; in the process, certain legal schemes and arrangements may stand out as comporting particularly well with therapeutic interests, and others may seem less satisfactory from a therapeutic viewpoint. If the therapeutically-appropriate legal arrangements are not normatively objectionable on other grounds, those arrangements may point the way toward law reform.

David B. Wexler & Bruce J. Winick, *Therapeutic Jurisprudence as a New Research Tool*, *in* ESSAYS IN THERAPEUTIC JURISPRUDENCE 303 (David B. Wexler & Bruce J. Winick eds., 1991).

[152]  Wexler, *supra* note 151, at 281.

[153]  David B. Wexler, *Therapeutic Jurisprudence and Changing Conceptions of Legal Scholarship*, 11 BEHAV. SCI. & L.. 17, 21 (1993).

[154]  *See supra* note 43 and accompanying text.

[155]  The social work profession now has an expanded role relative to many family legal proceedings:

As the number of families going through the legal process has increased, social workers have become involved in an attempt to make the process less adversarial so that family ties can continue. Counselors and therapists, who worked in roles supportive of the adjudicative function, have become more central to the family dissolution process.

Cahn, *supra* note 57, at 1091-92 (footnote omitted).

[156]  FINEMAN, *supra* note 60, at 90; *see also* WEITZMAN, *supra* note 23, at 16-17 (discussing the efforts in California in the early 1960s of Professors Herma Hill Kay and Aidan Gough to restructure the divorce process to reduce hostility and to create a Family Court to "help couples divorce with the least possible harm"). *But see, e.g.*, J. Herbie DiFonzo, *No-Fault Marital Dissolution: The Bitter Triumph of Naked Divorce*, 31 SAN DIEGO L. REV. 519, 520 (1994) (proposing that "[t]herapeutic divorce represented compelled nondivorce, holding families together through 'directive' psychiatry").

[157]  FINEMAN, *supra* note 60, at 151; *see* J. Herbie DiFonzo, *Coercive Conciliation: Judge Paul W. Alexander and the Movement for Therapeutic Divorce*, 25 U. TOL. L. REV. 535 (1994) (detailing the historical development of therapeutic divorce reform and early family courts and suggesting why the effort stalled); DiFonzo, *supra* note 156, at 520 (tracing the origins of the no-fault divorce movement and the history of conciliation courts as precursors to more recent family courts).

[158]  FINEMAN, *supra* note 60, at 151.

[159]  *Id.* at 152.

[160]  DiFonzo, *supra* note 157, at 575.

[161]  Wexler & Winick, *supra* note 151, at 309, 317.

[162]  Town, *supra* note 146, at 3, 21.

[163]  FINEMAN, *supra* note 60, at 164.

[164]  DAVID B. WEXLER, THERAPEUTIC JURISPRUDENCE: THE LAW AS A THERAPEUTIC AGENT 18 (1990).

[165]  Ralph Cavanagh & Austin Sarat, *Thinking About Courts: Toward and Beyond a Jurisprudence of Judicial Competence*, 14 L. & SOC'Y REV. 371, 395 (1980). The authors criticize adjudication as a proper method of fact-finding in "related-party" cases. *d.* at 396.

[166]  *Id.* at 399, 400.

[167]  *Id.* at 401.

[168]  Wexler & Winick, *supra* note 149, at 981.

[169]  *Id.* at 1004.

[170]  James Garbarino et al., *Social Policy, Children, and Their Families*, in CHILDREN AND FAMILIES IN THE SOCIAL ENVIRONMENT 271, 291 (James Garbarino et al. eds., 2d ed. 1992); *see also* Weinstein, *supra* note 38, at 254 ("Increasingly, we depend on the secular legal system to tell us how to live.").

[171]  Garbarino et al., *supra* note 170, at 275-76 ("For our purposes, a policy is a statement or a set of statements intended to guide decisions, activities, or efforts that generally describe either desired (or undesired) outcomes and/or desired (or undesired) methods of achieving them."); *see also* DONALD L. HOROWITZ, THE COURTS AND SOCIAL POLICY 56 (1977) (defining social policy as "policy designed to affect the structure of social norms, social relations, or social decisionmaking"); Opening Remarks of Clark C. Abt, *in* THE USE/NONUSE/MISUSE OF APPLIED SOCIAL RESEARCH IN THE COURTS 1 (Michael J. Saks & Charles H. Baron eds., 1978) (arguing that judicial intervention in social policy has been increasing to encompass social problem solving); MORONEY, *supra* note 12, at

2 ("[S]ocial policy is concerned with a search for and an articulation of social objectives and the means to achieve these.").

[172] *See* King, *supra* note 148, at 9; *see also* Younger, *supra* note 148, at 501-02.

[173] *See* HENGGELER & BORDUIN, *supra* note 123, at 28; *see also* Wexler & Winick, *supra* note 149, at 984 ("If the therapeutically appropriate legal arrangements are not normatively objectionable on other grounds, those arrangements may point the way toward law reform.") (footnote omitted).

[174] James Garbarino & S. Holly Stocking, *The Social Context of Child Maltreatment, in* PROTECTING CHILDREN FROM ABUSE AND NEGLECT: DEVELOPING AND MAINTAINING EFFECTIVE SUPPORT SYSTEMS FOR FAMILIES 1, 6 (James Garbarino & S. Holly Stocking eds., 1980).

[175] *See* James Garbarino & Florence N. Long, *Developmental Issues in the Human Services, in* CHILDREN AND FAMILIES IN THE SOCIAL ENVIRONMENT 231, 232 (James Garbarino et al. eds., 2d ed. 1992) ("The term 'human services' encompasses a broad range of activities, programs, and agencies designed to meet the physical, intellectual, and social-emotional needs of individuals and families. These services are encountered primarily in microsystems ... or mesosystems (e.g., referral or liaison between agencies).")

[176] Garbarino & Stocking, *supra* note 174, at 4.

[177] *Id.* at 3.

[178] *Id.* at 5.

[179] Robert F. Peckham, *A Judicial Response to the Cost of Litigation: Case Management, Two-Stage Discovery Planning and Alternative Dispute Resolution*, 37 RUTGERS L. REV. 253, 255, 256 (1985). "A judge's duty has never been purely adjudication. Judges have long engaged in case and calendar management as well as court administration, mediation, regulation of the bar, and other professional activities." *Id.* at 261; *see also* Judith Resnik, *Managerial Judges*, 96 HARV. L. REV.. 374 (1982). Several justifications exist for the increasing use of alternative dispute resolution techniques in family law:

Although thus far change exists more in the literature than in practice, the appropriate role in family law for extra-judicial procedures such as mediation, arbitration, and representation of both spouses by a single attorney is a subject of great interest. Several factors account for this development. First, courts' resources have been strained by a dramatic increase in the amount of family litigation, and judicial time for the resolution of these disputes is seriously inadequate. Second, the capacity of adversary proceedings (the litigational model used in the United States) to handle these matters in a humane and effective fashion continues to be seriously questioned. Finally, the financial costs of litigation have become so burdensome that many people seek less costly alternatives.

Bruch, *supra* note 122, at 115 (footnote omitted). An examination of the form of state statutes regarding custody mediation provides an example of how widespread the use of alternative dispute resolution techniques in family law has become:

The majority of the [state] statutes [regarding custody mediation] are [ [ [sic] discretionary in nature, allowing for mediation upon the recommendation of the court or the request of one of the parties. Only eight states, including California, require the mediation of all contested custody issues. Some states are still in the process of implementing pilot programs in order to evaluate the effectiveness of custody mediation prior to a full-scale commitment.

Dane A. Gaschen, Note, *Mandatory Custody Mediation: The Debate over Its Usefulness Continues*, 10 OHIO ST. J. ON DISP. RESOL.. 469, 472 (1995) (finding that approximately 60% of the states have some form of custody mediation statute). On the other hand, judges must understand the social science research documenting the coercive and anti-therapeutic nature of alternative dispute resolution techniques in some circumstances, such as actions involving victims of domestic violence and their abusers. *Cf.* Grillo, *supra* note 62, at 1584-85 (discussing the role of mediation in situations involving victims of domestic violence).

[180] Melton, *supra* note 7, at 2003. The conclusion that judges in family legal proceedings already affect participants' behavior seems inescapable:

Because judges presumably are affecting therapeutic and rehabilitative consequences anyway, a therapeutic jurisprudence approach would suggest that, while they remain fully cognizant of their obligation to dispense justice according to principles of due process of law, judges should indeed try to become less lousy in their inescapable role as social worker.

Wexler, *supra* note 151, at 299.

[181] RUBIN & FLANGO, *supra* note 45, at 3.

[182] Melton, *supra* note 7, at 2004, 2044 n.272 (discussing the need for citizen advisory groups to provide input to the courts).

[183] *Id.* at 2004; *see also* Harry D. Krause, *Child Support Reassessed: Limits of Private Responsibility and the Public Interest, in* DIVORCE REFORM AT THE CROSSROADS 166 (Stephen D. Sugarman & Herma Hill Kay eds., 1990). Some fear, however, that courts may become too much like human services agencies if they attempt to perform these functions:

Retooling the judicial process to cope with the new responsibilities of the courts means enhancing their capacity to function more systematically in terms of general categories that transcend individual cases. Some such innovations are required. And yet, it would seem, there is a limit to the changes of this kind that courts can absorb and still remain courts…. The danger is that courts, in developing a capacity to improve on the work of other institutions, may become altogether too much like them.

HOROWITZ, *supra* note 171, at 298.

[184] *See* MORONEY, *supra* note 12, at 13 (defining social services "as those services designed to aid individuals and groups to meet their basic needs, to enhance social functioning, to develop their potential, and to promote general well-being") (footnote omitted).

[185] Melton, *supra* note 7, at 2001; *see also* Resnik, *supra* note 179, at 438-40 (discussing the issues of alternative dispute centers and agency adjudication). Many barriers exist to attempts by courts and agencies to coordinate efforts to serve families:

Agencies and organizations often jealously guard their organizational turf and may be reluctant to relinquish some of the control they have over clients in traditional one-to-one relationships. Practitioners may be unwilling to share their functions with non-professionals. They may see central figures in personal social networks as incapable of dispensing help to needy families. New approaches that work to strengthen personal social networks may appear to be luxuries that most agencies cannot afford. What is more, efforts to promote and strengthen personal social networks raise the issues of confidentiality, autonomy, and privacy.

Garbarino & Stocking, *supra* note 174, at 11.

[186] Melton, *supra* note 7, at 2047.

[187] Americans tend to believe that reliance on social services or reliance on others for assistance constitutes an admission of failure:

It is apparent that all families make use of (and many more are in need of) some form of outside help in raising their children, yet we still maintain a myth of self-sufficiency. Since in reality we *are* dependent on each other, it makes little sense to perpetuate the myth that we are not. Valuing independence stigmatizes those individuals who use family services as well as those individuals who provide them. A new concept of the way in which families (and individuals) should interact with each other and the other elements of society is imperative. Why not acknowledge the interdependence that already exists? Why not see it as positive?

James Garbarino et al., *Who Owns the Children? An Ecological Perspective on Public Policy Affecting Children, in* LEGAL REFORMS AFFECTING CHILD & YOUTH SERVICES 43, 46-47 (Gary B. Melton ed., 1982) (footnote omitted).

[188] Anne Marie Tietjen, *Integrating Formal and Informal Support Systems: The Swedish Experience, in* PROTECTING CHILDREN FROM ABUSE AND NEGLECT: DEVELOPING AND

MAINTAINING EFFECTIVE SUPPORT SYSTEMS FOR FAMILIES 15, 17 (James Garbarino & S. Holly Stocking eds., 1980).

[189] *See* Edward F. Hennessey, *The Family, the Courts, and Mental Health Professionals*, 44 AM. PSYCHOLOGIST 1223, 1224 (1989) (advocating the need for therapeutic services due to the traumatic nature of many divorce and custody matters, as well as the importance of the fundamental familial rights courts must address in these cases); *see also* Peter Salem et al., *Parent Education as a Distinct Field of Practice: The Agenda for the Future*, 34 FAM. & CONCILIATION CTS. REV. 9 (1996) (examining issues of professional responsibility, accountability, standards, and procedures for the proliferation of parent education programs developed to help families deal with the difficult impact of separation and divorce, as well as the need for these programs to be court connected). "Most parent education programs are court connected in the sense that much of their support and referrals come from judges who hear cases arising out of separation and divorce. The legal system needs assistance in enabling parents to help their children." *Id.* at 18.

For examples of existing educational programs designed specifically to assist participants in family legal proceedings, see Larry Lehner, *Education for Parents Divorcing in California*, 32 FAM. & CONCILIATION CTS. REV. 50 (1994) (describing a variety of court-connected educational programs for family law litigants in California); Virginia Petersen & Susan B. Steinman, *Helping Children Succeed After Divorce: A Court-Mandated Education Program for Divorcing Parents*, 32 FAM. & CONCILIATION CTS. REV. 27 (1994) (discussing a mandatory parent education program in Ohio for divorcing couples with children, the goals of which include providing parents information about how to help their children with the divorce process, about divorce-specific resources and services, about options for problem solving, and about how to remain independent of the court); Carol Roeder-Esser, *Families in Transition: A Divorce Workshop*, 32 FAM. & CONCILIATION CTS. REV. 40 (1994) (describing a court-connected mandatory divorce orientation program in Kansas that focuses on the psychological, social, legal, and child-related effects of divorce, as well as enumerating optional educational programs on other topics, including step parenting, grandparents' visitation, and single parenting); Andrew Schepard, *War and P.E.A.C.E.: A Preliminary Report and a Model Statute on an Interdisciplinary Educational Program for Divorcing and Separating Parents*, 27 U. MICH. J.L. REFORM 131 (1993) (describing a court connected interdisciplinary parent education program in New York for parents involved in custody, child support, and divorce and separation, and detailing the cooperation among the courts, mental health professionals, and educators); Bill Miller, *Divorce's Hard Lessons: Court-Ordered Classes Focus on the Children*, WASH. POST,, Nov. 21, 1994, at A1, A12 (describing parent education programs in Maryland, Virginia, and Washington, D.C.).

For a discussion of court-based mediation programs, see Milne, *supra* note 65, at 68-69. *See also* ROBERT A. BARUCH BUSH, MEDIATION INVOLVING JUVENILES: ETHICAL DILEMMAS AND POLICY QUESTIONS 45 (1991) (discussing the use of mediation in disputes wherein one of the parties is a juvenile).

[190] Melton, *supra* note 7, at 2045.

[191] *See* HOROWITZ, *supra* note 171, at 298 ("The danger is that courts, in developing a capacity to improve on the work of other institutions, may become altogether too much like them.").

[192] *Id.* at 34.

[193] *Id.* at 35.

[194] *Id.* at 45.

[195] *Id.* at 51.

[196] *Id.* at 298.

[197] Younger, *supra* note 148, at 501.

[198] Ramsey & Kelly, *supra* note 77, at 685.

[199] Younger, *supra* note 148, at 501 (footnote omitted).

# [3]

# Rights Myopia in Child Welfare

## Clare Huntington

### Introduction

One of the central debates in family law focuses on the proper balance between parents' rights and children's rights. Although this debate plays out in numerous and varied contexts, including child custody,[1] religious freedom,[2] immigration proceedings,[3] education,[4] criminal law,[5] and the participation of the United States in international treaties,[6] the debate is particularly vociferous and the stakes especially high in the context of the child welfare system. In that context, the debate between advocates of parents' rights and children's rights is charged and polarized. Elizabeth Bartholet, for example, contends that a pervasive "blood bias" in the child welfare system sacrifices children's futures.[7] She alleges that the state is overly deferential to parents' rights and far too unwilling to remove children from homes where they have been abused or neglected.[8] To Dorothy Roberts, on the other hand, the state intervenes too readily, especially in the lives of African American families. Roberts argues that the disproportionate number of African American children in the child welfare system leads to African American families being "systematically demolished."[9]

To be sure, the debate between advocates of parents' rights and children's rights is complex. Those who promote children's rights do not uniformly favor state intervention. For example, some scholars and advocates contend that the unwarranted removal of a child from her biological parent is as much a violation of the rights of the child as of the parent.[10] In this way, the debate could more accurately be described as one between family preservationists (those who disfavor state intervention with a bias toward removal) and child protectionists (those who favor aggressive state intervention, even if it leads to removal).

Regardless of the frame, the debate misses the mark because it mistakenly privileges rights. As currently implemented, the rights-based model of child welfare protects neither parent nor child in the typical case. To give just three examples: First, despite parents' rights, there is substantial evidence that official decisions are often driven by racial biases and political expediency. Second, procedural safeguards and court adjudications that are designed to protect rights often do not lead to careful, reliable decisions. Third, state intervention to protect a child's right to be free from abuse and neglect may be essential in some cases, but also comes at a high cost to the child in the typical child welfare case.

Moreover, adding resources to the current system will not "fix" it because this will not resolve the fundamental problems associated with a myopic focus on rights within the child welfare system. The dominant conception of rights assumes the rights bearer is an autonomous individual seeking freedom from the state. Parents in the child welfare system need more than autonomy. They need concrete assistance. Children also need assistance, although most do not need state intervention in the form it is now provided. Thus, rights obscure the role of poverty in abuse and neglect, and relying on rights does not ensure poor parents will receive the help they need. Additionally, rights will never be the primary way to produce good results for families because the rights-based model creates, or at least perpetuates, an adversarial process for decisionmaking. This adversarial process impedes the thoughtful group collaboration among parents, children, and the state that is essential to devising beneficial solutions.

Indeed, the adversarial system, which is a direct outgrowth of a focus on rights, disserves the goals of both preservationists and protectionists. Preservationists contend that a misconstrued articulation of children's rights and de-emphasis of parents' rights results in too much intervention in the home in the form of removal (or threatened removal). Child protectionists claim that too much emphasis on parents' rights and a misconstrued articulation of children's rights results in too little intervention in the home. The reality is that the emphasis on rights has led to the wrong kind of involvement in the lives of troubled families, resulting in over- and underprotection of everyone's rights and a serious misallocation of resources. In this way, rights have created a largely ineffective process for addressing child abuse and neglect.

A new model, and a new process to implement that model, is needed. In searching for this new model, I contend that the central question is not where to draw the line between preservation and protection (the concern that animates the debate over parents' rights and children's rights), but rather how best to help families address the serious problems underlying child abuse and neglect.

To this end, in lieu of a rights-based model, I argue that a problem-solving model would better serve the goals of the child welfare system. In this new model, the substantive goals of the child welfare system – to promote family preservation and ensure the safety of children – would remain, but the means for achieving these goals would be different. The new model would focus on solving the problems underlying the abuse and neglect, viewing such abuse and neglect largely as products of poverty, not parental pathology. Additionally, the problem-solving model would generate a new process that would foster collaboration between the state and families.

Thus, at heart this Article is about the relationship between legal models and the processes that different models generate. To put it most simply, a rights-based model leads to an adversarial process, whereas a problem-solving model leads to a collaborative process. I argue the latter is better suited to serving the interests of both parents and children.

Although a number of collaborative processes could satisfy the problem-solving model, in this Article I focus on one especially promising process: family group conferencing. A form of restorative justice, family group conferencing is a legal process for resolving child welfare cases without relying on a family court judge as the decisionmaker. After a report of child abuse or neglect has been substantiated, the state convenes a conference with immediate and extended family members, and other important people in the child's life, such as teachers or religious leaders, to decide how to protect the child and support the parents. At the conference, the family and community members devise a plan for protecting the child and addressing the issues that led to the abuse and neglect, such as substance abuse, lack of housing, or inadequate child care. The participants of the family group conference and the state then work together to provide necessary supports to the family. By concentrating on the underlying problems, family group conferencing both focuses on the root causes of abuse and neglect and also fosters collaboration among parents, children, and the state.

\* \* \* \*

## II. Limitations of the Rights-based Model

Despite the theoretical promise of parents' rights and children's rights (both preservationist and protectionist strains), rights do not sufficiently protect parents or children. A solely rights-based approach to the issues that surface in the child welfare system is misguided and, for the majority of cases, fails to devise effective solutions for parents or children. This part explores why this is, first identifying three failures of rights as implemented, and then examining two conceptual shortcomings of rights.

Before exploring the limitations of rights in the child welfare system, however, I want to clarify the cabined nature of my critique. First, I limit my critique to the context of the child welfare system. For example, I do not intend to undervalue the importance of rights to claims of racial and gender equality.[97] Second, parents' rights and preservationist children's rights play a crucial role in the child welfare system, creating an important divide between the state and the family. I do not advocate weakening this divide such that it is easier for the state to insert itself into the lives of families, especially poor families.[98] Instead, my argument concerns the state's interaction with families who are already in the system. The argument assumes the state already has demonstrated an adequate need to intervene. My point is that some families face real problems – substance abuse, seriously inadequate housing, lack of appropriate child care – and that these problems can lead or contribute to child abuse and neglect. The issue is how the state will address these problems. In such cases, a myopic focus on rights risks obscuring the larger picture of the issues affecting families in the child welfare system, in turn doing a considerable disservice to both parents and children. Thus, my critique is largely about the incompleteness of parents' rights and children's rights, not the absolute disutility of such rights.

### A. The Failure of Rights as Implemented

This subpart sets aside the question of the utility of rights as a conceptual matter, and instead examines the rights-based model as it is currently implemented. Looking at rights through this real world lens, I conclude that a solely rights-based system does not produce good results for parents or children. I focus on three main limitations of rights as implemented: the failure of rights to protect sufficiently against racially and politically driven decisionmaking, the limited effectiveness of procedural safeguards and court adjudications, and the high cost to children of state intervention.

Rights do not protect against racially and politically driven decisionmaking. As implemented, rights do not prevent state intervention based on impermissible grounds, such as race. It is undisputed that racial disparities in the child welfare system exist and are marked. For example, in 2002, although African American children accounted for 15 percent of all children in the U.S., they accounted for 25 percent of substantiated maltreatment reports.[99] By contrast, white children accounted for 79 percent of all children and 51 percent of substantiated reports.[100] African American children enter foster care at a higher rate[101] and leave at a lower rate.[102]

The cause of these racial disparities is a hotly contested issue. Some scholars contend the disparities are due to racial bias.[103] Indeed, there is evidence that African American children are removed at greater rates than similarly situated white and Latino children,[104] and receive less effective services.[105] Other scholars contend that the disparities are explained by differential poverty rates.[106] If the disparities are the result of racial bias, then it is clear that, as implemented, parents' rights and preservationist children's rights are not sufficiently protecting African American families from such bias. If the disparities are due to poverty, rights are still not the proper tool for protecting parents and children.[107]

Additionally, removal of children is often heavily influenced by political and social forces. For example, there is evidence that foster care placements soar in the aftermath of well-publicized cases of abuse,[108] and placement rates vary from state to state, even when the states are geographically proximate, and economically and politically similar.[109] State agencies also are more likely to err on the side of caution when determining if abuse or neglect has occurred, thus leading to the removal of many children who could have stayed home.[110] If rights were sufficiently protective in practice, such variances would not occur because only considerations pertaining to particular parents and children, not external political and social factors, would affect the decision.

Procedural safeguards and court adjudications are insufficiently protective of parents. Procedural safeguards that should, in theory, guard against improper removals are virtually meaningless for many parents because they are often bypassed in real life. For example, most procedural protections, such as the assistance of counsel, are not triggered during the early and often dispositive stages of a case.[111] Parents often consent to a "voluntary" arrangement, agreeing to participate in specified programs and sometimes placing a child with an extended family member, in exchange for the state not placing the child in foster care.[112] Or a parent may agree to the placement of a child with child protective services for up to six months, during which period there is no court review.[113] Although these cases are ultimately reviewed by a court, any unnecessary placement negatively affects both parent and child.[114]

If and when a parent makes it into court, she is unlikely to receive meaningful review of her case. Lawyers for parents often do not provide adequate representation,[115] and most courts simply do not have sufficient time or resources to dedicate to these cases. Consider one anecdotal description of family court:

> In many jurisdictions, particularly those in large urban areas, the courts are overwhelmed by the size of their caseloads: Overtaxed judges hear "lists" of up to 100 cases a day, giving each case a maximum of five minutes. Families are sworn in en masse at the bar of the court, with little sense that what they say to the judge thereafter constitutes sworn testimony, rather than a free-for-all conversation. Judges bark at the parties, calling parents "Mom" or "Dad," rather than by their names. Orders typically are entered without any articulation of findings of fact, conclusions of law, or even a recitation of the relevant legal standards in justification. If a party determines that she needs more than five minutes of the court's attention to resolve a disputed issue – even an issue as important as whether a child should remain in foster care, whether a parent should be allowed to visit her child, or whether the state should be required to provide the parent with supportive services – she will have to wait months to get a new date in court.[116]

Thus, although parents' rights theoretically entitle parents to certain procedural safeguards and court review of the state's actions, in practice these entitlements offer little protection due to "voluntary" arrangements, overburdened courts, and poor counsel.

The state intervention required to enforce protectionist children's rights comes at a high cost to children. Protectionist children's rights, while appealing in theory, do not necessarily protect children. To begin, despite the widespread appointment of guardians ad litem and the changes required by ASFA, the child welfare system does not serve the vast majority of children well. As discussed more fully below, only about 10 percent of cases in the child welfare system involve severe abuse or neglect.[117] For these children, removal and placement in a foster home is likely the best outcome because of the danger in the home. But for the remaining cases, although some intervention may be necessary, intervening by removing the child and placing her in foster care comes at high cost.

In addition to the pain associated with the (even temporary) loss of a biological family, consider the impact on a child of living in foster care. Once a child is placed in foster care, she is likely to remain there for nineteen months, with a substantial likelihood she will remain in care for three, four, or even five years.[118] Approximately half of the children in foster care return to their biological families, but of the remaining children, only 18 percent are adopted; the remainder live with relatives, are emancipated, or live in legal limbo.[119] Children who are freed for adoption often must wait years[120] before being adopted because there are not enough adoptive families.[121] Therefore, adoptions do not keep pace with the terminations of parental rights.

Children in foster care face many difficulties, both while in care and later as adults. A child in foster care is often moved from one home to another.[122] Even if eventually reunified with a biological parent or placed in an adoptive home, children who were once in foster care typically suffer economic, educational, and psychological hardship.[123] Indeed, a recent study found the rate of post-traumatic stress disorder (PTSD) among adults previously placed in foster care to be twice as high as the incidence in combat veterans.[124] In addition to PTSD, former foster care children suffer from depression, social phobia, panic syndrome, and anxiety disorders.[125] Even if the removal is temporary, the experience of being removed from a home is deeply traumatizing to a child.[126]

These studies often do not control for prior abuse or neglect. Thus, it could be argued that the poor outcomes are a result of abuse and neglect at the hands of the original parent and not because of the subsequent placement into foster care. At the very least, however, it is clear that foster care does not improve the lives of most of the children placed in that system. And there is good reason to believe that foster care is a contributing factor to the poor outcomes studied. While in foster care, there is substantial evidence that children are at risk for additional abuse, particularly sexual abuse. For example, a study in Maryland found that foster families were more likely to be reported for physical abuse, sexual abuse, and neglect than nonfoster families.[127] Of the abuse and neglect occurring in foster care, nearly half (48.7 percent) involved sexual abuse.[128] In addition, children in foster care are likely to suffer from medically related neglect. From a sample of foster children in California, New York, and Pennsylvania, the U.S. General Accounting Office estimated that "12 percent of young foster children received no routine health care, 34 percent received no immunizations, and 32 percent had at least some identified health needs that were not met."[129]

In sum, any theory of protectionist children's rights necessarily entails greater state intervention in the family, and research demonstrates that such intervention comes at a very high cost to the well-being of children. For children who have suffered severe abuse and neglect at the hands of their biological parents, the foster care system may well be a better alternative. But for children who are removed from their homes for less serious abuse or neglect, placement in the foster care system is seldom a good solution. Although it is tempting to idealize a better home for the child – a loving, stable home with supportive adults – foster care too often fails to provide children with such homes. Further, the experience of being removed from the original home is typically so debilitating, and the ill effects are so long-lasting, that even a supportive foster home cannot compensate for the devastating experience of removal and the loss of a family.

* * * These are just three of the problems with the rights-based model as currently implemented. Certainly others exist.[130] One question, then, is whether these problems could be fixed while still retaining the rights-based model. It could be argued that an infusion of resources into the child welfare system would correct these problems by, for example, providing adequate counsel for parents and sufficient time for judges to hear cases. While it is possible that additional resources or other changes would at least mitigate the problems, such changes would not address the more fundamental, conceptual shortcomings of rights. It is to these shortcomings that I now turn.

*B. The Conceptual Shortcomings of Rights*

Regardless of the available resources, a solely rights-based framework is inadequate to address the problems in the child welfare system for two central reasons. First, rights assume autonomy, and most parents in the child welfare system need tangible assistance rather than autonomy.[131] In this way, rights obscure the role of poverty in the child welfare system. Second, rights create a win/lose mentality that fuels an adversarial process and an adversarial relationship between parents and the state, rather than fostering the true collaboration needed to address the difficult issues facing families.

Rights value autonomy, not assistance, and thus obscure the role of poverty. The common conception of rights is that rights-bearers are "separate, autonomous, and responsible individuals entitled to exercise rights and obliged to bear liabilities for their actions."[132] This conception of rights does not advance the interests of children in the child welfare system because children simply do not benefit from this sort of autonomy. Although there is certainly a range of capabilities among children, depending at least on age and individual development, it is a truism that most children rely on adults for their daily needs. They are not autonomous legally or practically.[133]

Perhaps surprisingly, adults involved in the child welfare system also do not fall within, and are not served by, the dominant understanding of an autonomous rights-bearing individual. As Jennifer Nedelsky argues, it is a fundamental misconception of human nature to view individuals as wholly separate from one another and from the state. Contending that the dominant conception of rights is one-sided in its emphasis on individualism, rather than relationships,[134] she identifies our dependency relationships – between parents and children, students and teachers, and state and citizens – as essential to fostering the real autonomy needed in a democratic society (the ability to engage in the polity).[135] To Nedelsky, the question is how to structure rights such that they foster these autonomy-enhancing relationships.[136] Nedelsky contends that the dominant conception of rights, which is based on a model of "rights as trumps,"[137] has limited utility for advancing certain goals.[138] She urges instead a model of rights as relationships, in which "we always try to get people to see the patterns of relationship that a proposed law or interpretation will foster."[139] In the "rights as relationship" model, rights are viewed as a means for structuring relationships,[140] and thus rights should be formulated in a manner that fosters beneficial relationships.[141] By unveiling "the relational consequences of certain forms of rights," Nedelsky aims to help "people see how different policies or legal interpretations will actually affect people and the ways they live together."[142]

Similarly, Mary Ann Glendon notes that the current conception of rights, in which a lone, autonomous rights-bearer asserts an absolute right to do as she pleases, ignores both relationships and responsibility.[143] For example, the motorcyclist who chooses not to wear a helmet because it is her right to make her own choices about her body ignores the impact of an injury on family, friends, and dependents, and on society through the cost of medical care.[144] The dominant view of rights "promotes unrealistic expectations, heightens social conflict, and inhibits dialogue that might lead toward consensus, accommodation, or at least the discovery of common ground."[145] And this has far-reaching effects: "Our simplistic rights talk regularly promotes the short-run over the long-term, sporadic crisis intervention over systemic preventive measures, and particular interests over the common good."[146] For Glendon, it is not the existence of rights per se that creates the problem, but rather the valorization of rights without concomitant responsibilities.[147]

Applying these insights to the child welfare system, it becomes apparent that the dominant model of rights does little to protect the interests of parent and child. The autonomy principle embodied in parents' rights and preservationist children's rights is important in that it requires the state to satisfy certain threshold criteria before intervening in the life of a family.[148] But the benefit of the autonomy principle may end there. I focus on the point after child abuse and neglect has been identified and ask how the state should address this abuse or neglect. I assume that there are real problems facing poor families and that something should be done to address these problems. Thus, it is not simply a question of asserting autonomy – "state, go away" – but rather, once the state is present, ascertaining the most beneficial relationship between the state and families. I believe this is achieved by helping parents address the underlying causes of the abuse and neglect. When rights are conceived as freedom from the state (the traditional concept of autonomy), the need of parents and children to receive something from the state is obscured.

To elaborate, poor parents need the state. There is a widespread misconception that the child welfare system intervenes only where there is evidence of severe abuse and neglect. In reality, although such cases receive tremendous publicity, they are not the norm, constituting approximately 10 percent of all cases.[149] By contrast, approximately 50 percent of all cases involve poverty-related neglect,[150] which typically involves substance abuse,[151] inadequate housing,[152] or inappropriate child care arrangements.[153] (The remaining 40 percent fall somewhere in between, involving abuse or neglect that is not considered severe and does not require intervention by the criminal justice system but still rises above the level of poverty-related neglect.)[154]

The correlation between poverty and involvement in the child welfare system is striking.[155] Noted child welfare researcher Duncan Lindsey has concluded that "inadequacy of income, more than any other factor, constitutes the reason that children are removed."[156] Negative changes in income, especially when that income is derived from welfare benefits, have been shown to increase levels of child welfare involvement.[157] A national study of the incidence of abuse and neglect concluded that children from families with incomes of less than $ 15,000 a year were forty-four times more likely to be neglected than children from families with income levels at or above $ 30,000.[158] The study concluded that the findings could not be explained entirely by the supposition that "children in lower income families more frequently come to the attention of ... community professionals."[159] Using data from Illinois, California, and North Carolina, the U.S. Department of Health and Human Services found that between 68 and 71 percent of children entering foster care had previously received federal welfare benefits or had been part of the Medicaid program.[160]

Some states explicitly exempt poverty as a ground for a finding of neglect,[161] but others do not.[162] Although the issues associated with poverty-related neglect, such as substance abuse, poor housing, and inappropriate child care, are serious problems, the child welfare system does not address these underlying poverty issues.[163] Rather, operating with limited resources, the system preemptively removes children from their homes.[164] For these poverty-related neglect cases – again, half of all children in foster care – studies have found that placement in foster care is not the proper solution.[165] Instead, treating the underlying issues is a better approach. Although substance abuse is difficult to treat, and relapse is highly likely,[166] housing supports can play a key role in helping parents break the cycle of addiction and enabling them to care for their children again.[167]

To be sure, there are multiple, interrelated risk factors for child welfare involvement,[168] and the connection between the factors and the involvement is not always clear. For example, homelessness is a very strong predictor of involvement in the child welfare system. Thirty-seven percent of families who have had one instance of homelessness become involved (although do not necessarily have their children removed) with the child welfare system, as compared with 9 percent of low-income families who have homes.[169] This pattern may reflect conditions related to homelessness, such as severe poverty and domestic violence. It may be explainable by referrals to shelters as part of service plans by child welfare agencies, or the greater scrutiny by child protective services of families in shelters. Or it may simply flow from the detrimental effect of homelessness on a parent's ability to raise a child effectively, and the compromise to children's development flowing from the upheaval of homelessness.[170]

I do not mean to imply that poor parents have their children removed simply because the parents are poor. Rather, my point is that poverty is a fundamental underlying issue and that the state should address the deep-seated problems associated with poverty, rather than "assisting" poor parents by removing their children. The question is how best to address these problems.

I believe a rights-based model of child welfare does not help parents or children because the model obscures the real issue of poverty by placing a premium on autonomy rather than assistance. Although a parent may wish the state to leave her alone and let her raise her child, if she is unable to do so because of poverty, then to truly exercise the right to the care and custody of her child, she may need the assistance of the state.[171] Similarly, children also need something from the state, but not necessarily the interventions they currently receive. The enforcement of protectionist children's rights requires adult intervention – it is the right to receive something rather than the right to be left alone. But what children currently receive is, in most cases, not helpful because the intervention is simply removal and placement in the foster care system (with its attendant risks), rather than an attempt to address the underlying issues.[172]

Rights create a zero-sum mentality, thus fostering an adversarial process and adversarial relationships. The child welfare laws are designed to be implemented in courts, which operate on the adversarial model. Thus, it is not surprising that rights become the focus of court proceedings. As described above, parents' rights and preservationist children's rights, on the one hand, are pitted against protectionist children's rights, on the other, in a zero-sum fashion.[173] The court becomes the distributor of rights, fueling a win/lose mentality among the parties. That most cases are not litigated does not diminish this mentality as settlements are, of course, conducted in the shadow of the rights-based system.

Setting aside the vast and rich literature written on this topic in the field of alternative dispute resolution, and focusing only on the child welfare system, it is clear that the adversarial process is a poor means for resolving the issues facing families. As noted above, only about 10 percent of the cases in the child welfare system involve severe abuse. In these cases, it is a fair claim that the rights of a parent who has severely abused or neglected a child and who wishes to retain custody of that child may be at odds with the right of the child to a safe home. This situation likely does pit the right of the parent squarely against certain rights of the child. In these relatively few cases I do not argue that the conception of rights creates a conflict between parent and child, but rather that there almost certainly is a conflict between the rights of parent and child. This dispute may well be best settled in court because the adversarial relationship between the parties is relatively clear.[174] But in the remaining cases, and in particular the approximately 50 percent of poverty-related neglect cases, the substantive rights of parent and child are not necessarily at odds with each other.

In less serious abuse and neglect cases, and especially in poverty-related neglect cases, helping a parent address the economic, psychological, and social issues that led to the abuse or neglect would help both parent and child. Put another way, the traditional assumption that a parent will act in her child's best interest cannot be truly tested without first helping the parent, because she may not be able to act in her child's best interest without substantial support from the state. For example, a parent may not be able to afford adequate housing without a subsidy. But this inability to provide adequate housing does not necessarily mean the parent is unwilling to act in the child's best interest, rather that she needs help doing so. In this way, the zero-sum orientation of the child welfare system obscures the alignment of interests between parent and child.

Such alignment does exist. In the typical child welfare case, parents and children share an interest in addressing the issues that led to the abuse or neglect. This observation is not the simple conclusion that parents and children share an interest in preventing unwarranted intervention,[175] which is certainly true, but rather that even where intervention is required, that is, where there is some abuse or neglect, the interests of parent and child may still be aligned. The parent has an interest in retaining custody of the child, and the child has an interest in the parent receiving help such that the child can remain safe and in the parent's home.

Thus, what is needed in the majority of cases is not an adversarial proceeding, but rather a process that facilitates thoughtful group collaboration among parents, children, and the state to address the underlying issues related to the abuse and neglect. The rights-based model – with its inevitable win/lose mentality – impedes this collaboration.[176]

* * * There is a fundamental mismatch between rights as conceived and implemented and the needs of parents and children. Thus, legal scholars should not look to rights as the primary ground for reforming the child welfare system. In the next part, I explore a model of child welfare that would shift rights to the background and focus instead on the problems facing families.

*Clare Huntington, J.D., is Associate Professor of Law at the University of Colorado School of Law.*

# Notes

[1]  See, e.g., Mary Ann Mason, The Custody Wars: Why Children Are Losing the Legal Battle, and What We Can Do About It 65-92 (1999) (arguing that the law privileges parental rights, vis-à-vis children's rights, in custody determinations).

[2]  See, e.g., James G. Dwyer, Parents' Religion and Children's Welfare: Debunking the Doctrine of Parents' Rights, 82 Cal. L. Rev. 1371 (1994) (arguing for the complete dismantlement of parents' rights, and instead using children's rights as the basis for protecting the interests of children, recognizing only a child-rearing privilege in parents).

[3]  See, e.g., David B. Thronson, Kids Will Be Kids? Reconsidering Conceptions of Children's Rights Underlying Immigration Law, 63 Ohio St. L.J. 979 (2002) (arguing that immigration law is decidedly not child-centered and instead relies on outdated notions of children as property, wards of the state, and mini-adults).

[4]  See, e.g., Barbara Bennett Woodhouse, Speaking Truth to Power: Challenging "The Power of Parents to Control the Education of Their Own," 11 Cornell J.L. & Pub. Pol'y 481 (2002) (arguing for children to have education rights apart from their parents, such as a voice in the decision whether to home school or receive sex education).

[5]  See, e.g., Jennifer M. Collins, Crime and Parenthood: The Uneasy Case for Prosecuting Negligent Parents, 100 Nw. U. L. Rev. (forthcoming 2006) (arguing for a child-centered view of the prosecution of parents who negligently leave children in cars, resulting in death).

[6]  See, e.g., Barbara Bennett Woodhouse, From Property to Personhood: A Child-Centered Perspective on Parents' Rights, 5 Geo. J. Fighting Poverty 313 (1998) (arguing that U.S. opposition to the U.N. Convention on the Rights of the Child has its roots in the protection of parents' rights, which in turn, has its roots in the view of children as property).

[7]  See Elizabeth Bartholet, Nobody's Children: Abuse and Neglect, Foster Drift, and the Adoption Alternative 7 (1999).

[8]  Id.

[9]  Dorothy Roberts, Shattered Bonds: The Color of Child Welfare, at viii (2002).

[10]  See infra text accompanying notes 75-79.


[97]  See, e.g., Catharine A. MacKinnon, Sex Equality 216-47 (2001) (setting forth cases recognizing the right to sex equality); Kimberlé Williams Crenshaw, Race, Reform, and Retrenchment: Transformation and Legitimation in Antidiscrimination Law, 101 Harv. L. Rev. 1331, 1356-58 (1988) (critiquing critical legal scholars for discounting the importance of rights to advancing claims of racial equality).

[98]  See Appell, supra note 43, at 686 (critiquing various proposals to weaken parents' rights by arguing that such proposals do not sufficiently protect families who are most vulnerable to state intervention).

[99]  Children's Bureau, U.S. Dep't of Health & Human Servs., Children of Color in the Child Welfare System: Perspectives From the Child Welfare Community 3 (2003).

[100]  Id.

[101]  Eight African American children for every 1000 enter foster care, versus three white children for every 1000. See Richard Wertheimer, Youth Who "Age Out" of Foster Care: Troubled Lives, Troubling Prospects, Child Trends Res. Brief (Child Trends, Washington, D.C.), Dec. 2002, at 1, 2 (citing U.S. Dep't of Health & Human Servs., Green Book 2000).

[102]  Thirty-three percent of African American children left foster care in 1999 versus 53 percent of white children. See id. at 1.

[103]  See Roberts, supra note 9, at 47.

[104]  See id. at 47-49.

[105]  See Children's Bureau, supra note 99, at 8.

[106]  Naomi Cahn, while agreeing with Roberts that African American children are overrepresented in the child welfare system, argues that this overrepresentation could be attributed to poverty and not racial bias because the poverty rate for African American households is almost double the rate for white households. See Naomi Cahn, Race, Poverty, History, Adoption, and Child Abuse: Connections, 36 Law & Soc'y Rev. 461, 474-75 (2002). Roberts rebuts the poverty explanation by arguing that poverty cannot account for the overrepresentation of African American children because equally poor Latino children are less likely to be involved in the child welfare system than their African American counterparts. See Roberts, supra note 9, at 48. She notes that African American and Latino children in San Diego, for example, have a similar socioeconomic status, but their rates of representation in the child welfare system are very different. Latino children were involved in the system "at a rate identical to their proportion of the population [however] African American children were overrepresented in foster care at a rate six times their census proportion." Id. (citing Ann F. Garland et al., Minority Populations in the Child Welfare System: The Visibility Hypothesis Reexamined, 68 Am. J. Orthopsychiatry, 142, 145-46 (1998)). Moreover, the relationship between poverty and racism is complex. See, e.g., Michael Katz, Reframing the Class Debate, in A New Introduction to Poverty: The Role of Race, Power and Politics 59 (Louis Cushnick & James Jennings eds., 1999).

[107]  See infra text accompanying notes 155-172.

[108]  See John Courtney et al., Aggressive Prosecutions Flooding the System, Child Welfare Watch (Ctr. for an Urban Future, New York, N.Y.), Winter 1999, at 4, 4 (documenting a 55 percent increase in filings of neglect cases and a 57 percent increase in filings of abuse cases from 1995 to 1998 following the well-publicized death of Elisa Izquierdo, a six-year-old girl subjected to fatal abuse by her mother).

[109]  See id.

[110]  See Guggenheim, supra note 39, at 194. Guggenheim states:

Courts and government reports alike regularly conclude that the current scheme results in a bias toward over-reporting and over-labeling child abuse and neglect. Indeed, one federal study found that investigators are more than twice as likely to "substantiate" a case erroneously than to mislabel a case "unfounded." Moreover, many studies have found that as many as two-thirds of those cases labeled "substantiated" do not involve serious charges.

Id. Peggy Cooper Davis and Gautam Barua describe what they termed the "sequentiality effect" of custodial decisionmaking in the child welfare system, arguing that decisions made at one stage of the proceedings will be repeated and reinforced at later stages in the proceeding, regardless of the correctness of the first decision. See Peggy Cooper Davis & Gautam Barua, Custodial Choices for Children at Risk: Bias, Sequentiality, and the Law, 2 U. Chi. L. Sch. Roundtable 139, 146 (1995). Davis and Barua further conclude that "interim decisions [in child welfare proceedings] are more likely to err on the side of intervention" and removal of the child, therefore this bias persists and is compounded as the case proceeds. Id. at 157.

[111]  For example, initial investigations of abuse and neglect, which are often conducted by caseworkers with minimal or nonexistent training, put parents at a disadvantage. See Duncan Lindsey, The Welfare of Children 7 (2d ed. 2004); Emily Buss, Parents' Rights and Parents Wronged, 57 Ohio St. L.J. 431, 433 (1996). Knowing that their ability to retain custody of a child is at stake, parents often cooperate with the investigation rather than resisting it from the start. See id. Parents do not have the assistance of counsel or the oversight of a judge when responding to the investigations. See id. at 434.

[112]  See Buss, supra note 111, at 434.

[113]  See id.

[114]  See Lindsey, supra note 111, at 171 (finding that parents who have their children placed in foster care are less likely to receive the services they needed in the first place, thus exacerbating the problem). Buss concurs, observing:

While these cases will eventually be reviewed by a court, the damage to the parents and child of an inappropriate removal will already have been done. At a minimum, the families will have suffered up to six months of inappropriate separation. At a maximum, the removal will accelerate whatever problems the parents were having and undermine an already troubled relationship between parent and child.
Buss, supra note 111, at 434.

[115] Although there are notable exceptions, many appointed counsel provide poor representation. See Buss, supra note 111, at 437.

[116] Id. at 434-35 (footnotes omitted). But see Amy Sinden, "Why Won't Mom Cooperate?": A Critique of Informality in Child Welfare Proceedings, 11 Yale. J.L. & Feminism 339, 376-96 (1999) (describing the dangers of informal dispute resolution processes in child welfare and arguing in favor of, at least in the absence of a better alternative, the current procedural safeguards).

[117] See infra text accompanying notes 149-154.

[118] Although the average stay in foster care is nineteen months, 11 percent of children remain for two to three years, 11 percent remain for three to four years, and 9 percent remain in care for five or more years. See Nat'l Adoption Info. Clearinghouse, U.S. Dep't of Health & Human Servs., Foster Care National Statistics 4 (2003).

[119] Fifty-five percent of the children who leave foster care return to live with their biological families, 18 percent are adopted, 11 percent live with a relative or guardian, 8 percent are emancipated, 4 percent have legal guardians, and the remainder are in legal limbo. See AFCARS FY 2003 Estimates, supra note 16, at 3. The children in "limbo" were transferred to another agency or were runaways. See id. An emancipated child in the context of child welfare means a child who is not adopted or reunited with a biological parent, but rather moves from foster care to independent living. In 2001, 19,000 children "aged out" of foster care, becoming "emancipated" adults. See Wertheimer, supra note 101, at 1.

[120] In 2003, there were 119,000 children awaiting adoption. See AFCARS FY 2003 Estimates, supra note 16, at 4. Children waited an average of forty-four months for an adoptive home after parental rights were terminated, see id., and a significant portion of children waited even longer (23 percent waited thirty-nine to fifty-nine months, and 24 percent waited sixty months or longer), see id. The report defines "children waiting to be adopted" as those "who have a goal of adoption and/or whose parental rights have been terminated. Children 16 years old and older whose parental rights have been terminated and who have a goal of emancipation have been excluded from the estimate." Id.

[121] For example, in 2003, although 68,000 children had their parental rights terminated, only 50,000 were adopted out of foster care. See id. at 3, 5.

[122] See Pew Comm'n on Children in Foster Care, Fostering the Future: Safety, Permanence and Well-Being for Children in Foster Care 9 (2004) (reporting that in 2002, 44 percent of children exiting foster care lived in one home, 22 percent lived in two homes, 27 percent lived in three or more homes, and 10 percent lived in five or more homes).

[123] Children in foster care exhibit significantly more behavioral and adaptive functioning problems than children in the general population. See June M. Clausen et al., Mental Health Problems of Children in Foster Care, 7 J. Child & Fam. Stud. 283, 284 (1998). Seventy-five to 80 percent of school-aged children in foster care score in the problematic range of behavior problem and social competence domains of the Child Behavior Checklist. See id. at 292. Furthermore, children who have been placed in foster care are also at risk of developmental problems, such as gross motor, fine motor, and cognitive delays. See Molly Murphy Garwood & Wendy Close, Identifying the Psychological Needs of Foster Children, 32 Child Psychiatry & Hum. Dev. 125, 126 (2001). The long-term outcomes are particularly poor for children emancipated from foster care (youth who are not adopted or reunited, but rather transition from foster care to independent living). About half of these children do not finish high school, have histories of job instability, and are paid less than their nonfoster care peers. See Richard P. Barth, On Their Own: The Experiences of Youth After Foster Care, 7 Child & Adolescent Soc. Work J. 419-40 (1990); Ronna J. Cook, Are We Helping Foster Care Youth Prepare for Their Future?, 16 Child. & Youth Servs. Rev.

213-29 (1994); Mark E. Courtney et al., Foster Youth Transitions to Adulthood: A Longitudinal View of Youth Leaving Care, 80 Child Welfare 685 (2001); Mark E. Courtney et al., Midwest Evaluation of the Adult Functioning of Former Foster Youth: Outcomes at Age 19 (2005), available at http://www. chapinhall.org/article_abstract.aspx?ar=1355&L2=61&L3=130 (last visited Dec. 15, 2005). As many as 25 percent report being homeless for at least one night, see id. at 710; 40 percent report receiving some sort of welfare, see Cook, supra, at 219-20; and, perhaps most troubling, 60 percent of young women leaving foster care were pregnant or already parenting within twelve to eighteen months after leaving the foster care system. See id. at 222.

[124] Press Release, Casey Family Programs, Former Foster Children in Washington and Oregon Suffer Post Traumatic Stress Disorder at Twice the Rate of U.S. War Veterans, According to New Study (Apr. 6, 2005) (on file with author).

[125] Id. This is not surprising given that, on average, children in foster care experience more than fourteen environmental, social, biological, and psychological risk factors that make them vulnerable to psychological problems. See Garwood & Close, supra note 123, at 126 (citing M.B. Thorpe & G.T. Swart, Risk and Protective Factors Affecting Children in Foster Care: A Pilot Study of the Role of Siblings, 37 Canadian J. Psychiatry 616 (1992)).

[126] See generally 3 John Bowlby, Attachment and Loss 7-14, 397-411 (1980); 2 id. at 13, 245-57 (1973); 1 id. at 27-30, 330 (1969) (documenting the psychological and emotional trauma to a child separated unnecessarily from her parent); Wendy L. Haight et al., Parent-Child Interaction During Foster Care Visits, 46 Soc. Work 325, 337-38 (2000) (reporting that a study on parent-child visitation during separation indicates the importance of reducing the time the parent and child are separated because of the disruptive impact of the separation on the parent-child relationship, and the risk of attachment related issues for the child).

[127] See Mary I. Benedict et al., Types and Frequency of Child Maltreatment by Family Foster Care Providers in an Urban Population, 18 Child Abuse & Neglect 577, 581 (1994) ("[F]oster families were almost seven times more likely to be reported for physical abuse as compared to families in the community...[and] had a four-fold greater risk of report for sexual abuse. The same families were almost twice as likely to be reported for neglect than nonfoster families."); see also id. at 577-85.

[128] See Mary I. Benedict et al., The Reported Health and Functioning of Children Maltreated While in Family Foster Care, 20 Child Abuse & Neglect 561, 563 (1996). The perpetrator was a foster father or other foster family member in more than two-thirds of the incidents and another foster child in the home in 20 percent of the incidents. See id.

[129] U.S. Gen. Acct. Off., Foster Care: Health Needs of Many Young Children Are Unknown and Unmet, GAO1 HEHS-95-114, at 2 (Washington D.C. May 26, 1995).

[130] For example, the rights-based system leads to a one-size-fits-all child welfare system, rather than context-driven decisions. See Ross, supra note 61, at 178-79, 192-93. Concepts of rights determine standards of removal of children. If preference is given to parents' rights and preservationist children's rights, then children will be removed only in extreme circumstances. If preference is given to protectionist children's rights, then children will be removed more frequently. As legal scholars have noted, this is a question of whether the system should be overinclusive or underinclusive. See Margaret F. Brinig & F.H. Buckley, Parental Rights and the Ugly Duckling, 1 J.L. & Fam. Stud. 41, 59 (1999) (noting that a disabled child is more likely to be abused than a nondisabled child, particularly if an unrelated adult is in the house, and concluding that taking disability "into account will increase the costs of over-inclusiveness: more disabled children will be taken from fit parents. But as we believe that present termination rules are too lax, we suggest that under-inclusiveness costs, including permanent damage to children, are a far greater concern than those of over-inclusiveness."). But the requirement that the system choose between removing too many children or too few children hardly seems like the best way to design a system. The relevant question should be what is best for this family. It may be that due to a particular history of relapse from substance abuse, a child should be removed more readily than a one-

size-fits-all standard would permit. Conversely, where there is a particularly strong relationship between a parent and child, despite maltreatment of that child, there may be compelling reasons for keeping that family together, with adequate safeguards for the child. Although the current rights-based system could, in theory, permit individualized decisionmaking, it does not. This is because theories of rights drive legal standards, and also because in practice the state uses boilerplate approaches to working with families. See, e.g., Annette R. Appell, Protecting Children or Punishing Mothers: Gender, Race, and Class in the Child Protection System, 48 S.C. L. Rev. 577, 583 (1997); see also Roberts, supra note 9, at 79.

[131] To be clear, I do not mean that the parents' rights doctrine should be abrogated for such parents. But rather that these parents need more social and economic supports from the state so that they can enjoy the same autonomy in decisionmaking afforded more economically stable parents. I intend to explore this issue more fully in a separate article.

[132] Minow, supra note 45, at 15; accord Mary Ann Glendon, Rights Talk: The Impoverishment of Political Discourse 47-75 (1991) (discussing the dominant paradigm of the lone rights-bearing individual).

[133] See Minow, supra note 45, at 18. Minow notes:

To the extent that the dominant conception of rights presumes both autonomy and a direct relationship between the individual and the state, rights for children are even more problematic than rights for adults. Conceptually and practically, children in our society are not autonomous persons but instead dependents who are linked legally and daily to adults entrusted with their care.

Id.

[134] See Jennifer Nedelsky, Reconceiving Rights as Relationships, 1 Rev. Const. Studies/Rev. d'Études Constitutionnelles 1, 7-8 (1993).

[135] See id. As Nedelsky explains the relationship between rights and autonomy,

[t]here is the idea that rights are barriers that protect the individual from intrusion by other individuals or by the state. Rights define boundaries others cannot cross and it is those boundaries, enforced by the law, that ensure individual freedom and autonomy. This image of rights fits well with the idea that the essence of autonomy is independence, which thus requires protection and separation from others. My argument is that this is a deeply misguided view of autonomy. What makes autonomy possible is not separation, but relationship.

This approach shifts the focus from protection against others to structuring relationships so that they foster autonomy. Some of the most basic presuppositions about autonomy shift: dependence is no longer the antithesis of autonomy but a precondition in the relationships–between parent and child, student and teacher, state and citizen–which provides the security, education, nurturing, and support that make the development of autonomy possible.

Id.

[136] See id. at 8 ("The constitutional protection of autonomy is then no longer an effort to carve out a sphere into which the collective cannot intrude, but a means of structuring the relations between individuals and the sources of collective power so that autonomy is fostered rather than undermined.").

[137] Id. at 6-8, 14, 17-18 (discussing this model and noting origins of phrase in Ronald Dworkin's work).

[138] Jennifer Nedelsky, The Practical Possibilities of Feminist Theory, 87 Nw. U. L. Rev. 1286, 1295-96 (1993).

[139] Id. at 1296. Nedelsky addresses the importance of framing arguments, noting the costs of using available legal doctrines rather than creating institutions that could resolve "problems in a genuinely feminist framework." Id. at 1287-89.

[140] In Nedelsky's view, this is a descriptive rather than a normative statement. See Nedelsky, supra note 134, at 13 ("[W]hat rights in fact do and have always done is construct relationships–of power, of responsibility, of trust, of obligation.").

[141] See Nedelsky, supra note 138, at 1289-90.

[142] Id. at 1296, 1300. Martha Minow also has addressed the importance of relationships to rights. She argues that the current conception of rights divides the world into winners and losers and that in this act of dividing, we overlook relationships. See Martha Minow, Making All the Difference: Inclusion, Exclusion, and American Law 1-4 (1990). She argues neither for a wholesale abandonment of rights nor for business as usual. See id. at 15-16. Minow acknowledges that a critical examination of rights is essential because legal rules enforce patterns of private power, and thus the pressing question is "what relationships [do] existing rights establish between the rights-bearing individual, the government, and other people? If a right protects liberty, whose liberty does it protect and at what cost to whom?" Id. at 283.

[143] See Glendon, supra note 132, at 45-46.

[144] See id.

[145] Id. at 14.

[146] Id. at 15.

[147] See id. at 5, 45.

[148] See supra note 30 (setting forth standards).

[149] See Waldfogel, supra note 11, at 124-25 (citing a study finding that approximately 10 percent of the cases in the child welfare system involve child abuse and neglect warranting criminal charges).

[150] See id. at 125.

[151] U.S. Dep't of Health & Human Servs., Blending Perspectives and Building Common Ground: A Report to Congress on Substance Abuse and Child Protection ch. 4 (1999), available at http:// aspe. hhs.gov/hsp/subabuse99/subabuse.htm (last visited Dec. 15, 2005) ("Most studies find that for between one third and two-thirds of children involved with the child welfare system, parental substance abuse is a contributing factor. Lower figures tend to involve child abuse reports and higher findings most often refer to foster care.").

[152] At the extreme–inadequate housing that endangers children–housing problems can lead to the removal of children. See, e.g., Oregon Dep't of Human Servs., Foster Care Trends 4 (2003) (finding that inadequate housing was a factor for 7.7 percent of children entering foster care in Oregon). And inadequate housing is a major issue for returning children placed in foster care to their biological parents. See Martin Guggenheim, Somebody's Children: Sustaining the Family's Place in Child Welfare Policy, 113 Harv. L. Rev. 1716, 1724 (2000) (citing a study of D.C. foster care system that concluded 33-50 percent of the children in foster care could be returned to their parents if the parents had adequate housing).

[153] See Waldfogel, supra note 11, at 124-25.

[154] See id. at 124. Although these categories are not perspicuous, distinctions among cases can be made, and it is clear that only a small percentage of cases fall into the severe category.

[155] See, e.g., Lindsey, supra note 111 (finding that the major determinant of children's removal from their parents' custody was not the severity of child maltreatment but unstable sources of parental income); Christina Paxson & Jane Waldfogel, Work, Welfare, and Child Maltreatment 1, 22-27 (Nat'l Bureau of Econ. Research, Working Paper No. 7343, 1999) (reporting their finding that "higher rates of poverty resulted in higher rates of substantiated reports of abuse and neglect").

[156] Lindsey, supra note 111, at 175.

[157] Paxson & Waldfogel, supra note 155, at 2; see also Kristen Shook, Does the Loss of Welfare Income Increase the Risk of Involvement With the Child Welfare System? 12 (Joint Ctr. for Poverty Research, Working Paper No. 65, 1999), available at http://www.jcpr.org/wpfiles/shook.pdf? CFID=27 61642&CFTOKEN=31487985 (documenting a study of welfare recipients in the Chicago metropolitan area).

[158] See Andrea J. Sedlak & Diane D. Broadhurst, U.S. Dep't of Health & Human Servs., Third National Incidence Study of Child Abuse and Neglect 5-50 (1996).

[159] Id. at 5-51.

[160] U.S. Dep't of Health & Human Servs., Dynamics of Children's Movement Among the AFDC, Medicaid, and Foster Care Programs Prior to Welfare Reform: 1995-1996, at 9 tbl. 1 (2000). A similar study was undertaken by the Joint Center for Poverty Research. See Kristen Shook, Assessing the Consequences of Welfare Reform for Child Welfare, Poverty Res. News (Northwestern Univ./Univ. of Chicago Joint Ctr. for Poverty Research), Winter 1998, at 8 (describing a relationship between children who had received Aid to Families with Dependent Children and placement in foster care).

[161] See, e.g., D.C. Code Ann. §16-2301(9)(A)(ii) (Lexis 2005); Fla. Stat. Ann. §39.01(30)(f) (West 2005); N.Y. Family Ct. Act §1012(f)(i)(A) (McKinney 2005).

[162] See, e.g., Ariz. Rev. Stat. Ann. §8-201(21) (2004); Ga. Code Ann. §49-5-180(5)(B) (2004); S.D. Codified Laws §§26-8A-2(4) & (5) (2004). The studies finding that children are removed due to poverty do not specify whether this happens only in states that permit such removals.

[163] Typically, the case plan for the parent is a "pretyped, generic form[ ] that obligate[s] the mother to submit to drug tests, go to counseling, submit to psychological evaluations, attend parenting classes, and visit the child." Appell, supra note 130, at 583.

[164] See Buss, supra note 111, at 433-34; Cynthia R. Mabry, Second Chances: Insuring That Poor Families Remain Intact by Minimizing Socioeconomic Ramifications of Poverty, 102 W. Va. L. Rev. 607, 616-24 (2000).

[165] See Lindsey, supra note 111, at 166; see also Waldfogel, supra note 11, at 78. I do not mean to minimize the consequences of severe neglect. Indeed, severe neglect accounted for 35.6 percent of the 1500 abuse and neglect deaths in 2003. See Child Maltreatment, supra note 17, at 55-56. Moreover, as Waldfogel notes, the poverty-related neglect cases are not unimportant as some of them may be early warning signs of a situation that may escalate, or the signs of minor maltreatment may reflect undetected chronic abuse or neglect. See Waldfogel, supra note 11, at 125. But the question this Article asks is whether for the typical lower-risk case, foster care is the appropriate "service" to help this family.

[166] See Dennis M. Donovan, Relapse Prevention in Substance Abuse Treatment, in Drug Abuse Treatment Through Collaboration: Practice and Research Partnerships That Work 121 (James L. Sorenson et al. eds., 2003). Donovan observes:

Relapse is a common outcome following the initiation of abstinence, whether the abstinence was initially achieved with or without formal treatment. The rates of relapse associated with alcohol, cocaine, heroin, and other drugs of abuse are quite high, with some estimates suggesting that 60% or more of individuals relapse after stopping their substance use.

Id. (citation omitted); see also id. at 122 (noting that relapse is a natural and normal part of recovery).

[167] See Hilary Waldman, A Second Chance as Mom: State Helps Troubled Parents Succeed by Providing a Home, and Advice, Hartford Courant, July 3, 2005, at A1 (describing a "Supportive Housing" program in Connecticut and early indications that permanent housing makes all the difference to successful drug treatment).

[168] See, e.g., Jocelyn Brown et al., A Longitudinal Analysis of Risk Factors for Child Maltreatment: Findings of a 17-Year Prospective Study of Officially Recorded and Self-Reported Child Abuse and Neglect, 22 Child Abuse & Neglect 1065, 1070-72 (1998) (discussing risk factors for abuse and neglect, and finding that different combinations of factors are associated with physical abuse, sexual abuse, and neglect). Maternal sociopathy and maternal youth were associated with all types of child maltreatment; poverty and large family size were strongly associated with neglect; low maternal involvement, early separation from a mother, and perinatal problems were associated with physical abuse; a child's gender and disability, a deceased parent, and living with a stepfather were associated with sexual abuse. See id. at 1073. Additionally, this study demonstrates that the greater the number of risk factors, the greater the likelihood for maltreatment. See id. at 1074 (finding that with no risk factors, the likelihood of maltreatment was only 3 percent; the presence of four or more risk factors raised the likelihood of maltreatment to 24 percent). Finally, the study concludes that low-income families may have higher

rates of physical abuse and neglect (although not sexual abuse) than families with greater income levels, and that this conclusion is not a result of biased reporting, investigation, or substantiation. See id. at 1066, 1074.

[169]  See Jennifer F. Culhane et al., Prevalence of Child Welfare Services Involvement Among Homeless and Low-Income Mothers: A Five-year Birth Cohort Study, 30 J. Soc. & Soc. Welfare 79, 89-91 (2003). Another indicator was the number of children in the families: Among homeless women, 24 percent of women with one child were involved in the child welfare system, whereas 54 percent of women with four children or more were involved with the child welfare system. See id. at 92-93.

[170]  See id. at 91.

[171]  I do not mean to imply that poor parents have no need for the rights of decisionmaking that more affluent parents enjoy. Indeed, poor parents still need deference to their parental decisionmaking. Thus, my claim may be better stated as one for autonomy and assistance. This dual need is the subject of a future article.

[172]  The argument that society should help, not punish, poor parents is not new. As Dorothy Roberts described in a recent article, after the Civil War, African American women, who were excluded by white women from child-saving campaigns, created their own movement by forming clubs and church groups designed to address the well-being of children. See Dorothy E. Roberts, Black Club Women and Child Welfare: Lessons for Modern Reform, 32 Fla. St. U. L. Rev. 957, 957-58 (2005). Instead of focusing on particular cases of abuse or neglect, this movement addressed the well-being of all children, and also tried to support, rather than penalize, mothers, believing that assisting mothers would assist the children. See id. at 958, 963-71.

[173]  See, e.g., Ross, supra note 61, at 176 ("In child welfare disputes, protections accorded to one party–parent, state, child or foster parent–almost inevitably diminish the substantive interests of another."). In this context I do not mean to include all rights, such as the right to present evidence or receive notice of a hearing. Rather, my point is that the broader conception of rights–solicitude for either the parent or the child, preservation or protection–presents a zero-sum situation.

[174]  As noted in the Introduction, I am not here resolving this question. Rather, my intent is to take these cases out of the equation in my attempt to determine the best legal model (and process to implement that model) for the majority of cases in the child welfare system.

[175]  See, e.g., Santosky v. Kramer, 455 U.S. 745, 760 (1982) ( "[U]ntil the State proves parental unfitness, the child and his parents share a vital interest in preventing erroneous termination of their natural relationship.").

[176]  On a related point, the individualist thinking fostered by rights does a disservice to children by excluding a "family systems" orientation to resolving family problems. Long-espoused by social workers, family systems theory proposes that the family is a living entity, with each part dependent on the other. The only way fully to understand an individual is to look at her in the context of her family and to understand the interaction of the family. See Salvador Minuchin, Families and Family Therapy 9 (1974); Stephen J. Schultz, Family Systems Therapy: An Integration 16-17 (1984). To help a child, the whole family must be treated. In the view of family systems theory, the clash between parents' rights and children's rights simply misunderstands the problem: It is not a question of parent or child. Rather, the only possible solution must involve parent and child. Cf. Susan L. Brooks, A Family Systems Paradigm for Legal Decision Making Affecting Child Custody, 6 Cornell J.L. & Pub. Pol'y 1 (1996) (discussing the need for a family systems approach to resolving child custody disputes).

# Part II
# Court Processes and Structure

# A: Historical Overview

# [4]

# The Evolving Judicial Role in
# Child Custody Disputes:
# From Fault Finder to Conflict Manager
# to Differential Case Management

## Andrew Schepard

## I. Introduction

The judiciary's role in divorce related child custody disputes has been transformed in the latter half of the twentieth century in response to the changing characteristics of American families, changing perceptions of the needs of children, and an overwhelming case load increase. The transformation occurred in two distinct phases, and a third is currently in process.

In Phase I, from the late 1960s (the beginning of widespread "no fault" divorce) to 1980, the child custody court was a fault finder functioning through adversary procedure. The court's job was to identify a single custodial parent and assign that parent primary legal rights to the child after a trial about which parent was a better custodian for the child.

Phase I courts conceived of a custody dispute much like a will contest. The parents' marriage, like the decedent, was dead. Parents, like the heirs, were in dispute about the distribution of one of the assets of the estate – their children. The Phase I court's role was, after trial, to determine which heir/parent was more morally or psychologically worthy to control the children. The goal of the proceeding was a one time determination of custody "rights" which created "stability" for the future management of the asset. The winner was, however, largely predetermined by gender biased substantive standards that eliminated the seeming indeterminancy of the "best interests" test. Once the court distributed custody rights, its role in facilitating the ongoing process of reorganizing the child's relationships with both parents was over, except for enforcement or modification of its initial award, tasks also accomplished through adversary process.

Phase I courts did not survive the advent of mass "no fault divorce," the associated increase in disputes about children, the drive against gender bias in the legal system, and, most significantly, the increasing evidence that the child's well-being after divorce generally is promoted by reduced parental conflict and continuing relationships with both. American society became more tolerant of divorce as a necessary evil in promoting adult happiness. It also came to recognize, however, that for children divorce is a process of redefining relationships over a long period of time – not the death of the family, but an occasion for its reorganization.

Custody courts responded by redefining themselves as conflict managers rather than fault finders, Phase II in their late twentieth century evolution. Courts became the apex of a multi faceted dispute resolution system that encourages out-of-court agreement on parenting plans. Court-affiliated education programs, mediation, and legal rules which reward post divorce and separation cooperation between parents are the core of a newly created settlement culture, and trials are a last resort for particularly troublesome cases.

A Phase II custody court can be analogized to a bankruptcy court supervising the reorganization of a potentially viable business in current financial distress. The business is raising children and the parents – the managers of the business – are in conflict about how that task is to be accomplished. The court's aim is to get the managers to voluntarily agree on a parenting plan rather than impose one on them. The court uses education and mediation to facilitate voluntary agreement. The court ratifies the parties' agreements and only decides issues that the parents cannot decide themselves. The court has an ongoing role in managing parental conflict; parents have continuing access to the settlement processes if future disputes arise or modification of the parenting plan is necessary because of changed circumstances.

The Phase II managerial court better serves the needs of most parents and children in divorcing families than its Phase I fault finding predecessor. The need for transformation of the judicial role in custody disputes, however, is not over. Phase III in the continuing evolution of the judicial role in child custody disputes is for courts to recognize that not all divorce related custody disputes are the same. High conflict cases – roughly defined as those involving repeated relitigation, family violence, child abduction, mental illness, or drug or substance abuse – require special treatment. The disproportionate judicial resources such cases consume create a temptation to include them in the settlement culture of Phase II. Phase II mediation and education programs are, however, not tailored to include such families. The special risks high conflict divorces pose to children and vulnerable family members make it imperative that they are identified through careful screening, that existing programs are adopted for them and that mental health resources are available for such families.

Overall, Phase III custody courts need to establish differential case management plans (DCM) for high conflict cases. These plans should develop criteria to "triage" these particularly difficult cases early in their judicial life cycle without burdening the great percentage of reasonably cooperative divorcing parents with unduly intrusive state intervention. Court-affiliated parent education and mediation must be adapted to account for the risks that high conflict disputes create for physical and emotional safety of children and parents. Mental health and child protection systems must be integrated into the DCM plan. DCM plans also must create an expedited, actively managed dispute resolution plan for the chaotic and conflicted families involved in high conflict cases to insure that someone in authority monitors the behavior of parents and the welfare of their children.

The first part of this article is a condensed history of the evolution of the judicial role in divorce and custody cases from fault finder to conflict manager. The second part describes the need for and the mechanisms of a plan for DCM of high conflict divorce-related custody disputes. It first summarizes some available data on high conflict divorces and their effects on children. It then describes a high conflict family, a composite drawn from actual cases. Finally, the article identifies several of the core principles that should govern how that family is treated by the judicial system – court unification, differential diagnosis, and multiple dispute resolution and treatment options.

## II. From Fault Finder to Conflict Manager

Before describing the transformation in the custody court's role from fault finder to conflict manager and beyond, it is important to note that it is a transformation of ideas that different states have implemented with different levels of operational enthusiasm and resource commitments. The transformation is far from complete at an operational level in the day to day resolution of custody disputes in courthouses throughout the nation. Rather, as will be seen, California has been at the forefront of change, and other states like Oregon, Washington, and New Jersey are also far along. New York, in contrast, continues to support a more adversarial child custody dispute resolution system. It does not mandate mediation of custody disputes,[1] does not have legislation or court rules authorizing courts to require attendance at parent education programs,[2] and does not mention the need for a child to have relationships with both parents following divorce in its custody statute.[3]

It is also important to note that the transformation from fault finder to conflict manager paralleled a period of great instability in American family life as reflected in official divorce statistics, court filings, and the social attitudes toward divorce that lie beneath them. Between 1950 and 1997, the divorce rate in the United States rose from 2.6 per 1,000 people to 4.3 per 1,000 people, with a peak of 5.3 per 1,000 people in 1981.[4] Between 1951 and 1999, the number of children annually involved in divorce climbed from approximately 6.1 per thousand to 16.8 per thousand[5] (which translates to about 1,005,000 per year), a fundamental change in the way children experience growing up in American society.[6] Almost half of United States first marriages end in divorce and 65% of those couples have minor children.[7] "Parents with young children are the fastest growing segment of the divorcing population, presently constituting the majority of those who are divorcing in the 1990s."[8] At least 40% of today's young adult women are likely to divorce sometime in their lives.[9]

The increase in divorces affecting children parallels an increase in court filings arising from changes in family composition. The number of divorce and custody related disputes filed in state courts has increased enormously in recent years. According to the National Center for State Courts, "domestic relations cases are the largest and fastest-growing segment of state court civil caseloads. In 1995, 25 percent of total civil filings, over 4.9 million, were domestic relations cases. The total number of domestic relations cases increased 4.1 percent since 1994 and 70 percent since 1984."[10] Divorces registered an 8% increase from 1988 to 1995 while custody cases increased 43% in that same period.[11] It is also important to note that a large percentage of the increase in custody cases are disputes between parents who were never married. Even though the divorce rate has stabilized in recent years, the number of custody disputes reaching court has grown, largely because of the increase in disputes between never married parents.[12] Disputes about children resulting from divorce and separation are the largest category of family related filings in the New York court system (child support is the first with child custody a close second).[13]

To me, as will be described, the transformation in the judicial role from fault finder to conflict manager is based on a policy judgment shared by legislators and the judiciary that children's best interests generally are promoted by parental conflict reduction and continuing relationships with both parents after family reorganization. A more cynical person might, however, view the transformation as a necessity for judicial survival – an adaptation to cope with an exponentially increased workload in a time of limited resources rather than a philosophical shift. The cynic would argue that the court system would break down if all of the child related divorce cases filed had to be tried and that judges are happy to delegate responsibility for family matters to settlement processes because they do not want such cases on their dockets. It is difficult to convince a cynic that her "realistic" view of human motivation has no basis. Interviews and discussions with many judges and family court personnel, however, have convinced me that most courts have embraced a better vision of children's best interests in moving from Phase I to Phase II. In any event, the operational result is the same no matter what the reasons are for it.

### A. Phase I: No Fault Divorce and the Sole Custody System

Until the second half of the twentieth century, only virtuous spouses could get divorces and "the divorce laws of every state assumed an adversary proceeding between spouses in which the plaintiff had to prove the defendant's 'fault'."[14] Today, every state has a no-fault divorce ground.[15] Overall, the philosophical shift to no-fault divorce has been described by one scholar as a "silent revolution" which took place without extended public debate or dramatic political controversy.[16]

Ironically, the silent revolution began in California in the 1960s as an effort to preserve marriages and reduce divorce, not to make family dissolution easier. Liberalized grounds for divorce were, in the conception of the no-fault divorce revolution's designers, tied to the creation of an expert family court one of whose goals was to scrupulously examine whether couples did indeed have "irreconcilable differences" and to reconcile as many couples as possible.[17] Politics and budgetary limitations, however, intervened, and only one half of the plan was ever implemented. The family court was never created while the liberalized grounds for divorce were. In effect, adults gained freedom to divorce without state scrutiny of their family life. The result was what my colleague J. Herbie DiFonzo has called the triumph of "naked divorce" – "no fault divorce on demand"[18] in many states.

The no-fault divorce revolution was not, however, linked to changes in thinking about the court's role in the child custody dispute resolution process. Even after no-fault divorce, custody courts awarded sole custody to one parent after a highly adversarial trial in contested cases. Children remained a prize to be won by casting aspersions on the other spouse in a courtroom. The result was that while fault was de-emphasized in the grounds for divorce, it remained the dominant criteria in the custody determinations which resulted from it.

Ostensibly, the substantive standard for custody determinations in Phase I was the indeterminate "best interests of the child" test. What the court really did, however, was to determine which of the contestants was the "better parent" and award all custody rights to her leaving the other parent legally marginalized with "visitation." The justification for the sole custody award was to create "stability" for the child and the legal system by identifying a "primary parent," thus supposedly authoritatively ending the possibility of future disputes.

In actual operation, the "tender years" doctrine filled in the indeterminacy of the "best interests" test in most cases involving younger children – mother won unless she was unfit. This standard placed a tremendous premium on one spouse demeaning the other in the courtroom, particularly fathers demeaning mothers. Custody trials were thus relatively rare because most of the time the outcome was preordained; few fathers wanted to invest the financial and emotional resources to contest in what was likely to be a losing battle. When trials occurred, however, they were intense acts of adversarial battle involving counter accusations of unfitness that would have qualified as grounds for divorce under the repealed fault regime.

The social and constitutional revolution against gender discrimination that began in the 1970s, however, also began to draw the sole custody system into question.[19] As mentioned earlier, divorce became a predictable event in the life cycle of American families, and the social stigma associated with it began to decrease. The entry of women into the workplace in massive numbers undercut the tender years doctrine's economic underpinnings, as many mothers were no longer willing or available to stay home with the children. Fathers began to perceive they had a chance to win a custody dispute and began to assert "rights" to the custody of their children in larger numbers. Most states eliminated the tender years doctrine in name if not necessarily in operation. The courts were faced with more disputes to resolve at the same time they lost their lodestone doctrine that provided certainty in decision-making and reduced the number of cases.

Into the breach rode mental health experts who sought to fill the gap in the sole custody system created by the demise of the tender years doctrine with gender neutral standards based on their expertise in assessing the child's best emotional interests. The most notable attempt was Goldstein, Freud, and Solnit's "psychological parent" test.[20] Goldstein, Freud, and Solnit urged courts to, above all, create emotional stability for children caught between warring parents by making a final and decisive determination of custody rights to one parent or the other. In this respect their goal was the same as the fault-based/tender years doctrine system, but their test was based on a vision of a child's mental health. Working from a psychoanalytic framework, Goldstein, Freud, and Solnit defined the task for divorce courts in resolving child custody disputes as identifying the single parent with whom the child had primary psychological relationships. Stability of the child's emotional relationship with that parent was so important to Goldstein, Freud, and Solnit that they advocated granting the psychological parent the power to preclude the other parent from even visiting with the child for fear it would cause emotional conflict.[21] No court, however, took the policy of stability that far, although the thinking behind it on the importance of emotional stability for the child caught in the turmoil of divorce was enormously influential. The importance of stability for the child also often served as a mental health surrogate for the "tender years" doctrine, as during this period mother was still usually the child's caretaker and many thought her the child's "psychological parent."

The "psychological parent" test appropriately focused courts on the emotional meaning of custody decisions for the child and the importance of stability in the child's emotional life amid the turmoil of family reorganization. Goldstein, Freud, and Solnit, however, formulated their standard based largely on clinical observations of the problems of children in foster care and first applied it to custody contests between the foster family and the child's natural parent. Children in foster care placed there by a natural parent are often shifted from one foster care giver to another and do not have day-to-day relationships with their natural parents for extended periods of time. Mental health experts are thus rightly concerned that a foster child forms a secure emotional attachment with at least one adult, an attachment which the legal system should give a very high priority to protecting.

Maintaining stability of relationships with the only adult with whom the child has emotionally bonded, however, is not the only mental health value in the divorce setting. Identifying a single psychological parent is a quite different and more difficult (some might say impossible) task to accomplish in divorce compared to the foster care setting.[22] The child of divorce, unlike the child in foster care, usually has two involved parents; each can plausibly claim important emotional attachments to the child. Generally, each parent sees the child on a daily basis and neither has placed the child in the care and control of the other.

Setting the court's task as identification of the child's single "psychological parent," moreover, did nothing to change the adversarial procedure used to conduct the "best interests" inquiry in divorce related custody cases; it simply shifted the dialogue from fault language to a mental health framework. The custody trial remained a "winner take all" contest, albeit one enriched with the often conflicting testimony of mental health experts. Parents vigorously disputed which of them had closer emotional bonds with their child while also contesting which was more morally fit to parent. Mental health experts (particularly those hired by one side or the other) sometimes went beyond the available empirical data and their limited capacity to predict the future in making conclusions about which parent should have sole custody to serve the child's best interests.[23]

The Phase I court was, in effect, prepared to declare one parent more important in the life of the child in the name of creating legal and emotional stability for the child. Both types of stability required a judicial choice of one parent over the other. The court's determination did not focus on maintaining a major role for the visiting parent in the life of the child or on long term management of the conflict between the parents so the child could maintain a relationship with both. "Stability" required that the legal death of the marriage because of divorce resulted also in a custody decision that came close to declaring one parent legally and emotionally dead to the child. The court's role was to preside over a family dissolution, not its reorganization. As late as 1978, in considering whether a court should award joint custody over the objections of one parent in a high conflict divorce case,[24] the New York Court of Appeals (its highest court) stated that "divorce dissolves the family as well as the marriage, a reality that may not be ignored."[25]

## B. Phase II: Joint Custody, Mediation and Parent Education

For many American children, however, the "reality that may not be ignored" was that they needed a different approach to child custody decision making than that provided by Phase I courts. Serious rethinking of the judicial role in custody disputes began when evidence began to accumulate showing that for the child, divorce may be the legal dissolution of a marriage, but is certainly not the dissolution of the importance of parent-child or parent-parent relationships. Research suggested that divorce was not, as had been optimistically assumed, a benefit for most children, but potentially the beginning of a downhill spiral with serious emotional, educational, and economic consequences. Research also established that involved fathers played a role in child development that was different from, but as important as, the role of mothers. Rather than needing a stable relationship with a single psychological parent, children generally had important emotional relationships with both parents before divorce and benefitted if such relationships continued after divorce.[26]

These research findings strengthened the resolve of fathers to seek custody, particularly after the demise of the tender years doctrine. Popular culture began to reinforce the notion that fathers could be nurturing parents and should assert custody rights.[27] These forces and the influx of cases that resulted caused a substantive and procedural transformation of the child custody dispute resolution process from fault finding and adversarial procedure to cooperative parenting and alternative dispute resolution.

Beginning in the late 1970s, many courts authorized joint custody using their common law powers. Additionally, the number of states authorizing joint custody by statute increased enormously, from three in 1978 to an overwhelming majority today.[28] The change in substantive legal doctrine was what two commentators have called a "small revolution . . . in child custody law" – enactment of joint custody or "friendly parent"[29] provisions of various levels of operational effect. The statutes vary in strength from making joint custody following divorce a presumption, a preference, or simply a possibility for parents who do not agree to their own parenting plans.[30] Whatever their strength, however, all joint custody statutes constitute a radical break with the sole custody system. All elevate the child's maintaining relationships with both parents after divorce to an important goal of public policy, one often in conflict with the "stability" that was the goal of the Phase I fault finding court.

The joint custody revolution also required a rethinking of the procedural role of the custody courts. That role had to be broader than simply declaring the marriage dead and distributing the assets with a final order. A core insight of modern developmental psychology is that children have different needs and different relationships with their parents at different stages of their emotional maturation. Parental conflict after divorce also ebbs and flows over time. To serve the child's best interest in maintaining relationships with both parents after divorce, courts had to help parents manage the different stages of their conflict and development. They had to recognize, in effect, that for parents and children divorce is a process of adjustment, not a single event encapsulated in a court order. The New Jersey Supreme Court encapsulated this philosophy when it specifically rejected the notion of the New York Court of Appeals that "divorce dissolves the family as well as the marriage. Both the legislation and the case law of this state are designed to encourage parent-child interaction following divorce. This policy is based on the best interests of the child and not on any notion of parental rights."[31]

From the early 1980s on, the critical question for judicial administration became how courts could implement the policy of encouraging continued contact with both parents. Fortunately, the philosophy and procedure of judicial dispute resolution began to shift at about the same time as the movement to encourage relationships with both parents after divorce gathered steam. Courts became more and more interested in "alternative" methods of dispute resolution such as mediation and arbitration, "a reference to the use of these processes in place of litigation."[32] The landmark national event in the increased judicial consciousness of ADR was the 1976 Pound Conference sponsored by the American Bar Association at which leading judges and lawyers expressed deep concern about expense and delay in the justice system in all cases. Professor Frank Sander, Reporter for the Pound Conference's follow-up task force, projected a powerful vision of the court as not simply "a courthouse but a dispute resolution center where the greivant, with the aid of a screening clerk, would be directed to the process (or sequence of processes) most appropriate to a particular type of case."[33] ADR processes – particularly mediation – were thought to be better for litigants with who had to have continuing relationships after the trial was over, as it emphasized their common interests rather than what divided them.

Custody cases were an obvious category of disputes that required not just a "courthouse, but a dispute resolution center." Children in general needed continuing relationships with both parents; parents, in turn, needed a procedural forum to work out their disagreements for the benefit of the child rather a courtroom for adversarial combat which further alienated them from each other.[34] The substantive law movement toward post-divorce cooperative parenting found its procedural partner in the ADR movement. California mandated mediation of child custody disputes in 1980, the event which most clearly marks the beginning of Phase II in the evolution of the judicial role.[35] Many states followed California's lead. A 1995 count by the National Center for State Courts estimated that 200 court-connected programs existed in 38 states, with 33 states having court rules or statutes mandating mediation in child custody disputes.[36]

Despite opposition and natural problems of growth and development,[37] mediation has proved itself generally well suited for the emerging role of dispute resolution forum of choice for encouraging a child's relationship with both parents following divorce.[38] It is confidential, so parents' negative statements about each other do not reach the public forum of a court and their families, friends, and neighbors. Mediation offers parents the possibility of self-determination, the ability to voluntarily formulate their own post divorce parenting plan rather than have a court impose one on them. Many states offer it at low or no cost to parents, saving both the parents' and the courts' resources.[39] "In California, about 20-30% of the total population of separating families file in court to resolve their disputes over the care and custody of their children and are mandated to use mediation. Mediation attains full resolution in one-half, and partial resolution in two-thirds, of all custody and access disputes that enter into court."[40] In addition to resolving disputes, mediation generally results in greater consumer satisfaction, less expense and better parent-child and parent-parent relationships compared to adversary litigation.

Consumer satisfaction with custody mediation is not a surprising finding, given parents' highly negative views of their experiences in family courts. Parents often feel that after the litigation process starts, it quickly caroms out of control. Decisions are made for them – by lawyers and judges and custody evaluators – rather than by them.

A national commission recently reported survey results in which 50-70% of parents characterized the legal system to be "impersonal, intimidating, and intrusive."[41] A recent empirical study of a sample of divorcing parents and their children about their attitudes toward their lawyers confirmed these findings. It reported "an overall consensus that the attorneys' roles and responsibilities in the divorce process are not translating into actual practice. The parents and children did not feel they had adequate representation through guidance, information, attention or quality of service."[42] Parents in the survey felt the process was too long and never finalized, too costly, inefficient, taking control of their lives.[43] "Many of the parents did recognize that they were already feeling angry and hostile, but 71 percent of them maintained the legal process pushed those feelings to a further extreme."[44] Higher number of ethics complaints seem to be filed against divorce lawyers than lawyers in other fields of practice,[45] another rough reflection of public dissatisfaction with the adversary process. The Oregon Task Force on Family Law, a legislatively authorized interdisciplinary reform group,[46] summed up public dissatisfaction after extensive public hearings on that state's divorce system:

> The divorce process in Oregon, as elsewhere, was broken and needed fixing. Lawyers, mediators, judges, counselors and citizens in Oregon agreed that the family court system was too confrontational to meet the human needs of most families undergoing divorce. The process was adversarial where it needn't have been: All cases were prepared as if going to court, when only a small percentage actually did. The judicial system made the parties adversaries, although they had many common interests.

> The Task Force found that the sheer volume of cases was causing the family court system to collapse. Too often, children were treated like property while parents clogged the courts with bitter fights over money, assets and support. The combative atmosphere made it more difficult for divorcing couples to reach a settlement and develop a cooperative relationship once the divorce was final.[47]

Mediation looks very good in contrast to the adversarial litigation system. Studies report that mediation parents reach resolution of their disputes more quickly than litigation parents, taking less than half the time and less cost to produce a parenting plan.[48] Even mediation parents who fail to reach agreement are more likely to settle prior to trial than litigation parents. Mediated agreements also tend to be more specific and detailed than those negotiated by attorneys alone.[49] Studies also report that mediated agreements result in higher rates of children's contact with both parents following divorce and higher rates of compliance with parenting plans and child support agreements compared to agreements reached by negotiations in the shadow of the adversarial process.[50]

Beginning in the early 1990s, educational programs joined mediation as an important service that courts made available to parents.[51] Virtually no court-affiliated educational programs for parents existed in 1960. Today, court-affiliated education is part of the child custody dispute resolution process in most states, as revolutionary a development as no fault divorce, joint custody, and mandated mediation. A recent survey computed a 180% increase in such programs between 1994 and 1998.[52] Forty-five states as of this writing have enacted legislation or court rules authorizing courts to require parents to attend such programs.[53]

The rapid grass roots development of court-affiliated educational programs for divorcing families indicates an emerging national consensus that family courts should have a strategy that encourages parents to reduce and manage their conflicts, not just serve as a forum for litigating about them.[54] Court-affiliated programs typically educate parents about the legal process of divorce and separation, the impact of divorce on the adults involved and, most important, the impact of divorce on their children and how parents can make the transitions easier for them.[55] Parents and judges have been quite enthusiastic about educational programs, and there is some preliminary evidence that parental attitudes and behavior improve as a result of attendance.[56]

Phase II of the transformation of the court's role in divorce related custody disputes accomplished a great deal. During Phase II, divorce became a predictable event in the life cycle of American children and lost its social stigma. Courts broke the stranglehold the sole custody system and adversary procedure had on judicial thinking about children's best interests and the nature of dispute resolution in custody disputes that was inconsistent with the nature and incidence of family reorganization in modern American life. Judicial policy makers appropriately constructed a dispute resolution system on the premise that the problems for children did not result from their parents' divorce per se, but came about because parents put their children in the middle of their continuing conflict. The Phase II managerial court embraced the substantive and procedural changes that encouraged continuing relationships between both parents and their children and helped parents manage their conflict responsibly.

*     *     *     *

*Andrew Schepard, J.D., is Director of the Center for Children, Families and the Law and Professor of Law at Hofstra University School of Law in Hempstead, New York.*

**Notes**

[1]    The first comprehensive statutory proposal for mediation of child custody disputes in New York grew out of a study in the 1980s by the New York State Law Revision Commission for which Professor Linda Silberman of New York University Law School and I were co-consultants. *See Recommendations of the Law Revision Commission to the 1985 Legislature Relating to the Child Custody Decision-Making Process*, 19 COLUM. J.L. & SOC. PROBS. 105 (1985). The Legislature did not enact the proposal in the face of opposition from the matrimonial bar and womens' lawyers groups. Bills are regularly introduced to require mediation of child custody disputes in New York, but so far, none has passed.

[2]    New York does, of course, have parent education programs, including P.E.A.C.E. (Parent Education and Custody Effectiveness) of which I am one of the founders. *See* Andrew Schepard, *War and P.E.A.C.E.: A Preliminary Report and a Model Statute on an Interdisciplinary Educational Program for Divorcing and Separating Parents*, 27 U. MICH. J.L. REFORM 131, 155 (1993) [hereinafter Schepard, *War and P.E.A.C.E.*]. Judicial referrals to parent education programs in New York, however, are not presently authorized by court rules or legislation. New York's Office of Court Administration has introduced legislation to remedy the situation. *See* S. 587-B, 222d Leg., Reg. Sess. (N.Y. 1999). Arkansas, in contrast, has recently joined the 44 other states that have enacted court rules authorizing courts to require parents to attend education programs as part of the divorce process. *See* Act of Mar. 18, 1999, No. 704 (codified at ARK. CODE ANN. § 9-12-322 (LEXIS Supp. 1999)). *See also* Debra A. Clement, *1998 Nationwide Survey of the Legal Status of Parent Education*, 37 FAM. & CONCILIATION CTS. REV. 219, 221 (1998) (providing a list of the other 44 states).

[3]    The only specific factor that the court must consider in a child custody dispute in New York is an allegation of domestic violence. *See* N.Y. DOM. REL. LAW § 240.1(a) (McKinney 1999). In contrast, Arkansas recently amended its child custody standards to require the court to consider the child's need for frequent and continuing contact with both parents and proven allegations of domestic violence in making a custody order. *See* ARK. CODE ANN. § 9-13-101 (a)-(c) (LEXIS Supp. 1999). *See* IRA MARK ELLMAN ET AL., FAMILY LAW: CASES, TEXT, AND PROBLEMS 672-73 (3d ed. 1998) (providing a brief description of and citations to statutes and articles describing the national trend to joint custody). After comprehensive study, a Special Joint Committee on Joint Custody and Access of the Canadian Parliament recently proposed that "[t]he willingness and ability of each of the parties to facilitate and encourage a close and continuing relationship between the child and the other parent" be added as a factor for courts to consider in their multi-factored child custody analysis, along with "[a]ny proven history of family violence" perpetrated by an applicant. SPECIAL JOINT COMMITTEE ON CHILD CUSTODY AND ACCESS OF THE PARLIAMENT OF CANADA, REPORT: FOR THE SAKE OF THE CHILDREN 45 (1998) [hereinafter CANADIAN PARLIAMENT CUSTODY REPORT].

[4]    UNITED STATES CENSUS BUREAU, STATISTICAL ABSTRACT OF THE UNITED STATES, VITAL STATISTICS 75 (1999). The divorce rate recently declined slightly and is presently at the lowest annual rate in two decades. This recent decline, however, must be measured against a 67% increase in the divorce rate between 1970 and 1990.

[5]    ELLMAN ET AL., *supra* note 3, at 240.

[6]    *See* Andrew Schepard, *Parental Conflict Prevention Programs and the Unified Family Court: A Public Health Perspective*, 32 FAM. L.Q. 95, 98-100 (1998) [hereinafter Schepard, *Conflict Prevention Programs*].

[7]    *See* National Center for Health Statistics, Centers for Disease Control, *Advance Report of Final Divorce Statistics*, 1989 & 1990 (visited Mar. 3, 2000) <http://www.cdc.gov/nchswww/products/pubs/pubd/mvsr/supp/44-43/mvs43_9s.htm>.

[8]    Marsha Kline Pruett & Tamara D. Jackson, *The Lawyer's Role During the Divorce Process: Perceptions of Parents, Their Young Children and Their Attorneys*, 33 FAM. L.Q. 283, 284 (1999).

[9]    Richard E. Behrman & Linda Sandham Quinn, *Children and Divorce: Overview and Analysis*, THE FUTURE OF CHILDREN: CHILDREN AND DIVORCE, Spring 1994, at 5.

[10]   BRIAN J. OSTROM & NEIL B. KAUDER, EXAMINING THE WORK OF STATE COURTS, 1995: A NATIONAL PERSPECTIVE FROM THE COURT STATISTICS PROJECT 39 (1996).

[11]   *See id.* at 40.

[12]   *See* Schepard, *Conflict Prevention Programs, supra* note 6, at 100.

[13]   *See* Judith S. Kaye & Jonathan Lippman, *New York State Unified Court System Family Justice Program*, 36 FAM. & CONCILIATION CTS. REV. 144, 145 (1998). The authors are the Chief Judge and the Chief Administrative Judge of the Courts of the State of New York.

[14]   ELLMAN ET AL., *supra* note 3, at 191.

[15]   *See* ELLMAN ET AL., *supra* note 3, at 201. There are, of course, important differences between types of no-fault divorce statues. *See id.* Some states have eliminated fault grounds entirely and make their sole ground for divorce "irreconcilable differences," "incompatibility," or some variation thereof. Id. Other states simply add a no-fault ground like living "separate and apart" for a period of time (often relatively lengthy like 18 months or so) to familiar fault grounds like "adultery" and "cruel or inhuman treatment." Id. The requirement of a lengthy period of separation or a formal separation agreement as a condition of no-fault divorce "may be sufficient to persuade parties to seek divorce on fault grounds instead." Id.

[16]   *See generally* HERBERT JACOB, SILENT REVOLUTION: THE TRANSFORMATION OF DIVORCE LAW IN THE UNITED STATES (1988).

[17]   *See* MAX RHEINSTEIN, MARRIAGE, STABILITY, DIVORCE AND THE LAW 373-81 (1972).

[18]   J. HERBIE DIFONZO, BENEATH THE FAULT LINE: THE POPULAR AND LEGAL CULTURE OF DIVORCE IN TWENTIETH CENTURY America 145, 170 (1997).

[19]   *See* Andrew Schepard, *Taking Children Seriously: Promoting Cooperative Custody After Divorce*, 64 TEX. L. REV. 687, 669-702 (1985) (historical overview of the development of child custody standards) [[hereinafter Schepard, *Taking Children Seriously*].

[20]   JOSEPH GOLDSTEIN ET AL., BEYOND THE BEST INTERESTS OF THE CHILD 37-38 (1973).

[21]   *See id.* at 38.

[22]   See Schepard, *Taking Children Seriously, supra* note 19, at 710-715, for a discussion of the limitations of the sole "psychological parent" test in a divorce and custody context.

[23]   A graphic illustration of how adversarial procedure and the sole custody system stretched the limits of credibility of mental health experts in the 1970s is the transcript of the custody hearing in *Rose v. Rose*, extensively excerpted in JUDITH AREEN, FAMILY LAW: CASES AND MATERIALS 488-574 (4th ed. 1999). Partisan witnesses and experts for each side repeat accusations of parental incompetence and infidelity and grandparent meddling worthy of a daytime soap opera. Goldstein himself testifies on behalf of the father, asserting the primacy of his emotional bond with the child without interviewing any of the parties or the child. It suffices to note that the Rose parents, their expert witnesses, and their lawyers were also in deep dispute about whether the mother or the father was the child's "psychological parent." Mother had the closest relationship with the child until she attempted suicide. Father-and most significantly, the paternal grandmother-took over care of the child during the mother's recovery period. Much of the transcript is devoted to attempts by each parent to bolster evidence of the child's psychological attachment to him or her and to minimize and disparage the child's psychological attachment to the other with the help of hired experts. None of the mental health experts interviewed all relevant family members. The only confident conclusion one can draw from the transcript on this point is the not surprising one that the child had psychological attachments to both sides and their extended families. The whole trial seems a sad exercise in futility and revenge. For a discussion of the limits of the empirical evidence on the effects of divorce on children in making mental health assessments in individual cases, see GARY B. MELTON ET AL., PSYCHOLOGICAL

EVALUATIONS FOR THE COURTS: A HANDBOOK FOR MENTAL HEALTH PROFESSIONALS AND LAWYERS 192-93 (2d ed. 1997).

[24] *See* Braiman v. Braiman, 378 N.E.2d 1019 (N.Y. 1978) (resulting from a custody modification brought by father two years after a separation agreement was entered into giving mother custody; mother accused father of gambling and physical abusiveness while father accused mother of sexual promiscuity; after award of joint custody in lower court father denied mother visitation in violation of court orders; mother disappeared for a period of time).

[25] *See id.* at 1022.

[26] A major landmark in the evolution of thinking about the effects of divorce on children was the publication of the first longitudinal study of fifty families experiencing divorce in Marin County, California. *See generally* JUDITH S. WALLERSTEIN & JOAN Berlin KELLY, SURVIVING THE BREAK-UP: HOW CHILDREN AND PARENTS COPE WITH DIVORCE (1980). Other social science researchers also made major contributions to our understanding of the problem. See Schepard, *Taking Children Seriously, supra* note 19, at 703-08, for a summary of the empirical literature through the middle of the 1980s. For an updated summary, see Schepard, *Conflict Prevention Programs, supra* note 6, at 96-105.

[27] The defining even in popular culture legitimizing fathers' claims to custody was the enormously popular Academy Award winning movie, KRAMER VS. KRAMER (Columbia 1979). Ironically, the movie relied on the discredited "tender years" doctrine to create dramatic tension; mother (played by Meryl Streep), who had abandoned her child and agreed to sole custody for the father (played by Dustin Hoffman), actually had a weak case for modification of the initial agreement. She was awarded sole custody after trial on the basis of the tender years doctrine which had been declared unconstitutional by New York courts several years before. Moreover, the film was woefully inaccurate in its depiction of the adversarial process in child custody cases-the child was, for example, never interviewed by a mental health expert. The parents in the end chose to voluntarily establish a custody arrangement rather than adhere to the one favoring the mother that had been ordered by the court, perhaps foreshadowing the judicial system's increasing emphasis on parental rather than judicial decision making in child custody disputes. *See* David Ray Papke, *Peace Between the Sexes: Law and Gender in* Kramer vs. Kramer, 30 U.S.F. L. REV. 1199 (1996).

[28] *See* ELLMAN ET AL., *supra* note 3, at 673.

[29] Elizabeth Scott & Andre Derdeyn, *Rethinking Joint Custody*, 45 OHIO ST. L.J. 455, 456 (1984).

[30] *See* ELLMAN ET AL., *supra* note 3, at 673 (citing Doris Freed & Henry Foster, *Family Law in the 50 States*, 22 FAM. L.Q. 367, 467 (1989)). By 1989, 34 states had joint custody statutes of one sort or another. *See* ELLMAN ET AL., *supra* note 3, at 673. *See also* ELLMAN ET AL., *supra* note 3, at 673-75, for various state statutes which describe different state policies towards joint custody. The authors of this well respected family law case book conclude their survey of state statutes on joint custody as follows: "[s]ome [states] simply allow joint custody; others require it to be considered[;] ... whether special findings are required if joint custody is (or is not) ordered, and the extend to which the details of a joint custody arrangement are left up to the parents themselves." *Id.* at 675.

[31] Beck v. Beck, 432 A.2d 63, 66 n.3 (N.J. 1981).

[32] STEPHEN GOLDBERG ET AL., DISPUTE RESOLUTION: NEGOTIATION, MEDIATION, AND OTHER PROCESSES 7 (3d ed. 1999).

[33] *See id.* (citing Frank E.A. Sander, *Varieties of Dispute Processing*, 70 F.R.D. 111 (1976)).

[34] *See* Schepard, *Taking Children Seriously, supra* note 19, at 756-59, for a 1986 discussion of the benefits of mediation in child custody disputes.

[35] *See* Susan C. Kuhn, Comment, *Mandatory Mediation: California Civil Code Section 4607*, 33 EMORY L.J. 733 (1984). The mandatory mediation statute was originally enacted as part of the

California Civil Code. *See* CAL. CIV. CODE § 4607 (West 1983). Today, it is part of the California Family Code. *See* CAL. FAM. CODE § 3170-3171 (West Supp. 1999).

[36]   *See* Peter Salem & Ann L. Milne, *Making Mediation Work in a Domestic Violence Case*, 17 FAM. AD. 34, 34 (1995).

[37]   Some suggested, for example, that mediation is not in the best interests of women because they have fewer resources and are more likely to make compromises for the sake of their children than men and thus are easy targets for unscrupulous manipulation. *See* Penelope Eileen Bryan, *Reclaiming Professionalism: The Lawyer's Role in Divorce Mediation*, 28 FAM. L.Q. 177 (1994). There are case histories to support such concern (as there are case histories of women being traumatized by courts and unscrupulous lawyers) but little systematic empirical evidence that women fare worse in mediation than litigation or negotiations in the adversarial system. In most studies, men and women express approximately equal satisfaction with mediation as a dispute resolution process. Furthermore, women report that mediation is helpful to them in "standing up" to their spouses, and rated themselves more capable and knowledgeable as a result of participation in mediation. *See* Joan B. Kelly, *A Decade of Divorce Mediation Research*, 34 FAM. & CONCILIATION CTS. REV. 373, 377-78 (1996) (describing numerous studies); Carol J. King, *Burdening Access to Justice: The Cost of Divorce Mediation on the Cheap*, 73 ST. JOHN'S L. REV. 375, 441 (1999) (summarizing the results of a survey of mediation participants in two Ohio judicial districts by reporting that "[t]he data [from the study] does not support the fears that women feel disadvantaged in mediation").

[38]   *See* Andrew Schepard, *Supporting Parent-Clients in Mediation of Child Custody Disputes*, 10 PRAC. LITIGATOR 7 (1999).

[39]   Problems in the delivery of mediation services to the large population of divorcing and separating parents continue to exist. One major problem, of course, is how to fund mediation services in an era of tight judicial budgets. For a discussion of the available alternatives, see King, *supra* note 37. Another problem is the creation of generally recognized standards of practice and professionalism for mediators, a task in which the family mediation community is currently engaged. *See Draft Model Standards of Practice for Divorce and Family Mediators*, 38 FAM. & CONCILIATION CTS. REV. 106 (2000).

[40]   Janet R. Johnston, *Building Multidisciplinary Professional Partnerships with the Court on Behalf of High Conflict Divorcing Families and Their Children: Who Needs What Kind of Help?*, 22 U. Ark. LITTLE ROCK L. REV 451 (2000).

[41]   UNITED STATES COMMISSION ON CHILD AND FAMILY WELFARE, PARENTING OUR CHILDREN: IN THE BEST INTERESTS OF THE NATION. A REPORT TO THE PRESIDENT AND CONGRESSS 38-39 (1996).

[42]   Pruett & Jackson, *supra* note 8, at 306.

[43]   *See* Pruett & Jackson, *supra* note 8, at 299-300.

[44]   Pruett & Jackson, *supra* note 8, at 298.

[45]   *See* Stephen Labaton, *Are Divorce Lawyers Really the Sleaziest?*, N.Y. TIMES, Sept. 5, 1993, § 4 (Week in Review) at 5.

[46]   Working in tandem with the Future of the Courts Committee, the Oregon Legislature established the bipartisan interdisciplinary Task Force on Family Law which can well serve as a model for other states considering divorce and custody reform. *See* William Howe III & Maureen McNight, Oregon *Task Force on Family Law: A New System to Resolve Family Law Conflicts*, 33 FAM. & CONCILIATION CTS. REV. 173 (1995). See also Schepard, *Conflict Prevention Programs, supra* note 6, at 124-26, for a description of the Task Force and its work in rethinking the adversarial system of divorce.

[47]   Oregon TASK FORCE ON FAMILY LAW, FINAL REPORT TO GOVERNOR JOHN A. KITZHABER AND THE Oregon LEGISLATIVE ASSEMBLY 2 (1997).

[48]   *See* Kelly, *supra* note 37, at 376-77.

[49]   *See* Kelly, *supra* note 37, at 373 (short summary of research results with citations).

[50]   *See* Peter A. Dillon & Robert E. Emery, *Divorce Mediation and Resolution of Child Custody Disputes: Long Term Effects*, 66 AM. J. OF ORTHOPSYCHIATRY 131, 132-33 (1996).

[51]   *See generally* Schepard, *War and P.E.A.C.E., supra* note 2; Schepard, *Conflict Prevention Programs, supra* note 6.

[52]   *See* Margie J. Geasler & Karen R. Blaisure, *1998 Nationwide Survey of Court-Connected Divorce Education Programs*, 37 FAM. & CONCILIATION CTS. REV. 36 (1999).

[53]   *See supra* note 2 and sources cited therein.

[54]   *See* Schepard, *Conflict Prevention Programs, supra* note 6, at 124.

[55]   *See* Geasler & Blaisure, *supra* note 52, at 51.

[56]   See Schepard, *Conflict Prevention Programs, supra* note 6, at 118-21, for a summary of research findings.

# B: Problem-solving Courts

# [5]

# Problem-solving Courts: A Brief Primer

## Greg Berman and John Feinblatt

*This essay traces the history of problem-solving courts (including drug courts, community courts, domestic violence courts and others), outlines problem-solving principles, and answers a basic set of questions about these new judicial experiments: Why now? What forces have sparked judges and attorneys across the country to innovate? What results have problem-solving courts achieved? And what – if any – trade-offs have been made to accomplish these results?*

The past decade has been a fertile one for court reform. All across the country, courts – in concert with both government and community partners – have been experimenting with new ways to deliver justice. This wave of innovation goes by many names and takes many forms: Domestic violence court in Massachusetts; drug court in Florida; mental health court in Washington; community court in New York. Each of these specialized courts targets different kinds of concerns in different kinds of places. And yet they all share a basic organizing theme: a desire to improve the results that courts achieve for victims, litigants, defendants, and communities.

"Problem-solving courts" are still very much a work in progress. As yet, there is no clearly articulated definition or philosophy that unites all of those who espouse or practice problem-solving justice. Viewed in the aggregate, however, it is possible to identify several common elements that distinguish problem-solving courts from the way in which cases are typically handled in today's state courts. Problem-solving courts use their authority to forge new responses to chronic social, human, and legal problems – including problems like family dysfunction, addiction, delinquency, and domestic violence – that have proven resistant to conventional solutions. They seek to broaden the focus of legal proceedings, from simply adjudicating past facts and legal issues to changing the future behavior of litigants and ensuring the future well-being of communities. And they attempt to fix broken systems, making courts (and their partners) more accountable and responsive to their primary customers – the citizens who use courts every day, either as victims, jurors, witnesses, litigants, or defendants.

The proliferation of problem-solving courts raises some important questions: Why now? What forces have sparked judges and attorneys across the country to innovate? What results have problem-solving courts achieved? And what – if any – trade-offs have been made to accomplish these results?

This article is an attempt to begin to answer these questions. It traces the history of problem-solving courts, outlines a basic set of problem-solving principles, and poses a set of questions that are worthy of further study as problem-solving courts move from experiment to institutionalization.

*        *        *        *

Problem-solving courts are a response to the frustrations engendered by overwhelmed state courts. They are an attempt to achieve better outcomes while at the same time protecting individual rights. While drug courts, community courts, domestic violence courts, mental health courts, and other problem-solving initiatives address different problems, they do share some common elements:

- *Case Outcomes*
  Problem-solving courts seek to achieve tangible outcomes for victims, for offenders, and for society. These include reductions in recidivism, reduced stays in foster care for children, increased sobriety for addicts, and healthier communities. As Chief Judge Kaye has written, " ... outcomes – not just process and precedents – matter. Protecting the rights of an addicted mother is important. So is protecting her children and getting her off drugs" (1999:13). Protecting the rights of an addicted mother is important. So is protecting her children and getting her off drugs" (1999:13).

- *System Change*
  In addition to re-examining individual case outcomes, problem-solving courts also seek to re-engineer how government systems respond to problems like addiction, mental illness, and child neglect. They promote reform outside of the courthouse as well as within. For example, family treatment courts that handle cases of child neglect have encouraged local child welfare agencies to adopt new staffing patterns and to improve case management practices.

- *Judicial Monitoring*
  Problem-solving courts rely upon the active use of judicial authority to solve problems and to change the behavior of litigants. Instead of passing off cases to other judges, to probation departments, to community-based treatment programs – judges at problem-solving courts stay involved with each case even after adjudication. Drug court judges, for example, closely supervise the performance of offenders in drug treatment, requiring them to return to court frequently for urine testing and courtroom progress reports.

• *Collaboration*
  Problem-solving courts employ a collaborative approach, relying on both government and nonprofit partners (i.e., criminal justice agencies, social service providers, community groups, and others) to help achieve their goals. For example, many domestic violence courts have developed partnerships with batterers' programs and probation departments to help improve the monitoring of defendants.

• *Non-Traditional Roles*
  Some problem-solving courts have altered the dynamics of the courtroom, including, at times, certain features of the adversarial process. For example, at many drug courts, attorneys (on both sides of the aisle) work together to craft systems of sanctions and rewards for offenders in drug treatment. Problem-solving courts often engage judges in unfamiliar roles as well, asking them to convene community meetings or broker relationships with social service providers.

The cumulative impact of these changes has been significant, and not just on the judges and lawyers who staff problem-solving courts. Problem-solving courts are still relatively new, but there are signs that they have begun to have a tangible impact on thousands of victims, defendants, and community residents. These include domestic violence victims who have been linked to safe shelter, residents of high-crime areas who no longer have to avoid local parks at night, formerly addicted mothers who have been reunited with their children, and mentally ill defendants who have received meaningful treatment for the first time.

## V. RESULTS

Rigorous, independent evaluations of problem-solving courts are just starting to emerge, but the early results have been promising. As the most well-established brand of problem-solving court, drug courts have the longest track record. The evidence shows that drug courts have achieved solid results with regard to keeping offenders in treatment, reducing drug use and recidivism, and saving jail and prison costs.

The most authoritative review of drug courts is a meta-analysis by Columbia University's National Center on Addiction and Substance Abuse (CASA) that looked at fifty-nine independent evaluations covering forty-eight drug courts throughout the country (Belenko 1998). Among other findings, this study revealed that drug court participants are far more likely to successfully complete mandated substance abuse treatment than comparable participants who seek help on a voluntary basis. One-year treatment retention rates are 60 percent for drug courts, compared to 10 to 30 percent among voluntary programs (Belenko 1998:29-30). In addition, the CASA analysis found that defendant drug use and recidivism are substantially reduced during the period of drug court participation (ibid.:36). While less conclusive, there is also evidence to suggest that the benefits of drug court participation do not end when a defendant graduates from the program. According to the CASA study, drug court participants have lower *post-program* re-arrest rates as well. Of nine drug court evaluations that used a comparison group, eight found positive recidivism results (ibid.:39-41).

In addition to these impacts on participants, the CASA meta-analysis found that drug courts generated significant cost savings. In general, incarceration is far more costly than treatment. As a result, drug courts save money even after accounting for administrative costs. A study of the Multnomah County, Oregon drug court found that, over a two-year period, the court had achieved $2.5 million in criminal justice cost savings, based on 440 participants (ibid.:34). Additional savings outside the criminal justice system – reductions in victimization, theft, public assistance, and medical claims were estimated to be an additional $10 million (ibid.:34).

The most detailed evaluation of a community court is the National Center for State Courts's recently published assessment of the Midtown Community Court. The National Center's team of researchers found that the court had helped reduce low-level crime in the neighborhood: Prostitution arrests dropped 63 percent, and unlicensed vending dropped 24 percent (Sviridoff et al. 2000: 155). The compliance rates for community service at Midtown were the highest in New York City – an improvement of 50 percent. Supervised offenders performing community service contributed more than $175,000 worth of labor to the local community each year.

Just as important, preliminary findings from a telephone survey of five hundred area residents suggest that the Midtown experiment has made an impression in the court of public opinion. Sixty-four percent of the respondents said that they were willing to pay additional taxes for a community court. And according to evaluators, these results have been achieved without sacrificing efficiency. In fact, by keeping defendants and police officers in the neighborhood instead of transporting them to the downtown courthouse, the Midtown Court cut the time between arrest and arraignment in 1994 by 45 percent (ibid.:203).

Less is known about the impacts of domestic violence courts, family treatment courts, mental health courts, re-entry courts, and other newer forms of problem-solving justice. Their self-reported results are, perhaps predictably, encouraging – improved services for victims of domestic violence, reductions in probation violations, and increased numbers of defendants receiving needed treatment. Whether these findings will withstand the rigors of independent evaluators remains to be seen. The days ahead will see the completion of several important evaluations of problem-solving courts, including a national, multi-site review of domestic violence courts by the Urban Institute.

## VI. TENSIONS

The preliminary results of problem-solving courts have earned these projects high marks from many corners, including elected officials, the press, and funders. They have also fueled the field's rapid expansion. Good initial results do not insulate problem-solving courts from criticism, however. After all, the problem-solving reform efforts of the last several years have taken place within a branch of government that is understandably cautious about innovation. Core judicial values – certainty, reliability, impartiality, and fairness – have been safeguarded over many generations, largely through a reliance on tradition and precedent. As a result, efforts to introduce new ways of doing justice are always subjected to careful scrutiny. Problem-solving courts are no exception to this rule, nor should they be. Critics have questioned both their results (Hoffman 2000) and their ability to preserve the individual rights of defendants (Baar 2000). While the academic literature on problem-solving courts is still emerging, it seems clear that there are a number of areas of potential tension between this new brand of jurisprudence and standard practice in state courts:

• *Coercion*
   What procedures exist to ensure that a defendant's consent to participate in a problem-solving court is fairly and freely given? Are problem-solving courts any more coercive than the current practice of plea bargaining that resolves the large majority of criminal cases in this country?

• *Zealous Advocacy*
   Is advocacy in a problem-solving court more or less zealous than in a traditional court? How should attorneys measure their effectiveness? To what extent do problem-solving courts actually help attorneys – both prosecutors and defenders – realize their professional goals?

• *Structure*
   Do problem-solving courts give greater license to judges to make rulings based on their own idiosyncratic world views rather than the law? Or, with their pre-determined schemes of graduated sanctions and rewards, do problem-solving courts actually limit the discretion of judges and provide more uniform justice than conventional courts?

• *Impartiality*
   As judges become better informed about specialized classes of cases, is their impartiality affected? As they solicit the wisdom of social scientists, researchers, and clinicians, are they more likely to become engaged in ex parte communication?

• *Paternalism*
   Are problem-solving judges imposing treatment regimes on defendants without reference to the complexity of individuals' problems? Do problemsolving courts widen the net of governmental control? Or are they simply efforts by judges and attorneys to focus more constructively and humanely on the underlying problems of the people who come to court?

• *Separation of Powers*
   Do problem-solving courts inappropriately blur the lines among the branches of government? As judges become involved in activities like convening, brokering, and organizing, are they infringing upon the territory of the executive branch? Are they, in effect, making policy? Or are judges simply taking advantage of the discretion they have traditionally been afforded over sentencing in order to craft more meaningful sanctions?

There are several important realities to keep in mind as one attempts to make sense of these tensions. The first is context. When weighing the merits of any reform effort it is always important to ask the question: compared to what? Proponents of problem-solving courts have been adamant about not allowing critics to pick apart these new initiatives by comparing them to an idealized vision of justice that does not exist in real life. They point to the fact that the large majority of criminal, housing, and family court cases today are handled in courts that

Roscoe Pound and John Marshall would scarcely recognize. Judge Judy Harris Kluger, the administrative judge for New York City's criminal courts, has described standard practice in the state courts: " ... for a long time, my claim to fame was that I arraigned 200 cases in one session. That's ridiculous. When I was arraigning cases, I'd be handed the papers, say the sentence is going to be five days, ten days, whatever, never even looking at the defendant" (Berman 2000:81). Under these circumstances, it is fair to question the extent to which many frontline state courts measure up to their own ideals of doing justice. While the excesses of today's "McJustice" courts do not justify any and all reform efforts, they do help to explain why so many judges and attorneys have been attracted to new ways of doing business. And they provide a valuable context for evaluating the merits of problem-solving courts.

In addition, any effort to separate the wheat from the chaff with problemsolving courts must take into account what might be called the "shoddy practice effect." Put simply, some of the concerns raised by critics of problemsolving courts are a response to the failings of individual judges, attorneys, and courtrooms, rather than an indictment of anything intrinsic to problem-solving courts. These concerns include courts that have been created without any consultation with the local defense bar; courts that have failed to offer specialized training to the attorneys that work within them; courts in which defendants are not given a meaningful opportunity to raise factual and Fourth Amendment defenses; courts in which "back-up" incarceration sentences for defendants who fail to comply are considerably longer than the sanctions that the defendant would have originally faced; and courts that have done little to ensure that social service interventions are effective and culturally appropriate.

While serious, these are all issues that might reasonably be resolved by better planning and the development and dissemination of best practices. In fact, there are already signs that problem-solving innovators in the field are beginning to adapt their models to address these issues. For example, problem-solving courts in Seattle and Portland have instituted structures that give defendants several weeks to test out treatment while their cases are still pending. Defendants can use this period to decide whether to opt into or out of the program, while their defense attorneys can use the time to investigate the strength of the case against their clients (Feinblatt & Denckla 2001).

## VII. FAIRNESS

Not all questions about problem-solving courts can be explained away by bad practice or the widespread problems of today's mill courts, however. The most pointed critiques have asked whether problem-solving courts' emphasis on improving case outcomes and protecting public order has come at the expense of the rights of defendants (Baar 2000). Are problem-solving courts fair? Have they fundamentally altered the rights protections typically found in today's criminal courts? Courts have traditionally relied on zealous advocacy as a bulwark against these kinds of concerns, so the role of attorneys at problem-solving courts is an issue that merits special scrutiny (Feinblatt, Berman & Denckla 2000). Michael Smith of the University of Wisconsin Law School has been particularly vocal in articulating the importance of advocates to problem-solving courts:

"One of the things that judges and courts are particularly good at when they're not just milling people is fact-finding. But a fact-finding court is heavily reliant on advocates if it's any good .... If we don't figure out a way to take advantage of that, then we're not going to have very good problem-solving courts. The courts will be no better than the social service clinics, which have failed to address these problems. So the adversary system and the presence of defense counsel are of enormous value in problem solving." (Berman 2000:83)

The nature of advocacy in problem-solving courts is the subject of some debate. Some look at the "team approach" of drug courts, where all of the courtroom players work together to support a defendant's participation in treatment, and declare that defense attorneys have abdicated their role as forceful advocates on behalf of their clients. Others argue that adversarialism is alive and well in problem-solving courts. They point to the fact that throughout the adjudication process – up until a defendant decides, by virtue of pleading to reduced charges, to enter treatment – prosecutors and defenders in problem-solving courts typically relate to one another as they always have: as adversaries. In addition to contesting the merits of each case, advocates in drug courts also argue about eligibility criteria, the length of treatment sentences, and appropriate treatment modalities (Feinblatt, Berman & Denckla 2000).

In general, what is different about problem-solving courts are the activities that take place after adjudication, as judges and attorneys become engaged in the ongoing monitoring of defendants instead of leaving this job to, probation departments or community-based organizations or – in all too many cases – to no one at all. (It is worth noting that some drug courts and community courts – and many domestic violence courts – depart from the standard problem-solving model, mandating defendants to pre-trial rather than post-disposition interventions. These courts may raise additional questions from those concerned with due process protections.) As John Goldkamp of Temple University has observed, "Generally, adversarial procedures are employed at the screening and admission stage ... and at the conclusion of drug court when participants are terminated and face legal consequences or graduate. During the drug court process, however, formal adversarial rules generally do not apply" (Goldkamp 2000:952). As Goldkamp's formulation makes plain, by and large, problem-solving courts seem to emphasize traditional due process protections during the adjudication phase of a case and the achievement of tangible, constructive outcomes post-adjudication. In doing so, problem-solving courts have sought to balance fairness and effectiveness – the protection of individual rights and the preservation of public order (Feinblatt, Berman & Denckla 2000).

To what extent have problem-solving courts achieved this delicate balancing act? It varies from jurisdiction to jurisdiction. And it depends upon the perspective of the person asking the question. Conversations about the fairness of problem-solving courts often spark a Rashomon effect, with judges having one response, prosecutors another, and defenders yet a third.

There is little doubt that the tensions between problem-solving courts and conventional state courts are felt particularly acutely by defenders. There is an almost palpable sense of ambivalence on the part of many defenders toward problem-solving courts. After all, defense attorneys have been arguing for years that courts should make more aggressive use of drug treatment, mental health counseling, and other alternative sanctions. Problem-solving courts have begun to deliver on this expectation, but at the cost of greater state involvement in the lives of their clients. Are there any historical antecedents that might guide defenders as they wrestle with competing professional goals? What are their ethical obligations to their clients, given the changing judicial landscape? Is there a need for new standards of effective lawyering at problem-solving courts? These are issues that merit deeper investigation and additional scholarship.

## VIII. CONCLUSION

Now is an important moment to begin to look at the questions raised by problem-solving courts. Problem-solving courts have achieved a kind of critical mass. They are no longer just a set of isolated experiments driven by entrepreneurial judges and administrators. According to John Goldkamp:

> "[W]hat we have now is not a bunch of little hobbies that judges have in isolated jurisdictions, but rather a paradigm shift that larger court systems are trying to come to grips with. They're at your door step. The question isn't:
> Gosh, are courts supposed to be doing this? It's: What are you going to do about it? How does it fit in? It's no longer a question of whether this should have been invented. They're here." (Berman 2000:85)

Problem-solving courts have begun to spark the interest of not just frontline practitioners, but the chief judges and administrators who make decisions about court policies and court operations. The signs are unmistakable. Problem-solving courts continue to multiply. California and New York are overhauling the way that their courts handle drug cases. And the Conference of Chief Justices and the Conference of State Court Administrators have passed a joint resolution that pledges to "encourage the broad integration, over the next decade, of the principles and methods employed in problem solving courts into the administration of justice" (2000:2-3).

Formal institutionalization of any new idea does not come easy, however. If problem-solving courts are to accomplish this goal – if they truly hope to infiltrate the mainstream of thinking about law and justice in this country they must begin to preach to the unconverted. This means reaching out to the skeptics and the uninitiated within state courts – defenders concerned about due process protections, administrators worried about the allocation of limited resources, and prosecutors and judges who see nothing wrong with the way they have been doing their jobs for years. And it means reaching outside of the system as well – to law schools and bar associations and elected officials. In the process, advocates of problem-solving courts must tackle some of the policy and procedural concerns that have been outlined in this article. And they must begin to think through the problems of "going to scale," that is, of how small-scale experiments can be translated into systemwide reform.

These are not insignificant challenges, to be sure. But, given the tangible results that the first generation of problem-solving courts have achieved reduced recidivism among drug-addicted offenders, reduced probation violation and dismissal rates in domestic violence cases, and improved public safety (and confidence in justice) in communities harmed by crimethey are challenges well worth pursuing.

*Greg Berman, B.A., is Director of the Center for Court Innovation in New York City and the co-author of Good Courts: The Case for Problem-Solving Justice (The New Press, 2005).*

*John Feinblatt, J.D., is the Founding Director of the Center for Court Innovation in New York City. Since 2002, he has served as Criminal Justice Coordinator for the Mayor of the City of New York.*

## References

BAAR, CARL (2000) "The Role of the Courts: Two Faces of Justice." Paper presented at Third National Symposium on Court Management, 13-18 August 2000, Atlanta.

BELENKO, STEVEN (1998) "Research on Drug Courts: A Critical Review," *National Drug Court Institute Review 1(1):1-42.*

-- (1999) "Research on Drug Courts: A Critical Review, 1999 Update," *National Drug Court Institute Review 2(2):1-58.*

BERMAN, GREG (2000) "What Is a Traditional Judge Anyway?: Problem Solving in the State Courts," *Judicature 84:78-85.*

BOLDT, RICHARD C. (1998) "Rehabilitative Punishment and the Drug Treatment Court Movement," *Washington University Law Quarterly 76:1205-1306.*

CONFERENCE OF CHIEF JUSTICES AND CONFERENCE OF STATE COURTS ADMINISTRA-TORS (2000) "CCJ Resolution 22 COSCA Resolution for In Support of ProblemSolving Courts," *Journal of the Center for Families. Children and the Courts 2:2-3.*

FEINBLATT, JOHN, and GREG BERMAN (200 I) "Community Courts: A Brief Primer," *U.S. Attorney Bulletin 49(1):33-38.*

FEINBLATT, JOHN, GREG BERMAN, and AUBREY FOX (2000) "Institutionalizing Innovation: The New York Drug Court Story," *Fordham Urban Law Journal* 28:277-92.

FEINBLATT, JOHN, GREG BERMAN, and DEREK DENCKLA (2000) "Judicial Innovation at the Crossroads: The Future of Problem-Solving Courts" *Court Manager* 15(3):28-34.

FEINBLATT, JOHN, GREG BERMAN, and MICHELE SVIRIDOFF (1998) "Neighborhood Justice at the Midtown Community Court." In *Crime and Place: Plenary Papers of the 1997 Conference on Criminal Justice Research and Evaluation.* Washington, D.C.: U.S. Dept. of Justice, Office of Justice Programs, National Institute of Justice.

FEINBLATT, JOHN, and DEREK DENCKLA (2001) "What Does It Mean to Be an Effective Lawyer: Prosecutors and Defenders in Problem-Solving Courts," *Judicature 84:206-14.*

GOLDKAMP, JOHN S. (2000) "The Drug Court Response: Issues and Implications for Justice Change," *Albany Law Review: 63:923-61.*

GOLDKAMP, JOHN S., and DORIS WEILAND (1993) *Assessing the Impact of Dade County's Felony Drug Court.* Washington D.C.: U.S. Dept. of Justice, Office of Justice Programs, National Institute of Justice.

HOFFMAN, MORRIS B. (2000) "The Drug Court Scandal," *North Carolina Law Review* 78:1437-1534.

HORA, PEGGY FULTON, WILLIAM G. SCHMA, and JOHN T. A. ROSENTIIAL (1998) "Therapeutic Jurisprudence and the Drug Treatment Court Movement: Revolutionizing the Criminal Justice System's Response to Drug Abuse and Crime in America," *Notre Dame Law Review 74:439-537.*

KAYE, JUDITH s. (1999) "Making the Case for Hands-On Courts," *Newsweek* 11 October: 13.

KNIPPS, SUSAN K., and GREG BERMAN (2000) "New York's Problem-Solving Courts Provide Meaningful Alternatives to Traditional Remedies," *New York State Bar Journal* 72(5):8-10.

LEE, ERIC (2000) *Community Courts: An Evolving Model.* Washington, D.C.: U.S Dept. of Justice,

Office of Justice Programs, Bureau of Justice Assistance.

NATIONAL CENTER FOR STATE COURTS (1997) *Child Protection Orders: The Benefits and Limitation for Victims of Domestic Violence.* Williamsburg, Va.: National Center for State Courts.

NATIONAL INSTITUTE OF JUSTICE (1998) *Arrestee Drug Abuse Monitoring (ADAM) 1997 Annual Report on Adult and Juvenile Arrestees.* Washington, D.C.: U.S. Dept. of Justice, Office of Justice Programs.

NEW YORK STATE COMMISSION ON DRUGS AND THE COURTS (2000) *Confronting the Cycle of Addiction and Recidivism: A Report to Chief Judge Judith S. Kaye.* Albany: New York State Commission on Drugs and Courts.

OFFICE OF JUSTICE PROGRAMS DRUG COURT CLEARINGHOUSE AND TECHNICAL ASSISTANCE PROJECT (1999) *Looking at a Decade of Drug Courts: Rev. 1999.* Washington, D.C. : Justice Programs Office, School of Public Affairs, American University. Online at < http://www. american.edu/justice/decadel.htm > .

-- (2000) *Summary of Drug Court Activity by State and County.* Washington, D.C.: Justice Programs Office, School of Public Affairs, American University. Online at < http://www.american.edu/justice/ drgchrt1.pdf>.

OSTROM, BRIAN J., and NEAL B. KAUDER (eds.) (1998) *Examining the Work of State Courts, 1998: A National Perspective from the Court Statistics Project.* Williamsburg, Va.: National Center for State Courts.

ROTTMAN, DAVID, and PAMELA CASEY (1999) "Therapeutic Jurisprudence and the Emergence of Problem-Solving Courts," *National Institute of Justice Journal* (July): 12-20.

ROHDE, DAVID (1999) "Crackdown on Minor Offenses Swamps New York City Courts," *New York Times,* 2 February:Al.

STURM, SUSAN P. (1997) "From Gladiators to Problem-Solvers: Connecting Conversations about Women, the Academy and the Legal Profession," *Duke Journal of Gender Law & Policy 4:119-47.*

SVIRIDOFF, MICHELE, DAVID B. ROTTMAN, BRIAN OSTROM, and RICHARD CURTIS *(2000) Dispensing Justice Locally: The Implementation and Effects of the Midtown Community Court.* Amsterdam: Harwood Academic Publishers.

TSAr, BETSY (2000) "The Trend Towards Specialized Domestic Violence Courts: Improvements on an Effective Innovation," *Fordham Law Review 68:1285-1327.*

WEXLER, DAVID B., and BRUCE J. WINICK (1991) "Therapeutic Jurisprudence as a New Approach to Mental Health Law Policy Analysis and Research," *University of Miami Law Review 45:979-1004.*

WRIGHT, MARTIN (1996) *Justice for Victims and Offenders: A Restorative Justice Response to Crime.* 2d ed. Winchester, U.K.: Waterside Press.

ZEIDMAN, STEVEN M. (1998) "To Plead or Not to Plead: Effective Assistance and Client-Centered Counseling," *Boston College Law Review 39:841-909.*

## Laws Cited

1994 Crime Act, 42 USC § 13701.

# [6]

# Fixing Families:
# The Story of the Manhattan Family Treatment Court

## Robert Wolf

*This is no ordinary day in court. For one thing, the jury box is overflowing with people, many of them clutching bouquets of flowers. And the gallery is packed. There are television cameras, too, plus a large table near the judge's bench full of cake and soda. But the most unique feature is the children. They're doing their best to be quiet, with their hands in their laps, but periodically one chases another down an aisle, another shouts a greeting to a familiar face, and an infant cries for a moment before a bottle or a soothing bounce restores calm.*

*There is no trial today, no special hearing, no stream of arraignments. Today is graduation day. The 22 people sitting in and around the jury box are parents who lost their children because they were abusing drugs. But they don't abuse drugs anymore. They've gone through drug treatment, learned parenting skills, and had vocational training as part of a unique judicial experiment, the Manhattan Family Treatment Court. They are the second group to graduate from the court, which was created in March 1998 in response to long-standing problems that many urban family courts face: parents who don't follow through on court orders to participate in drug treatment and children languishing in foster care for years on end.*

*The Manhattan Family Treatment Court has so far been remarkably successful, sending hundreds of parents into long-term drug treatment, building their skills as parents, and reuniting drug-free parents with their children in record time. In New York City's child welfare system, the average foster-care stay is about four years – an eternity in the life of a child. The family treatment court has reduced the average stay to about a year for children whose parents have successfully completed the court's program. In cases where parents haven't been successful, the court has taken an average of 13 months to begin termination of parental rights or permanently place the children in the home of a relative – far more quickly than in the past.*

*But the court is not just about numbers. It's about changing lives, a reality reflected again and again in the words of the 22 parents who graduate today. Says one: "My life has changed in that I don't live in darkness anymore. I don't feel destitute. Today I can smile from my heart and know that living a life without drugs is a beautiful life. I owe this to God and the court for giving me the opportunity to be a better mother."*

*This article tells the court's story – from its planning through its first two years of operation – in the words of the people who run it and participate in it. Its story provides valuable lessons for anyone grappling with some of the seemingly intractable problems that arise when drug addiction and families collide.*

## THE CRACK EPIDEMIC

The family treatment court's story begins with crack cocaine. Beginning in the early 1980s, the crack epidemic fueled a huge rise in child protective cases. By the end of the decade, neglect filings, which previously had been only a small percentage of New York City's family court caseload, had quadrupled.[1] By the mid-1990s, three-fourths of suspected child abuse and neglect cases in the city involved substance-abusing parents.[2]

This flood of cases "strained the resources of child protective agencies," New York State Chief Judge Judith S. Kaye said in a speech in 1997. "The highly addictive nature of crack demanded intensive services, yet gaps in service delivery and case supervision were rampant. As a result, more children entered foster care, more stayed longer, and more saw adoption as their only hope of a permanent home. The family court thus also found itself engaged in human recycling – placing a child born with a positive toxicology for cocaine in foster care one year, followed by another 'positive tox' sibling placed in care the next."[3]

The sad reality was that more and more children every year were going into foster care while proportionally fewer were getting out. Between 1985 and 1991 the number of children in foster care nearly tripled in New York City, from about 17,000 to 50,000, while the average length of stay in foster care leapt from 1.81 years in 1985 to 4.5 years by 1997.[4]

The protracted stays in foster care were a clear sign that the system was failing. Caseworkers from the Administration for Children's Services (ACS), the city's child protection agency, removed children from the homes of substance-abusing parents and made referrals to drug treatment. Judges backed up the caseworkers with court orders requiring parents to complete drug treatment as a condition of their children's return. Yet despite ACS's and the court's good intentions, there was little monitoring except at court appearances, which could be up to a year apart. "Caseworkers would make a referral for drug treatment and leave it up to the parent to follow up," says Judge Gloria Sosa-Lintner, a family court judge since 1988 and the founding judge of the Manhattan Family Treatment Court. "It's like telling someone who's very sick to go on their own to see the doctor. They may get there, or they may not."

Cases remained open for years with little progress toward resolution. "What had been happening with most drug cases, and most cases for that matter, was that they would drag on with long periods between court appearances, and no progress was being made toward permanency for the child," explains Ray Kimmelman, an attorney with ACS. "It was sort of potluck what would happen on any court date. The judge would ask, 'What's happening with services?' And ACS would say the mother has not complied and the judge would adjourn it for another day. Cases would drag on and on until we finally gave up and had to file a termination-of-parental-rights petition."

Judges were forced to make heart-rending decisions about a family's fate: Should a parent's rights be terminated, or should the parent be given another chance to become sober? Should a child be freed for adoption or wait another year on the dimming hope his parent might get clean? These decisions were made more difficult when key information was missing. Often a case had been transferred among so many lawyers and caseworkers that it was impossible to know with confidence how and why parents had failed to comply with the court's orders: Was it because they were truly beyond reform, or had the system failed to get them the help they needed?

Blaming ACS, the agency charged with linking parents to drug treatment and other services, became a popular pastime. Yet the problem was clearly systemic. Everyone was stretched too thin. What was needed was a way to help respondents get off drugs and become competent parents, but that required time, money, and expertise, which the parents' attorneys, ACS caseworkers, and the court – already over-whelmed by the swollen caseload – lacked. Meanwhile, the ones who suffered the most – the children – were the least capable of doing anything about it.

## THE SEARCH FOR A SOLUTION

In 1997, Chief Judge Kaye launched a statewide initiative to revamp family court. The initiative, called the "Family Justice Program," opened family court to the public and called for fundamental changes in the family court structure. As part of her plan, Judge Kaye asked the Center for Court Innovation, the court's research and development arm, to develop a new kind of family court that could better handle cases of child neglect involving charges of drug abuse. That effort began in early 1997, even before the enactment of the federal Adoption and Safe Families Act, which required states to implement regulations to speed permanency decisions for children in foster care.

The New York State Unified Court System had tackled similar problems in the past with its Center for Court Innovation. By the time it began working on the Manhattan Family Treatment Court, it had already developed a range of successful problemsolving courts, including the award-winning Midtown Community Court, which focuses on quality-of-life crimes in the heart of Manhattan, and the Brooklyn Treatment Court, which links felony drug offenders with substance abuse treatment.

At the planning table in Spring 1997 were top family court judges and their law clerks; Judge Sosa-Lintner, who had been chosen to preside over the newly formed court; court clerks; and planners from the Center for Court Innovation. But quickly the planning group expanded to include administrators and attorneys from ACS, the Juvenile Rights Division of the Legal Aid Society (which represents children), and the Assigned Counsel Panel (a collection of private attorneys paid by the court to represent parents).

Expanding the planning group proved crucial. "We realized that without the sign-on of participating agencies like Legal Aid, ACS, and the Assigned Counsel Panel, it wouldn't work. So we began the first of many, many meetings that we like to think of as true collaborative efforts," says Rosemarie Wyman, then-law clerk to Judge Michael Gage, administrative judge of the New York City family court at the time. "At first people wore their own hats, and then over time there came to be a real feeling that we are in this together and we must work together. People became much more forthcoming about problems they anticipated with the court or other concerns they might have."

## OUTLINING THE PROBLEM

Before developing a new court model, planners carefully outlined what they felt was wrong with the current system. Among the problems they identified were:

* **Lack of information.** Most cases passed through at least several ACS caseworkers, so it was nearly impossible to know which caseworker was in charge at any given time. The system diffused responsibility among so many caseworkers that no one person could be relied on for accurate and up-to-date information.

* **Lack of accountability.** ACS or the foster-care agency with which it had contracted often did not follow up on social service referrals or see to it that visitation plans were fulfilled. Moreover, parents could give almost any excuse for why they had not entered treatment or why the treatment failed, and the court had no way to assess their veracity.

* **Delay.** Court dates could be anywhere from three months to a year apart. "Everyone was frustrated because there was always a lapse in time before we found anything out. A judge orders treatment but the parent doesn't go. That takes a few months. Then another referral is made and for some reason that doesn't work out. Months can go by before anyone knows," recalls attorney Pauline Gray of the ACS Division of Legal Services.

* **Lack of services.** Although ACS was charged with making referrals to social services, overburdened caseworkers sometimes lacked the knowledge and resources to make appropriate referrals and follow through to see they were carried out. "In my experience, [ACS] caseworkers are overwhelmed and lack the skills to identify what a parent really needs and locate a program that meets those needs," says Ron Richter, who heads up the Manhattan Juvenile Rights Division of the Legal Aid Society. "It was frustrating to me because I had clients who wanted to return home to their parents, and the parents were strung out year after year after year, and the agency would say, 'We're making referrals, we're making referrals ...' There was a devastating lack of connection between parents and appropriate services, and nobody was doing anything about it. It was maddening, it was sad."

## THE DRUG COURT MODEL

Faced with the challenge of working with drug abusers in family court, planners looked to the model of a "drug court," a judicially supervised treatment program that has had a solid track record of helping offenders achieve sobriety. The nation's first drug court was started in Florida in 1989, but by 1997 there were hundreds of drug courts in operation around the country.

New York City's first drug court experiment, the Brooklyn Treatment Court, was launched in April 1996 and had already shown in its first year that it could successfully get felony offenders off drugs through a rigorous course of court-mandated drug treatment and close court supervision, including frequent visits to the court for drug testing and intensive case management.

Like all drug courts, the Brooklyn Treatment Court is informed by an understanding of the process of recovery from drug addiction. As such, it doesn't instantly kick participants out if they relapse. Rather, it accepts that relapse is sometimes a part of the recovery process. To teach participants that their actions have consequences, the court responds to relapses with graduated sanctions – for example, having participants spend two full days observing in court and then writing an essay about it. The court also uses rewards – applause in the courtroom, less-frequent court appearances – to encourage those who are doing well.

Interestingly, the Brooklyn Treatment Court's own experience indicated the possible need for a drug court in the family court setting. About 14 percent of the Brooklyn court's participants had already lost custody of children before entering the treatment court. The question then arose, If the parents had been placed in a drug court earlier – well before their drug abusing led to a felony drug arrest – would they have been able to keep their children?

## ANSWERING A NEED

The drug court model addressed many of the problems in the family court system that planners had identified. The model improved accountability by requiring participants to return frequently to the court for drug testing, and by using sanctions and rewards. Frequent court appearances and intensive case management helped supply the court with accurate and up-to-date information. And participants received better services with the help of court caseworkers, who thoroughly assessed their needs and then referred them to appropriate services.

Placing drug-abusing parents in a drug court seemed a natural fit, yet planners weren't convinced it would work. Drug courts were created in criminal settings. Would they work as well in a family-court setting, which has different procedures and measures of success? In a criminal drug court, for instance, the ultimate reward is a clean criminal record; but in family court, the final reward is usually family reunification. Furthermore, to "graduate" from a criminal drug court, all you need do is follow the court's orders and stay clean and sober for a sufficient length of time. But in family court, "drug free" can't be the only measure. Respondents must also be what the court calls a "good-enough parent." That means having hard-to-measure qualities like parenting skills and an ability to manage anger, plus adequate housing and a source of income. There are other considerations as well, depending on the case. For instance, the court will not return a child to a home that has a history of domestic violence unless the abuser is no longer present.

One of the biggest differences between a civil family court and a criminal court is leverage. New York City's family court lacks the coercive power of a criminal drug court, which can use jail as a tool to support treatment – either as a sanction when a participant is chronically noncompliant or as punishment when a defendant fails the program entirely and a criminal sentence is imposed. In theory, a family court judge can put respondents in jail, but as a matter of practice it's never done in New York City.

A criminal drug court can also hold defendants in jail until arraignment, which ensures that case managers can at least approach them to explain the drug court option. But in family court, respondents are not held pending their first appearance. (In practice, this has meant that 20 percent of the parents who are initially deemed eligible to participate in family treatment court never show up, so they never learn what the court has to offer.)[5]

Court Coordinator Raye Barbieri observes that family treatment court wouldn't be able to attract parents if jail were ever an option for those failing in treatment, especially if traditional family court in New York City, as a matter of judicial custom, never exercised that option. "If we exposed our voluntary participants to jail, we wouldn't have any participants," Barbieri says. Further, notes Emily Sack, a deputy director at the Center for Court Innovation, "we felt we didn't want to create a situation where they'd be facing a much larger penalty than they'd face in other parts of the family court."

Planners ultimately decided that the drug court model – adapted to a civil setting – was the right way to go. Family court may not wield jail as a "stick," but the promise of family reunification had been and would continue to be a strong incentive for parents to cooperate. Parents know that if they succeed in rehabilitation, their children will be returned to them, and if they don't, their rights as parents will be irrevocably severed. As family treatment court graduate Steven Kemp, 37, says, "When you go through what I went through – to have them physically take your kids away – that's motivation enough. You don't wish it on your worst enemy."

## CRITERIA FOR PARTICIPATION

One of the early questions planners had to answer was, Whom would the court admit? Some at the table suggested accepting, at least until the court gained more experience, only the so-called cream of the crop – those clients who were new to the family court system and relatively new drug abusers, such as women who for the first time had a child born with a positive drug toxicology. But people representing the experience of the Brooklyn Treatment Court cautioned that "it isn't always first-time people who do better in treatment. The Brooklyn Treatment Court found that folks who have a more serious drug problem and have hit bottom sometimes do better," Sack explains.

Planners ultimately tried to balance these two views by picking parents who, as Judge Sosa-Lintner puts it, "had some chance of success without limiting it to those with positive tox babies." They also decided to focus on neglect cases only – as opposed to more serious cases involving abuse, which were thought to exceed the rehabilitative scope of a treatment court. The neglect allegations, of course, had to include drug abuse, but other forms of neglect, such as medical or educational neglect, could also be part of the case. They also placed other limits: no allegations of domestic violence, no overt signs of mental illness, no more than one other child already in foster care, and then not for more than three years. Planners decided that as the court gained in experience it would broaden its criteria in phases to accept more participants and more complicated cases. (In a later phase, for instance, the court began taking cases involving allegations of domestic violence and extended the foster-care limit to five years.)

## RECONCILING DIFFERENT VIEWS

The planning phase lasted a year, during which time a long list of issues was worked out, from graduation criteria to staffing to the frequency of court appearances. But the process wasn't easy. One of the biggest challenges for planners was reconciling the disparate views and interests of the many players in a family court. Unlike a criminal court, in which the primary players are the prosecution and the defense, child protective cases in family court have three "sides" – the respondent, the child, and ACS, all of whom have their own attorneys and agendas; in addition, caseworkers at ACS and at individual foster-care agencies who directly supervise foster-care placements are major players in each case.

At first, there were some who doubted that an experimental treatment court could be fair to all sides. Attorneys for the children thought the court was being "designed to go easy on the respondents," says Brad Martin, an attorney with the Juvenile Rights Division of the Legal Aid Society. "I think people from my office expected, incorrectly as it turned out, that the kids from the beginning of the case would be home with the parents, that they'd never be removed." The parents' attorneys took the opposite view: that the court would drive the case like "a runaway train toward termination and adoption," Barbieri recalls.

Parents' lawyers were also dubious of the court's value to their clients. On the one hand, supportive services to help their clients get off drugs and be reunited with their children were an obvious plus. On the other, what if the parent failed in treatment after repeated tries? The only practical defense in proceedings to terminate parental rights is that "[ACS] didn't do enough to reunite the family," explains attorney Edwinna Richardson, who represents parents. In family treatment court, however, parents were going to be given intensive assistance, "making it impossible to establish that the agency didn't work diligently," Richardson says.

With the passage of the Adoption and Safe Families Act, which required states to implement regulations to expedite permanency decisions for children in foster care, attorneys like Richardson decided that their clients needed all the help they could get. "The truth is that parents are going to have to rehabilitate quickly or they'll lose their children," Richardson observes. And after working with the court for two years, "I have reconciled myself that the best way parents will have a chance to get their children back is if they participate in the family treatment court. It's not very difficult to terminate parental rights to begin with, and under the new laws this is the only place we have a chance to have parents reunified with their children."

## ADMISSION OF NEGLECT

Planners decided that respondents would have to admit to the substance abuse charges against them (typically child neglect due to substance abuse) as a requirement for entering the treatment court. This was done not only to save time (because hearings to reach a finding of neglect could easily take more than three months), but also to increase the chances of a participant's success in treatment.

The Brooklyn Treatment Court found that placing participants in drug treatment immediately – at most a few days after arrest – increased the likelihood that they would succeed in treatment. So the Brooklyn court has participants, as a requirement of admission into the program, admit guilt upfront. Their sentences are deferred and the cases are subsequently dismissed upon successful completion of the treatment program. Failure in the program brings a prearranged jail sentence. With the plea agreement behind them, the adversarial elements of the case are eliminated and everyone can focus on the participants' recovery.

Admissions are also a clinical requirement for treatment. "Clinically you can't engage someone in the treatment process until they've admitted they have a drug problem," explains Barbieri, who worked in the Brooklyn court before she became coordinator of the family treatment court.

The idea of parents' admitting blame within days of their first court appearance was at first hard for parents' attorneys to accept – after all, no attorney wants a client to automatically cede any rights. Yet they ultimately agreed to the plan because they recognized that they could advise clients facing weak cases to decline participation in family treatment court.

Richardson and her peers on the Assigned Counsel Panel were also concerned about court caseworkers' assessing their clients' suitability for the program. What if the parents make admissions that could be used against them later if they decide not to participate in the treatment court? And what if their clients say something with criminal repercussions – what would prevent the district attorney from getting this information? The parents' attorneys finally went along when, after much negotiation, it was agreed that the assessment would be kept confidential and not be used against respondents if they opted out of the family treatment court.[6]

## RESOURCE COORDINATOR

In March 1998, the Manhattan Family Treatment Court opened for business. And while its courtroom on the ninth floor of the Manhattan Family Court's black granite office tower looks much like any other in the building, it is immediately apparent to an observer that what goes on here isn't business as usual.

While in many courtrooms long pauses are customary as people shuffle through stacks of folders for information and unanswered questions lead to adjournments, Resource Coordinator Scott Brown hands everyone in the treatment court an update on each respondent on the day's calendar. The updates list the respondents' days clean, their progress in treatment, the results of drug tests, information about their drug treatment programs, the status of their visits with their children, and any issues of concern – basically all the information needed to make sure each appearance is productive.

Brown amplifies the written update by telling the judge at the beginning of each respondent's appearance the recommendations of treatment providers and court staff regarding sanctions and rewards, phase advancements, treatment, and the delivery of other services.[7] After the hearing he updates providers and court caseworkers on the judge's decisions. "As resource coordinator, I'm the eyes and ears for the clinical team in the courtroom," Brown says.

The resource coordinator spares case managers the need to appear in court, allowing them to devote all their time to working with clients. Without the resource coordinator, case managers would be placed in the awkward position of "telling" on their clients. "When you look at the client-and-case-manager relationship, it's probably not the best thing to go to court and drop the hammer on the client or sing his praises to the judge and then six months later have to do a 180," Brown observes.

Brown also works closely with two liaisons from ACS. The liaisons are based at the court and stand in for individual ACS caseworkers during court appearances. The liaison position was created to make sure the court always has the most current information from ACS and foster-care agency caseworkers. The liaisons also convey court orders back to ACS.

ACS attorney Pauline Gray says the wealth of information in the court-room makes her "feel more comfortable with the decisions that are made. Because of frequent court appearances, it's very obvious what the plan should be. There are no adjournments for adjournment's sake. You always have enough information to go forward."

## THE JUDGE

The treatment court is in session four afternoons a week. Judge Sosa-Lintner, who juggles a caseload in traditional family court as well, was its sole presiding judge for nearly two years. Sosa-Lintner, who didn't know anything about drug courts when first assigned to the project in the preplanning stage, is now clearly used to her role as judge, cheer-leader, and critic.

She adapts her tone and demeanor to each respondent, smiling as she congratulates a parent who is doing well and then a few minutes later becoming stern as she questions a mother who has apparently lied about her drug use. The mother, who tested positive for alcohol, claimed that she hadn't had a drink but admitted to taking four Tylenol 3s because of surgery-related pain. "Do you have any idea how you could take four Tylenol 3s and not test positive for opiates, but test positive for alcohol?" Judge Sosa-Lintner asks. "You better watch what you take and learn to tolerate pain more."

The judge doesn't hesitate to spell out the consequences to parents who are backsliding, pointedly reminding them that they can lose their children forever if they don't sober up. To one mother she says flatly, "You have to decide if you want your children back home or if you want to do drugs. Your kids are young, but they're not that young ... you don't want them to end up in the foster-care system, do you?"

Parents, even those who have relapsed, say they like Judge Sosa-Lintner's style. "She knows me upfront," says Lillian Harris as she waits to see the judge. Harris, who was about to be ordered into a new treatment program after a relapse, says that when she entered court, "I was just mean and arrogant" and rebelled against the court and treatment. At one point, Judge Sosa-Lintner ordered her to write an essay about her anger. "Now I'm learning to be more friendly," Harris says.

## DEALING WITH RELAPSE

Despite Judge Sosa-Lintner's stern approach, she and Judge Sheldon Rand, who began sharing the treatment court's calendar with her in January 2000, understand that treatment is a long process and that relapse is, in many cases, inevitable. "The reality is that some of our clients do well for a while and then relapse. My experience has been that the judges in family treatment court tend to give the parents more chances than other family court judges because they're more knowledgeable about drug addiction," Richardson, who represents parents, says. "And they're seeing a case very frequently, so they're more familiar with each parent, whereas other judges will see parents every year or every few months at the outset of a case and won't have a personal connection."

Judge Sosa-Lintner also offers generous encouragement to those who succeed. After their first 90 days sober, she typically gives respondents a journal in which she writes a congratulatory inscription. The judge is not alone in offering congratulations, however. Sometimes, at the judge's urging, everyone in the courtroom breaks out into applause. And sometimes, on their own, courtroom players offer words of support. At the conclusion of an appearance by a mother who had trouble staying sober but now had 65 "clean" days under her belt, ACS attorney Pauline Gray told the judge, "I'm glad that she's back on track."

## VISITATION

Judge Sosa-Lintner says that she isn't ordering anything different from what judges in other family courts order. What's different is that through frequent court visits she's ensuring that her orders are enforced. "I'm guaranteeing compliance, and I do it by having them in the courtroom," she says.

Judge Sosa-Lintner is concerned not only with the respondents' sobriety, but also with the status of the children. Is the foster-care placement working out? Are the children getting the supportive services they need? And, at the top of her list, are visitations being carried out as prescribed by her orders?

Unlike other family courts, family treatment court micromanages visitation schedules. "Typically, visitation schedules are left to ACS to figure out. We do it on the record because information gets lost otherwise," Barbieri explains. If there is a problem with visitation – perhaps a residential drug program does not let a participant leave for visits, or perhaps the parent is simply failing to show up – the frequent court appearances ensure that the judge promptly hears about the problem.

Statutes require a minimum of biweekly supervised visits. But the treatment court tries to move quickly to weekly visits when they are clinically appropriate. For the children's attorneys this took some getting used to. "It was a bit of an attitude shift for us," law guardian Brad Martin concedes. "They move very quickly toward long visits, unsupervised visits, weekend visits. We had to swallow hard and go along with it."

## THE CLINICAL OFFICE

Much of what goes on at the family treatment court takes place three stories below the courtroom in the court's clinical office. It's there that parents are first given a thorough psychosocial assessment, both to determine eligibility and to develop an initial treatment plan. Once they are in the program, participants regularly visit the clinical office to meet with their case managers, get referrals to social services, and provide urine samples for drug tests. The clinical office also hosts a support group for parents once a week.

As part of the court's monitoring process, parents must meet with their case managers before every court appearance. In advance of these appointments, case managers talk with the off-site treatment counselors to find out how the parents are doing. The treatment providers also regularly fax over progress reports that include attendance records and drug-test results.

Parents are tested every time they come to court. Positive test results inevitably lead to discussions about what in the parents' life led them to use drugs. "The case managers probe to find out what the issues are," Brown says.

## FAMILY GROUP CONFERENCING

The court hired a family facilitator in December 1999 to help involve extended families in permanency planning. "Family is broadly defined," says the facilitator, Lisa Horlick. "It can be a sister, mother, brother, father, roommate, girlfriend – basically anyone concerned about the children. Families are sometimes overlooked, and yet they're a resource for permanency planning."

The family conferences have three main goals: to identify ways to support ongoing sobriety, to develop family support for speedier reunification, and to think about ways to prevent children from later developing their own substance abuse problems. Horlick says the conferences provide "a window into the family's life outside of family court, which gives us a way to make a more accurate assessment of their needs."

In one family conference, a mother talked with her two sisters about her drug problem. The sisters didn't understand why the mother had trouble putting down drugs and were very angry that she had relapsed. Horlick talked to them about the nature of drug addiction and the role the sisters might play if the children were returned to the mother. "The family was able to offer love and support, but they also came to an understanding that they might offer respite care for the children if the mother was feeling overwhelmed," Horlick says. "That way, they could play a part in relapse prevention, be her support team."

In another conference, a mother met with her 16-year-old daughter. Horlick helped them talk about the daughter's fears about returning home and discuss what rules would be in the home, including what the girl's curfew would be and the chores she would be expected to do. Horlick also gave the daughter a questionnaire that could help the court identify services, such as summer camp or tutoring, that might help make the reunification process easier. "We want to make transitions smoother to help keep at-risk kids out of trouble and to avoid a relapse by the parent," Horlick explains.

## TEAM APPROACH

The court has tried to create a team out of the court's many players. Even when the project was still in development, planners were careful to allow everyone a chance to express his or her thoughts and then move ahead only after all those involved had reached at least a tentative consensus.

The court hosts troubleshooting meetings once a month. Representatives from the court, ACS, the various attorneys, and the judges attend. Matters like changing the admission criteria, altering the court's hours, or experimenting with warrants have topped the agenda at various meetings.[8] Because everyone is permanently assigned to the court (or, in the case of members of the Assigned Counsel Panel, spend a significant amount of their time there), they have a depth of experience that allows them to speak knowledgeably about court operations. It also helps save time in the courtroom. "You don't waste time with attorneys advocating for positions that are not reasonable," Gray observes. "We have a lot of cases every day, and having a fixed staff helps it go quickly."

For some, the idea of working so collaboratively in a courtroom was an entirely new concept. "The whole idea of a team goes against my instinct as a defense attorney," Richardson says. "Frankly, my client could care less about what the team thinks. And technically my obligation is to the client. But even though the team concept has always seemed a bit mushy to me, the reality is that the goals we all have are fairly similar – almost always it's to reunify the family."

One of the payoffs of the team approach is a more efficient calendar. Judge Sosa-Lintner has instructed attorneys to confer among themselves before each case and bring before her only the issues she needs to focus on. For example, Michael Wroblewski represented a woman with 200 days clean, who had been reunified with her children on a trial basis for 60 days when she relapsed. Wroblewski, with attorneys from ACS and Legal Aid, worked out an arrangement that allowed her to keep the children but required her to be in treatment five days a week. Thus, the issue didn't have to be debated before the judge. As it turned out, the mother got back on the sober path and ultimately graduated from the program.

## PARENTS' PERSPECTIVE

For many parents family treatment court is an easy choice. "They told me what the process was and, in comparison to what I knew of from hearsay about regular court, it was not something I had to think about. I chose family treatment court right away," explains a 35-year-old female graduate, who asked that her name be withheld. When she entered court, she was still in denial about her drug abuse, even as she admitted in court that she had a problem. "When I started, I was still thinking pot wasn't drugs," she says. ACS opened her case after she had been arrested for smoking marijuana on a street corner with her 2-year-old son at her side. "I was thinking, 'I'm going through all this for a joint?'"

Cynthia Bruno, another graduate, had similar thoughts at the outset: "I thought the system was wrong for taking my son. He was clean, had enough clothes, and got to school on time, but then I realized it was only a matter of time before he wouldn't be clean and wouldn't have enough clothes and, God forbid, got hurt."

Like Bruno, most parents come to see that, in fact, they do have a drug problem. And while many get through treatment without a relapse, others backslide. When that happens, participants are usually glad they're in the treatment court. "I was coming for six months and my urine tests were still dirty. I was smoking crack, but they didn't give up on me," Kindel Williams, 34, says. "They always continued to encourage me to find some other way of looking at treatment."

Williams started in an outpatient program, but it didn't work. "I didn't bother to go," she says. While she was using, she got pregnant, which marked a turning point. "I knew I didn't want this child getting hooked up with the system." The court placed her in a residential parent-child program for eight months, and Williams finally sobered up. When she was discharged, the court linked her with a babysitting service so she could continue to attend the program as an outpatient. Williams has done so well that she also works at the program on a part-time basis.

Now, almost two years after entering the court, Williams is thinking about pursuing trial custody of her first child, a daughter currently living with a relative. Williams says she feels lucky that she ended up in family treatment court. In addition to giving her a number of chances, the court offered "consistency, which is what you need when you try to overcome addiction," Williams says.

Many parents say they welcome the court's close scrutiny. Steven Kemp, the 37-year-old father of a 1-year-old girl and a 4-year-old boy, says he liked the frequent court dates. "I enjoyed going to court because the judge could see I was improving every time. It gave me motivation," explains Kemp, who "graduated" from the court in March 2000.

And while program graduates say the court's support has helped them get sober, the biggest factor that helped them quit drugs, many say, was their kids. "When my kids were removed it was devastating," Lisa Heard, a graduate, says. "I swore I'd never go through that again."

## CHALLENGES

Of course, the court has experienced challenges in its first two years. In some instances, family court clerks did not understand some of the screening criteria and referred inappropriate cases or failed to send appropriate ones. Despite admission criteria against it, occasionally the court has admitted a parent with a serious mental health problem, which has posed a challenge for placement, since few programs treat both mental illness and drug addiction.

The program has also pointed up deficiencies elsewhere. While the creation of the ACS liaison has greatly improved the agency's communication with the court, there are still internal communication problems to be worked out, ACS attorney Ray Kimmelman says. "Each of our cases involves a caseworker in a private agency plus a caseworker at ACS in a field office plus the liaison who stands up in court. We still sometimes have problems with sharing information as to how visits are going and how the drug treatment program is going and if there are relatives who can take the kids. These are the systemic problems that show up in every case, but in family treatment court it shows up in even greater relief because you don't have weeks and weeks between appearances to fix the problem."

The court has also had to deal with limited resources. Because of a growing caseload in family court and the departure of a judge, the entire family court calendar in Manhattan has been readjusted. Judge Sosa-Lintner's time in the treatment court was reduced from 50 percent to 20 percent so she could take on more of the crushing caseload in regular family court. And although she was joined by Judge Rand, he, too, can give only 20 percent of his time. "In essence, we have fewer judicial resources than when we started," Barbieri says. Despite that, the court has been able to increase its caseload, and planners expect that it will soon be expanded to a full-time courtroom.

## NEW ROLES

Perhaps one of the greatest challenges is the need for court players to adapt to new roles. The judges have seen the most changes in their work. Judge Sosa-Lintner has gone from being a lone figure on the bench to a team player by joining in the trouble-shooting meetings, hosting informational lunches with treatment providers, and giving presentations about the court to ACS workers, foster-care associations, and local bar associations.

Other judges sometimes criticize her for "coddling" drug abusers and running a court that is too "social work oriented," she says. "There's a perception the court is holding hands too much, but the respondents will learn a lot better if you hold their hand. We're not coddling, we're monitoring, we're keeping control of the situation. You can't fix a problem if you don't know about it for three months."

But the judges aren't the only ones in new roles. Everyone has had to make adjustments. The children's attorneys, for instance, now have more time to counsel their clients. "Our role is often to secure compliance with court orders and hold the commissioner of child welfare's feet to the fire," Ron Richter, a law guardian, says. "In family treatment court, because cases are on so frequently and because the court staff is also advocating for the family's needs, there's less of a role for us to play in terms of compliance and more of a role for us to play as legal counselor for the children. We see the children more often, and we have a greater role in picking service providers and working out visitations."

## LOOKING TO THE FUTURE

The Manhattan Family Treatment Court has demonstrated that a drug court can work in the family court setting. With intense court monitoring and links to supportive services, the court has been able to rehabilitate drug-abusing parents and reunite, after its first two years, 30 respondents with 72 children. The respondents had an average of 439 days sober upon "graduation," and the average length of time their children spent in foster care was 11 months – far less than the citywide average of four years. This represents a savings in financial as well as human terms, since the city has so far saved hundreds of thousands of dollars in foster-care expenses. By the start of its third year, the court had worked with 277 respondents representing 243 families and 453 children. With an average of 68 percent of its clients in compliance with court mandates, the court is poised to reunite many more parents with their children in the near future.

The court expects in its third year to face a new challenge: difficult decisions about termination of parental rights. During its first two years, 28 parents failed. But all the cases were clear-cut: the parents had either dropped out of the program altogether or had been unable to put together even a bare minimum of sober days. Now, as the mandates of the Adoption and Safe Families Act come into play, the court will begin to grapple with cases that fall in a grayer area, involving parents who have had longer stretches of sobriety and shown a great deal of effort but still haven't been able to make enough progress to be reunited with their children. "There are parents who haven't been able to put together more than two or three months of sobriety," Barbieri explains. "What makes it difficult is the relationship with the client and the emotional investment the team has made in the person, but like the judge says, at some point you have to fish or cut bait. Ultimately, the child's developmental clock has to prevail."

While the Manhattan Family Treatment Court continues to develop and meet new challenges as they emerge, plans are under way to begin replicating the model in other parts of New York City's family court, starting in the borough of Queens, where a planning team has already been named. For other jurisdictions interested in the treatment court's model, lack of resources is a likely obstacle. Treatment courts require extra staff and more time from the schedules of judges, lawyers, and other court players because of the intensity of the case management and the frequency of court visits. But when grappling with tight budgets, jurisdictions should also weigh the financial savings from shortened stays in foster care and, even more importantly, the savings in social capital when fractured families are made whole.

For people long familiar with business as usual, the Manhattan Family Treatment Court has drawn no shortage of praise.

Edwinna Richardson, a lawyer who represents parents, calls it "a bright light in my family court life. Some of my colleagues are still skeptical and laugh at me, and think it's not a real court, but I say, 'I'm sorry, I have many parents who've gotten their kids back.'"

Ron Richter, the law guardian, calls it "a ray of sunshine in my eight years of experience in family court." He continues: "The most compelling advantage to the whole model is that children's attorneys are able to observe parents become an advocate for their child. You start out with a parent who doesn't know what's going on, and over time, week by week and month by month, they become transformed. You're seeing them so frequently you're actually watching the improvement before your very eyes. It makes you a lot more confident in the parents who are participating successfully, and that encourages reunification. You have a much better sense of the person because you see them so much, and you're getting updated reports constantly."

But the speakers most persuasive about the work of the treatment court are the parents themselves. A mother of two children, ages 2 and 4, wrote in her "graduation application" about the lessons she's learned since entering the court: "I have come a long way now since last year. I have maintained myself to stay sober, and I learned that no matter how much pressure you have in your life, you have to deal with it the right way and that drugs are not the answer. My children are very special to me and I love them very much. Now I think about my future with them. I'm very thankful to this court for giving me a second chance, for giving me the benefit of the doubt."

Another graduate wrote that she appreciated the court because "they want you to get your family back. I feel good that they encourage my sobriety and they support you, make you feel good about being clean and staying that way. I have an older daughter [who] was very ashamed of me and now she is very proud of me and my relationship with her is very good and I treasure that."

And still another graduate – a mom with three kids – wrote: "When my children [were] removed ... I thought I would die. I had a [hole] in my heart no other mother could possibly feel. ... I took it as an act of God stopping me from hitting rock bottom. It was a strange blessing. The only choice I had was family treatment court, because if I had gone to trial God knows how long my beautiful boys would have been in the system. ... All I can say is, thank God for family treatment court, I could not have done it without them."

*Robert Wolf, B.A., is Director of Communications at the Center for Court Innovation in New York City.*

## Notes

[1] Judith S. Kaye, Changing Courts in Changing Times: The Need for a Fresh Look at How Our Courts Are Run, Tobriner Lecture, Hastings Law School (Nov. 3, 1997).

[2] *Id.*

[3] *Id.*

[4] *Id.*

[5] Even though about 20 percent of people never show up, this is significantly lower than the usual family court average, which is about 35 percent. Raye Barbieri, coordinator of the Manhattan Family Treatment Court, thinks this is because ACS and the court's case managers do extra outreach to bring parents in. "We badger a lot," Barbieri says.

[6] Although the district attorney could potentially seek the information by subpoena, the parents' lawyers decided not to let this possibility stand in the way of the court's creation. They vowed to protest vigorously if there was a problem. And, in two years, there hasn't been. "The reality is the family treatment court has been very protective of our clients' rights," Richardson says.

[7] Participation in the treatment court is divided into three phases. Participants complete Phase One after they have gone 120 days without using drugs and have met other requirements, like eight satisfactory supervised visits with their children and regular attendance in court. Participants appear in court every two weeks in Phase One, but in Phases Two and Three, participants return to court only once a month. In the later phases, parents not only work on their sobriety but also take parenting skills classes and participate in educational or vocational programs.

[8] The family treatment court briefly experimented with issuing warrants to bring in parents who missed court dates. The warrants were in effect only during court hours to ensure that parents were brought to court immediately and not held in jail. In addition, a stay was issued for five days so that the parents' attorneys could have time to track down their clients themselves. But the warrant experiment failed when the police, short of resources and occupied with what they felt were more urgent matters, failed to execute them.

# C: Unified Family Courts

# [7]

# The Failure of Fragmentation:
# The Promise of a System of Unified Family Courts

## Catherine J. Ross

## I. Introduction

It seems a kind of poetic injustice that courts hearing matters concerning children and families in most states appear to be "stepchildren" of the justice system. Unfortunately, they are not stepchildren in the modern, positive sense, where the children become part of a resilient hybrid family, but rather in the classic sense of Hansel and Gretel, whose stepmother abandoned them in the forest. Under this analogy, the idealized figure of justice holding the scales is the biological mother who died in childbirth, the father who provided financial resources to the family died after remarrying, and the stepmother directs her limited resources to raising her own biological children-preferred matters such as commercial litigation and criminal prosecutions. In contrast, the courts that hear cases about children and families are truly disfavored. Fragmented and lacking resources, they are places in which only relatively few, exceptionally dedicated, legal professionals wish to spend their careers.[1]

To make matters worse, many lawyers, judges, and legal scholars dismiss cases involving child custody, distribution of middle class marital assets, deadbeat dads, overwrought spouses, and impoverished children as having little theoretical legal significance. That negative appraisal is wrong in at least two respects.

First, family matters that bring people to courts raise theoretically complex issues of vulnerability, autonomy, and paternalism. The potential for state intervention in intimate life appears here in its most powerful form. Legal, political and social debates about such matters as the status of women and children, the tensions between the rights of parents and the state's interests in protecting children, and the legitimacy of state intrusion, whether regarded as benevolent or not, play out in concrete form affecting real people in these cases. Moreover, the emotional dynamic behind many family cases may mask the fact that controversies decided in family courts often require complex doctrinal analysis. Judges presiding over family matters must frequently consider the interaction among governing local, state, and federal law, including statutes, regulations, case law, and even constitutional issues.[2] Nor could the cases have greater ultimate significance. Indeed, domestic relations cases frequently involve children whose future is in the hands of the court through no fault of their own.

Second, cases that at first glance may appear prosaic, and overly fact-specific, turn out to be the point of contact with the justice system that frames the average citizen's experience and understanding of courts, and their respect for, or alienation from, the legal system in its entirety. The justice system gains or loses legitimacy, depending on the extent to which people feel that: (1) the justice system has helped them resolve disputes that they were unable to handle without outside intervention; (2) decision-makers listened to them and understood the complexity of the issues that brought them there; and (3) the legal system crafted responsive solutions to their problems. Perceptions of the legal system have real consequences. Where judges are able to avoid the appearance of arbitrariness and create a hearing that takes the voices of all parties into account, they reinforce the legitimacy of the justice system and improve the likelihood of genuine compliance with court orders and treatment plans.[3]

In this article, I focus primarily on these more practical concerns, rather than on the first set of lofty, theoretical, and jurisprudential matters. Specifically, Part II presents an overview of the failures of fragmented judicial systems to deliver either efficient or equitable justice to families. Part III lays out the rationales for a unified family court by exploring four essential components of any unified family court system, suggesting the likely impact of structural reforms in these areas on families and children: (1) comprehensive jurisdiction; (2) structure and administration; (3) specialized training; and (4) comprehensive services, including prevention. It then considers the potential offered by transforming those fragmented forums into unified family courts and some of the concrete steps needed to attain that goal.

*       *       *       *

## II. Stepchild of the Justice System: Disjointed, Discordant Courts

Despite the prevalence of cases involving families, and the dramatic significance of the outcome of such cases to the litigants' lives, the courts that handle these cases are usually understaffed, by both judges and support staff, under-funded, fragmented, disorganized, and at or near the bottom of the judicial status hierarchy. Such courts are frequently viewed as the "despised, entry-level 'kiddie court'" from which many judges wish to escape.[4] Family courts in most states conjure up overcrowded facilities lacking the veneer of civility, let alone majesty, whose chaotic site itself speaks volumes to the frequently downtrodden and almost always traumatized families that pass through them. Unfortunately, too many stakeholders in the legal system, including some judges, "believe that matrimonial cases clog up the judicial system, taking valuable time away from more important and more legitimately public matters."[5]

## III. Beyond Fragmentation: The Critical Components of Unified Family Courts

In response to the manifest failures of fragmented courts for families discussed in Part II, court reform efforts around the country have recently emphasized the promise of unified family courts. Chief Justice Shirley Abrahamson of the State of Wisconsin, asked to summarize the most important developments in state justice, responded that "many are coming to believe that family legal problems can best be addressed through a holistic approach," represented by a growing interest in unified family courts.[22] This trend is witnessed in a spate of activity at the state and local levels: pilot projects,[23] judicially initiated court reform,[24] and statewide discussions.[25]

The concept of unified family courts is not new.[26] In the last few years, however, more and more states have created, initiated, or experimented with, some version of unified family court in all or part of their jurisdictions. According to the most recent data, eleven states currently have courts that they label "unified family courts."[27]

Intensifying interest in unified family courts does not, of course, occur in a conceptual vacuum. Unified family courts are part of a broader emerging interest in "community justice." Community justice involves new ways of thinking about the justice system, particularly the criminal justice system, with an emphasis on problem solving, responsiveness to citizen concerns, individual responsibility, and coordination of the range of service systems available in the community.[28]

Drug courts, for example, reflect many of the same concerns that motivate the current interest in unified family courts and parallel them in many respects.[29] Most persons who have substance abuse problems do not pay the price alone. Drug abuse has numerous adverse effects on all family members. According to the Child Welfare League of America, at least half of all child abuse and neglect cases involve an adult substance abuser.[30] Drug courts emphasize treatment instead of prison sentences for users, with the threat of prison as a sturdy stick to promote treatment. Drug courts reduce drug abuse and related crime dramatically; they also save taxpayers money, because the cost of treatment averages $5,000 less per participant than the cost of jail.[31] The strategy, like that of unified family courts, uses the court's authority to bring together all of the persons and agencies who need to work cooperatively to effect behavioral change, with the court insuring follow through and coordination.[32] A drug court is sometimes thought of as a specialized unified family court, that is, a unified family court with limited jurisdiction.

That definition in itself, however, may raise as many questions as it answers, because even in the eleven states that have unified family courts, the nature of those courts varies widely.[33] Courts with similar characteristics, and outsiders observing them, routinely disagree about whether they would label each court a "unified family court." In part, the problem of devising a simple definition reflects the reality that no one system is perfectly adapted to all jurisdictions or all communities.[34]

The elusiveness of a concise definition of a unified family court is best captured by the fable of the three blind men, each of whom accurately described an elephant from his own vantage point: one feeling the trunk, a second tusk, and the third a hind leg. The resulting argument among the three resembles the range, and intensity, of opinions on this subject.

## A. The Four Components of a Unified Family Court

Despite the range of opinions about crafting a definition, four critical components stand out as essential to a genuine unified family court system: (1) comprehensive jurisdiction; (2) efficient administration designed to support the concept of "one family, one team"; (3) broad training for all court personnel; and (4) comprehensive services. A functional exploration of each of the component parts individually enhances our understanding of the essential characteristics of unified family courts, and, in turn, of their potential to deliver efficient, equitable justice to families.

### 1. COMPREHENSIVE JURISDICTION

Given the harmful effects of fragmentation, it should come as no surprise that broad jurisdiction lies at the heart of any unified family court. A unified family court system ideally combines all of the essential elements of traditional family and juvenile courts into one court system, at the level of the highest court of the general trial division. Unified family courts should be at the highest trial court level because that status affects the court's ability to command necessary resources, as well as to attract and retain well qualified personnel.[35]

Only broad jurisdiction promises an integrated approach to interrelated problems in the same family.[36] Experts agree that the subject matter jurisdiction of unified family courts should be extensive. The American Bar Association has long endorsed jurisdiction for unified family courts that includes:

> [j]uvenile law violations; cases of abuse and neglect; cases involving the need for emergency medical treatment; voluntary and involuntary termination of parental rights proceedings; appointment of legal guardians for juveniles; intrafamily criminal offenses [including all forms of domestic violence]; proceedings in regard to divorce, separation, annulment, alimony, custody and support of juveniles; proceedings to establish paternity and to enforce [child] support ....[37]

The National Council of Juvenile and Family Court Judges amplified this definition at its 1990 conference on unified family courts by recommending that such courts contain within their ambit all matters affecting families and children: all aspects of divorce, as well as dependency, children and other persons in need of services, delinquency and other violations such as juvenile traffic matters including driving while intoxicated, status offenses (i.e., behavior that violates the law only when committed by a minor, such as incorrigibility or truancy), guardianship and conservatorship, matters involving mental incompetency and mental health including civil commitment and confinement, and legal-medical issues such as right-to-die, living wills, and emancipation of minors.[38] Inclusive jurisdiction would also encompass related courts of special jurisdiction, such as those established by federal legislation to reduce the backlog of child support cases.[39]

Although the aspirational jurisdiction described above includes jurisdiction over intra-family criminal offenses, relatively few jurisdictions grant their unified family courts original jurisdiction over such cases.[40] Some skeptics fear that if unified family courts have jurisdiction over criminal offenses, whether domestic violence, sexual abuse, or delinquency, the therapeutic inquiries and proposals in such courts may suggest to perpetrators that the offenses are less serious than those heard in criminal courts. They worry that the perpetrator may be seen as a person needing treatment, and the punishment will not be proportionate to the offense.[41] But this need not be so. As I have argued elsewhere, therapeutic justice is not incompatible with retributive justice where retribution is called for. Indeed, proportionate punishment may be a necessary precondition for rehabilitative efforts in certain circumstances.[42]

Labeling a court as a "family court," or even a "unified family court," does not resolve the underlying problems that result when that court lacks an essential element of jurisdiction. Broad jurisdiction is key to being able to perform the function of a unified family court. The confusion about labels is perhaps best captured by the State of New York's recent response to a questionnaire about unified family courts. The official who spoke on behalf of the court administration explained that "yes," New York has a "Family Court." But, she continued, the one word answer called for by the questionnaire is misleading. When the state legislature created the "Family Court" in 1962, it excluded matrimonial and probate matters, including guardianship of minor children, from that court's jurisdiction. Matrimonial matters, including divorce, annulment and separation, are handled in Supreme Court, a higher status court than family court, while the family court handles numerous related matters such as child support and custody, visitation and domestic violence, as well as juvenile dependency and delinquency. To remedy what it identifies as the resulting "fragmentation," the Office of Court Administration is seeking a constitutional amendment that would create a "comprehensive Family Division of the State Supreme Court," that is, a genuine unified family court at the level of the state's highest trial court.[43]

## 2. STRUCTURE AND ADMINISTRATION

Besides jurisdiction, the most important aspect of the unified family court is "one family, one judge," sometimes reframed as "one family, one team."[44] The major legal organizations that have endorsed the concept of unified family courts have largely recognized this goal.[45] The reasoning is that only continuity before one decision-maker who hears all related legal problems can ensure that each family is viewed as a whole. Continuity provides the decision-maker with a broad perspective on interrelated family problems that can prove indispensable to crafting solutions appropriate to the particular family. Chief Justice Abrahamson has explained that while

> [t]here are different kinds of unified family courts[,] [t]he underlying concept is that a family is often involved in multiple proceedings in different courts in the same jurisdiction.... In the unified family court approach, the various court divisions that adjudicate family problems are consolidated into a single operation so that one judge handles all matters relating to a particular family.[46]

Even if the principle of one judge, one family is realized, that judge will not be able to do what judges do best-resolve issues properly determined by the adversary process and fashioning appropriate remedies-unless many other reforms are in place. Judges are seriously overburdened: they hear too many cases; too few judicial slots exist, in many jurisdictions; too many of those slots lie unfilled; and judges do not have sufficient support personnel. For example, in New York City where family court judges handle one case from start to finish and often hear subsequent cases involving the same family, a recent study found that there were only forty-one judges available to hear over 225,000 cases a year, yielding roughly 5,500 cases a year per judge, resulting in what the authors termed "assembly-line justice."[47]

Each court needs an intake team and a case manager for every family in order to relieve the judges of burdensome administrative work that currently eats away at their scarce time. Courts should have well-trained resource personnel at all levels, including magistrate hearing-officers, special masters, mediators, court clerks, social workers, and other service providers, who can perform triage. The ratio of support staff to judges may seem very high; in New Jersey, for example, the 106 judges in the unified family court system in 1996 were supported by over 1,600 staff members.[48] Staff members, however, normally earn far less money than judges, so it has been fiscally prudent to rely on staff where a system can do so without sacrificing due process rights.[49]

New York State has recently established what it believes to be the first specialized "Family Drug Treatment Court," in Suffolk County, that includes many of the essential features of a unified family court, except comprehensive jurisdiction. Perhaps most importantly, the presiding judge expects to handle a light case load, about 100 cases in the first year, so that she can supervise each one closely. "The court staff is being trained about drug and alcohol treatment. A case manager will coordinate services for each family and track their progress.... 'Transportation, day care-whatever it is that [the parent] needs to be rehabilitated-'" will be provided.[50]

Investment in computers and a modern case-tracking system is also essential.[51] The pressures on family courts to function more efficiently will undoubtedly intensify as efforts to speed decisions about families become more prevalent, and in response to emerging federal laws and regulations. For example, the recently enacted "Adoption and Safe Families Act of 1997" requires that children in foster care receive permanent placements after fifteen months.[52] This limitation on the length of foster care placements will require courts to handle the most complex cases swiftly and to oversee agency compliance with the law.[53]

Judges can focus on complex cases by, among other things, delegating to others matters that can safely be handled by alternative forms of dispute resolution. If handled properly, many or most of these cases need never reach a judge. Many of the recurrent issues in family courts, such as visitation, custody, and even financial support, frequently benefit from mediation, because, unlike the adversary process, mediation generally does not inflame hostility between the parties, and frequently results in better compliance, reducing the likelihood of a return to court. Of course, effective mediation requires sophisticated court intake to identify which matters are appropriate for dispute resolution. For example, cases involving domestic violence are usually not appropriate candidates for mediation because of the imbalance of power in the relationship and the risk of escalated violence outside of the process.[54] Mediation also requires flexibility, and sensitivity to varied ethnic and family cultures. Where families volunteer to participate in mediation that proves to be unsuccessful, they should receive priority on the court docket so that they are not penalized by going to the end of the line. Just as in the case of criminal offenses heard before a unified family court, the diversion from litigation to alternate dispute resolution should not be interpreted as suggesting that issues resolved without litigation are any less significant than those that proceed to trial.

Uncontested private matters, such as uncontested divorces, adoptions, or paternity decrees that make up the preponderance of domestic relations matters, should be heard by magistrates who would issue appropriate orders.[55] Such a system would leave judges more time for the complex decisions, like those that arise from bitterly contested custody disputes or an action to terminate parental rights.[56]

The system also benefits members of the matrimonial bar, who may discover advantages for both their clients and their own practices in a successful unified family court system. According to Judge Robert Fall, who has served in the New Jersey unified family courts for over a decade, matrimonial lawyers in that state who were "very reticent" about the transition to a unified court system came to support it. They learned that their clients would be happier and better served under the new system, they themselves would "do a better job," and, as a result of having happier clients in a more efficient system, make a better living, because they would have fewer clients who refused to, or couldn't afford to, pay disproportionately high legal bills, such as those that mount up in the non-unified Pennsylvania system.[57]

## 3. SPECIALIZED TRAINING

Social, medical, and psychological considerations intersect with traditional legal analysis in many cases concerning families. The conventional court is not necessarily well suited to deal with these issues, nor does traditional legal training prepare court personnel to do so.[58] Judges and others who work with families in the court system need intensive training in issues delegated to other professions. Because considerations of child development, varying cultural norms, service delivery choices, and social work and medical terminology coalesce with legal analysis so frequently in cases about children and families, every person who works in a unified family court, from clerks to intake personnel to case managers to lawyers and judges, requires specialized training. Ideally, that training should be provided when people begin their jobs, and continue on an ongoing basis, keeping personnel conversant with emerging knowledge, and helping them to achieve greater sophistication in their work.

Despite the transparent need for training, family court judges in many traditional jurisdictions assume their robes with little or no special expertise.[59] Training serves several integrated purposes: it will help legal personnel understand more about topics, such as child development, that are essential to sound resolution of many family cases; and, it will enable legal personnel to seek more focused guidance from other professions and evaluate the resulting advice more effectively.

Inter-professional training should prepare lawyers and judges to know what questions to ask professionals from other fields, how to frame those questions to help clarify their understanding of specialized issues, and how to interpret the responses they receive in applying the legal analysis that ultimately governs a court's decision.[60] Such sensitivities may help courts to reduce the harmful effects of their involvement in family problems. Unified family courts offer a fresh chance for the legal system to embrace Mary Ann Glendon's observation "that family members may need nurturing environments as much as they need rights."[61] Of course, the parties need rights, too.[62]

In a similar vein, training will help court personnel to understand that the best outcome for some families may be to avoid reaching a hearing at all. Training in the appropriate use of alternative dispute resolution is a critical aspect of the move toward unified family courts. It should be noted that in most jurisdictions, if not all, reliance on mediation is growing, regardless of the court structure.

Finally, training and refresher courses, combined with ongoing support, should improve the performance of legal personnel by helping them to avoid problems such as "burn-out." All family courts take a toll on judges. The work is often painful and draining. "I cry in there," says Miami Juvenile Court Judge Cindy Leberman, "but I try not to let people see me.... We cry at least once a week, often from something a child says."[63] Even in the New Jersey unified family court system, a well-respected judge says that work "wring s her out" so that "by the end of the court day, she has nothing left to give."[64] The competence, self-image, and attitude of court personnel may significantly affect how well any court system functions. As one judge reported regarding the effect of reform in the family court system, one of the key elements contributing to an improved justice system is "me. My attitude."[65]

Sophisticated training for court personnel, greater reliance on the contributions of other professions, and the effort to create a nurturing environment in court do not, however, substitute for adequate protection of the legal rights and interests of the children and adults who appear before a unified family court. Great care must be taken to avoid the excesses of the pre-*Gault* juvenile court, compared by Justice Fortas to a "kangaroo court."[66] At a minimum, unified family courts must balance their inherent flexibility with respect for the recognized rights of the parties who appear before them.[67]

## 4. COMPREHENSIVE SERVICES

Even if all of the improvements discussed above were implemented overnight in every jurisdiction in the United States, they would not offer a panacea for the broader societal problems that exacerbate family difficulties-problems including poverty, inadequate housing, education or child care, and the numerous other underlying social problems that no family court can change at their roots. But just as the special nature of the problems that arise in unified family courts require special training, as discussed above, so too, solutions to those problems require courts be able to connect families to vital services they need.[68] Courts must also serve as preventive centers which help people learn to resolve their own family problems without resorting to court.[69]

In *America's Children at Risk,* we summarized the problem as follows:

> Families in crisis are often faced with a service system that is bewildering, difficult to navigate, fragmented, and indifferent to their concerns-at a time when they are least equipped to handle more stress and badly need help.... Too often, children and parents don't receive the services they need

(even if those services are ordered by a court), cannot find transportation to services, encounter poor quality services, or are placed on a long waiting list.[70]

To address these inadequacies, the ABA policy on unified family courts (adopted in 1994) called for "[p]rovision and/or integration of comprehensive services and other assistance, as appropriate, for children and families in the courts."[71] Many proponents of unified family courts urge that services be onsite to facilitate accessibility and accountability. As Jeffrey Kuhn makes clear, the essential elements of services tied to the unified family court are comprehensiveness and speedy access, as soon as possible after the family's problems are made known to the court.[72]

Proper training of court personnel can help to insure that families are connected to the most appropriate services. As one unified family court consultant explains:

> [W]hen people come to the courthouse and they need services, nine times out of ten they are not direct[ed] appropriately. If they just knew where to go and what form to fill out and who to talk to, 90% of the problem would be resolved in terms of the ability of the system to deliver the services that the family requires.[73]

Where resources are available, courts may provide what are known as "soft" services, such as counseling. Unified family courts may also cooperate with and coordinate philanthropic or volunteer efforts available in the community.[74] Alternative dispute resolution, where appropriate, may be offered by the court along with education on how to use it. Pro se litigants, common in domestic relations matters, may be helped to represent themselves by informational kiosks, standardized forms, and well-trained court personnel who answer questions.

Services such as education programs for children in divorcing families benefit recipients of all social classes. The National Council of Juvenile and Family Court Judges recently awarded its "Unique and Innovative Project Award" to "Children Cope With Divorce," a curriculum that educates parents about how to help their children adjust to the changes that accompany divorce. That curriculum, which currently serves children in portions of thirty-eight states, is used, for example, in Tulsa, Oklahoma, and four surrounding counties where it is mandatory for all divorcing couples with children and is provided free of charge through a United Way member agency.[75]

Unified family courts can also order what are known as "hard" or "concrete" services, such as subsidized housing needed to avoid breaking up a family. Some observers worry that court orders for hard services, and even for some specialized treatment programs, may force agencies to spend money that the legislature may not have appropriated.[76] The concern reflects a legitimate awareness of limited resources, and of the separation of powers, but it is misplaced.

In the 1990 case of *Tilden v. Hayward,* for example, the Chancery Court of Delaware held that homeless plaintiffs had no cause of action in seeking declaratory and injunctive relief, ordering the state to provide housing assistance to *all* child welfare clients experiencing housing problems. Nonetheless, the court emphasized that Family Court (in Delaware, a unified court) not only had the power to, but also is required as a matter of law, to make a factual determination in each *individual* case regarding whether the state had met its statutory obligations to "make reasonable efforts" to keep families together before placing children in foster care.[77] "Reasonable efforts," the court held, included efforts to obtain adequate housing for the family where the family court exercised its discretion to mandate such efforts.

Similarly, appellate courts in several other states have recently held that a juvenile court judge's power to review the status of a minor in state custody includes the power to order a specific treatment plan,[78] and that a family court may order a state department to provide housing if it finds that lack of housing is "the primary factor in preventing reunification" where children are in foster care.[79] Presumably, the same reasoning would apply to prevent a child's initial placement outside his or her home where services and subsidies remove the need for such placement. As an intermediate appellate court in the State of Washington explained, a juvenile court is inherently empowered to address the needs of the child and family appearing before it:

> not with the tools of appropriation and administration that are more adapted to other branches of government, but by means of its authority as a court. The court has indisputable authority over the parties, as well as statutory authority to require that an individualized treatment plan proposed for a child do a better job of meeting critical needs. The court has power to compel the attendance in the courtroom of the caseworker, or her supervisor, or even the Secretary of the Department, as frequently as necessary until the agency acts with the urgency and effectiveness that the particular needs of the children demand.[80]

The decisions discussed above are drawn from a mixture of jurisdictions, some of which have and some of which lack unified family courts. Thus, they make clear that all of the component parts of a unified family court do not need to be implemented at once to improve justice to families.

Even in states with well-established unified family courts, however, resources seldom meet the level of minimal reasonable demands. One recent, well-publicized case from New Jersey, a national leader in unified family courts, illustrates the problem. Fifteen year old Sam Manzie was ready for release from a crisis center, but his parents did not want him to come home and asked the judge to send Sam to a residential facility. The family, which had recently learned of Sam's sexual involvement with a forty-five year old man, described Sam as depressed, in a rage, and violent. He was not going to school. The rage continued despite a regime of psychotropic drugs. His parents and sister were afraid of him; the parents told the court they loved Sam but could not control him. Mr. Manzie begged the court for help. He explained that his medical insurance would not cover the residential care that Sam's counselors recommended.

The judge, however, reduced the issue to one question: "The question is ... do we have the resources to accommodate that; and, the answer is no, okay. We don't have the resources to accommodate an inpatient ... program ...."[81] Just before the judge announced that he was going to send Sam home with his parents, encouraging them to seek intensive counseling, but not providing it by court order, the judge said, "Nobody here is going to like what I'm going to do.... And the reason you're not going to like it, is because it's not what I want and it's not what you want."[82] The judge emphasized that the "premise" underlying his decision was that the services Sam needed were "not readily available here today, and we have to do the best we can with what we have...."[83] The judge was right about at least one thing: nobody liked his decision. Days later, according to prosecutors, Sam murdered an eleven-year-old neighbor and stuffed the body in a suitcase.[84]

The flaw in the handling of Sam's case was not caused only by a lack of adequate funds or programs. It stems, in part, from the emphasis that our justice system traditionally places on individuals as atomized and self-determining. In contrast, social science literature indicates that while "the family is the first important influence on children, ... children and families are interactive members of a large system of social institutions. If we imagine the child to be at the center of a set of concentric circles, then the family is the first circle, the community is next, and the nation and its policies are the outermost circle."[85] This view of the relatedness of children, families, and community proves significant not only in how we think about preventing a major crisis, like the one that occurred in Sam Manzie's case, but also in how we approach preventing children and families from falling into such crises at all. Authorities from many fields uniformly recognize two pervasive deficiencies in service systems for children and families: first, that the programs are narrowly defined, thus serving only narrow categories of children, depending on the labels assigned to them; and, second, that as a consequence, services are fragmented, even when delivered by court order.[86] This fragmentation, in part, accounts for the court's inability to help Sam in time to save his young neighbor's life, and his own.

Another problem is that no reliable predictor can tell a judge how dangerous any given child is to her or himself, family or community. No single risk factor is determinative. Yet social science research has identified several factors that negatively influence a child's developing social and intellectual competence and sense of well-being, which in turn affect the risk of delinquent behavior. Such studies strongly suggest that intervention efforts must begin early and continue in the daily context of the child's family life. One well-regarded clinical study showed that ten years after low-income, inner-city families received a wide range of preventive services, the children in the study "required *fewer* remedial and support *services, including court hearings,* at an average savings of $1,120 each per academic year" when compared to a control group that did not receive preventive intervention (emphasis added).[87] To the extent that courts have early contact with families at risk, courts should be able to help those families obtain the preventive services they need, as well as reactive or emergency services.

The four components of a unified family court system, comprehensive jurisdiction, a structure that supports one team for each family, specialized training, and comprehensive services, offer the building blocks through which to enhance the likelihood of effective justice in matters concerning families. No system, however, lacks imperfections of its own. Although I focus on the promise offered by unified family courts, I am aware of the risks inherent in concentrating power, authority, and discretion in one judge, especially since family cases rarely reach appellate courts. Efforts to craft, implement, and oversee unified family courts should be informed by the lessons of excesses of the juvenile justice system when it lacked the balance required by individual rights as enunciated by *In re Gault* and its progeny-and to the extent that it still suffers from a lack of meaningful process.[88]

\*   \*   \*   \*

*Catherine J. Ross, J.D., Ph.D., is Professor of Law at the George Washington University School of Law in Washington, D.C.*

*I thank George Washington University Law School, especially Dean Jack Friedenthal, for research support; Naomi Cahn and Patricia Hanrahan for their comments; and Amber Heinze for her capable research assistance.*

## Notes

¹   *See* Naomi Cahn, *Family Law, Federalism and the Federal Courts,* 79 IOWA L. REV. 1073, 1091 (1994), on the traditionally low status accorded family courts in the state judicial systems.

²   Barbara Bennett Woodhouse, *A Public Role in the Private Family: the Parental Rights and Responsibilities Act and the Politics of Child Protection and Education,* 57 OHIO ST. L.J. 393, 407 (1996) (*citing* AMERICAN BAR ASSOCIATION PRESIDENTIAL WORKING GROUP ON THE UNMET LEGAL NEEDS OF CHILDREN AND THEIR FAMILIES, AMERICA'S CHILDREN AT RISK: A NATIONAL AGENDA FOR LEGAL ACTION, 53-54 (1993) [hereinafter AMERICA'S CHILDREN AT RISK]).

³   Catherine J. Ross, *From Vulnerability to Voice: Appointing Counsel for Children in Civil Litigation,* 64 FORDHAM L. REV. 1571, 1619, 1619 n.280-81 (1996).

⁴   Jan Hoffman, *Judge Hayden's Family Values,* N.Y. TIMES MAG., Oct. 15, 1995, §§ 6, 44, 46.

⁵   Jana B. Singer, *The Privatization of Family Law,* 1992 WIS. L. REV. 1443, 1507 (*citing* Martha L. Fineman, *Dominant Discourse, Professional Language, and Legal Change in Child Custody Decisionmaking,* 101 HARV. L. REV.. 727 (1988)).

²²   Symposium, *The Future of State Supreme Courts as Institutions in the Law: Roundtable Supreme Courts as Sources of Legal Change,* 72 NOTRE DAME L. REV. 1193, 1199 (1997).

²³   See, e.g., Art Barnum, *Judge to Try "Better Way" to Family Justice; Dupage to Debut New Domestic Court,* CHI. TRIB.. Dec. 30, 1997, 1 (discussing a pilot project receiving technical support from the ABA Project on Communities, Families and the Justice System).

²⁴   *See, e.g.,* JANET FINK, NEW YORK STATE UNIFIED COURT SYSTEM, RESPONSE TO QUESTIONNAIRE FROM THE JUDICIAL COUNCIL OF CALIFORNIA, FAMILY AND JUVENILE LAW ADVISORY COMMITTEE (Oct. 6, 1997) (on file with author).

²⁵   *See, e.g.,* AMERICAN BAR ASSOCIATION, JUST SOLUTIONS: SEEKING INNOVATION AND CHANGE IN THE AMERICAN JUSTICE SYSTEM 45 (1994) (unified family courts received the "resounding endorsement" of conferees from around the country); FRANKLIN COUNTY [Massachusetts] FUTURES LAB TASK FORCE, MOVING TO A PREFERRED FUTURE: A REINVENTING JUSTICE ACTION PLAN, 30, 49 (1995).

²⁶   The first unified family court was created in Cincinnati, Ohio, in 1914. Nearly half a century later statewide systems were established, first in Rhode Island (1961), then in Hawaii (1964), South Carolina (1968), the District of Columbia (1970), and Delaware (1971). These "pioneer" efforts were followed by expansion into the state courts for Louisiana, New Jersey, Florida, Vermont, Virginia, Kentucky, and parts of other states. *See* Barbara A. Babb, *Where We Stand: An Analysis of America's Family Law Adjudicatory Systems and the Mandate to Establish Unified Family Courts,* 32 FAM. L.Q. 31 (1998), for a summary of jurisdictions that have all or some of the attributes of a unified family court.

²⁷   Babb, *supra* note 26, at 38.

²⁸   Jeffrey Tauber, *Community Policing and Drug Courts: Working Together Within a Unified Drug Court System* (forthcoming, draft on file with author). *See also* Gordon Bazemore & Dennis Maloney, *Rehabilitating Community Service: Toward Restorative Justice Sanctions in a Balanced Justice System,*

58 FED. PROBATION 24 (1994); GORDON BAZEMORE, BALANCED AND RESTORATIVE JUSTICE FOR JUVENILES: A NATIONAL STRATEGY FOR JUVENILE JUSTICE IN THE 21ST CENTURY (The Balanced and Restorative Justice Project, Florida Atlantic University, Sept. 1995).

[29]   Since the creation of the first drug court in 1989, 171 drug courts have been established around the country, with another 100 being planned. In addition, 25 drug courts are dedicated to juvenile offenders, and at least 40 more juvenile drug courts are in development. *Drug Strategies, Stopping the Cycle in Drug Court, in* KEEPING SCORE 23 (1997).

[30]   CHILD WELFARE LEAGUE OF AMERICA, CHILD WELFARE FACT SHEET (on file with author), *citing,* M.M. Dore et al., *Identifying Substance Abuse in Maltreating Families: A Child Welfare Challenge, in* CHILD ABUSE AND NEGLECT, at 531-43 (1995).

[31]   *Drug Strategies, supra* note 29.

[32]   Tauber, *supra* note 28.

[33]   *See* Babb, *supra* note 26.

[34]   *See ABA Policy,* 32 FAM. L.Q. 1; Jeffery A. Kuhn, *A Seven-Year Lesson on Unified Family Courts: What We Have Learned Since the 1990 National Family Court Symposium,* 32 FAM. L.Q. 67 (1998).

[35]   *See* Robert W. Page, *Family Courts: An Effective Judicial Approach to the Resolution of Family Disputes,* 44 JUV. & FAM. CT. J. 1, 8 (1993).

[36]   AMERICA'S CHILDREN AT RISK, *supra* note 2, at 53-54 (describing the current patchwork approach that applies in many jurisdictions), *cited in, inter alia,* Woodhouse, *supra* note 2, at 406-07 (explaining how one incident may lead to simultaneous proceedings before a domestic relations court, a dependency court, a special court dealing with domestic violence, and a criminal court, each of which may issue overlapping and conflicting orders); *and* Paul A. Williams, *A Unified Family Court for Missouri,* 63 UMKC L. REV. 383, 387 (1995).

[37]   INSTITUTE OF JUDICIAL ADMINISTRATION/AMERICAN BAR ASSOCIATION, JUVENILE JUSTICE STANDARDS RELATING TO COURT ORGANIZATION, Standard 1.1 Part 1, 5 (1980) (approved by the ABA House of Delegates in 1980).

[38]   SANFORD N. KATZ & JEFFREY A. KUHN, RECOMMENDATIONS FOR A MODEL FAMILY COURT: A REPORT FROM THE NATIONAL FAMILY COURT SYMPOSIUM, Recommendations 13-17 (National Council of Juvenile and Family Court Judges, May 1991).

[39]   The Social Security Act, Pub. L. No. 103-66, § 13712, 107 Stat. 649 (as codified in 42 U.S.C. § 670). Delaware and Rhode Island, for example, have incorporated child support enforcement courts (known as "IV-D courts") into their long established unified family court systems.

[40]   *See* Babb, *supra* note 26, at 42.

[41]   *See, e.g.,* Billie Lee Dunford-Jackson et al., *Unified Family Courts: How Will They Serve Victims of Domestic Violence?,* 32 FAM L.Q. 131 (1998) (enumerating such concerns and explaining how unified family courts can respond to them).

[42]   *See* Ross, *supra* note 18, at 1040-41, 1044-51.

[43]   RESPONSE TO QUESTIONNAIRE, *supra* note 24.

[44]   *See* Kuhn, *supra* note 34, at 67, 77-79 (for an explanation of how this concept has evolved during the last seven years).

[45]   The organizations that endorse the concept of unified family courts include the American Bar Association, National Council of Juvenile and Family Court Judges, Association of Family and Conciliation Courts, Conference of State Court Administrators, National Association of Counsel for Children, National Association of Women Judges, and National Judicial College. While the ABA Policy, for example, does not expressly call for "one judge, one family," the accompanying report emphasizes the importance of "one judge, one family" as a goal for most jurisdictions. *See* American Bar Association Steering Committee on the Unmet Legal Needs of Children, *One Judge, One Family: One Staff, One*

*Family, in* REPORTS WITH RECOMMENDATIONS TO THE HOUSE OF DELEGATES: 1994 ANNUAL MEETING, § 10C, 5 (1994).

[46]   Symposium, *supra* note 22, at 1199.

[47]   THE FUND FOR MODERN COURTS, THE GOOD, THE BAD AND THE UGLY OF THE NEW YORK CITY FAMILY COURT: A CITIZEN'S COURT MONITORS ASSESSMENT OF THE COURT AND RECOMMENDATIONS FOR IMPROVEMENT 6, 9 (Sept. 1997).

[48]   New York Colloquium of the Second World Congress on Family Law and the Rights of Children, *Comments of Jeffrey A. Kuhn, in* CHILDREN AND FAMILIES IN COURT-A UNIFIED SYSTEM (Transcript), at 23 (UNICEF, N.Y., Sept. 12, 1996).

[49]   AMERICA'S CHILDREN AT RISK, *supra* note 2, at 54.

[50]   Bruce Lambert, *A Court Aims at Roots of Child Neglect: On Long Island, New Program Takes on Parents' Substance Abuse,* N.Y. TIMES, Dec. 12, 1997, at B17.

[51]   AMERICA'S CHILDREN AT RISK, *supra* note 2, at 53-54; Woodhouse, *supra* note 2, at 407.

[52]   Adoption and Safe Families Act of 1997 § 103, Pub. L. 105-89, 111 Stat. 211, Nov. 19, 1997 (requiring concurrent planning for adoption of children who have been in foster care for 15 out of 22 consecutive months).

[53]   *Id.* at § 305(a)(3), 42 U.S.C. § 629(b). For a discussion of the complexities of child welfare cases, see Mark Hardin, *Child Protection Cases in a Unified Family Court,* 32 FAM. L.Q. 147 (1998).

[54]   *See* Dunford-Jackson et al., *supra* note 41; Lisa G. Lerman, *Mediation of Wife Abuse Cases: The Adverse Impact of Informal Dispute Resolution on Women,* 7 HARV. WOMEN'S L.J.. 57 (1984); Trina Grillo, *The Mediation Alternative: Process Dangers for Women,* 100 YALE L.J. 1545 (1991).

[55]   The vast majority of domestic relations matters are resolved by the parties before trial and merely require a judicial decree to become effective. *See* Ross, *supra* note 3, at 1583 (*citing* Sanford N. Katz, *The Judge and Child-Custody Decision-Making in the United States, in* FRONTIERS OF FAMILY LAW, 187, 188 (David Pearl & Ros Pickford, eds., 1995)). Before such orders are issued, however, intake workers and case managers should inquire carefully to insure that uncontested private matters really are uncontested rather than resulting from an uneven distribution of power among the parties.

[56]   *See* AMERICA'S CHILDREN AT RISK, *supra* note 2, at 54. *See also* AGENDA FOR JUSTICE, *supra* note 8.

[57]   New York Colloquium, *supra* note 48, at 38.

[58]   One promising trend is the development of inter-professional training programs at the graduate level. Such programs may involve students and professors from law, education, social work, psychology, and the medical sciences. Two good examples are the Boston College Center for Child, Family, and Community Partnerships (Chestnut Hill, Massachusetts), and the Civitas programs at Loyola and other universities. Graduates of such programs should be able to work well together as professionals, in part because they will understand the capabilities and limitations of the other professions. For example, based on my own experiences in inter-professional settings, nonlawyers do not immediately understand that the lawyer's code requires him or her to focus on the identified client's rights and interests rather than on the interests of the family group, whereas a social worker, for example, might consider the needs of all of the family members collectively. For additional programs at law schools, *see* Bruce A. Green & Bernardine Dohrn, *Foreword: Children and the Ethical Practice of Law,* 64 FORDHAM L. REV. 1281, 1287 n.12 (1996).

[59]   Hoffman, *supra* note 4, at 48.

[60]   AMERICA'S CHILDREN AT RISK, *supra* note 2 at 55.

[61]   MARY ANN GLENDON, THE TRANSFORMATION OF FAMILY LAW: STATE, LAW, AND FAMILY IN THE UNITED STATES AND WESTERN EUROPE 308 (1989).

[62]   *See infra* at 22, 28; and Hardin, *supra* note 53.

[63]   Bill Hewitt, *A Day in the Life,* PEOPLE WEEKLY MAG., Dec. 15, 1997, 48, 50 (cover story reporting on 24-hours observing the child protection system around the country).

[64]    Hoffman, *supra* note 4. Judge Hayden has since been appointed a U.S. district judge.

[65]    John Gibeaut, *Nobody's Child,* A.B.A.J., 44, 50 (Dec. 1997) (quoting one formerly frustrated dependency court judge regarding changes in an improved system in Florida).

[66]    *In re* Gault, 387 U.S. 1, 28 (1967).

[67]    *Id.*; Hardin, *supra* note 53.

[68]    Kuhn, *supra* note 34, at 67, 69.

[69]    Andrew Schepard, *Parental Conflict Prevention Programs and the Unified Family Court: A Public Health Perspective,* 32 FAM. L.Q. 95 (1998).

[70]    AMERICA'S CHILDREN AT RISK, *supra* note 2, at 47.

[71]    *See ABA Policy, supra* note 34.

[72]    *See* Kuhn, *supra* note 34.

[73]    New York Colloquium, *Comments of Jeffrey A. Kuhn, supra* note 48, at 29.

[74]    For a broad survey of examples, *see* CENTER FOR THE STUDY OF SOCIAL POLICY, CHILDREN IN THE HALLS OF JUSTICE: A REPORT ON CHILD CARE IN THE COURTS (June 1995).

[75]    *See* Family and Children's Service, *Helping Children Cope with Divorce Program Receives National Award* (press release) (Oct. 8, 1997); interview with Millie Otey, Member of the ABA Steering Committee on the Unmet Legal Needs of Children (Oct. 10, 1997) (document on file with author). For an in-depth discussion of parent education programs, *see* Schepard, *supra* note 69, at 106-29.

[76]    This explains the language in the ABA Policy on Unified Family Courts specifying that a "unified children and family court [sic] must have all authority which is supported by its constitutional, statutory and equitable powers to order other government agencies, e.g. housing authorities, mental health agencies, etc., to provide services to families." *ABA Policy, supra* note 34, ¶ 2.

[77]    Tilden v. Hayward, CIV. A. No. 11297, 1990 WL 131162 (Del. Ch., Sept. 10, 1990). The court noted that, absent violation of clear statutory requirements,

> [c]ourts are not empowered to redress every social and economic malady. Courts are not legislatures.... [T]he economic wisdom of [spending many times more on foster care for children than it would cost to provide housing for the family] is an issue for the elected representatives of the people, not for those fortunately placed members of the legal profession who are not democratically accountable.

*Id.* at 1990 WL 131162, *17.

[78]    S.G. v. Prince William Co. Dep't of Soc. Servs., 488 S.E.2d 653 (Va. Ct. App. 1997) (a juvenile court may order the state to provide and pay for specific residential treatment for a child adjudicated as dependent).

[79]    *In re* Nicole G., 577 A.2d 248, 250-51 (R.I. 1990) (expressly rejecting the state's contention that the unified family court lacks authority to order a state agency to provide housing subsidies or to adopt other individualized plans that would "divert" resources from its "primary mission").

[80]    *In re* J.H. v. S.H., 880 P.2d 1030, 1034 (Wash. Ct. App. 1994) (upholding an order to provide housing for a homeless family, but reversing the lower court's use of contempt powers invoked by implication rather than expressly).

[81]    *In re* S.M., FJ-1125-98-N (N.J. Super. Ct. Ch. Div. Sept. 24, 1997), transcript of Hearing before the Hon. James N. Citta (on file with the author).

[82]    *See id.* at 12.

[83]    *See id.* at 17.

[84]    *See, e.g.,* Nina Burleigh, *The Killer Next Door,* N.Y. TIMES MAG., Dec. 8, 1997, 52, 57; Terry Pristin, *New Jersey Daily Briefing: Family Sought to Commit Boy,* N.Y. TIMES, Oct. 4, 1997, at B1.

[85]    Elizabeth F. Emens, Nancy W. Hall, Catherine Ross & Edward F. Zigler, *Preventing Juvenile Delinquency: An Ecological, Developmental Approach, in* CHILDREN, FAMILIES AND

GOVERNMENT: PREPARING FOR THE TWENTY-FIRST CENTURY 308, 313 (E.F. Zigler et al., eds., 1996).

[86]    *See* Mark Soler, *Re-Imagining the Juvenile Court, in* CHILD, PARENT AND STATE: LAW AND POLICY READER 596, 601-02 (S. Randall Humm et al., eds., 1994).

[87]    Emens et al., *supra* note 85, at 321 (describing the Yale Child Welfare Research Program). *See also* David L. Olds et al., *Long-term Effects of Home Visitation on Maternal Life Course and Child Abuse and Neglect: Fifteen-Year Follow-up of a Randomized Trial,* 278 JAMA No. 8, 637 (Aug. 27, 1997) (presenting data supporting the recommendation of the U.S. Advisory Board on Child Abuse and Neglect that home visitation services be provided routinely to all parents of newborns). *Compare* the discussion of prevention with regard to marital dissolution *in* Schepard, *supra* note 69, at 107-21.

[88]    *See In re* Gault, 387 U.S. 1 (1967); Ross, *supra* note 18, at 1040; PATRICIA PURITZ ET AL., A CALL FOR JUSTICE: AN ASSESSMENT OF ACCESS TO COUNSEL AND QUALITY OF REPRESENTATION IN DELINQUENCY PROCEEDINGS (American Bar Association 1995)(surveying the failure to achieve the the right to counsel guaranteed to minors in Gault).

# [8]

# Unified Family Courts:
# Tempering Enthusiasm with Caution

## Anne H. Geraghty and Wallace J. Mlyniec

*Much has been written about the potential success of unified family courts. Unified family court proponents share great optimism and enthusiasm for what they see as a solution to several of the problems facing court systems today. This enthusiasm should be applauded. As with any reform, however, unified family court advocates must stop to consider the possible drawbacks to the system that they propose; otherwise, they might end up with a system that is the same or worse than the one that they were attempting to fix. This article highlights several of the potential problems with unified family courts. It is not a condemnation of unified family courts per se; it is simply a suggestion that reformers proceed with their eyes open, taking time to consider the potential drawbacks of the unified family court system before using valuable resources for its implementation.*

## I. INTRODUCTION

The movement to create unified family courts, although not new,[1] has gained momentum during the past 12 years.[2] The momentum is generated in large measure by the perceived failures of the currently configured juvenile courts and child welfare systems. Criticism regarding the way families and children are treated in court comes from social workers, legislators, lawyers, and judges. The critics span all political parties. Moreover, newspaper stories recounting the courts' inability to resolve complicated family and children's issues are common, and the tragedies that sometimes result from those failures make the current court system easy prey for critics.

Proponents of the unified family court believe that many, if not all, of the current system's shortcomings can be remedied by bringing all matters touching on family issues into one unified court. That court would investigate and resolve not only the dispute that brought a family into the court system but also all other family problems that might be related to the dispute. This is a tall order, indeed, but the enthusiasm that the proponents have for the unified court, and their faith in its ability to provide creative solutions to the complex dynamics of dysfunctional, disintegrating, and troubled families, is impressive. Our goal in this article is not to discourage attempts to improve courts or help troubled families and children. Our goal is only to temper the enthusiasm and faith of unified court proponents and to urge reformers, law teachers, judges, practitioners, and policy makers to be cautious as they debate the issues regarding unified family courts. Enthusiasm and faith are important when embarking on reform. So is hope; but none necessarily translates into effective policy, teaching, or practice. We hesitate to call this essay a critique. We prefer to consider it a reflection on caution by people who have studied, taught, and practiced family and juvenile law. One of us has done these things for a long time. One brings a newer, younger perspective to this issue.

We offer seven observations about the unified family court system. First, history suggests that the unified family court idea is not new; proponents of the early juvenile court movement advanced similar ideas about therapeutic justice, comprehensive jurisdiction, and an expanded role for the judiciary. These earlier reforms became increasingly oppressive for the children involved in juvenile court systems until the Supreme Court intervened and mandated new legal protection.[3] Second, we question the propriety of the one judge-one family model offered by some unified family court proponents. Although it may result in increased court efficiency, such efficiency may not be a compelling enough goal to overcome the due process concerns that arise with judicial overfamiliarity with cases. Third, although the concept of therapeutic justice sounds beneficial, it diverts judicial attention from the court's basic role as a forum for resolving disputes. Fourth, unified family courts create difficult legal issues by mixing the civil and criminal jurisdiction of a court. Fifth, we wonder whether the money spent to create and implement unified family courts would be better spent by fixing other systemic problems that bring families into court in the first place or by offering better treatment options to families once they come into the legal system. Sixth, it is not clear that the new courts being created in various states today are really unified courts at all. It appears that the term "unified family courts" has become a catchall phrase used by policy makers to garner support for weak reforms to existing systems. Finally, we point out that despite all of the literature on unified family courts no studies have been conducted to date that compare the effectiveness or the quality of justice unified family courts provide with the systems that they are designed to replace. Policy makers, judges, court reformers, and advocates of the unified family court system should be wary of making unsubstantiated claims of potential success. Before spending valuable time, resources, and money on an idea that is supported only by anecdotal evidence, policy makers should carefully assess whether unified family courts really can make the lives of families better in the long run.

We believe, like the proponents of unified family courts, that the current legal system for intervening in the lives of families and children needs to be improved. As such, we consider them allies in a unified cause. We question, however, whether their proposed cure will really result in more justice for troubled families or merely more efficiency for the professionals in the system.

## II. DEFINING THE UNIFIED FAMILY COURT

Supporters use the term *unified family court* liberally.[4] In fact, there is no agreed-on definition of what family courts are or how they differ from many of the existing court systems that they are meant to replace. Most definitions proposed for family courts, however, do have characteristics in common.[5]

First, unified family courts should have comprehensive jurisdiction over a range of family law matters, including marriage, divorce, domestic violence, and criminal assault stemming from abuse, juvenile justice, and child welfare cases.[6] In practice, however, many jurisdictions pick and choose which categories of cases to include.[7] Second, unified family courts aim to increase efficiency and to decreasing the stress on families by implementing a one judge-one family system. Proponents cite several benefits to this approach: ensuring that judges have experience and training in family law matters, reducing the need for families and children to appear in duplicative hearings for multiple family matters, preventing the possibility of conflicting court orders, and increasing familiarity between the judge and the family. Third, family courts should focus on resolving disputes through "therapeutic justice" rather than through coercive or punitive measures.[8] To this end, unified family courts aim to provide coordinated holistic services including counseling, alternative dispute resolution, and drug treatment to address the physical and mental needs of the family. To best dispense these services, family court judges and staff members must receive comprehensive training, aimed at creating a team of family specialists.[9] Court administrators focus on the development of coordinated case management procedures to ensure that cases proceed smoothly and efficiently through the system.[10] Finally, unified family courts should be housed in one building, a "one stop shopping center,"[11] so that people do not need to travel to various locations to deal with multiple, but related, issues.

In this article, we assume that we are dealing with a unified family court with truly comprehensive jurisdiction, incorporating everything from divorce and domestic violence to criminal prosecutions for domestic abuse, neglect, and adoption to juvenile delinquency. We acknowledge that some proponents of unified family courts have argued for a more limited jurisdiction, for example, removing domestic violence or criminal cases from unified family court jurisdiction. Although limiting jurisdiction in this way would render inconsequential some of the reflections made in this article, there are several observations that are relevant to all unified family court models, regardless of the scope of jurisdiction. For example, ridding the unified family court of criminal jurisdiction does not eliminate concerns about the one judge-one family model or about the use of therapeutic justice in the resolution of family disputes. In other words, we are not attempting to pinpoint a particular model of unified family court in this article; but rather we are simply providing observations that may apply to a spectrum of unified family court models that exist today.

## III. HAVE WE DONE THIS BEFORE? A LOOK AT THE HISTORY OF THE JUVENILE COURT MOVEMENT IN AMERICA

History is a significant factor in any analysis of a proposed reform. We should not teach the value of unified family courts or make them a policy objective without understanding the history of other social movements that have tried to achieve similar goals. The maxim that "history repeats itself" has some reality when thinking about complex and political social justice issues. In a recent evaluation of the sad history of New York's child welfare system, Nina Bernstein warned that "the two-hundred year history of American child welfare is littered with programs once hailed as reforms and later described as harmful or ineffective, only to emerge again in the guise of new solutions to past failures."[12] History tells us that the idea of the unified family court is not a new concept; it is an idea that we already have tried and have altered substantially because it has harmed the very people that it was designed to help.

The Pre-*Gault* juvenile court was, in essence, a kind of unified family court.[13] Perhaps it was not quite as unified as that envisioned today, but its founders had goals that were similar to the goals of today's proponents of unified family courts. The Progressive Reformers who established the first juvenile courts aimed at stabilizing the family unit,[14] similar to the emphasis of the therapeutic model in family law situations.[15] The Progressives wanted to provide an individualized response to each child and created courts that focused on treatment and rehabilitation rather than punishment,[16] akin to unified family courts' proponents focus on "individualized justice."[17] Judges in the original juvenile courts were supposed to be experts in juvenile justice issues, who could function as benevolent and kind substitute parents for children in need.[18] The one judge-one family model aimed to create well-trained judges knowledgeable about the problems of children and families in need.[19] This system enables judges to make detached, rational decisions based on what is best for each individual family.[20]

Perhaps the most significant parallel between the Progressives and those in favor of unified family courts is the strong sense of optimism about their causes. Optimism is important to any reform, and we applaud the energy and dedication that unified family court proponents bring with them into the debate. For the Progressives, however, a similar optimism has resulted in a failure to see some of the near-fatal flaws in the juvenile court structure that they created.[21] We wonder whether the same flaws exist in the unified family court.

As we all know, the Pre-*Gault* juvenile court became a nightmare. The services that it offered often resulted in very coercive sanctions against children and families.[22] Justice was quite irrational and subject to the personality of the particular judge who presided.[23] Due process was secondary to the subjective evaluation of what the judge believed was in the child's "best interests."[24] This meant that judges could choose to detain a child indefinitely without offering the benefit of presenting or rebutting evidence, cross-examining witnesses, or even providing notice of the charges.[25] It took 70 years to reverse some of the worst aspects of that great social movement, partially because few people questioned the propriety of the juvenile court system.[26] People assumed that the juvenile court was an enlightened idea and that the Progressives had discovered the key to reforming juvenile justice. They seldom looked behind the theory to the reality of the court.

History has shown that many aspects of the law, especially due process, "get in the way" when people certain of their own convictions seek to help other people. If we are to learn from history, we should always be vigilant in the face of blind optimism and demand more than mere assertion when reformers argue that they have found a miracle cure for legal or social problems. Policy makers should remain mindful of Justice Brandeis's warning that

> experience should teach us to be most on our guard to protect liberty when the government's purposes are beneficent. Men born to freedom are naturally alert to repel invasion of their liberty by evil-minded rulers. The greatest dangers to liberty lurk in insidious encroachment by men of zeal, well-meaning but without understanding.[27]

The history of social welfare experiments is replete with high-sounding ideas implemented without consideration of Justice Brandeis's warning. Liberty and fairness concerns have been shoved aside in the past to make way for reformers' good intentions. Policy makers should look at the past and ask whether the proposed reforms are actually new, whether they have been tried before under a different guise, and whether they have failed. The similarity between the unified family courts and the juvenile courts of the past suggests the danger that we may not be considering history's lessons.

## IV. THE ONE JUDGE-ONE FAMILY MODEL: IS THIS WHAT WE REALLY WANT?

One of the tenets of the unified family court movement is that there should be one judge to conduct all proceedings involving the same family; i.e., the one judge-one family model. Proponents cite many potential benefits of assigning one judge to hear all of the cases involving a single family. The primary assertion is that it can make the family court process more efficient[28] by eliminating duplicative hearings, decreasing the potential for conflicting orders issued by different judges, streamlining the services offered to families in need, and preserving judicial resources.[29] This efficiency will then produce more just results.

While efficiency is laudable, it should not be placed above fundamental due process concerns. The one judge-one family model makes it difficult to preserve due process protections.[30] When a person is charged with a crime, he or she requires an unbiased resolution of guilt or innocence. In most cases, we prevent juries from knowing a person's previous social history to ensure that the jury will not be swayed by that information.[31] While the law assumes that judges can separate admissible from inadmissible information,[32] there is little to guarantee this premise.[33] Laypeople find this premise absurd.[34] In other contexts, our legal system recognizes that judges cannot be expected to compartmentalize information and make objective decisions without considering inadmissible evidence.

The drafters of the Bill of Rights required juries in serious criminal[35] and civil[36] cases specifically because they felt that 12 people were better equipped to dispense justice than "could one official wearing the black robe of a judge."[37] Juries were created specifically to protect the people from the tyranny of a single government official.[38] If we believed that judges were perfect dispensers of justice, then we would not need a jury system at all.

Similarly, rules of evidence keep inadmissible evidence from juries.[39] We keep irrelevant evidence from a jury because we understand that jurors are unable to ignore that evidence in arriving at a verdict. Yet, we currently expect judges to do what citizens cannot. The fear that inadmissible, damning evidence about extraneous material will corrupt a verdict is very real.[40] It is true that many juvenile courts, especially those in rural areas, have few judges and thus know something about the personal histories of people brought before the court. Because of this problem, some statutes proscribe the court from looking at social information prior to determining guilt or innocence.[41] Policy makers should look to minimize the risk of corrupted verdicts rather than expand that risk, especially when so many different causes of actions are combined.

The danger of judicial overfamiliarity can occur in civil as well as criminal cases. Imagine two parents accused of abusing their children, facing the loss of their children in neglect proceedings and possible termination of parental rights.[42] One of the parents has fought the system every step of the way, whereas the other has been more cooperative and willing to submit to court mandated services. Later, the parents are involved in a domestic violence case in which each claims that the other was the aggressor. In a nonunified family court adhering to basic rules of evidence, the judge hearing the domestic violence case would not be able to hear evidence about the parents' behavior in the therapeutic aspects of the abuse and neglect proceeding because the behavior is not relevant to the ultimate legal question of whether one parent is guilty of domestic violence. In a unified family court, where both cases appear before the same judge, it would be nearly impossible for the judge to disregard the conduct of each parent in the therapeutic aspects of the abuse and neglect case when considering each parent's credibility in the domestic violence case. At some subconscious level, almost any judge would take the earlier behavior into account.

Even some of the strongest advocates of unified family courts have expressed concern over this weakness in the one judge-one family model,[43] although few have provided satisfactory responses. Some commentators have urged blind faith; we should simply trust that judges will be able to do their jobs fairly.[44] History and human nature show us that this is unrealistic. Other solutions suggested by commentators include judicial recusal at the parties' initiative[45] or asking for voluntary waivers of individual rights in exchange for additional social services or lesser sanctions.[46] Again, these suggestions are not viable and suggest coercion rather than therapeutic intervention. Litigants before family courts are in positions of relative powerlessness. Allowing them to request recusal assumes that they will make such decisions for the right reasons and at the right times. In reality, litigants, even those represented by counsel, make decisions for a multitude of reasons, but they are all related to self-interest. They may decide not to make a request for recusal either because they fear reprisals from the judge (who holds a huge amount of power over their families) or because they simply are not aware of their right to do so. Moreover, litigants should not have to waive fundamental rights in exchange for services. Fundamental rights are fundamental because they come without strings attached. Litigants should be entitled to them irrespective of the court's desire to provide needed social services.

The most common suggestion for resolving problems resulting from the one judge-one family model is to use a one *team*-one family approach, relying on magistrate judges, mental health professionals, or caseworkers when sensitive issues are at stake.[47] This suggestion ignores the court's important dispute resolution function. Moreover, it is not clear how a family court without a one judge-one family model can be called a unified family court at all. If families must go to multiple judges or court personnel for each matter in which they are involved, a core feature of the unified family court disappears. Once the one judge-one family model is abandoned, the family court is no different, other than in name, from the courts they were designed to replace.

One of the rationales for the one judge-one family model is that it prevents judicial burnout by allowing judges to become specialists and by keeping them actively involved with families.[48] The one judge-one family model could actually have an opposite effect.[49] Judges may burn out more quickly hearing difficult family cases day in and day out, or they may become the judicial tyrants that social workers describe today when discussing judges in single-judge juvenile courts.[50] There is no doubt that there are many people who are both skillful jurists and who have an abiding interest in these cases. They may be able to remain in the court for many years. On the other hand, there is little evidence that a large number of experienced judges, well versed in the law and procedure generally, want to leave the rotation of a court of general jurisdiction to take an assignment limited to family cases. Moreover, juvenile courts often have been thought of as training grounds for judges as they seek better positions. There is no guarantee that this can change. Nor is there great evidence that the good lawyers who practice in this area will want to be judges. If they do, that can further diminish the small cadre of good lawyers practicing in this generally low paid part of the legal profession.[51]

Families that must submit to a burned-out judge or one ill prepared for the task of curing family dysfunction may be worse off than they would have been in a court or general jurisdiction. In a general jurisdiction court, they would have a chance of appearing before multiple judges, some of whom may not have experienced the same level of burnout. Realizing this possibility, many advocates have suggested that judges rotate from the family court bench periodically.[52] This solution, however, seems to contradict completely the underlying goals of the one judge-one family model. As soon as judges are transferred, families have to adjust to new judges and face the same possibilities of duplicative orders, and judicial resources are not conserved.

## V. THE PROPER ROLE OF COURTS IN FAMILY DISPUTES: SOCIAL CONTROL OR FAMILY COUNSELOR?

A court is, at its core, an instrument of social control. What it does best is resolve disputed factual issues at a point when the litigants cannot resolve them by themselves. Courts gain control over these acrimonious situations only through the threat or reality of coercion. Thus, courts are generally seen as an option of last resort, somewhere for people to go to resolve serious disputes without resort to violence, and a place where society can assert its control over behavior that it considers too egregious to go unpunished. Most people who appear before a court do not wish to be there, and would have chosen another form of dispute resolution had it been possible.

The concept of therapeutic justice, central to the operation of the unified family court, is premised on the view that courts can be more than instruments of social control. Proponents of therapeutic justice believe that a court can work with families to provide positive, lasting resolutions to family problems.[53] Seeing the traditional adversarial system as a process that splinters rather than heals family relationships, adherents seek alternative solutions for preserving family coherence.[54] In the world of therapeutic justice, judges work with caseworkers, psychologists, doctors, and family members to resolve family conflicts through counseling, mediation, and other nonpunitive measures. Judges are supposed to consider more than a discrete factual dispute. They are to look at the family's environment, existing support structure, and cultural context when making decisions.[55]

Despite these promising theories, there are at least two problems with the therapeutic justice model. First, it ignores the fact that sanctions given out by the court, whether or not called "therapeutic," are inherently coercive. Second, the focus on therapy may divert the court from its fundamental role as a forum for dispute resolution.

Most litigants involved in the family court system do not see the therapeutic justice system as particularly benign. For the most part, poor people are brought into the court system against their will, very often without lawyers.[56] They are often unaware of their legal rights but believe that failing to cooperate fully with judicial orders and demands from social workers can result in serious negative consequences. They seldom come to the court voluntarily, looking for holistic services or for assistance from mental health professionals. They are there because someone charged them with being bad parents, with committing a crime, or with abusing their significant other. There is nothing consensual about this process. In this setting, the therapeutic service contracts that social workers and judges enforce on these families are not truly voluntary. Compliance is usually gained by the threat of coercive sanctions. Parents know that if they fail to do what the powerful players in the system think they should do, they will go to jail or lose their children. Thus, they often go through the motions of compliance simply to have their children returned or to avoid going to prison, rather than from a genuine desire to seek help or treatment.[57] In this context of coercive therapy, compliance with a list of programs takes precedence over more important questions about the families' wishes, whether services will actually help families, or the best way to resolve the dispute in question.[58]

People can only be helped if they want to be helped. They will accept help by a court if they believe they are being treated fairly.[59] Poor people do not perceive that they are being heard in family courts, not because of the structure of the court, but because the value system that supports it does not resonate with the value system of the people coming before it.[60] Moreover, many of these psychological and underlying personal relationship problems exist because people are poor or are being viewed by the court system from a perspective that is different from that of the community in which the litigants reside.[61]

Therapeutic remedies are inherently suspect because they do not start with the worldview of those who must comply with them. Instead, they take on the perspective of the social science researcher who has structured his research and collected data in the context of his own perceptions and biases.[62] Judges and caseworkers also approach the social science data with their own cultural biases, applying social science findings according to their own personal views.[63] We do not mean to ascribe bad motives to judges and social workers. We do mean to imply that litigants and the official players in the family court system often view the world differently and that court orders usually reflect the worldview of the more powerful players. Thus, reliance on social science data in fact may be used to justify an outcome that is really based on a judge's cultural belief.[64] These cultural beliefs may also have subtle (and often not so subtle) racial undertones, resulting in the disparate treatment of Black families.[65] For example, stereotypes of Black single mothers as weak and irresponsible may prompt a judge to remove a child from the custody of a poorer Black family while offering therapeutic treatment to a middle-class White family under the same circumstances.[66] In other words, judicial discretion to dispense therapeutic justice may result in disparate treatment for similarly situated families, even though an intent to do so is lacking.[67]

From the therapeutic justice perspective, social problems are to be solved; dispute resolution seems secondary. In most legal cases, however, allegations are contested. If so, resolution of the dispute should be the court's primary focus. Litigants should not be coerced into admitting culpability to obtain the services that other people think they need. For example, many parents must confess to abuse or neglect before the state offers them services.[68] The result occurs in juvenile delinquency proceedings; poor children must be adjudicated delinquent and possibly removed from their homes before they have access to the types of services that wealthier families are able to afford on their own.[69] Judges rendering guilt or innocence decisions in domestic abuse cases, or neglect/no neglect findings may also be vulnerable to this temptation. If they know that a finding against a parent is the only way to obtain needed services for a child or family, they may be more willing to make such a finding.[70] There is real danger that this tendency can become more pronounced in a court that focuses on therapeutic justice. This shift in focus has serious consequences. Juveniles may be committed and sent to juvenile prison, and parents may have to suffer the stigma of being branded neglectful or even have their children taken away to obtain help; yet, the actual dispute in question is minimized. Litigants suffer major repercussions without a proper inquiry into basic questions of culpability. When this occurs, well-intentioned efforts at therapeutic justice backfire and become the vehicles for injustice.

Proponents of the unified family court claim that they do not want the court to become a social agency.[71] However, under the system they propose, adjudication of the original dispute seems to be a minor part of the process. This may very well occur in today's juvenile court, but it can only get worse in a court focused on therapeutic justice. Many advocates of family courts see the court as a centralized place where services are coordinated, doled out, and monitored. Judges are supposed to take service providers to task when they are ineffective, ensure that duplicative services are not given by different agencies, and watch family members to make sure that they are taking part in required treatment.[72] It is questionable whether this is really a proper role for judges or whether this function might be handled more appropriately by a centralized agency in charge of family services. There is also little evidence that judges are uniquely qualified to handle these burdensome and largely administrative tasks. Perhaps judicial time and resources can be better spent resolving factual and legal disputes. Well-functioning child welfare agencies are-or at least they should be-better equipped to provide solutions to the underlying problems that give rise to these disputes. In today's juvenile courts, judges spend a considerable amount of time trying to coordinate the services that families are to receive across agencies.[73] Like current judges, the single judge in the unified family court can continue to be at the mercy of the child welfare professionals in the system. It is difficult to believe that one judge with a large caseload can be responsible for so many lives.

Perhaps the better way to approach family problems is to offer services and counseling before family disputes become serious enough to require court intervention. One of the greatest criticisms of the services we offer families is that they are not triggered until families are already steeped in serious crises.[74] In a time of shrinking judicial resources, it seems strange that the courts should be the first resort rather than the last resort for families. People should not have to go to court to get help. Although the justice system may facilitate such assistance, the court's primary role should be to resolve disputes and exercise governmental authority fairly.[75] Perhaps a better focus of resources, then, should be on reforming and strengthening preventive services for families rather than on reforming existing court structures.

## VI. MIXING CRIMINAL AND CIVIL JURISDICTIONS

Even the staunchest supporters of the unified family court movement recognize the many problems inherent in mixing criminal and civil jurisdictions. These problems have led many jurisdictions to create family courts that do not include criminal jurisdiction.[76] Many supporters have expressed concern about the role of therapeutic justice in the criminal context.[77] A family court that is focused on therapeutic and rehabilitative justice may be more lenient on criminal offenders than they would be otherwise, and such leniency may have the effect of decriminalizing serious offenses.[78] Such a system fails to hold offenders accountable, frustrates victim's rights, and may result in disparate treatment of offenders. Focusing on therapeutic justice may also shift focus away from the adversarial process to which the criminal defendant is entitled and induce him or her to accept a guilty plea when innocent just to obtain social services.[79] Some commentators also believe that since judges are already overburdened by the huge caseloads in the family court setting, switching between civil and criminal rules of procedure and standards of proof will make their job even more difficult.[80] It also will create serious due process concerns if criminal defendants do not receive the same level of procedural protections that they would have in criminal court. Criminal courts also require resources such as cells, additional guards, space for jury trials, bail hearings, and specialized criminal procedures that civil courts do not require.[81] The potential efficiency gains promised for unified family courts may not be sufficient to offset the space and personnel requirements that may accompany these extra protections.[82] Finally, the concerns that arise out of the one judge-one family model are of particular concern in the context of mixed criminal and civil jurisdictions. The more serious the offense, the less likely it is that a judge will be able to disregard that offense in making a later decision. For example, it is more difficult to ignore prior criminal acts when making a child custody decision than it is to ignore a prior divorce proceeding.

These questions are posed starkly when policy makers consider whether domestic violence cases should be included in the jurisdiction of a unified family court. Many domestic violence advocates believe that a rehabilitative model is inappropriate in domestic violence cases. They fear that unified family courts will be more lenient toward abusive partners than would a traditional criminal court[83] and that the ultimate effect of including domestic violence in a unified family court would be tantamount to decriminalizing the offense.

> The abuser's access to the children endangers rather than nourishes them; the imbalance of power between abuser and victim transforms alternative dispute resolution into yet another weapon in the abuser's arsenal; and striving for family preservation confronts the victim with Hobson's choice of remaining in a potentially lethal setting in order to continue living with her children or abandoning them and her home.[84] Mediation, a potentially useful dispute resolution device in some contexts, is also considered counterproductive in the domestic violence setting, where courts are focused on keeping the abuser away from family members rather than on trying to bring them together.

Finally, people tend to react strongly to domestic violence cases. Judges may have a very difficult time disregarding a past domestic violence judgment when making decisions in later cases.

> Criminal proceedings are charged with emotion and the separation of custody, support and visitation matters in another court at a later time may be preferable because few judges can remain objective while considering the case of a severely bruised victim the morning after the incident.[85] Judges are human, and it would be difficult for any person to ignore such an emotional case in evaluating a new set of facts. Someone who has been involved in a domestic dispute may, therefore, be at an automatic disadvantage at a hearing to set child support.

Although these concerns are particularly strong in the domestic violence context, they apply to the problems of mixing criminal and civil jurisdictions in any context. Civil and criminal cases are different. They have different goals, different rules of procedure, different rules of confidentiality, and different outcomes. Given these variations, policy makers may wish to consider keeping criminal and civil jurisdictions separate when structuring new unified family courts.

## VII. PAYING FOR UNIFIED FAMILY COURTS

Money counts. No matter what new legal structures we create to improve the lives of families and children, they cost money. Policy makers must determine the best investment to achieve the ultimate goals of maintaining a well-functioning court system and strong, stable families. The public money dedicated to a unified court system may divert resources from other governmental priorities. Legislators may take money from other parts of the social network that support needy families to fund the new court. Perhaps better results may be obtained if the money dedicated to the court was spent improving the daily lives of families and children. We seldom have met parents or children who want to be involved in the family court or who would have to be there if their life chances had been better. Money that is available to build more courtrooms, appoint new judges and clerks, and hire more experts might be better spent creating better lives for disadvantaged people, or at least delivering better services to those who get caught up in our current family court systems.[86]

The money a county spends on a new court system may also come from the budget of the existing court system. Current complaints about court resolution of family issues-conflicting orders, too many and duplicative hearings, failure to communicate, lack of ADR programs, and a lack of expertise in judges and court personnel,[37] do not necessarily suggest a need for a new family court system. They may suggest that the administrative and judicial operation of the entire court system needs improvement. Jurisdictions that have these kinds of problems when processing their family cases probably have the same problems throughout their entire court system. When money counts, one must decide whether it is better to create a whole new system to fix one part of the court or to fix the entire court system.

According to family court proponents, the creation of a unified family court in a particular jurisdiction will increase efficiency,[88] reduce delay, create opportunities for alternative dispute resolution, and increase overall client satisfaction.[89] Problems such as these are not unique to family cases. If they exist in one part of a court, they probably exist throughout the entire court system. Fixing one part of an inefficient court system may prove to be only a temporary improvement. If the culture of a local legal system permits such problems to exist, it takes a great deal of faith to believe that the culture may not, in time, create the same problems in a new unified family court system. Furthermore, even if these problems are remedied, it is not clear that they can create better results. Unified family courts by themselves cannot stem the increase in caseloads. They can have no effect on the life chances of the litigants prior to the time a case is filed. Nor will families face fewer complex problems just because court process and jurisdiction have been unified and the court becomes more efficient. Poor education, dwindling housing stock, mental illness, drug use, crime, and crumbling neighborhoods are all beyond the reach of the court. Nor can a court force the executive and legislative branches of government to create more and better services. Before expending huge amounts of money to create new court systems, policy makers must ask themselves whether a unified family court can solve the problems existing in their particular jurisdictions or whether better results can be obtained by other investments.

The District of Columbia's new unified family court system demonstrates some of the problems of resource allocation. The District of Columbia has had a Family Division in a court of general jurisdiction that has worked fairly well for many years. It also has a child welfare system that is badly in need of repair. Problems with the child welfare system have been illustrated with tragic clarity in 2000 when a child, Brianna Blackmond, was murdered after being returned to an abusive stepparent.[90] Outraged federal lawmakers,[91] seeking to prevent such occurrences in the future, have chosen to reform the District of Columbia court system, rather than to look carefully at the entire child protection system. In their enthusiasm for change and with faith that a new unified court can eliminate such tragedies, advocates and policy makers have ignored the fact that the preventive programs and treatment programs of the District of Columbia are in disarray or nonexistent. They have ignored the fact that the former Family Division has had a drug court and a domestic violence program that has provided therapeutic services. They have ignored the fact that many lawyers believed that the only part of the family law apparatus that has worked well is the court system. So in January 2002, Congress replaced the D.C. Superior Court Family Division with a unified family court housed within the Superior Court.

Despite great fanfare, the differences between the new unified family court and the former family division are small. The implementing legislation provides the structure for a one judge-one family system and adds new judges and judge magistrates.[92] It also provides for cases to be transferred into the new family court system and for a change in name from the family division to the family court.[93] It requires 3-year judicial rotations rather than the former customary 1-year rotation.[94] On the other hand, it permits criminal and civil domestic violence cases to be tried in other divisions of the D.C. Superior Court.[95] The judges themselves realize the limitations in the one judge-one family model and are struggling to ensure that verdicts are not contaminated by inadmissible evidence. These small and probably ineffective changes cost $18 million.[96]

It is difficult to determine how these minor changes in court structure can provide more just results in the District of Columbia court system when the systemic problems in the provision of prevention and treatment services remain elusive and ultimately outside of the court's power. For now, the new legislation has caused only confusion in the court system and has split the child welfare and juvenile delinquency lawyers into opposing groups. It remains to be seen whether this cost is justified or whether these resources can be better spent elsewhere.

## VIII. THE RISK OF BECOMING A POLITICAL PANACEA

Unified family courts have been so widely discussed and accepted that they risk becoming an easy political "solution" to systemic problems that poor families face. Policy makers have used the term *unified family court* to describe a myriad of reforms that range from a comprehensive restructuring of the court system to simple changes. The general definition of a unified family court includes five elements: (a) comprehensive jurisdiction, (b) a one judge-one family system, (c) a therapeutic justice approach, (d) training of judges and court personnel, and (e) coordinated case management procedures. Despite reliance on these five elements, the only true defining characteristic of a family court is comprehensive jurisdiction. Without comprehensive jurisdiction, it is difficult to have a unified family court.

This raises two distinct issues. First, in responding to criticism of the unified family courts, advocates often are willing to abandon comprehensive jurisdiction to focus on other goals, including therapeutic justice and coordinated case management,[97] while still clinging to the term unified family court to describe their efforts. In reality, they are not advocating for a unified family court but for a series of reforms in an existing court structure.[98] The momentum of the unified family court movement and the unchecked enthusiasm of politicians and supporters make the concept of the unified family court a seemingly quick solution to all existing family court problems.[99] By using the term loosely, legislators are able to gain political support without having to institute any real reform.

Second, although comprehensive jurisdiction is the only defining characteristic of the unified family court, legislative activity suggests that comprehensive jurisdiction is not necessarily so crucial to achieve the other goals that unified family courts seek to achieve. In other words, why is "therapeutic justice" an element that has to be unique to unified family courts? There is no evidence to suggest that courts with broad jurisdiction over family cases are any better at handing out therapeutic justice than other courts. Likewise, better training for court personnel and case management do not follow automatically from comprehensive jurisdiction. Moreover, if the public believes that all family problems can be solved with the creation of a unified family court, advocates for children and families may move on to other problems and ignore persistent cracks in the family court system.

## IX. THE SEARCH FOR PROOF: WHAT EVIDENCE DO WE HAVE THAT UNIFIED FAMILY COURTS WILL DO IT BETTER?

There is very little, if any, evidence that unified family courts are able to achieve their stated goals. Our search of the literature has found little more than anecdotal evidence about the likely success of the unified family court.[100] Several authors have cited the lack of a comprehensive evaluation to determine that family courts are accomplishing their stated goals.[101] Some new studies exist concerning the administrative effectiveness of the court,[102] and some states have done self-assessments of their new systems.[103] But no one, to our knowledge, has shown that the unified family court can or will produce better justice than is currently provided by current court systems.

Our literature search found a great deal of enthusiasm by supporters of the court. Indeed, the enthusiasm we found mirrors, often in very similar terms, the enthusiasm of Jane Addams, Judge Lindsey, and the other Progressive Reformers of the 1890s as they began to develop their new juvenile court.[104] Unfortunately, enthusiasm alone is not enough to justify the cost and administrative burden of rearranging this country's court systems.[105]

## X. CONCLUSION

Our goal in this article is not to condemn the notion of a unified family court but to suggest that there is scant evidence to show that it can produce better results than current functioning courts of general jurisdiction and to propose questions that policy makers must address before they invest in such a system.

We are willing to accept that we might be totally wrong about our fears. Perhaps our hopes and faith have been dashed too many times to invest anew in another reform, even one that might succeed. On the other hand, new initiatives should not be implemented unless there is some basis to predict that they will succeed. We believe that the case for unified family courts, as defined by their proponents, has not yet been made. As legislators consider new policy initiatives and law professors begin to teach about the unified family court, we suggest that the enthusiasm and hope of the new reformers be tempered with a little caution.

*Anne H. Geraghty, J.D., is Pro Bono Counsel in the Chicago office of DLA Piper.*

*Wallace J. Mlyniec, J.D., is the Lupo-Ricci Professor of Clinical Legal Studies and Director of the Juvenile Justice Clinic at Georgetown University Law Center in Washington, D.C.*

Authors' Note: *The authors would like to thank Professors Abbe Smith and Deborah Epstein at Georgetown, Robert Schwartz at the Juvenile Law Center, and Professor Paul Holland at the University of Michigan for their helpful comments on earlier drafts of this article. This article is an expanded version of a presentation at the Association of American Law Schools Section on Family and Juvenile Law Panel on Court Reform, Family Law and the Role of Teaching and Scholarship at the AALS 2002 meeting in New Orleans on January 4, 2002.*

## Notes

[1]   The family court movement began at the same time as the juvenile court movement. The first juvenile court was founded in Chicago, Illinois. The first court with broad jurisdiction over family issues was formed in Cincinnati in 1914. Barbara A. Babb, *Where We Stand: An Analysis of America's Family Law Adjudicatory Systems and the Mandate to Establish Unified Family Courts*, 32 FAM. L.Q. 31, 35-36 (Spring 1998).

[2]   The endorsement of unified family courts by the American Bar Association (ABA) in 1980 and the Council of Juvenile and Family Court Judges in 1991 highlighted and legitimated the movement. See ABA Joint Commission of Juvenile Justice Standards (Standard 1.1, Part 1) (1980); ABA reaffirmed in 1994; Sanford N. Katz & Jeffrey A. Kuhn, *Recommendations for a Model Family Court: A Report from the National Family Court Symposium*, National Council of Juvenile and Family Court Judges, May 1991.

[3]   In re Gault, 387 U.S. 1 (1967). Even earlier, Dean Roscoe Pound had likened the powers of the Juvenile Court to the Star Chamber. Forward to YOUNG, SOCIAL TREATMENT IN PROBATION AND DELINQUENCY (1937).

[4]   "The term 'Family Court' is used by many courts 'without any thought about what the term includes substantively or procedurally.'" Victor Eugene Flango, *Creating Family Friendly Courts: Lessons from Two Oregon Counties*, 34 FAM. L.Q. 115, 117 (Spring 2000), quoting Robert Page, *Family Courts: A Model for an Effective Judicial Approach to the Resolution of Family Disputes*, in ABA Summit on Unified Family Courts; Exploring Solutions for Families, Women and Children in Crisis (1998), at A3.

[5]   *See, e.g.*, PATRICIA A. GARCIA, AMERICAN BAR ASS'N, UNIFIED FAMILY COURTS: JUSTICE DELIVERED (2001) (attempting to define and summarize the major characteristics of unified family courts).

[6]   Flango, *supra* note 4 at 115; Jeffrey A. Kuhn, *Unified Family Courts: A Discussion Paper*, available at http://ubmail.ubalt.edu/~cshafer/lsr_kuhn_. htm; Catherine J. Ross, *The Failure of Fragmentation: The Promise of a System of Unified Family Courts*, 33 REV. JUR. U.I.P.R. 311, 320-21 (1999); GARCIA, *supra* note 5.

[7]   *See* D.C. Family Court Statute, Pub. L. 107-114, 115 Stat 2100, Jan. 8 2002, sec. 2 d (permitting the domestic violence jurisdiction to opt out of the unified family court).

[8]   *See generally*, Barbara A. Babb, *An Interdisciplinary Approach to Family Law Jurisprudence: Application of an Ecological & Therapeutic Perspective*, 72 IND. L.J. 775 (Summer 1997).

[9]   Kuhn, *supra* note 6.

[10]   *Id.*

[11]   *Id.*

[12]   NINA BERNSTEIN, THE LOST CHILDREN OF WILDER, xii (2001).

[13]   Many of the early juvenile courts had broad jurisdiction. For example, under the Illinois Juvenile Court Act of 1899, juvenile courts heard not only criminal cases involving minors but also dealt with abuse and neglect. DEAN J. CHAMPION, THE JUVENILE JUSTICE SYSTEM: DELINQUENCY, PROCESSING AND THE LAW, 14-15 (1992). Generally, pre-Gault juvenile courts had jurisdiction over

delinquency, dependency, and neglect cases. CHRISTOPHER P. MANFREDI, THE SUPREME COURT AND JUVENILE JUSTICE, 29-30 (1998). Some early juvenile courts also had jurisdiction over cases involving widow's pension, adoption, truancy, contributing to the delinquency of a minor, and commitment of minors to institutions for the mentally ill or retarded. DAVID J. ROTHMAN, CONSCIENCE AND CONVENIENCE: THE ASYLUM AND ITS ALTERNATIVES IN PROGRESSIVE AMERICA, 237 (1980).

[14]   *See* ROTHMAN, *supra* note 13 at 215.

[15]   Babb, *supra* note 8 at 800.

[16]   ROTHMAN, *supra* note 13 at 207-211.

[17]   *Id.*; "The unified family court recognizes the individual dignity of all persons and does not settle for simply forcing change in a family member's behavior by threatening with the power of the judicial system." Kuhn, *supra* note 9.

[18]   ROTHMAN, *supra* note 13 at 217.

[19]   Ross, *supra* note 6 at 324-25.

[20]   Carol R. Flango, *Family Focused Courts*, 2 J. OF THE CENTER FOR FAMILIES, CHILDREN & THE CTS. 99, 99-100 (2000) (assuming that judges will be able to make informed decisions that address the needs of families); H. Ted Rubin, *Families in Court: Will a Family Court do it Better?* 16 BEHAV. SCI. & THE L.. 169, 176 (1998) (asserting that a single judge presiding over all family matters will be able to make better decisions for a family because he will be better informed about that family's needs).

[21]   ROTHMAN, *supra* note 13 at 213-14. ("[The juvenile court] seemed so capable of solving the problem of delinquency without sacrificing anyone's interests that reformers did not anticipate any objections.")

[22]   Overall, punishments in juvenile courts tended to be harsher than those given out in their general jurisdiction predecessors because of the increased use of probation as a means of rehabilitation; a child would often receive probation in juvenile court for a case that would have been dismissed in a regular court. This practice of providing probation meant that the children were involved in the court system for a long time and that they had criminal records earlier in their lives. *Id.* at 255-57. *See generally*, Holland & Wallace J. Mlyniec, *Whatever Happened to the Right to Treatment: The Modern Quest for a Historical Promise*, 68 TEMPLE L.R. 1791 (1995).

[23]   *See generally*, ROTHMAN, *supra* note 13 at 236-60 (1980) (describing early juvenile courts as centered around a "cult of judicial personality").

[24]   CHAMPION, *supra* note 13 at 304.

[25]   *Id.* at 308.

[26]   The first juvenile court was established in Chicago in 1899. Sixty-eight years later, the U.S. Supreme Court finally recognized the flaws with the existing juvenile court structure and mandated that children have a right to an attorney, the right to notice of charges, the right to confront and cross-examine witnesses, and the right against self-incrimination. In re Gault, *supra* note 1.

[27]   Olmstead v. United States, 48 S. Ct. 564, 572-73 (1928) (Brandeis, J., dissenting).

[28]   Proponents are concerned about efficiency because they believe most families are likely to be involved in multiple matters within the family court system. One study found that in child abuse and neglect cases, 18% of litigants had been previously involved in divorce cases, 15**ad been involved in juvenile delinquency matters, and 15**ad been previously involved in another instance of child abuse and neglect. Of juvenile delinquency cases surveyed, 27% of juveniles had been involved in divorce cases, 22**ad been involved in child abuse and neglect, and 13**ad had siblings involved in juvenile delinquency cases. Victor Eugene Flango & H. Ted Rubin, *How Is Court Coordination of Family Cases Working?* 33 THE JUDGE'S JOURNAL 10, 15 (Fall 1994). The same study cautions, however, that some judges do not wish to be involved with the same families, especially in delinquency matters, because they are concerned that familiarity with family history may color their decisions. *Id.* at 36.

[29] For a discussion of the proposed benefits of the one judge-one family model, *see generally* Babb, *supra* note 1 at 32; Kuhn, *supra* note 9.

[30] Once again, the history of the pre-Gault juvenile court provides useful lessons here. Before Gault, the lack of procedural protections offered to children gave judicial personality the deciding factor in any given case. Some judges were stern, some were lenient, some preferred incarceration, while others focused on holistic remedies. Procedures such as sentencing guidelines, the presence of a jury, or the right to appeal did not exist to even the playing field for children as they did for adults. *See* ROTHMAN, *supra* note 13 at 238-39. Similarly, combining the jurisdiction of several courts so that a single judge hears multiple cases within a single family is tantamount to removing one crucial procedural protection that would otherwise promote uniformity in decision making. In a unified family court, families are not given the opportunity to play the judicial lottery, whereby they may be stuck with the wrong judge in one case but can be sure that they may get the right judge in the next case. Instead, if they get the wrong judge, there is little that can be done. "God help the family that gets stuck with the wrong judge-forever!" Jay Folberg, *Family Courts: Assessing the Trade-Offs*, 37 FAM. & CONCILIATION CTS. REV. 448, 451 (October 1999).

[31] For example, character evidence is generally inadmissible in a criminal trial. Fed. R. Evid. 404.

[32] Harris v. Rivera, 454 U.S. 339, 346 (1981).

[33] Flango & Rubin, *supra* note 28 at 36 (noting that some judges do not wish to be involved with the same families, especially in delinquency cases, because they are concerned that knowledge of family history may color their decisions).

[34] In Duncan v. Louisiana, 391 U.S. 145 (1968), the Supreme Court noted that the framers provided a right to a jury to protect against "compliant, biased, or eccentric judges."

[35] U.S. CONST., amend VI.

[36] U.S. CONST., amend VII.

[37] WILLIAM L. DWYER, IN THE HANDS OF THE PEOPLE, 70 (2002).

[38] *Id.*

[39] *See, e.g.*, FED.R EVID. 104(c), requiring that hearings on the admissibility of confessions be conducted outside of the presence of the jury.

[40] *See* Martin Guggenheim & Randy Hertz, *Reflections on Judges, Juries, and Justice: Ensuring the Fairness of Juvenile Delinquency Trials*, 33 WAKE FOREST L. REV. 553, 571 (1998) (noting that one of the major factors that may sway judicial opinion in a juvenile court proceeding includes hearing extraneous, inadmissible evidence).

[41] *See* D.C. Code Ann. § 16-2319 (a) (2001) prohibiting the judge from viewing a social investigation until after a finding of guilt in a delinquency case.

[42] The authors would like to thank Professor Paul Holland of the University of Michigan Law School for providing us with this hypothetical.

[43] *See, e.g.*, Carol R. Flango, *supra* note 20 at 99-100; Rubin, *supra* note 20 at 174.

[44] *See* Folberg, *supra* note 30 at 451 (asserting his faith in the American judge and pointing out that judicial bias is a potential critique of the entire legal system rather than something that is unique to unified family courts). Folberg asserted that constitutional review is available as a remedy when violations do occur. However, it seems contrary to our system to assert that the Constitution can only remedy violations that have already occurred, rather than acting as a preventative tool.

[45] Rubin, *supra* note 20 at 174; Folberg, *supra* note 30 at 174.

[46] *Id.*

[47] *See, e.g.*, Jeffrey A. Kuhn, *A Seven-Year Lesson on Unified Family Courts: What We Have Learned Since the 1990 National Family Court Symposium*, 32 FAM. L.Q. 67, 76-77 (Spring 1998).

[48] *Id.* at 67, 75.

[49] *Id.*

[50]   Professor Mlyniec has trained social workers for many years. They have constantly complained that there was no law in their court other than the opinions of the single judge of their court. *See also*, Victor Eugene Flango, *supra* note 4 at 123. ("What is the balance point between having judges remain on the family bench long enough to master the specialized legal knowledge necessary to make quality decisions, and deciding so many of these emotionally charged cases for so long that a more general perspective is lost?")

[51]   It is also true that the quality of practice by lawyers in family courts has been less than outstanding.

[52]   Rubin, *supra* note 20 at 174 (1998) (noting that Hawaii's family courts provide for periodic rotation of their judges).

[53]   "The goal of therapeutic jurisprudence suggests a need to restructure the law and the legal process by applying behavioral science knowledge to accomplish therapeutic outcomes without interfering with traditional notions of justice." Babb, *supra* note 8 at 799.

[54]   *Id.* at 803.

[55]   *Id.* at 804.

[56]   Almost half of all family law litigants are not represented by counsel. Babb, *supra* note 1 at 32 (citations omitted).

[57]   David Wexler has hypothesized that the legal system may actually encourage unnecessary mental health treatments that exacerbate problems in many settings. For example, he suggests that the availability of an incompetence to stand trial doctrine prompts some people to play into mental health problems to avoid punishment. David B. Wexler, *An Introduction to Therapeutic Jurisprudence*, in ESSAYS IN THERAPEUTIC JURISPRUDENCE 17,21 (David B. Wexler & Bruce J. Winick, eds., 1991). This suggests that people may be willing to use treatments that the system offers to obtain a desired result rather than as a genuine means of healing family problems.

[58]   "Compliance overshadows the child's needs or parent's ability to care for the child or even the truth of the original charges of maltreatment. The issue is no longer whether the child may be safely returned home, but whether the mother has attended every parenting class, made every urine drop, participated in every therapy session, shown up for every scheduled visitation, arrived at every appointment on time, and always maintained a contrite and cooperative disposition." DOROTHY ROBERTS, SHATTERED BONDS: THE COLOR OF CHILD WELFARE, 80 (2002).

[59]   TOM R. TYLER, ET AL., SOCIAL JUSTICE IN A DIVERSE SOCIETY 75-102 (1997) (discussing findings that people are more willing to accept legal decisions if they are perceived as fair).

[60]   "Multiculturalism will create problems if it creates psychological boundaries between groups that must interact in society." If people do not believe that they are being heard because of cultural differences, they come away from interactions "feeling dissatisfied and angry." *Id.*

[61]   *See* Gary B. Melton, *Children, Families and the Courts in the Twenty-First Century*, 66 S. CAL. L. REV. 1993, 2021 (1993) (arguing that family courts should be sensitive to cultural differences in decision making).

[62]   Babb, *supra* note 8 at 796.

[63]   *Id.*

[64]   Psychological evaluations, for example, can provide a purportedly objective basis for removing children from a home. Any psychological evaluation can reveal signs of anxiety, hostility, depression, or improper attitude, especially when the subject has gone through the traumatic and frustrating experience of losing her children. The psychological evaluation also provides a surreptitious way of keeping custody of children because of poverty without saying it.
      ROBERTS, *supra* note 58 at 40.

[65]   For example, Black children are more likely than White children to be separated from their parents once they become involved with the child welfare system. *Id.* at 16-17; it has been suggested that misperceptions of Black culture and tradition have lead to some of these disparities because courts and

caseworkers use White, middle-class families as the yardstick for measuring model family behavior. *Id.* at 59.

⁶⁶    Social workers and probation officers preconceptions often color their decisions. In a study by George Bridges and Sara Streen, one probation officer described two boys without criminal histories charged with first-degree robbery as follows: This robbery was very dangerous as Ed confronted the victim with a loaded shotgun. He pointed it at the victim and demanded money be placed in a paper bag .... There is an adult quality to this referral. In talking with Ed, what was evident was the relaxed and open way he discussed his lifestyle. There didn't seem to be any desire to change. There was no expression of remorse from the young man. There was no moral content to his comment.-about Ed, an African American youth, who robbed a gas station with two friends. Lou is the victim of a broken home. He is trying to be his own man, but ... is seemingly easily misled and follows other delinquents against his better judgment. Lou is a tall emanciated little boy who is terrified by his present predicament. It appears that he is in need of drug/alcohol evaluation and treatment.-About Lou, a white youth, who robbed two motels at gunpoint, cited in Hoyt et al., 8 Pathways to Juvenile Detention Reform, Reducing Racial Disparities in Juvenile Detention, A Project of the Annie Casey Foundation 2002.

⁶⁷    ROBERTS, *supra* note 58 at 39 (noting that, "when middle-class parents send their children to school without breakfast as they rush off to work in the morning, it is not seen as neglect requiring supervision by child welfare authorities").

⁶⁸    *Id.* at 83.

⁶⁹    *Id.* at 219.

⁷⁰    Martin Guggenheim & Randy Hertz, *supra* note 40 at 570.

⁷¹    Babb, *supra* note 15 at 799 (noting that therapeutic justice models are designed not to "interfere with traditional notions of justice").

⁷²    Kuhn, *supra* note 47 at 79 (noting that the judicial function in a one team-one family model includes "calendar coordination and case monitoring").

⁷³    Courts are becoming more and more involved in coordinating services across agencies to ensure that families receive the treatment that they need. Carol R. Flango, *supra* note 20 at 102; Flango described the court's role in this respect as one of "neutral arbiter," mediating between competing social service agencies and holding them accountable for failure to provide quality, timely services. *Id.*

⁷⁴    ROBERTS, *supra* note 58 at 90.

⁷⁵    Gary B. Melton, *supra* note 61 at 2047.

⁷⁶    Victor Eugene Flango, *supra* note 6 at 119-20 ("in practice, most family courts do not hear intra-family criminal cases at all or, if they do, hear only misdemeanors") (citations omitted).

⁷⁷    *Id.* at 119.

⁷⁸    Victor Eugene Flango, *supra* note 6; *see also* Kuhn, *supra* note 9.

⁷⁹    ROBERTS, *supra* note 58 at 83. *See generally*, Section V, infra.

⁸⁰    Rubin, *supra* note 43 at 174 (1998).

⁸¹    Victor Eugene Flango, *supra* note 6 at 119.

⁸²    *See* Kuhn, *supra* note 9.

⁸³    Victor Eugene Flango, *supra* note 6 at 120.

⁸⁴    Billie Lee Dunford-Jackson et al., *Unified Family Courts: How Will They Serve Victims of Domestic Violence?* 32 FAM. L.Q. 131, 132 (1998).

⁸⁵    National Center for Juvenile Justice, *Ohio Family Court Feasibility Study: Final Report*, 60 (1997).

⁸⁶    For example, Indiana chose not to "reinvent the wheel" when it came to family law cases by establishing a new unified family court. Instead, Indiana targeted its resources at providing specialized services to families who were in the most need of specialized services. Frances G. Hill, *What Is a Family Court, and What's in it for the Lawyer?* 44 RES GESTATE 26 (November 2000).

⁸⁷    Folberg, *supra* note 44 at 450.

[88]   We have seen through recent reforms in adoption practices that efficiency is not always the best goal when it comes to helping children. In an effort to "free up" children for adoption and increase permanent placements for children in foster care, several states have relaxed standards for termination of parental rights. The reform did have the effect of making more children available for adoption, but the number of adoptions did not increase. The result was that more children were permanently separated from their families and were indefinitely placed in the limbo of foster care. Reformers had failed to look at the big picture, and children suffered as a result. *See* Martin Guggenheim, *The Effect of Recent Trends to Accelerate the Termination of Parental Rights of Children in Parental States*, 29 FAM. L. Q. 121, 135 (1995) (noting that "a well-intentioned desire to serve the best interests of children appears to have resulted in needless destruction of families without providing any offsetting gains").

[89]   *See e.g.* Kuhn, *supra* note 47 (discussing the proposed benefits of unified family courts).

[90]   *A Lesson from Brianna*, Washington Post, Jan. 29, 2002, at A 18.

[91]   The District of Columbia's unique political status under the U.S. Constitution gives the U.S. Congress plenary authority over its system of government.

[92]   Pub. Law 107-114, Stat. 2100 (2002).

[93]   *Id.*

[94]   *Id.*

[95]   *Id.*

[96]   *D.C. Family Court Funding Splits Officials*, Washington Post, Sept. 22, 2001, at B02m.

[97]   *See, e.g.*, Victor Eugene Flango, *supra* note 6 at 199 (noting that many court systems have chosen not to incorporate criminal cases into their unified family court systems).

[98]   In describing the current family court project in Indiana, Frances G. Hill said that,

the Indiana Family Court Project is more about changing our mind-set in family law litigation than structural change in the court system. It does not envision a building or room labeled family court. It is not dependent upon one judge (or set of judges) hearing only family law cases.

Hill, *supra* note 86. Family courts also have been defined as "a court hearing cases involving children and families with a consumer orientation," whether with or without comprehensive jurisdiction. Carol R. Flango, *supra* note 20. When the basic framework of the comprehensive jurisdiction model is washed away, it is simply not clear how these reforms can be deemed as unified family court projects at all.

[99]   Ross, *supra* note 19 at 321 (warning that the mere label of a family court does not resolve problems; the court must have comprehensive jurisdiction to be a true unified family court).

[100]   *See, e.g.*, Folberg, *supra* note 44 (asserting that family courts are effective because he has seen no evidence that family courts are abandoned once they are put into place and because he is not aware of any due process or ethics challenges to unified family courts); Rubin, *supra* note 43 at 177 (stating that that satisfaction with unified family courts is quite likely, without citing to case studies. "Likely, a survey of court clients would find a general preference for ongoing hearings before the same judicial officer. Likely, different family members would prefer not to give the family's chapter and verse over and over again to different judicial officers").

[101]   *See* Kuhn, *supra* note 47 at 82. ("Court and legislative leadership request, with increasing frequency, evidence that family courts deliver what they promise before mandating their creation or investing in them. Therefore, family court performance programs have become a necessity."); Sanford L. Braver, Melanie C. Smith, & Stephanie R. DeLusé, *Methodological Considerations in Evaluating Family Court Programs: A Primer Using Divorced Parent Education Programs as a Case Example*, 35 FAMILY AND CONCILIATION COURTS REVIEW 9 (January 1997) (stressing the need for evaluation of family courts and outlining a potential model for evaluation); Rubin, *supra* note 43 (noting that although there has been much anecdotal evidence, hope and blind faith surrounding family courts, no objective studies confirm their effectiveness); Carol R. Flango, *supra* note 20 at 103 ("Creating a family court does not automatically guarantee that service delivery will be efficient and effective. Evaluation

is needed to see where success is achieved and where opportunities for improvement persist"); Victor Eugene Flango, *supra* note 6 at 131 (finding that courts must be willing to experiment with the unified family court model and to adapt it to the particular needs of each individual jurisdiction).

[102] For example, studies conducted in Hawaii and Rhode Island looked at the timeliness of court decisions, the length and depth of court hearings, and whether the one judge-one family system had been implemented. *See* Mark Hardin, *Child Protection Cases in a Unified Family Court*, 32 FAM. L.Q. 147, 185-91 (1998).

[103] *See, e.g.*, Hunter Hurst & Gregg Halemba, National Center for Juvenile Justice, *Ohio Family Court Feasibility Study, Phase Two Final Report: Assessment of Family Court Pilot Initiatives* (2001).

[104] *Compare* Julian Mack, *The Juvenile Court*, 23 HARV. L. REV.. 104, 118 (1909) (implementing a juvenile court with a single judge "may prove to be the best solution to a difficult problem, combining as it does the possibility of a quick disposition of the simpler cases in many sections of a large city or county, with a unity of administration through the supervisory power of a single judge"), with Folberg, *supra* note 44 at 449 (arguing that "coordination and efficiency can be achieved by one judicial manager for one file, no matter how thick and complex its contents. The long-term societal benefits and savings may be considerable").

[105] "A review of the literature on unified family courts reveals much passion advocating unified family courts, but without a more specific discussion of the conditions under which family courts are appropriate. Family courts are often presented as the only alternative to the current system. This alternative presumes that one specialized court system fits all circumstances." Victor Eugene Flango, *supra* note 6 at 119.

# D: Family Mediation

# [9]

# Divorce Mediation: Research and Reflections

## Robert E. Emery, David Sbarra and Tara Grover

*Mediation and other forms of alternative dispute resolution (ADR) grew rapidly in the last few decades as a result of high divorce rates, frequent conflicts between parting parents, the resulting administrative burden on courts, and especially concerns about damaging effects on children and postdivorce family relationships. This article focuses on our longitudinal research involving randomized trials of mediation and adversary settlement to support the conclusions that mediation can: (1) settle a large percentage of cases otherwise headed for court; (2) possibly speed settlement, save money, and increase compliance with agreements; (3) clearly increase party satisfaction; and (4) most importantly, lead to remarkably improved relationships between nonresidential parents and children, as well as between divorced parents--even twelve years after dispute settlement. The key "active ingredients" of mediation are likely to include: (1) the call for parental cooperation over the long run of co-parenting beyond the crisis of separation, (2) the opportunity to address underlying emotional issues (albeit briefly), (3) helping parents to establish a businesslike relationship, and (4) the avoidance of divisive negotiations at a critical time for family relationships. We call for more research on mediation and other forms of ADR, as well as a renewal of the excitement and optimism of the "first generation" of mediators, qualities that are "active ingredients" in any successful social or psychological intervention.*

In the last few decades, mediation and other forms of alternative dispute resolution (ADR) for disputes between divorcing, divorced, or never-married parents have spread rapidly, particularly for conflicts involving custody and other issues about children. The growth of mediation followed increasing rates of divorce in the United States and elsewhere in the industrialized world, and was motivated by a general dissatisfaction with the traditional adversary methods for settling these disputes through attorney negotiations or litigation. Advocates promised that mediation and other forms of ADR would achieve the two broad, but not always fully compatible, goals of making dispute resolution both more efficient and increasingly family friendly.

*Resolving Family Conflicts*

Motivated by research showing that many harmful effects of divorce on children were due to exposure to and involvement in parental conflict (Emery, 1982), we embraced the promise of mediation (Emery & Wyer, 1987a) and developed a court-based custody mediation program in the mid-1980s, one of the first such programs in Virginia. Two unique features distinguished our efforts from most mediation programs. First, our objective from the beginning was to evaluate the effectiveness of mediation in comparison to adversary settlement, and, in fact, we were able to obtain random assignment to one or the other alternative, a powerful and critically important scientific control. Second, our mediation process was short-term so as to be practical for court programs, yet our mediation style also was informed by therapeutic considerations, including our own unique psychological conceptualizations (Emery, 1994, 2004). Thus, our intervention contained elements of both problem solving and therapeutic mediation.

In this article, we focus on the rationale, theory, and twelve years of longitudinal follow-up research from our program. We highlight the surprisingly large benefits we found for mediation when compared to adversary settlement even twelve years later. We also offer some reflections about the critical "active ingredients" of mediation, and make suggestions about needed research on ADR in family conflicts. Consistent with our emphasis and with other articles in this special issue, our primary concern is whether and how ADR can promote family well-being as opposed to the potential benefits of ADR for the administration of justice. We use our own work to highlight key themes, findings, and issues rather than extensively reviewing the entire literature. However, we do incorporate the results of other's research, particularly to bolster, challenge, or fill in gaps in our own findings.

## WHY MEDIATE DIVORCE AND CUSTODY DISPUTES?

### *RATES OF DIVORCE AND DIVORCE CONFLICT*

Why has ADR for divorce disputes grown so rapidly? The increase in divorce is one main reason. Divorce rates escalated rapidly in the United States beginning in the late 1960s, a trend that foreshadowed similar increases in other English-speaking countries and throughout most of the industrialized world (Pryor & Rodgers, 2001; Emery, 1999). Since the early 1980s, divorce rates in the United States have flattened and even declined somewhat, yet the plateau reached is a high one. More than 40% of first marriages in the United States are still predicted to end in divorce (U.S. Bureau of the Census, 1992). Not only does divorce remain frequent, but other demographic trends, particularly increased rates of nonmarital childbearing and cohabitation (parenting arrangements that are known to be less stable than marriage), appear to account for much of the apparent decline in divorce. If people who cohabit and/or have children outside of marriage had not "selected out" of marriage, there would be little or no decline in American divorce.

Some break-ups are amicable and even beneficial; however, many are acrimonious, some intensely so. One thorough survey of divorces in two California counties found that 25% involved either substantial or intense conflict, and 24% required the involvement of a professional other than the parties' lawyers (a mediator, evaluator, or judge) to reach settlement

(Maccoby & Mnookin, 1992). There are no reliable data on the frequency or intensity of legal and personal disputes that develop between formerly amicable parents as time passes and circumstances change (e.g., remarriage, relocation) or on disputes between never-married parents, but experience suggests that both are frequent. Thus, not only are parental separation and divorce common, but they are commonly accompanied by serious conflict between former partners who remain parents.

From the perspective of increasing the efficiency of the administration of justice, increasing rates of divorce, high conflict, and the resulting cost in terms of time and money (for the courts and the parties involved) are prime reasons for promoting mediation and other forms of ADR. From the perspective of creating more family-friendly intervention programs, the more important concern has been how children and postseparation family relationships are affected by divorce, parental conflict, and adversary settlement procedures.

## EFFECTS OF DIVORCE AND PARENTAL CONFLICT ON CHILDREN

Different experts have vehemently contended either that children from divorced families are at substantial risk for psychological problems or that they are overwhelmingly resilient. While we do not have the space to elaborate on these conflicting points of view here, we do want to note that elsewhere we have offered what we view as an empirically based resolution to the great divorce debate. Research consistently shows that, while divorce is associated with an increased risk for a variety of emotional and behavioral problems, *most* children from divorced families are resilient, that is, they do not suffer from serious psychological problems (Emery, 1999; Emery & Forehand, 1994). Yet, we also find that even among highly resilient youth, many report substantial and continuing "pain" about their parents' divorce, for example, feeling that they had a harder childhood than most kids or wondering if their father even loves them (Emery, 2004; Laumann-Billings & Emery, 2000).

Our reinterpretation of the divorce debate is that it stems from conflicts in preferred research methods. Most empirical researchers have focused on mental health measures, but overlooked children's emotional pain. Most clinical investigators, in contrast, have emphasized children's pain while missing the backdrop of children's overall successful coping. Our view is that most children from divorced families are resilient, but their resilience is not invulnerability. Children's resilience often is accompanied by painful feelings about present relationships, unhappy memories of the past, and important worries about the future. We believe that pain is not pathology, but we also believe that pain is psychologically important. Recently, figures in the divorce debate have voiced agreement with our findings and reinterpretation of research (Kelly & Emery, 2003; Wallerstein, 2003).

Less controversial and more directly relevant to the promise of ADR is that research consistently shows that certain family characteristics predict increased emotional problems among children in separated or divorced (or married) families. Our analysis of this extensive research literature has led us to conclude that four potentially modifiable aspects of family relationships are most important to children's mental health in divorce (Emery, 1999): (1) an authoritative relationship with at least one parent, (2) mild parental conflict or conflict that does not involve the children, (3) economic stability, and (4) a good relationship with the other parent. We rank these four family characteristics in order of their importance for children's mental health, but our goal in mediation and elsewhere is, if possible, to promote all four aspects of family relationships after separation and divorce.

Elsewhere we have reviewed the extensive field and laboratory research that led us to these conclusions (Emery, 1999), but space allows us only to make two commonsense observations here. First, conflict is not inherently "bad," something to be avoided at all costs. Conflict often is unavoidable and it can be constructive. In disputes between parents, the keys are to: contain conflict between parents, manage its emotional and physical expression, present a united front to the children and about childrearing, keep children out of the middle of parental disputes, and work toward resolving the conflicts (Emery, 2004). Second, many of the destructive effects of *not* managing conflict are commonsensical. All too often, professionals who work with separating parents witness each party's deliberate subversion of the other, their direct and indirect manipulations of the children, and their deteriorated parenting, for example, trying to "win" children's loyalty by indulging them materially or by giving them inappropriate autonomy. No business would succeed in such a state of conflict and disorganization, and it is hardly surprising that the arrangement works poorly for the business of raising healthy children after divorce.

## *EFFECTS OF ADVERSARY DISPUTE RESOLUTION ON CHILDREN AND FAMILY RELATIONSHIPS*

An assumption underlying the promotion of mediation and other forms of ADR from the "family friendly" perspective has been that adversary settlement procedures continue, exacerbate, or even create conflict between parents. This assumption seems reasonable given that, as the name "adversary process" clearly indicates, legal settlement in American law is based on a model of formalized competition. Mediation, by contrast, embraces a more informal, cooperative approach to dispute resolution. Even though, as noted earlier, most custody disputes are negotiated outside of court and often with relatively little conflict (Maccoby & Mnookin, 1992), experiences with "hardball" attorney negotiations and acrimonious court hearings make assumptions about the adverse consequences of legal procedures on divorcing families seem reasonable. However, what was and remains most striking to us about the assumptions concerning the damaging effects of legal procedures is that they largely continue to be assumptions. There is a startling absence of empirical research, not only with regard to ADR, but even more so when it comes to traditional court practices in relation to separation and divorce.

## EMPIRICALLY COMPARING MEDIATION AND ADVERSARY SETTLEMENT

Random assignment to alternative conditions is the key to any research designed to compare the effectiveness of alternative "treatments" whether the alternatives are mediation versus litigation or the antidepressant Prozac versus a placebo medication (a sugar pill). Logically and statistically, random assignment, assigning study participants to one condition or the other by the flip of a coin, overcomes the real-life complication that parents who are cooperative are likely to want to mediate, while parents who are hostile beforehand are likely to want to fight out their differences through lawyers or in court. When random assignment is used correctly, the procedure allows scientists to conclude that the different treatments caused different outcomes among the participants in the study. Without random assignment, we know that the alternative treatments may be correlated with different outcomes, but the differences may have been there to begin with, as with cooperative couples choosing mediation and angry couples choosing adversary settlement.

We viewed random assignment as essential to our research and randomly assigned families in our study in the following manner. When parents petitioned a Juvenile and Domestic Relations Court in Virginia for a contested custody hearing, we approached families at random, asking them either to try our program of mediation as an eleventh hour settlement attempt (and also to let us study them) or to participate in a study of the court (i.e., to continue with adversary settlement, but let us study them). A key to the success of random assignment was obtaining a high degree of agreement to participate. In the end, 71% of the families agreed to try mediation, and 84% of the families agreed to participate in the court study. These rates were imperfect, but we found no differences between those who accepted and those who rejected participation (Emery, Matthews, & Wyer, 1991). In our view, the rates are as high as we could expect in the real world, and they are far higher than what was obtained in the other major study of custody mediation that attempted random assignment (Pearson & Thoennes, 1984). Another major study comparing comprehensive divorce mediation and adversary settlement could not attempt random assignment, but instead controlled for selection differences as best as possible using statistics (Kelly, 1990). (See Braver & Smith, 1996 and West & Sagarin, 2000 for detailed discussions of the randomized invitational design.) Finally, we successfully followed a large percentage of study participants over twelve years, and carefully examined possible differential attrition between the mediation and adversary settlement groups that might have compromised our long-term results (but apparently did not; Emery et al., 2001).

While random assignment is a notable strength of our research, we should also note an important limitation: we studied a fairly small sample (thirty-five mediation families, thirty-six litigation families) in only one court, in one state, using one program of mediation limited to child-related disputes (we did not mediate alimony or property settlement) to work with high-conflict parents who were almost all young and low-income (Emery & Wyer, 1987b; Emery et al., 1991). Put another way, our research shows the kinds of results that mediation *can* cause relative to adversary settlement, but it does not show what mediation *will* produce in another setting, when financial matters are included, following another model of mediation, and/or in the hands of mediators who might not be as enthusiastic and committed as we believe we were in initiating our project. With these strengths and qualifications as a backdrop, we can turn to the findings of our research and of other investigators whose findings can ease some concerns about the cautions we have offered.

*SETTLEMENT RATES*

One of the most basic questions to ask about mediation is whether it helps parents to settle disputes versus only adding another impediment to the settlement process. We can state this important concern the way some skeptical lawyers put it to us, "Sure. You'll settle some disputes with mediation, but we settle disputes too. Oftentimes we only file a petition for a hearing in order to 'up the ante' in our negotiations."

The lawyers' point is well taken, and we found support for their claim. Over a quarter of the cases in our adversary group (recruited at the time of filing for a judicial hearing) did settle before the court hearing. However, 72% of cases randomly assigned to the adversary settlement group did appear in front of a judge, while only 11% of cases randomly assigned to mediation appeared in front of a judge. This difference is statistically significant and substantively important. We found that cases randomly allowed to continue with litigation were nearly seven times more likely to be settled by a judge as were the cases assigned at random to mediation. In fact, we found that even when mediation did not end in a settlement (we settled 80% of our cases in mediation), parents often settled outside of court with the aid of their lawyers (Emery et al., 1991). Again, it is important to underscore that our research design allows us to conclude that mediation caused this very large difference in settlement patterns.

*Settlement Rates in Other Programs*
Do our results generalize to other settings? Evidence from other programs indicates that our rate was at the high end, as settlement rates typically range from 50 to 80% (Kelly, 1996). Importantly, however, good settlement rates among families petitioning for a contested custody hearing have been found in large samples. For example, one study of California's program of mandatory mediation for disputed custody found that, of 1,388 cases, 46% settled within two weeks of their first mediation while 20% scheduled appointments for further mediation (Depner, Cannata, & Simon, 1992). In one recent study using random assignment, notably higher agreement rates were found for families ordered into mediation sooner in the legal process (Zuberbuhler, 2001), an important finding consistent with the common view that it is more difficult to cooperate once parents have moved too far down the litigation path.

*A Proviso*
While it is obviously important that mediation can and does produce substantial rates of agreement between parents who have failed to settle outside of court, we want to point to a qualification concerning settlement rates. We do not believe that settlement rates are the only, or the most important, index of the success of mediation. In fact, this is where the administration of justice and family-friendly goals of mediation can be in conflict. Higher settlement rates keep more families out of court, but we are concerned that an overemphasis on settlement can make mediation less family-friendly as mediators feel pressured to become more coercive and less facilitative in order to maximize the likelihood of settlement.

**TIME, COST, AND COMPLIANCE**

We found that parents settled their disputes in about half the time when assigned to mediation versus adversary settlement (Emery et al., 1991). Other researchers have not yet adequately addressed this question (Beck & Sales, 2001). In studying the related issue of cost, some investigators have found that mediation is less expensive than adversary legal settlement

(Kelly, 1991; Pearson & Thonnes, 1989) but others have not (Walker, McCarthy, & Timms, 1994). We did not investigate this issue in our study.

Another hope expressed by advocates of mediation is that, in contrast to adversary settlement, parents will adhere to the agreements they reach in mediation both because the process is more cooperative and because parents will feel increased "ownership" over agreements they reach on their own. We did find a trend for greater compliance with child support orders among nonresidential parents who mediated, although noncompliance was quite high in both groups (Emery, Matthews, & Kitzmann, 1994). Others also have found higher rates of compliance with various aspects of separation agreements (Irving & Benjamin, 1992; Irving, Benjamin, Bohm, & MacDonald, 1981; Kelly, 1990; Pearson & Thoennes, 1989), although the evidence is somewhat mixed and parents who mediate may actually use court services more often (Jones & Bodtker, 1999). We suggest, however, that repeated use of court services may be a positive, not a negative, outcome for mediation.

*Two Provisos*
Although it appears that compliance is greater with mediated than adversary agreements, we believe that this is a topic that requires more extensive research. We also want to indicate that we view it as a success, not a failure, when parents return to mediation, and when an agreement is updated and changed using cooperative negotiation methods. Parents' and children's circumstances change following separation and divorce, and this means that agreements often must change too. In fact, we view it as essential that parents view their parenting plan as a living agreement, and encourage parents to return to mediation either as needed or perhaps once at the beginning of every "semester" in their children's lives (before school in the fall, after the first of the new year, and before summer school vacations). In fact, in the twelve-year follow-up of our sample, we found that parents who mediated made more changes in their agreements in comparison to parents in the adversary settlement group. The changes hardly represented chaos for these families. The average number of changes was only 1.4 over a twelve-year period for the mediation group compared to rare changes (.3 on average) in the adversary settlement group. Most of the changes were made informally, thus it would seem that parents who mediated flexibly accommodated important changes in their own and their children's lives.

## PARTY SATISFACTION

A question we studied extensively was whether parents would prefer the mediation process over adversary settlement or whether they would favor one dispute resolution alternative in some respects, but not in others. Our consistent finding was that, on average, parents did prefer mediation to adversary settlement and this held true both on items assessing the assumed strengths of mediation (e.g., Your feelings were understood) and the assumed strengths of adversary settlement (e.g., Your rights were protected). On both types of items, mediation consistently came out ahead. Furthermore, we found that parents were more satisfied with mediation than with adversary settlement six weeks after dispute resolution (Emery & Wyer, 1987b; Emery, Matthews, & Wyer, 1991), a year and a half later (Emery, Matthews, & Kitzmann, 1994), and twelve years following the initial settlement (Emery et al., 2001). Many other researchers report finding greater satisfaction with mediation in comparison to adversary settlement, and in general, parties report a high degree of satisfaction with mediation (Beck & Sales, 2001; Jones & Bodtker, 1999; Kelly, 1996). Thus, we are confident that mediation produces higher levels of satisfaction than adversary methods based on our own findings and those of others.

*Satisfaction Differences for Mothers and Fathers?*
In our research, we often found greater differences in satisfaction with mediation over adversary settlement for fathers than for mothers. In fact, we found greater reported satisfaction among mothers in the adversary group on two items assessing whether they won or lost what they wanted (Emery & Wyer, 1987b). We want to review our findings on this point in some detail here as we have elsewhere (Emery et al., 1991; Emery, 1994), because some have suggested that our results bolster the claim that mediation is harmful to women (e.g., Grillo, 1991).

We disagree with this conclusion based on two aspects of our results that are apparent upon closer inspection. First, mothers in our mediation group could not be more satisfied than mothers in our adversary settlement group because the adversary settlement mothers were very happy (see Figure 1). Technically, this is called a "ceiling effect"--mothers in the adversary group were already at the top of our scales, so there was no way for the mothers in the mediation group to score higher than them. In fact, Figure 1, which portrays the extent to which mothers and fathers in mediation or litigation felt that their "rights were protected" and a careful inspection of virtually all of our results show that mothers were very satisfied whether they mediated or continued with adversary settlement, as were fathers who mediated. Consistently, the outlying and unhappy group in our studies was fathers who continued with adversary settlement.

There were good reasons for this pattern of results based on our findings and on the predominant views of fathers and parenting in Virginia during the time of our study. Mothers almost always won full legal and physical custody in the adversary settlement group, while mediation gave fathers more of a "voice" in the process and more joint legal (but not physical) custody (Emery et al., 1991; Kitzmann & Emery, 1993). Against a different legal and social backdrop in California during roughly the same time, Kelly and her colleagues found that both mothers and fathers were more satisfied with mediation than with adversary settlement (Kelly & Gigy, 1989; Kelly & Duryee, 1992).

The second aspect of our data that causes us to conclude that they do not show that mediation is "bad" for women is based on further analysis of our findings about perceptions of winning and losing. As is well known, mediation promotes a "win-win" mentality while adversary settlement takes a "win-lose" approach. Our results for the items favoring women in the adversary group seem consistent with this pattern. In the adversary group, women report high levels of winning while men report low levels. In the mediation group, by contrast, both women and men are closer to the middle, perhaps indicating greater compromise in this group (see Figure 1). In fact, we found strong evidence for this interpretation. In the adversary group, mothers' and fathers' scores were negatively correlated: The more mothers felt they won, the less fathers felt they won (win-lose). In the mediation group, mothers' and fathers' scores were positively correlated, the more mothers felt they won, the more fathers felt they won too (win-win) (Emery et al., 1991).

## FAMILY RELATIONSHIPS AND PSYCHOLOGICAL ADJUSTMENT

Our major hope for mediation was and continues to be that the more cooperative alternative will have a more positive (or less negative) effect on postseparation family relationships and the psychological well-being of parents and children. Although we did find that reduced parental conflict in either the mediation or litigation group predicted improved psychological adjustment among children a year and a half after dispute settlement (Kitzmann & Emery, 1994), we generally were disappointed by the lack of immediate and short-term effects of mediation on family relationships and psychological health. We found no differences in relationship quality or psychological well-being in comparing the mediation and adversary settlement groups immediately after dispute resolution (Emery et al., 1991) or one year later (Emery et al., 1994).

This circumstance changed dramatically when we conducted our twelve-year follow-up study. In initiating this research, we hypothesized that the broader family-friendly benefits of mediation might not be obtained until some time later, particularly after the crisis phase of separation and divorce had ended. Although our hypothesis seemed reasonable, we frankly were skeptical when we began the long-term follow-up, especially since very few psychological interventions have been shown to produce positive effects many years later. We, therefore, were both surprised and very pleased when our research uncovered that mediation led to several substantial long-term benefits for parents and children, particularly for the relationships between children and nonresidential parents, and between the parents themselves.

Increased contact between nonresidential parents (mostly fathers) and children proved to be one notable and very important benefit of mediation. Contact between divorced fathers and their children is distressingly infrequent, and contact decreases as time passes after a martial separation (Seltzer, 1991). We believe that one very important reason for this unfortunate pattern is that many adults manage the grief, hurt, and pain of a divorce the way most people deal with lost love affairs: They exclaim, "I never want to see you again!" and eventually fulfill the threat (Emery, 2004). The problem with this common reaction, however, is that partners who are also parents end up divorcing their children as well as their former spouse. We view mediation as a forum for renegotiating relationships as well as negotiating agreements (Emery, 1994), and wondered if our approach to ending the spousal, but not the parental, relationship would make a difference years later.

The data portrayed in Figure 2 indicate that being randomly assigned to mediation versus adversary settlement did indeed make a substantial difference in nonresidential parent--child contact twelve years later. Thirty percent of nonresidential parents who mediated saw their children once a week or more twelve years after the initial dispute in comparison to only 9% of parents in the adversary group. At the opposite extreme, 39% of nonresidential parents in the adversary group had seen their children only once or not at all in the last year compared to 15% in the mediation group. These differences are both substantively important and statistically significant (Emery et al., 2001).

We found even larger differences for telephone contact, perhaps a better measure of nonresidential involvement given the geographic mobility of parents over twelve years, as well as of children who, at the time of the twelve-year follow-up, ranged in age from adolescents to young adults. In the mediation group, 54% of nonresidential parents spoke to their children on the telephone once a week or more often in contrast to 13% in the adversary group. Once again at the opposite extreme, 54% of nonresidential parents in the adversary settlement group had not spoken with their children on the telephone in the last year, or had done so only once, in comparison to 12% in the mediation group. These differences are statistically significant (Emery et al., 2001), and in many ways, they are startling. An average of five hours of mediation (Emery et al., 1991) caused these huge differences in contact twelve years later.

The greater contact between nonresidential parents and their children did not increase parental conflict, despite there being more opportunities for them to fight. In fact, when parents mediated rather than continuing with the legal action over their children, twelve years later the residential parent reported that the nonresidential parent was (statistically and substantively) significantly more likely to discuss problems with the residential parent. In addition, the nonresidential parent had a greater influence on childrearing decisions, and was more involved in the children's discipline, grooming, moral training, errands, holidays, significant events, school or church functions, recreational activities, and vacations (Emery et al., 2001). Very few psychological interventions have been shown to produce such positive outcomes so many years later, even with the investment of large amounts of time, not a mere five hours.

In concluding our overview of research findings, we should note one area where our research did not show differences between mediation and adversary settlement. We found no group differences in the mental health of parents or children twelve years after dispute resolution based on whether they mediated or proceeded with adversary settlement. The limited power of our study to detect significant effects, along with some of our unpublished results, suggest possible explanations for this null result and offer the hope that mediation might benefit children's mental health. Mediation also might improve mental health outcomes, if packaged with other effective interventions that specifically target psychological outcomes, such as parenting or children's groups (Pedro-Carroll & Alpert-Gillis, 1997; Wolchik et al., 2002). On the other hand, it might be too much to expect mediation to cause dramatic improvements in children's or parents' mental health. Years of therapy and/or of treatment with psychoactive medication have not been shown to lead to improved mental health twelve years after intervention ends. The reduced court hearings, increased satisfaction, and dramatically improved family relationships caused by five hours of mediation over the course of twelve years is an incredible benefit for a brief intervention.

## WHAT WORKED?

Our research shows that mediation caused several important and often sizeable differences relative to adversary settlement both from the perspective of increasing the efficiency of the administration of justice and especially benefiting postseparation family relationships. What our research does not and cannot show is what elements of mediation (or of adversary settlement) were most important in producing these results, especially the effects we found twelve years later. However, we do have some speculations about the "active ingredients" in mediation that some may find valuable now and, we hope, others will want to test empirically. We should note that we have elaborated elsewhere, in detail, on the ideas we summarize below (Emery, 1994, 2004).

## TAKING THE LONG VIEW

Many advocates of mediation suggest that cooperation is the strongest active ingredient in ADR relative to adversary settlement. We agree that the cooperative approach is important, yet our naïve hopes of how we might easily promote cooperation among separating parents were crushed early in our enterprise. The families we worked with were high-conflict, and our mediation sessions often were riddled by tension, anger, and outright hostility. We studied parents who had failed to reach an agreement on their own, were requesting judicial intervention, and were assigned to mediation at random. We found them; they did not find us. Our experience in conducting mediation tells us that we did not turn warring parents into pacifists.

So what did mediation do to promote cooperation? We believe it helped parents to see the need for cooperation over their children in the long run, even if cooperating seemed impossible in the midst of the crisis of separation. We believe that mediation helped parents to begin to take the long view of their relationship. They were divorcing each other, but they would be parents forever. Since they would have to deal with each other for this reason, we think the parents learned that they better begin to find a way of doing so now. Our research suggests it may have taken years for the parents to really learn this lesson, but eventually they did learn it.

## EDUCATION ABOUT EMOTIONS

We believe an equally, or even more, important aspect of the mediation process, at least as we practiced it, was that it provided an opportunity to educate parents about emotions--the children's and especially their own. The way we practice, the education in mediation is not a detached lesson (as it might be in a divorce education seminar), but a very real and emotional experience. While there are many subtle aspects to our goals and techniques, two examples illustrate the general approach.

As one example, the mediators would often use their own emotional reactions (we used male--female co-mediator teams in our research) to reflect the children's experience of their parents' conflicted relationship. For example, a mediator might say, "I feel tense and jumpy just sitting in this room with you. When you start to fight, I want to either yell or run away. I wonder how your children feel, since they're sitting in this same middle position day in and day out."

Our second example of emotional education in mediation involved the parents expressing anger and redirecting their attention to the hurt and grief that underlies much of the anger in separation and divorce. We often followed an angry outburst between the parents with an individual caucus and found that, for many parents, anger quickly dissolved into tears of desperation over the end of the marriage. These parents admitted that they were hurting, grieving, and hoping to reconcile or to punish their ex, and that these feelings and motivations fueled much of their anger (Emery, 2004). In plumbing parents' emotional depths, our goal was not to be therapeutic; we did not expect them to resolve their grief while working out an agreement. However, we did want our clients to begin to understand the emotions lying behind their anger, get help and support elsewhere, and find a way to control their feelings as best as possible to be able to work out a parenting plan in mediation.

## BUSINESSLIKE BOUNDARIES

We believe that encouraging former partners to develop businesslike boundaries around their ongoing co-parenting relationship was a third key component to our approach to mediation. Most of the broken relationships that preceded these custody disputes were one-sided. Thus, there was a leaving and a left party (Emery, 1994, 2004). Having completed much of their grief in anticipation of the end of the relationship, leavers often hoped to "be friends" with their former partners. Of course, this familiar hope was a hurtful and impossible idea for the left party who wanted to be either intimates or enemies. Our solution to this central dilemma was to encourage a type of relationship that neither party wanted: a more formal, businesslike relationship as opposed to either a friendship or an intimate relationship.

We developed several techniques to help parents get more distance from each other, and thereby reduce conflict, facilitate grieving, and improve parenting and co-parenting. For example, we urged parents to follow co-parenting rules rigidly (including the terms spelled out in their legal agreement) and to communicate with each other briefly, only as necessary, and strictly about the children. In our view, developing these kinds of distant, businesslike boundaries is the most workable alternative to splitting up the "natural" way, that is, not seeing or talking to the ex (and therefore not working together as co-parents) for a very long time.

## AVOIDING BECOMING ADVERSARIES

As a final point, we might note that perhaps mediation produces none of these (or other) benefits. Perhaps the most important benefit of mediation is that it keeps parents from following an adversarial route, one that can cause severely strained relationships to deteriorate further, perhaps irreparably. The hurt, anger, and injustice of divorce are powerful and understandable emotions, and strong motivations for wanting to tell your former partner (literally or metaphorically), "I'll see you in court!" We see relatively few problems with responding to divorce emotionally if no children are involved. However, perhaps the gulf created by these divisive feelings only grows wider in the adversary system, and the primary, but hardly unimportant, benefit of mediation is to prevent the wound of divorce from growing bigger.

## A LOOK TO THE FUTURE

We are excited about the challenge and prospects of mediation and of other forms of ADR for divorcing parents, and feel satisfaction in the efforts we have made in conceptualizing the divorce process and especially in conducting empirical research on mediation and adversary settlement. We are far from fully satisfied with our own work or with the state of the field, however, and suggest that our efforts are not the final word, but only an opening paragraph. We briefly note some topics and issues for further research and practice that seem most pressing to us.

## MORE RESEARCH ON OUTCOMES

As we noted at the beginning of this article, our research shows what mediation can do in one program, not what mediation will do in practice. We need more research on how mediation and adversary procedures work in different settings, against various legal backdrops, and among large groups of people of diverse backgrounds. Researchers also need to investigate new interventions with divorcing parents using methodologically rigorous designs. ADR topics that merit immediate, additional, and objective research attention include divorce education programs, parenting coordinators, and collaborative law.

## MORE RESEARCH ON PROCESS AND PROCEDURE

In addition to better documenting of the relative outcomes of traditional and ADR procedures, more research is needed on the process of dispute resolution and what does and does not work. One line of research in this regard is to analyze actual mediation sessions, mediator styles, and the interactions of the parties (Bickerdike & Littlefield, 2001). Another line of research needed involves contrasting alternative approaches to ADR, for example, completing randomized trials, comparing mediation that does or does not directly involve children (McIntosh, 2000), or comparing the outcomes of problem solving versus therapeutic mediation. Randomized trials also can and should be used to document the outcome of alternative ADR policies and procedures, for example, comparing mediation that is confidential with mediation where recommendations are made to the court if no agreement is reached.

## MAINTAINING ENTHUSIASM, EXCITEMENT, AND COMMITMENT

In our view, perhaps the biggest challenge facing the field of mediation and ADR in divorce is fostering and nurturing mediators' enthusiasm, excitement, and commitment. Mediation is hard work, and many of the rewards of mediation are intrinsic, not extrinsic. As with any new intervention, moreover, part of the success of mediation over the last few decades surely owes to the fact that it was new. Much of what makes mediation (or any new intervention) successful is high expectations, dedication, and high hopes for being able to help.

We believe this to be true for us, as well as for the practice of mediation more widely. Many of the positive benefits we found for mediation probably are partially attributable to our enthusiasm and excitement, our belief that mediation could make things better for divorcing families, and our willingness to go the extra mile to try to make that happen. We hardly believe we were alone in these hopes. However, many from the first generation of mediators have passed by, and more are not far from the exit (the senior author included). Can the next generation carry the flag of this now not-so-new intervention with enthusiasm, excitement, and commitment, entering the fray of separation and parental conflict because someone needs to get in the middle in order to get children out of the middle?

*Robert E. Emery, Ph.D., is Professor of Psychology and Director of the Center for Children, Families and the Law at the University of Virginia.*

*David A. Sbarra, Ph.D., is Assistant Professor of Psychology at the University of Arizona.*

*Tara Grover, B.S., is a graduate student in clinical psychology at the University of Virginia.*

Author Note: *We are grateful to the William T. Grant Foundation for their ongoing support of this research.*

## References

Beck, C.J.A., & Sales, B.D. (2001). *Family mediation: Facts, myths, and future prospects.* Washington, DC: American Psychological Association.

Bickerdike, A.J., and Littlefield, L. (2000). Divorce adjustment and mediation: Theoretically grounded process research. *Mediation Quarterly, 18,* 181–201.

Braver, S.L., and Smith, M. (1996). Maximizing both external and internal validity in longitudinal true experiments with voluntary treatments: The "combined modified" design. *Evaluation and Program Planning, 19*(4), 287–300.

Caprez, J.V., and Armstrong, M.A. (2001). A study of domestic mediation outcomes with indigent parents. *Family Court Review, 39,* 415–430.

Depner, C.E., Cannata, K.V., and Simon, M.B. (1992). Building a uniform statistical reporting system: A snapshot of California Family Court services, *Family and Conciliation Courts Review, 30,* 185–206.

Emery, R.E. (1982). Interparental conflict and the children of discord and divorce. *Psychological Bulletin, 92,* 310–330.

Emery, R.E. (1994). *Renegotiating family relationships: Divorce, child custody, and mediation.* New York: Guilford.

Emery, R.E. (1999). *Marriage, divorce, and children's adjustment.* (2nd ed.). Thousand Oaks, CA: Sage.

Emery, R.E. (2004). *The truth about children and divorce: Groundbreaking research and advice for dealing with the emotions so you and your children can thrive.* New York: Viking/Penguin.

Emery, R.E., and Forehand, R. (1994). Parental divorce and children's well-being: A focus on resilience. In R. J. Haggerty, L.R. Sherrod, N. Garmezy, and M. Rutter (eds.), *Stress, risk, and resilience in children and adolescents: Processes, mechanisms, and interventions* (pp. 64–99). London: Cambridge University Press.

Emery, R.E., Laumann-Billings, L., Waldron, M., Sbarra, D.A., and Dillon, P. (2001). Child custody mediation and litigation: Custody, contact, and co-parenting 12 years after initial dispute resolution. *Journal of Consulting and Clinical Psychology, 69,* 323-332.

Emery, R.E., Matthews, S.G., and Kitzmann, K.M. (1994). Child custody mediation and litigation: Parents' satisfaction and functioning a year after settlement. *Journal of Consulting and Clinical*

*Psychology, 62,* 124–129.

Emery, R.E., Matthews, S., and Wyer, M.M. (1991). Child custody mediation and litigation: Further evidence of the differing views of mothers and fathers. *Journal of Consulting and Clinical Psychology, 59,* 410–418.

Emery, R.E., and Wyer, M.M. (1987a). Divorce mediation. *American Psychologist, 42,* 472–480.

Emery, R.E., and Wyer, M.M. (1987b). Child custody mediation and litigation: An experimental evaluation of the experience of parents. *Journal of Consulting and Clinical Psychology, 55,* 179–186.

Grillo, T. (1991). The mediation alternative: Process dangers for women. *Yale Law Journal, 100,* 1545–1610.

Irving, H.H., and Benjamin, M. (1992). An evaluation of process and outcome in a private family mediation service. *Mediation Quarterly, 10*(1), 35–55.

Irving, H.H., Benjamin, M., Bohm, P., and MacDonald, G. (1981). *Final research report.* Toronto, Canada: Provincial Court (Family Division).

Jones, T.S., and Bodtker, A. (1999). Agreement, maintenance, satisfaction and relitigation in mediated and non-mediated custody cases: A research note. *Journal of Divorce and Remarriage, 32*(1/2), 17–31.

Kelly, J.B. (1990). *Final report. Mediated and adversarial divorce resolution processes: An analysis of post-divorce outcomes.* Corte Madera, CA: Northern California Mediation Center (on file with the authors).

Kelly, J.B. (1991). Parent interaction after divorce: Comparison of mediated and adversarial divorce processes. *Behavioral Sciences and the Law, 9,* 387–398.

Kelly, J.B. (1996). A decade of divorce mediation research: Some answers and questions. *Family and Conciliation Courts Review, 34,* 373–385.

Kelly, J.B., and Duryee, M.A. (1992). Women's and men's views of mediation in voluntary and mandatory mediation settings. *Family and Conciliation Courts Review, 30,* 34–49.

Kelly, J.B., and Emery, R.E. (2003). Children's adjustment following divorce: Risk and resilience perspectives. *Family Relations, 52,* 352–362.

Kelly, J.B., and Gigy, L. (1989). Divorce mediation: Characteristics of clients and outcomes. In K. Kressel and D.G. Pruitt (eds.), *Mediation research* (pp. 263–283). San Francisco: Jossey-Bass.

Kitzmann, K.M., and Emery, R.E. (1993). Procedural justice and parents' satisfaction in a field study of child custody dispute resolution. *Law and Human Behavior, 17,* 553–567.

Kitzmann, K.M., and Emery, R.E. (1994). Child and family coping one year following mediated and litigated child custody disputes. *Journal of Family Psychology, 8,* 150–159.

Laumann-Billings, L., and Emery, R.E. (2000). Distress among young adults from divorced families. *Journal of Family Psychology, 14,* 671–687.

Maccoby, E.E., and Mnookin, R.H. (1992). *Dividing the child: Social and legal dilemmas of custody.* Cambridge, MA: Harvard University Press.

McIntosh, J. (2000). Child-inclusive divorce mediation: Report on a qualitative research study. *Mediation Quarterly, 18,* 55–69.

Pearson, J., and Thoennes, N. (1984). *Final report of the divorce mediation research project.* Denver, CO (on file with the authors).

Pearson, J., and Thoennes, N. (1989). Divorce mediation: Reflections on a decade of research. In K. Kressel and D.G. Pruitt (eds.), *Mediation research* (pp. 9-30). San Francisco: Jossey-Bass.

Pedro-Carroll, J., and Alpert-Gillis, L. (1997). Preventative interventions for children of divorce: A developmental model for 5 and 6 year-old children. *Journal of Primary Prevention, 18,* 5–23.

Pryor, J., and Rodgers, B. (2001). *Children in changing families. Life after parental separation.* Oxford: Blackwell.

Seltzer, J.A. (1991). Relationships between fathers and children who live apart: The father's role after separation. *Journal of Marriage and the Family, 53,* 79–101.

Somary, K., and Emery, R.E. (1991). Emotional anger and grief in divorce mediation. *Mediation*

*Quarterly, 8,* 185–198.

U.S. Bureau of the Census. (1992). *Marriage, divorce, and remarriage in the 1990's.* (Current Population Rep. No. 23–180). Washington, DC: U.S. Government Printing Office.

Walker, J., McCarthy, P., and Timms, N. (1994). *Mediation: The making and remaking of cooperative relationships. An evaluation of the effectiveness of comprehensive mediation.* Newcastle: Relate Centre for Family Studies, Newcastle University.

Wallerstein, J.S. (2003). Children of divorce: A society in search of policy. In M.A. Mason, A. Skolnick, and S.D. Sugarman (eds.), *All our families: New policies for a new century* (pp. 66–95). New York: Oxford University Press.

West, S.G., and Sagarin, B.J. (2000). Subject selection and loss in randomized experiments. In L. Bickman (ed.), *Contributions to research design: Donald Campbell's legacy* (Vol. 2). Thousand Oaks, CA: Sage.

Wolchik, S.A., Sandler, I.N., Millsap, R.E., Plummer, B.A., Greene, S.M., Anderson, E.R., et al. (2002). Six-year follow-up of preventive interventions for children of divorce. A randomized controlled trial. *Journal of the American Medical Association, 288,* 1874–1881.

Zuberbuhler, J. (2001). Early intervention mediation: The use of court-ordered mediation in the initial stages of divorce litigation to resolve parenting issues. *Family Court Review, 39,* 203–206.

# [10]

# Bring in the Lawyers:
# Challenging the Dominant Approaches to
# Ensuring Fairness in Divorce Mediation

Craig McEwen, Nancy Rogers and Richard Maiman

## INTRODUCTION

Mandatory divorce mediation[1] is under attack. According to some critical commentators, divorce mediation reinforces bargaining imbalances between parties and places women at a disadvantage.[2] Professor Penelope Bryan, for example, concludes that there is an "insidious nature of mediation" for divorcing women and that "those who structure court affiliated programs, as well as mediators, now should recognize their complicity in the continued oppression of women and their dependent children."[3] She and other critics charge that mandatory mediation programs[4] represent an unnecessary step that leaves divorcing parents unprotected by lawyers and makes the divorce process less fair. Bryan claims that mediation "exploits wives by denigrating their legal entitlements, stripping them of authority, encouraging unwarranted compromise, isolating them from needed support, and placing them across the table from their more powerful husbands and demanding that they fend for themselves."[5] Professor Trina Grillo contrasts mediation with the litigation process, in which she says people believe that "what transpires is at least partially a matter of right and justice."[6] As a consequence, critics argue, the courts should never mandate divorce mediation.[7]

Mediation proponents respond that mandatory mediation can produce results as fair as or more fair than those achieved through a traditional divorce system, and they praise mediation's benefits as compared to litigation.[8] To insure fairness, however, proponents sometimes advocate regulation.[9] Under this view, the elaborate scheme of statutes and court rules enacted to ensure that mediation is "done right"[10] should produce uniformly high quality, and thus fair mandatory divorce mediation. This "regulatory" approach to mandated mediation often includes mediator duties to assure fairness (such as a duty to assure a balanced dialogue); exemption of some cases from compulsory mediation; limitation of the scope of discussion during sessions to custody and visitation issues; requirement of advanced degrees and mediation training for mediators; requirement that the parties' lawyers and the court review mediated agreements; and prohibitions against the mediator making recommendations to the court.[11]

This "regulatory" approach to assuring fairness in divorce mediation contrasts with the "voluntary participation" approach often favored by those most critical of mediation.[12] Unlike the "regulatory" approach, the "voluntary participation" approach leaves courts without authority to compel the parties to attend mediation sessions.[13] Under this approach, the parties presumably decide whether to go to mediation based upon how well they believe they will fare. The assurance of fairness then rests on their ability to choose. Thus, the "voluntary participation" approach sometimes entails very little regulation of the mediation process.

In this Article, we argue that the debate about fairness in divorce mediation, as well as the resulting legal schemes based on either the "regulatory" or "voluntary participation" approaches, results from the view that one must choose between a "lawyered" process ending in the courtroom, and an informal, problem-solving process involving parties but not lawyers in the mediation room. In our view, this dichotomy has unnecessarily narrowed the policy choices underlying mediation schemes, because it assumes that lawyers either cause conflict or act as mouthpieces for clients with a cause;[14] that the divorce process is one in which, absent mediation (where lawyers do not appear), aggressive lawyers contest custody cases at hearings;[15] and that mediators either protect parties' interests or pressure them toward a particular (and sometimes unjust) settlement.[16]

We challenge these assumptions and the two approaches in statutes and court rules that follow from them – the "regulatory" and the "voluntary participation" approaches. We argue that the mediation scheme in Maine, where attorneys participate regularly and vigorously in mandated divorce mediation, provides a third avenue – one we call the "lawyer-participant" approach. Research evidence about this third approach undermines the assumptions that have confined the debate about fairness.[17] Although several jurisdictions have employed the "lawyer-participant" approach,[18] it has not been considered viable because of the widely shared, but flawed, assumptions about mediation and the divorce process. In this Article we critique these assumptions and seek to demonstrate that the "lawyer-participant" approach in fact promotes fairness more effectively than the two dominant legal schemes for divorce mediation.

Part I reviews in greater depth the debate about fairness in divorce mediation. In Part II, we examine the merits and weaknesses of the two primary contending approaches in mediation statutes, the "regulatory" and "voluntary participation" approaches. In Part III, we identify in detail the four "myths" that confine the debate to the two dominant approaches, and, in Part IV, we examine the perceptions and experiences of Maine divorce lawyers in an effort to challenge these myths. Ultimately, in Part V, we reject as flawed both the "regulatory" and the "voluntary participation" approaches to protecting fairness in divorce mediation and instead advocate Maine's "lawyer-participant" approach. In doing so, we side with the mediation critics in their skepticism about the capacity of the regulatory approach to insure fairness, but we also side with mediation advocates who believe that mediation holds promise for improving the divorce negotiation process without sacrificing fairness.

## I. THE "FAIRNESS" DEBATE

Mediation critics claim that mandatory mediation, even if regulated, is less fair than trial.[19] In contrast, mediation proponents contend that the judicial system is itself destructive and thus introduces an unfairness of sorts.[20] For instance, mediator John Haynes begins his book, Divorce Mediation, with the assertion, "The pain, anger, and frustration of divorce are frequently exacerbated by the legal process as it presently works."[21] Furthermore, he argues, "much of the decision making is taken out of the hands of the clients, as the attorneys engage in battle within the legal system."[22] Similarly, Dean Jay Folberg argues that family law and court procedures are often used "coercively to supplant family self-determination."[23] He states, by contrast, that mediation enhances "self determination," and public support for it affirms "the dignity and importance of the family."[24]

Empirical studies provide little help in resolving the debate whether mediation is fair.[25] Professor Grillo, for example, dismisses as inadequate studies of party perceptions of fairness.[26] Instead, Professors Grillo and Bryan point to research about women's inferior societal position or gender roles and power and infer that mediation places women at a disadvantage.[27] Alternatively, they cite egregious examples of divorce mediation in which parties, particularly women, are isolated from counsel and face pressures and threats from both their spouses and the mediator.[28] They contend that mediators, intent upon settlement, force the weaker party to concede to facilitate agreement.[29] Under this view, inequalities in power and exposure to settlement pressures in an informal process such as mediation promote coerced and unfair outcomes. Mediation critics also claim that mediators favor joint custody and press for solutions that split the children's lives between the parents, leaving unsettled the division of economic benefits.[30] Under this view, because one party (presumably the mother) will actually take major responsibility for the children, even equal division of child support typically is economically unfair to the woman.[31] The critics seem to believe that these arguments should shift the burden of persuasion in the fairness debate to advocates of mandatory mediation. In their view, advocates have not met this burden and mediation should be completely voluntary, if it is used at all.[32]

Mediation advocates, however, confidently refer to the empirical evidence regarding parties' perceptions of mediation and dismiss the critics' examples as exceptional and not reflective of good mediation practice.[33] Using anecdotes, they contend that well-trained, sensitive, ethical mediators compensate for power imbalances between parties, do not exert pressures to settle, and remain impartial, freeing the parties to accept or reject agreements.[34] "Good" mediation practice, according to Professor Joshua Rosenberg, does not permit mediators to advise judges how to decide cases that do not settle, because doing so would exert settlement pressure on the parties.[35]

Although they believe that mediation is usually fair, many mediation proponents take seriously concerns about the exceptional dangers of unfairness. They advocate assuring fairness in mediation by regulating the process to assure qualified mediators use appropriate procedures.[36] Regulation is seen as the "fail-safe" mechanism of mandatory mediation, the safety net that provides the final protection against unfairness.

What do mediation critics and proponents mean by "fairness" in the context of divorce mediation? They seem to refer to several aspects of procedural fairness, and appear to link them to outcome fairness. Procedural aspects of fairness in divorce mediation[37] commonly include balanced bargaining between parties;[38] a "level playing field" in the mediation process;[39] self-determination by parties without undue settlement pressures or imposition of a mediator's values;[40] and consideration of the children's interests.[41] Commentators on divorce mediation seem especially concerned with those bargaining imbalances that may reflect differences in power between men and women, because these may lead to negotiated results that favor men.[42] Bargaining imbalances thus produce "unfair results" unless mediators can overcome them.[43] If mediators intervene too strongly to balance differences between parties, however, they may actually tilt the "level playing field" that "neutral" mediators arguably establish.[44] When the circumstances of mediation permit a mediator to impose his or her preferences for an outcome on the parties – as when mediators make recommendations to the triers of fact – settlement pressures not only violate the principle of self-determination, but also may destroy a "level playing field" and produce unfair results, at least when these pressures affect parties differently.[45] Court procedures that penalize the recalcitrant party or that impose costs that one party can bear with more ease than the other can also lead to arbitrary and unequal pressures to capitulate.[46]

Although an unfair process would produce unfair outcomes, commentators differ sharply about whether there exist standards for evaluating the fairness of outcomes. For some mediation advocates, fair outcomes are in the eyes of the beholder – if parties believe the outcome to be fair, then it is.[47] For others, fair settlements must creatively incorporate a variety of values and goals, rather than exclusively legal ones, and parties should arrive at them without pressure.[48] Some would also add that fair results work in favor of children's interests.[49] For some mediation critics, however, fair settlements mirror likely court rulings rendered after a contested hearing.[50] Any outcome departing from that standard means that one party relinquished too much.

Sometimes, commentators include "party empowerment" as another aspect of fairness,[51] but they differ on how to achieve it.[52] For mediation critics, legal advocacy and court hearings equalize power and diminish pressures for settlement.[53] They view lawyers particularly as buffers between demanding spouses and intimidated clients.[54] Lawyers insure that parties understand the alternatives to settlement. For some mediation advocates, however, legal advocacy and decision making diminish party autonomy and freedom – and thus "empowerment" – by allowing lawyers and courts to shape decisions using legal rules in a way that may have little relationship to the parties' priorities, needs, and interests.[55]

At the extremes, these two views of outcome fairness and empowerment lead mediation critics to advocate against settlement and mediation proponents to oppose trials.[56] An intermediate position, typically supported by commentators from both camps, involves determining how far a settlement departs from one that informed, unpressured parties would have reached absent mediation.[57]

Because comparisons with adjudication are difficult,[58] a rough comparison to settlement resulting from negotiation outside mediation represents a practical definition of fairness. In fact, the benchmark standard of fairness used by some commentators is the lawyer-to-lawyer negotiation. For example, Professor Bryan states that "lawyers have a professional obligation to pursue and protect the client's interests during negotiations. The lawyer advocate also insulates the disadvantaged wife from her husband and prevents the tangible, intangible, and sex role differences between them from dictating the terms of the agreement."[59] Women's rights advocate Laurie Woods notes that negotiations between lawyers take place with access to applicable laws and knowledge of both the capacity to secure discovery and the alternatives to settlement.[60] Academics point out the role of lawyers as effective advocates for battered women.[61] The critics appear to accept the view of Professors Robert Mnookin and Lewis Kornhauser: that with represented parties "the outcome that the law will impose if no agreement is reached gives each parent certain bargaining chips - an endowment of sorts."[62] Obviously, lawyers vary in ability and expertise, but this is the sort of variance that operates as well in other parts of the disputing process, such as trial.

Clearly, fairness in divorce mediation concerns both critics and advocates. Most embrace a comparable notion for fairness – that is, mediation should approximate the results achieved in lawyer-to-lawyer negotiation. Even when they embrace this mainstream definition of fairness, however, their commentary about how best to insure fairness in mediation has been constrained by common assumptions about the absence of lawyers, the similarity of all mediation programs, the role that lawyers would play if present, and the role of trial as the alternative to mediation. The same faulty assumptions have also confused the analysis of the dominant "regulatory approach," to which we now turn.

## II. EVALUATING THE TWO DOMINANT STATUTORY APPROACHES

The two dominant statutory schemes of mediation – the "regulatory" approach and the "voluntary participation" approach – reflect the debate over fairness in divorce mediation. The "regulatory" approach requires divorcing parents to attend an introductory session on mediation or mediation itself,[63] and the process is highly regulated in an effort to make it fair, despite the usual absence of lawyers at mediation sessions. The "voluntary participation" approach enables the parties to choose whether to participate in an introductory session or mediation session. Because lawyers will not attend mediation sessions, parties should opt not to participate if they anticipate conditions that will lead to unfairness.

In this section, we explain why the efforts to add regulations or remove compulsion in order to make mediation fair are not only ineffective, but also introduce significant costs. In doing so, we measure the fairness against lawyer-to-lawyer negotiations, a process few commentators question.[64]

## A. The "Regulatory" Approach

Early divorce mediation statutes were simple. They authorized the courts to require divorcing parents to appear for mediation of custody or visitation disputes before an impartial mediator.[65] That was all. Over the last decade and in the context of the debate about the fairness of mandatory mediation, regulatory schemes accompanying the authority to compel participation have emerged and burgeoned.[66] At present, numerous statutes, supplemented by court rules, reflect in varying degrees the dominant scheme for regulating court-directed mediation.[67]

Under the dominant regulatory scheme, mediation is a negotiation that the mediator guides. The lawyers usually will not attend the mediation session or will attend in silence. Statutes in California, Kansas, and Wisconsin permit exclusion of lawyers from mediation sessions.[68] In some Arizona courts, counsel can confer with the mediator at the beginning, but can be excluded thereafter.[69] In some other jurisdictions, parties have a right to bring their lawyers,[70] although in Florida the lawyers may be instructed to speak only privately to their clients.[71] Research indicates that in most jurisdictions, lawyer participation is the exception.[72]

The typical rationale for excluding lawyers is that they "spoil" mediation: lawyers will interfere with candid expressions by the parties and thwart a problem-solving style of negotiation.[73] Statutes reflect this by highlighting problem solving by the parties[74] and emphasizing that the parties themselves should speak in mediation.[75]

As discussed above, most commentators would not find such extensive regulation necessary to ensure fairness if lawyers attended and participated in mediation, because the process then would become the equivalent of lawyer-to-lawyer negotiation in terms of fairness.[76] To obviate potential unfairness in the absence of attorney representation, commentators have advocated regulating the mediator and the mediation procedures.[77] In this section, we discuss whether each of the varying forms of regulating divorce mediation is likely to contribute to fairness in the absence of lawyers, and we examine the probable costs of regulation in terms of other mediation goals.

### 1. Mediator Duties Regarding Fairness

Some statutes and court rules make the mediator accountable for the fairness of the mediation process and result. Mediators often must encourage the parties to consult with their lawyers before signing a mediated agreement.[78] In some jurisdictions, mediators must ensure that the parties make factual disclosures to each other.[79] The mediator must define or explain the mediation process, fees, and limitations.[80] In Iowa, the mediator must "assure a balanced dialogue," and in Florida a "balanced process," although these terms are left undefined.[81] In California, the mediator must be "vigilant" about power imbalances,[82] "conducting negotiations in such a way as to equalize power relationships between the parties."[83] Elsewhere, the mediator must terminate the mediation in certain situations, such as when the parties cannot "participate meaningfully" or "harm" will result,[84] or when the mediator believes this to be the case[85] or believes that the agreement would be unconscionable.[86]

In addition, the mediator commonly must assess and sometimes advocate for the best interests of the children.[87] For example, Iowa divorce mediators must ensure that participants "consider fully the best interests of any affected child and that they understand the consequences of any decision they reach concerning the child."[88]

In some jurisdictions, there is no apparent sanction for breaching these mediator duties and no indication that the duties create defenses to enforcement of a settlement agreement. Civil liability is not a risk in jurisdictions providing immunity for negligent acts.[89] In several jurisdictions, however, the duties are accompanied by a risk of liability[90] and even sanctions.[91] In Florida, for example, a mediator who violates statutory duties may lose the certification to receive court referrals, may be required to pay costs, or may receive other sanctions.[92]

Nonetheless, there is little reason to believe that these mediator duties ensure fairness. Miranda-type warnings do little to address critics' concerns about bargaining imbalances and pressures to settle that might produce settlements placing at least one party in a worse position than would have resulted from lawyer-to-lawyer negotiations. Although the broader requirements imposed upon mediators respond to critics' concerns, they implicitly demand that mediators play a quasi-judicial function, in conflict with their mediary role and without guidance as to the meaning of "harm," "power imbalance," or "balanced dialogue."[93] Aside from highlighting conflict between the mediator's role in assisting settlement and the demands to promote fairness, the effect of such duties is unclear. As Professor Robert A. Baruch Bush has noted regarding mediator standards generally, "Where the mediator is confronted ... with the need to choose between two values, like fairness and self-determination, the codes typically contain provisions that, read together, tell her to choose both."[94] Even if mediators are eager to comply with their broad duties, they may not have sufficient information to do so. Mediators do not hear the witnesses or make factual findings, and often do not talk with the children.[95] Furthermore, if mediators are not eager to comply, it is not likely that the parties can show that they violated the duty, even if sanctions are available. One is reminded of Lerner's lyric

'A law was made a distant moon ago here, A law was made a distant moon ago here, July and August cannot be too hot; And there's a legal limit to the snow here in Camelot.'[96]

Thus, the primary virtue of legislating such mediator duties is to instill optimism in the rule-maker or legislator.

Because provisions of mediator accountability are unlikely to be effective, and because they are unnecessary if the parties bring their lawyers to the session, it is important to examine the costs of mediator duties. By analogy, one can examine commentary on the cost of defensiveness in the medical field, which argues that warnings, disclosures, and additional tests result in expenses for the patient and government and physician unwillingness to accept certain cases.[97] If the threat of accountability is taken seriously, mediators may react in similar fashion, issuing warnings, insisting on written acknowledgements, and taking only "low-risk" cases. In this event, the spontaneity, simplicity, and availability of the mediation process will likely fade, a particularly dear cost because these aspects of mediation make it more effective than traditional court processes in engaging parties actively and assisting in identifying creative solutions.[98] Given low prospects for ensuring fairness, mediator duties seem like a costly placebo.

## 2. Case Selection

If one accepts that unfairness in lawyerless mediation stems in part from bargaining imbalances, it follows that the process becomes more fair if courts exclude cases from mediation that are likely to involve such imbalances.[99] Presumably, fairness would also be enhanced if the courts similarly excluded cases involving parties who are particularly susceptible to mediator pressures.[100] Mediation statutes identify several classes of parties who might be subject either to imbalances or mediator pressure: victims of domestic violence; persons with substance abuse or mental health problems; and persons who fit in a more general category of bargaining disadvantages.[101] Domestic violence exclusions have been the primary subject of debate and regulation.[102]

The problem with exclusion as a means to achieve fairness is the difficulty in predicting whether and how power imbalances will appear or when the mediator will pressure a party to settle. Scholars of the negotiation process note that power shifts frequently during negotiation.[103] Based on studies of mediation transcripts, Janet Rifkin, Sara Cobb, and Jonathan Miller observe that the mere order of presentation of the opening stories in the mediation may impact significantly on bargaining advantage and thus outcomes.[104] Ethnic identifications between mediators and parties may also affect outcomes.[105] The imbalances probably shift according to the issue under discussion as well as the order of proceedings.[106] Power shifts may also occur if there is a sense of guilt or lack of knowledge on particular issues. Thus, it is difficult to predict power imbalances either by category of case or by individual in advance of the mediation session.[107]

Even if one focuses only on imbalances stemming from domestic violence, the problems arising in implementing case selection by statute or court rule become apparent. Statutes employ three primary means to exclude domestic violence cases from mediation: categorical prohibition, case-by-case screening by the court,[108] and exclusion by the court upon a party's motion and special showing.[109] Each of these methods proves problematic.

Categorical exclusions from mediation are "blunt instruments." Research and experience indicate that they may lead to underinclusion of cases, particularly when such exclusions are based only on court pleadings.[110] In a pilot study of 261 contested custody cases in three Ohio courts, parties alleged violence in the pleadings twenty-six percent to thirty percent of the time.[111] A much higher proportion, however, fifty-one percent of the eighty-nine respondents to surveys and forty-five percent of those interviewed by employees of one court, said that their marriage had been violent.[112] Elsewhere, interviews show a higher incidence of violence reported to court personnel than alleged in pleadings.[113]

Procedural hurdles that serve to curb misuse of categorical exclusions lead to further underinclusion. Legislators appear hesitant to exclude cases from mediation solely on the basis of a statement of abuse to a court counselor. In fact, they seem to worry that permitting exclusion based on allegations in the pleadings will lead to misuse and overexclusion.

Thus, some statutes do not provide for exclusion from mediation solely because of reported violence.[114] In California, for example, cases receive special treatment only if parties allege domestic violence under penalty of perjury.[115] Some statutes require a finding of probable cause,[116] a showing to the satisfaction of the court,[117] or a finding that the violence occurred.[118] Although the reaction to possible bogus claims is understandable, this higher threshold widens the gulf between actual violence cases and those cases that are excluded from mediation. A conservative estimate based on the Ohio data[119] indicates that almost fifty percent of domestic violence cases are excluded where something more formal than the victim's statement to a counselor is required.

The substantiation requirement also adds to cost, because it introduces additional court processes prior to mediation. This also probably interferes with early mediation scheduling. By adding cost and introducing delay, substantiation may destroy the cost-effectiveness of mediation for the parties and allow conflicts to escalate.

Categorical case exclusion would seem to be relatively cost-free if based solely on a party's statement. Reliance on the statements alone, however, might result in substantial overexclusion, and cases that could be mediated fairly would not enter the process.[120] One study indicates that four-fifths of the divorce mediation couples had families with serious substance abuse, child abuse, or family violence situations.[121] Given the view that lawyer advocacy helps balance power in cases of abuse,[122] blanket categorical exclusion would be unnecessary if lawyers participated actively in mediation and if provisions were made for separating the parties in mediation upon request.

Individual case assessments by court personnel have been touted as a means to identify instances of domestic violence and to predict whether the violence will present serious bargaining imbalances.[123] We do not have research on which to evaluate the success of case assessment in excluding cases that involve substantial bargaining imbalances. As we discussed above, however, it is difficult to predict how the negotiations, and thus bargaining power, will play out in mediation.[124] In addition, high-quality screening is costly. In one Ohio court, for example, a full-time equivalent mediation professional assessed 594 cases in the course of a year and recommended against mediation in only fifteen percent of the cases.[125] In contrast, during the same time in another Ohio court, the equivalent of one mediation professional provided free mediations in about seventy-five cases, resulting in almost one-half of them settling.[126]

Similar arguments about under- and overinclusion and costs could be made for other types of bargaining imbalances, such as those created by persons who are risk averse or have low aspirations. Case selection is thus questionably effective in achieving the same level of fairness as in lawyer-to-lawyer negotiations, and it is costly. Categorical exclusions are likely either to vastly over- or underexclude or to add delay and cost. Individual assessment, the method most likely to be effective, requires expending staff resources that could otherwise be used to offer free mediation.

## 3. *Issue Limitations*

Commentators state that bargaining imbalances are more likely to cause harm if parties discuss economic as well as child status issues during the mediation.[127] Justifications for this assertion vary. One commentator contends that an aggressive parent will demand economic concessions in exchange for allowing the other parent more access to or rights concerning the children.[128] Separating economic issues from child custody and visitation issues in the mediation process presumably averts these inappropriate trade-offs. Other commentators add that the legally-naive party faces the greatest disadvantage in the negotiation of economic issues, where legal advice, higher education, and experience make choices more informed.[129] One also argues that lawyers will resist mediation if non-lawyer mediators "handle" economic issues.[130] Most statutes authorize mandatory mediation only for contested custody and visitation issues, probably to prevent linking these to economic issues, to reduce bargaining imbalances, and to avoid resistance from the bar.[131] In two states, separate mediation programs, staffed by attorney-mediators, are authorized for economic issues.[132]

The statutes that purport to separate economic from custody/visitation issues probably do not succeed in actually severing these issues or in preventing parties from linking them.[133] Dean Folberg suggests that we must "romanticize" to believe these issues are not considered together.[134] In fact, despite statutory language limiting mediation to custody and visitation issues, a recent national survey indicates that, in a substantial number of programs, mediators are likely to discuss child support.[135] Some private mediators consider other economic issues so intertwined with custody that they now consider them together.[136] Professor Grillo points out that joint custody arrangements often assume equal financial obligation when, in fact, one parent usually has the major care responsibilities and thus financial burdens,[137] creating economic implications when custody is resolved. In sum, it is doubtful whether issue limitations in fact circumscribe discussion of financial matters or prevent parents from linking them together inappropriately.

There is reason to doubt whether those seeking custody will be forced to trade financial support for custody. A recent study of California divorce cases found "no statistically persuasive evidence that mothers who experienced more legal conflict had to give up support to win the custody they wanted."[138] Sociologist Jessica Pearson also characterized "custody blackmail" as a "relatively rare phenomenon."[139]

Given doubts about the need for and effectiveness of issue limitations, it is important to assess their costs. One important cost is the apparent inference by lawyers that they need not attend the mediation sessions, thus creating risks of unfairness. After reviewing selected state statutes and court rules governing lawyer participation in divorce mediation, Professor John McCrory concluded that lawyer participation depends on the scope of the issues subject to mediation, with lawyers more actively participating when mediation addresses property and financial issues.[140] An analysis of data on court-connected mediation programs supports McCrory's view.[141] It reveals that lawyers participate in only thirty-eight percent of the programs that mandate custody mediation but participate in ninety-one percent of those mandatory programs that touch on economic issues in addition to custody and visitation.[142]

Another cost is in the effectiveness of mediation. A British study of marital conciliation reports more satisfaction and greater savings when the mediation included all issues in the divorce,[143] – a logical result considering that mediated settlement removes the need for further proceedings, other than presenting the agreement for court approval. If the mediation addresses only custody matters, however, then either a court or the parties with their lawyers must separately craft the financial terms of the divorce. In addition, British and Canadian researchers suggest that settlements of isolated issues, such as child custody, will not endure as long as more comprehensive settlements.[144]

Issue limitations thus do not seem to solve the problem for which they were designed – avoiding linkage between economic and custody issues. They may be based on faulty premises of custody blackmail. They tend to discourage lawyer attendance, thus eliminating a promising fairness protection. Furthermore, they are costly in terms of party expenditures, party satisfaction, and compliance.

### 4. Mediator Qualifications

In the early days of divorce mediation, there were few, if any, legal qualifications for divorce mediators.[145] For example, mediators could be court employees or volunteer retirees who had impressed a court administrator as fit for the job. Like negotiators – and, indeed, like judges – mediators were thought to vary in ability, but not in easily quantifiable terms.

Now, the quality or fairness of mediation is treated as a direct product of the mediator,[146] and mediator qualifications, set by statute or rule, commonly include educational degrees and specialized training.[147] In a number of jurisdictions, mediators who receive court referrals must have post-baccalaureate degrees.[148] The advanced degree may be in one of a variety of fields, such as law, mental health, or accounting.[149] The mediation training requirement is often described in terms of hours of class, usually forty hours, sometimes by a trainer who has met yet another set of certification requirements.[150] Occasionally, the rules require continuing education.[151] There have also been proposals to add or substitute skills testing.[152] These statutes and rules aim to screen out all but the "good mediator,"[153] who will then protect the parties against unfairness.[154]

There is reason to be skeptical about whether mediator qualifications, particularly those requiring educational degrees, substantially contribute to the fairness of the process. Research on mediator qualifications has failed to show a correlation between the mediator's education and rough indicators of performance, such as settlement rates or satisfaction by the parties.[155] The content of the required education also provides little reason to predict that mediator qualifications affect bargaining imbalances.[156] Law and accountancy programs require few, if any, courses that develop qualities that might make mediators effective at promoting fairness, such as ability to perceive and understand power imbalances, demonstrate empathy, show sensitivity to diverse values, and distance the mediator's values from the issues.[157] Indeed, some commentators and researchers raise concerns about the powerful influence of the mediator's professional ideology on the parties' decisions.[158]

Enhanced educational qualifications may carry a variety of costs. A "blue ribbon" commission of dispute resolution professionals warns that high educational qualifications may produce a contracting pool of mediators who lack diversity and who charge higher fees.[159] Already, there is anecdotal support for this. For example, private mediators in Florida receiving court referrals usually charge $125 per hour for several hours of mediation.[160] Florida requires advanced degrees. In Maine, by contrast, mediators are paid $ 50 per mediation.[161] Maine does not have such educational requirements. Furthermore, some rural counties may be unable to operate mediation programs, because no one in the community meets the educational qualifications. In addition, varying qualifications may restrict mediators from handling cases in other jurisdictions.[162]

In sum, mediator qualifications can be costly. They may serve other purposes,[163] but they are not needed to preserve fairness if lawyers attend mediation sessions, and they are probably ineffective at insuring fairness if lawyers do not attend.

### 5. Lawyer and Court Review of Mediated Agreements

Mediated agreements regarding children do not become final until the court approves them.[164] In some jurisdictions, mediators must also advise the parties to seek attorney review of the settlement before execution of the mediation agreements.[165]

Court review has traditionally been viewed as a check on only the most egregious and obvious unfairness, because the judge receives only the written result of negotiations and has no advocate for non-signature.[166] Professors Robert Mnookin and Lewis Kornhauser point out that the "sheer quantity of cases that a judge must oversee" makes it impractical for a judge to attend to cases prone to injustice.[167] Nonetheless, court approval costs the parties relatively little and does not hamper the effectiveness of the mediation process. Thus, we see little reason to change this requirement.

By contrast, lawyer review of mediation agreements appears to present better prospects for meaningful protection. Lawyers, however, express frustration over their limited ability to advise on these agreements, because they do not witness the give-and-take of the negotiations that created them and lack access to the information needed to evaluate properly alternatives to settlement.[168] One commentator warns of legal malpractice liability for advice under these circumstances.[169] Some lawyers refuse to provide opinions because they believe that they cannot competently do so under the circumstances.[170] The Boston Bar Association approved the process of attorney review of mediated agreements, but warned, "A separation agreement cannot really be evaluated by one who has not participated in the negotiations leading to it and, therefore, cannot judge whether it appropriately reflects the views, needs, strengths, and weaknesses of each of the parties."[171]

While providing limited help in assuring fairness, post-mediation lawyer review is a costly process. The more thorough the review, the more costly it will be. Lawyers who are uncertain about whether the agreement represents the best possible result may recommend against execution, perhaps unnecessarily scuttling the client's best option. Even the possibility of frequent lawyer consultation does not seem to avert rejections of tentative agreements. In fact, mediators view lawyer recommendations against signing tentative mediation agreements as a significant problem.[172] Thus, the cost and effort of the mediation may be lost when lawyers do not participate. In sum, required lawyer review is a costly and less effective alternative to lawyer attendance.

*6. No Recommendation by the Mediator to the Court*
Some of California's domestic relations courts allow the mediator to make a recommendation to the court if the parties fail to reach a settlement during mediation.[173] This procedure enables the mediator to threaten a recalcitrant party with a negative report. Professor Grillo most recently attacked this kind of settlement pressure.[174] "Blue ribbon" reports on mediation by members of the dispute resolution profession have also criticized this approach.[175] Though mediator recommendations have become a highly visible target through Grillo's article and other reports, court rules more often eschew mediator recommendations to the court, and some statutes specifically prohibit these.[176]

The prohibitions against mediator recommendations remove a potential source of pressure to settle and, thus, of unfairness. As such, these laws serve a valuable function, regardless of whether lawyers attend the mediation sessions, and we strongly support them. They do not, however, address bargaining imbalances that may exist even in jurisdictions where the mediators do not provide recommendations.[177]

The "regulatory" approach attempts to insure fairness in the absence of lawyer participation in mediation sessions. Only one type of regulatory provision – judicial review – is relatively low in cost. Only one type of provision – prohibition of mediator reports on the merits – seems likely to increase the fairness of divorce mediation. The others – issue limitations, case selection procedures, high mediator qualifications, mediator duties, and lawyer review – threaten to make mediation more expensive and, in some cases, more rigid and less effective, with little prospect of positive effects on fairness. In short, substituting regulation for lawyer-participation threatens to undermine important qualities of mediation without doing much to insure fairness.

In addition, regulation fails to address the deepest concerns of critics of mediation – that even the best mediators can never be "neutral" and will play a powerful role in shaping outcomes [178] that may create disadvantages for the parties. Lawyers who participate in mediation can address these concerns. Lawyer representation does not guarantee equity, but critics of mediation tend not to criticize as unfair divorce outcomes resulting from lawyer negotiations. Their confidence in lawyer-negotiated outcomes suggests a general agreement that attorney representation provides the best insurance of fairness that we know. The research in Maine, discussed below, indicates that in practice, lawyers play just such a role in protecting client interests in mediation.

*B. The "Voluntary Participation" Approach*

Some commentators argue that mediation will be more fair if legislators or courts simply eliminate the compulsion to participate.[179] Presumably, if parties choose to use mediation, those who do will be informed, and their rights will not be jeopardized, even though lawyers generally will not attend the mediation sessions. These commentators thus advocate against mandatory participation.

There is reason to doubt, however, whether lawyers can predict when they need to attend to protect their clients against unfairness.[180] Furthermore, a voluntary system that lacks lawyer participation presents the risk that lawyers will encourage mediation to resolve the problems they dislike or feel uncomfortable handling. In Maine, as elsewhere, lawyers encourage divorcing clients to do part of the negotiating themselves.[181] Thus encouragement appears much more likely on some issues (the division of personal property and visitation schedules) and for some clients (those with less income).[182] Such encouragement probably stems from a concern about controlling costs, especially when there are insufficient resources to pay attorneys. It also arises from a desire by some lawyers to avoid "pots and pans issues."[183] According to these lawyers, these matters do not require legal expertise, unlike matters involving real property, alimony, and pensions. Parties, however, may well need as much support and guidance on these issues as they do on more legally relevant topics, but may find themselves referred either to party-to-party negotiation or mediation without lawyers, if it is available.[184] Thus, a statutory approach that relies wholly on voluntary participation may indirectly exacerbate problems of unfairness by delegating difficult and important "nonlegal" issues to mediation without lawyers present.

Voluntary participation, as a means of assuring fairness, may also entail costs if voluntary mediation programs are party-paid. This makes mediation an option primarily for the well-to-do. For instance, in an Ohio study of contested cases, while only forty percent of all divorcing parties with contested cases had incomes over $20,000, seventy-three percent of those attending voluntary, party-paid mediation had incomes over $20,000.[185]

Experience indicates that mediation does not occur frequently unless states require that parties participate or require attendance at a session where parties are urged to participate.[186] One parent may reject the option when it is (or because it is) favored by the other parent. At least one of the parties rejected even free mediation services in half of the cases reported by one custody mediation study[187] and even more in another.[188] Thus, if reduced use of mediation constitutes a cost,[189] voluntary mediation carries with it an additional disadvantage.

Under the voluntary approach, parties would rarely use mediation and would have little assistance of counsel when they did. Requiring the divorcing parties to attend a mediation session at which their lawyers actively participate would seem to promote fairness more effectively. Regulators and commentators, however, assume that this would destroy mediation. Furthermore, those advocating voluntary mediation often assert that trial will obviate fairness concerns, assuming trial is the alternative to attending mediation sessions.[190]

Such assumptions as these have artificially limited the examination of alternatives for promoting fairness in divorce mediation. Consequently, the debate about fairness has revolved around the "regulatory" approach and the "voluntary participation" approach, neither of which satisfactorily addresses fairness. These limiting assumptions, however, prove to be inaccurate.

We turn now to evidence showing that the assumptions that the two dominant approaches present are myths. This opens up a third policy choice – the "lawyer-participant" approach.

## III. ASSUMPTIONS UNDERLYING THE DOMINANTAPPROACHES

Four assumptions are implicit in the two dominant statutory approaches to assuring fairness in mediation, and also in the commentary for and against mandatory mediation: (1) lawyers do not attend mediation sessions but do attend trials; (2) divorce mediation sessions are all alike; (3) lawyers spoil mediation if they attend and participate in the sessions; and (4) trial represents the typical alternative to mediation. We address the assumptions in turn, and in the next section show them to be myths.

### A. The Disappearing Lawyer

Critics and proponents of mediation alike see the absence of lawyers as a defining aspect of divorce mediation.[191] According to mediation advocate Joshua Rosenberg, for example, "Admittedly, one significant difference between court hearings and most mediation sessions is the presence of attorneys at one and not the other."[192] Case summaries of "ideal" mediations by a number of commentators describe sessions without lawyers present.[193] A diminished role for lawyers is indeed one of the goals of some divorce mediation advocates.[194] For example, after describing a structured mediation process for divorce, O.J. Coogler asks, "What is there for the lawyer to do when mediation is completed?"[195] His answer is, " "Not much.' ... Even if the divorce is handled by an attorney, it is a ministerial ritual for which only a very nominal fee can be charged."[196] Under the dominant view, the parties' lawyers may consult before or after the session, perhaps even by phone during it, but they disappear when the parties sit down with the mediator.[197]

Statutory provisions in several states that permit exclusion of lawyers from mediation reinforce the presumption of attorney non-involvement.[198] Even where attorneys may attend,[199] they generally do not.[200] It is possible that they have accepted mediation sessions as being outside their turf or believe that mediation covers issues not squarely within their legal expertise.

It should not be surprising, therefore, that lawyers are notably absent in the commentary on what occurs during divorce mediation sessions.[201] Research about divorce mediation focuses largely on the experience of the parties and seldom mentions lawyers.[202] Popular accounts adopt this view as well: "[Mediation] does, of course, represent a trade-off. A couple in mediation forgoes a lawyer's advocacy in return for avoiding a lawyer's friction."[203] Although most books about divorce mediation practice list "lawyers" briefly in the index, they figure in the text most prominently as lawyer-mediators, as promoters of the adversarial climate, or as reviewers of mediation agreements.[204] One book even lists "legal advice" as a subheading under "Obstacles to Successful Mediation."[205]

Critics of mediation also assume that lawyers do not participate in mediation. They see the results, however, as bad rather than good.[206] For them, lawyers who protect clients from domination at all other points in the divorce process disappear into the shadows during mediation except to advise clients on the wisdom of agreements reached. Bryan, for example, asserts, "Negotiating lawyers rely upon these legal entitlements and divorce agreements reflecting them, thereby loosening the control men traditionally wield over economic resources and the socialization of children [but] ... mediation [without attorneys] unobtrusively reduces this threat to patriarchy by returning men to their former dominant position."[207] Thus, critics believe that the absence of lawyers in mediation and their ineffectiveness in advising parties about mediation agreements precludes effective advocacy and fails to protect legal rights in mediation. Professor Grillo starkly poses the dilemma resulting from the presumed absence of lawyers from mediation. She states that "the choice presented today is between an adversary process with totally powerful legal actors, in which clients never speak for themselves (and often do not know what is going on), and a mediation process in which they are entirely on their own and unprotected."[208]

## B. Mediation as Monolith

Much commentary treats mediation generically, as if all mediation was alike.[209] Many critics of mediation offer as prototypical the mediation programs of one jurisdiction.[210] Professor Grillo, for instance, draws her examples from a county in California that follows the minority rule of permitting the mediator to make disposition recommendations to the court if the parties fail to reach agreement.[211] Professors Bryan and Martha Fineman assume a generic, lawyerless mediation, in which the mediator is a mental health or social work professional who lacks financial sophistication and who holds a bias toward joint custody.[212] This runs counter to studies that show no mediator bias toward joint custody,[213] and to the reality that there are thousands of divorce mediators who are not mental health or social work professionals.[214]

Supporters of mandatory mediation also treat mediation generically in their aspiration to a world of uniformly "good" mediators. They argue that "bad mediation" is an aberration that training and tighter or better regulation can cure.[215]

## C. Lawyers as Spoilers

Laws that regulate mandatory mediation seem designed to protect the parties' interests in the absence of their lawyers. This regulatory approach implies that the easy solution – encouraging lawyer presence – must be avoided because lawyers negatively affect mediation.[216] For example, Professor Rosenberg argues against lawyer involvement in mediation because the advocacy role that attorneys play may promote reluctance "to explore helpful and creative solutions. Possibilities that might help both parties could be permanently lost."[217] Professor Thomas Carbonneau warns that adversarial attorney interaction in divorce mediation "threatens to compromise the viability of the process," adding that lawyers who do not agree with mediation goals are "likely to become a dysfunctional element in the process, not only jealous of its intrusion into their domain of competence, but also unable to adapt professionally to a situation of controlled and defused, rather than polarized and contentious, conflict."[218] Mediation proponents also suggest that lawyer participation may reduce commitment to, and thus compliance with, the settlement reached.[219]

Critics of mediation also assume that lawyers would "spoil" the mediation process.[220] Because they see the virtues of a lawyered process, but believe that lawyers and mediation are incompatible, they give little attention to lawyer presence as a protection against unfairness.[221]

## D. Mandated Mediation Versus Trial

Much of the current debate about the fairness of mediation presupposes a choice between trials and mediations, although some critics such as Professor Bryan,[222] some advocates such as Blades,[223] and some researchers such as Chandler[224] recognize that most divorce cases settle.[225] Thus, Professors Grillo and Rosenberg debate whether judges or mediators are more biased and whose biases are more consequential.[226] Proponents sell mediation as a way for parties to control their own fate.[227] By contrast, critics deride mediation because it removes the opportunity to have a judge find on behalf of a weaker party.[228]

Mandatory mediation programs have been instituted for "contested" custody or divorce proceedings.[229] As the California statute makes clear, the goal of mediation is to "reduce acrimony ... [and] develop an agreement."[230] Mediation advocates assume that mediation – when it works – largely replaces trial or hearing with settlement.[231] Proponents celebrate this consequence. They believe court contests harm parties and children, and find judicial decisions frequently inadequate for dealing with the complex and highly individual needs of divorcing parties and their children.[232] That presumed consequence is consistent with the claims that mediation saves money for the parties and reduces the burden on the courts. [233]

In sum, the four assumptions underlying the dominant regulatory approaches are rarely challenged in the debate about mandated divorce mediation. If they are accurate, there may be only two viable alternative solutions to the universally acknowledged problem of unfairness – the "voluntary participation" approach and the "regulatory" approach. But if these assumptions are myths, as we argue they are, options for insuring fairness can be more broadly examined. In fact, lawyers can and do participate in mediation sessions more often than they appear in trial; mediation can look very different from state to state and mediation to mediation; lawyers can and do assume constructive roles in mediation as advocates without undermining the party-centered goals of mediation;[234] and mediation can, and in some places does, complement negotiation more often than it substitutes for trials.

To buttress these challenges to the four assumptions, we turn to a detailed case study of the experience of lawyers who play an active role in mandated divorce mediation.

* * * *

## V. BRING IN THE LAWYERS

Absent the faulty assumptions discussed above, one can look anew at a regulatory scheme in which lawyers participate in mandatory mediation. This scheme achieves fairness primarily by encouraging lawyers to attend and participate. Legislators could accomplish this result by prohibiting exclusion of lawyers from mediation sessions and, in fact, broadening the issues covered in mediation to include matters of real property, alimony, and other financial issues that stimulate lawyer participation. This scheme includes only two other key regulatory provisions – court review of mediated agreements and a prohibition against the mediator's recommendation to the court. It is possible that some extra provision for domestic violence cases, such as the right to refuse joint sessions with the attacker, ought to be included as well.

## A. Compared to the "Regulatory" Approach

Most fairness concerns evaporate if lawyers attend mediation sessions with the parties or if the parties opt out of the process when unrepresented.[320] Less intrusive regulations, such as judicial review of agreements, prohibition of settlement pressures, and provisions for unrepresented parties, may moderate the remaining fairness issues. The detailed rules of the "regulatory approach" largely become unnecessary to preserve fairness if lawyers are present.

By encouraging lawyer presence and permitting modification of the mediation ground rules, this scheme is more flexible and certain in responding to the problems of bargaining imbalances and mediator pressures. Especially given the unpredictability and changing situational character of these challenges to fairness, the presence of lawyers in the process can assure necessary help in those unpredictable circumstances. The Maine research shows that with lawyers present as advisors and potentially as spokespersons, the risks of unfairness decline, even in the most unbalanced situations. By permitting adjustment of the mediation process (for example, allowing shuttle mediation), mediation can be tailored to fit particular relationships and issues in each case.

Lawyers prevent or moderate the effects of a face to face encounter with an abuser, thus diminishing the likelihood of unfairness in domestic violence cases. Maine lawyers attending mediation sessions with their clients report arranging separate sessions, time-outs, and other measures to protect their clients. Past violence, which may be a key factor in determining whether the parties will submit to an unfair settlement or will be forced into a frightening situation,[321] becomes less of a bargaining factor if the parties attend with their lawyers.[322] Lawyers can advise clients to avoid settlements that will allow further opportunities for abuse, or that are unlikely to be obeyed, or that are bad deals.[323] Lawyers can also advise their clients to terminate mediation sessions. Although some suggest that mediation should also be avoided because divorce settlement condones violence,[324] research indicates that in the prime alternative to mediation – negotiation – settlements occur with about the same frequency as in mediation.[325] Thus, in domestic violence cases, mediation probably encourages settlement more quickly rather than more often.

Issue limitations also become unnecessary if lawyers attend and can advise on economic trade-offs and legal issues. There is no more danger in combining the issues in mediation than exists if disposition of all issues occurs outside of mediation.

So, too, an assumption that lawyers will be absent underlies reliance on mediator qualifications as a means to ensure fairness. Absent lawyers, mediators must have at least some of the skills and knowledge that lawyers would otherwise provide.[326] In fact, Maine divorce lawyers acknowledge that they sometimes get poor mediators. In these cases, the lawyers simply take charge and use the sessions as four-way negotiation sessions. Although mediator qualifications involving advanced educational degrees may help increase settlements or party confidence, they are unnecessary to protect against unfairness under the "lawyer-participant" approach, because mediators need not substitute their knowledge for that of lawyers. Lawyers can intervene (as discussed above) to compensate for inferior mediators and can request their removal.

Mediator duties to appraise parties of various legal rights, to terminate mediation, and to moderate bargaining imbalances also rest on the assumption that lawyers are absent in mediation. Obviously, requirements for post-mediation review of settlements by lawyers rest on the assumption that the lawyer does not take part in the give-and-take of negotiations.

In other words, lawyer participation reduces substantially the need for regulation. Probably, a mediation model should allow domestic violence victims to opt out of joint sessions. This model should also prohibit mediator recommendations to the court. Such low-cost requirements as court review of the agreement and brief mediation training should be incorporated into this third model. Finally, because this model assumes lawyer participation, perhaps unrepresented parties should be able to avoid mediation.

Our opposition to regulation by court rule or statute in order to achieve fairness is not an opposition to good management and supervision of mediation programs. Such management probably should insure periodic training, discussion of issues of practice, and efforts at quality control. In attempting to insure quality, mediation programs should make use of such devices as peer evaluation and attorney commentary. Regulation, however, differs from management because regulation imposes rigid and categorical obligations and thus introduces unnecessary costs and inflexibility.

## B. Compared to the "Voluntary Participation" Approach

The "voluntary participation" approach to assuring fairness assumes that lawyers can and will predict in advance whether unfairness will occur at a mediation session.[327] Under this approach, however, the lawyer still is not present if an unexpected problem arises during a session. The "lawyer-participation approach," by contrast, does not compel the lawyer and party to take risks based solely on a prediction regarding the course of negotiations. Also, the "lawyer-participation" approach makes greater use of mediation, because lawyers who can attend mediation sessions will more likely recommend that their clients participate in such sessions. Finally, with lawyers participating, the courts can, without undue concerns about fairness, compel a reluctant party to attend, thereby increasing the use of mediation.

## C. Concerns About the "Lawyer-Participant" Approach

Critics of mandatory mediation will still question what requiring parties to participate in mediation adds to a lawyer-guided settlement or trial process.[328] Mediators may still question whether the lawyer-participant approach, although fair, provides worthwhile benefits for the parties. At base, these reactions stem from the myths discussed and dismissed above. The remaining concerns of mediation critics and advocates about this third regulatory model can be summarized in five questions. First, does mediation add anything to the lawyer-to-lawyer negotiation that usually would otherwise occur? Second, does requiring participation undermine self-determination in the litigation process? Third, does lawyer participation increase the cost of the mediation process? Fourth, what happens in cases in which both sides are not represented by counsel? Fifth, and finally, does lawyer-participant mediation constitute "real mediation"? The research in Maine provides a basis for answering these questions.

*1. Mediation Versus Negotiation*
One might ask whether lawyer-participant mediation differs from lawyer-to-lawyer negotiation. As described below, Maine divorce attorneys believe that mediation improves negotiation because, in their view, it increases efficiency, decreases communication problems, enhances client involvement and understanding of the process, increases information for attorneys, and dignifies the divorce process for many clients.[329]

Unlike many of the theoretical models of negotiation, actual negotiations over divorce cases are discontinuous and fragmented.[330] By gathering everyone together at the same place and time to give sustained attention to settlement, the "months [or more] of diddling back and forth between lawyers"[331] can be diminished:

Years ago, there wasn't any real alternative. You make me a proposal. I get the letter. I send it to my client. The client reviews. The client comes on back into the office, we look at it together, and then I make a counter-proposal. And you get this . . . round robin thing that is going back and forth like this. And often, very time consuming. A lot of opportunity for miscommunication.[332] Each of the events in the negotiation round robin may be separated by days or even weeks as lawyers play telephone tag with each other and with clients. Frequently, one party simply fails to respond at all, dragging out an already protracted process. At each step, distracted lawyers and anxious parties must get up to speed on the issues and possible settlement. Simply by assembling the parties, mediation in Maine streamlines the negotiation process.

Mediation also provides direct communication between the two lawyers and the two parties, and thus insures that nothing will be "lost in the translation":

I think people regard mediation as a good place to do their negotiations and get them over with in one or two sessions. Everybody's there. You don't have to say, "Well, I've got to ask my client." If there's any confusion, they're both there to talk about it. They're both there to disagree, so you don't lose. . . . Something isn't lost in the translation.[333]

It gets them face to face with the other side. It eliminates all the rumors. They tell me what their spouse said their lawyer said; all that smoke is gone when we sit down in mediation.[334]

If I think the attorney on the other side is being the difficult one, if my client keeps saying, "I'm sure my ex, my soon-to-be ex, wouldn't be saying those kinds of things," gives me an opportunity in mediation to make our pitch, make our fair arguments, so that the clients hear, and it's not always straight through me [and the other lawyer].[335] At the least, the mediation process alters the dynamics of the communication in negotiation. Instead of a process in which client A talks to lawyer A who talks to lawyer B who talks to client B and then back again, all actors are present to listen and to speak to one another. This benefit, of course, would exist if lawyers and clients met without the assistance of a mediator, but in practice such four-way talks do not occur frequently unless scheduled through mediation.[336] Several Maine lawyers explained why. They had doubts that such four-way talk would work out with attorneys they did not know well and trust. In addition, lawyers expressed concern about creating situations where client emotions could run high without a helping hand to guide and channel those emotions productively.

Apart from inefficiency and inaccuracy in communication, a lawyer-run negotiation can also create tension in the relationship between lawyer and client. Almost every attorney whom we interviewed attempted to keep clients fully informed of the progress of their cases by sending them copies of all or most correspondence and informing them of any offers received. Yet, lawyers frequently reported that clients felt left out and uninformed:

If you're negotiating, and you're doing letters, which I hate to do already . . . and phone calls, and you're meeting with lawyers, the client's going to get the sense of "Wait, who's doing this anyway? I didn't say I would do that." And so [mediation] is a way of covering your tail and involving your client and being efficient about getting a resolution.[337] In the episodic, lawyer-run negotiation, clients who play a passive and consultative role may believe that their lawyers are doing little and resent the diminished participation in and control over their case. The direct engagement of parties and concentrated attention to negotiation that mediation provides can thus improve lawyer-client relationships as well as efficiency and communication.

Lawyers also report that participation in mediation permits them to glean additional information that increases their capacity to serve as advisors to and advocates for clients. First, mediation provides attorneys an opportunity for contact with and first-hand assessment of the other party, something that rarely occurs otherwise. Over one-third of the Maine divorce attorneys whom we interviewed commented on this value of the mediation process, often characterizing it as "discovery":[338]

Also going is like early discovery, you get a sense of the other person, and where they're at, and you get a sense of like issues that pop up that maybe you don't know about and then, like, your client gives you one story and now you hear the other story and if you're not there you don't hear the other story.[339]

That's one thing about mediation. If they do talk, the other party, not their attorney, does talk, you can kind of understand where they are coming from. Then you can kind of judge the ways that you are going to present yourself to this person.[340] The exposure of lawyers to the other spouse in mediation also helps each attorney to assess that person independent of the potentially inaccurate reports of both their client and the opposing lawyer.[341] The conventional insulation from the other spouse may at times contribute to contentiousness or compromise the capacity of a lawyer to advise her client well.

Lawyers hear their [client's] side of the story, and they start from that, and they believe in their side of the story, and they never really understand or fully accept the other side, the other view of the same situation. If you hear it from the other lawyer, you don't believe in it as thoroughly as if you're sitting there [in mediation], and the lawyer and client are spelling it out in a way that you have to sit there and absolutely listen, and you can't interrupt, and it really gets spun out.[342] When attorneys cannot "size up" the other party directly, they may be less effective in assessing the other spouse's priorities and needs, a practice widely viewed as essential to effective negotiation.[343]

Typically, arm's-length negotiation leaves little room for divorcing husbands and wives to hear each other out in a relatively safe setting. Either lawyers take over the communication, or direct interactions between the parties are heated and unproductive.[344] Mediation provides a setting for communication between parties that settlement does not, a setting in which parties can and do discuss and explain needs and problems and express anger and disappointment with the other party,[345] not just exchange demands and positions:

Sometimes the parties don't talk and [mediation means] maybe listening and maybe hearing, that maybe makes sense, hearing the other side. I think it's important to hear the other side.
[346]

[M]y experience has been that sometimes that room is the first time that clients have been face to face, or it's one of the few times they have the opportunity to be face to face, and they need to get some stuff off their chests and it can be done in that setting safely and usefully.
. . .[347]

[T]his is the only opportunity I have to have him sitting there listening to my client's point of view. He's probably never done it in his life. Now he's got someone who's describing what her life is going to be like; going through her budget. This is what expenses are going to be; she's going to have to move out . . . . This is what your family, the people that you are responsible for, the people that you married and loved for fifteen years, this is how they are going to be living. This is what they are going to be living on.[348]

Mediation, unlike negotiations, is a dignified process that engages the divorcing parties and gives them a chance to tell their story, not only to their spouse but to someone "official":

Mediation introduces the supposedly neutral party and what a lot of divorce clients want is the opportunity to tell the story to somebody else and get it out of . . . their system.[349]

I think that it also gives people the sense that they've had, maybe not so much as their day in court, but they at least feel as if another person has heard their side of the story. And that the other side, the other attorney has heard their side.[350]

[Mediation] is definitely something out of the ordinary. You are not just sitting having coffee in your attorney's office, and the two attorneys aren't just whacking each other on the back and saying "Oh well, I see you have a new tree in the corner of your office or . . . ." You know it's definitely a separate, formal procedure, and I think that in going through a divorce it's very important the people have marked guideposts and milestones. . . . When [couples] separate, many times that's not so. They just go into court and have five minutes in front of a judge – boom, boom – my lawyer says this, his lawyer says this, we signed a piece of paper – it's as if you're just left in the middle of a hurricane, whereas at mediation it is a formal marking of the occasion and the system is participating . . . .[351] A central conclusion from the research about procedural justice is that people value highly the opportunity to voice their grievances and to be heard in a dignified setting.[352] Many Maine lawyers see divorce mediation not only as a way of improving efficiency in negotiation, but also as a way of formalizing and dignifying the process for clients. Lawyer-participation in mediation thus appears to add substantial "value" to lawyer-to-lawyer negotiation.

A by-product of lawyer participation is its effect on lawyers even when not in mediation. By changing the structure for negotiation through the addition of mediation involving parties and attorneys, lawyer behavior may change over time. As discussed above, there is some evidence that Maine lawyers, for example, are significantly more willing to endorse "reaching a settlement fair to both parties" as the goal of negotiation – compared to "getting as much as possible for their client" – than a comparable group of New Hampshire lawyers who had no experience participating in court mandated mediation.[353] Furthermore, the use of the formal legal process – such as discovery requests and motions to compel – declined significantly in Maine after the introduction of mediation while increasing in neighboring New Hampshire. One plausible interpretation of these changes and differences is that Maine lawyers have learned in mediation to assist clients in achieving their goals in a more cooperative fashion.[354]

### 2. Mandated Lawyered Mediation and Self-Determination

Maine mandates mediation.[355] Lawyers may not simply select mediation voluntarily to enhance the negotiation process. Requiring lawyer participation in Maine might appear to burden substantially both lawyers and clients.[356] In practice, however, mandatory divorce mediation in Maine permits considerable flexibility and does not appear to undermine free choice regarding settlement.

The general practice in the use of mediation varies from court to court. In some courts, lawyers routinely request mediation soon after filing, while in others local culture encourages mediation requests only when initial efforts at negotiation reveal problems in achieving settlement. Because of its costs, lawyers are less likely to routinely request mediation in cases where the parties have few resources.[357]

From the perspective of clients, mediation in Maine simply appears as another step in the divorce process – often described by lawyers as an important opportunity – rather than as a special burden. In fact, having incorporated mediation into their practices, Maine divorce lawyers report that they typically describe the process, seriously examine settlement options and approaches, and preach mediation's virtues to clients in preparing them to undertake the process:

[I] explain that we can take breaks and discuss things and that they don't have to reach any agreement if they don't want to, that most people are happier if they agree to something rather than having it imposed upon them.[358]

I explain what the process is and what I tell them is that my view of a good mediation is a free-wheeling discussion where you can feel free to say anything . . . . As far as my client goes, I tell them the best thing that could happen is if you guys could get it all out and walk out of the room with an agreement.[359] Belief in mediation's potential assistance in negotiation leads eighty-five percent of the Maine divorce lawyers whom we interviewed to request mediation even in cases not involving children.[360] In their vital role as translators and interpreters of the legal process, lawyers convey to their clients a realistic view of the process, but one which emphasizes the opportunities mediation provides rather than the burdens it imposes.

The slight imposition, as perceived by the parties' lawyers, seems even less significant compared with the benefits. Without mandatory mediation, settlement discussions are unlikely to occur as frequently, because both sides – rather than one – have to agree to participate. By requesting mediation in Maine's mandatory system, one side can bring a reluctant party to the negotiation table.[361]

Sometimes, you cannot get the other lawyer to make a commitment, you can't, they just want to march right into court, and [mediation] gets the other side to see that, that their own lawyer is [sort of avoiding the case].[362]

[Without mediation] you cannot force the other party to sit down with you face-to-face and discuss the issues.[363]

Furthermore, compulsion to participate removes one tactical concern of the party requesting mediation. With mandated mediation, the other side will not view a proposal that the parties seek mediation as a sign of weakness or as a rush to settle. Rather, parties will view such requests as either routine or as a sign that the requesting party wants to proceed to trial and needs to get past the mediation stage.[364]

In addition, lawyers indicate that mandated mediation focuses the lawyers and parties to settle earlier than would otherwise occur. The pressures of managing a law practice, of handling a heavy caseload, and of responding to court deadlines make it difficult for lawyers to pursue sustained efforts to settle a single case. By scheduling mandated mediation, lawyers create a settlement event and deadline.

[Mediation] moves the process along because it, for the unprepared attorney, it forces the attorney to become prepared, or at least to come to face the fact, that, okay, we're going to have to deal with these issues in this divorce.[365]

[M]ost lawyers tend not to get ready until they have to . . . [that is] sitting down [and] focusing on what the issues are. And mediation helps to speed up that process because they've got to be prepared for that mediation.[366] The mediation event may also move indecisive clients to make decisions they have been reluctant to make.

And it also helps, I think, to get the parties ready in a sense, to be prepared for mediation they really have to give the matters some thought, think about what they truly want, what they expect out of the process, and it causes them to focus on the real issues that they might otherwise have been ignoring or just refusing to come to grips with . . . . [367] Lawyers often request mediation quite early in the case. The scheduled mediation date then prompts case preparation and serious involvement in negotiation.

Finally, required participation brings cases to mediation that profit from the process but would not have gone to mediation in a voluntary system. In fact, the experience of many Maine lawyers challenges the argument that the parties may know something that the "state" does not about the value of mediation.[368] Attorneys report that they were often mistaken in their predictions about the uselessness of mediation for particular cases:

Other times it's just because, well, we're gonna have to go through mediation because this one issue involving custody is just not going to be resolved, but we've got to go to mediation before we can have a hearing so we've got to go through the motions somewhat, but sometimes you get fooled and things get worked out at the mediation.[369]

I'm growing increasingly of the opinion that they're productive even in those case where I've said, "No way!"[370]

A lot of times you'll end up with a case that doesn't look like it's going to settle, or people think that it won't. . . . But I also realize a lot of those cases do settle in mediation. Very extreme cases will settle in mediation, maybe even after one session.[371] If left alone to screen which cases should enter mediation, lawyers might not guess well about when it may be useful.

The major impact of a mandated mediation program, such as Maine's, is to structure and improve settlement negotiations. What remains is the argument that mediation is an unnecessary and costly procedure. Fifty-three percent of the Maine lawyers interviewed reported that mediation was sometimes a wasted step "on the way to trial," while forty-seven percent felt that this happened rarely or not at all. In some situations, this argument may trump all others.[372] If settlement rates drop or if the expense of mediation climbs, mandatory mediation may not be worth it, on balance. Thus, courts should monitor their mandatory mediation programs and should change or abandon them when they are not a net benefit or when their cost constitutes a barrier to trial for some parties.

*3. Cost and Lawyer Presence*

Does lawyer presence make mediation more costly? Research done in programs without lawyer presence indicates that, on the average, the parties save if they settle through mediation and do not pay more if they attend mediation and do not settle.[373] Some might argue that lawyer presence changes the calculus by making mediation more costly. The Maine lawyers whom we interviewed were almost evenly split on the question of whether mediation increased the costs of divorce.[374]

We think there is a sound argument that the cost on average is about the same for those who undergo mediation under either the "regulatory" approach or the "lawyer-participant" approach. With lawyers present, the sessions can take place early in the case and can address all issues in the divorce. Research in Canada indicates that parties in programs mandating mediation of all issues save costs, whereas no such savings result in programs that mediate only custody issues.[375] Pearson's review of fifteen divorce mediation studies concludes that private programs offering mediation of all divorce issues achieve the greatest cost saving for the parties.[376]

Furthermore, even with lawyers absent, parties incur substantial legal fees connected with mediation. Presumably, fees for consultation before, during, and after mediation (a mean fee of about $1500 per person in one California study)[377] should be lower if lawyers attend.

Mediators are not required to have substantial educational qualifications in Maine, and the mediator's fee is therefore likely to be low. Court mediator fees of $60 per party for the entire mediation in Maine (with the mediator paid $50)[378] compare favorably with fees of about $125 per hour (paid directly to the mediator) in those Florida jurisdictions that refer parties to private mediators who must meet higher qualifications.[379] One private mediation center in California charged an average mediation fee of $2224 in the late 1980s.[380]

Other cost-related factors deserve mention. When lawyers attend, courts do not need to hold special conferences to assess the case before assignment to mediation, eliminating attendant costs to parties, perhaps including attorney costs. Lawyer attendance renders unnecessary the post-mediation agreement review by the attorney, and the lawyers will not need to advise against signature, thus requiring a costly reconvening of mediation.[381] Attorney presence in mediation may reduce the need for discovery and may narrow the issues, even if the parties do not settle. In Maine, the use of discovery requests and motions to compel for contempt and for temporary support declined significantly after mandatory mediation involving lawyers began.[382] In other words, there is reason to believe that mediation does not simply add a step to an otherwise unaltered litigation or settlement process; instead, mediation involving lawyers changes those processes substantially, making them more efficient and less costly.

It also seems likely that mediation with lawyers can occur more expeditiously than mediation without them. Lawyers assist in clarifying information, consult with and advise clients on the spot, and help identify unaddressed issues. Absent lawyer participation, mediation experts advise a series of sessions with time for consultation between them.[383] By contrast, Maine divorces cases typically require only a single session.[384]

In sum, the research in Maine offers promise that mandatory mediation, even with lawyers attending, on average does not increase costs and that mandatory mediation does not decrease the possibility of affordable trials.

## 4. Fairness for Unrepresented Parties

The typical party to a divorce proceeding is represented only if the case is contested. A recent study of divorce in sixteen urban areas indicates that one or both parties was unrepresented in anywhere from fifty-three percent to eighty-eight percent of the cases, with an average across areas of seventy-two percent.[385] The authors of this study conclude that many divorce litigants represent themselves because "substantial percentage of divorces are uncontested, and most parties have meager property or financial assets. These cases are simple and, with a little guidance, the parties can obtain a divorce without incurring a few hundred dollars of lawyer's fees."[386] These conclusions parallel those described earlier for Maine. Clearly, case duration and the likelihood of motions – both good indicators of contest – are substantially greater for two-lawyer cases than for single-lawyer cases, and are greater for single-lawyer cases than for no-lawyer cases. Thus, even given the empirical reality that most divorcing parties have no legal representation, it is far more likely that parties have attorneys in contested cases.

The courts mandate mediation only in contested cases.[387] Because parties are usually represented in contested cases, mediated cases are particularly likely to involve parties with lawyers. A study of three urban domestic relations courts in Ohio indicated that in 247 contested custody cases, about ninety-five percent of the parties had lawyers.[388] In Maine, we estimate from docket records that eighty percent of all mediation cases involved two lawyers. Thus, the nature of selection into mandatory mediation insures that disproportionate numbers of cases involve counsel when compared to the total population of divorce cases. But not all do.

A system for insuring fairness that rests largely on the participation of lawyers, of course, would appear to fall short when parties are unrepresented. Clearly, when lawyers are not representing parties to mediation, they cannot be present to assist them and protect their rights. Although we lack research on this point, we suspect that problems of inequity in bargaining power would be more pronounced and the potential for unfairness greater in negotiations conducted in the absence of a mediator. The mediator can set ground rules, prevent interruption, serve as a drafter, and in other ways moderate the effects of aggressive negotiation on a weaker party. Thus, even weak mediation may be better than leaving the parties alone to work out a settlement, perhaps with one party negotiating, pro se, with the other party's lawyer.

In addition, the regular presence of lawyers in mediation sessions may provide training, education, and a regular check on inappropriate mediator conduct that may in turn improve the quality and fairness of mediation in cases where attorneys are not present. Lawyers might effectively contribute to a system of supervision and quality control of mediators that would be far more effective than rules and qualifications in rooting out ineffectiveness. As experienced users of many mediators, lawyers' confidential judgments of mediator competence could be a far better device for assessing quality than a collection of responses from divorcing parties who only have the one experience to judge.

Still, the research provides little guidance about whether the greater prospect of unfairness for pro se litigants argues in favor of giving those litigants an opportunity to "opt out" of mandatory mediation.[389] The pro se party who opts out would be left to his or her own devices. Because the most likely alternative to mediation is negotiation, those who opt out would presumably face negotiating with the other party's lawyer or directly with the other party. If they are not permitted to opt out, however, the "regulatory" approach is not likely to assure fair mediation. Furthermore, the regulation is likely to be costly for the bulk of the mediation parties who have lawyers. Thus, an "opt out" provision for pro se parties may be the best alternative for the present.

### 5. Is This "Real Mediation"?

To the divorce mediation traditionalists, lawyers attend judicially-hosted settlement conferences but not mediation sessions, and Maine mediation may thus seem more like facilitated pretrial settlement conferences and less like mediation sessions. These traditionalists may say that sessions involving lawyer participation do not constitute "real mediation."

What is meant by "real" in this context? If "real" references active participation by the divorcing parents, the research suggests that party participation can be maintained, even with lawyers present.[390] If "real" describes an opportunity for expression of emotions, there is also evidence that this occurs in Maine mediation.[391] If it describes an opportunity to listen, research indicates that this occurs in the largely joint sessions in Maine.[392] The same is true for a focus on the parties' interests,[393] for a problem-solving approach to negotiations,[394] and for opportunities for integrative solutions.[395] Settlement rates resemble those in programs where lawyer attendance is the exception. Over fifty percent of all Maine mediations result in settlement.[396] Two Florida counties in which parties typically have lawyers with them during mediation have settlement rates of seventy-five percent and sixty-nine percent; six Florida counties in which parties attend without lawyers in ninety percent or more of the cases have settlement rates of forty-nine percent, sixty-five percent, sixty-eight percent, sixty-eight percent, sixty-eight percent, and eighty-seven percent.[397] The agreements endure at least in the short term. In Maine, only one percent of the mediated agreements fail to survive long enough to become court judgments.[398] "Real" may also refer to confidentiality, and Maine mediation sessions are privileged.[399]

In short, divorce mediation involving lawyers resembles the mediation described in the literature,[400] with a few exceptions. First, mediation tends to take less time.[401] Second, "lawyer-participant" mediation sends fewer fees to mediators and more fees to lawyers, probably with approximately the same total expense by divorcing parents.[402] Third, mediators tend not to be lawyers or mental health professionals.[403] Fourth, there seem to be more assurances of fairness.[404]

Ultimately, the needs of divorcing families and the indicia of fairness in the process ought to be key factors in defining mediation procedures. Lawmakers should discard traditional mediation, even if it seems more "real" or satisfying to the mediator, if it fails to serve the families' needs or ensure fairness. The courts call upon mediators to serve these aims rather than to create satisfying professional goals for themselves. Thus, the value of the procedures should not depend on whether mediation professionals view them as producing "real mediation."

## CONCLUSION

Critics and proponents of mandatory divorce mediation recognize potential for unfairness in its use. They should also realize that the remedy is that lawyers should participate, along with their clients, in mandatory divorce mediation. Alternative approaches – the "voluntary participation" and "regulatory" approaches – are ineffective and costly. Furthermore, the assumptions underlying these dominant approaches are myths.

With lawyers present and participating, the concern for fairness no longer justifies heavy regulation or confining mediation to voluntary participants. Lawyer participation in the mediation sessions permits intervention on behalf of clients and buffers pressures to settle. Lawyers may also counsel clients to moderate extreme demands. In addition, once lawyers become accustomed to mediation, lawyer involvement in mandated mediation does not appear to prevent the meaningful participation of parties or inhibit emotional expression between spouses.[405]

With mediation covering a broad scope of issues and with lawyers in attendance, the parties probably will pay more for lawyers and less for mediators. Overall costs, however, will probably remain unchanged because settlements are more likely to be comprehensive and less likely to fall victim to negative reviews by a non-participating lawyer. In addition, mediation with lawyers may reduce discovery costs. What the parties will get is likely to be a fair process in which lawyers intervene to protect against pressures from the other party, the process, or the mediator. They are also likely to get a more spontaneous mediation, unfettered by a web of regulation or defensive mediators. They will enjoy, as compared with parties in a system without mandatory mediation, a greater likelihood of having the opportunity to express themselves and to listen to discussions regarding matters of utmost concern. About one-half the time, they can expect to secure a settlement earlier in the process than would otherwise be the case.

Bringing the lawyers into mandatory mediation will permit the repeal of numerous statutes and a reduction in court rules. Furthermore, it will ease fairness concerns as a reason not to compel participation in mediation. The revised regulatory approach preserves the widespread use and flexibility of the mediation process without undue risk of unfairness.

*Craig McEwen, M.A., Ph.D., is the Daniel B. Fayerweather Professor of Political Economy and Sociology and Senior Faculty Fellow in the Center for the Common Good at Bowdoin College in Maine.*

*Nancy Rogers, J.D., is Dean and Moritz Chair in Alternative Dispute Resolution at the Michael E. Moritz College of Law at Ohio State University.*

*Richard Maiman, Ph.D., is Professor of Political Science at the University of Southern Maine.*

**Notes**

¹     Commentators define mediation as a process in which a person not involved in a dispute helps the disputing parties negotiate a settlement. The mediator has no authority to issue a binding award in the event that the parties do not reach a settlement. Jay Folberg & Alison Taylor, Mediation 7-9 (1984); Nancy H. Rogers & Richard A. Salem, A Student's Guide to Mediation and the Law 3 (1987).

²     See Penelope E. Bryan, Killing Us Softly: Divorce Mediation and the Politics of Power, 40 Buff. L. Rev. 441, 441-46 (1992); Trina Grillo, The Mediation Alternative: Process Dangers For Women, 100 Yale L.J. 1545, 1547, 1549-51 (1991); see also Martha A. Fineman, The Illusion of Equality: The Rhetoric and Reality of Divorce Reform 144-46 (1991) (contending that mediation harms women because of its bias in favor of shared custody); Andre G. Gagnon, Ending Mandatory Divorce Mediation For Battered Women, 15 Harv. Women's L.J. 272, 272-73 (1992) (asserting that mediation puts battered women at risk for more abuse); Robert Geffner & Mildred D. Pagelow, Mediation and Child Custody Issues in Abusive Relationships, 8 Behav. Sci. L. 151 (1990) (arguing that mediation's premise of equal power between parties is false); Mary P. Treuthart, In Harm's Way? Family Mediation and the Role of the Attorney Advocate, 23 Golden Gate U. L. Rev. 717, 721-31 (1993) (asserting that the inequality inherent in our culture disadvantages women in mediation); Laurie Woods, Mediation: A Backlash to Women's Progress on Family Law Issues, 19 Clearinghouse Rev . 431, 435 -36 (1985) (arguing that mediation harms women, trivializes family law issues, and provides fewer safeguards for the parties than litigation).

³     Bryan, supra note 2, at 523; see also Woods, supra note 2, at 435 (arguing that mediation trivializes domestic disputes and removes legal protection for battered women).

⁴     Mandatory mediation programs currently operate in about one-eleventh of the nation's domestic relations courts. Jessica Pearson, Family Mediation, in National Symposium on Court-Connected Dispute Resolution Research 55, 55 (Susan Keilitz ed., 1994).

⁵     Bryan, supra note 2, at 523.

⁶     Grillo, supra note 2, at 1559.

⁷     See supra note 2 and accompanying text (citing critics who assert that mediation reinforces power differentials to the detriment of women).

⁸     For writings that generally find divorce mediation fair, see Florence Bienenfield , Child Custody Mediation: Techniques For Counselors, Attorneys and Parents 2-4 (1983); Thomas E. Carbonneau, Alternative Dispute Resolution: Melting the Lances and Dismounting the Steeds 170-72 (1989); O.J. Coogler, Structured Mediation in Divorce Settlement 1-2 (1978); Robert Coulson, Fighting Fair: Family Mediation Will Work for You 5-6 (1983); Stephen K. Erickson & Marilyn S.M. Erickson, Family Mediation Casebook: Theory and Process 1-5 (1988); John M. Haynes & Gretchen L. Haynes, Mediating Divorce: Casebook of Strategies for Successful Family Negotiations 13-16 (1989); Howard H. Irving, Divorce Mediation: A Rational Alternative to the Adversary System 22-26 (1980); Howard H. Irving & Michael Benjamin, Family Mediation: Theory and Practice of Dispute Resolution (1987); John A. Lemmon, Family Mediation Practice (1985); Lenard Marlow, Divorce and the Myth of Lawyers (1992); Donald T. Saposnek, Mediating Child Custody Disputes 17-22 (1983) [hereinafter Saposnek, Custody Disputes ]; Mary A. Duryee, Mandatory Mediation: Myth and Reality, 30 Fam. & Conciliation Cts. Rev. 507 (1992); W. Richard Evarts & Frances H. Goodwin, The Mediation and Adjudication of Divorce and Custody: From Contrasting Premises to Complementary Processes, 20 Idaho L. Rev . 277, 282-83 (1984); H. Jay Folberg, Divorce Mediation – A Workable Alternative, in Alternative Means of Family Dispute Resolution 11, 26-30 (1982); Joshua Rosenberg, In Defense of Mediation, 33 Ariz. L. Rev. 467, 487-91 (1991); Donald T. Saposnek, Clarifying Perspectives on Mandatory Mediation, 30 Fam. & Conciliation Cts. Rev . 490, 501 (1992) [hereinafter Saposnek, Mandatory Mediation]; Gary A. Weissman & Christine Leick, Mediation and Other Creative Alternatives to Litigating Family Law Issues, 61 N.D. L. Rev. 263, 279-80 (1985). See generally Stephen Goldberg et al., Dispute Resolution:

Negotiation, Mediation, and Other Processes 292-425 (2d ed. 1992) (collecting commentary on the fairness of mediation); Frank Gibbard & Fred Hartmeister, Mediation and Wyoming Domestic Relations Cases – Practical Considerations, Ethical Concerns and Proposed Standards of Practice, 27 Land & Water L. Rev. 435, 465-66 (1992) (concluding that mediation reduces acrimony between the parties and presents a beneficial alternative to litigation); Mark C. Rutherford, Lawyers and Divorce Mediation: Designing the Role of "Outside Counsel," Mediation Q., June 1986, at 17, 19-21 (discussing the benefits of mediation relative to litigation).

[9]     Richard A. Gardner, Family Evaluation in Child Custody Mediation, Arbitration, and Litigation 513-16 (1989); Diane Neumann, How Mediation Can Effectively Address the Male-Female Power Imbalance in Divorce, 9 Mediation Q .227, 238 (1992); Saposnek, Mandatory Mediation, supra note 8, at 491; Margaret L. Shaw, Mediator Qualifications: Report of a Symposium on Critical Issues in Alternative Dispute Resolution, 12 Seton Hall Legis. J. 125, 125-27 (1988); see also New York Law Revision Comm'n, Recommendation of the Law Revision Commission to the 1985 Legislature Relating to the Child Custody Decision-Making Process , reported in 19 Colum. J.L. & Soc. Probs . 105, 130 (1985) (recommending that the New York legislature adopt statewide standards for mediation); Thomas A. Bishop, Mediation Standards: An Ethical Safety Net, Mediation Q. , June 1984, at 5, 12 (advocating standard mediation settings); John A. Fiske, Divorce Mediation: An Attractive Alternative to Advocacy, 20 Suffolk U. L. Rev. 55, 62 (1986) (identifying minimum standards for divorce mediation); Rutherford, supra note 8, at 22-23 (arguing for the development of ethical standards).

[10]    For a list of statutes related to divorce mediation, see Nancy H. Rogers & Craig A. McEwen, Mediation: Law, Policy, Practice app. B (2d ed. 1994). For a review of the prevalence of domestic court mediation programs, see Linda R. Singer, Settling Disputes: Conflict Resolution in Business, Families, and the Legal System 37 (1990) (estimating 10% of domestic courts had mediation). For a review regarding Great Britain, see John M. Eekelaar & Robert Dingwall, The Development of Conciliation in England, in Divorce Mediation and the Legal Process 3-22 (Robert Dingwall & John Eekelaar eds., 1988) [hereinafter Divorce Mediation ]. For a review regarding Canada, see C. James Richardson, Court-Based Divorce Mediation in Four Canadian Cities: An Overview of Research Results 8-9, 15-19 (1988).

[11]    See infra part II.A (analyzing the "regulatory approach" to mediation).

[12]    See infra part II.B (discussing the "voluntary participation" approach to mediation).

[13]    Statutes employing this framework include Alaska, Michigan, and Wyoming. See Alaska Stat. s 25.24.140 (1991) (providing that the court may order the parties to engage in mediation if both parties agree); Mich. Comp. Laws Ann. s 552.513(1) (West 1993) (providing that the court may not require the parties to meet with a mediator); Wyo. Stat. s 1-43-101 (1994) (containing no provisions regarding mandated mediation or regulation of the mediation process). Often states do not specifically authorize voluntary mediation programs, presumably because there is no perceived need to regulate them.

[14]    See infra text accompanying notes 216-221 (discussing the "lawyers as spoilers" assumption).

[15]    See infra text accompanying notes 191-208 (discussing the "disappearing lawyer" assumption); infra text accompanying notes 222-234 (discussing the "mediation versus trial" assumption).

[16]    See infra text accompanying notes 209-215 (discussing the "mediation as monolith" assumption).

[17]    See infra note 243 and accompanying text (describing study of Maine divorce lawyers).

[18]    The National Center for State Courts in Williamsburg, Virginia, maintains a State ADR Program Database [hereinafter NCSC Database] that includes responses to standardized reporting forms of directors of approximately 1100 court-connected or court-referred dispute resolution programs in the United States. The Database is regularly updated. The data reported here were supplied to us in fall 1991 by Kenneth Pankey of the NCSC. All of the summaries of the data are based on our computations, not those of the NCSC.

[19]    See supra note 2 (citing sources).

²⁰   Patricia Vroom et al., Winning Through Mediation: Divorce Without Losers, in Alternative Means of Family Dispute Resolution 3, 4 (1982) ( "Mediation builds relationships, unlike the adversarial approach, which destroys them.").

²¹   John M. Haynes , Divorce Mediation 3 (1981).

²²   Id. at 5.

²³   Jay Folberg, A Mediation Overview: History and Dimensions of Practice, Mediation Q ., Sept. 1983, at 3, 10.

²⁴   Id.; see also Vroom et al., supra note 20, at 5-7 (noting growing support for mediation and its positive impact on the family).

²⁵   Considerable research reports that both men and women perceive mediation as fair. See, e.g., Jeanne A. Clement & Andrew I. Schwebel, A Research Agenda for Divorce Mediation: The Creation of Second Order Knowledge to Inform Legal Policy, 9 Ohio St. J. on Disp. Resol. 95, 98-99 (1993) (reporting high satisfaction rates from parties who participate in mediation); Jessica Pearson, The Equity of Divorce Mediation Agreements, 9 Mediation Q. 179, 191, (1991) (finding no evidence that women settling through mediation fared worse financially than those who settled without mediation, but noting difficulty in comparing outcomes). These perceptions might not reflect the actual outcomes.

²⁶   Grillo, supra note 2, at 1548-49.

²⁷   Id. at 1601-07; see also Bryan, supra note 2, at 481-98 (discussing how sex role ideology affects divorce mediation).

²⁸   See Bryan, supra note 2, at 491-93; Grillo, supra note 2.

²⁹   Bryan, supra note 2, at 446-98, 523; Grillo, supra note 2, at 1610.

³⁰   Fineman , supra note 2, at 146-48; Bryan, supra note 2, at 491-95.

³¹   Grillo, supra note 2, at 1570-72.

³²   Gagnon, supra note 2, at 291; Grillo, supra note 2, at 1610.

³³   E.g., Duryee, supra note 8, at 507-11, 513 -16; Rosenberg, supra note 8, at 467-73, 504 -06.

³⁴   Linda K. Girdner, Custody Mediation in the United States: Empowerment or Social Control, 3 Can. J. Women & L. 134, 152-54 (1989); see also Duryee, supra note 8, at 513 -15 (discussing training only).

³⁵   Rosenberg, supra note 8, at 473.

³⁶   Gardner , supra note 9, at 513 -16, 607; Ann Milne & Jay Folberg, The Theory and Practice of Divorce Mediation: An Overview, in Divorce Mediation: Theory and Practice 19-20 (Jay Folberg & Ann Milne eds., 1988); Neumann, supra note 9, at 231-32; Shaw, supra note 9, at 125.

³⁷   Jay Folberg, Divorce Mediation: Promises and Problems, in Goldberg et al. , supra note 8, at 308, 309-10.

³⁸   Gagnon, supra note 2, at 274; Geffner & Pagelow, supra note 2, at 155-157; Treuthart, supra note 2, at 719, 728-29; see also Robert H. Mnookin, Divorce Bargaining: The Limits on Private Ordering, 18 U. Mich. J.L. Ref. 1015, 1017 (1985) (posing questions designed to address bargaining imbalances).

³⁹   Saposnek , Custody Disputes , supra note 8, at 257-78.

⁴⁰   Gwynn Davis & Marian Roberts, Access to Agreement: A Consumer Study of Mediation in Family Dispute 74-75 (1988); Robert Dingwall, Empowerment or Enforcement? Some Questions About Power and Control in Divorce Mediation, in Divorce Mediation , supra note 10, at 150; Gagnon, supra note 2, at 274; Geffner & Pagelow, supra note 2, at 155-57; Girdner, supra note 34, at 152; Grillo, supra note 2, at 1593. But see Bryan, supra note 2, at 515 (asserting that parties will not reach a fair settlement in abuse cases unless monitored by the court).

⁴¹   Saposnek, Custody Disputes, supra note 8, at 118-34, 257-78. Some statutes require mediators to discuss or advocate the children's interests in mediation. Mnookin, supra note 38, at 1017.

⁴²   Examples of bargaining imbalances include different knowledge of finances, different experience in negotiation, and intimidation of one by the other. These differences are said to lead to

unfair apportionment of property and custody arrangements that favor one party. Folberg, supra note 8, at 12, 26; Treuthart, supra note 2, at 728-29.

43 Unfortunately, there is little agreement about how to define bargaining imbalances, identify them in practice, or understand the degree to which they relate to such characteristics as gender differences among parties in conflict. For example, Erickson and Erickson argue that power and power imbalances are largely in the eye of the beholder. Erickson & Erickson , supra note 8, 173-93.

44 For a critique of mediator neutrality, see Sara Cobb & Janet Rifkin, Practice and Paradox: Deconstructing Neutrality in Mediation, 16 Law & Soc. Inquiry 35, 36-39 (1991). For research on the mediator's influence, see Dingwall, supra note 40, at 166.

45 Bryan, supra note 2, at 523; Grillo, supra note 2, at 1610.

46 See Gagnon, supra note 2, at 286-87, 292.

47 See Rosenberg, supra note 8, at 487-88 (asserting that mediators are able to guide parties to an appropriate understanding of fairness).

48 See Marian Roberts, Mediation in Family Disputes 103-09 (1988); Stephen K. Erickson, The Legal Dimensions of Divorce Mediation, in Divorce Mediation: Theory and Practice , supra note 36, at 105, 106-07; Leonard L. Riskin, Toward New Standards for the Neutral Lawyer in Mediation, 26 Ariz. L. Rev. 329, 330 (1984); see also Margaret F. Brinig & Michael V. Alexeev, Trading at Divorce: Preferences, Legal Rules and Transactions Costs, 8 Ohio St. J. on Disp. Resol. 279, 292 (1993) (noting a distinction between what parties want and what the courts can provide).

49 Mnookin, supra note 38, at 1031-35; Saposnek, Mandatory Mediation, supra note 8, at 491-93.

50 See Woods, supra note 2, at 435-36.

51 Gardner , supra note 9, at 504; Girdner, supra note 34, at 141-42, 147-51.

52 For a challenge to the concepts of empowerment in mediation, see Jonathon G. Shailor, Empowerment in Dispute Mediation 135-36 (1994).

53 Gagnon, supra note 2, at 273.

54 Grillo, supra note 2, at 1597.

55 Erickson, supra note 48, at 106; Fiske, supra note 9, at 59; see also Diane Trombetta, Custody Evaluation and Custody Mediation: A Comparison of Two Dispute Interventions, in Therapists, Lawyers, and Divorcing Spouses 65, 69-70 (Esther O. Fisher & Mitchell S. Fisher eds., 1982) (discussing differences between the major tenets of mediation and other forms of intervention).

56 Similarly, if one demands complete equality between parties as a prerequisite for fairness – as some critics appear to – one must inevitably reject the fairness of mediation or negotiation. In reality, the parties to settlement have different values and priorities. For mediation advocates, this is a virtue. Gary J. Friedman & Margaret L. Anderson, Divorce Mediation's Strengths, in Divorce Mediation Readings 81, 81-82 (1985). In fact, it is the very existence of differing values and priorities that sometimes permits each to gain by settling. See, e.g., Haynes , supra note 21, at 5 (concluding that when a mediator focuses couples on ways to achieve individual goals, it is possible to achieve a win-win situation). To adopt this position one must of course assume that the alternative to mediation is legal advocacy and that legal advocates equalize the positions and resources of parties.

57 Susan L. Keilitz et al., Multi-State Assessment of Divorce Mediation and Traditional Court Processing 37 (1992); Pearson, supra note 4, at 73-76.

58 Pearson, supra note 25, at 191.

59 Bryan, supra note 2, at 519-20.

60 Woods, supra note 2, at 435. The presence of lawyers in mediation would not necessarily respond to Woods's other critique of mediation, namely that it "trivializes family law issues by relegating them to a lesser forum," one which "diminishes the public perception of the relative importance of laws addressing women's and children's rights ... by placing these rights outside society's key institutional system of dispute resolution – the legal system." Id.

[61]  Karla Fischer et al., The Culture of Battering and the Role of Mediation in Domestic Violence Cases, 46 S.M.U. L. Rev. 2117, 2153 (1993).

[62]  Robert H. Mnookin & Lewis Kornhauser, Bargaining in the Shadow of the Law: The Case of Divorce, 88 Yale L.J. 950, 968 (1992).

[63]  We do not distinguish between mandatory attendance at an introductory session or at mediation itself because the parties do not seem to perceive a distinction. Jeanne Clement et al., Descriptive Study of Children Whose Divorcing Parents Are Participating in Voluntary, Mandatory or No Custody/Visitation Mediation 16 (1993) (reporting that 82.4% of Columbus, Ohio, parties ordered to an assessment felt pressured to attend mediation).

[64]  Bryan, supra note 2, at 519-23; Woods, supra note 2, at 435. There is both research and commentary raising questions about the fairness and adequacy of lawyered negotiation outside of the divorce process. For example, research on negotiation of tort cases suggests that plaintiffs do better the more they participate in the process. Douglas Rosenthal , Lawyer and Client: Who's In Charge? 38-56 (1974). Similarly, clients lose control of their cases in the typical lawyer-to-lawyer negotiation, which excludes them. Stephen Bundy, The Policy in Favor of Settlement in an Adversary System, 44 Hastings L.J. 1, 46-47 (1992); Robert J. Condlin, Bargaining in the Dark: The Normative Incoherence of Lawyer Dispute Bargaining Role, 51 Md. L. Rev. 1, 29-30 (1991). These authors, however, simply point out that negotiation can be improved; they do not contend that negotiated settlements are less fair than adjudicated judgments.

[65]  E.g., Colo. Rev. Stat. s 14-10-129.5(1) (1987 & Supp. 1994); Fla. Stat. Ann. s 61.183 (West Supp. 1995) (effective Oct. 1, 1986); Iowa Code Ann. s 598.41(2) (West Supp. 1994) (enacted in 1984).

[66]  In 1986, California amended its statutes to require the California Judicial Council to adopt standards regarding equalization of power and safeguarding children's rights and interests and to provide special provisions for domestic violence cases. Cal. Fam. Code ss 3180-85 (West 1994). Colorado amended its statutes in 1992 to exclude domestic violence cases upon request and to deal with cases involving other situations of unfairness. Colo. Rev. Stat. s 13-22-311 (Supp. 1994). In 1992, the Florida Supreme Court adopted Rule 10.060 of its Rules for Certified and Court-Appointed Mediators dealing with power imbalance. Fla. R. for Certified & Court Appointed Mediators 10.060 [hereinafter Fla. Mediators R.]. The Indiana Supreme Court promulgated rules on alternative dispute resolution in 1992, giving mediators certain duties regarding fairness. Ind. R. Alt. Disp. Resol. 2.7(D). In 1986, the Iowa Supreme Court adopted rules requiring family mediators to assure a "balanced dialogue" and to assume other duties related to fairness. Iowa R. Prac. for Lawyer Mediators in Fam. Disp. 5(B) [hereinafter Iowa Mediator R.], reported in Iowa Code Ann. s 598 App. (West Supp. 1994). In Missouri, the rules of civil procedure deal with fairness in family mediation. Mo. R. Civ. P. 88.07(b). New Jersey also deals with fairness in the rules of civil procedure. N.J. R. Gen. Appl. 1:40-4(e). The Oklahoma Supreme Court, in 1989, adopted a Code of Professional Conduct for mediators, requiring mediators to end the mediation under certain circumstances related to fairness. Okla. R. & Proc. for Disp. Resol. Act app. A [hereinafter Okla. R. for Disp. Resol.], reported in Okla. Stat. Ann. tit. 12, s 37 app. (West 1993).

[67]  Seventeen states have mandatory mediation that is more heavily regulated than in other states, in an attempt to achieve fairness. The regulations and the states adopting them are listed in Appendix A, infra.

[68]  Cal. Fam. Code s 3182 (West 1994); Kan. Stat. Ann. s 23-603(a)(6) (West 1988); Wis. Stat. Ann. s 767.11(10)(a) (West 1993).

[69]  Ariz. Super. Ct. R. Local Prac., (Maricopa Cty.) R. 6.8(e), (Pima Cty.) R. 8.7, (Pinal Cty.) R. 4.2(4), (Yavapai Cty.) R. 10.2, reported in 17B Ariz. Rev. Stat. Ann. (West 1988).

[70]  Alaska Stat. s 25.24.060(c) (1991 & Supp. 1994); Del. Fam. Ct. Civ. R. 16; N.D. Cent. Code s 14-09.1-05 (1991).

[71]  Fla. Stat. Ann. s 44.1011(d) (West Supp. 1995).

[72] Data from the NCSC Database indicate that 14% of the programs reported lawyer participation in most mediation sessions. See NCSC Database, supra note 18. Sometimes lawyer attendance varies widely, even within a particular state. For example, in three Florida counties, attorneys attended the sessions in less than 10% of the cases, while in one county attorneys were present in 98% of the cases mediated. Jennifer L. Mason & Sharon B. Press, Florida Dispute Resolution Ctr., Florida Mediation/ Arbitration Programs: A Compendium 4-5 to 4-7 (1991).

[73] See infra text accompanying notes 216-221 (exploring the "lawyers as spoilers" assumption).

[74] Cal. Fam. Code s 3161 (West 1994) ("The purposes of the mediation proceeding are as follows: (a) To reduce acrimony that may exist between the parties, (b) To develop an agreement ... ."); La. Rev. Stat. Ann. s 9:352 (West 1991) (same); Minn. Stat. s 518.619(1) (1994) (same); N.C. Gen. Stat. s 50-13.1(b) (Supp. 1994) (instructing mediators to provide "nonadversarial setting that will facilitate ... cooperative resolution"); Wash. Rev. Code Ann. s 26.09.015(1) (West Supp. 1995) (asserting that mediation can reduce acrimony).

[75] Alaska Stat. s 25.24.060(c) (1991 & Supp. 1994); Del. Fam. Ct. Civ. R. 16; Fla. Stat. Ann . s 44.1011(d) (West Supp. 1995); N.D. Cent. Code s 14-09.1-05 (1991); Or. Rev. Stat. Ann. s 107.785(a) (Butterworth 1990).

[76] But see Penelope E. Bryan, Reclaiming Professionalism: The Lawyer's Role in Divorce Mediation, 28 Fam. L. Q . 177, 222 (1994). Professor Bryan argues that mediation "cools out" the lawyer, a phenomenon not confirmed by our research in Maine. See infra part IV.B (documenting lawyers' advocacy during mediation).

[77] See Gardner , supra note 9 at 513-16, 607; Gagnon, supra note 2, at 291-93; Neumann, supra note 9, at 231; Saposnek, Mandatory Mediation, supra note 8, at 491-92. See generally Edward F. Hartfield, Qualifications and Training Standards for Mediators of Environmental and Public Policy Disputes, 12 Seton Hall Legis. J. 109, 124 (1988) (concluding that personal qualifications, temperament, and personality may be the most significant aspects for consideration); Shaw, supra note 9, at 136 (concluding that guidelines for selecting and developing mediators should be measured in terms of human skills and demonstrated performance rather than technical or theoretical parameters).

[78] Fla. R. Civ. P. 1.740(f); Iowa Mediator R. , supra note 66, R. 6; Kan. Stat. Ann. s 23-603 (1988); La. Rev. Stat. Ann. s 9:353B (West 1991); Minn. Stat. s 518.619(7) (1994); Mo. R. Civ. P. 88.06(c); Neb. Rev. Stat. s 25-2913(6) (Supp. 1994); Nev. R. Prac. for 8th Dist. 5.70(c); N.D. Cent. Code s 14-09.1-07 (1991); Utah Code Ann. s 30-3-29(1) (Supp. 1994); Wis. Stat. Ann. s 767.11 (West 1993).

[79] Iowa Mediator R. , supra note 66, R. 4; Kan. Stat. Ann. s 23-603(a)(7) (1988).

[80] Cal. Standards of Jud. Admin. s 26(b), reported in Cal. Civ. R. app. (West Supp. 1994); Fla. Mediators R., supra note 66, R. 10.100; Iowa Mediator R. , supra note 66, R. 1; Kan. Stat. Ann. s 23-603 (1988); Mo. R. Civ. P. 88.06(a).

[81] Iowa Mediator R. , supra note 66, R. 5; Fla. Mediators R., supra note 66, R. 10.060.

[82] Cal. Standards of Jud. Admin. s 26(h), reported in Cal. Civ. R. app. (West Supp. 1994).

[83] Cal. Fam. Code s 3162(b)(3) (West 1994).

[84] Kan. Stat. Ann. s 23-604(b) (1988); see also Iowa Mediator R. , supra note 66, R. 1 (requiring mediator to terminate mediation if party or mediator cannot participate in good faith); Okla. R. for Disp. Resol., supra note 66, app. A at (B)(1)(e)(1) (requiring termination if continuation would cause harm or prejudice).

[85] Kan. Stat. Ann. s 23-604(b) (1988); Mo. R. Civ. P. 88.07(b); Neb. Rev. Stat. s 25-2913(4) (Supp. 1994); see also N.J. R. Gen. Appl. 1:40-4(e)(1) (providing circumstances when mediator should terminate mediation).

[86] Mo. R. Civ. P. 88.07(b); Neb. Rev. Stat. s 25-2913(4) (Supp. 1994).

[87] Cal. Fam. Code s 3180(b) (West 1994) ("The mediator shall use his or her best efforts to effect a settlement ... in the best interests of the child."); Iowa Mediator R., supra note 66, R. 3 (requiring that the mediator shall ensure that the parties "consider fully the best interests of any affected child"); Kan.

Stat. Ann. s 23-603(a)(8) (1988) (requiring that the mediator shall "ensure that the parties consider fully the best interests of the children").

[88]    Iowa Mediator R. , supra note 66, R. 1

[89]    Colo. Rev. Stat. s 13-22-305(6) (Supp. 1994); Fla. Stat. Ann. s 44.107 (West Supp. 1995).

[90]    Del. Super. Ct. Interim R. 16.2(f); Fla. Mediators R. , supra note 66, R. 10.220, R. 10.230.

[91]    Fla. Mediators R. , supra note 66, R. 10.240; N.H. Rev. Stat. Ann. s 328-C:7 (Supp. 1993).

[92]    Fla. Mediators R. , supra note 66, R. 10.240.

[93]    See Joseph B. Stulberg, The Theory and Practice of Mediation: A Reply to Professor Susskind, 6 Vt. L. Rev . 85, 91-97 (1981) (profiling mediator functions).

[94]    Robert A.B. Bush, The Dilemmas of Mediation Practice 30 (1992).

[95]    Cf. Gary Paquin, Protecting the Interests of Children in Divorce Mediation, 26 J. Fam. L. 279, 310 (1987- 88) ("[M]any private mediators usually never even see the children ....")

[96]    Alan J. Lerner & Frederick Lowe , Camelot (Chappell & Co., 1967).

[97]    See Barry R. Furrow et al., Health Law 163 (2d ed. 1991); Harvard Medical Practice Study, Patients, Doctors, and Lawyers: Medical Injury, Malpractice Litigation, and Patient Compensation in New York 9 -10 (1990).

[98]    Folberg, supra note 23, at 9-11; Pearson, supra note 4, at 61-65, 68-69.

[99]    Ngoh Tiong Tan, Developing and Testing a Family Mediation Assessment Instrument, Mediation Q. , Spring 1988, at 53, 55.

[100]    Gagnon, supra note 2, at 291- 92 ("If there is reason to believe that there is current physical abuse or that the women fears for her own or her children's safety due to a history of domestic abuse, mediation is not appropriate.").

[101]    Ariz. Rev. Stat. Ann. s 25 -381.23 (West 1991) (undue hardship); N.C. Gen Stat. s 50 -13.1(c) (Supp. 1994) (drug, alcohol, mental health, spousal abuser or neglect); Or. Rev. Stat. Ann. s 107.179(3) (Butterworth 1990) (emotional distress); Utah Code Ann . s 30 - 3 -22 (Supp. 1994) (undue hardship, abuse, substance abuse, and mental illness); Wis. Stat. Ann. s 767.11(8) (1993) (undue hardship); see also infra note 102 (citing statutes that exclude cases involving domestic abuse)

[102]    Colo. Rev. Stat. s 13 -22-311(1) (Supp. 1994) (excluding cases with domestic abuse); Fla. Stat. Ann. s 44.102(2)(b) (West Supp. 1995) (excluding case if significant history of violence would compromise mediation); La. Rev. Stat. Ann. tit. 9, s 363 (West Supp. 1995) (excluding case if court finds that family violence exists); Md. R. Spec. P. S73A(b)(2) (excluding case if there is genuine issue of physical or sexual abuse of party or child); Minn. Stat. s 518.619(2) (1994) (excluding cases with probable cause of domestic abuse); Nev. Rev. Stat. Ann. s 3.500(2)(b) (Michie Supp. 1993) (allowing exclusion of case with a showing of child abuse or domestic violence); N.J. R. Gen. Appl. 1.40 -5, -7; N.C. Gen. Stat. s 50 -13.1(c) (Supp. 1994) (excluding cases with allegations of party or child abuse); N.D. Cent. Code s 14 - 09.1- 02 (1991) (excluding case if issue of abuse); Ohio Rev. Code Ann. s 3109.052(A) (Anderson Supp. 1993) (providing that conviction or determination that parent perpetrated abusive act is a factor in deciding whether mediation is appropriate); Utah Code Ann. s 30 -3 -22 (Supp. 1994) (excluding case if mediation participation would cause undue hardship or threaten health or safety); see Fischer et al., supra note 61, at 2173; see also Desmond Ellis, Comment, Marital Conflict Mediation and Post-Separation Wife Abuse, 8 Law & Ineq. J. 317, 339 (1989 - 90) ("[M]ediation is inappropriate in the presence of pre-separation abuse and alcohol and/or drug abuse.").

[103]    David A. Lax & James K. Sebenius , The Manager as Negotiator 119 - 44 (1988).

[104]    Janet Rifkin et al., Toward A New Discourse for Mediation: A Critique of Neutrality, 9 Mediation Q. 151 (1991).

[105]    Michele Hermann et al. , The Metro Court Project Final Report 137-48 (1993).

[106]    Melvin Eisenberg, Private Ordering Through Negotiation: Dispute Settlement and Rulemaking, 89 Harv. L. Rev. 637, 638 - 65 (1976).

[107] For a discussion on power shifts during mediation sessions, see Albie Davis & Richard A. Salem, Dealing With Power Influences in Mediation of Interpersonal Disputes, Mediation Q. , Dec. 1984, at 17, 17.

[108] Okla. R. for Disp. Resol. , supra note 66, R. 8B; Wis. Stat. Ann. s 767.11(8)(b) (West 1993).

[109] N.C. Gen. Stat. s 50 -13.1(c) (Supp. 1994) (allowing waiver of mandatory mediation for "good cause," including "undue hardship," allegations of substance or family abuse, or emotional problems); Or. Rev. Stat. Ann. s 107.179 (Butterworth 1990) (permitting waiver if court "finds that participation ... will subject the party to severe emotional distress"); Utah Code Ann. s 30 -3 -22(1) (Supp. 1994) (permitting waiver if attendance would pose a threat to mental or physical health or safety); Wis. Stat. Ann. s 767.11(8) (West 1993) (permitting court to waive attendance if it would cause "undue hardship" or "endanger the health or safety" of a party).

[110] Maine Court Mediation Serv., Mediation in Cases of Domestic Abuse: Helpful Option or Unacceptable Risks, The Final Report of the Domestic Abuse and Mediation Project 26 -29 (1992) (relating experience about reluctance of victims to reveal abuse); Clement et al. , supra note 63, at 20 -21 (discussing research about differences between allegations in pleadings and statements to court personnel).

[111] Clement et al. , supra note 63, at 20 -21.

[112] Id.

[113] One study found that in Alaska, in 61% of eligible cases, one divorcing party said in an interview that violence had occurred. Susanne D. DiPietro, Alaska Child Visitation Mediation Pilot Project, Report to the Alaska Legislature i (1992).

[114] Minn. Stat. s 518.619(2) (1994) (requiring probable cause that abuse occurred); Ohio Rev. Code Ann. s 3109.052(A) (Anderson Supp. 1993) (requiring conviction or determination in another proceeding).

[115] Cal. Fam. Code s 3181(a) (West 1994).

[116] Minn. Stat. s 518.619 (1994).

[117] La. Rev. Stat. Ann. s 9:363 (West Supp. 1995)

[118] Ohio Rev. Code Ann. s 3109.052(A) (Anderson Supp. 1993).

[119] Clement et al. , supra note 63, at 20-21.

[120] See DiPietro , supra note 113, at i-ii (reporting that, as the result of various exclusions, only 20 cases of a potential 475 cases screened and 125 cases deemed eligible for mediation services actually reached mediation; domestic violence allegations excluded 61%, despite statements by victims that they wanted to try mediation).

[121] Pearson, supra note 4, at 71 (citing Charlene E. Depner et al., Building a Uniform Statistical Report System: A Snapshot of California Family Court Services, 1989 Fam. Conciliation Cts. Rev. 30).

[122] Fischer et al., supra note 61, at 2153.

[123] Linda Girdner, Mediation Triage: Screening for Spouse Abuse in Divorce Mediation, 7 Mediation Q. 365, 376 (1990).

[124] Fischer et al., supra note 61, at 2155.

[125] Telephone Interview with Jessica Shimberg, Director of Mediation, Franklin County Common Pleas Court, Domestic Relations Division (Mar. 4, 1994).

[126] Telephone Interview with Michele McFarland, Director of Mediation Services, Lucas County Common Pleas Court (Mar. 4, 1994).

[127] Bryan, supra note 2, at 496 - 97; Gagnon, supra note 2, at 292.

[128] See Ann Milne, Mediation -- A Promising Alternative for Family Courts, 1991 Juv. & Fam. Cts. J. 61, 68.

[129] Bryan, supra note 2, at 449; Treuthart, supra note 2, at 735-36, 752.

[130] Singer , supra note 10, at 42.

[131] Appendix A pt. D and Appendix B pt. D list 27 statutes of this type. See Cal. Fam. Code s 3170 (West 1994); Md. R. Spec. P. S73A(c)(2); Mich. Comp. Laws Ann. s 552.531 (West Supp. 1994); Mo. R. Civ. P. 88.03; Nev. Rev. Stat. Ann. s 3.500(2)(a) (Michie Supp. 1993); N.C. Gen. Stat. s 50 - 13.1(b) (Supp. 1994); Or. Rev. Stat. Ann. ss 107.179, 107.765(1) (Butterworth 1990) (requiring written approval of parties or counsel); S.D. Codified Laws Ann. s 25 - 4 -56 (Supp. 1994); Utah Code Ann. s 30 -3 -25 (Supp. 1994) (permitting mediation of property division if related to custody); Wis. Stat. Ann. s 767.11(9) (West 1993) (limiting issues mediated unless parties agree in writing to broaden issues); see also Ohio Rev. Code Ann. s 3109.052 (Anderson Supp. 1993) ("[T]he court may order parents to mediate ...."). But see Minn. R. Gen. Practice 310.04 (allowing mediator to address all issues unless limited by court order); N.D. Cent. Code ss 14 - 09.1- 01, - 02 (1991) (allowing mediation to include support).

[132] Cal. Fam. Code s 20034 (West 1994); Mich. Ct. Spec. Proc. R. 3.211.

[133] Severing issues, even if possible, may not be a good idea, inasmuch as "simultaneous exploration of custody and financial matters significantly increases the total number of potential solutions available." Irving & Benjamin , supra note 8, at 134.

[134] Folberg, supra note 8, at 33-34.

[135] See generally Susan Myers et al., Court-Sponsored Mediation of Divorce, Custody, Visitation and Support: Resolving Policy Issues, 13 State Ct. J. 24 (1989) (indicating custody issues are commonly discussed despite statutory prohibitions).

[136] Irving & Benjamin , supra note 8, at 134; Folberg, supra note 8, at 33 -34 ("As much as we would like to romanticize parenting and separate children's needs from the financial needs of parents, we know that custody and the attendant financial arrangements represent some trade offs in the minds of the divorcing parties that we can only pretend to keep separate.").

[137] Grillo, supra note 2, at 1571; see also Bryan, supra note 2, at 492 (discussing how mediators' assumptions that husband and wife are equal gives men an advantage in the custody process).

[138] Eleanor Maccoby & Robert Mnookin, Dividing the Child 273 (1992).

[139] Pearson, supra note 4, at 20.

[140] John P. McCrory, Legal and Practical Issues in Divorce Mediation: An American Perspective, in The Role of Mediation in Divorce Proceedings: A Comparative Perspective 142, 150 -52 (Vermont Law Sch. Dispute Resolution Project ed., 1987).

[141] Craig A. McEwen et al., Lawyers, Mediation and the Management of Divorce Practice, 28 Law & Soc'y Rev. 149, 181 (1994) (analyzing data collected by the National Center for State Courts).

[142] Id.

[143] Anthony Ogus et al., Report to the Lord Chancellor on the Costs and Effectiveness of Conciliation in England and Wales 219, 264, 385 (Conciliation Project Unit, Univ. of Newcastle Upon Tyne 1989).

[144] Id. at 264, 385C; Richardson , supra note 10, at 45.

[145] California, for example, provided that the mediator could be an employee of the court, probation department, mental health agency, or any other person designated by the court. Cal. Fam. Code s 3164 (West 1994) (formerly Cal. Civ. Code s 4607 (effective 1980)).

[146] See Gardner , supra note 9, at 513 -26 (discussing disadvantages of mediation).

[147] See infra Appendix A pt. A (listing statutes).

[148] Cal. Fam. Code ss 1815, 3155 (West 1994); Fla. Mediators R. , supra note 66, R. 10.010(b); Idaho R. Civ. P. 16(j)(6); La. Civ. Code Ann. art 9, s 356 (West 1991) (permitting experience as substitute); Mo. R. Civ. Proc. 88.05; N.J. R. Gen. Appl. 1:40 -20 (experience may sometimes substitute); N.C. Gen. Stat. s 7A- 494(c) (1994); Utah Code Ann. s 30 -3 -27 (West Supp. 1994).

[149] Fla. Mediators R. , supra note 66, R. 10.010(b) (master's or higher in behavioral sciences, or a physician, lawyer, or accountant); La. Civ. Code Ann. art. 9, s 356 (West 1991) (attorney, master's in counseling, social work); Mich. Comp. Laws Ann. s 552.513(4) (West 1988 & Supp. 1994) (psychologist, master's in counseling, social work, behavioral science, attorney, or five years of experience); Mo. R.

Civ. P. 88.05 (graduate degree in behavioral science, attorney); N.J. R. Gen. Appl. 1:40 -10 (master's in behavioral science or other training or experience); N.C. Gen. Stat. s 7A- 494(c) (1994) (master's degree in human relations discipline); Utah Code Ann . s 30 -3 -27 (Supp. 1994) (psychiatrist, social worker, family therapist, attorney).

[150]    Cal. Standards of Jud. Admin. s 26(b), reported in Cal. Civ. R. app. (West Supp. 1994); Del. Super. Ct. Interim R. 16.2(g) (25 hours); Fla. Mediators R. , supra note 66, R. 10.010(b) (40 hours in program certified by court); Ind. R. Alt. Disp. Resol. 2.5 (40 hours); Mich. Comp. Laws Ann. s 552.513(4) (West 1988 & Supp. 1994) (40 hours); Minn. Stat. s 518.619(4) (1994) (40 hours); Neb. Rev. Stat. s 43 -2905(1) (1993) (60 hours); N.H. Rev. Stat. Ann. s 328 -C:5 (Supp. 1993) (48 hours and 20 hours in internship); N.C. Gen. Stat. s 7A- 494(c)(2) (1994) (40 hours in program approved by court); Ohio R. Super. Ct. C.P. 81 (40 hours); Tex. Civ. Prac. & Rem. Code s 154.052 (West Supp. 1995) (40 hours); Utah Code Ann. s 30 -3 -27 (Supp. 1994) (40 hours); Wis. Stat. Ann. s 767.11(4) (West 1993) (25 hours).

[151]    Okla. R. for Disp. Resol. , supra note 66, R. 11B.1.

[152]    Test Design Project, Interim Guidelines for Selecting Mediators 1-2 (1993). For a series of articles critiquing the guidelines, see 9 Negotiation J. 309 -53 (1993).

[153]    See Gardner , supra note 9, at 504.

[154]    Cf. Gagnon, supra note 2, at 292 (advocating ending mandatory divorce mediation for domestically abused women).

[155]    Jessica Pearson & Nancy Thoennes, Divorce Mediation Research Results, in Divorce Mediation: Theory and Practice , supra note 36, at 429, 435-41 (comparing lawyers and mental health professionals); see also Singer, supra note 10, at 41 (finding no evidence tying mediators' educational qualifications to performance).

[156]    But see Gardner , supra note 9, at 522-23 (asserting that many years of professional experience make a difference).

[157]    Commission on Qualifications, Society of Professionals in Dispute Resolution, Qualifying Neutrals: The Basic Principles 9 (1989); Test Design Project , supra note 152, at 5-6; see also Singer , supra note 10, at 41 (suggesting familiarity with divorce law and basic counseling techniques as primary qualifications).

[158]    Fineman , supra note 2, at 145-47; Gardner , supra note 9, at 524 (warning against mental health professionals with a classical psychoanalytical orientation as custody mediators); Bryan, supra note 2, at 490; David Greatbatch & Robert Dingwall, Selective Facilitation: Some Preliminary Observations on a Strategy Used by Divorce Mediators, 23 Law & Soc'y Rev. 613, 613-16 (1989); Marian Roberts, Systems or Selves? Some Ethical Issues in Family Mediation, 1990 J. Soc. Welfare L. 6, 14.

[159]    Commission on Qualifications , supra note 157, at 5.

[160]    Telephone Interview with Sharon Press, Director, Florida Dispute Resolution Center, Florida Supreme Court (May 10, 1993).

[161]    Telephone Interview with Paul Charbonneau, Director, Court Mediation Services, Augusta, Maine (Mar. 8, 1994).

[162]    For an analogy to social worker regulation, see David A. Hardcastle, Public Regulation of Social Work, 22 Soc. Work 14, 19 (1977).

[163]    For example, some qualifications may affect settlement rates or public perception of programs.

[164]    E.g., Unif. Marriage and Divorce Act s 306(a)-(c), 9A U.L.A. 216-17 (1987).

[165]    La. Civ. Code Ann. art. 9, s 353 (West 1991); Wis. Stat. Ann. s 767.11(12) (West 1993).

[166]    Bryan, supra note 2, at 519; Folberg, supra note 8, at 24; Mnookin & Kornhauser, supra note 62, at 993 ; Pearson, supra note 25, at 194.

[167]    Mnookin & Kornhauser, supra note 62, at 993.

[168]    Pearson, supra note 25, at 194.

[169]    Rutherford, supra note 8, at 24.

[170]  See generally Bryan, supra note 2, at 515-19 (discussing this dilemma).

[171]  Boston Bar Ass'n, Op. 78 -1 (1979), reprinted in 5 Fam. L. Rep. (BNA) 2606-07 (May 29, 1979).

[172]  Stephen K. Erickson & Marilyn S. McKnight, Divorce Mediation: Strategies For Breaking Impasse, in ABA Options For All Ages, Family Dispute Resolution 55, 58 (Velitta F. Prather ed., 1990).

[173]  This process is in place in San Francisco and 32 other California counties. Cal. Fam. Code ss 3163, 4351(f) (West 1994) (providing authority for local court rules). One commentator suggests that Massachusetts probate courts follow this procedure as a matter of practice. Gagnon, supra note 2, at 279.

[174]  Grillo, supra note 2, at 1554-55.

[175]  Center for Dispute Resolution & The Institute of Judicial Administration, National Standards for Court-Connected Mediation Programs Recommendation 9.4 (1992); Society of Professionals in Dispute Resolution, Mandated Participation and Settlement Coercion: Dispute Resolution as it Relates to the Courts Recommendation 3, at 16-17 (1991).

[176]  Minn. Stat . s 518.619(6) (1994) (unless parties agree otherwise); N.D. Cent. Code s 14 - 09.1-08 (1991); Ohio Rev. Code Ann. s 3109.052(B) (Anderson Supp. 1993); Or. Rev. Stat. Ann. s 107.765(2) (Butterworth 1990).

[177]  See supra note 176 (citing statutes).

[178]  Cobb & Rifkin, supra note 44, at 60-62; Greatbatch & Dingwall, supra note 158, at 614-16.

[179]  Gagnon, supra note 2, at 291; Geffner & Pagelow, supra note 2, at 157; Treuthart, supra note 2, at 777 (arguing that mandatory mediation is a "contradiction in terms").

[180]  See supra text accompanying notes 103-107 (discussing the difficulty of predicting when lawyer's presence is necessary to protect party).

[181]  The New Hampshire lawyers interviewed were as likely as Maine lawyers to report that their clients negotiated some part of the divorce agreement. Divorce Lawyer Interview Data, infra note 243; see also Howard S. Erlanger et al., Participation and Flexibility in Informal Processes: Cautions From the Divorce Context, 21 Law & Soc'y Rev. 585 (1987) (critiquing informal divorce settlement).

[182]  Lawyers whose clients were generally upper middle class were far less likely to report that their clients frequently did most of the negotiating (9%) while those with a range of clients or largely working class clients reported more often that clients frequently did most of the negotiating (25%). Divorce Lawyer Interview Data, infra note 243.

[183]  For example, in commenting on what went on at mediation a handful of lawyers interviewed in connection with the authors' research noted observations such as the following: "But then there are some things, if they're talking about visitation times, if they're talking about dividing up the personalty, I don't need to be there for that." Interviews, infra note 243, No. 28. "What's a lawyer going to do with pots and pans? Why should a lawyer get involved whether it's Friday at five or Sunday at six? That's ridiculous, I mean clients aren't babies." Id. No. 29. See also infra note 244 (presenting percentages of representation in New Hampshire cases).

[184]  We found, for example, that those New Hampshire attorneys we interviewed who expressed an interest in the potential of mediation generally viewed it either as an alternative for potential clients to lawyer representation or as an adjunct to representation where parties could be sent on their own to work out these "pots and pans" issues, including visitation. Typical New Hampshire lawyers who worked with a voluntary, private system of divorce mediation were two who observed: "The only time I encouraged them to do mediation is on the issue of visitation." Interviews, infra note 243, No. 112. "Not on the financial aspects. I don't mind, too much, mediation in terms of visitation or mediation in terms of personal property." Id. No. 133.

[185]  Clement et al. , supra note 63, at 17.

[186]  Jessica Pearson, An Evaluation of Alternatives to Court Adjudication, 7 Just. Sys. J. 420, 426 -29 (1982).

[187]  Pearson & Thoennes, supra note 155, at 431.

[188]  DiPietro , supra note 113, at ii.

[189]  See infra text accompanying notes 329-354 (comparing mediation with negotiation).

[190]  See supra part II.B (discussing the "voluntary participation" approach).

[191]  Erickson & Erickson , supra note 8, at 173; Gardner , supra note 9, at 504-05; Irving , supra note 8, at 83; Bryan, supra note 2, at 515 -19; Folberg, supra note 8, at 11, 13; Geffner & Pagelow, supra note 2, at 156; Grillo, supra note 2, at 1581.

[192]  Rosenberg, supra note 8, at 500.

[193]  Gary J. Friedman , A Guide to Divorce Mediation 67-293 (1993) ; Haynes & Haynes , supra note 8; Irving & Benjamin , supra note 8, at 79-111; Janet R. Johnston & Linda E.G. Campbell, Impasses of Divorce: The Dynamics and Resolution of Family Conflict 198-244 (1988); Marlow , supra note 8, at 144-50.

[194]  See Marlow , supra note 8; Victoria Solomon, Divorce Mediation: A New Solution to Old Problems, 16 Akron L. Rev. 665, 669 -70 (1983); Weissman & Leick, supra note 8, at 266-67.

[195]  Coogler , supra note 8, at 91.

[196]  Id.

[197]  Rutherford, supra note 8, at 23 -34.

[198]  See, e.g., Cal. Fam. Code s 3182 (West 1994); Fla. R. Civ. P. 1.720(d); Kan. Stat. Ann. s 23 - 603(a)(6) (1988); Wis. Stat. Ann. s 767.11(10)(a) (West 1993); see also text accompanying notes 68-72 (discussing limited role for lawyers).

[199]  Alaska, Delaware, and North Dakota prohibit exclusion of lawyers from divorce mediation sessions. Alaska Stat. s 25.24.060(c) (1991); Del. Fam. Ct. Civ. R. 16(b)(1); N.D. Cent. Code s 14 - 09.1- 05 (1991). A report of The Society of Professionals in Dispute Resolution has recommended against exclusion. Society of Professionals in Dispute Resolution , supra note 175, at 2-3, 18.

[200]  NCSC Database, supra note 18.

[201]  Among the critics, see Fineman , supra note 2; Bryan, supra note 2; Fischer et al., supra note 61, at 2117, 2172 (asserting that excluding lawyers increases unfairness in domestic violence cases); Grillo, supra note 2; M. Laurie Leitch, The Politics of Compromise: A Feminist Perspective on Mediation, Mediation Q. , Winter 1986/Spring 1987, at 163; Woods, supra note 2, at 435. Among the proponents, see Joan Blades, Family Mediation: Cooperative Divorce Settlement 50 (1985); Coogler , supra note 8, at 23 -38; Haynes & Haynes , supra note 8; Michelle Deis, California's Answer: Mandatory Mediation of Child Custody and Visitation Disputes, 1 Ohio St. J. on Disp. Resol .149, 152-55; Milne & Folberg, supra note 36, at 6 - 9; Rosenberg, supra note 8; Saposnek, Mandatory Mediation, supra note 8.

One of the reasons for the presumption that lawyers will be absent has been the preoccupation with private, voluntary mediation. According to Kelly's and Gigy's study of private divorce mediation clients, 81% went to mediation in order to "reduce contact with lawyers and court." Joan B. Kelly & Lynn L. Gigy, Divorce Mediation: Characteristics of Clients and Outcomes, in Mediation Research 263, 270 (Kenneth Kressel et al. eds., 1989). As states have turned to public, mandatory mediation, these presumptions have turned up variously in policies and policy discussions of the proper role of lawyers in mediation. Some of the myths of mediation have developed out of and in response to the early marketing of private, voluntary, attorney-free divorce mediation as a better way to handle divorces than adversarial processes.

[202]  E.g., Pearson & Thoennes, supra note 155 (discussing results of two major research projects).

[203]  Peggy Clausen et al., Divorce American Style, Newsweek , Jan. 10, 1983, at 42, 45. But see Ted Gest, Divorce: How the Game Is Played Now, U.S. News & World Rep. , Nov. 21, 1983, at 39, 41 ("[M]ediation does not necessarily save money, because couples are advised to hire their own attorneys on top of paying the mediator.").

[204]  See Blades, supra note 201, at 50, 238 (mentioning lawyers also participate in exceptional cases); Coogler, supra note 8, at 27-28; Erickson & Erickson, supra note 8, at 129; Milne & Folberg, supra note 36, at 13-15; Saposnek, Mandatory Mediation, supra note 8. Several of these authors, however, note the potential value of lawyer participation in mediation, in cases that have reached impasse.

[205]  Lemmon, supra note 8, at 107-08.

[206]  See Martha Fineman, Dominant Discourse, Professional Language, and Legal Change in Child Custody Decision-Making, 101 Harv. L. Rev. 727, 774 (1988); Woods, supra note 2, at 435. In a recent article, Professor Bryan urges lawyers to participate in mediation for "high risk clients." Bryan, supra note 76, at 208.

[207]  Bryan, supra note 2, at 443-44.

[208]  Grillo, supra note 2, at 1609.

[209]  See Gardner, supra note 9, at 503 - 04; Bryan, supra note 2, at 447- 48; Evarts & Goodwin, supra note 8, at 279 - 80; Geffner & Pagelow, supra note 2, at 155 -56; Grillo, supra note 2, at 1547-51, 1610.

[210]  Bryan, supra note 2, at 447- 48; Grillo, supra note 2, at 1551-55.

[211]  Grillo, supra note 2, at 1551-55. For a criticism of Professor Grillo on this point, see Duryee, supra note 8, at 513. See generally supra notes 173-176 and accompanying text (discussing Grillo's criticism of California domestic relations courts).

[212]  Bryan supra note 2, at 491; Fineman, supra note 206, at 765-66, 774.

[213]  Maccoby & Mnookin, supra note 138, at 290; Pearson, supra note 4, at 67

[214]  Approximately 1250 mediators who are members of the Academy of Family Mediators are attorneys. Telephone Interview with Linda Wilkerson, Executive Director, Academy of Family Mediators (Mar. 18, 1994).

[215]  Girdner, supra note 34, at 152-55; Hugh McIsaac, Reducing the Pain of a Child Custody Struggle, 14 Fam. Advoc. 26, 29, 56 (1992); Rosenberg, supra note 8, at 469-70.

[216]  Gardner, supra note 9, at 51 -15; Marlow, supra note 8, at 69-80.

[217]  Rosenberg, supra note 8, at 500. But see Saposnek, Mandatory Mediation, supra note 8, at 496 (indicating a change in his views to favor greater involvement of lawyers in family mediation).

[218]  Carbonneau, supra note 8, at 174.

[219]  See Sheila D. Isbell, The Attorney's Role in Mediation and Conciliation of Domestic Disputes: An Overview, 12 Law & Psychol. Rev .167, 169 (1988).

[220]  Bryan, supra note 2, at 445 n.7; Grillo, supra note 2, at 1548 (extolling party control in decision making).

[221]  But see Bryan, supra note 76, at 208; Grillo, supra note 2, at 1597-1600 (discussing exceptions).

[222]  Bryan, supra note 2, at 445 n.8.

[223]  Blades, supra note 201, at 10.

[224]  David B. Chandler, Violence, Fear, and Communication: The Variable Impact of Domestic Violence Mediation, 7 Mediation Q. 331, 332 (1990).

[225]  Folberg, supra note 8, at 12 ("Divorce mediation ... has been proposed as an alternative to traditional judicial intervention and divorce litigation."); Weissman & Leick, supra note 8, at 268-69; Terri Garner, Comment, Child Custody Mediation: An Alternative To Litigation, 1989 J. Disp. Resol. 138, 148-49.

[226]  Grillo, supra note 2, at 1588-90; Rosenberg, supra note 8, at 488-89.

[227]  Marlow, supra note 8, at 174; Diane Neumann, Divorce Mediation 49 (1989).

[228]  Grillo, supra note 2, at 1559.

[229]  Rogers & McEwen, supra note 10, s 7:01.

[230]  Cal. Fam. Code s 3161 (West 1994).

[231] Fiske, supra note 9, at 57-61; Jay Folberg, Mediation of Child Custody Disputes, 19 Colum. J.L. & Soc. Probs. 413, 419-21 (1985); Rosenberg, supra note 8, at 471-74.

[232] Bienenfield , supra note 8, at 155; Gardner , supra note 9, at 508-12; Rutherford, supra note 8, at 19-21; Weissman & Leick, supra note 8, at 279.

[233] Deis, supra note 201, at 161, 163.

[234] See Evarts & Goodwin, supra note 8, at 295-97 (discussing the role of lawyers as negotiators).

[319] Galanter makes a similar point about alternative dispute resolution generally. Marc Galanter, Compared to What? Assessing the Quality of Dispute Processing, 66 Denv. U. L. Rev. xi, xiii-xiv (1989).

[320] It should be noted that mediation may provide important, if imperfect, protections for unrepresented parties who otherwise would negotiate on their own or, for the pro se party, who would face a represented spouse in negotiation. See infra part V.C.4 (discussing unrepresented parties).

[321] But see Chandler, supra note 224, at 344 (reporting findings that women who reported spouse abuse did not enter unfair agreements). In an Ohio study, women who reported domestic violence settled at about the same rate as those who did not and were no more likely to report pressure to settle. Furthermore, settlement rates for those reporting violence were slightly lower in mediation than in negotiation without mediation. Clement et al. , supra note 63, at 20-21.

[322] There are, however, sometimes concerns or fear simply as a result of the meeting, but arguably this can be handled by separate sessions.

[323] Cf. Geffner & Pagelow, supra note 2, at 155-157 (arguing that ineffective assistance of counsel often disadvantages battered women in the mediation process).

[324] Treuthart, supra note 2, at 726 (arguing mediation fails to hold an abuser accountable for his actions).

[325] Clement et al. , supra note 63, at 20.

[326] There may be reasons for qualifications apart from fairness concerns, such as enhancing the acceptance of a program. These are beyond the scope of this Article.

[327] See supra part II.B (discussing the "voluntary participation" approach to mediation).

[328] Bryan, supra note 76, at 208.

[329] See infra text accompanying notes 330-354 (setting forth lawyers' descriptions of their experiences with mediation).

[330] For a similar assertion on regular civil cases, see Herbert M. Kritzer, Let's Make a Deal: Understanding the Negotiation Process in Ordinary Litigation 30-41 (1991).

[331] Interviews, supra note 243, No. 227.

[332] Id. No. 216.

[333] Id. No. 209.

[334] Id. No. 17.

[335] Id. No. 201.

[336] Judith Ryan, Mediator Strategies for Lawyers, 30 Fam. & Conciliation Cts. Rev. 364, 364-69 (1992).

[337] Interviews, supra note 243, No. 10.

[338] Divorce Lawyer Interview Data, supra note 243.

[339] Interviews, supra note 243, No. 26.

[340] Id. No. 209.

[341] In addition, attorneys report learning more from and about their own clients through the mediation process:

[Mediation] gives you an opportunity to evaluate the other party as to whether they're going to be a good or a bad client and also to see whether or not there are some things that your client has not told you about. You sit down, your client has said, "Well, it's going to be this, that or the other," and all of a sudden, here's the other party saying, "Well, how about the John Deere tractor," you know .... And you turn to your client and say, "Let's step outside. What's this all about?" Id. No. 2. According to another attorney, "[I]t's amazing what comes out at mediation. I mean, I get surprises at mediation when clients divulge things that I had no idea were there ...." Id. No. 44.

Factual information about her client's case is not the only potential byproduct of mediation for a lawyer. A divorce attorney can also evaluate a client's potential as a witness at trial:

[Mediation] sometimes gives me the first opportunity to see how my client reacts, not in court, but in court-like situations, where the client is confronted with the other party and the other attorney and the mediator. So it gives me a barometer of the client's possible reaction if we do litigate. Id. No. 222. Maine lawyers perceive mediation as providing a context to learn more about their own clients as well as about the other party with the result that they can better advise about settlement possibilities and about the likelihood of success in a contested hearing.

[342]    Id. No. 203.

[343]    See, e.g., Roger Fisher & William Ury, Getting to Yes: Negotiating Agreement Without Giving In 40-55 (1991) (asserting that effective negotiation focuses on interests); Roy J. Lewicki & Joseph A. Litterer, Negotiation 69-71 (1985) (explaining that information about an opponent's objectives and needs is crucial to the formulation of a successful negotiation strategy).

[344]    Erlanger et al., supra note 181, at 590-96.

[345]    Professor Grillo has suggested that anger is best expressed through the lawyer as surrogate or "mouthpiece." Grillo, supra note 2, at 1573 ("The parties' anger is expressed in a formal, contained way through the ritualized behavior of the lawyers."). Neither the typical divorce trial nor the even more typical divorce negotiation, however, provides much room for the lawyer to deliver for the client. Few avenues exist in negotiation – except nasty letters – because a lawyer cannot talk directly with the other spouse if he or she is represented. In addition, our interviews suggest that divorce lawyers generally try to resist voicing client anger themselves because it diminishes their ability to be "reasonable lawyers."

Moreover, attorneys often discourage the expression of anger even in the privacy of their own offices. For example, lawyers frequently point out that they cannot do anything about the client's feelings and that each emotional outburst costs the client considerable money in lawyer's fees.

Under these circumstances, mediation provides a more likely outlet for expression of anger than either trial or negotiation.

[346]    Interviews, supra note 243, No. 28.

[347]    Id. No. 21.

[348]    Id. No. 225.

[349]    Id. No. 218.

[350]    Id. No. 41

[351]    Id. No. 4.

[352]    See e.g., E. Allan Lind & Tom R. Tyler, The Social Psychology of Procedural Justice 101- 06 (1988) (arguing, generally, that the opportunity to speak enhances one's experience of procedural fairness); E. Allan Lind et al., In the Eye of the Beholder: Tort Litigants' Evaluations of Their Experiences in the Civil Justice System, 24 Law & Soc'y Rev. 953, 980-983 (1990) (asserting that procedural formality enhances the parties' satisfaction with the proceeding).

[353]    McEwen et al., supra note 141, at 176-80 (comparing data from Maine and New Hampshire court dockets).

[354]    See supra part IV.B.3 (asserting that Maine lawyers, rather than acting as "spoilers," promote successful mediation and settlement).

[355]    Me. Rev. Stat. Ann. tit. 19, s 752 (West Supp. 1994).

[356]    Indeed, only a small minority of Maine lawyers (four percent) indicated interest in abandoning mandatory mediation altogether. The major concerns about the mandate, even among some of its

supporters, were that it imposed added costs and that it sometimes demanded mediation in cases where failure was inevitable.

[357] The discretionary character of these choices is, in practice, suggested by the fact that the proportion of cases entering mediation dropped from about 28% to around 21% after the initiation of a $60 fee for the mediation service. See 1989 Annual Report , supra note 268 (author's calculations).

[358] Interviews, supra note 243, No. 7.

[359] Id. No. 213.

[360] Divorce Lawyer Interview Data, supra note 243.

[361] These problems prevent lawyers from regularly using four-way conferences of attorneys and clients. Additional resistance to four-way meetings is generated by the special character of divorce cases. According to one lawyer: "A lot of lawyers were very skittish about the emotions that get generated in a divorce case and as a rule would never sit down and have that kind of meeting [four-way conferences of lawyers and clients] in a divorce case." Interviews, supra note 243, No. 56.

However, a few lawyers report that they have developed a level of trust with a few other attorneys so that they regularly schedule such meetings. Erlanger, Chambliss, and Melli take a different view of such four-person conferences, describing them as a device to pressure clients into settlements. Erlanger et al., supra note 181, at 593.

[362] Interviews, supra note 243, No. 28.

[363] Id. No. 23.

[364] See Deanne Siemer, Perspectives of Advocates and Clients in Court-Sponsored ADR, in Goldberg et al., supra note 8, at 423, 425 (arguing that "[l]awyers may hold back from offering settlement alternatives so as not to appear too ready to compromise").

[365] Interviews, supra note 243, No. 237.

[366] Id. No. 8.

[367] Id. No. 32.

[368] Grillo, supra note 2, at 1582 ("It is presumptuous to assume that the state has a better idea than the parties themselves about whether mediation will work in their particular case.").

[369] Interviews, supra note 243, No. 256.

[370] Id. No. 32.

[371] Id. No. 209.

[372] Divorce Lawyer Interview Data, supra note 243.

[373] Jessica Pearson & Nancy Thoennes, Mediation Versus the Courts in Child Custody Cases, 1 Negotiation J. 235, 241-42 (1985); see Joan Kelly, Is Mediation Less Expensive? Comparison of Mediated and Adversarial Divorce Costs, 8 Mediation Q. 15, 23-25 (1990).

[374] Divorce Lawyer Interview Data, supra note 243.

[375] Richardson , supra note 10, at 40, 45.

[376] Pearson, supra note 4, at 62.

[377] Kelly, supra note 373, at 15.

[378] Telephone Interview with Paul Charbonneau, Director, Court Mediation Services, Augusta, Maine (Mar. 8, 1994).

[379] Telephone Interview with Sharon Press, Director, Florida Dispute Resolution Center, Florida Supreme Court (May 10, 1993).

[380] Kelly, supra note 373, at 15.

[381] See Pearson, supra note 25, at 194 (reporting occasional need to revise agreements based on attorney feedback).

[382] During the same period, discovery requests and motions of various kinds increased in neighboring New Hampshire, a state without mandatory mediation.

[383] There may be other values in scheduling multiple sessions over time, but they seem to be less significant as a means to reach settlement, as multiple sessions were often not needed in Maine to settle a case.

[384] Richard Wagner, Mediated Divorces Last – At Least to the Bench, 6 Negotiation J. 47, 47 (1990).

[385] Goerdt , supra note 245, at 48, 61-63.

[386] Id. at 63.

[387] Rogers & McEwen , supra note 10, s 7:01.

[388] Clement et al. , supra note 63, at 15.

[389] Colo. Rev. Stat. s 19 -3 -310.5(3) (Supp. 1994) (permitting pro se litigants to opt out of neglect/dependency mediation).

[390] See supra part IV.B.3.c (asserting that lawyer presence does not preclude parties from actively participating in mediation).

[391] See supra part IV.B.3.c.

[392] See supra part IV.B.3.c.

[393] See supra part IV.B.3.a (discussing effect of lawyer participation on settlement).

[394] See supra part IV.B.3.a (discussing lawyer's role in facilitating settlement).

[395] See supra part IV.B.3.a.

[396] Orbeton & Charbonneau, supra note 268, at 64-65.

[397] Mason & Press , supra note 72, at 4-5 to 4-7, 4-10.

[398] Orbeton & Charbonneau, supra note 268, at 67. But see Wagner, supra note 384, at 50 (noting a 10% rate of challenge to mediated agreements in Lewiston, Maine).

[399] Me. R. Evid. 408(b) (disallowing admissibility of conduct or statements by parties or mediator during court-sponsored domestic relations mediation sessions).

[400] See, e.g., Weissman & Leick, supra note 8, at 279-80 (describing advantages of mediation).

[401] Orbeton & Charbonneau, supra note 268, at 64-67 (reporting that mediation resolved 56% of cases studied; most cases took only one mediation session); Pearson & Thoennes, supra note 155, at 432 (reporting that an average mediation in the private sector takes 8.7 hours and requires an average of 6.2 sessions; the average mediation in the public sector takes 6.3 hours and requires an average of 3.4 sessions).

[402] See supra text accompanying notes 373-383 (discussing costs of mediation with lawyers present).

[403] Court Mediation Serv., Maine Judicial Dep't, Ten Years of Progress: The Court Mediation Service 1977-1987 at 10-13 (1988); Telephone Interview with Paul Charbonneau, Director, Maine Court Mediation Service, Portland, Maine (Apr. 19, 1995) (indicating that mediator qualifications are similar to those reported in 1988).

[404] See supra text accompanying notes 320-326 (discussing how lawyer presence reduces risks of unfairness).

[405] Moreover, involvement has generated a favorable view by lawyers toward mediation and may alter attitudes about negotiation outside of mediation. McEwen et al., supra note 141, at 177-79.

# [11]

# Yes, No, and Maybe:
# Informed Decision Making about Divorce
# Mediation in the Presence of Domestic Violence

## Nancy Ver Steegh

**Introduction**

All happy families are like one another; each unhappy family is unhappy in its own way.[1]

Divorce mediation in the context of domestic violence is one of the most controversial issues in family law today. Some believe that mediation is never appropriate when domestic violence has taken place, and others believe that it is always appropriate and should be mandatory.[2] These views can be reconciled by taking a third approach, that mediation is sometimes appropriate but that this decision must be made on a case-by-case basis in consultation with the abuse survivor.

The central premise of this article is that victims of domestic violence should have the opportunity to make an informed choice about which divorce process – mediated or adversarial – will best meet the needs of their families. Because families are different and because both adversarial and mediated proceedings vary in quality and accessibility, decisions about what process to use must be made on an individual basis in light of the real, not theoretical, options available to the family. The article uses social science research to (1) establish that families experience different types of violence and consequently differ from each other in ways that are significant for choosing a divorce process; (2) provide objective information on how mediation and the adversarial process compare in terms of overall effectiveness, satisfaction rates, and compliance with agreements or orders; and (3) evaluate the extent to which commentators' fears about mediation and domestic violence have been substantiated. The article analyzes this information and suggests factors, both individual and systemic, to be considered in choosing a divorce process. Finally, the article discusses specific practice safeguards and makes recommendations for future change.

\* \* \* \*

M. Gender

Because the adversary system sometimes has failed to protect the interests of women and battered women in particular,[282] some believe that mediation embodies a style of conflict resolution that is more compatible with women's world view and "ethic of care."[283] Others have expressed grave concern about the use of mediation in divorce cases generally and most especially in cases where there is a history of domestic violence. These concerns are explored in the next section.

## VI. Divorce Mediation When Domestic Violence Is an Issue

Although mediation provides a desirable alternative for many families, there are serious concerns about its use in cases of domestic violence. Some of these concerns arise from the mediation process itself and others stem from the varying quality of the conducted mediation.[284]

*A. Reasons Why Mediation Might Never Be Appropriate*

*1. Is Mediation Too Private?*

Privacy and confidentiality are critical aspects of the mediation process. Both are necessary to encourage full disclosure and candid problem solving.[285] Some women's advocates, however, are troubled by the private nature of mediation. After years of working to have domestic violence dealt with as a crime, they see mediation as potentially returning the issue "back into the shadows."[286] Because criminal prosecution sends a public message to the abuser that his behavior is unacceptable, advocates fear that the abusers in mediation will not be held accountable for the abuse.[287] Similarly, they fear that if these cases are removed from the courts, new favorable legal precedents will not be established.[288]

Two factors mitigate these concerns. First, divorce mediation need not supplant the use of the criminal system.[289] If an abuse survivor chooses to do so, she can file criminal charges, pursue a protective order, and mediate the divorce. Use of the criminal courts is not an exclusive remedy. Second, a growing body of evidence suggests that applying criminal sanctions may not deter further abuse. Rather, in some cases, criminal charges have been correlated with an increased likelihood of a recurrence of abuse.[290] Consequently, each victim must make an individual assessment of whether the abuser will be deterred from further violence by criminal prosecution. Either way, she could proceed with mediation.

Proponents of mediation argue that the privacy of the process and the neutrality of the mediator increase the likelihood that the abuser will admit the abuse and accept help.[291]

> The adversarial approach to spousal abuse often actually encourages the husband to deny his past abusive behavior because his defense attorney will assist him in denying the offense . . . . In mediation, the mediator and the couple can immediately deal with the abuse because the neutral role of the mediator takes away the need for the mediator to be a judge determining what happened in the past and allows the mediator to focus on steps to remove any possibility of future allegations or

occurrences of abuse.[292] Some batterers may respond more constructively if they perceive that they are being listened to, treated fairly, and given clear expectations for future behavior.[293] This does not mean that abuse should ever be tolerated or negotiated.[294]

Although more research is needed in this area, there is some evidence that mediation prevents future violence.[295] Researchers Ellis and Stuckless report that voluntary multi-session mediation is more effective in preventing future violence than either coerced mediation or lawyer negotiations.[296] Interestingly, they found that the preparation of affidavits with "hurtful" content may have undermined lawyers' efforts to end the abuse.[297]

Some mediators specifically recommend that a protective order be pursued simultaneously with mediation and that the mediation sessions be used to reinforce the boundaries set in the order.[298]

Until more is known about which abusers are likely to offend again and under what circumstances, the abuse survivor ought to have an expanded, not more limited, array of options including both civil and criminal sanctions.

*2. Are Power Imbalances Insurmountable?*
The potential difference in power between the victim and the abuser is a major concern when mediation is being considered or conducted.[299]

a. The Issue of Power Imbalance in Nonviolent Relationships
Power involves the potential for one party to impose his or her will upon the other party.[300] Power can shift and change and is not an all or nothing attribute.[301] It can spring from different capacities such as one's belief system, personality, self-esteem, gender, selfishness, force, income/assets, knowledge, status, age, and education.[302] In divorce, power generally corresponds with who originated the divorce, who has the more favorable legal case, who feels more guilty, and who has the stronger lawyer or support system.[303] Power need not be entirely competitive in nature; rather, in a cooperative relationship, each party benefits from enhancing each other's power.[304]

Power imbalances occur to some extent in all divorce mediation, even when violence is not a factor.[305] Despite the fears of commentators, research shows that women do not necessarily wield less power in the mediation process.[306]

Women often find mediation to be empowering. They report that participation in mediation enhances their ability to stand up for themselves, assume responsibility for themselves,[307] solve problems,[308] and express their views.[309] Most women studied prefer mediation[310] and their satisfaction levels are not associated with power related marital issues such as abuse, who won arguments, or difficulty being heard.[311]

Of course, some women do report being pressured into agreements by their husbands, being uncomfortable with expressing their feelings, and feeling tense, angry, confused, and overwhelmed during the mediation process.[312] Research has shown that these women tend to terminate the mediation rather than submit to agreements they deem unfair.[313]

Feeling pressure to settle has been more strongly associated with poor communication throughout the marriage than the presence of domestic violence.[314] However, even though abuse is "an unreliable indicator" of power imbalance,[315] there may still be an association and this is cause for concern.[316]

b. The Problem of Power Imbalance in Cases of Domestic Violence

In cases where domestic violence has taken place, there has already been a severe abuse of power and the consequent power imbalance can make mediation impossible.[317] Barbara Hart argues that cooperation between spouses when domestic abuse had occurred is "an oxymoron."[318] Others agree that especially where there has been a culture of battering coupled with severe abuse, the power imbalance is too great to be overcome in mediation.[319] Victims may fear retaliatory violence if they disagree with the abuser,[320] thus making negotiation impossible.[321] This is described by Leigh Goodmark:

> Memories of the batterer's power, and the way he used that power, trigger fear of the abuser. As one abused women noted, "When he had power over me, he didn't have to exert himself. The more powerful I become [in getting away from him], the more irrational he becomes. I wonder, would he hurt me physically?" These memories may render the victim inarticulate or angry, making it difficult for her to express her position during mediation. The victim may feel pressure to settle or to compromise, continuing to believe that the abuse . . . will stop if she simply decreases her demands.[322] Research does bear out some of these concerns. A 1995 study found that abused women perceive themselves as having less power than women who have not been abused; they were more likely to think that the abuser could "out-talk" them, had "gotten back at them" previously, and said they were afraid to "openly disagree" for fear of retaliation.[323] Interestingly, the authors also made some contrary discoveries as well.

> However, there were no significant differences for abused and nonabused women on four personal empowerment items: (a) giving in just to stop dealing with the abuser, (b) feeling guilty for asking for the custody and visitation that they wanted, (c) perceived ability to speak up for themselves about custody and visitation wishes, and (d) getting what they wanted in disagreements.[324] Other studies report that abuse survivors are able to negotiate effectively[325] and are not at a disadvantage in mediation because of power imbalances.[326] These favorable findings may be related to the mediator screening for abuse and carefully monitoring relative power levels.[327]

Despite the contrary indications found in the research, power imbalance is an important consideration in deciding whether mediation is appropriate. The extent of the problem varies with the individual couple.[328] As discussed previously, women who are dealing with ongoing and episodic male battering or psychotic and paranoid reactions as defined by Johnston and Campbell, may have more difficulty mediating.[329] Similarly, women suffering from "battered women's syndrome" or PTSD may have difficulty standing up for themselves. However, some abuse survivors are able to state their own needs and problem solve effectively.[330]

At the other extreme, some have argued that men are disadvantaged in mediation because of women's greater power with respect to children, their relationship-oriented negotiation style, and sometimes their ability to "tell a better story."[331]

Each couple differs with respect to power imbalance and relative power levels may change throughout the relationship. The power imbalance inherent in domestic violence will render some abuse survivors unable to mediate. However, this assumption cannot be made for all couples who have had violent incidents. Capacity to mediate can only be assessed on an individual level. However, if the couple and the mediator proceed with the mediation, the mediator needs to remain especially alert for power imbalances and be prepared to deal with them. In addition to viewing each couple as unique when deciding whether the mediation process is appropriate, it is important to ask, as Folberg and Milne do, "Compared to what?"[332]

\* \* \* \*

### 3. Mediation Triage

As noted previously, mediation should never proceed against the wishes of the abuse survivor.[418] However, even when the victim wants to mediate, there are some conditions under which many mediators will not agree to mediate. For this reason, the Model Standards specifically state that some domestic violence situations "are not suitable for mediation because of safety, control, or intimidation issues."[419]

Experts agree that some categories of domestic violence cases should never be mediated. Erickson and McKnight find mediation inappropriate when (1) the abuser discounts the victim and refuses to acknowledge how his behavior affects her, (2) abuse is ongoing between mediation sessions, (3) either client is carrying a weapon or attempts to mediate while drinking or using drugs, or (4) either party continues to violate the mediation ground rules.[420]

Linda Girdner writes that cases should be excluded from mediation when abuse and/or control are central to the relationship to such an extent that the parties are unable to differentiate their interests, the abuser does not accept responsibility for his behavior, and the victim fears retribution.[421] These conditions render the couple unable to negotiate. In addition, Girdner cautions against mediation when weapons are involved and/or the abuser has fantasies of killing the victim and children or committing suicide.[422] These exclusions are similar to those recommended by Johnston and Campbell. In a similar vein, Elizabeth Ellis suggests that **mediation may** go forward if the violence has been brief, was instigated by the wife, and/or began only after the separation.[423]

Because abuse can differ widely in "form, duration, and severity," the existence of violence creates a red flag for the mediator signaling a need for a closer look at the victim's ability to negotiate and the level of the abuser's denial and control.[424]

If there has been abuse but the identified prohibitions are absent, mediation might proceed, but only under stringent conditions. These include use of a specially trained mediator, a specialized process, and agreed upon safety protocols.[425]

### 4. Context and Making Informed Decisions

The abuse survivor is more familiar with her situation than anyone. Consequently, all process decision-making should start and end with her. She will have the best information on the following topics and should consider the following questions.

The Abuse. As discussed previously, there is a continuum of abuse and the experience of each victim is unique. What is the history with respect to the severity, frequency, and amount of abuse? How recently has the abuse occurred? Is there a pattern? Is there a culture of battering with systematic domination and control by the batterer?[426]

Immediate Safety Issues. The abuse survivor cannot make any decisions until she is safe. Has the couple separated? Is the abuse ongoing? If so, referrals should be made to community resources and the victim should consider pursuing a protective order and/or pressing criminal charges.

Status of the Abuse Survivor. Is she ready and able to make decisions? What does she want to happen? Is she interested in counseling? Does she need medical treatment for PTSD?

Likely Behavior of the Abuser. The abuse survivor is usually very knowledgeable about how the abuser is likely to respond to a protective order, criminal charges, and/or mediation. The point of this discussion is not to put his needs before hers, but to anticipate and avoid future abuse.

Need for Future Contact. If the couple has children, especially young ones, there will be some form of future contact that must be carefully structured.

Resources. What resources does the victim have? Can she afford to be represented by an attorney? Is she connected to an advocate or other support system? Are there other time and cost issues?

All of these factors can point in different directions and this makes decision- making difficult. For example, if the abuse survivor is seriously traumatized, has no children, and can afford an attorney, she may elect to proceed through the court system. On the other hand, if the abuse has been less severe and only took place around the time of the separation, if she has small children, and if she cannot afford an attorney, exploring mediation might make sense. Most abuse survivors will fall between these two scenarios and their decisions will be more complex.

Beyond individual considerations, divorce process decisions must be made within a larger context. Ideally the abuse survivor should have access to information about the quality and approach of the court system as well as the particular mediation process. Whatever process is chosen, state law will inform the ultimate outcome. The abuse survivor should be aware of whether the law provides a rebuttable presumption against custody awards to batterers or whether custody decisions are made in accordance with the "best interests" standard. The survivor might also want to consider whether joint custody is the norm.

If the abuse survivor enters the adversarial system, she should know whether the judge is likely to be informed about domestic violence issues. If she enters mediation, she might consider whether she will have access to a mediator or co- mediators who are experienced and specially trained to mediate domestic violence cases. The survivor should also learn whether the mediation will cover all topics and involve multiple sessions.

The quality of the process may be of more significance than the process itself. Poorly conducted mediation could be more dangerous than when unrepresented parties appearing before a well-trained and sensitive judge. In reality, there is not always a clear choice between mediation and the adversarial process. For example, a well-structured, cooperative two-attorney negotiation is more like mediation than a contested trial. Consequently, each abuse survivor must individually evaluate her actual options.

### VII. Safeguards for Mediating in the Context of Domestic Violence

If the couple and mediator agree to proceed with mediation, the Model Standards provide that safety precautions be taken. These include the following:

D. If domestic abuse appears to be present the mediator shall consider taking measures to insure the safety of participants and the mediator including, among others;

1. establishing appropriate security arrangements.

2. holding separate sessions with the participants even without the agreement of all participants;

3. allowing a friend, representative, advocate, counsel, or attorney to attend the mediation sessions;

4. encouraging the participants to be represented by an attorney, counsel or an advocate throughout the mediation process;

5. referring the participants to appropriate community resources; and

6. suspending or terminating the mediation sessions, with appropriate steps to protect the safety of the participants.

E. The mediator should facilitate the participants' formulation of parenting plans that protect the physical safety and psychological well-being of themselves and their children.[427]

A. Procedures and Ground Rules

As noted previously, the time of separation is potentially one of the most dangerous for the abuse survivor.[428] Research shows that 73% to 96% of mediation programs use special techniques and procedures when mediating cases involving domestic violence.[429] For example, physical safety can be enhanced by providing separate waiting rooms, staggering arrival and departure, and providing an escort to and from the car.[430]

*Nancy Ver Steegh, J.D., is Professor of Law at William Mitchell College of Law in St. Paul, Minnesota.*

## Notes

[1]    Leo Tolstoy, Anna Karenina 17 (1961).

[2]    Compare Carrie-Anne Tondo, et al., Mediation Trends, 39 Fam. Ct. Rev. 431 (2001) (arguing that mediation is never appropriate), with Penelope E. Bryan, Reclaiming Professionalism: The Lawyer's Role in Divorce Mediation, 28 Fam. L. Q. 177, 203-05 (1994) (arguing that mediation is always appropriate) [hereinafter Reclaiming Professionalism].

[282]    See Vincent, supra note 211, at 282.

[283]    See McCabe, supra note 228, at 471-72 (discussing Carol Gilligan, In A Different Voice: Psychological Theory and Women's Development 24-63 (1993)); Vincent, supra note 211, at 257-58 (citing Nancy G. Maxwell, The Feminist Dilemma in Mediation, in International Review of Comparative Public Policy, 4 Family Law and Gender Bias: Comparative Perspectives 67-68 (Nicholas Mercuro & Barbara Stark, eds., 1992)).

[284]    Stephen K. Erickson & Marilyn S. McKnight, Mediating Spousal Abuse Divorces, 7 Mediation Q. 377, 379 (1990) (emphasizing that mediators must have "special skills . . . tailored to the complex dynamic of spousal abuse." The role of the mediator is to help set "new rules" to eliminate spousal abuse.).

[285]    Mary Pat Treuthart, In Harm's Way? Family Mediation and the Role of the Attorney Advocate, 23 Golden Gate U. L. Rev. 717, 730 (1993).

[286]    Goodmark, supra note 147, at 24; Sarah Krieger, The Dangers of Mediation in Domestic Violence Cases, 8 Cardozo Women's L.J. 235, 240-41 (2002). See also Winner, supra note 149, at 182-84 (discussing the imbalance of power in divorce mediation).

[287]    Kerry Loomis, Comment, Domestic Violence and Mediation: A Tragic Combination for Victims in California Family Court, 35 Cal. W. L. Rev. 355, 367 (1999).

[288]    Goodmark, supra note 147, at 24; Laurie Woods, Mediation: A Backlash to Women's Progress on Family Law Issues, 19 Clearinghouse Rev. 431, 431 (1985).

[289]    See Ann W. Yellott, Mediation and Domestic Violence: A Call for Collaboration, 8 Mediation Q. 39, 39-42 (1990).

[290]    See Janell D. Schmidt & Lawrence W. Sherman, Does Arrest Deter Domestic Violence?, in Do Arrests and Restraining Orders Work? 49 (Eve S. Buzawa & Carl G. Buzawa eds., 1996).

[291]    Luisa Bigornia, Alternatives to Traditional Criminal Prosecution of Spousal Abuse, 11 J. Contemp. Legal Issues 57, 60-61 (2000); Rimelspach, supra note 103, at 102; Yellott, supra note 289, at 43.

[292]    Erickson & McKnight, supra note 284, at 385.

[293]    Marilyn McKnight, Mediating in the Shadow of Domestic Violence 50 (1997); Holly A. Magana & Nancy Taylor, Child Custody Mediation and Spouse Abuse: A Descriptive Study of Protocol, 31 Fam. & Conciliation Cts. Rev. 50, 54 (1993). But see Reclaiming Professionalism, supra note 2, at 205 (asserting that in cases of domestic abuse, "mediation is a power choice").

[294]    Mary A. Duryee, Guidelines for Family Court Services Intervention When There Are Allegations of Domestic Violence, 33 Fam. & Conciliation Cts. Rev. 79, 82 (1995).

²⁹⁵ Kelly, supra note 207, at 381; Linda Perry, Mediation and Wife Abuse: A Review of the Literature, 11 Mediation Q. 313, 322 (1994); Rimelspach, supra note 103, at 103. See Ellis & Stuckless, supra note 72, at 61; Kelly Rowe, Comment, Limits of the Neighborhood Justice Center: Why Domestic Violence Cases Should Not Be Mediated, 34 Emory L.J. 855, 883-84 (1985) (citing a study in which 70% of those contacted reported no further problems).

²⁹⁶ Ellis & Stuckless, supra note 72, at 61-62.

²⁹⁷ Id. at 62; Jessica Pearson, Mediating When Domestic Violence Is a Factor: Policies and Practices in Court-Based Divorce Mediation Programs, 14 Mediation Q. 319, 329 (1997) (noting that the court system is often counterproductive because couples have to deal with each other after "trashing" each other in pleadings).

²⁹⁸ Erickson & McKnight, supra note 284, at 386.

²⁹⁹ Telser, supra note 142, at 973.

³⁰⁰ Scott H. Hughes, Elizabeth's Story: Exploring Power Imbalances in Divorce Mediation, 8 Geo. J. Legal Ethics 553, 574 (1995) (citing Max Weber, Law in Economy and Society 323 (1954)).

³⁰¹ Diane Neumann, How Mediation Can Effectively Address the Male-Female Power Imbalance in Divorce, 9 Mediation Q. 227, 229 (1992).

³⁰² Id. at 229.

³⁰³ Id. at 236-37.

³⁰⁴ Stephen K. Erickson & Marilyn S. McKnight, Power Imbalance in Mediation: Showstopper or Opportunity 5 (1998) [hereinafter Power Imbalance].

³⁰⁵ Id. at 2. See Ellis & Stuckless, supra note 72, at 5-6.

³⁰⁶ See Multi-State Assessment, supra note 229, at 30; Kelly, supra note 207, at 378. See also McCabe, supra note 228, at 480 ("[M]ediation offers women an opportunity to step out of their socialized image and speak for themselves.").

³⁰⁷ Beck & Sales, supra note 146, at 1037; Kelly, supra note 207, at 378.

³⁰⁸ Vincent, supra note 211, at 278. See Roselle Wissler, Study Suggests Domestic Violence Does Not Affect Settlement, Disp. Resol. Mag., Fall 1999, at 29.

³⁰⁹ King, supra note 113, at 444; Wissler, supra note 308, at 29.

³¹⁰ Multi-State Assessment, supra note 229, at 30; Pearson & Thoennes, supra note 204, at 440-41.

³¹¹ Beck & Sales, supra note 146, at 1037.

³¹² Joan B. Kelly et al., Mediated and Adversarial Divorce: Initial Findings from a Longitudinal Study, in Divorce Mediation: Theory and Practice 469 (Jay Folberg & Ann Milne eds., 1988); Kelly & Gigy, supra note 21, at 279; Pearson & Thoennes, supra note 204, at 440-41.

³¹³ David B. Chandler, Violence, Fear, and Communication: The Variable Impact of Domestic Violence on Mediation, 7 Mediation Q. 331, 343-44 (1990).

³¹⁴ Beck & Sales, supra note 146, at 1037; Pearson & Thoennes, supra note 204, at 440; Vincent, supra note 211, at 277.

³¹⁵ Pearson, supra note 297, at 324.

³¹⁶ Vincent, supra note 211, at 278-79.

³¹⁷ Reclaiming Professionalism, supra note 2, at 203; James Martin Truss, The Subjection of Women . . . Still: Unfulfilled Promise of Protection for Women Victims of Domestic Violence, 26 St. Mary's L.J. 1149, 1186 (1995).

³¹⁸ Barbara J. Hart, Gentle Jeopardy: The Further Endangerment of Battered Women and Children in Custody Mediation, 7 Mediation Q. 317, 320 (1990).

³¹⁹ Reclaiming Professionalism, supra note 2, at 203-04.

³²⁰ Barbara Hart, Battered Women and the Criminal Justice System, in Do Arrests and Restraining Orders Work?, 98-99 (Eve S. Buzawa & Carl G. Buzawa eds., 1996).

³²¹ Holly Joyce, Comment, Mediation and Domestic Violence: Legislative Responses, 14 J. Am. Acad. Matrimonial L. 447, 453 (1997).

[322]   Goodmark, supra note 147, at 22.

[323]   Girdner, supra note 24, at 13; Lisa Newmark et al., Domestic Violence and Empowerment in Custody and Visitation Cases, 33 Fam. & Conciliation Cts. Rev. 30, 57 (1995).

[324]   Newmark et al., supra note 323, at 57. See generally Multi-State Assessment, supra note 229.

[325]   Wissler, supra note 308, at 29.

[326]   Pearson, supra note 297, at 327.

[327]   Ellis & Stuckless, supra note 72, at 80.

[328]   Joyce, supra note 321, at 457.

[329]   Johnston & Roseby, supra note 47, at 42.

[330]   McCabe, supra note 228, at 476-77.

[331]   Macoby & Mnookin, supra note 115, at 95-96; Randy Frances Kandel, Power Plays: A Sociolinguistic Study of Inequality in Child Custody Mediation and a Hearsay Analog Solution, 36 Ariz. L. Rev. 879, 896 (1994); Lenard Marlow, Samson and Delilah in Divorce Mediation, 38 Fam. & Conciliation Cts. Rev. 224, 224 (2000); McCabe, supra note 228, at 477; Vincent, supra note 211, at 278.

[332]   Mary Ann Mason, The Custody Wars: Why Children are Losing the Legal Battle, and What We Can Do About it 154 (1999); Grobe, supra note 209, at 17.

[418]   Girdner, supra note 24, at 20.

[419]   Model Standards of Practice for Family and Divorce Mediation, Standard XC; Introduction to the Model Standards, supra note 201, at 20-21.

[420]   Erickson & McKnight, supra note 284, at 387.

[421]   Girdner, supra note 24, at 21-22.

[422]   Linda K. Girdner, Mediation Triage: Screening for Spouse Abuse in Divorce Mediation, 7 Mediation Q. 365, 374 (1990).

[423]   Ellis, supra note 22 at 77.

[424]   Pearson, supra note 297, at 324.

[425]   Girdner, supra note 24, at 20-21; Erickson & McKnight, supra note 284, at 387.

[426]   Gerencser, supra note 223, at 59.

[427]   Model Standards of Practice for Family and Divorce Mediation Standard, Standard XD (2001).

[428]   Rimelspach, supra note 103, at 98.

[429]   Pearson, supra note 297, at 326; Thoennes et al., supra note 364, at 19-20.

[430]   Fuller & Lyons, supra note 214, at 926; Zylstra, supra note 366, at 277.

# [12]

Rights Myopia in Child Welfare:
A Problem-solving Model:
The Example of Family Group Conferencing

Clare Huntington

\* \* \* \*

### III. A Problem-solving Model: The Example of Family Group Conferencing

Thus far I have described the rights-based model governing the child welfare system and explored the considerable limitations of this model. Because the current system – and the academic debate about how to fix it – is so dominated by rights, other possible models are largely unexplored. But an alternative model is needed because the solution to child welfare will never be found solely in rights. A new model would acknowledge a parent's need for assistance – thus creating a better frame for the issues facing families in the child welfare system – and would foster collaboration, not adverseness, between the state and families. It would be a problem-solving model.

Carrie Menkel-Meadow first coined the term "problem-solving model," noting that it reflected a move in negotiation away from adversarial, zero-sum thinking.[177] As she stated, a "problem-solving model seeks to demonstrate how negotiators ... can more effectively accomplish their goals by focusing on the parties' actual objectives and creatively attempting to satisfy the needs of both parties, rather than by focusing exclusively on the assumed objectives of maximizing individual gain."[178] As Robert Mnookin and his coauthors state, "at its core, problem-solving implies an orientation or mindset – it is not simply a bundle of techniques."[179] In this Article, I use the term "problem-solving" both in the sense it is used in the world of alternative dispute resolution, and also more generally to describe a model of child welfare that focuses proactively on the problems facing families, rather than on allocating blame for abuse and neglect.

A number of collaborative processes may satisfy the problem-solving model,[180] but one in particular seems promising. Family group conferencing, a radical departure from the adversarial process, has been used successfully in child welfare in a number of countries and embodies a problem-solving approach to child welfare. To show concretely the problem-solving model in practice, this part describes the theory and practice of family group conferencing. I offer this discussion of family group conferencing as simply one example of a collaborative process. My point is not that family group conferencing is perfect, or that it is the only process that embodies a problem-solving model of child welfare. Rather, I argue that family group conferencing represents a different approach to child welfare than the adversarial process born of the rights-based model, and that such approaches are very promising.

## A. Origins, the Process, and Theoretical Underpinnings

Family group conferencing[181] is part of the broader restorative justice movement, which seeks to reform the justice system to incorporate victims and to allow the offender to "restore" the status quo.[182] Although largely focused on criminal justice, the restorative justice movement has also addressed other systems, including child welfare. In that context, family group conferencing is the practice of convening family members, community members, and other individuals or institutions involved with a family to develop a plan to ensure the care and protection of a child who is at risk for abuse or neglect.[183]

Simplified descriptions of two cases, one receiving traditional child welfare services and one receiving a family group conference, illustrate the marked differences between the two approaches. In a child welfare case under the current system, after the state agency receives a credible report of child abuse or neglect sufficient to warrant removal, a caseworker goes to the home and assesses the danger to the child. Assuming the caseworker finds sufficient evidence of such danger, the caseworker removes the child and places her in foster care pending a more thorough investigation. The state agency then files a petition in court seeking temporary custody of the child. The child is assigned a guardian ad litem to represent her interests. The caseworker then develops a case plan for the parents, requiring the parents to, for example, obtain drug treatment and attend parenting classes. If the parents do not comply with this case plan within the specified period, generally twelve to eighteen months, then the state agency files for a petition for the termination of parental rights. If the court agrees that parental rights should be terminated, the child is freed for adoption. The majority of decisions in this model are made by professionals: caseworkers, therapists, guardians ad litem, and judges.

In a family group conferencing case, the story and decisionmakers are decidedly different.[184] In a typical family group conferencing case, after receiving a report, a social worker conducts an initial investigation to determine if there has been abuse or neglect. If the social worker concludes there is evidence of abuse or neglect, she refers the case to a coordinator, who has the authority to convene a family group conference. The coordinator contacts the parents, the child,[185] extended family members, and significant community members who know the family. Before the conference, each potential conference participant meets separately with the coordinator to learn about the process. In these meetings, the coordinator screens for potentially complicating factors, such as a history of domestic violence,[186] to determine whether the case is appropriate for family group conferencing and, if so, what additional supports may be needed for the participants.

There are three stages of the conference. In the first stage, the coordinator and any professionals involved with the family, such as therapists, teachers, and the investigating social worker, explain the case to the family. In the second stage, the coordinator and professionals leave the room while the family and community members engage in private deliberation. During the private deliberation, the participants acknowledge that the child was abused or neglected and develop a plan to protect the child and help the parents. After the participants reach an agreement, they present the plan to the social worker and coordinator, who likely have questions for the participants. Parents, custodians, social workers, and coordinators can veto the plan produced by the conference and refer the case to court.[187] In practice, this rarely occurs: The participants come to a decision, and the social worker and coordinator accept the plan (perhaps with a few changes) if it meets predetermined criteria. The coordinator writes up the plan, sends it to all participants, and then sets a time for a subsequent conference to assess developments in the case.

The plan typically includes a decision about the safety of the child, including whether the child should be placed outside of the home for a certain period of time, and, if so, with whom. If the child is placed outside the home, she is almost invariably placed with a relative or other conference participant. The plan also identifies the services and supports needed by the parents. Finally, the plan determines which participants will both help the family and also check in on a regular basis to ensure the child is safe and the parents are complying with the plan.

As is apparent from this description, five principles characterize the philosophy of family group conferencing. First, children are raised best in their own families. Second, families have the primary responsibility for caring for their children, and these families should be supported, protected, and respected. Third, families are able to make reliable, safe decisions for their children, and families have strengths and are capable of changing the problems in their lives. Fourth, families are their own experts, with knowledge and insight into which solutions will work best for them. Finally, to achieve family empowerment, families must have the freedom to make their own decisions and choices.[188]

As one of its proponents has stated, "family group conferences amount to a partnership arrangement between the state, represented by child protection officials; the family; and members of the community, such as resource and support persons; with each party expected to play an important role in planning and providing services necessary for the well-being of children."[189] Family group conferences are not a means for child protection officials to relinquish their responsibilities, but rather are a different method for exercising those responsibilities. The intent is to strike a balance between the interests of child protection and family support. Family group conferencing represents a radical reorientation of child protection:

Many child protection approaches attempt to enforce community standards (accountability) but lack any way for the community to reach out and weave the family back into the community fabric with the development of shared, voluntary commitments to community standards. Consequently, those strategies often create short-term relief, but do not change behavior in the long term. Those strategies also rely heavily on outside enforcers, the professional system, to solve the problem.[190]

Family group conferencing originated with the Maori and other First Nations around the world, and New Zealand was the first country to incorporate the process into its laws.[191] To avoid the removal of Maori children to non-Maori families, and to incorporate Maori traditions of involving extended family members in decisionmaking, legislative changes were made to New Zealand's child welfare system in the Children, Young Persons, and Their Families Act of 1989.[192] The changes were in response to several government reports documenting discrimination against Maori families in the child welfare system.[193] The legislative changes were not limited to Maori families. Rather, the law required that all substantiated cases of child abuse and neglect be referred for family group conferencing.[194] The premises of family group conferences resonated with the idea, long-espoused by social workers, "that lasting solutions to problems are ones that grow out of, or can fit with, the knowledge, experiences, and desires of the people most affected."[195]

There are four hallmarks of the family group conferencing process (and these hallmarks reflect the principles set forth above).[196] First, the process is intended to find and build on a family's strengths, rather than to place blame.[197] One method for achieving this is to focus on the problem, rather than the person, and to concentrate on healing.[198] Although the current system is supposed to preserve families, in practice social workers often do not look for the strengths in a family and instead focus on the dysfunctional elements.[199] Thus, family group conferencing facilitates a strengths-based practice because it requires the family and community to look within to find solutions.[200] Second, the process respects and values important cultural practices of the relevant community.[201] Third, the process involves the extended family and community.[202] Those individuals with information to share, individuals who love the child, and individuals with a stake in the outcome are all included in the conference.[203] Finally, the process views the community as a resource for the family.[204]

In addition to the four hallmarks of family group conferencing, there are several key features of the process that set it apart from other alternative dispute resolution methods and are essential for its success. These key elements include sufficient preparation of the participants by the coordinator (often a total of thirty-five hours of preparation per conference[205]), private family time without professionals present, consensus on the plan, and monitoring and follow-up by the conference participants and the state.[206]

Although no country other than New Zealand requires the use of family group conferencing, many countries have started to experiment with it.[207] In the United States, child welfare agencies have been experimenting with family group conferencing since the early 1990s.[208] Although its use is by no means widespread, states and localities are using some version of it with increasing frequency.[209] Notably, in the United States, social workers, rather than lawyers and legislators, have pushed for its adoption.[210]

## B. Early Empirical Research

Studies on programs implemented around the world and in the United States demonstrate that family group conferencing has had substantial success in improving child welfare systems.[211] First, studies suggest, but are not uniform in concluding, that families who participate in family group conferences have lower levels of subsequent abuse and neglect than the typical child welfare case.[212] This may be due in part to the way family group conferences enlist family members in monitoring the safety and welfare of children.[213]

Second, research indicates that in the vast majority of cases families are able to devise a plan for the care and protection of their children.[214] Family members, including fathers, participate in numbers far greater than in the traditional child welfare model.[215] Caseworkers report that the plans devised by the participants often require more of the parent than the agency typically would.[216] Conference participants play an active role in finding a solution for the troubles facing the family by providing, for example, child care, home furnishings, transportation, housing, and help with managing the household. [217] Although participating family members have multiple problems, including substance abuse and histories of violence, these participants are able to create thoughtful and detailed plans to keep the children safe.[218] These plans draw on familial and professional resources.[219] An evaluation of a Washington project demonstrated that the family group conferences resulted in detailed plans drawing on the families' expertise about their children and their own resources. The plans also drew on social service supports, but as requested and defined by the families. To use the vernacular of family group conferencing, the process and results were "family-centered."[220] The conferences were based on a "strengths-based practice," focusing not on pathology and dysfunction, but rather on resilience and potential for development and success.[221]

Third, participants report satisfaction with the process and result.[222] For example, one mother described her experience as follows:

> There comes a time when you think "I can take control now" and that's when I think the normal way of running social services departments falls down. Yes people come initially because they do need a certain amount of support and a certain amount of help. But if you go on trying [to] nursemaid and suffocate that person then their growth isn't going to take place. The social services, the way it's run at the moment actually doesn't allow the person who has to ... take control, they're very reluctant to give that person back the control of the family. So social services becomes the head of the family, and the mother and the father, or one of them, becomes more or less like a child themselves, and they regress into no responsibility, because they're instructed all the way, what their responsibilities are. But they are not actually helped to rebuild their confidence to enable them to take up the full responsibility.[223]

Fourth, there is evidence that family group conferencing fosters development of a strong support network within the child's extended family and community. For example, when the plan does recommend placement outside of the immediate family, children are more often placed with extended family members.[224] In the Washington project, 77 percent of children who were placed outside of the home as a result of the family group conference were placed with relatives, whereas only 27 percent of children not in family group conferencing but in need of out-of-home placement were placed with relatives.[225] In New Zealand, 95 percent of all children who are removed from their homes are placed with a relative.[226] The process also fosters stronger ties between the family and the community. Research has demonstrated that ties to the community are particularly important to help an at-risk child overcome difficult family circumstances and that emotional support outside of the immediate family can be a crucial protective factor for children who grow up in high-risk environments.[227]

Finally, to the extent the process prevents the placement of children in the foster care system, it could well generate significant savings for federal, state, and local governments.[228] In fiscal year 2002, the total cost of child welfare spending from federal, state, and local government sources was $22.2 billion.[229] Of this amount, $ 10 billion was spent on out-of-home placements.[230] Family group conferencing could incorporate poverty-related programs already in place that are more cost-effective than foster care. For example, Connecticut has been experimenting with a Supportive Housing program in which the state partners with a private social services agency to provide both permanent housing and intensive social services to rebuild families. In one illustrative case, a mother had six children in foster care, at a total cost to the state of $60,000. Once provided permanent housing and intensive supports, she was able to regain custody of her children and keep them out of foster care. The cost of this program was $ 11,000 for the support services and approximately $5500 for the housing.[231]

Of course, the economic benefits of family group conferencing present a complex issue. For example, relatives caring for children in the current system still receive foster care payments from the state. To the extent children are placed with relatives through a family group conference, presumably such payments would continue. Additionally, the services requested from the family group conference come with their own substantial price tag. My intent here is not to conduct a definitive cost-benefit analysis of family group conferencing versus traditional child welfare services, but rather simply to raise the point that vast sums of money are spent on the current child welfare system, but with very poor results. The question is how better to allocate these resources.

Despite these five successes of family group conferencing, there are important criticisms of the theory and the appropriateness of the process. First, one concern is whether a family challenged by tough issues can make its own decisions. Advocates of family group conferencing contend that there are healthy parts of families traditionally labeled dysfunctional, and functioning conference participants, found in the extended family or community, can help the family make decisions.[232] If the community is dysfunctional as well, the coordinator can bring in members from a larger community where there are resources.[233] In this way, family group conferencing is able to adapt to each family's decisionmaking abilities.

Second, scholars have identified process concerns for women in alternative dispute resolution settings, noting, for example, that the flexibility and lack of legal constraints can recreate existing power imbalances.[234] Of particular concern is a victim of domestic violence, who, through an alternative dispute resolution process, may be required to interact, or, worse, compromise, with her batterer. In the context of family group conferencing, there is considerable disagreement on the propriety of the process when there is a history of domestic violence. New Zealand mandates its use for all cases, including those with a history of domestic violence, and some experts support this practice, arguing that with proper protections for the victim, family group conferencing can work effectively.[235] Other experts, however, view family group conferencing as being appropriate only "as a final step in a limited number of domestic violence cases ... after safety mechanisms are first set in place that can be enforced through court sanctions" and that "for the incidence of domestic violence to be curtailed, clear and unambiguous messages must be given by our legal system that such violence is wrong."[236] Although protections offered by legal representation are absent in family group conferencing, there are advocates for women and children within the conference. "Support persons" are identified by the coordinator for both adult and child victims and these persons are supposed to protect victims who are emotionally and physically vulnerable.[237] Additionally, in some programs, lawyers, guardians ad litem, and court-appointed special advocates participate in the conference.[238]

Third, there is a debate about the types of cases appropriate for family group conferencing. New Zealand has determined that all cases of child abuse and neglect are appropriate for family group conferencing, but some countries have chosen not to use it for cases involving child sexual abuse.[239] The argument against addressing child sexual abuse in a family group conference is that the dynamics of sexual abuse can run across generations and reflect a deep denial within the family, thus undercutting the ability of family members in the conference to acknowledge the abuse and adequately protect the child.[240] On the other hand, there may be some role for family group conferencing in cases of child sexual abuse,[241] although it is important to note that child sexual abuse cases differ radically from the typical abuse or neglect case.[242]

* * * Family group conferencing holds great potential for the child welfare system. Although it may be no panacea for the very difficult issues facing the system, the relevant question is whether family group conferencing, and a problem-solving model more generally, is a marked improvement over the current legal framework, which clearly is not serving the interests of parents or children.

## IV. Beyond the Myopia of Rights

The basic interests underlying rights – that the state should not intervene in a family absent a showing of parental unfitness, and that children should be safe in their homes – should be retained in any legal model. But these interests are best protected by shifting our focus from rights to problem-solving. We should stop calibrating the proper balance between parents' rights and children's rights, and instead move beyond a fixation on rights as the savior of parents and children. In particular, I argue that we should pull decisionmaking authority away from distributors of rights, that is, the courts, and put it back in the hands of families and communities. A problem-solving model would protect the substantive interests of both parents and children by moving away from a process where rights dominate and focusing, in the vast majority of cases, on how to help parents overcome the underlying issues that led to the abuse and neglect. The family group conferencing process exemplifies the problem-solving model of child welfare. It is clear that such a model has significant advantages over the current rights-based model.

A. Benefits of the Problem-solving Model

A problem-solving model for the child welfare system does not abandon the interests underlying parents' rights and children's rights – the interest in family integrity and being free from abuse and neglect. These substantive interests still lie at the heart of the child welfare system. But the process for protecting these interests is not cast in terms of rights. As the rhetoric of rights recedes, the specific procedures designed to protect the interests are relinquished in favor of a more fluid process. In the problem-solving model, the first question is how to meet the needs of and safeguard the child as well as support the parents. In this way, the model does not assume a conflict between preservation and protection. Rather, the task is to widen the lens and see who has a role in creating the problem and who can help resolve it.

As a first step, and as discussed above, it is important to distinguish among the types of cases in the child welfare system, separating the approximately 10 percent of egregious cases from the remaining 90 percent of cases.[243] This filtering would lead to a better allocation of the limited resources in the child welfare system. The state could focus its investigative resources on the egregious cases, and the court system could target its limited resources appropriately. If a family court had to reach decisions in only 10 percent of its current caseload, the court could devote the necessary time to determining the best outcome for these families. Not only would judges be focused, but limited resources, such as adequate counsel for parents, would be more available. Thus narrowed, in these egregious cases, the rights of parents and children would be better protected in practice. After segregating the egregious cases, the problem-solving approach could be adopted for the remaining cases. I now turn to a detailed discussion of the benefits of the problem-solving model.

1. More Protection in Practice

As described in Part II, the rights-based model, as implemented, fails to protect parents and children in three important ways: It does not safeguard against racial and politically driven decisionmaking; it does not offer procedures and court adjudications that lead to considered, careful decisions; and it requires state intervention that often comes at a high cost to the well-being of children. The problem-solving model – and here I refer to the specific process of family group conferencing – is greatly superior to the rights-based model with respect to these three practical concerns.

First, family group conferencing protects the interests of parents and children in unnecessary removals because it better guards against racial bias and politically motivated decisionmaking. Implicit in the decision to remove a child and ultimately terminate parental rights is a cultural judgment by those with the authority to decide the child's future – child protective services and the family court. In family group conferencing, these decisions are made by (more) culturally sensitive actors.[244] If family members and community representatives assess a family's well-being, that assessment likely will come less laden with the racial, class, and cultural biases of the predominantly white and middle class child welfare system.[245] And because decisionmakers are not agency officials, there will not be the same tendency to overreach in the aftermath of well-publicized abuse and neglect cases. To be sure, child protective services could initiate more investigations in the wake of well-publicized cases, but the family group conference would decide for itself if removal was necessary, thus acting as an important check on the agency.

Second, family group conferencing is not dependent on adequate counsel or a court with sufficient time and resources to determine a beneficial outcome. Rather, in family group conferencing, the participants can deliberate at their own pace. It also accounts for the multifaceted human problems that may not lend themselves to court-determined solutions.[246] In family group conferencing, professionals do not provide a solution, rather, the individuals involved in the problem devise the solution. One advocate of family group conferencing describes the theory as follows:

> The relationships between all the parties, and out of which the problems have arisen, are so numerous and ever-changing, and so interconnected that it is folly to believe that outsiders to those relationships could ever "know" them in a way that permits either accurate prediction or predictable intervention. The only ones who might have a chance at that are the parties themselves. For that reason it is they who must pool their perceptions of the relationships, of the problems arising within them, then search together for ways in which each of them, according to their own skills and inclinations, can make different and better contributions.[247]

It is precisely this personal expertise that is lost in the current system.

Third, the safety of children is better protected through family group conferencing because it leads to fewer removals and more placements with family members, while still ensuring that children are not abused or neglected. In the ideal model of family group conferencing the conference occurs before removal, thus the risk of damaging the bond between parent and child by preemptive removal is minimized. Children are not removed until the family group conference determines that is the proper course of action. Certainly difficult cases exist, such as substance abuse, where drug treatment can take years and relapse is highly likely.[248] However, if the family group conference is able to devise a solution that both ensures the parent will obtain treatment and the child will be protected, perhaps by placing the child with a close relative, then a conflict between parent and child does not necessarily exist. Continued contact between parent and child during treatment will maintain the bond, but the child's needs will still be met in the alternative home.

Finally, family group conferencing has additional practical benefits. For example, it gives greater voice to extended family and community members in the decisionmaking process. The current legal framework does not account for the reality of children's lives, in which many individuals beyond parents may play important roles. If we continue to adhere to the parents' rights and children's rights model, then it becomes necessary to determine who can assert parental rights, and important to limit that right to a defined set of individuals. Family group conferencing, by contrast, allows multiple adults to participate in decisionmaking relevant to the child's life, accounting for what is in fact a broader range of individuals with a stake in the child.[249] Thus a child's relationships with these individuals will be accounted for in the decision without the necessity of assigning parental rights to a limited group or abrogating those rights in favor of alternative adults. Likewise, a strength of family group conferencing is that it acknowledges the importance of a child's connection to her community and reinforces those community ties. As noted above, these connections may make the difference in the life of an at-risk child.[250]

## 2. A More Apt Theoretical Framework

My two central theoretical concerns with a rights-based model – that it privileges autonomy while undervaluing assistance, thus failing to account for the important role of poverty in child abuse and neglect, and that it generates adversarial processes and relationships – are also better addressed in a problem-solving model.

First, the problem-solving model is a more apt framework for implementing Jennifer Nedelsky's model of rights, in which the relevant question is how to structure rights such that they foster desirable relationships. In this new model, rather than asserting a right of autonomy from the state, the parent asserts a claim for assistance from the state.[251] This dependency on the state is intended to foster true autonomy for the parent – ultimately the ability to care for a child without state support. This assistive approach of the problem-solving model[252] is more protective than the rights-based model because offering meaningful assistance to parents, such as job training, drug treatment, or subsidized housing, does far more to vindicate the rights recognized by the Supreme Court than a five-minute court hearing with poor counsel after children already have been removed from the home.[253] Moreover, parents are invested in the solution because they chose it themselves. Indeed all conference participants have this "buy-in," which would not happen to the same degree if the solution was imposed by the state, either through a social worker or the court.

This recognition of the need for assistance, not simply autonomy, better acknowledges the role of poverty and creates a more accurate frame for the issues facing families in the child welfare system.[254] This frame will, in turn, reorient the substance of the child welfare system. As opposed to intervening to "rescue" a child and offering minimal, and often ineffective, services to the parent, the process of family group conferencing is a means for families to articulate what supports they need to function better, and an opportunity for the child welfare system, extended families, and the community to provide those supports. Although the risk factors for abuse and neglect are complex, they are not unknown, and can be addressed.

Changing the frame for the child welfare case could help reorient society's views of abuse and neglect away from the view that abuse and neglect are products of parental pathology, and toward a view of social responsibility, where a broader group – both the immediate community and the state – claims responsibility for the larger circumstances that led to the abuse or neglect.[255] Noted child welfare researcher Duncan Lindsey has described the "residual" nature of the child welfare system as one where the system intervenes in the lives of a subset of low-income families, those who experience, or are at great risk for, abuse and neglect, rather than intervening and offering services to all families who suffer from poverty.[256] In this way, the child welfare system views abused and neglected children apart from the society that helped create their circumstances.[257] Family group conferencing can help bridge this divide. It is not a radical reordering of our social system to redistribute wealth, but rather one step toward greater social responsibility for responding to the environment that led to the abuse or neglect.

Family group conferencing itself will not solve poverty. To the extent the needed services, such as subsidized housing, job training, or effective treatment for substance abuse problems, are not provided or available, family group conferencing will have limited utility. Thus, a ready criticism of family group conferencing is that even if it does focus the system on poverty, the resources to address the underlying issues may be unavailable.

There are two answers to this criticism. The family group conference would at least identify the real problem, instead of, for example, a caseworker removing a child for inadequate housing and referring the parent for parenting classes. In the family group conference, all would agree that the family needs help with housing. This focus would be a sea change from the current system, which typically does not meaningfully address the underlying causes of abuse or neglect.

Additionally, highlighting the real needs of the families involved in the child welfare system may require society to acknowledge these needs and thus reorder our social policies. This orientation is a far cry from the current trend of limiting benefits to low-income families, but this reorientation would at least force an honest public debate about whether society indeed wants to help reduce child abuse and neglect. In other words, if the question is whether the state should provide economic benefits to parents who abuse or neglect their children, the answer likely is no. But if the question is whether society wants less child abuse and neglect, the answer likely is yes. If reducing child abuse and neglect requires providing parents with adequate economic support, such as subsidized housing and child care, then society may view the provision of such supports more openly.[258] Moreover, if the political will is there, and if family group conferencing delivers on the promise of fewer out-of-home placements, then some of the $22 billion currently spent on the child welfare system[259] could be redirected toward direct economic support for poor families, such as subsidized child care.

Second, family group conferencing facilitates a collaborative, not adversarial, relationship between parents and the state. The state is helping a parent resolve the underlying issues leading to the abuse or neglect, rather than trying to establish parental unfitness. In other words, the starting point is the assumption that the interests of the state, parents, and children are aligned: All would benefit from helping the parents overcome the issues facing them and be better able to parent.[260] This will further support the move in the child welfare field among social workers to recognize the strengths of biological families and to try and work with them to preserve families.[261]

The problem-solving model as embodied in family group conferencing also fosters better relationships between parents and children because it is a legal framework that draws on the widely-respected "family systems" theory, which posits that the most effective intervention for a child occurs when the whole family is treated.[262] Family group conferencing does not isolate the child from the parent and determine whose interests should prevail, but rather assumes that the family, who played a role in the problem, can also play a role in a solution. Susan Brooks describes the five attributes of a legal framework that would reflect family systems theory: (1) identifying the members of the family system, (2) considering the mutual interests of all the members, (3) maintaining family ties and continuity, (4) emphasizing the present and future, rather than past misdeeds, and (5) focusing on a family's strengths.[263] Family group conferencing fits this bill. Instead of interrupting the important bond between parent and child, family group conferencing reinforces that bond, while still acknowledging that something has gone awry between parent and child. Children need a process that ensures their safety while simultaneously recognizing the complexity of family problems, the importance of original families, and the need for assistance to address underlying social and economic issues.[264]

*Clare Huntington, J.D., is Associate Professor of Law at the University of Colorado School of Law.*

## Notes

[177] See Carrie Menkel-Meadow, Toward Another View of Legal Negotiation: The Structure of Problem Solving, 31 UCLA L. Rev. 754, 755-58 (1984).

[178] Id. at 758; accord Carrie Menkel-Meadow, When Winning Isn't Everything: The Lawyer as Problem Solver, 28 Hofstra L. Rev. 905, 906 (2000) ( "[P]roblem solving negotiation means that the parties can do better than they might otherwise do, especially if they are employing an unnecessarily unproductive adversarial approach.")

[179] Robert H. Mnookin et al., Beyond Winning: Negotiating to Create Value in Deals and Disputes 315 (2000).

[180] Indeed, many courts self-identify as problem-solvers, using an interdisciplinary approach to the complex interaction of multiple problems, such as substance abuse, crime, and child abuse. See, e.g., Judith S. Kaye, Changing Courts in Changing Times: The Need for a Fresh Look at How Courts Are Run, 48 Hastings L.J. 851, 859-62 (1997). Kaye describes the Family Treatment Court in Manhattan's family court system, in which

the court is no longer a remote adjudicator but is heading a problem-solving team. The problem solving is on two levels. In any particular case, the court will be asking what do we do to get this particular parent off drugs. But on a larger scale, the court will be taking a leadership role in seeing that all the players--from Medicaid eligibility specialists to private foster care agencies to drug treatment providers to child welfare agency case-workers--work together.

Id.; see also Jane M. Spinak, Adding Value to Families: The Potential of Model Family Courts, 2002 Wis. L. Rev. 331, 332-33, 367-74 (describing the successes of model courts, including the Manhattan Family Treatment Court, but also noting the failure of such courts to focus on family integrity).

[181] "Family group conferencing" is the term used in New Zealand. As the practice has spread around the globe, alternative terms, and alternative practices, have emerged. For simplicity, this Article uses the term family group conferencing.

[182] Mark S. Umbreit, What Is Restorative Justice?, in Ctr. for Restorative Just. & Peacemaking, U.S. Dep't of Justice, Family Group Conferencing: Implications for Crime Victims 1 (2000); accord John Braithwaite & Heather Strang, Restorative Justice and Family Violence, in Restorative Justice and Family Violence 1, 4 (Heather Strang & John Braithwaite eds., 2002) ("The most general meaning

of restorative justice is a process where stakeholders affected by an injustice have an opportunity to communicate about the consequences of the injustice and what is to be done to right the wrong."). But see Mike Doolan, Restorative Practices and Family Empowerment: both/and or either/or?, Family Rights Newsletter (2003), available at http:// fp.enter.net/restorativepractices/au05/au05_doolan1.pdf (challenging the idea that family group conferencing is akin to restorative justice because the latter is focused on the victim and restoring the harm, whereas the former is focused on empowering the family). Family group conferencing differs from therapeutic jurisprudence, in which judges take a more active role in the lives of litigants, such as ensuring that drug addicts are attending drug rehabilitation treatment programs, rather than simply adjudicating guilt and innocence. By contrast, family group conferencing seeks to avoid court involvement altogether. Family group conferencing also differs from dependency mediation in that the latter concerns negotiations regarding matters pending before a court. See Susan M. Chandler & Marilou Giovannucci, Family Group Conferences: Transforming Traditional Child Welfare and Policy Practice, 42 Fam. Ct. Rev. 216, 217-18 (2004).

[183] See Gale Burford & Joe Hudson, General Introduction: Family Group Conference Programming, in Family Group Conferencing: New Directions in Community-Centered Child and Family Practice, at xix (Gale Burford & Joe Hudson eds., 2000) [hereinafter Family Group Conferencing]. Although not addressed in this Article, family group conferencing is also used for juvenile offenses. See Umbreit, supra note 182, at 2 (describing the process for addressing crimes of juveniles).

[184] The following description draws on a number of sources, including Hardin et al., supra note 12, at 3-5; Paul Adams & Susan M. Chandler, Building Partnerships to Protect Children: A Blended Model of Family Group Conferencing, 40 Fam. Ct. Rev. 503, 505-06 (2002); Jolene M. Lowry, Family Group Conferences as a Form of Court Approved Alternative Dispute Resolution in Child Abuse and Neglect Cases, 31 U. Mich. J.L. Reform 57, 66-76, app. (1997); Allison Morris, Children and Family Violence: Restorative Messages From New Zealand, in Restorative Justice and Family Violence, supra note 182, at 89, 99-101; Barbara White Stack, CYF Program Allows Mother to Take Fate Into Own Hands, Pittsburgh Post-Gazette, Dec. 20, 2003, at B1.

[185] If the child is developmentally able to participate in the family group conference, the coordinator will meet with the child. If the child is not able or willing to participate, the coordinator will still at least see the child.

[186] For a discussion of domestic violence and family group conferencing, see infra notes 235-238 and accompanying text.

[187] This is the New Zealand model. See Hardin et al., supra note 12, at 4 ("A number of people have the legal right to veto the family's decision. This group includes parents, custodians, social workers, care and protection coordinators, and children's lawyers.").

[188] Donald N. Duquette, Non-adversarial Case Resolution, in Child Welfare Law and Practice: Representing Children, Parents, and State Agencies in Abuse, Neglect, and Dependency Cases 354 (Marvin Ventrell & Donald N. Duquette eds., 2005).

[189] See Burford & Hudson, supra note 183, at xix.

[190] Kay Pranis, Conferencing and the Community, in Family Group Conferencing, supra note 183, at 40, 44. One of the premises of family group conferencing is that families involved in the child welfare system do better when they have input into the decisions affecting them. See Burford & Hudson, supra note 183, at x. Family group conferences "are predicated on the belief that, given the right information and resources, families will make better decisions for themselves than professionals....The approach attempts to change the relationships between families and professionals, moving families from passive recipients of 'professional wisdom' to front-line decision-makers for their children." See Paul Nixon, Building Community Through Family Group Conferences: Some Implications for Policy and Practice, in Am. Humane Ass'n, 1999 Family Group Decision Making National Roundtable Proceedings and International Evaluation Conference: Summary of Proceedings 3, 3 (1999). Some proponents make even broader claims, contending that family group conferencing "is a process for acknowledging and then

transforming conflict within and between people." David Moore & John McDonald, Guiding Principles of the Conferencing Process, in Family Group Conferencing, supra note 183, at 49, 49 (emphasis omitted).

[191]  See Mike Doolan & Pam Phillips, Conferencing in New Zealand, in Family Group Conferencing, supra note 183, at 193.

[192]  See Children, Young Persons, and Their Families Act of 1989 §428, 1989 S.R. No. 24 (N.Z.); Doolan & Phillips, supra note 191, at 193-97.

[193]  Catherine Love, Family Group Conferencing: Cultural Origins, Sharing, and Appropriation--A Maori Reflection, in Family Group Conferencing, supra note 183, at 15, 15-16; see also Hardin et al., supra note 12, at 5 ("As in the United States, a very disproportionate number of children involved in the New Zealand child welfare system have non-European origins.").

[194]  Children, Young Persons, and Their Families Act of 1989 §§17-18.

[195]  Burford & Hudson, supra note 183, at xxiii.

[196]  These hallmarks are not unique to family group conferencing and are found in many alternative dispute resolution and problem-solving processes. See, e.g., Roger Fisher et al., Getting to Yes: Negotiating Agreement Without Giving In 17-39 (2d ed. 1991) (discussing the need to focus on the problem, not the person); Jeanne M. Brett, Culture and Negotiation, 35 Int'l J. Psychol. 97 (2000) (describing the importance of incorporating the relevant culture and values of participants); Lawrence E. Suskind, Consensus Building and ADR: Why They Are Not the Same Thing, in The Handbook of Dispute Resolution 361-62 (Michael L. Moffitt & Robert C. Bordone eds., 2005) (describing a consensus-building approach to problem-solving as one that is more inclusive than court-based procedures, which include only the parties themselves, not all the stakeholders).

[197]  See Chandler & Giovannucci, supra note 182, at 219; Linda Richardson, Family Group Decision Making: Transforming the Child Welfare System by Empowering Families and Communities, in Am. Humane Ass'n, supra note 190, at 39, 39-40.

[198]  Pranis, supra note 190, at 42-44; Rupert Ross, Searching for the Roots of Conferencing, in Family Group Conferencing, supra note 183, at 5, 12 ("Relational justice tries to move [away from stigmatizing a perpetrator], to convince people that they are more than their antisocial acts, that they can learn how to respond in better ways to the pressures that affect them day to day."). It is this aspect of family group conferencing, and, more broadly, restorative justice, that often causes advocates for women and children concern. See infra notes 234-238 and accompanying text.

[199]  For example, in Alabama, biological parents brought a class-action lawsuit challenging that state's child welfare practices because the state did not do enough to help families or protect children from abuse or neglect. The parties agreed to a settlement in 1991 requiring Alabama to completely reform its child welfare system. See Bazelon Ctr. for Mental Health Law, Making Child Welfare Work: How the R.C. Lawsuit Forged New Partnerships to Protect Children and Sustain Families 5 (1998); Erik Eckholm, Once Woeful, Alabama Is Model in Child Welfare, N.Y. Times, Aug. 20, 2005, at A1. The consent decree required the state to provide services based on the strengths of children and parents and that families be preserved whenever possible. See Bazelon Ctr. for Mental Health Law, supra, at 51. One of the major barriers to this change was overcoming the views of the social workers, who were used to perceiving deficits, not strengths, in biological families. See id.

[200]  See Lowry, supra note 184, at 65-66; Richardson, supra note 197, at 39-40; Robert Victor Wolf, Promoting Permanency: Family Group Conferencing at the Manhattan Family Treatment Court, 4 J. Center for Families, Child. & Cts. 133, 134 (2003).

[201]  See Ross, supra note 198, at 5.

[202]  See Chandler & Giovannucci, supra note 182, at 219.

[203]  As one practitioner stated, "anybody who's going to be involved--or be an obstacle--in planning for the children" should attend the conference. See Wolf, supra note 200, at 137. Although community

may be an amorphous concept, proponents of family group conferencing contend that such ambiguity does not present a problem in practice. For example, Kay Pranis contends that

> [m]uch has been written about the meaning of "community" and lack of clarity is often cited as a problem, which must be solved before we can proceed to work with communities. Practical experience demonstrates otherwise. Communities themselves do not worry much about academic definitions. They soon define themselves based on the issue at hand.

Pranis, supra note 190, at 40. This inclusiveness overlaps with Woodhouse's model of generism, which grants parental rights to individuals who have established their ability and desire to take responsibility for a child, rather than relying on mere biology. See supra notes 86-88 and accompanying text.

[204] Chandler & Giovannucci, supra note 182, at 219.

[205] See Lisa Merkel-Holguin, Diversions and Departures in the Implementation of Family Group Conferencing in the United States, in Family Group Conferencing, supra note 183, at 224, 224-25 (finding that adequate preparation for conferences is essential and that this typically involves twenty-two to thirty-five hours of work for the coordinator).

[206] See Joan Pennell & Gale Burford, Widening the Circle: Family Group Decisionmaking, 9 J. Child & Youth Care 1, 8-9 (1994); Laura Mirsky, Family Group Conferencing Worldwide: Part One in a Series, Restorative Practices eForum, Feb. 20, 2003, at 1, available at http:// iirp.org/library/fgcseries01. html (last visited Dec. 15, 2005).

[207] See, e.g., Peter Marsh & Gill Crow, Family Group Conferences in Child Welfare (Olive Stevenson ed., 1998) (discussing family group conferencing in Great Britain); Paul Ban, Family Group Conferences in Four Australian States, in Family Group Conferencing, supra note 183, at 232; Knut Sundell, Family Group Conferences in Sweden, in Family Group Conferencing, supra note 183, at 198.

[208] See Wolf, supra note 200, at 134-35. There are three main types of "family involvement" programs in the U.S., each falling along a continuum from simple involvement to complete empowerment. First, a form of family group conferencing that very closely resembles the New Zealand model, as of 2003 had been adopted in hundreds of communities in thirty-four states. See Lisa Merkel-Holguin & Leslie Wilmot, Analyzing Family Involvement Approaches, in Widening the Circle: The Practice and Evaluation of Family Group Conferencing With Children, Youth, and Their Families 186 (Joan Pennell & Gary Anderson eds., 2005). Second, family team conferencing, first begun in Alabama as a result of a lawsuit challenging child welfare practices, involves family members as part of a team to make decisions. See id. at 186-87. Although the family members do not have private family time, as in family group conferencing, the practice is reported to offer meaningful involvement for the family. See id. Finally, team decisionmaking offers families the opportunity to participate in decisionmaking, although without the level of involvement as the other two models provide. The extended family is not necessarily involved, and one of the main goals is bringing in a variety of professionals to ensure that the social worker is not making a decision alone. See id.

[209] See Burford & Hudson, supra note 183, at xxiv; Merkel-Holguin, supra note 205, at 224 (reporting that in 1995, approximately five communities used family group conferencing; by 1999, over one hundred communities used it); Larry Graber et al., Family Group Decision-Making in the United States: The Case of Oregon, in Family Group Conferences: Perspectives on Policy and Practice 180 (J. Hudson et al. eds., 1996).

[210] See Lowry, supra note 184, at 83.

[211] See, e.g., Gary R. Anderson & Peg Whalen, Identifying Short-Term and Long-Term FGC Outcomes, in Widening the Circle, supra note 208, at 134-36; Carol Lupton & Paul Nixon, Empowering in Practice? A Critical Appraisal of the Family Group Conference Approach 119-37, 155-77 (1999); Carol Lupton et al., Univ. of Portsmouth, Family Planning: An Evaluation of the Family Group Conference Model 43-68, 105-19 (1995); Marsh & Crow, supra note 207, at 96. For a good discussion of the challenges of evaluating alternative processes like family group conferencing and the importance

of doing so, both to the practice of family group conferencing and for persuading policymakers to adopt family group conferencing, see Gordon Bazemore & Jeanne B. Stinchcomb, Restorative Conferencing and Theory-based Evaluation, in Family Group Conferencing, supra note 183, at 284. Of course it is possible that selection bias played a role in the generally positive outcomes described in these studies. But this is not a risk in New Zealand, where family group conferencing is mandated for all child welfare cases and thus where a "cherry picking" phenomenon is highly unlikely.

[212]  See Nancy Shore et al., Long Term and Immediate Outcomes of Family Group Conferencing in Washington State, Restorative Practices eForum, Sept. 10, 2002, at 1, available at http://fp.enter.net/restorativepractices/fgcwash.pdf. Shore reports:

> Children who had a conference experienced high rates of reunification or kinship placement, and low rates of re-referral to CPS. These findings generally remained stable as long as two years post-conference. This study, the longest long-term follow-up study of FGC published to date, suggests that FGCs can be an effective planning approach for families involved with the public child welfare agency, resulting in safe, permanent plans for children at risk.

Id.; Joan Pennell & Gale Burford, Family Group Decision Making: Protecting Women and Children, 79 Child Welfare 131, 145-47 (2000) (finding a decrease in abuse and neglect after a family group conference: The number of events triggering intervention declined from 233 to 117 for participating families; by contrast, nonparticipating families experienced an increase in triggering events from 129 to 165); see also Charles E. Wheeler & Sabrina Johnson, Evaluating Family Group Decision-making, The Santa Clara Example, Protecting Children: FGDM Research and Evaluation (Am. Humane Ass'n, Denver, CO), 2003, at 65, 68; Nat. Council of Juvenile & Family Court Judges, Empowering Families in Child Protection Cases: An Implementation Evaluation of Hawai'i's 'Ohana Conferencing Program, 7 Technical Assistance Bull., Apr. 2003. But see Knut Sundell & Bo Vinnerljung, Outcomes of Family Group Conferencing in Sweden: A 3-Year Follow-Up, 28 Child Abuse & Neglect 267, 282-83 (2004) (noting higher rates of re-referral for child welfare agencies following a family group conference than comparison group, but also noting multiple explanations for higher rates).

[213]  See Hardin et al., supra note 12, at 87 ("[T]he coordinators felt that family group conferences can enhance the safety of the child because they set up more whistleblowers who can be involved with the family far more frequently than any professionals.").

[214]  See Burford & Hudson, supra note 183, at xxi.

[215]  See William Vesneski & Susan Kemp, The Washington State Family Group Conference Project, in Family Group Conferencing, supra note 183, at 312, 315; Shore et al., supra note 212, at 5 (noting that in service plans, 80 percent of parents mentioned mental health services, 61 percent mentioned substance abuse treatment or prevention, 61 percent mentioned behavioral interventions [anger management, domestic violence services, parenting, and stress management classes], and 30 percent mentioned housing resources).

[216]  See McElroy & Goodsoe, supra note 12, at 5-6.

[217]  See Richardson, supra note 197, at 45.

[218]  See Vesneski & Kemp, supra note 215, at 315, 318.

[219]  See id.

[220]  See id. at 315-19.

[221]  See id. at 320-22.

[222]  See Burford & Hudson, supra note 183, at xxi. For example, an evaluation of the Arizona Department of Economic Security's Family Group Decision Making program reported that 94 percent of respondents expressed satisfaction with the process and outcome immediately following the meeting. See Ariz. Dep't of Econ. Sec., Family Group Decision Making: Third Annual Evaluation Report 2 (2003).

[223]  Marsh & Crow, supra note 207, at 169-70.

[224]  See Burford & Hudson, supra note 183, at xxi.

²²⁵  See Vesneski & Kemp, supra note 215, at 319-20.

²²⁶  See Margaret Zack, Program Will Try to Place Abused Kids With Relatives--It Aims to Cut Time in Shelter or Foster Care, Star Trib. (Minneapolis), July 6, 1999, at 1B.

²²⁷  See Emmy E. Werner, Children of the Garden Island, Sci. Am., Apr. 1989, at 106 [hereinafter Werner, Garden Island]. A thirty-year study of 698 infants on the Hawaiian island of Kauai demonstrated the importance of the community to such children. See id. at 106, 108-10; Emmy E. Werner, High-Risk Children in Young Adulthood: A Longitudinal Study From Birth to 32 Years, 59 Am. J. Orthopsychiatry 72, 74 (1989) [hereinafter Werner, High-Risk Children]. The two principal goals of the study were "to assess the long-term consequences of prenatal and perinatal stress and to document the effects of adverse early rearing conditions on children's physical, cognitive and psychosocial development." Werner, Garden Island, supra, at 106. The study evaluated the children both during the prenatal period and then after birth at ages one, two, ten, eighteen, and thirty-two. See id. One-third of the children were classified as high-risk because of exposure to perinatal stress and other factors such as poverty, an uneducated parent, an alcoholic or mentally ill parent, or divorce. See id.; Werner, High-Risk Children, supra, at 73. Despite these stressful events, one out of three of the children in the high-risk category developed into competent, caring adults. See Werner, Garden Island, supra, at 108; Werner, High-Risk Children, supra, at 73. The research indicated that emotional support outside of the immediate family greatly contributed to their resiliency. See Werner, Garden Island, supra, at 108-10; Werner, High-Risk Children, supra, at 74. While growing up, these children had at least one close friend, they relied on kin, neighbors, teachers, or church groups for support, and they participated in extracurricular activities. See Werner, Garden Island, supra, at 108-10; Werner, High-Risk Children, supra, at 74.

²²⁸  A tentative analysis of family group conferencing in the United Kingdom postulated that there were "probable" or "possible" savings for the state in using family group conferences, due to reduced court costs, lower re-abuse rates, and more stable placements. See Marsh & Crow, supra note 207, at 172; see also Chandler & Giovannucci, supra note 182, at 222. Chandler and Giovannucci note:

> The child placement data from Minnesota and Arizona for those cases where the FGC was used seems to point to a trend whereby children's out-of-home placements are either less restrictive or avoided entirely. From this information, one could deduce that a reduction in overall cost to the child welfare system for placement-related services might offset the costs associated with an FGC program. Further analysis is likely to assist and inform programs in demonstrating these cost benefits.

Id.

²²⁹  See Cynthia Andrews Scarcella et al., The Cost of Protecting Vulnerable Children IV: How Child Welfare Funding Fared During the Recession 6 (2004).

²³⁰  See id. at 10.

²³¹  See Waldman, supra note 167. Although reports do not describe the cost of the housing voucher, the average subsidy costs the federal government $457 per month, see Office of Pol'y Dev. & Research, U.S. Dep't of Housing & Urban Dev., Costs and Utilization in the Housing Choice Voucher Program 34 (2003), for a total cost of $5484. See also Interagency Council on Supportive Housing and Homelessness, Report to the Hon. M. Jodi Rell, Gov., State of Conn. 4 (2005) (describing the cost of Supportive Housing versus alternatives, and noting the connection between homelessness and foster care placement).

²³²  Moore & McDonald, supra note 190, at 50.

²³³  Id.

²³⁴  See, e.g., Trina Grillo, The Mediation Alternative: Process Dangers for Women, 100 Yale L.J. 1545, 1555-1607 (1991); see also Penelope E. Bryan, Killing Us Softly: Divorce Mediation and the Politics of Power, 40 Buff. L. Rev. 441, 454-56 (1992). Bryan states:

> Research on marital negotiations shows that the greater income and education and the higher occupational level of husbands, compared to wives, confers upon husbands greater power over routine decisions....[U]nless the mediator intervenes, the husband's greater tangible resources

will grant him the lion's share of power in divorce negotiations, particularly over critical financial issues.
Id. Of course we should be mindful of these critiques. Nonetheless, family group conferencing still holds considerable promise, especially for those women who currently have very little voice in the typical, adversarial child welfare proceeding. See supra text accompanying notes 111-116 (discussing practical problems with poor counsel and cursory legal proceedings).

[235] See, e.g., Joan Pennell & Gale Burford, Family Group Decision-Making and Family Violence, in Family Group Conferencing, supra note 183, at 171. John Braithwaite has asserted that "court processing of family violence cases actually tends to foster a culture of denial, while restorative justice fosters a culture of apology," and that an apology, "when communicated with ritual seriousness, is actually the most powerful cultural device for taking a problem seriously, while denial is a cultural device for dismissing it." John Braithwaite, Restorative Justice and Social Justice, 63 Sask. L. Rev. 185, 189 (2000).

[236] Ruth Busch, Domestic Violence and Restorative Justice Initiatives: Who Pays if We Get It Wrong?, in Restorative Justice and Family Violence, supra note 182, at 223-24. Busch argues that safety, not reconciliation, should be the primary goal, see id., and that "[t]here are grave risks in assuming that all relationship conflicts can be patched by consensus. Since the consensual resolution of conflict requires an attitude of 'give a little, take a little' to reach an agreement, there are risks in translating these principles unthinkingly into relationships affected by violence." Id. at 228. However, Busch commends the Pennell and Burford model for

> its emphasis on protection of victims through extensive pre-conference preparation, through ensuring that victims will not be isolated or silenced during conference, the researchers' willingness to use the criminal justice system's protections when necessary, their commitment to ongoing monitoring and evaluation of families who have been through the conferencing process--these demonstrate that restorative justice processes may be useful in some domestic violence cases, at a late stage, after safety issues have been dealt with, in conjunction with other measures also aimed at providing safety and autonomy for victims.

Id. at 246-47.

[237] See Merkel-Holguin, supra note 205, at 227; Gale Burford et al., Measures to Ensure the Safety of Family Members Participating in the Family Group Decision Making Project, in Manual for Coordinators and Communities: The Organization and Practice of Family Group Decision Making 91 (1995). Some communities also offer support persons for offenders.

[238] See Merkel-Holguin, supra note 205, at 227.

[239] See id. at 225.

[240] See id.

[241] Some advocates contend that the offender apologizing to the victim, and the victim having the opportunity to tell the offender about her experience of the offense, can help heal sexual abuse. See Terry S. Trepper, The Apology Session, in Treating Incest: A Multiple Systems Perspective 93 (Terry S. Trepper & Mary Jo Barrett eds., 1986); see also Hardin et al., supra note 12, at 22-23. Hardin writes:

> [T]here are at least two major reasons for using family group conferences in all sexual abuse cases. The first is that the mother should not be left alone to protect the child and to decide whether or not to side with the father against the child. Second, there should be more rigor in making sure that all family members are properly informed about the nature of the situation, [and thus protected from the perpetrator].

Id. Moreover, distinguishing cases presents difficulties because some cases that appear to present "only" physical abuse or neglect may well involve sexual abuse as well, a fact that comes to light during the process. See Gale Burford & Joan Pennell, Family Group Decision Making: New Roles for 'Old' Partners in Resolving Family Violence: Implementation Report Summary 19 (Memorial Univ. of Newfoundland, Inst. Soc. & Econ. Research 1996).

²⁴² See supra note 19 (discussing the distinct characteristics of sexual abuse).

²⁴³ See Ross, supra note 61, at 192 (discussing the need to distinguish cases with "a more sensitive filtering system, in which neglect that does not result in serious harm or danger would trigger benefits in the form of services, rather than potentially unwarranted removal"). This segregation builds on the relatively new practice in child welfare of "differential response." Recognizing that cases vary and thus that different responses are appropriate for different cases, this practice uses an "assessment-oriented approach" for those cases where abuse and neglect are suspected or known, but are considered less severe; for cases of severe abuse and neglect, the traditional investigative (and adversarial) process is used. See Schene, supra note 13, at 4-6. Thus, although critics may contend that the state cannot distinguish among the types of cases, such a process is already in place and being used with some success. See id. at 4-5 (describing a Minnesota study on the benefits of differential response).

²⁴⁴ See Marian S. Harris & Ada Skyles, Working With African American Children and Families in the Child Welfare System, in Race, Culture, Psychology and Law 98-99 (Kimberly Holt Barrett & William H. George eds., 2005) (calling for greater cultural competence among child welfare professionals working with African American families in the child welfare system). Of course family group conference participants would have their own biases and cultural values, but at least these biases would be more endogenous than those of social workers and judges who are not part of the community. Moreover, the decisions of the family group conference will be more contextualized because the participants actually know the family.

²⁴⁵ In the Indian Child Welfare Act of 1978 (ICWA), Congress recognized these cultural judgments and, fearing the ramifications of such judgments--the removal of children from Indian homes and their placement in non-Indian families--devised a statutory scheme that more heavily favors parental rights by permitting the removal of an Indian child only upon a showing of "clear and convincing evidence," ICWA, Pub. L. No. 95-608, §102(e), 92 Stat. 3071 (1978) (codified at 25 U.S.C. §1912(e) (2000)), and the termination of parental rights only upon a showing of evidence beyond a reasonable doubt ☐that the continued custody of the child by the parent or Indian custodian is likely to result in serious emotional or physical damage to the child. Id. §102(f) (codified at 25 U.S.C. §1912(f) (Supp. 2002)). These standards are much higher than those used for non-Indian child welfare cases. See supra note 30.

²⁴⁶ See Gregory Firestone & Janet Weinstein, In the Best Interests of Children: A Proposal to Transform the Adversarial System, 42 Fam. Ct. Rev. 203, 203 (2004) ("[T]he adversarial, rights-based model typically fails to serve the interests of children and families and may be more harmful than beneficial to children relative to other possible methods of dispute resolution."); John E.B. Myers, Children's Rights in the Context of Welfare, Dependency, and the Juvenile Court, 8 U.C. Davis J. Juv. L. & Pol'y 267, 281 (2004) (arguing that family courts are unable to solve "complex human problems" through an adversarial process).

²⁴⁷ Ross, supra note 198, at 13.

²⁴⁸ See supra text accompanying note 166.

²⁴⁹ See Buss, supra note 40, at 29 (noting that the classic frame of parent versus state "oversimplifies the field of potential competitors considerably," notably excluding extended family members).

²⁵⁰ See supra note 227 (discussing the Kauai study).

²⁵¹ Of course this is a complex issue. I do not, here, frame this as a right to assistance, largely because the U.S. legal system, at least constitutionally speaking, generally does not confer positive rights--our liberty is negative. Although my preference would be for a legally enforceable right to assistance from the state, because I think this so unlikely to happen, I state the right here as a "claim," thus diluting its power but also giving it a greater chance for recognition. I intend to explore this issue more fully in a subsequent article. In addition to the legal question of whether the parent has a right to receive support from the state, there are a host of practical questions. How much can the parent claim from the state? Should the state set a dollar limit on what it owes the parent? What if the state refuses to provide the requested supports, perhaps because of an independent determination that such supports will not help

the family? Rather than explore these issues at length here, I only note that these are the right questions to be asking

[252] I am aware of the potential for increased state control of poor families in such a model, see, e.g., Appell, supra note 43, at 765-69 (describing the importance of rights to poor families to prevent the state imposing its own view of acceptable parenting and family forms); Katherine M. Franke, Taking Care, 76 Chi-Kent L. Rev. 1541, 1541 (2001) (noting that the "delicate act of translation--from private need to public obligation--demands acute sensitivity to the ways in which public responsibility inaugurates a new and complex encounter with a broad array of public preferences that deprive dependent subjects of primary stewardship over the ways in which their needs are met"). I intend to explore this issue more fully in a subsequent article.

[253] See Lindsey, supra note 111, at 318-19 (proposing "two simple programs" to end child poverty: a child allowance from the government to raise children and effective child support programs, combined with universal child care); Roberts, supra note 9, at 268 (arguing for addressing family poverty by increasing the minimum wage, creating jobs, establishing national health insurance, providing high-quality subsidized child care, and increasing the supply of affordable housing). In this Article I emphasize the role of the state in assisting families, but one of the benefits of family group conferencing is that it identifies the hidden resources of families and communities.

[254] Family group conferencing is still relevant and beneficial for economically stable families. For example, the process provides them with greater decisionmaking authority than in a court-centric system.

[255] See Guggenheim, supra note 39, at 181-85 (discussing the origins of child protection as part of an attempt to address child poverty, but describing political changes in the twentieth century, particularly the 1970s, that led away from framing child abuse as a product of greater social ills).

[256] See Lindsey, supra note 111, at 18. This is not true for child sexual abuse, which spans all classes. See supra note 19. Annette Appell argues that this view of child abuse is part of a larger discourse that locates responsibility for poverty and its related problems in the individual, rather than society. See Annette R. Appell, Disposable Mothers, Deployable Children, 9 Mich. J. Race & L. 421, 421 (2004). Appell writes:

> The dominant discourse about poverty and racism has changed significantly in the past decade to reflect a view that poverty, problems attendant to poverty, and racial affiliation are matters of individual choice that have individualized solutions. In this discourse, poverty, homelessness, child neglect, and economically blighted and isolated communities reflect personal pathology; White supremacy is a relic and all race distinctions are bad. These beliefs are manifested in federal legislation that limits welfare benefits, promotes adoption of poor children, and removes barriers to transracial adoption. A common denominator of this legislation is the notion that poor (Black) families are pathological so they should be discouraged from having children and the children that they do have would be better off with other parents.

Id.

[257] See Lindsey, supra note 111, at 2 n.1

[258] It could also be argued that the costs of the child welfare system far outweigh the costs of providing economic supports to families. See supra text accompanying notes 228-231. Moreover, in the long-term, the costs associated with the poor outcomes for children in foster care–increased involvement in the criminal justice system, lower rates of employment, higher rates of teen pregnancy–also argue in favor of investing sooner rather than later. Cf. Clare Huntington, Welfare Reform and Child Care: A Proposal for State Legislation, 6 Cornell J.L. & Pub. Pol'y 95, 110-11 (1996) (addressing the costs associated with not investing in child care).

[259] See supra note 229 and accompanying text.

[260] There will be cases where a party engages in strategic behavior or acts deceptively, or the interests of the parties do conflict. I do not mean to gloss over these realities of human behavior. Rather, I

intend to highlight the orientation of a problem-solving model: The model assumes it is at least possible that the parties can work together toward a mutually beneficial outcome.

[261]   See Schene, supra note 13, at 6. New York City has made this change on a policy level, reducing by half the number of children in foster care, and statistics appear to support the conclusion that this shift has not compromised the safety of those children not placed in foster care. See Fernanda Santos, Placements in Foster Care Are at Lowest Since Mid-80's, N.Y. Times, Oct. 23, 2005, at A33. City officials attribute the reduction to a strong economy, a decline in the use of crack cocaine, and an explicit policy adopted by the Administration for Children's Services (ACS) that strives to keep children in their own families. See id. The city offers substantial supports to parents, such as counseling, housing aid, and substance abuse treatment. See id. A policy emphasizing preservation is always vulnerable, however, as evidenced by the debate following a recent death of a child returned to his mother by the ACS. See Leslie Kaufman, Mother of Boy Who Died Was Trained, Agency Says, N.Y. Times, Nov. 10, 2005, at B3; Leslie Kaufman, Baby Drowned as Mother Listened to CD's, Prosecutor Says, N.Y. Times, Nov. 9, 2005, at B1. Of course this shift is not complete around the country. For example, in Alabama, it took a consent decree to get social workers to start working with biological families, rather than simply to dismiss such families as dysfunctional. See supra note 199. Certainly the current legal framework, as embodied in the Adoption and Safe Families Act (ASFA), does not facilitate this social work approach. See supra text accompanying notes 59-62 (describing ASFA).

# [13]

# Why Won't Mom Cooperate?
# A Critique of Informality in Child Welfare Proceedings

## Amy Sinden

### Introduction

Reams of paper have been filled with the ruminations of countless judges and legal scholars on the subject of criminal procedure. It is the central concern of four of the ten constitutional amendments that make up the Bill of Rights. It is a major course offered at every law school. And it is the paradigmatic context in which we frame much of our debate about the relationship between the state and the individual in a democratic society.

But there is another system that exists in every county across the country, in which the state hauls private citizens into court against their will, accuses them of acts that trigger severe social reprobation, and threatens them with a deprivation of liberty that, for many people, strikes at the very core of their identity and threatens to remove the most profound source of purpose, fulfillment, and happiness from their lives. This is the child welfare system. Yet despite the indisputable importance of the interests at stake, judges and scholars have devoted relatively little attention to the procedures employed by the courts that decide whether to remove children from their homes when their parents are accused of abuse or neglect.[1]

The Constitution, of course, guarantees procedural rights to more than just criminal defendants. It accords a right of "due process of law" to all those whom the government deprives of life, liberty, or property. The procedural due process ideal embodied in this constitutional phrase encompasses two fundamental goals: first, to promote accurate decision-making, and second, to provide the "opportunity to be heard." In child welfare cases, both of these goals are particularly compelling. When the courts make inaccurate decisions the results can be tragic. Inaccuracy in one direction may result in a child suffering serious injury in her home. Inaccuracy in the other direction may result in a child being wrenched from a healthy and loving family. Additionally, the gravity of the charge – there is perhaps no more socially abhorrent act than the mistreatment of one's children – demands that courts give the accused ample opportunity to be heard in defense of her reputation and dignity. In this Article I will examine the procedures employed in child welfare cases and consider the extent to which such procedures achieve these two goals.

I draw on feminist theory to inform my analysis for two reasons. First, the vast majority of the parents caught up in the child welfare system are women.[2] Second, the liberty interest at stake – the relationship with one's child - is central to female identity, at least as it has been culturally constructed.[3] Surprisingly, despite the enormous number of women acutely affected by the child welfare system, feminist legal scholarship on the subject is virtually non-existent.[4] I suspect this is due, at least in part, to the fact that the child welfare system does not fit neatly within the established framework of feminist thought.

Feminist discussions of child abuse almost always lump it together with the abuse of women by husbands and boyfriends under the rubric of "domestic violence."[5] With battered women as their paradigm,[6] feminists have aligned themselves with women and children as the victims of domestic violence, and against the male perpetrators.[7] Based on this model of the heterosexual, two-parent, nuclear family, feminists have fought – with a great deal of success – against the traditional liberal notion of the family as a closed private unit,[8] immune from public scrutiny or state intervention, viewing that notion as a mechanism that has served to perpetuate the power of male heads of household over women and children. Rejecting the traditional liberal focus on protecting the individual against intrusion by the state, feminists have instead viewed the state as an ally, seeking state intervention into the family to regulate violence in the private sphere.

Due in part to the efforts of feminists, every state now has an extensive legal and bureaucratic child welfare system designed to protect children from abuse and neglect at the hands of their parents.[9] The irony, of course, is that the vast majority of the families subjected to government scrutiny and control under this system are not traditional male-headed nuclear families, but single mothers and their children.[10] Because the child welfare system affects almost exclusively poor and minority communities,[11] however, it is outside the personal experience of most feminist theorists.[12] This may also explain, in part, the extent to which feminists have viewed the issue of child abuse from the top down – succumbing to the temptation to fit it into the existing theoretical paradigm that has developed around the issue of domestic violence, rather than looking up from the bottom - grounding theory in the experiences of those women whose lives are directly affected by the child welfare system.[13]

Paradoxically, a feminist analysis of the procedures employed in child welfare cases appears to point in two diametrically opposite directions. On one hand, a feminist critique of the value system that ranks autonomy over connection and the public over the domestic sphere supports the argument that the loss of the care and companionship of one's child constitutes as grievous a deprivation of liberty as imprisonment. Under standard due process principles, this leads to the conclusion that a high level of procedural protection and formality is appropriate in these proceedings.

On the other hand, the same strand of feminism that offers this critique of values has also questioned the assumption embedded in our due process jurisprudence that formal methods of dispute resolution are superior to informal ones and that disputes involving more important interests therefore warrant more formal procedures. Some feminists reject formal adversarial processes as reflective of a one-sided male norm and promote instead a "female" mode of problem solving that emphasizes cooperation, relationships, and mediation.[14] Many in the child welfare system embrace this notion of a kinder, gentler, female mode of dispute resolution with particular enthusiasm because they view these disputes as centering on "women's issues" of children, family, and emotions.

This conflict illustrates both the power and the danger of the feminist critique of values and the importance of remaining vigilant to the feminist commitment to grounding theory and generalization in concrete experience and particularized context. We can dislodge this theoretical logjam only by carefully examining the practical implications of de-formalization in child welfare cases in light of a thorough understanding of the particular incentives and power dynamics influencing individual behavior in these proceedings. This closely grounded look reveals that de-formalization of these proceedings is actually antithetical to feminism's paramount concern with equalizing power imbalances and undermines the goals of due process by disempowering mothers, generating false agreements, and increasing the risk of inaccurate fact-finding.

This Article proceeds in three parts. Part I provides an overview of the existing system. First, it describes the statutory and constitutional standards governing procedure in child welfare cases. It then describes the pressures toward further de-formalization that come from both within and outside the system. Part II examines how courts analyze the procedural due process issues raised in child welfare proceedings. Part IIA critiques the assumption, evident in much of the case law, that the deprivation of liberty caused by the forcible separation of parent and child is less grievous than the deprivation of liberty caused by imprisonment in a criminal case. Part IIB examines how altering that assumption to treat the deprivation of liberty at stake in a child welfare case as equivalent to that in a criminal case would affect the overall due process calculus in these cases. Part III then questions the assumption, implicit in the traditional due process framework, that formal procedure is better than informal procedure and that stronger interests demand more formal procedures. Looking contextually at how formality and informality play out amidst the peculiar power dynamics and incentive structures of the child welfare system, I conclude that, in most instances, formality better serves the outcome and process goals of the procedural due process ideal.

I. The Existing System: Intermediate Due Process Protection and the Pressure for Further De-Formalization.

We can envision various types of adjudicative proceedings on a scale from less to more formality. Informal processes that provide relatively few procedural safeguards and protections occupy one end of the scale. The criminal system, with its elaborate set of formal rules and procedures, occupies the other end of the scale. As a matter of constitutional and statutory law, courts and legislatures generally have located child welfare cases at an intermediate point on this scale.[15]

From outside this statutory and constitutional scheme, there is significant pressure to further de-formalize these proceedings.[16] That pressure comes from two sources. First, a subtle dynamic arises on a day-to-day level in these cases, due in part to the prevalence of social work discourse and the tendency of the participants to view these cases in therapeutic rather than legalistic terms. This dynamic implicitly suppresses rights talk and discourages the participants from taking advantage of those procedural protections that do exist. Second, an explicit movement among some commentators and reformers is currently promoting the adoption of informal, non-adversarial alternative dispute resolution mechanisms in child welfare cases. Before describing these pressures toward de-formalization, I will provide a brief overview of the stages of a child welfare case and the governing substantive and procedural standards.

A. The Anatomy of a Child Welfare Case

At the core of the child welfare system are the state-administered child welfare agencies charged with protecting children from abuse and neglect.[17] These state agencies typically employ hundreds of social workers to investigate reports of suspected child abuse and neglect and work with families when such reports are substantiated. These agency social workers usually serve as case managers, contracting with other private non-profit agencies to provide particular services, such as intensive social work or foster care.[18]

The typical case proceeds as follows. First, a hotline administered by the child welfare agency receives an anonymous report of suspected child abuse or neglect.[19] The agency then assigns a social worker to investigate the report. The social worker begins by knocking on the family's door and attempting to interview the parent and other adults that live in the household, as well as the child who is the subject of the report.[20] If the child attends school, the social worker may go to the school to interview her. Depending on the nature of the allegations, the social worker may also talk to school personnel, medical providers, neighbors, or others who may have relevant information.

Based on her investigation, the social worker then makes one of several decisions. She may determine that the alleged abuse or neglect did not occur and close the case.[21] Or she may determine that it did occur but did not sufficiently endanger the child to warrant removing the child from the home. In that case she will usually seek to have the family placed under agency supervision to provide those social services she thinks will help to alleviate the problem she has identified. Or, if she determines that some one in the home has perpetrated abuse or neglect sufficient to endanger the safety of the child, she may seek to have the child removed from the family and placed in foster care.[22]

Under any of these scenarios, the social worker can seek court intervention at various stages of the case if the parent does not accede voluntarily to the social worker's plan. If, when the social worker first knocks on the family's door, the parent refuses to let her in, refuses to talk to her, or refuses to allow her to talk privately with the child, the social worker may ask the agency's attorneys to file a petition seeking a court order compelling the parent to cooperate with the investigation. If the social worker completes her investigation and determines that the family needs agency supervision and services but the parent refuses to submit to supervision or cooperate with the provision of services, the social worker may ask the agency's attorneys to file a petition seeking court-ordered supervision of the family.[23]

Finally, if the social worker concludes that the situation warrants the removal of the child from her parents, the social worker will try to accomplish this in one of two ways. First, she will try to convince the parent to sign a voluntary placement agreement.[24] Such an agreement will typically authorize the state to keep the child in foster care for some specified amount of time (30 days to six months), at the expiration of which a court hearing will be scheduled to determine whether the placement should continue.[25] Second, if the parent refuses to consent to placement, the social worker will seek to have the agency's attorneys petition the court to remove the child.

Child welfare agencies often remove children from their homes on an emergency basis. All states authorize social workers (or in some instances police) to immediately remove children from their homes where they are deemed to be in imminent danger.[26] In some states the social worker must first obtain an ex parte order from a judicial officer, and in others the social worker acts independently in making the initial removal decision.[27] In either case, the court holds a preliminary hearing at which the parents are entitled to appear (often called a "detention" hearing) within a proscribed period of time, generally ranging from three days to six days, but sometimes as long as two weeks.[28] At this hearing, the court addresses only the limited issue whether the evidence warrants holding the child in foster care until a full hearing can be held.

Once in court, and following any preliminary hearing on emergency removal, cases usually proceed in two phases. At the first phase, in some states termed the "adjudicatory" hearing, the court determines whether the allegations of abuse or neglect rise to a level warranting state interference with the parent-child relationship and, if so, whether they are true.[29] If the court finds that the state has made a sufficient showing on these issues, it makes a finding to that effect, in some jurisdictions termed an "adjudication of dependency."[30] If the court makes such a finding, it then moves on to the second phase, usually termed the "dispositional" hearing. At this hearing the court determines where the child should be placed.[31] Choices may include leaving the child in the home with agency supervision and provision of services, placement in foster care, or placement with a relative or friend.

It is important to note that, while these proceedings involve the custody of children, their substantive standards differ fundamentally from those that govern custody disputes between parents. In the latter case, the dispute is between private parties, each of whom stands in the same legal relationship to the child, and the governing substantive standard is the "best interests of the child."[32] A dependency case, in contrast, pits parent against state. This raises the specter of state interference with the fundamental civil rights of private citizens. In this context, courts reject a best-interests-of-the-child standard because it would allow the state to interfere in private family functioning simply because the parents were not providing the best possible care.[33] Especially in light of the indeterminacy of the best interests standard and its vulnerability to distortion by cultural and class bias,[34] such a standard would clash irreconcilably with our political system's commitment to individual freedom.[35]

For these reasons the state must meet a higher standard to interfere in family functioning. At the adjudicatory phase, the state must show parental unfitness by proving acts or omissions on the part of the parent that bring the child within the statutory definition of a "dependent" child or a "child in need of assistance."[36] Even at the dispositional stage, after the court has already made a finding of parental unfitness, some states require a stronger showing than the best interests of the child in order to remove a child from her parents.[37]

Following a dispositional hearing, the court reviews the case periodically, often every six months.[38] Except in certain exceptional cases of severe abuse, once a child is placed outside the home, state agencies must make "reasonable efforts" to reunify children with their families in order to receive federal funding for foster care.[39] Accordingly, when a child welfare agency first removes a child, the agency social worker meets with the parent and draws up a plan for reunification of the family. This plan specifies steps the parent needs to take and services the agency needs to provide to meet that goal.[40] Tasks identified for the parent may include completing a parenting course or a program of mental health or drug treatment, or finding a suitable place to live. Services to be provided by the agency may include referrals to or payments for drug or mental health treatment or logistical or financial help finding housing.

If reunification does not occur within a certain period of time, the agency may try to have the child adopted. This requires the agency's lawyers to first petition the court for an order terminating the natural parent's rights. To obtain such an order, the agency must generally prove in court that the parent is unable or unwilling to care for the child presently and in the foreseeable future.[41] With the passage of the Adoption and Safe Families Act of 1997, the pressures on agencies to move quickly toward termination of parental rights once removal has occurred have increased substantially. Under the Act, the agency must file a petition for termination twelve months after placement in most instances.[42] Where the court finds "aggravated circumstances," the agency must move for termination in just 30 days.[43]

State statutes and case law interpreting constitutional due process protections direct trial courts to conduct dependency and termination proceedings at an intermediate level of formality. These proceedings therefore include most of the standard trappings of the traditional adversarial model of dispute resolution. The state must set forth its allegations in a petition and serve it on the parent. Cases are heard by judges. Witnesses testify under oath. A court reporter transcribes the proceedings. Rules of evidence apply, with some exceptions. The parties may be represented by lawyers and may appeal adverse decisions.

However, parents in dependency and termination proceedings do not receive many of the procedural rights that criminal defendants – even those facing minor charges – enjoy. Thus, as a matter of federal Constitutional law, an indigent parent in a dependency or termination case has no right to appointed counsel.[44] A number of states provide a right to appointed counsel by statute,[45] but even in those states, courts have held that parents have no right to effective assistance of counsel because the right to counsel is not constitutionally mandated.[46] An indigent parent facing termination of parental rights has a right to a free transcript on appeal but she does not have this right in a dependency proceeding.[47] The constitutionally required standard of proof in a termination of parental rights proceeding is the intermediate clear and convincing evidence standard.[48] The civil "preponderance of the evidence" standard of proof governs dependency proceedings in many states.[49] Although termination and dependency cases generally provide the parent an opportunity to confront and cross-examine witnesses (with exceptions for child witnesses), courts in many instances apply relaxed evidentiary rules.[50] For example, many jurisdictions allow social workers' hearsay reports to be admitted into evidence.[51] Courts do not construe the due process rights of parents and children in dependency and termination proceedings to include rights analogous to the criminal prohibition on double jeopardy or the right against self-incrimination contained in the Fifth Amendment.[52] Courts do not require social workers investigating reports of child abuse to comply with the Fourth Amendment's warrant and probable cause requirements before searching a home,[53] and no exclusionary rule limits the admissibility of improperly obtained evidence.[54]

But we cannot glean the full of flavor of the system that actually confronts a mother accused of child abuse from case books and statutes. Overlaying the constitutional and statutory procedural scheme is a subtle dynamic arising in the day-to-day human interactions within the child welfare system that implicitly suppresses rights talk and discourages parties from using those procedural protections that are available to them. The next section attempts to describe that dynamic.

## B. The Implicit Promotion of Informalism in Dependency Proceedings

A woman who has been subpoenaed to court to answer charges that she mistreats her children maneuvers up the wide stone staircase at the entrance to the family court building in Philadelphia – children, stroller, diaper bag in tow – where she is greeted by a long line of adults and children waiting to be admitted through a metal detector. Professional looking people with briefcases rush past the line and pass quickly around the metal detector with a smile and a nod from the guard. After about forty-five minutes, the woman finally reaches the front of the line, her children nervous and whining. The guard opens her bags and examines their contents. When he comes to the sandwiches she has packed for the children, he sets them aside with a gruff "sorry, no food in the courtrooms or waiting rooms." She starts to protest that her three-year-old and five-year-old are already getting fidgety and won't last without something to eat if she has to stay past noon and that she doesn't have money to buy them something, but the guard has already waived her through and turned his attention to the next family in line...

She leads her children in the direction the guard indicated, diagonally across the lobby to where she sees lots of people coming in and out of a short corridor. The corridor leads to a large square windowless room filled with rows of wooden chairs and a din of voices punctuated periodically by a crying child or an adult's angry shout. There are perhaps 200 people in the room; most of the chairs are taken. Some sit staring vacantly into space. Others try to comfort crying children. Others sit huddled in groups. Around the perimeter, groups of people stand talking. Some are laughing, others talk intently. Some write on pads of paper while they talk. Others carrying files or briefcases push through as if in a hurry. Our visitor unfolds her subpoena. It says report to courtroom I by 9:00 a.m. After waiting in line it is now almost 10:00, but she can't see any sign indicating she's in the right place. At one end of the room there are two desks with chairs behind them, but the chairs are empty. She approaches a woman in a silk dress who sits next to one of the desks concentrating on a file. The woman looks up from her file and points vaguely to a door. "The court officer should be coming out in a while. Check in with him. He'll probably have a blue jacket on." She turns back to her file. The visitor spots a few empty chairs in the middle of the row. Squeezing past with her children, she reaches them and sits down with a sigh, looking nervously at the door for someone with a blue jacket... [55]

The day-to-day proceedings in child welfare cases are shaped in large part by the prevalence of "repeat players": professionals who appear repeatedly in the same forum on many different cases. [56] Indeed, it is not unusual for the lawyers for all sides - parents, children, and state child welfare agencies – to all be specialists, handling child welfare cases exclusively or nearly exclusively. A special unit of the city solicitor's or state attorney general's office typically "prosecutes" these cases on behalf of the child welfare agency. Since the vast majority of families in the system are poor, where parents and children receive representation at all, it is usually from legal aid or public defender organizations with specialized units of lawyers who handle these cases exclusively. Court systems also often assign particular judges and magistrates to specialize in this area. Finally, a host of social workers regularly appear in court on multiple cases. They may work for the government child welfare agency or for private social service agencies that contract with the state to provide foster care and/or in home services. Thus, it is common for everyone involved in a case – except for the parents and children who are its objects – to be repeat players, familiar with each other and familiar with the workings of the system.

This specialization no doubt proves useful in that professionals develop the expertise necessary to handle cases effectively and efficiently. The dominance of repeat players, however, can also create a "clubby" atmosphere, in which all of the individuals in the courthouse – from the lawyers and social workers to the judges, their courtroom deputies, stenographers and clerks – have well-established relationships and a kind of collegiality that comes from daily contact.[57] This atmosphere fosters the development of a set of unwritten rules and shared expectations that govern the expected and accepted behavior of players in the system. Familiarity and collegiality can become a cliquishness in which newcomers and outsiders feel an intense pressure to conform to established rules of behavior in this "microsocial" setting.[58] For those who would depart from established norms, the phrase "things just aren't done that way around here" becomes a familiar refrain.

A mother subpoenaed to court on allegations of abuse or neglect is likely to feel particularly vulnerable and insecure as she enters this environment. In light of the allegations against her, she may be especially eager to be accepted and viewed as normal and respectable. She may be particularly sensitive to any cues she receives from professionals as to how she should act to fit in with the norms of this microsocial setting. Race and class often exacerbate this outsider dynamic. The professionals in the system are by and large well-educated, middle-class, and predominantly white. Meanwhile, many of the accused parents and their children are members of racial minority groups and virtually all are extremely poor with little formal education.[59]

In the negotiations leading up to and surrounding courtroom proceedings, a mother may often find herself the only outsider in a room full of professionals. Indeed, the sheer number of lawyers and social workers involved in a single family's case can be mind-boggling. In addition to the state agency social worker, there may be a social worker from a private agency contracted to provide more intensive social work services to the family, a social worker with the foster care agency (or in cases with more than one child in different foster homes, several social workers from different foster care agencies), a social worker working for the child advocacy organization, a guardian ad litem, a court-appointed special advocate,[60] a lawyer representing the state child welfare agency, a lawyer representing the child, a lawyer representing the mother, and in some cases a lawyer representing one or more fathers or other involved family members. With some exceptions, all of these people speak with the intonation and dialect of the professional, educated class. This is usually not the native tongue of the mother. Additionally, as in any insular microsocial setting in which a limited group of people interact repeatedly, a host of catch phrases, acronyms, short-hands, and jargon develop that are unknown to outsiders.

Social work norms and discourse predominate in this setting. Perhaps this is due to the considerable power wielded by social workers, who initially exercise the discretion as to whether the coercion of the court process will be invoked against a family and to whom judges are often inclined to defer once a case gets to court. Perhaps it is also attributable to the tendency of both lawyers and social workers to view these cases in therapeutic terms, as an emotional crisis or breakdown in communication, rather than a legal question about whether the allegations of abuse are true and warrant state intervention.[61]

In any case, the predominance of social work norms and discourse creates significant pressure on parents to resolve these cases through non-adversarial, informal means. Social workers are trained to be effective by building non-adversarial relationships characterized by cooperation and trust. From a social worker's point of view, she fails professionally if her relationship with her client becomes adversarial. While lawyers' training steeps them in the discourse of individual rights and prepares them to operate in formal, procedure-bound environments, social workers are steeped in the discourse of relationships and cooperation and trained to value informality over formality as a means of gaining trust and building rapport.

A key word in the prevailing social work discourse is thus "cooperation." This word often forms the focal point of the meetings and conversations that take place in the hallways of the courthouse: "If mom would just cooperate ..." Running as an undercurrent to this refrain are powerful cultural stereotypes and expectations attached to motherhood. Mothers are supposed to be nurturing, loving, and above all protective of their children. Conflict is viewed as harmful to the child, and therefore the mother accused of child abuse who creates conflict by failing to "cooperate" harms her child a second time.[62] This language of "cooperation" cloaks the substantial power differential that exists between the child welfare agency and the accused mother. The word "cooperation" implies a collaboration between equals in which each party contributes and makes compromises. In the child welfare context, however, "cooperation" is frequently just a code word for the parent doing whatever the social worker tells her to do.

Where there is disagreement between the parties, it is the mother, not the social worker, who is labeled "uncooperative," and therefore blamed for creating conflict.

Another common element of this social work discourse is the claim: "we're all really on the same side; we just want what is best for the children." By creating an illusion of shared goals, this claim makes cooperation the obvious best solution. Two people working toward a shared goal clearly work more effectively if they cooperate. Conflict is again subverted and the power dynamic hidden. The fallacy, of course, is that this claim treats the "best interests of the child" as some objectively determinable absolute, when in fact it is an extremely malleable and subjective standard.[63] In fact, the parent and the agency social worker may have two entirely different ideas of what is in the child's "best interests." In such a case, their goals are not shared and "cooperation" may be an impossibility.[64]

These dynamics - operating either within the hallways of the courthouse or in families' homes or social workers' offices before court involvement has even been initiated - create pressure to cooperate rather than to assert rights, and to resolve cases through a process of compromise and agreement rather than through litigation. This is not simply to say that the parties tend to resolve these cases through negotiation rather than contested hearings. Where negotiation occurs against the backdrop of the formal procedures and rights afforded by the adversarial process, it reflects - at least roughly - the likely outcome of that process. Accordingly, such negotiation is a product of the formal rules and procedures that would apply if the case went to a hearing.[65] For example, a litigant might gain concessions from her opponent by pointing out in negotiations that a particular witness's testimony would be barred as hearsay, and thus gain the protection against unreliable evidence afforded by the rules of evidence without actually invoking those rules in a contested hearing.

But the dynamics I describe above do more than simply push participants to resolve cases through negotiated settlement rather than trial. Instead, they serve to devalue and suppress rights talk, treating any effort to frame problems in an adversarial context as unmotherly and harmful to the child. Accordingly, they discourage participants from asserting, either in negotiations or contested hearings, the rights and procedural protections that are available to them. As such, these dynamics push the actual day-to-day functioning of these proceedings to an even lower level of formality than that proscribed by the due process analyses of courts and legislatures.

C. The ADR Movement

In addition to these implicit pressures that operate on a day-to-day level to de-formalize the existing adversarial system, there is currently a movement to explicitly de-formalize the child welfare court system by introducing alternative dispute resolution ("ADR") mechanisms, primarily mediation.[66] A number of jurisdictions in California, Oregon, Kansas, Illinois, Connecticut and elsewhere have established pilot programs in dependency court mediation.[67] These programs usually allow cases to be referred to mediation at any stage of the proceeding[68] by order of the court or agreement of the parties. A trained mediator, or sometimes a male-female mediator team, meets with the parties and other interested persons. The participants discuss the case and attempt to reach an agreement. The mediator acts as a facilitator, not a decisionmaker, remaining neutral and helping the participants to communicate effectively. There are relatively few rules. No relevancy or hearsay standards limit the range of subjects that can be discussed.[69] No rules limit who can participate. Foster parents, extended family members, and service providers, all of whom would be excluded from adversarial proceedings as nonparties, are often included in mediation at the discretion of the mediator.[70] Attorneys may or may not be included.[71] All mediation participants are bound to keep statements made during mediation confidential, except for information that requires a mandated reporter to report new allegations of child abuse or neglect.[72]

Proponents of mediation cite a number of benefits in addition to its ability to ease crowded dockets.[73] Mediation is said to encourage participation by parents by giving them a sense of inclusion, validation, and empowerment.[74] This decreases the likelihood that parents will withdraw from the process and leave their children feeling rejected.[75] The parties' sense of inclusion and investment in the process is also said to give mediated agreements a greater chance of long-term success.[76] But primarily, mediation is touted as an antidote to the adversarial process, which is viewed as inherently destructive to families and harmful to children.[77] The adversarial process is said to break down communication, polarize disputants, create hostility, and "tear at the thin fabric that holds these families together."[78] Indeed, one pilot program makes the extraordinary claim that the "adversarial process can be as traumatic [to children and families] as the child abuse and neglect which brought the child to the attention of the juvenile justice system."[79] Mediation, in contrast, is presented as an alternative that opens lines of communication, promotes sharing of information and joint problem solving, and assists the participants in reaching mutually beneficial and constructive solutions.[80]

\* \* \* \*

A. De-formalization of Child Welfare Cases: The View from the Ground

We can ask two basic questions about process. First, does it produce good outcomes? And, second, apart from outcomes, how does the process itself affect the participants?[167] With respect to outcomes, the obvious goal is factual accuracy. Because the goal of a child welfare proceeding is ultimately prospective – the protection of the child – factual accuracy in this context really means making accurate predictions about the future. Without getting into debates about whether psychologists can accurately describe a child abuser profile or whether other reliable methods might exist for predicting abuse before it happens, I will proceed from the proposition that regardless of the substantive standard applied, this prediction must be made on the basis of factual findings about past events, whether those events are actual incidents of abuse or neglect or parental actions or behaviors that can be strongly correlated with abuse or neglect. Good outcomes, then, depend on accurate factual determinations about past events.

A just outcome requires more than accurate fact finding, however. Once factual findings have been made, a second layer of decision making situates those facts among legal categories. In the child welfare context, this involves determining whether any acts of abuse or neglect the court finds to have occurred are severe enough to warrant state intervention or removal. We want this level of decision making to lead to outcomes that are fair and just, i.e., that comport with principles of equality and liberty. This means we want results that, first, are consistent – such that similar fact patterns lead to similar decisions about removal (the equality principle) - and, second, reflect our collective judgment about when sub-optimal treatment of a child rises to a level warranting state intervention or removal (the liberty principle).

Next, under the heading of "process values," we ask whether the process treats participants with dignity, gives them a sense that they are participating in and contributing to the decision making process, promotes a perception among participants that the process is fair, and preserves relationships between the parties. This set of questions arises out of two important insights about procedure. The first is a recognition that processes themselves, as well as outcomes, affect individuals in important ways.[168] The second is a recognition that in order for a dispute resolution system to have legitimacy, the participants must perceive it as fair and that participants' perceptions about the fairness of a process are to some degree distinct from their level of satisfaction with the outcome.[169] This concern is related to the outcome question, since participants who perceive a process as fair are more likely to comply with its outcomes.

Thus, when we ask whether formal or informal processes "work," we are really asking about the extent to which the processes serve or disserve the two outcome goals – I will call them "factual accuracy" and "just results" – as well as "process values." In the following sections I will examine the extent to which formality and informality serve or disserve each of these goals in the context of child welfare proceedings and attempt to identify the conditions under which each type of process is most and least successful in meeting these goals.

1. Factual Accuracy

Her dirty blond pony-tail danced behind her head as she talked, her face red with agitation. "That child welfare lady said it would be okay – she said she was my friend - now she's taking my baby." The case was in court for a review hearing. This young mother had been under agency supervision for a number of months, but the relationship between her and the social worker had been amicable. There had never been any allegations that Sheila hurt her baby, just that she was young, living in an apartment with no heat or hot water, with insulation and wires hanging from the ceiling, and that her baby had been born with severe medical problems. Her social worker had been friendly and helpful, negotiating with the landlord, and now the apartment was being fixed. Her baby had been in the hospital for a month and now was being released, though he'd still be on an apnea monitor. Her social worker was telling her that she couldn't bring the baby home because there was still no heat or hot water in her apartment and that he would be placed in a foster home. Sheila didn't want to bring him home because the apartment was still in bad shape, but her mother was willing to take him until the repair work was finished. She didn't see why her baby should be cared for by a stranger when his grandmother was willing.

Sheila and I made our way through the crowded waiting room and found the agency social worker talking to the child advocate. I presented Sheila's plan to them. The social worker's resistance was immediate and unyielding: "The grandmother hasn't been trained on the apnea monitor so the hospital won't release the baby to her anyway." The child advocate chimed in: "Besides, we don't know anything about this grandmother. Who is she? We'd have to at least send someone out to see her house first and I know I can't do that until next week."

I suggested to the social worker that maybe the hospital could train the grandmother to use the apnea monitor. Did she know how long the training would take? Had she talked to anyone at the hospital to find out what they thought of the grandmother? The social worker said she had talked to the hospital staff several days ago and they had made it very clear that the baby would only be released to some one with the proper training. "I've found an excellent medical foster home and they're willing to take him today." The child advocate nodded and smiled encouragingly at Sheila.

I had been feeling Sheila's frustration building and now it broke. "Why you talking about foster care? My baby don't need to be with a bunch of strangers when his own grandmother can take him." The social worker gave her a big grin. "Now mom, there's no need to get excited. You know we all just want what's best for your baby. This foster home is very nice. And it will only be for a month or so until we can get those repairs finished. Remember what we talked about. Let's keep our eye on the ball and try not to get distracted by these silly details. Lets all try to work together." Sheila's face was red and her voice shrill with anger. "But you ain't working with me! I tol' you my mom could take him but you don't care. You just tryin' to steal my baby!" Her eyes brimming with tears, Sheila turned and walked off. The social worker looked at me disapprovingly. "You know, until you got involved, Sheila was being very cooperative."

I found Sheila in a corner, still fighting back tears. "I guess I better go along coz if that lady gets mad at me, I'll never get my baby back." I explained that we could also put a case on and let the judge decide but that we would need more evidence. "Do you think the people at the hospital would support your mother taking the baby?" Sheila looked up, despondent. "I don't know. They seemed nice I guess."

I went to a phone and called the hospital. When I finally got through, the hospital social worker and attending physician gave rave reviews of Sheila and the grandmother. Both had been visiting regularly, were very bonded to the child and understood the seriousness of his condition. Sheila had made a mature judgment that she shouldn't take the baby home right now, but the grandmother was willing. They had given the grandmother the training and were planning to send the baby home with her today. I explained what was going on and the hospital social worker agreed to come to the courthouse at 4:00 to testify if necessary...

The formal adversarial process is designed to produce accurate decisions by bringing out all relevant facts and limiting bias and prejudice. Because adversaries each present their position in an attempt to persuade the judge to rule in their favor, each side is motivated to ferret out all the evidence that supports its position. Each side is also motivated to view its opponent's evidence critically and to undermine it through cross-examination and the introduction of contradictory evidence or evidence showing bias or lack of credibility. This motivation is critically important, particularly in a system in which professionals are juggling high caseloads. The parties' adoption of a conciliatory stance toward each other raises the danger that they will accept statements uncritically and fail to seek out contradictory evidence.

The formal rules that govern trial procedure also help to assure accuracy. Witnesses testify under oath under threat of penalty for perjury. The judge excludes unreliable evidence, like hearsay, as well as evidence likely to cause prejudice. The requirement that judges state the basis for their decisions helps to ensure that decisions are based on a rational view of the evidence and not on prejudice or bias. Numerous rules governing judges' conduct in adversarial proceedings encourage impartiality and the appearance of impartiality. Thus, judges sit higher than and at some distance from the parties, and usually address only the lawyers. When they do address the parties directly they do so formally and on the record. And they do not communicate with one party out of the presence of the other party.[170]

Of course, these mechanisms are far from perfect, and it is beyond question that trials can and often do reach inaccurate results skewed by judges' prejudice and partiality.[171] Where decision making occurs without these formal constraints, however, it is even more susceptible to being swayed by prejudices, stereotypes, and snap judgments based on innuendo and rumor. Mediators are trained to maintain impartiality and neutrality, but because their role is to facilitate communication between the parties rather than to judge, they do not maintain the same kind of physical and psychological distance from the parties that judges do. They sit closer to the parties, talk to them directly in an informal style, and may speak to one party without the presence of the other and without subsequently relating to the other what was said. This more intimate and informal setting may make mediation "an environment in which prejudices can flourish."[172]

The danger that prejudice or incomplete or unreliable information will distort decisions is particularly acute in the emotionally-charged arena of dependency and termination cases. Where so much is at stake – the suffering of children – the players in the system are all the more likely to make snap judgments based on gut feelings and instinct and to cut corners in an attempt to manipulate decisions to conform to their own view of the right outcome.[173] Imagine, for example, a social worker who is convinced in his gut that a mother is severely beating her child. Maybe it is because the look in her eyes is exactly the same one he saw in another mother who seriously injured her child after he failed to act quickly enough. In the face of such a feeling, imagine how tempted the social worker must be to remove the child immediately without bothering to confirm all the facts – to perhaps accept at face value the estranged father's hearsay statement that the doctor had said the broken bone could only have been the product of abuse. Because of these pressures, the evidentiary constraints and protections against bias and prejudice afforded by formality are particularly important in the child welfare context.

On the other hand, proponents of de-formalization claim that the adversarial process heightens distrust among the parties, encouraging them to be evasive and to use procedural maneuvering to avoid disclosing information.[174] By removing the adversarial edge, they argue, informal proceedings encourage participants to be more open and honest, thereby increasing factual accuracy.[175]

There are two problems with this analysis. First, it fails to take account of the substantial disparity of power between the state and the parent in a child welfare proceeding. At least since Miranda v. Arizona,[176] we have recognized that informality in the context of the power imbalance that exists when the state elicits information from an individual under a palpable threat of a substantial deprivation of liberty (there, physical restraint - here, removal of child) is a recipe for coercion and that such coercion can actually result in inaccurate information being elicited.[177]

Second, the argument that informality increases honesty and accuracy assumes that formal adversarial processes create conflict where otherwise there would be community and shared interests.[178] More often than not, however, in a child welfare proceeding conflict inheres in the substantive postures of the parties and precedes any choice of procedure. Where the state attempts to remove a child from a parent, the parent will almost always be opposed. Moreover, the central issue in a dependency or termination case – the welfare of the child – is frequently fraught with sufficient ambiguity that it accommodates multiple reasonable yet conflicting points of view. Usually the interests of the parties only appear to be shared when expressed in abstract terms, like, "we all want what's best for the child."[179] But at the concrete level - which is the level at which decisions must be made – the interests of the parties become decidedly adverse, the state viewing removal as "best for the child" and the parent viewing preservation of the family unit as "best for the child." In such a situation, where conflict is inherent and the power imbalance between the parties substantial, the process is unlikely to create conflict where none existed before. The more significant danger is that the process will mask the conflict that does exist by discouraging the weaker party from expressing her true feelings or position, encouraging her instead to "go along to get along."

2. Just Results

The court officer catches me looking harried between cases. There is another detention hearing and the mother is here, he tells me, but don't worry about picking it up - there's an agreement. I'm tempted to take his word for it and focus instead on the five other cases I have scheduled for today, one of which is threatening to blow up into a last minute trial for which I am not prepared. Instead, I pull an empty yellow pad out of my brief case, take a deep breath and walk over to the group indicated by the court officer. Two well-dressed African-American women sit talking in low voices. A young man sits next to them listening. He is also African-American, perhaps in his late 20's, neatly dressed in jeans and a polo shirt, with a county child welfare agency badge hanging from a chain around his neck. I ask for the mother by the name given me by the court officer, and one of the women identifies herself. I briefly explain who I am and ask her to talk to me in private. She glances questioningly at the man with the tag, who raises his eyebrows and shrugs. Looking bewildered, she follows me to another corner of the waiting room, out of earshot of the others.

She tells me she moved to Philadelphia several months ago from Virginia with her three-year-old daughter. She has no close connections here – a few cousins – but she moved to try to get away from her old community, to try to kick her cocaine habit, and to start a new life. She's been living in a small, privately run shelter for three months. The people there have been very supportive, and she had been clean since she moved in – until two days ago when she screwed up. She left the shelter in the afternoon. She left her daughter with another resident, telling her she was doing errands and would be back in an hour. She went to northeast Philly to find one of her cousins, hoping to borrow some money. She found him, but he's heavily into crack. One thing led to another, she ended up using again, and she didn't get back to the shelter until after midnight. By that time, the shelter had called the child welfare agency and her daughter had been taken into custody.

The next day she called the number on the card left by the social worker who took her daughter, and eventually was able to get through to him - the man with the tag. He told her that she needed to get six months of drug treatment before she could get her daughter back and asked if she had any relatives who could take her daughter during that time. She arranged with him to send her daughter to live with her mother-in-law in Virginia while she goes into inpatient drug treatment in Philadelphia. He told her she will get her daughter back in 6 months.

"What do you want?" Her expression is blank, uncomprehending. "I'm gonna send my daughter down to Virginia so I can go into treatment and kick my habit and learn to be a good mother." "And is this the way you want to do that?" Again, a blank stare, no response. "Pretend the worker didn't tell you what you have to do. How would you want to deal with this problem if it was entirely up to you?" She looks confused and startled, as if she's so used to thinking within the confines of what she has been told is permissible that the concept of thinking about what she wants is entirely foreign.

Eventually, she expresses to me that she's terrified of leaving her daughter for six months - terrified that her daughter will feel abandoned, terrified that her mother-in-law won't treat her daughter well, terrified that her mother-in-law will try to get permanent custody, terrified that being separated from her daughter will make it harder to give up the habit. It is seeing her daughter's face every morning that gives her the resolve to keep fighting her addiction. When I suggest the idea of a drug program where she could live with her daughter, she brightens considerably for a moment, but then looks doubtful. Someone at her shelter had suggested that, but her social worker said it wasn't possible. She seems unsure whether to trust me or her social worker, who are now saying contradictory things...

Formality incorporates a number of mechanisms designed to promote just outcomes in terms of both consistency with each other (the equality principle) and consistency with collective norms (the liberty principle). First, formal processes generally require judges to explain the bases for their decisions.[180] This requires the judge to be able to defend her decision as consistent with past cases and consistent with collective norms. It also facilitates public scrutiny of decisions for conformance with equality and liberty principles.[181] Second, formal processes require the application of formal rules and standards, which helps to promote consistency, both among cases and with collective norms. A system of formal rules and legal standards provides a mechanism for the articulation of a collective standard through legislative and judicial action. These standards are applied to decisions in individual cases to ensure consistency of individual outcomes with the collective norms reflected in those standards.[182]

In this context, for example, the collective judgment about the balance between individual liberty and social welfare that has been made by state legislatures and courts generally requires a showing of parental unfitness and actual harm to the child before a child can be removed from her family.[183] Informal processes, however, tend to devalue the kind of formal legalistic analysis that requires precise application of legal standards in favor of vague therapeutically-styled generalizations about the "best interests of the child."[184] This highly contingent social standard is essentially indeterminate and particularly susceptible to bias and prejudice.[185] Its dominance in the therapeutic discourse that reigns in informal proceedings leads to results that are inconsistent with each other (disserve the equality principle) and inconsistent with collective norms (disserve the liberty principle).[186]

Rather than reflecting collective or democratically determined norms, informal proceedings tend to produce results that reflect the disparity of power between the parties.[187] Decisions are based on the extent to which each side is willing to compromise rather than on a neutral evaluation of evidence and arguments. While they are not perfectly effective, formal processes are designed to equalize power disparities between the parties to some degree.[188] Each party (theoretically) has an attorney, versed in the language and rules of the forum, and formal rules limiting the evidence and arguments that can be presented are applied equally to both sides.[189] Informal proceedings provide no equivalent check on power imbalance.

In child welfare cases, where the individual is pitted against the vast power and resources of the state, the power imbalance is particularly extreme. And in the vast majority of cases, the fact that the parent is female, poor, uneducated, and nonwhite, exacerbates this inherent power disparity.[190] Parents frequently come to court unfamiliar with the system, unversed in the prevailing professional discourse, unaware of their legal rights, eager to prove themselves respectable, rational, reasonable, and cooperative, and eager to please the agency social worker, whom they (rather accurately) perceive as enormously powerful.[191] Moreover, when a parent first comes to court, the social worker is often the only familiar face she sees. What passes for an agreement may often be the parent's capitulation to the agency's wishes out of intimidation and coercion.[192] Even where coercion is not intentional on the part of the social worker, parents are often too quick to accede to the agency social worker's suggested resolution of their case,[193] resulting in false agreements that do not accurately reflect either the result that would have been achieved in court or our society's chosen balance between intervention and family privacy.[194]

Proponents of de-formalization, however, argue that informal proceedings lead to more just outcomes because when parties are not locked in an adversarial win/lose posture and are able to step back from the rhetoric of blame and rights that dominates formal proceedings, they are able to find a third way – creative solutions that meet all parties needs.[195] Certainly it is possible to imagine such a dynamic producing positive results in a child welfare case. A mediation process may encourage the parties to think outside the box of the adversarial paradigm that insists on winning and defines winning narrowly: for the parent, a dismissal; for the agency, placement of the child in foster care. Instead, in the non-confrontational, needs-centered atmosphere of mediation, the mother may be able to admit that she needs drug treatment while communicating to the agency the sincerity of her desire to improve and the strength of her bond with her child. The agency may be able to re-frame its position from insisting on foster care to simply needing assurance that the child will be safe. Out of this softening of positions the possibility for a third way – placement of the mother and child together in a mother-child drug treatment program – might arise.

But in the child welfare context, the vast disparity in power between the parties distorts this process. Too often informality results in the weaker party – the parent – simply capitulating to the agency rather than pushing the agency to find the creative third way. The "win-win" solution so frequently touted by the proponents of informality requires a creative tension between the parties that tends to arise only when the parties are roughly equally matched in power. Otherwise there is no leverage to dislodge the stronger party from its position. This is particularly true in the child welfare context where the agency's position can often be well entrenched. First, because the agency inevitably equates its own win with the best interests of the child, it may often approach a dispute resolution proceeding with the intransigence of those who believe they are "on the side of the angels." Secondly, in the child welfare context, the creative third way often involves the agency providing some innovative service to the family that allows the parent and child to stay together while addressing the problem that led to the agency's involvement – for example a mother-child drug treatment program, a supervised group home for teenage mothers, or financial assistance in obtaining housing. But these solutions are usually more costly than the standard package of services and require initiative on the part of the agency social worker. Unless the parent has sufficient power to exert some leverage on the agency, such solutions are frequently out of reach. Parents can sometimes exert leverage in a formal adversarial process by seeking a court order compelling the agency to provide innovative services in order to fulfill its legal mandate to make reasonable efforts to preserve the family.[196] No such leverage is available in an informal proceeding, however.

Additionally, the "win-win" solution depends on the parties having a set of shared values so that there is some set of cultural norms in common that can form a basis for agreement.[197] Otherwise informality will simply result either in a stand-off or in the weaker party capitulating to the cultural norms of the more powerful party.

3. Process Values

a. Children

Advocates of deformalizing child welfare proceedings often point to the negative effects that formal, adversarial processes can have on children. Certainly, a number of aspects of the process can cause emotional trauma to children who are old enough to have some awareness of its meaning.[198] First, there is the disruption, uncertainty, and anxiety of knowing that strangers are making decisions about where and with whom they will live. Second, there is the trauma of being questioned by strangers about the personal details of family life, and possibly being asked to recount some painful or embarrassing event. Third, there is the stress of being put in the middle of a dispute and perhaps pressured by each side or pushed to say things that might betray a parent. And fourth, there is the fear and intimidation invoked by the formal courtroom setting.

For the most part, however, these factors arise from the very fact that there is a dispute rather than the process used to resolve it. Whether the process involved is formal or informal, a child old enough to have awareness of it will be affected by the knowledge that the adults in her life are in crisis and that decisions that profoundly affect her are being made by strangers – whether a judge or a group of social workers or lawyers who meet in a mediation session. Moreover, informal process does not remove the necessity of having strangers question the child or the possibility that the two sides to the dispute will pressure the child, either subtly or explicitly, to take sides or betray a loved one. Indeed, to the extent that informality is generally less successful than formality at lessening the power disparity between the parties, informality may actually increase the likelihood that a parent – feeling powerless to effect the process though legitimate channels – might resort to illegitimate means, like pressuring the child, in a desperate attempt to sway the decision making process.

Before a case ever gets to a court or an ADR process, the child may already have been interviewed several times by teachers, medical personnel, or social workers. Once in court (or ADR) the child will be interviewed again by a child advocate, if one is appointed.[199] If the case is one in which the child's version of events is critical to the factual determination at issue, the child is likely to be interviewed by others as well, whether the process is formal or informal. These may include the state's lawyer, the parent's lawyer, and the judge or mediator. The difference between a formal and informal proceeding is primarily that testimony before a judge in a formal proceeding requires the simultaneous presence of the attorneys and the court reporter, which will usually add up to at least five people. An informal process, on the other hand, might allow the child to be interviewed individually or in smaller groups.[200]

The relative formality of the courtroom atmosphere, however, is of limited consequence in the context of a child's testimony, which usually occurs in the judge's chambers. Most judges try hard to set an informal tone that will put the child at ease, perhaps giving the child a toy to play with and starting out by asking non-threatening questions and explaining the process in language appropriate to the child. Most judges also keep a tight rein on counsel, keeping cross-examination short and cutting off questioning that becomes hostile or aggressive in tone. Certainly, the judge's black robes, the court reporter, the air of deference to the judge's authority, and the inevitable lawyerly discourse all lend an atmosphere of formality that may be intimidating to a child. It is also possible, however, that a child who is aware that the adults in her life are fighting over her and who feels profoundly affected by the dispute but powerless in the face of it may, in some instances, benefit from participating in an orderly, formal proceeding presided over by an authoritative decision maker to whom she has the opportunity to speak directly. Finally, it is important to note that even in formal adversarial systems, children do not usually testify.[201] Most cases are resolved through negotiation against the backdrop of formal rules and procedures, and even those that go to a hearing may not necessarily require the child's testimony. In short, while formal adversarial processes no doubt present risks to children, many of these risks are not obviated by de-formalization and may in many instances be overstated.[202]

b. Parents

Mediation and other informal processes are generally touted for their capacity to empower participants by giving them a sense of inclusion and participation. By dispensing with the intricate procedural rules and arcane language of the adversarial system, informal processes create a setting that is less intimidating and more accessible, allowing disputants to participate directly in the process. This is said to serve process values by according the participants the respect and dignity of speaking on their own behalf. Moreover, by promoting a sense of ownership in the decision making process, informality is said to increase the likelihood that participants will buy in to the agreements reached and comply with them over the long term.[203]

These process values, however, may be frustrated where informality is employed in child welfare cases. In Part IB, I described the dynamic that can arise in the microsocial setting of child welfare proceedings due to the prevalence of "repeat players," the dominance of social work norms and discourse, and the vast power disparity between the parties. Parents, as newcomers and outsiders, feel an intense pressure to conform to established rules of behavior. The therapeutic rhetoric of "cooperation" and the illusion of shared goals embedded in the repeated insistence that "we all want what is best for the child" subvert conflict, create an illusion of intimacy in which the power dynamic is obscured, and suppress any assertion of rights by the parent as unmotherly and creating conflict harmful to the child.[204] In this environment, informalism may often disable parents from even articulating their own point of view and instead push them into a position of passivity that is profoundly disempowering.[205] Similarly, the notion, promoted by some proponents of informality, that informal processes provide the parent a chance to "vent"[206] reveals a patronizing attitude toward parents – that their speech is purely emotive, serves only a therapeutic goal, and contributes nothing to the substantive decision being made.

Furthermore, it is not clear that formality is necessarily wholly disempowering to participants. The formality of the courtroom setting creates an aura of seriousness and gravity that can convey to a participant a sense that she and her case are considered important by the state. Additionally, while proponents of informality insist that representation by an attorney disempowers participants by disabling them from speaking in their own voice and on their own behalf,[207] I suspect that having an attorney speak on one's behalf can also be experienced as empowering, giving a parent a sense that she does not stand alone, that her position has legitimacy, and that it commands attention and respect from the judge.[208]

Informal proceedings are often promoted for their ability to preserve an ongoing relationship between the parties.[209] Even Richard Abel, who has been an outspoken critic of informality, supports this view. Abel suggests that we can gain important insight into the situations in which informal dispute resolution mechanisms are useful by examining the circumstances in which rich and advantaged members of society voluntarily choose them. Those are situations in which the disputants are of relatively equal power and wish to preserve an important relationship – for example, a businessman's dispute with a trading partner or disputes between divorcing spouses.[210]

In the child welfare context, the disparity in power between the parties may lessen informality's effectiveness in this regard. It is certainly possible to imagine situations in which an informal proceeding pressures the parent, as the weaker party, into suppressing her point of view in order to achieve agreement, thus creating unexpressed resentment that adversely affects the ongoing relationship. In such a situation, an adversarial courtroom battle might serve a cathartic function, after which the parent might feel that she had said her piece and be able to sit down and work with the agency social worker in accordance with the judge's order.[211] Nonetheless, with their emphasis on communication and meeting the parties' needs and their de-emphasis of blame and rights, informal processes in most instances probably tend to be more successful at preserving a functioning relationship between the parties during and following dispute resolution. As I discuss in the next section, however, the preservation of an ongoing relationship between the parties should not necessarily be a primary goal in child welfare proceedings, at least not at the initial stages.

In sum, the above discussion suggests that in the particular context of child welfare cases, informal procedures are unlikely overall to be as successful as formal ones in meeting the outcome and process goals of due process. The substantial power disparity between the parties, the emotionally charged nature of the subject matter, and the lack of a shared set of interests and values between the parties all tend to distort the decision making process. Traditional formal adversarial processes have mechanisms that, while far from perfect, are designed to combat the distortion caused by such conditions. But informality generally offers no equivalent protections. In the next section, I explore further why the particular dynamics of child welfare cases are so ill-suited to informality, particularly in comparison to domestic relations cases, in which the use of mediation is widespread.

B. The Domestic Relations Model: Mandatory Family Therapy as State Intrusion

Much of the rhetoric promoting the use of informal procedures in child welfare cases is borrowed from the domestic relations context, where mediation has been used extensively for many years in divorce and custody cases.[212] But the domestic relations paradigm cannot simply be transplanted to the dependency context. The alignment of the parties is fundamentally different.[213] Domestic relations cases involve disputes between private parties. There may be some disparity of power between them, and, indeed, many feminists have criticized the use of informal procedures in domestic relations cases for that reason,[214] especially in instances where the power disparity is particularly acute, like those involving battering.[215] Still, in domestic relations cases the vast power disparity between the individual and the state that exists in child welfare cases is absent. Moreover, in the domestic relations context, the parties have an existing intimate relationship which they entered into voluntarily and which they will often need to preserve – though in some altered form – in order to continue to share parenting responsibilities. Thus, often in a domestic relations case, determining accurately what occurred in some past event is less important than reaching a compromise that addresses both parties' needs and preserves a workable relationship for the future. Additionally the fact that there was at some point a voluntary intimate relationship between the parties indicates a set of shared values or at least a commitment to reconciling conflicting values.

The move to de-formalize child welfare cases attempts to squeeze these disputes into the domestic relations paradigm, locating them in the realm of family therapy rather than adjudication.[216] Thus, one particular mediation program is touted as "cathartic"[217] and as providing the parents a chance to "vent."[218] The issue is viewed not as whether the parent committed some act of child abuse or neglect that warrants state intervention, but how to facilitate communication between the participants and how to reach a compromise that meets all of their needs.[219] Principles of blame and rights are replaced with the rhetoric of compromise and relationship. The conflict is "styled as a personal quarrel, in which there is no right and wrong, but simply two different equally true or untrue views of the world."[220]

By identifying communication as the problem, however, the proponents of mediation presume that the state is entitled to have a relationship with the parent.[221] This involves two false assumptions: first, that all parents are guilty (i.e., intervention is warranted), and, second, that intervention is always helpful to a family (or at least not harmful).[222]

The first assumption is unwarranted because the parent may not have done the act of which she is accused, or the act she did do may not rise to the level of abuse or neglect warranting state intervention.[223] These are the first questions that a dependency proceeding must resolve. Though ultimately the aim of the dependency proceeding is prospective – to prevent harm to the child in the future – these initial determinations are essentially retrospective in nature. Since we cannot predict the future, we must rely on past events as predictors of likely future events. And only when past events are proven that show a likelihood of harm in the future, do we allow the state to intervene in the private functioning of families.[224] Thus, the initial inquiry is fact-based and retrospective, rather than an attempt to reach a middle ground between different sets of needs and emotions.

The second assumption is also unwarranted. Intervention - even at the level of simply talking - can be harmful in itself. Even if a child is not removed, the social worker's act of knocking on the door and questioning a parent about her family life, can be very harmful, undermining the parent's authority in the eyes of the child or making the child fearful of removal.[225] Certainly, in the criminal context we routinely recognize the dangers of state coercion that arise simply from forcing an individual to talk to a state official.[226] Similarly, the state is effecting an extraordinary intervention in the family relationship just by insisting that the state social worker and others have the right to participate in a conversation about the parents' day-to-day parenting activities.[227]

Thus, informal processes replace the initial factual adjudication of whether acts of abuse or neglect warranting state intervention actually occurred with a free-ranging family therapy session.[228] There is virtually no limit on the topics that can be discussed nor on the people who may be invited to join. Mediation programs typically give discretion to the mediator to invite people who are not parties to the case, including foster parents, extended family members, and members of the "community," such as a local church pastor.[229] Once these people are brought to the table, all become equal participants, entitled to have their "concerns" heard and their "needs" met. Rather than seeking to determine the truth of the allegations of abuse or neglect, the focus of the discussion becomes "finding solutions which meet the competing needs and interests of all parties."[230] Suddenly, the needs and interests of foster parents, aunts, uncles, grandparents, and social workers are placed on an equal footing with those of the parents and children.

But before the family is forced to participate in therapy, the process is supposed to first make a determination as to whether state intervention is warranted.[231] This stage has been skipped. In essence, the mediation session becomes the very state intrusion that the proceeding is supposed to determine whether or not to allow in the first place.[232]

## C. Possibilities for Successful Informality in Child Welfare?

The recurring theme that emerges from the above analysis is that informalism is particularly ill-suited to meeting the goals of procedure in situations involving gross disparities of power between the parties.[233] It also appears that formality is better at making accurate factual determinations and helping to assure consistent and just outcomes in an environment of moral and cultural diversity,[234] while informality is probably better at preserving an ongoing relationship between the parties.[235] In other words, informal processes work best under conditions of relative social equality, where there is community consensus about norms and values, and where preserving relationships in the future is more important than reaching accurate factual determinations about what happened in the past.[236]

Certainly the adjudicatory phase of a dependency proceeding or a termination of parental rights proceeding involves all the elements that make informality a bad strategy for achieving the outcome and process goals of procedure. The central issues in the dispute are retrospective and fact-based. The preservation of a relationship between the disputants is not paramount. In a dependency adjudiction, there is no pre-existing voluntary relationship between the family and the state, and it has not yet been established that such a relationship is warranted. In a termination case there may be a pre-existing relationship between the state social worker and the parent, but preservation of that relationship is of little relevance, since the state no longer seeks to provide rehabilitative help to the parent in any case. Finally, the power imbalance between the parties in both proceedings is extreme.

In the post-adjudicatory phases of a dependency case, however, the characteristics of the dispute are somewhat different. At the dispositional phase (where the court faces a decision about where the child should be placed, having already determined that abuse or neglect occurred) and at subsequent periodic review hearings, the case shifts from a retrospective, fact-based inquiry to a prospective inquiry into what steps the parent must take and what services the agency must provide to alleviate the conditions that led to placement. But perhaps the most important difference between an adjudicatory hearing and subsequent dispositional and review hearings is that in the latter the relationship between the state and the parent has been legitimized. An adjudication of dependency answers affirmatively the question whether state intervention is warranted, and the case then proceeds on the assumption that it is. Accordingly, the preservation of the relationship between the parent and the state social worker becomes a legitimate goal at the dispositional and review phases of a dependency proceeding and, indeed, an important factor in ensuring the success of the prospective rehabilitative plan.[237] Although the power disparity and the potential for dissensus on norms and values persists, the shift in the relative importance of retrospective fact-finding (formality's strength) vis a vis the preservation of relationships (informality's strength) may warrant a shift to less formal procedures at these stages of a dependency case.

Conclusion

Child welfare bureaucracies and court systems make thousands of decisions each day that profoundly effect the lives of millions of people, touching an aspect of life that many hold central to their identity. Too often, however, the policies and doctrines that shape the procedures by which these decisions are made are based on superficial reactions to the latest tabloid horror story about child maltreatment. Resistance to the adoption of formal procedures in these cases has frequently been justified by vague allusions to the need to avoid the harshness of the adversarial process in cases involving women and children and by reference to the questionable assertion that the deprivation of liberty effected by the forcible separation of parent and child is less grievous than the deprivation that is held up as the defining standard in questions involving procedure: criminal imprisonment. While a feminist critique of values can reveal the arbitrariness of the male norm embedded in such value judgments, it also forces us to question the traditional liberal notion that important interests demand formal procedures. Ultimately the question of procedure must be resolved through a contextual examination of the peculiar set of power dynamics and incentives that operate in child welfare cases.

I have argued that, at least in termination of parental rights cases and at the initial adjudicatory phase of dependency cases, traditional formal adversarial process offers the best hope of protecting against the distortions of power imbalance and the dangers of prejudice and snap judgments. I do not mean to argue that formality offers the perfect solution. My analysis has proceeded largely based on what is, with little speculation about what might be. By endorsing formality as the best among existing alternatives, I do not mean to suggest that a better third way might not be imagined.

*Amy Sinden, J.D., is Associate Professor of Law at the Beasley School of Law at Temple University in Philadelphia.*

**Notes**

[1]    My focus here is solely on civil, not criminal, child abuse and neglect proceedings. The name for these proceedings varies from state to state, but I will use the term "dependency" to refer to those cases in which temporary removal of children from their families is threatened, "termination" to refer to those cases where the state seeks to permanently sever a parent's relationship with her child, and "child welfare" to refer to both types of proceedings.

²   This is inevitable in light of the facts that women remain the primary caretakers of children in our culture and that single mothers are so prevalent. In the poor communities most affected by the child welfare system. Statistics maintained by the Philadelphia Juvenile Court on active dependency cases in 1997, for example, show that there were 4,975 cases involving mothers and only 1,694 cases involving fathers. See Philadelphia Juvenile Court, Active Dependent Case Appointments for Parents and Guardians (June 8, 1997) (on file with the Yale Journal of Law and Feminism). There may be overlap between these two numbers (i.e., cases involving both a mother and a father), but clearly most cases involve a mother and no father.

³   See generally Nancy Chodorow, The Reproduction of Mothering: Psychoanalysis and the Sociology of Gender (1978).

⁴   The existing literature mostly focuses on "bad mothers" and either explains their behavior as a rebellion against the patriarchy or excuses it based on the mother's brutalization at the hands of an abusive man. See, e.g., Marie Ashe, Postmodernism, Legal Ethics, and Representation of "Bad Mother," in Mothers in Law 142 (Martha Albertson Fineman & Isabel Karpin eds., 1995); Marie Ashe & Naomi Cahn, Child Abuse: A Problem for Feminist Theory, 2 Tex. J. Women & L. 75 (1993); Linda J. Panko, Legal Backlash: The Expanding Liability of Women Who Fail to Protect Their Children From Their Male Partner's Abuse, 6 Hastings Women's L.J. 67 (1995); Tonya Plank, How Would the Criminal Law Tret Sethe?: Reflections on Patriarchy, Child Abuse, and the Uses of Narrative to Re-Imagine Motherhood, 12 Wis. Women's L.J. 83 (1997); Dorothy E. Roberts, Motherhood and Crime 79 Iowa L. Rev. 95 (1993). The dearth of feminist literature on the child welfare system is especially glaring in light of the vast feminist literature on battered women.

⁵   See, e.g., Panko supra note 4; Bonnie E. Rabin, Violence Against Mothers Equals Violence Against Children: Understanding the Connections, 58 Alb. L. Rev. 1109 (1995).

⁶   See, e.g., Evan Stark & Anne H. Flitcraft, Women and Children at Risk: A Feminist Perspective on Child Abuse, 18 Int'l J. Health Services 97, 97 (1988) (explicitly "viewing child abuse through the prism of woman battering").

⁷   See supra note 5. Linda Gordon argues that the original nineteenth century movement against child abuse was an attack on patriarchal power--even though then, as now, single mothers were over-represented in child neglect cases. See Linda Gordon, Child Abuse, Gender, and the Myth of Family Independence: Thoughts on the History of Family Violence and its Social Control 1880-1920, 12 N.Y.U. Rev. L. & Soc. Change 523, 524, 527 (1983-84).

⁸   See Elizabeth M. Schneider, The Violence of Privacy, 23 Conn. L. Rev. 973, 973-94 (1991). This traditional notion of family privacy has its roots in the separate spheres ideology of the nineteenth century, under which women and children were viewed as properly confined to the domestic sphere of family life, while the public sphere of politics, business and government was the domain of men. Many feminists view this strict public/private dichotomy as a primary element of women's oppression, and thus see dismantling this distinction as necessary not only to open private family violence to public scrutiny but also to liberate women economically. See, e.g., Lucinda M. Finley, Transcending Equality Theory: A Way Out of the Maternity and the Workplace Debate, 86 Col. L. Rev. 1118, 1165 (1986). Dorothy Roberts, however, has pointed out that this analysis does not apply to African-American women, who have never been confined to the private sphere but have always been in the work force. While many white women have viewed work outside the home as a liberation from motherhood, African-American women have viewed the family as a refuge from an oppressive work environment. See Roberts, supra note 4, at 130; see also Schneider, supra at 994-99 (exploring ways in which privacy can be both affirming and oppressive to women).

⁹   See Martha Minow, Making All the Difference: Inclusion, Exclusion, and American Law 243-47, 250-51 (1990).

¹⁰   See supra note 2.

¹¹   See infra note 59.

[12] See Dorothy E. Roberts, Punishing Drug Addicts Who Have Babies: Women of Color, Equality, and the Right of Privacy, 104 Harv. L. Rev. 1419, 1471 (1991) ("The primary concern for white middle-class women with regard to child custody is private custody battles with their husbands following the termination of a marriage. But for women of color, the dominant threat is termination of parental rights by the state.").

[13] See Katharine T. Bartlett, Feminist Legal Methods, 103 Harv. L. Rev. 829, 849 (1990) (arguing that feminism was born out of the consciousness-raising method which "starts with personal and concrete experience, integrates this experience into theory, and then in effect, reshapes theory based on experience and experience based on theory.").

[14] See infra notes 160-63 and accompanying text.

[15] See infra Part IIA.

[16] Some scholars have observed a general trend in this direction in other areas as well. See, e.g., Judith Resnik, Whose Judgment? Vacating Judgments, Preferences for Settlement, and the Role of Adjudication at the Close of the Twentieth Century, 41 U.C.L.A. Rev. 1471, 1529 (1994) (noting trend in federal courts away from adjudication of disputes and toward resolution through settlement or ADR).

[17] See, e.g., N.Y. Soc. Serv. Law § 423 (1992); 23 Pa. Cons. Stat. Ann. § 6361 (1997).

[18] See, e.g., N.Y. Soc. Serv. Law § 423(2) (1992); 23 Pa. Cons. Stat. Ann. § 6378 (1997).

[19] See, e.g., N.Y. Soc. Serv. Law § 424(1) (1992); 23 Pa. Cons. Stat. Ann. § 6366 (1997). The majority of reports involve allegations of neglect rather than abuse. Nationwide statistics for 1996 show that only 36 percent of all substantiated or indicated reports of child abuse and neglect involved allegations of physical or sexual abuse. The rest involved neglect or "emotional maltreatment." See U.S. Dep't of Commerce, Statistical Abstract of the United States 227 (table 373) (1998).

[20] See, e.g., N.Y. Soc. Serv. Law § 424(6) (1992); 23 Pa. Cons. Stat. Ann. § 6368 (1997).

[21] See, e.g., N.Y. Soc. Serv. Law § 424(7) (1992); 23 Pa. Cons. Stat. Ann. § 6337 (1997).

[22] In some instances, where the perpetrator is not the primary caretaker of the child, the social worker may attempt to remove the perpetrator from the home instead of the child, either by agreement or by court order. In many such instances, however, the social worker is unwilling to take that approach to protecting the child because the non-caretaker perpetrator is romantically involved with the caretaker (usually the mother) and the social worker does not trust the caretaker to keep the perpetrator out of the home.

[23] See, e.g., N.Y. Soc. Serv. Law § 424(10), (11) (1992); 23 Pa. Cons. Stat. Ann. § 6370 (1997).

[24] See, e.g., N.Y. Soc. Serv. Law § 358-a, 384-a (1992); 55 Pa. Code § 3130.65 (1999). A surprisingly large percentage of foster care placements begin in this way. In some states, over 50% of the children in foster care were placed there through voluntary placement agreements. See Richard Wexler, Wounded Innocents: The Real Victims of the War Against Child Abuse 119 (1990). Especially since parents almost never have the benefit of legal counsel when signing these agreements, the practice raises substantial questions about coercion by agency social workers. See infra note 194 and accompanying text.

[25] Under the Adoption Assistance and Child Welfare Act of 1980, states lose federal foster care payments if a child remains in foster care under a voluntary placement agreement for more than six months without a judicial determination. See 42 U.S.C. § 672(e) (1994).

[26] See, e.g., N.Y. Soc. Serv. Law § 417(1)(a) (1992) (social worker authorized to take child into custody if reasonable cause to believe child in "imminent danger"); Vt. Stat. Ann. tit. 33, § 5510 (1991) (law enforcement officer authorized to take child into custody when reasonable grounds to believe child in immediate danger). Some states require a lesser standard than imminent danger. See, e.g., Okla. Stat. Ann. tit. 10, § 7003-2.1 (1998) (authorizing peace officer or employee of court to take child into custody without court order "if the child's surroundings are such as to endanger the welfare of the child").

[27] See, e.g., Mont. Code Ann. § 41-3-301(1) (1997) (emergency removal by social worker permitted without court order where child in immediate or apparent danger of harm); Conn. Gen. Stat. Ann. § 17a-101g(c), (d) (West 1998) (social worker authorized to remove child in immediate danger without

court order); Tex. Fam. Code Ann. § 262.101(1) (West Supp. 1998) (agency may request permission from court to take possession of child in emergency by showing, through affidavit, that child faces immediate danger to physical health or safety, or has been the victim of neglect or sexual abuse, and that continuation of child in the home is contrary to her welfare).

[28] See, e.g., 42 Pa. Cons. Stat. Ann. § 6332(a) (West Supp. 1999) (informal hearing must be held within 72 hours of removal); Wash. Rev. Code § 13.34.060(1) (1998) (hearing must be held within 72 hours, excluding Saturdays, Sundays, and holidays); Tex. Fam. Code § 262.103 (child may be held for up to 14 days without hearing) (West 1996). Note that if Saturdays, Sundays, and holidays are excluded from the 72-hour period, only parents whose children are taken on a Monday or a Tuesday have a right to a hearing in less than five days, and where holidays intervene, the period may be six days.

A "prompt" post-deprivation hearing is constitutionally required. See Sims v. State Dep't of Pub. Welfare, 438 F. Supp. 1179 (S.D. Tex. 1977) (when child taken into emergency custody, state must conduct full adversary hearing with adequate notice to parents within 10 days of removal), rev'd on other grounds sub nom., Moore v. Sims, 442 U.S. 415 (1979); In re R.G., 238 Neb. 405, 417 (1991) (14-day delay between removal of child and hearing did not violate parent's due process rights).

[29] See, e.g., 42 Pa. Cons. Stat. Ann. § 6335(a) (West Supp. 1999) (adjudicatory hearing within 10 days of detention hearing); Ill. Ann. Stat. ch. 705, § 405/2-14 (Smith-Hurd 1994) (adjudicatory hearing held within 90 days of preliminary hearing); Wash. Rev. Code § 13.34.070(1) (1998) (first hearing--termed "fact-finding hearing"--held within 75 days after filing of petition).

[30] See, e.g., Ill. Ann. Stat. ch. 705, § 405/2-21 (Smith-Hurd 1994); Pa. Stat. Ann. tit. 42, § 6341 (West Supp. 1999).

[31] See, e.g., Ill. Ann. Stat. ch. 705, § 405/2-22 (Smith-Hurd 1994); Wash. Rev. Code § 13.34.110 (1998); Pa. Stat. Ann. tit. 42, § 6341(d) (West Supp. 1999).

[32] See, e.g., Commonwealth ex rel. Pierce v. Pierce, 426 A.2d 555, 557 (Pa. Super. 1981).

[33] As the Superior Court of Pennsylvania put it over forty years ago:

It is a serious matter for the long arm of the state to reach into a home and snatch a child from its mother. It is a power which a government dedicated to freedom for the individual should exercise with extreme care, and only where the evidence clearly establishes its necessity....

A child cannot be declared "neglected" merely because his condition might be improved by changing his parents. The welfare of many children might be served by taking them from their homes and placing them in what the officials may consider a better home. But the Juvenile Court Law was not intended to provide a procedure to take the children of the poor and give them to the rich, nor to take the children of the illiterate and give them to the educated, nor to take the children of the crude and give them to the cultured, nor to take the children of the weak and sickly and give them to the strong and healthy.

In re Rinker, 117 A.2d 780, 783 (Pa. Super. 1955).

[34] See Lassiter v. Department of Social Servs., 452 U.S. 18, 45 n.13 (1981) (Blackmun, dissenting) (arguing that the best interests standard offers little guidance, which encourages judges to rely on their own personal values); Martha Fineman, The Illusion of Equality: The Rhetoric and Reality of Divorce Reform 107 (1991) (describing best interests standard as "amorphous, undirected, incomprehensible and indeterminate"); Peggy C. Davis, Use and Abuse of the Power to Sever Family Bonds, 12 N.Y.U. Rev. L. & Soc. Change 557, 559 (1984) (expressing doubt, based on author's experience as family court judge "whether I knew, or anyone knew, what precisely was in the best interests of the child").

[35] The Supreme Court has suggested in dicta that a best-interests-of-the-child standard at this phase would be unconstitutional. See Quillion v. Walcott, 434 U.S. 246, 255 (1978) ("We have little doubt that the Due Process Clause would be offended '[i]f a State were to attempt to force the breakup of a natural family, over the objections of the parents and their children, without some showing of unfitness and for the sole reason that to do so was thought to be in the children's best interest." ' (quoting Smith, 431 U.S. at 862-63 (Stewart, J., concurring))); s ee also Martin Guggenheim, The Political and Legal Implications

of Psychological Parenting Theory, 12 N.Y.U. Rev. L. & Soc. Change 549, 554 (1984) (arguing that state should intervene only to protect children from imminent risk of death or disfigurement).

[36] See, e.g. Md. Code Ann. § 3-801 (1999); Pa. Stat. Ann. tit. 42, § 6341(a) (West Supp. 1999). These statutory standards are typically very vague. For example, many states define a dependent child, at least in part, as a child "without proper parental care or control." See, e.g., Pa. Stat. Ann. tit. 42, § 6302 (West Supp. 1999). Numerous commentators have urged that such statutes be more narrowly drawn. See, e.g., Michael S. Wald, State Intervention on Behalf of "Neglected" Children: Standards for Removal of Children from their Homes, Monitoring the Status in Children in Foster Care, and Termination of Parental Rights, 28 Stan. L. Rev. 623 (1976).

[37] In Pennsylvania, for example, the state must show that removal is "clearly necessary." See In re Pernishek, 408 A.2d 872, 878 (Pa. Super. Ct. 1979).

[38] See, e.g., Ill. Ann. Stat. ch. 705, § 405/2-28 (Smith-Hurd 1994) (initial review hearing after 12 months, then every 6 months); Pa. Stat. Ann. tit. 42, § 63 (West Supp. 1999) (disposition reviewed every 6 months); N.Y. Soc. Serv. Law § 392 (1992) (disposition reviewed every 18 months).

[39] The Adoption Assistance Act of 1980 conditioned federal foster care payments to states on a requirement that state child welfare agencies make "reasonable efforts" to prevent the removal of children from their homes and to make it possible for children who have been removed to be returned to their families. See 42 U.S.C. § 671(a)(15)(1997). The Adoption and Safe Families Act of 1997, §103, Pub. L. 105-89, 111 Stat. 211, has created exceptions to the "reasonable efforts" requirement for certain categories of cases, including, among other things, where "aggravated circumstances," as defined by state law, are present and where parental rights to another child have already been terminated. See 42 U.S.C. § 671(a)(15)(D).

[40] See, e.g., Ill. Ann. Stat. ch. 325, § 5/8.2 (Smith-Hurd 1994); 55 Pa. Code § 3130.61 (1999).

[41] See, e.g., Ill. Ann. Stat. ch. 705, § 405/2-13, (4.5) (Smith-Hurd 1994); 23 Pa. Cons. Stat. Ann. § 2511 (1997).

[42] See 42 U.S.C. § 675(5)(c).

[43] See 42 U.S.C. § 671(a)(15)(E)(i).

[44] See Lassiter v. Department of Social Servs., 452 U.S. 18 (1981).

[45] See, e.g., Wash. Rev. Code § 13.34.090 (1998); Pa. Stat. Ann. tit. 42, § 6337 (West 1992). Some state constitutions also provide a right to counsel. See Danforth v. State Dep't of Health, 303 A.2d 794, 800 (Me. 1973).

[46] See, e.g., In re Ammanda G., 231 Cal. Rptr. 372, 374 (Ct. App.1986); Howell v. Dallas County Child Welfare Unit, 710 S.W.2d 729, 734-35 (Tex. Ct. App. 1986). But see In re Kristen H., 54 Cal. Rptr. 2d 722 (Cal. App. 1996) (parent in dependency proceeding may raise claim of ineffective assistance of counsel on appeal).

[47] See M.L.B. v. S.L.J., 519 U.S. 102 (1996).

[48] See Santosky v. Kramer, 455 U.S. 745 (1982). Although the Indian Child Welfare Act of 1978 and one state require proof beyond a reasonable doubt in termination proceedings, see 25 U.S.C. § 1912(f) (1999); State v. Robert H., 393 A.2d 1387, 1389 (N.H. 1978), the Supreme Court has held the clear and convincing evidence standard constitutionally sufficient, see Santosky, 455 U.S. at 769-70. Louisiana also required proof beyond a reasonable doubt, see La. Ch. C. Ann. § 1035 (West 1995), until the statute was amended in 1997 to require clear and convincing evidence. See La. Acts No. 256, § 1 (1997).

[49] See, e.g., Wash. Rev. Code § 13.34.130 (1998); Ind. Code Ann. § 31-34-12-3 (Michie 1997).

[50] See, e.g., Alsager v. District Court of Polk County, 406 F. Supp. 10, 24 (S.D. Iowa 1975) (admission of hearsay evidence in termination hearing held not to violate parents' procedural due process rights). Procedural rules may be relaxed as well. See, e.g., In re Maria F., 428 N.Y.S. 2d 425 (Fam. Ct. Bronx County 1980) (Family court judge has discretion whether to apply civil rules of procedure in a dependency case). Statutes often provide for an even further relaxation of evidentiary rules at the

dispositional hearing. See, e.g., Wash. Rev. Code § 13.34.120 (1998) (requiring court to consider social studies and reports at dispositional hearing); Pa. Stat. Ann. tit. 42, § 6341(d) (West Supp. 1999) ("[A]ll evidence helpful in determining the question presented ... may be received by the court ... even though not otherwise competent in the hearing on the petition.").

[51]   See, e.g., In re Malinda S., 51 Cal. 3d 368 (1990) (social worker's report admissible hearsay in dependency proceeding); Baxter v. Texas Dep't of Human Resources, 678 S.W. 2d 265, 267 (Tex. App. 1984) (same).

[52]   See, e.g., Jenks v. Hull, 1993 U.S. Dist. LEXIS 4706 (N.D. Cal. Apr. 7, 1993) (parents are not entitled to Miranda warnings before child taken into temporary custody).

[53]   See Darryl H. v. Coler, 801 F.2d 893 (7th Cir. 1986) (no warrant or probable cause required for search by child welfare agency social worker); New Jersey Div. of Youth & Family Servs. v. Wunnenburg, 167 N.J. Super. 578, 408 A.2d 1345 (App. Div. 1979) (probable cause not required for child welfare agency social worker's search of parent's home); Kohler v. State, 713 S.W.2d 141 (Tex. Ct. App. 1986) (Fourth amendment protections do not apply to searches conducted by child welfare agency social workers). While the Supreme Court has never addressed this issue, in Wyman v. James, 400 U.S. 309 (1971), the Court based its holding that a home visit by a welfare case worker did not constitute a search within the meaning of the Fourth Amendment in part on the "rehabilitative" character of welfare home visits and the need to protect dependent children. See Douglas Besherov, Juvenile Justice Advocacy: Practice in a Unique Court 142 (1974) (arguing based on Wyman that residence entries in the course of civil child abuse investigations are not "searches" governed by fourth amendment). But see Mark Hardin, Legal Barriers in Child Abuse Investigations: State Powers and Individual Rights, Wash. L. Rev. 493, 536-39 (1988) (arguing that child welfare agency social workers may constitutionally search home based on reasonable suspicion rather than probable cause, but that warrant should be required); Michael R. Beeman, Note, Investigating Child Abuse: The Fourth Amendment and Investigatory Home Visits, 89 Colum. L. Rev. 1034 (1989) (arguing that search warrants, issued under a flexible "reasonable cause" standard should be required before home searches by child welfare agencies).

[54]   See, e.g., In re Christopher B., 147 Cal. Rptr. 390 (Cal. Ct. App. 1978) (exclusionary rule does not apply in dependency proceedings); In re Diane P., 494 N.Y.S.2d 881 (N.Y. App. Div. 1985) (same); but see In re Melinda I., 488 N.Y.S.2d 279, 280 (N.Y. App. Div. 1985) ("[W]e conclude that evidence alleged to have been acquired illegally in violation of a person's constitutional rights may properly be the subject of a suppression motion in a civil child abuse or neglect proceeding.").

Courts also routinely apply a more lenient standard in evaluating due process vagueness challenges to civil child abuse statutes then they do to criminal statutes. See, e.g., Doe v. Staples, 706 F.2d 985, 988 (6th Cir. 1983) (noting "[w]hen a statute is not concerned with criminal conduct or first amendment considerations, the court must be fairly lenient in evaluating a claim of vagueness," court rejected vagueness challenge to statute authorizing removal of children from parent's custody without a prior hearing where "necessary for [the child's] welfare or in the interests of public safety"). But see Roe v. Conn., 417 F. Supp. 769, 777, 780 (M.D. Ala. 1976) (statute authorizing summary removal of child "if it appears that ... the child is in such condition that his welfare requires" held unconstitutionally vague); Alsager v. District Court of Polk County, 406 F. Supp. 10 (S.D. Iowa 1975) (termination of parental rights standards of "necessary parental care and protection" and "parental conduct detrimental to the physical or mental health or morals of the child" held unconstitutionally vague).

[55]   The passages in italics (here and infra at parts III(A)(1) and III(A)(2)) are based on my experiences representing parents in child welfare proceedings in Philadelphia. All are based loosely on actual events, but are offered as broad-brush illustrations, not as accurate historical accounts.

[56]   See generally Marc Galanter, Why the "Haves" Come out Ahead: Speculations on the Limits of Legal Change, 9 L. & Soc'y Rev. 95 (1974).

[57]   These are generalizations, of course, that do not necessarily hold true for all individuals in the system. In particular, attorneys for parents who attempt to make use of procedural protections and the

formal rules of the adversarial system on behalf of their clients may themselves be ostracized and treated as outsiders. See Sandra Anderson Garcia & Robert Batey, The Roles of Counsel for the Parent in Child Dependency Proceedings, 22 Ga. L. Rev. 1079 (1988).

[58]    Tina Grillo has discussed this informal law that evolves in "microsocial" settings in the context of divorce mediation proceedings:

The norms that govern microlegal systems are unwritten and often not consciously perceived, but they are always present. Violation of these norms may produce strong reactions. What makes such norms distinguishable from the mere "shoulds" of daily conversation is the presence of sanctions: additional communications which accompany the "shoulds" and which punish the deviant or reward the conformist. Many of these sanctions might appear trivial at first glance--for example, laughing at or dismissing someone--but they are powerful nonetheless. According to Michael Reisman, an actor enforcing norms within a micro-legal system is often both unaware of the nature of the system and oblivious to his own functional role in it. It is not the actor's motive or self-awareness that renders his reaction a sanction, but the effect of the reaction on those sanctioned.

Tina Grillo, The Mediation Alternative: Process Dangers for Women, 100 Yale L.J. 1545, 1556 (1991).

[59]    Statistics compiled by the U.S. Department of Health and Human Services Children's Bureau indicate that nationwide, 60 percent of the children in foster care are non-white. See <http:// www. acf.dhhs.govpt/programs/cb/stats/afcars/rpt0199/ar0199a.htm> (last visited January 19, 2000). A 1996 study by the U.S. Department of Health and Human Services National Center on Child Abuse and Neglect shows reports of child abuse and neglect to be "overwhelmingly concentrated among the lowest income families." Michael R. Petit & Patrick A. Curtis, Child Abuse and Neglect: A Look at the States, 1997 CWLA Stat Book 208 (1997); s ee also Santosky v. Kramer, 455 U.S. 745, 763 (1982) ("[P]arents subject to termination proceedings are often poor, uneducated, or members of minority groups."); Smith v. Organization of Foster Families for Equality and Reform, 431 U.S. 816, 833-35 (1977) (noting that children in foster care are disproportionately poor and non-white); Leroy H. Pelton, Child Abuse and Neglect: The Myth of Classlessness, in The Social Context of Child Abuse and Neglect 23, 24 (Leroy H. Pelton, ed. 1981) ("Every national survey of officially reported incidents of neglect and abuse has indicated that the preponderance of the reports involves families from the lowest socioeconomic levels."); Martin Rein, Thomas E. Nutt, & Heather Weiss, Foster Family Care: Myth and Reality, in Children and Decent People 27 (Alvin L. Schorr, ed. 1974) (families that receive child welfare services disproportionately lower class, lower income, and non-white); Dorothy E. Roberts, Racism and Patriarchy in the Meaning of Motherhood, in Mothers in Law: Feminist Theory and the Legal Regulation of Motherhood 224, 231-32 (Martha A. Fineman & Isabelle Karpin eds., 1995) (child welfare denies parental rights disproportionately to Black mothers).

[60]    See, e.g., Ill. Ann. Stat. ch. 705, § 405/2-17, 405/2-17.1, (4.5) (Smith-Hurd 1994) (providing for appointment of guardian ad litem and court-appointed special advocate to represent interests of child).

[61]    Cf. Martha Fineman, Dominant Discourse, Professional Language, and Legal Change in Child Custody Decisionmaking, 101 Harv. L. Rev. 727, 733, 744-45 (1988) (discussing similar phenomenon in private child custody cases).

[62]    See Grillo, supra note 58, at 1604 (observing in the context of divorce mediation that "the intimation [to a mother] that she is not being cooperative and caring or that she is thinking of herself instead of thinking selflessly of the children can shatter her self-esteem and make her lose faith in herself.").

[63]    Additionally, at least at the initial phases of the proceeding, it is not the correct legal standard. See supra notes 32-37 and accompanying text.

[64]    The illusion of intimacy and shared goals is also promoted by the common practice by the professionals in the system of referring to the accused mother as "mom." Whether it comes from a desire to build rapport or the inability of a professional juggling numerous cases to remember a particular

parent's name, to be the only participant referred to as "mom" in a room where everyone else is consulting files, carrying briefcases, handing out business cards, and being called by name is, no doubt, highly demeaning and disempowering. Moreover, by creating an illusion of intimacy--pretending we're all in the family--it contributes to the creation of an atmosphere in which secrets must be shared and dissent is unacceptable.

[65] See Robert H. Mnookin & Lewis Kornhauser, Bargaining in the Shadow of the Law: The Case of Divorce, 88 Yale L.J. 950, 978-80 (1979) (noting that "the rules and procedures used in court for adjudicating disputes affect the bargaining process that occurs ... outside the courtroom."). But see Owen M. Fiss, Against Settlement, 93 Yale L.J. 1073, 1076 (1984) (arguing against notion that settlement is simply a product of the parties' predictions of the outcome of trial).

[66] See, e.g., Gregory Firestone, Dependency Mediation: Where Do We Go from Here? 35 Fam. & Conciliation Cts. Rev. 223 (1997).

[67] See Julius Libow, The Need for Standardization and Expansion of Nonadversary Proceedings in Juvenile Dependency Court with Special Emphasis on Mediation and Role of Counsel, 44 Juv. & Fam. Court Ct. J. 3 (1993).

[68] See Nancy Thoennes, An Evaluation of Child Protection Mediaton in Five California Courts, 35 Fam. & Conciliation Cts. Rev. 184, 195 (1997) [[[hereinafter Thoennes, An Evaluation] (study showing mediation can produce agreements at any stage of a dependency proceeding--jurisdictional (adjudicatory), dispositional, or post-dispositional). Mediation of termination cases is less common, though it does occur. See Nancy Thoennes, Child Protection Mediation in the Juvenile Court, 33, No. 1 Judges' J. 14, 17 (1994) [hereinafter Thoennes, Child Protection Mediation].

[69] See Thoennes, An Evaluation, supra note 68, at 192 (mediation often addresses issues not legally in dispute).

[70] The dependency mediation guidelines for Alameda County, California, for example, allow the mediator to include "[a]ny other interested party ... whose involvement may facilitate decision making or resolution." Elizabeth M. Dunn, Alameda County Juvenile Dependency Mediation Program, Program Guidelines (1998) (on file with author) [hereinafter Program Guidelines]; see also Steve Baron, Dependency Court Mediation: The Roles of the Participants, 35 Fam. & Conciliation Courts Rev. 149, 158 (1997) ("the wider the net cast" with regard to involving other participants in mediation, the better); Hon. Leonard Edwards, Dependency Court Mediation, The Role of the Judge, 35 Fam. & Conciliation Cts. Rev. 160, 162 (1997) (social workers should "actively recruit the attendance and participation of other interested family or community members"); Marilou T. Giovannucci, Understanding the Role of the Mediator in Child Protection Proceedings, 35 Fam. & Conciliation Courts Rev. 143, 144 (1997) (foster parents, service providers, and others may be invited to participate in mediation); Thoennes, An Evaluation, supra note 68, at 185 ("[M] any individuals attended the mediation process who would not ordinarily be involved with a court hearing.").

[71] See Baron, supra note 70, at 149 (noting that some California mediation programs officially exclude attorneys while others include them); Edwards, supra note 70, at 162 (suggesting that mediation sometimes more effective without lawyers).

[72] See Baron, supra note 70, at 158; Edwards, supra note 70, at 162. This standard is often so vague as to make the confidentiality rule fairly toothless.

[73] See Thoennes, Child Protection Mediation, supra note 68, at 15; see also Jerold S. Auerbach, Justice without Law? Non-Legal Dispute Settlement in American Law 57 (1983) (arguing that, since the civil war, arguments in favor of ADR have primarily expressed a desire for judicial efficiency more than community justice).

Various efforts have been made by proponents of mediation to measure the "success" of pilot programs, see, e.g., Megan G. Orlando, Funding Juvenile Dependency Mediation through Legislation, 35 Fam. & Conciliation Cts. Rev. 196, 197 (1997), but an empirical measure of such an amorphous concept is, of course, elusive. Measuring the percentage of cases in which agreements are reached obviously leaves many questions unanswered. See Thoennes, An Evaluation, supra note 68, at 191. Surveys showing high rates of "satisfaction" among participants in mediation are also problematic. One study, for example, reported that parents were happy with one mediation pilot program because they actually got more face time with their lawyers than they had in the traditional adversarial system. This study suggests that the adversarial system that the mediation program replaced was severely broken: "In a system where attorneys admit they often appear in court before they know who their clients are mediation ensured parents got some undivided attention. Parents' attorneys also acknowledged that parents got a lot of practical information in mediation, which was important because not all attorneys take the time to answer questions and ensure that clients fully understand the situation." Id. at 190.

[74]    See Giovannucci, supra note 70, at 144; Nancy Thoennes, Child Protection Mediation: Where We Started, 35 Fam. & Conciliation Cts. Rev. 136, 137 (1997).

[75]    See Thoennes, supra note 74, at 137.

[76]    See Giovannucci, supra note 70, at 147; Edwards, supra note 70, at 161; Firestone, supra note 66, at 228.

[77]    See Giovannucci, supra note 70, at 144.

[78]    Thoennes, supra note 74, at 137. The assumption is made that "these families" involved in the child welfare system are all by definition in need of treatment. See infra text accompanying notes 221-32.

[79]    Program Guidelines, supra note 70; see also Fineman, supra note 61, at 754 ("The image of the legal system constructed by the helping professions is adversarial, combative, and productive of divisions, misunderstandings, and hostility;" mediation is seen as the cure --- serving to open up blocked channels of communication); Mumma, Mediating Disputes, 42 Pub. Welfare 22, 25 (1984) (asserting that "the litigation process is little more than an institutionalized form of emotional abuse to children"). Social workers and mediation advocates also believe that the antagonism between the parties in legal disputes is created by the adversary system and that therefore elimination of that system will eliminate antagonism. In the divorce context, see Meyer Elkin, Conciliation Courts: The Reintegration of Disintegrating Families 22 Fam. Coordinator 63, 70 (1973) ("The elimination of adversary proceedings eliminated adversary roles and therefore reduced the need to fulfill antagonistic roles and the need to strike out at each other"). In contrast, Richard Abel takes the position that mediation suppresses conflict. See infra notes 204, 206 and accompanying text.

[80]    See Lisa Merkel-Holguin, Putting Families Back into the Child Protection Partnership: Family Group Decision Making, 12 Protecting Children 4 (1996).

A parallel but largely separate reform movement called Family Group Decision Making ("FGDM") originated in New Zealand in the late 1980's and has recently been garnering attention in this country as well. See generally Marie Connolly & Margaret McKenzie, Effective Participatory Practice: Family Group Conferencing in Child Protection (1999); Bronwyn Dalley, Family Matters: Child Welfare in Twentieth-Century New Zealand (1998). It arose specifically in response to objections voiced by the indigenous Maori people to what they viewed as an imperialist and racist child welfare bureaucracy that was wrongly removing Maori children from their native communities and culture and denying Maoris the sovereign right to deal with child welfare issues in conformance with their own cultural traditions and standards. FGDM attempts to integrate the government child welfare system with a family-centered process modeled on traditional Maori methods of conflict resolution.

In this process, the child welfare agency convenes a meeting that includes the usual cast of professionals (social workers and possibly lawyers), family, extended family members and kin, tribal elders, and other community members (neighbors or clergy) that the family views as supportive. The participants open the meeting with traditional Maori "rituals of engagement," which include songs or incantations acknowledging the supernatural, the ancestors, and the living. See Harry Walker, Whanau Hui, Family Decision Making, and the Family Group Conference: An Indigenous Maori View, 12 Protecting Children 8, 9 (1996). The social worker who investigated the case then presents the basis for her concern about the family, but does not share any opinions or recommendations. The professionals and other non-family members then leave the room, leaving the family to discuss the case in private and develop a plan. Once the family has reached consensus, they invite the other participants back in the room and present and explain their plan. The agency, the parents, and the child's attorney each have veto power over the final plan, but they rarely exercise this power. In 90 to 95 percent of the cases, the participants reach agreement. See Lisa Merkel-Holguin, Putting Families Back into the Child Protection Partnership: Family Group Decision Making, 12 Protecting Children 4, 6 (1996).

A statute passed in New Zealand in 1989 requires all substantiated cases of abuse and neglect to be referred to FGDM. See id. at 5. Versions of this model have also been adapted for use in the United States. The main modification in many U.S. programs has been to keep the social workers and other professionals in the room for the entire meeting. See id. at 6; Ted Keys, Family Decision Making in Oregon, 12 Protecting Children 11 (1996).

The claimed benefits of FGDM are similar to those of mediation. The process is said to foster cooperation, collaboration, and communication and to avoid the negative effects of the adversary process on children and relationships. See Markel-Holguin, supra note 80, at 4. The proponents of FGDM also particularly stress its capacity to empower families and its sensitivity to cultural differences.

[167] See supra note 155.

[168] See Mashaw, supra note 134, at 50; Summers, supra note 155, at 3.

[169] See Tyler, supra note 155.

[170] In my experience, these formalities were not always observed by judges in child welfare cases. The therapeutic mindset that pressures participants to abandon procedural formalities in these cases can affect judges as well. Thus, ex parte communications and other irregularities were not uncommon.

[171] See Judith Resnik, On the Bias: Feminist Reconsiderations of the Aspirations for Our Judges, 61 S. Cal. L. Rev. 1877, 1907 (1988).

[172] See Richard Delgado, Fairness and Formality: Minimizing the Risk of Prejudice in Alternative Dispute Resolution, 1985 Wis. L. Rev. 1359, 1387-88 (1985); Grillo, supra note 58, at 1589-90 ("The very intimacy that renders mediation such a potentially constructive process may facilitate the mediator's projection of her own conflicts onto the parties.").

[173] See Delgado, supra note 172, at 1403 (arguing ADR poses heightened risk of prejudice when issue touches sensitive or intimate area of life).

[174] See supra notes 77-79 and accompanying text.[FN175]. See id.

[176] 384 U.S. 436 (1966).

[177] See id. at 515.

[178] Minow, supra note 9, at 291.

[179] Jean Koh Peters calls the "best interests of the child" the "looming legal standard" that tends to preoccupy judges and parties "throughout all phases of all [child welfare proceedings] ... even when, at a given phase of the proceeding, another standard, such as parental fault, is controlling." Jean Koh Peters, The Roles and Content of Best Interests in Client-Directed Lawyering for Children in Child Protective Proceedings, 64 Fordham L. Rev. 1505, 1515 (1996).

[180] See Owen Fiss, Against Settlement, 93 Yale L.J. 1073 (1984).

[181] Public scrutiny may be frustrated in many existing formal adversarial child welfare systems by rules that close these proceedings to the public and the press. Though appellant decisions will often be published (identifying the parties by initials to preserve confidentiality), trial level decisions are rarely in writing and thus escape public scrutiny altogether.

[182] In the context of welfare benefit programs, William Simon argues that formal legal rules are not actually effective in ensuring consistency with social norms because they are necessarily both over- and under-inclusive and preclude front line workers from exercising discretion to respond to the particularized needs and circumstances of claimants. See William H. Simon, Legality, Bureaucracy, and Class in the

Welfare System, 92 Yale L.J. 1198, 1227 (1983). More broadly, Simon argues that the formalization of public welfare programs as a result of the legal reforms of the 1960s and 1970s, which established welfare as a legal right and sought to rein in the discretion of front line workers, has not actually resulted in any improvement in the treatment of recipients. The pathology of condescending moralism that the legal reformers sought to eradicate has simply been replaced by a new set of pathologies stemming from the proletarianization and alienation of front line workers from the purposes of their work and from the recipients themselves.

As an alternative to formalism, Simon promotes "professionalism" as a mechanism for preventing abuses of state power. Front line social workers would exercise broad discretion but within a set of standards instilled through the course of professional training and socialization. Social workers would receive relatively high status and reward, would be "active participants in a vital professional culture," id. at 1242, and would participate in a collegial supervision process involving extensive review and dialogue between worker and supervisor regarding individual cases. See William H. Simon, The Invention and Reinvention of Welfare Rights, 44 Md. L. Rev. 1, 21 (1985).

Simon's critique of formality is not entirely transferable to the child welfare context. First, the level of rigidity and specificity in the formal rules governing public benefits programs--which often take the form of numeric formulas--go much further in constraining discretion than rules in the child welfare context probably ever could. Because of the complex nature of the judgments involved, child welfare workers--even when constrained by legal rules--retain enormous discretion. It is hard to imagine that the determinations involved in a child welfare case could ever be reduced to the kind of formulaic rules that would lead to the level of proletarianization and alienation of front line workers that Simon decries in the welfare benefits context. In that sense, the child welfare system perhaps already looks more like the system of professionalism that Simon promotes. Child welfare workers' level of prestige, education and engagement with the purposes of their work is no doubt considerably higher than that of the front line clerks employed in public benefits offices. Yet, while even higher levels of education, pay, prestige, and professionalism among child welfare workers would no doubt benefit these systems immensely, because of the peculiar dynamics of the child welfare system, I am skeptical that professionalism alone could ever provide the kind of check on arbitrary treatment that Simon envisions.

Simon describes a therapeutic relationship between social worker and client in which the autonomy of the client is the ultimate goal. See id. at 16. The social worker does not pretend to be a neutral faceless bureaucrat, but rather individualizes herself by expressing her own judgments about the client's best interests. This enables "the client to see the worker as a distinct individual capable of empathizing and feeling solidarity with her," but the social worker avoids the pitfalls of paternalism or coercion by honoring the client's choice should she decline to engage in dialogue or should she "express a decision contrary to the worker's judgment." Id. at 19. This latter aspect of the therapeutic relationship is, of course, far more problematic where the social worker is judging not only the client's interests but the client's child's interests, and thus may have to override the client's choice where, in the worker's judgment, it endangers the child.

In a response to Simon's 1983 article, Joel Handler made a similar observation on the limits of Simon's theory. He noted that home visits by welfare benefits caseworkers were usually "pleasant and attitudes toward the caseworker were positive," except in those instances in which the caseworker had control over something the client wanted. "[T]hen negative feelings arose--feelings of dependency and coercion." Joel F. Handler, Discretion in Social Welfare: The Uneasy Position in the Rule of Law, 92 Yale L.J. 1270 & n.1 (1983).

[183]   See supra notes 36-37 and accompanying text.

[184]   See, e.g., Hon. Leonard P. Edwards & Steven Baron, Alternatives to Contested Litigation in Child Abuse and Neglect Cases, 33 Fam. & Conciliation Cts. Rev. 275, 278, 279 (1997) ("[M]ediation should always focus on preserving ... the best interests of the children.").

[185]   See supra note 34. It also is not the correct legal standard. See supra notes 32-37 and accompanying text.

[186] The capacity for reforms labeled as purely procedural to effect changes in substantive law has been observed in other related contexts. See Fineman, supra note 61, at 760-65 (arguing that the procedural trend toward use of mediation in child custody disputes actually masks a change in substantive law toward a preference for joint custody); Martin Guggenheim, Reconsidering the Need for Counsel for Children in Custody, Visitation, and Child Protection Proceedings, 29 Loyola U. Chi. L. J. 299 (1998) (noting that advocates for children have sometimes sought indirectly to effect changes in substantive law with which they disagree by advocating for increased procedural rights for children).

[187] See Auerbach, supra note 73, at 59 ("Informality, in a social setting of disparate power relations, inevitably served the interests of the dominant group"); Richard Abel, Informalism: A Tactical Equivalent to Law, 19 Clearinghouse Rev. 375, 379 (1985)("[W]hen informality is freed from all formal constraints, law simply reflects the distribution of power in the larger society."); see also Fiss, supra note 180, at 1076 (settlements distorted by disparities in resources between parties).

[188] Cf. Fiss, supra note 180, at 1078 (Judgment "knowingly struggles against" inequalities between the parties, while settlement, which is based on bargaining, "accepts inequalities of wealth as an integral and legitimate component of the process.").

[189] See Auerbach, supra note 73, at 120 ("Court intervention is most appropriate in a setting where conflict occurs among unequal strangers, when a court can, at least in theory, rectify an imbalance by extending the formalities of equal protection to the weaker parties.").

[190] See supra note 59.

[191] See supra notes 55-65 and accompanying text.

[192] See id.

[193] Cf. Hardin, supra note 53, at 503 (noting the "inherently coercive nature of child abuse investigations" and suggesting that even a parent who is confident that her child has not been maltreated may feel even less free to refuse entry in a child abuse investigation than a typical suspect in a criminal investigation).

[194] This problem is particularly evident in the widespread practice of placing children in foster care through the mechanism of "Voluntary Placement Agreements" (VPAs). A VPA is a document signed by the parent voluntarily relinquishing temporary custody of her child to the agency. The agreement usually allows the agency to keep the child in foster care without a court hearing for 30 days to 6 months. Because it avoids the necessity of an emergency court hearing, VPAs are the preferred mechanism for placement by many social workers. In some states, more than half the children in foster care were placed there by a VPA. See Wexler, supra note 24, at 119. Parents almost never have the benefit of legal counsel when they sign VPAs and are frequently coerced into signing by social workers who threaten that the child will be placed for a longer time period or even permanently removed by court intervention if the parent does not sign. See Smith v. Organization of Foster Families, 431 U.S. 816, 833-34 (1977); In re Burns, 519 A.2d 638, 640-41 (Del.1986) (finding that 17-year-old mother signed VPA on understanding that if she did sign, her child would stay with her and if she did not, the court would take him away); In re David R., 420 N.Y.S.2d 675, 677 (N.Y. Fam. Ct. 1979) (involving a woman, fluent only in Spanish, who signed VPA in English without the aid of interpreter that relinquished custody of grandchild); Robert H. Mnookin, Foster Care--In Whose Best Interest?, 43 Harv. Educ. Rev. 599, 601 (1973); Musewicz, The Failure of Foster Care: Federal Statutory Reform and the Child's Right to Permanence, 54 S. Cal. L. Rev. 633, 639 (1981). An American Bar Association report in 1983 called coerced "voluntary" placement a "recurrent problem." See Diane Dodson, The Legal Framework for Ending Foster Care Drift: A Guide to Evaluating and Improving State Laws, Regulations and Court Rules 6 (Wash. D.C., Foster Care Project, National Legal Resource Center for Child Advocacy and Protection, American Bar Association, August 1983).

[195] See, e.g., Edwards & Baron, supra note 184, at 279-80 (by reducing resistance and defensiveness, mediation allows constructive communication and problem solving and permits consideration of options formerly ruled out or never considered); Thoennes, Child Protection Mediation, supra note 68, at 137

(mediation "identif[ies] mutually acceptable, but often nonobvious, solutions" and facilitates joint problem solving).

[196] See supra note 39.

[197] See Auerbach, supra note 73, at 16 ("Only when there is congruence between individuals and their community, with shared commitment to common values is there a possibility for [informal dispute resolution to achieve justice]."); Richard Abel, The Contradictions of Informal Justice, in The Politics of Informal Justice 285 (Richard Abel ed., 1983) (conflict in homogeneous societies reinforces shared norms by creating occasions on which they may collectively be asserted); William L.F. Felstiner, Influences of Social Organization on Dispute Processing, 9 L. & Soc'y Rev. 63 (1974) (mediation works best within small social groups where social and cultural norms and experiences are shared and where mediator understands the personal experiences and perspectives of the disputants). But see Grillo, supra note 58, at 1560 (suggesting mediation works better than adjudication in the environment of a pluralistic society with conflicting moral codes and values, because as long as both parties accept an agreement, no third party need decide which moral code governs).

[198] See Judith Masson & Maureen Winn Oakley, Out of Hearing: Representing Children in Care Proceedings (1999) (studying the experiences and views of children and their representatives in child welfare proceedings in England).

[199] In some instances, there may even be more than one individual serving in a child advocacy role, each of whom will interview the child. There may be some combination of a lawyer, a guardian ad litem, a social worker, and/or a volunteer from the Court Appointed Special Advocates program.

[200] The child advocate will usually want to be present while others interview the child in any case.

[201] It is also important to remember that most cases do not involve allegations of severe abuse. See supra note 19.

[202] Cf. Grillo, supra note 58, at 1609 n.293 (asserting that there is no evidence that children whose parents reach a mediated settlement are any better adjusted after divorce than those whose parents used traditional processes).

[203] See supra notes 74-76 and accompanying text.

[204] See supra text accompanying notes 62-64; Abel, supra note 197, at 271 ("Informalism ... disguis[es] the coercion that both stimulates resistance and justifies the demand for the protection of formal due process.").

[205] For a mother whose neglect or mistreatment of her children stems from depression, a legal process that makes passivity appear to be the best coping mechanism may be counterproductive from a therapeutic perspective. Cf. Grillo, supra note 58, at 1603 (discussing how mediation in divorce cases can be particularly "disastrous for a woman who embraces a relational sense of self"); Schneider, supra note 159, at 648 (suggesting assertion of rights can be transformative for many women).

[206] Thoennes, An Evaluation, supra note 68, at 187; see C. Moore, The Mediation Process 129-31 (1986); Donald T. Saposnek, Mediatinng Child Custody Disputes: A Strategic Approach 85-86 (1998); Abel, supra note 197, at 294 (noting that in some forms of informal dispute resolution, "the 'full airing' of the complainant's grievances becomes an end in itself"); Grillo, supra note 58, at 1575 (criticizing rhetoric of mediation that participants be permitted to "vent" as not taking anger seriously enough-- "anger that is merely vented has lost its potential to teach, heal, and energize").

[207] The attorney-client relationship, of course, embodies a significant and complicated power dynamic of its own. Lucie White has suggested that lawyers for the poor "inevitably replay the drama of subordination" in their own relationships with their clients. See Lucie E. White, Goldberg v. Kelly on the Paradox of Lawyering for the Poor, 56 Brook. L. Rev. 861 (1990).

[208] These are, of course, phenomena that are difficult to measure empirically. Mediation in child welfare cases has been touted as a success based on parents' self-reported satisfaction with the process. See Thoennes, An Evaluation, supra note 68, at 190. Of course, these reports must be viewed in the

context of the deficiencies of the court system to which mediation is being compared. See supra note 73.

[209] See Auerbach, supra note 73, at 102 (noting that commercial arbitration originally developed as an alternative to litigation within trade associations whose members engaged in continuous trade of particular products and within which "the value of an enduring commercial relationship far exceeded the value of a particular commodity"); Christine V. Harrington, Shadow Justice: The Ideology and Institutionalization of Alternatives to Court 99 (1985) (identifying the "central thesis" of the ADR movement as the notion that "conflict in continuing relationships is best dealt with in an informal setting"); Frank E. A. Sander, Varieties of Dispute Processing, 70 F.R.D. 111, 120 (1976) (noting that disputes between parties involved in long-term relationships are particularly amenable to mediation); Linda Silberman & Andrew Schepard, Court-Ordered Mediation in Family Disputes: The New York Proposal, 14 N.Y.U. Rev. L. & Soc. Change 741, 742 (1986) (arguing that mediation is particularly appropriate to divorce and custody cases because of its capacity to help parties resume a constructive relationship). Disenting in Goss v. Lopez, 419 U.S. 565, 593-94 (1975), Justice Powell decried the majority's decision to apply formal due process principles to public school discipline cases, precisely because he believed it would be unnecessarily destructive to the maintenance of an ongoing relationship between teacher and student.

[210] See Abel, supra note 187, at 381.

[211] Research has shown that people tend to accept the outcome of a given dispute resolution procedure if they perceive it as fair, and that people's perceptions of the fairness of a procedure is unrelated to the outcome (i.e., whether they win or lose). See Tyler, supra note 155, at 7.

[212] See Grillo, supra note 58, at 1552; Saposnek, supra note 206; Silberman & Schepard, supra note 209, at 741.

[213] See supra notes 32-37 and accompanying text.

[214] See Grillo, supra note 58.

[215] See supra note 165.

[216] See Keys, supra note 80, at 13 (noting that the Family Unit Meeting--a U.S. variant on Family Group Decision Making--grew out of family therapy).

[217] Thoennes, An Evaluation, supra note 68, at 191; see also Julius Libow, The Need for Standardization and Expansion of Nonadversary Proceedings in Juvenile Dependency Court with Special Emphasis on Mediation and Role of Counsel, 44 Juv. & Fam. Court J. 3, 10 (1993).

[218] Thoennes, An Evaluation, supra note 68, at 187.

[219] See Edwards, supra note 70, at 161-62; Thoennes, An Evaluation, supra note 68, at 192.

[220] Grillo, supra note 58, at 1560.

[221] See Abel, supra note 197, at 271.

[222] See Edwards, supra note 70, at 162 ("[M]ediation has never resulted in any harm.").

[223] See Wexler, supra note 24, at 124 (citing study that found that in half of all emergency removals there was no maltreatment).

[224] See supra notes 36-37 and accompanying text.

[225] Cf. In re T.D., 553 A.2d 979, 982 (Pa. Super. 1988) (noting that dependency proceeding may color a child's future attitude toward and relationship with parents); see also Goldstein, supra note 97, at 9, 25, 174-78 (Children "react even to temporary infringement of parental autonomy with anxiety, diminishing trust, loosening of emotional ties, or an increasing tendency to be out of control."); Joseph Goldstein, Medical Care for the Child at Risk: On State Supervention of Parental Autonomy, 86 Yale L.J. 645, 649-50 (1977) ("Court or agency intervention without regard for or over the objection of parents can only serve to undermine the familial bond which is vital to a child's sense of becoming and being an adult in his own right."); Murray Levine, A Therapeutic Jurisprudence Analysis of Mandated Reporting of Child Maltreatment by Psychotherapists, in Law in a Therapeutic Key 323, 330 (David B. Wexler & Bruce J. Winnick eds., 1997) (noting that the very appearance of a child welfare agency social

worker at the door of a family's home "raises the specter that children may be removed," and quoting one social worker who said, "[w]e terrorize people ... Just the thought of [the child welfare agency] frightens people.").

    [226] See Miranda v. Arizona, 384 U.S. 436 (1966).

    [227] See Richard Hofrichter, Neighborhood Justice and the Social Control Problems of American Capitalism: A Perspective, in The Politics of Informal Justice 239 (Richard Abel ed., 1982) (discussing "freewheeling therapeutic inquiry that characterizes mediation" and how openness of it magnifies extent to which state penetrates lives of disputants).

    [228] See Mumma, supra note 79, at 23 (contending that there is no distinction between mediation and therapy).

    [229] See Program Description, supra note 70.

    [230] Id.

    [231] See In re T.D., 553 A.2d 979 (Pa. Super. 1988).

    [232] See Hofrichter, supra note 227, at 239 ("Within the mediation session, many programs encourage disputants to 'tell their stories,' ventilate their feelings, and otherwise reveal details about their personal lives. The purpose is not to punish or reprimand but rather to understand the roots of the conflict. But this sort of therapeutic openness magnifies the extent to which the state penetrates the lives of disputants: Their deepest emotions and most personal problems become part of the process of conflict resolution. This intervention itself is regulation, regardless of its effect on the outcome."). Where state intrusion into the private lives of parents is explicitly coercive, there are constitutional limits. See In re T.R., 731 A.2d 1276 (Pa. 1999) (court's order compelling mother of dependent child to undergo involuntary psychiatric examination held unconstitutional).

    [233] See, e.g., Richard Abel, The Politics of Informal Justice 11 (1982).

    [234] See supra notes 170-97 and accompanying text.

    [235] See supra notes 209-11 and accompanying text.

    [236] These principles suggest that the Family Group Decision Making (FGDM) model, at least as practiced among the indigenous Maoris of New Zealand where it was originally developed, may provide one context in which informality can be successfully used in the resolution of child welfare disputes. See supra note 80. By shifting the locus of the dispute from the interface between state and individual to the relationships among family members, FGDM may make possible the kind of creative problem solving that depends on a community of shared norms and values and may lessen the degree to which power imbalance infects and distorts the process.

    The New Zealand model may be difficult, if not impossible, to replicate in this country. See Auerbach, supra note 73, at 100, 114 (suggesting that in the U.S. informal dispute resolution has "worked where it was indigenous to an immigrant community, but the attempt of legal professionals to impose it upon poor people was unsuccessful"); id. at 118-20 (discussing unsuccessful attempt in 1960s to transplant tribal dispute resolution mechanism used by indigenous Kpelle tribe of Liberia to urban American poor). In the pluralistic, fragmented culture of modern America, it is less clear that an allegedly abusive parent is likely to be part of a functioning community. But see Carol B. Stack, Cultural Perspectives on Child Welfare, 12 N.Y.U. Rev. L. & Soc. Change 539 (1984) (criticizing child welfare system for failing to take account of existing extended kinship networks in minority communities in the U.S.).

    [237] Some may argue that the use of adversarial processes at the adjudicatory phase will be so damaging to the relationship between social worker and parent that attempts to preserve that relationship through informal processes at the dispositional and review stages will be unavailing. Agencies may be able to address this problem, however, by assigning a different set of social workers to handle ongoing cases from those that handle investigations. To some degree, this problem is already alleviated by the widespread practice of state agency social workers contracting with independent agencies to provide ongoing services to families. Thus, following the initial investigation, agency social workers may act more as case managers than direct service providers.

# E: Managing High Conflict Cases

# [14]

# Parenting Coordination For High Conflict Families

## Christine Coates, Robin Deutsch, Hugh Starnes, Matthew Sullivan and BeaLisa Sydlik

The increasingly widespread use of parenting coordination to provide ongoing, intensive case management of higher conflict child custody cases recognizes the many advantages of this alternative dispute resolution (ADR) process in the family courts. The essential functions of the parenting coordination process are to create appropriate parenting plans; to build functional, enduring coparenting relationships; and to resolve ongoing coparenting disputes. In this article, an experienced multidisciplinary group from different jurisdictions across the United States examines a few of the most challenging issues that currently confront the field of parenting coordination. These include legal issues, such as the quasi-judicial authority of the parenting coordinator (PC) derived from statutory and legislative means, continuing jurisdiction of cases, and constitutional challenges. A description of cases that can benefit from the appointment of a PC is provided, as well as a judicial view of the pros and cons of the role. Essential aspects of the practice are discussed, including the importance of structure and boundaries, challenges to the use of the role, liability issues, and the PC's role in creating and managing collaborative teams to work on these cases. The article concludes with a vision of the future that highlights the need for research and training to responsibly advance this promising, emerging role.

The past two decades have seen a progressive development of alternative dispute resolution (ADR) processes within the family court system.[1] Across the spectrum of traditional family court procedures, alternatives have been developed to serve families such as at intake with family court orientation and parent education programs,[2] early in the process as disputes manifest with mediation services,[3] and with an increased focus on judicial case management and settlement processes prior to permitting litigation to proceed.[4] The widespread use of these ADR processes recognizes the court's efforts to assist families through the divorce transition not only by resolving disputes and creating appropriate parenting plans, but by also building functional, enduring coparent relationships.[5] This spectrum of alternative family court services, whether privately provided or in conjunction with the family court services, is based on collaborative rather than adversarial models and on interdisciplinary professional involvement that recognizes interparental conflict as the major source of detriment to children of divorce.

More recently, Parenting Coordination models have been added to the spectrum of ADR processes to provide intensive case management for chronically conflicted child custody situations.[6] In the early 1990s, this new professional role evolved independently in a couple of jurisdictions that were attempting to deal with high-conflict families. These high-conflict families, roughly 8% to 12% of divorcing parents, continued in chronic high-conflict postdivorce and relitigated frequently,[7] using a disproportionate amount of the court's time and resources. These parents also depleted their own economic reserves, reinforced their negative views of each other as enemies, and, most importantly, subjected their children to toxic conflict. Most of the disputes were minor, generated by one or both parents' need to control, punish, or obstruct the access of the other, such as one-time changes in the timeshare schedule, telephone access, vacation planning, and decisions about the children's after-school activities, health care, child care, and child-rearing practices.

In response to the frustration of judges that certain families were repeatedly returning to court to handle disputes about their parenting plans, a few courts began to delegate (with the consent of the parents) limited areas of authority over child custody issues to experienced mental health professionals and attorneys to settle parental disputes in an immediate, nonadversarial, court-sanctioned forum. The use of this new, quasi legal-mental health-ADR role that combined assessment, case management, mediation, and arbitration functions, began to spread and is now called Parenting Coordination[8] generically across states and provinces. In addition, the role of the Parenting Coordinator (PC)[9] has been increasingly specified and defined, with common standards of practice emerging across jurisdictions.[10] The use of parenting coordination has been cited in the literature as particularly useful in addressing difficult issues, such as child alienation,[11] and in monitoring and modifying parenting plans that need to evolve over time (e.g., with very young or special needs children or with parents who have serious issues that have restricted their parenting time).[12] Some suggest that PCs are also useful earlier in cases that appear conflicted either to assist with the development of parenting plans or in conjunction with custody evaluations, which often need intensive case management for several months during the time a custody evaluation is completed and litigated.[13]

The essential function of parenting coordination is to help families develop, implement, and monitor viable parenting plans. The proposed Florida Parenting Coordination statute provides a useful definition of parenting coordination when it states that

> Parenting Coordination is a process whereby an impartial third person called a parenting coordinator helps the parties to implement their parenting plan by facilitating the resolution of disputes between parents and/or legal guardians, providing education, making recommendations to the parties, and, with the prior approval of the parties and the court, making decisions within the scope of the court order of appointment.[14] PCs function outside the formal family court process, but they are accountable to the court; write and file their decisions as court orders, reports, or arbitration awards; and adhere to court rules and procedures, and their work (decisions and conduct) is subject to judicial and professional review.[15]

Although research is sorely lacking on the effectiveness of parenting coordination, there is evidence that the intervention can substantially reduce relitigation rates. In one California study, in the year prior to the appointment of a PC, 166 cases had 993 court appearances.[16] The same 166 cases had 37 court appearances the year following the appointment. Another survey found that the majority of parents working with a PC reported being satisfied and experiencing decreased conflict with the other parent.[17]

From a conceptual standpoint, the PC reinforces a parallel parenting model (low engagement, low conflict) by increasing the structure and detail of parenting plans and becoming the linkage between the parents for any interactions that become conflicted. This effectively disengages the parents from each other, allowing them to parent independently and use the PC for any remaining coparenting issues. This parallel structure of coparenting appears to be adequate to support children's positive postdivorce adjustment.[18] Through a variety of processes implemented by the PC (education, mediation, and arbitration), the parents ideally learn more functional dispute resolution strategies and conflict management that cannot occur through repeated exposure to the legal-adversarial process. At a minimum, the parents have a stable, knowledgeable, and readily accessible professional to resolve day-to-day disputes specified by the PC appointment order that otherwise would result in high interparental conflict to the detriment of the children involved.

In many jurisdictions, the scope of authority and areas of decision making of the PC tend to be limited and specified by the PC appointment order. Most jurisdictions impose limits on the PC's authority regarding custody determination, relocation, or substantial changes to the parenting plan. Similarly, most jurisdictions specify that the process is nonconfidential, that the PC has access to nonparties involved with the family (e.g., health and education professionals), the children, and any information necessary to execute his or her duties. The PC is often entitled to direct children and parents to obtain third-party services (e.g., counseling, drug testing and/or treatment, and parent education).[19]

This article will address a few of the most challenging issues that currently confront the field of parenting coordination. The Parenting Coordination role is facing legal challenges because the PC functions on the boundary of the legal and mental health paradigms and does not fit easily into the existing sanctioned family court roles, such as judge, attorney, guardian ad litem, custody evaluator, and mediator. Selected issues are next addressed from the practice-oriented point of view of those authors of this article who have experience with the role. Many more challenging issues exist, but space limitations allow only an overview of a few.

## I. LEGAL CHALLENGES

There have been several areas in which the PC model has been or may be the subject of legal challenge.

## DELEGATION OF JUDICIAL AUTHORITY

Parenting Coordination necessarily entails a varying degree of fact finding and issue determination in each case. The degree to which this is seen as a usurpation of the court's inherent decision-making authority depends on a jurisdiction's interpretation of applicable laws and the local legal culture. The more that third-party professionals (e.g., evaluators, mediators, therapists, special masters, and referees) are looked to for assessment of a family's situation and relied on for recommendations as to "best interest" determinations, the more likely the PC model will be accepted as yet another valuable intervention at the court's disposal to assist in dispute resolution.

*Legislative authority*. A grant of legislative authority to make PC appointments may lend credibility to the process, implying that the legal implications have been considered and agreed on by the stakeholders. In states where dissolution law is wholly statutory, such a grant may be indispensable. An Oregon appellate case, *Heinonen v. Heinonen*,[20] considered the threshold issue of whether a trial court can lawfully delegate to a "visitation specialist" its decision-making power in visitation and custody disputes where one or more parties object. Noting that the trial court's authority in dissolution proceedings is "wholly statutory," the court found that there was no Oregon statute that authorized the reference to a visitation specialist of custody and visitation modification issues. The court further opined that a difficulty with the order was that it invested the "visitation specialist" with absolute authority to resolve visitation conflicts and direct the parents' behavior without a vehicle for judicial review of the "visitation specialist's" findings or decisions.

Idaho state has adopted a rule of court[21] that specifically states, "*The appointment of a Parenting Coordinator does not divest the court of its exclusive jurisdiction to determine fundamental issues of custody, visitation, and support, and the authority to exercise management and control of the case.*" The rule further lists those issues that the PC may "determine" as distinguished from a list of issues that the PC may only "make recommendations to the court on." Such differentiation implies that the legislature found a dichotomy between what is an unlawful delegation of judicial authority versus what is not. The list of issues the PC could "determine" includes "minor alterations in parenting schedule ... which do not substantially alter the basic time share allocation" and "telephone communication with the children." Issues that the PC is limited to making recommendations to the court on include the following: (a) what parent may authorize counseling, treatment, and school selection for a child; (b) supervised visitation; (c) the need for a custody evaluation; (d) appointment of an attorney or guardian ad litem for a child; and (e) financial matters including support, insurance, and allocation of dependency exemptions.

*Limited reference of issues*. In California, the most prevalent statute used for parenting coordination appointments is the special master statute.[22] *California Evidence Code §730* provides for a delegation of court authority for a specific issue in a case where special expertise is required (i.e., mental health evaluation in high-conflict custody cases). The courts in California had routinely ordered parties into the special master process until the appellate court ruling in *Ruisi v. Theriot*.[23]

In *Ruisi*, the court's order provided that the special master "hear and consider any and all issues regarding custody." The court noted the basic constitutional principle that judicial power may not be delegated without statutory authority and held that a "general" reference to a third party empowered to make a conclusive determination without further action by the court required consent of both parties.

However, the *Ruisi* court further explained that a "special" reference, whereby a third party would make advisory findings that do not become binding unless adopted by the court after its independent review thereof, did not require consent of the parties. Where the parties do not consent, the authority of the trial court to refer any part of a case to a special master "is limited to particular issues" and "does not permit a reference of all the issues in an action." The court found that the trial court's order containing a "sweeping reference of 'any and all issues regarding custody'" was not limited to "strictly factual issues," as required by the applicable statute, and was overly broad.

Although it seems that the court's ruling in *Ruisi* would authorize a delegation of authority that is circumscribed to factual questions on specified controversies that are then subject to judicial review, this case has been interpreted by California courts such that the appointment of a special master requires the agreement of both parties.

*Opportunity for judicial review.* The cases above point to the opportunity for judicial review as being a touchstone in what may constitute a lawful delegation of authority versus what is an unlawful delegation of authority. Thus, many states have implemented PC procedure that provides for the court to review and approve a PC's recommendations and an opportunity for a dissatisfied party to object.

However, one state has provided that this is not sufficient in and of itself, at least with respect to arbitration. In the case of *Kelm v. Kelm*,[24] the Supreme Court of Ohio ruled that matters of child custody and parental visitation in domestic relations cases are not subject to arbitration and that the "authority to resolve disputes over custody and visitation rests exclusively with the courts." The Court reasoned that the use of arbitration to resolve such disputes conflicts with the duty of the domestic relations courts to protect the best interests of children.[25] The Court also opined that the opportunity for de novo judicial review of an arbitration award destroys the parties' expectation that an arbitration award will be final, is wasteful of time and duplicative of effort, and, thus, "it does not seem advantageous to the best interests of children that questions of custody be postponed."

## CONTINUING JURISDICTION

An increasingly thorny but important issue jurisdictions face when implementing the PC model is the concern that judges cannot appoint a PC whose intervention continues after the case has concluded. The reasoning is that the case is no longer pending. Generally, judges do not allow cases to remain open on their dockets after a final judgment is entered. A common court administration scenario where a dissolution judgment or parenting order has been filed and signed is for the case to be terminated on the judge's docket and the file closed. In many instances, the only way to reactivate a case is by one of the original parties filing a motion to invoke the continuing jurisdiction of the court.

Although this issue has not been specifically addressed as it pertains to parenting coordination, it has been considered in other related contexts. The court's decisions in these cases provide information as to how other jurisdictions might approach the "continuing jurisdiction" issue in a PC case.

*Continuing jurisdiction invoked by motion.* Several jurisdictions provide that while the jurisdiction of the court "continues" after judgment, it is "invoked" by a party's filing of a motion. In *Eden v. Eden*,[26] the concept of "continuing jurisdiction" was considered with respect to an appeal from a qualified domestic relations order (QDRO). The court noted that the continuing jurisdiction of the trial court over various domestic relations matters is authorized by statute, for example, the court retains jurisdiction to modify parental rights and responsibilities, child support, and visitation after entry of judgment (R.C. 3105.65). *Ohio Civil Rule 75(J)* provides that the continuing jurisdiction of the court is "invoked by motion filed in the original action." The court ruled on the appropriate statute for service of process to be applied where the continuing jurisdiction of a court to modify such orders has been invoked by the filing of a party's motion.

*Statutory authority.* In California, the special master model addresses the issue of continuing jurisdiction by appointing the parenting coordinator under *Code of Civil Procedure 638*. This law states that a referee appointed by agreement of the parties does not require that a case be open or that an action be pending before the court to function as a parenting coordinator in the case.

An Idaho statute, I.C. 32-717, appears to specifically confer "continuing jurisdiction" upon a trial court to "give such direction for the custody, care and education of the children of the marriage as may seem necessary or proper in the best interests of the children." The court may act both "before and after judgment." The statute does not specifically require a motion to "invoke" the continuing jurisdiction of the court.[27]

One other state has similarly legislated that "continuing jurisdiction" continues after entry of judgment and without the filing of a motion to "invoke" the court's authority. *Minnesota Statutes 2002, 518.1751*,[28] Parenting Time Dispute Resolution, explicitly states that the court may appoint a "parenting time expeditor" to resolve parenting time disputes *"while a matter is pending ... or after a decree is entered."* The appointment may be made at the request of either party, the parties' stipulation, or upon the court's own motion. A parenting time expeditor may be appointed to resolve a one-time parenting time dispute or to provide ongoing parenting time dispute resolution services. The statute directs that the appointment may be made without the necessity of the parties appearing in court by submitting a written agreement.

On the other hand, an Oregon appellate case, *Thomason v. Thomason*,[29] held that a trial court lacked authority to appoint an attorney for the children in a dissolution case postjudgment because no action was pending as required by the court's interpretation of the applicable statute. That statute specifically contained the language *"whenever a domestic relations suit ... is filed, or whenever a habeas corpus proceeding or motion to modify ... is before the court."*

The court determined that this language evidenced a legislative intent for a restricted grant of authority as to the timing for appointment of counsel for a child.

*"Continuing jurisdiction" language in appointing order.* In light of the *Thomason* case, *supra*, an Oregon jurisdiction has inserted the following language into its PC appointment order:

> *The court shall have continuing jurisdiction for purposes of modification, enforcement and clarification of the parent plan until the term of the coordinator has expired or the coordinator's appointment has otherwise been terminated, and all objections are resolved. The court's retention of jurisdiction does not affect the finality of the underlying judgment, which is intended by the court to be a final judgment under ORS 19.205.* This language may be sufficient, given there is no existing statutory authority to the contrary as there was in *Thomason*. In fact, the Oregon legislature recently amended existing law and provided by statute that PCs may be appointed for the purpose of *"monitoring compliance with court orders,"* and *"providing parents with problem solving, conflict management and parenting time coordination services or other services approved by the court,"* inferring that this authority extends postjudgment.[30] However, this language has not yet been reviewed and ruled on by the Oregon courts as of the date of this article.

## INFRINGEMENT OF CONSTITUTIONAL RIGHTS

The constitutionality of the Oklahoma Parenting Coordinator Act, 43 O.S.Supp 2001 120.1 et seq., has been questioned in a case currently pending before the Supreme Court of Oklahoma, *Barnes (now Hendrix) v. Barnes*.[31] Appellant (mother) claimed that the Act "is unconstitutional in requiring nothing more than a best-interest determination to infringe on a parent's fundamental right to make child-rearing decisions and in treating a divorced parent differently than a married parent." Although the Act provides that a party may object to the report of a parenting coordinator pursuant to 120.4 of the Act and thereby obtain a court review, the appellant cited the PC's "right to make binding decisions as to any problems relating to time spent with their child and to conduct any investigation with anyone, including the child, and to collect any records and any documents" as an infringement of a parent's fundamental child-rearing rights. Citing authority for the proposition that a court may not lightly replace a parent's decision with their own, appellant noted language from another state court case stating that "it does not serve the interests of the parties, the judiciary, or the public to require trial courts to 'micromanage' family decision making."[32] The appellant cited the U.S. Supreme Court's decision in *Troxel v. Granville*,[33] for the proposition "that a parent's interest in the care, custody, and control of her child is perhaps the oldest of the fundamental liberty interests recognized by this Court."[34] As of the writing of this article, there has been no decision by the Oklahoma Supreme Court.[35] The legislature, however, amended the Act in 2003 to require a finding of high conflict in addition to a finding of best interest.[36] The legislature further amended the statute to vest the trial court with exclusive jurisdiction over custody, visitation, and support, and the authority to exercise management and control of the case. The PC may only make temporary departures from the parenting plan if authorized by the court.[37]

## II. CHALLENGING ISSUES

## CASES THAT MAY BENEFIT FROM PARENTING COORDINATION

A proactive approach is used in some jurisdictions in which parenting coordination is ordered at the time of the entry of permanent orders in the event that the parents are unable to agree in the future about issues regarding the children. The judge, attorneys, or custody evaluators astutely recognize the signs of intractable long-term conflict and plan for it during the finalization of the divorce. More frequently, however, cases are usually referred to parenting coordination because they are chronically litigious and difficult to manage. These parents have often had several attorneys, evaluators, and mediators-professional hopping and shopping is rampant. Their court files are thick with motions, court appearances, and allegations of wrongdoing by the parents.

Parenting coordination may not be effective in cases in which a parent chronically refuses to follow court orders or has severe personality disorders, mental illness, or substance abuse. The PC may be able to protect the children from the impaired parent, but generally will serve more as a "thumb in the dike" rather than a change agent. The PC's function may become simply to arbitrate all parenting disputes when mediation, education, and coaching on appropriate coparenting have been ineffective.

## JUDICIAL SUPPORT

The authors of this article have found that most judges welcome parenting coordination. Judges recognize that it saves much court time and relieves the judge of much of the stress that the most conflicted cases inflict on the judge because the prospect of any acceptable resolution through formal court proceedings is so unlikely. Judges should support the PC process while still being neutral. When a PC is having a difficult time with one or both parties, the PC should be able to request a case management conference with the judge and all the parties. The PC should be able to present the problems and any suggestions for solutions to keep the process moving, and to expect that the judge will be supportive of the PC's position. If such difficult parties sense a lack of determination or vacillation on the part of the judge, they will likely dig their heels in and become even more difficult. On the other hand, the judge must be alert to listening for signs that this is a case in which the PC is not well matched with the parties, is using inappropriate techniques, does not have the necessary skills, or appears to be incurring higher fees than expected. Although the parenting coordination process is designed to operate outside the courthouse, reasonable oversight is necessary to maintain the integrity of the process, and the judge should be responsive to this need. Monitoring and ensuring the quality of PC appointees also needs to be a priority.

Judges who are supportive of this process can be very influential in its widespread use. Inquiries in appropriate cases as to the potential for the PC process will usually not fall on deaf ears. Attorneys can benefit because they can be relieved of some of their most nightmarish cases, and parents are usually eager to use a PC because they get prompter attention, and the attention comes from one who they may consider to be an authority figure. Each party usually assumes they will come out on top because they think they are right and that the other party is clearly in the wrong. For these reasons, the judge has fertile ground on which to sow the seeds of persuasion about the use of parenting coordination. One of the challenges, however, is to avoid overusing parenting coordination-every case does not need a PC.

Some judges may not be supportive of the PC process. Parties in such cases may consider asking for a referral to a general or special master or hearing officer. These quasi-judicial officers usually have a high caseload and are used to short hearings and often handle case management conferences. Thus, they may be more receptive to a referral to a PC. Usually, a judge will routinely accept a recommendation of a master or hearing officer.

## SELECTION OF A PC

Choosing cases that are amenable to this process should also be a priority; otherwise, considerable time and expense of all the parties will be wasted and the court will still wind up with the responsibility for achieving an outcome in the courtroom setting. Because the PC is working with some of the more difficult parties in the family law system, it is extremely important to match the right PC and the right PC process with the parties in the case. There should be some consideration given to the practice style and attitude of the attorneys, if any, in the case. Each PC has a different style and emphasis, and any hope for success with difficult parties demands close attention to matching all the personalities and processes. For instance, some PCs use an educational approach and seek to promote cooperation by educating the parents as to the developmental needs of children and the harm that is inflicted on the children by continual parental conflict. Parents who appear to be logical, well-motivated, highly moral, and secure in their personal life may respond to this approach even though personal dynamics have created an adversarial relationship with their ex-spouse. On the other hand, parties with emotional insecurities and less stable personal lives may need behavioral modification techniques, such as negative consequences for destructive or uncooperative behavior. This may be imposed by the PC if he or she has arbitration power, or the PC may make a recommendation to the judge for an appropriate sanction. Some PCs are more comfortable with and effective at using this stronger behavioral modification approach. The choice could also be as simple as choosing a male or female, depending on which gender can relate to or counter the more problematic parent. If attorneys are qualified to act as a PC, their status as authoritative figures may cause some parents to more quickly follow a suggested path of cooperation, whereas the same parents may tend to rebel against a (perceived) softer mental health professional. The concept of matching the PC to the parents may warrant some further consideration regarding who may act as a PC. If the qualifications and the discretion of the court are too limited, some potentially effective professionals may be excluded when they have exactly the right style and experience to handle the particular conflicted case. One approach would be to have established qualifications but allow the judge with the consent of the parties the ability to appoint any person deemed qualified by experience and training. Jurisdictions that have dealt with the issue of qualifications differ in the formality and extent of education and training required for the PC but have all generally looked first at areas of required expertise in developing qualifications.[38]

## MAINTAINING STRUCTURE AND BOUNDARIES

Another challenge that PCs face as they navigate the pulls for alignment, challenges to authority, and appeals for reprimand is to hold steady, maintaining neutrality and role definition. To avoid the difficulties of redefinition, retraction, and recoupment, articulating boundaries in writing and practice in the beginning and an ongoing basis is part of the management and educational role of the PC.

What forms of communication will be accepted? How will the PC respond to hostile communications, late payments, telephone calls, demands for an immediate response, weekend "emergencies," or unilateral requests? How will the PC react to individual therapeutic issues? If the issues center on a change in custody, how will the PC respond? These are the predicaments that the PC frequently faces. The initial agreement between the PC and the parents will outline many of these issues, but compelling clients can and will try to elicit a helping response or sympathetic ear that may ultimately lead to a violation of the agreement, dual role, or breach of neutrality.

Clarity of role is an essential topic for thought and discussion. Advocacy for any one member of the family is never acceptable. At the same time, working to help the family collaborate, resolve their own disputes, stay focused on the child, and understand the other parent and child's points of view is to in fact advocate for the family system as a workable, viable decision-making unit.

Although it is the PC's role to reduce tensions in the family and raise the parents' level of skill in collaborative planning for their children, it is not the role to provide therapeutic services beyond the identification of the impasses and individual issues that impede the parent's ability to stay focused on collaboration, other points of view, and the child's needs. The PC's role as practiced today requires multiple functions of assessment, education, mediation, and arbitration. This hybrid role needs definition and clarification for clients. Because the role of PC typically relies on mediation skills, the distinction between mediation and parenting coordination must be articulated at the outset of work with a family. Issues of confidentiality and reporting to the court can easily be confounded without careful review of the boundaries of the PC role.

The PC does not make custody recommendations. Doing so would compromise the PC's neutrality and ability to work in an ongoing basis with parents. It would also require the PC to take on an evaluative role, which may be considered a dual role. The PC helps implement, modify, and mediate parenting plans but does not substantially change the existing court order. That authority remains with the court. A frequent challenge is to identify the point at which the PC's role is no longer useful and/or a parent's request for a custodial change requires court intervention. In the initial agreement and discussion of role, the PC must make clear the issues that lead to court intervention or termination of role.

Because of the personality issues in many of these families, maintaining neutrality is often an ongoing challenge for the PC. Although it is often clear how one party may be experienced by the other, it is sometimes difficult to assess how one's own reactions may or may not be consistent with the child's experiences. Although a client can be difficult, inflexible, and challenging for the PC, that is not always the same experience for the child. The parent who demands a lot of attention to detail or requires what feels like constant responses may in fact be more relaxed and flexible with the child. Likewise, a compliant parent who seems to eagerly accept suggestions and responds to requests may be dependent on the child or engage the child in parentifying behaviors. However, the information at hand is a useful tool to educate a party about the impact of his or her behavior when the parent's observed behaviors are consistent with the reports from the other party and the children. The PC relationship becomes a training ground for maintaining appropriate boundaries within the family.

Setting limits about the kind of communication (phone, e-mail, fax); the number, length, and tone of messages; and the length and response time for interactions between the clients and between the clients and the PC sets the boundaries that hopefully can be generalized to other interactions within the family.

A number of states are exploring standards for PCs. Issues of training and qualifications, role definition and boundaries, confidentiality, informed consent, interventions and functions, boundaries of their court-ordered authority, procedures for documentation, and decision making are just some of the issues that need to be addressed. An Association of Family and Conciliation Courts (AFCC) Parenting Coordinator Task Force has recently been charged with the development of standards for PCs. These standards of professional conduct may also serve professionals in states where there is no statutory authorization or quasijudicial authority immunity for the PC as well as a model for states that are developing their own standards.

## TERMINATING THE PROCESS

Placing a specific duration for the process in the order of appointment is a good idea because it will focus the participants on a deadline and gives a good milestone for the court to assess whether the process is achieving the desired goal of resolving disputes and allowing the parties to proceed with a reasonable degree of cooperation to implement their parenting plan.

There may be cases where the judge will find the PC is not being cost-effective, is at odds with one of the parties, or uses methods the court is not comfortable with, and the deadline will furnish a graceful method of having the PC exit the case.

The judge usually wants to be supportive of the process and the PC, but there has to be an end to the process. There has to be monitoring by the court, but if the parties continue to come back to court frequently, or if one of the attorneys who does not believe in the process attempts to thwart it, the judge may have to acknowledge that a PC will not work for the case and terminate the process. Sometimes this is a bitter pill for the PC to swallow, particularly because a "helping professional" may desperately want to continue trying to obtain a beneficial result. In this instance, the judge may have to be the agent of reality and terminate the process that is not working.

## PRACTICAL CONSIDERATIONS FOR AVOIDING A SUCCESSFUL CHALLENGE TO THE USE OF A PC

The safest method of avoiding a legal challenge to the Parenting Coordination process is to gain the approval of the parties for using the process at the outset. If the parties stipulate to use the process, they could hardly be expected to challenge the power of the court to appoint a PC. If they also enter into an agreement as to who should serve as PC, they are less likely to challenge the actions of the person they selected, and the court is less likely to grant such a challenge.

The judge and the attorneys have the ability to "sell" the concept of a PC to the parents. This attempt to sell the process is not a gimmick or a devious approach; it is a good faith opportunity to help the parents through a process that is normally less expensive, faster, and more satisfactory to the parties. If they can gain at least a modicum of cooperation, the parents are able to be in control of the decision making. If there is a proactive approach by the judge, hopefully with the help and support of the attorneys (who may also want to get out of the case), the parties are usually very receptive. The idea of working outside the courthouse, with prompt access to a mental health or child development expert who is not in a judgmental position, appeals to even the most difficult parents. If the judge and the attorneys are unified in recommending this process, the parties tend to be receptive. If they stipulate to use the parenting coordination process, and to the appointment of a specific person as the PC, it will be much harder to successfully get the PC removed if one parent does not like the way the process is going.

Some of the most frequent reasons given for removing a PC are the following: allegations of bias, creation of conflict with the coordinator by refusing payment of the bill for services, or setting up conflict on implementation of the parenting plan by refusing to compromise or cooperate. The granting of arbitration powers to the PC, although often helpful in expediting resolution of minor disputes, can also carry a risk of a request for removal because of dissatisfaction with the decision. Thus, including this clause in the order of appointment should be carefully considered and probably only utilized where both parties agree to the grant of this power and have some reasonable potential for modest cooperation. The PC is more likely to avoid a challenge by being open and advising parties of their right to ask for a discharge of the PC at the beginning of the process, and by making certain that the process does not become an adversarial battle between the PC and one of the parties. If there is a court hearing on a motion to remove the PC, the greater the adversarial relationship between the PC and one party (however irascible), the more likely the court will conclude that the PC has lost his or her effectiveness and feel that removal is necessary.

## LIABILITY OF THE PC

Any professional can be sued for negligence by violating the standard of care for the particular profession. The professional can also be the subject of a complaint to any regulatory board governing their profession or removed from a voluntary professional organization. There is no effective method to prevent a disgruntled party from attempting one of these actions.

Court-appointed experts normally are accorded a quasi-judicial immunity for actions appropriately taken under the court's order. For a parenting coordinator, the risk is that because the order and the activities may not have a firm basis in any statute or case law and also are breaking new ground in professional duties by merging different functions, the court-expert type of quasi-judicial immunity may be in jeopardy. In other words, there may be no actual expert designation for these particular duties, or an appellate court may say the trial court had no authority to appoint. Having documented standards of conduct for PCs within a particular jurisdiction may be an important consideration in the quest to have the PC considered for expert witness quasi-judicial authority.

Other considerations for authority to appoint a parenting coordinator:

> 1. The PC might consider not serving unless the parties stipulate to the order with broad powers. Such a stipulation may insulate the PC from liability more than a court appointment without the parties' consent. 2. Acknowledge in the order that there is judicial or quasi-judicial immunity and that there will be no liability unless there is actual malice. Remember that public policy may be against such a limitation of liability. 3. Professional liability insurance is available in many jurisdictions, if there is some authority for the appointment of a PC. 4. Consider having the parties agree that the PC has the appropriate professional qualifications and skills for the appointment. This agreement should be reflected in the order of appointment. 5. Consider including the following language in an order appointing a PC: *It is the intent of this order to include the broadest possible authority for the parenting coordinator to facilitate the smooth and cooperative implementation of the parenting schedule for the full family's benefit under (the dissolution of marriage statute defining the need to avoid harm to the children in custody cases). Thus, the parenting coordinator may use the powers of a guardian ad litem for the child under (the state's guardian ad litem statute), where those functions will assist in carrying out this Court's adjudication of a parenting plan. It is also the intent of the Court that the parenting coordinator shall have full benefit of quasijudicial immunity as a Court-appointed expert and the immunity provisions provided for in (the state's guardian ad litem statute). The parties have stipulated to this appointment and the powers granted herein to the parenting coordinator, and that the person appointed has the requisite professional qualifications and professional skills to do the work required.* Reference to mediation or arbitration powers is not included in the above provision to avoid the appearance of inappropriate dual roles and the potential for conflicting ethical standards.

The suggestions and discussion above are general in nature and are intended to provoke thought and discussion. Any attempts to use these ideas should be with the advice and consultation of an attorney because of the sophistication of the legal concepts involved. It is suggested that the parenting coordinators, family law attorneys, and judges in a particular jurisdiction collaborate regarding the use of these ideas.

## COLLABORATIVE TEAMS AND THE PC

Attorneys, therapists, teachers, school administrators, and even child care workers and coaches can become caught in the interparental conflict in a way that compromises their intended functions. The polarizing pulls of high conflict can affect and align the most competent and well-intentioned professional with one parent's partial, often distorted perceptions of the problem.

When multiple professionals are involved with high-conflict families, collaboration and effective teamwork may not occur without coordination by one or more of the professionals.

In some of the more complex, high-conflict cases, the PC may serve the purpose of bringing the professionals together into a collaborative team to support the parents. A PC has four ingredients that are critical to managing collaborative teams: (a) comprehensive understanding of and exposure to the family and professional system, (b) the time and availability for intensive case management, (c) the authority to monitor and enforce compliance with professional interventions and to modify the parenting plan (if appropriate), and (d) conflict resolution skills. The role of the PC in managing a collaborative team includes responsibility for the following: (a) the team's composition, (b) the team's ongoing functioning, and (c) decision making as it relates to ongoing treatment and the parenting plan. A brief description of these aspects of the PC's role with collaborative professional teams follows.

*Team composition.* The PC ideally will design a therapeutic intervention that requires the least number of professionals for cost-effectiveness and to decrease the complexities of team functioning as more professionals involved in high-conflict cases are not necessarily better for the families. Often the PC may work in conjunction with a child therapist, family therapist, or coparent counselor, whereas in some cases, the team may include individual therapists for the child(ren), parents, and other experts (psychiatrists, special education professionals, etc.).[39] Ideally, the PC will have some input into the selection of professionals who will become involved in these cases. Team composition must take into account the needs and resources of the family and involve professionals willing to work in a role that may be different than a traditional therapeutic role.

*Responsibility for team functioning.* The PC is responsible for setting treatment goals (often assisted by recommendations in a custody evaluation report), providing a structure for systematic review and modification of those goals, establishing and maintaining communication channels (periodic team meetings, letters, two-way communication between particular team members, communication between team members and the parents). Clear structures for team functioning, supported by written contracts (court orders, confidentiality agreements with clients, written protocols provided to the team and parents), are essential to the functioning of the team. Careful consideration needs to be given to what information therapists keep confidential (not directly relevant to parenting and coparenting), what information they share with the team, what feedback the team provides the family members, and, if necessary, what information might be provided to the court. The PC should function as the team's exclusive linkage to any court proceedings to protect the professional relationships that team members have with family members. The PC's strategic management of information is the most powerful tool and biggest challenge to effective team treatment interventions.

Team roles and hierarchy need to be clearly defined and followed. Each team member needs to understand and act according to his or her agreed upon role in the family intervention. This includes the relationship with other team members, clients, and the legal process. The PC is the team leader, and although consensus is a preferred mode of decision making in teams (and often requires considerable dialogue), it is the PC's role to make decisions either when consensus is not reached by the team or it is inappropriate for team members to provide anything more than input from their perspective. These can be decisions about the treatment or decisions required to resolve disputes about parenting issues. The PC must develop the trust and confidence of team members so as not to undermine decisions made by the PC; otherwise, splitting of the team will result, collaboration will break down, and the team will begin to mirror the polarization in the family system. The PC also functions as a support base for the team members in their work with the family. When alliances become compromised between therapist and client, as often occurs in these cases, it is the PC's role to address compliance issues, such as failure to show for appointments or fee issues. In addition, joint meetings with the therapist and client may be necessary to shore up the therapeutic relationship and ultimately, efforts on the PC's part to protect professionals from involvement in litigation may be necessary. This protective and supportive function of the PC is appreciated by therapists and often essential for professionals who are willing to work with these difficult cases.

## III. VISION FOR THE FUTURE

Parenting Coordination is now practiced throughout North America. As is typical of new fields, there is ongoing discussion and collaboration among professionals from multiple disciplines. The issues revolve around the professional and ethical practices that provide due process and effective service for the families who are in need of the help of PC. Distinguishing the role, developing guidelines of practice and training, and managing risk are concerns for each state and province. Mentoring is one way for a new PC to get on-the-job training. The first few cases for a new PC would be a joint appointment with an experienced PC, which would provide protection for the neophyte and create a mentor-mentee relationship in the future. The AFCC Task Force on Parenting Coordination will be considering these issues and drafting model standards for professional conduct for PCs. Collaboration among mental health professionals, mediators, and lawyers is necessary to address these issues and design effective programs.

Although some states have PC legislation, others use court orders under another statute or under the mantle of inherent authority. For most states, there is no legal code that addresses the role and functioning of the PC. At this point in time, there is little consistency or clarity between states or even within a state as to the level of authority, relationship to the court, or due process issues especially related to gathering of evidence. Greater definition of the role, with a focus on the multiple functions a PC may employ and clarity about issues of confidentiality and due process, will be part of the continuing interdisciplinary conversation. Guidelines for practice emerging nationally from an interdisciplinary organization, such as AFCC, will provide a base from which states and provinces might create their own definition of the role of the PC. In addition, guidelines will be useful to professional organizations such as the American Psychological Association (APA), the American Bar Association (ABA), or the National Association of Social Workers (NASW) when they are called on to respond to complaints about PCs.

There is a major need for research of the effectiveness of this role for families. Research must focus on what kinds of families respond to Parenting Coordination and what specific functions may be more useful or effective than others. We need to answer the dual question of whether Parenting Coordination helps parents resolve their differences without returning to court, and what the outcomes of working with a PC are compared to those who continue to use the courts to help them resolve their differences.

Along with research into effectiveness of the role, there will be a need for continued emphasis on skill building for the PC practitioner. As with any new field, many practitioners will be attracted to the excitement of a new process for helping families in conflict, and some will be attracted to the opportunity to capitalize on the economic benefits of a new and trendy practice. There will be an increasing need to advance the skill levels of all practitioners through training, networking, and regulation by minimum educational and experience levels, and opportunity for fair resolution of grievances.

With greater definition and development of the PC role, as well as research that examines the efficacy of the role, funding for more families may become a reality. At this time, there are few opportunities for families without means to avail themselves of a PC. Until states find ways to incorporate PCs into the array of court-based services, these professionals will not be available to people who do not have financial resources for such services.

As all these trends and uncertainties play out, the PC process will likely take its place as a part of a larger landscape: a continuum of services to assist separating parents in coming to the most effective parenting plan for them in the least contentious manner. This larger landscape should encompass a substantial array of services that allow forming a triangle, with the apex being those cases requiring a decision by the judge in a contested hearing. The base of the triangle will be composed of the majority of cases in which the parents are able to come to a decision with minimal intervention. Such processes include educational programs, simple mediations, and four-way conferences with nonadversarial attorneys. As the triangle narrows, more intensive and intrusive forms of intervention are necessary, including case management hearings by the judge, difficult mediations, individual and group counseling, collaborative law cases, home studies, and custody evaluations. The parenting coordination process in its classic form fits closer to the apex because it is designed to deal with moderately to highly conflicted couples. In some jurisdictions, a demand is developing for using a PC to develop a parenting plan as opposed to implementing an existing parenting plan. This is symbolic of the larger landscape in which there is a constant search for alternatives to existing traditional methods of resolving parenting disputes. In the future, it is likely that attempts will be made to expand the role of the PC process as a part of the larger trend to find a greater variety of techniques that are effective in resolving parenting disputes.

*Christine Coates, J.D., is Adjunct Professor at the University of Colorado School of Law and an attorney in Boulder, Colorado.*

*Robin Deutsch, Ph.D., is a psychologist and the Director of Forensic Services of the Children and the Law Program in the Department of Psychiatry at Massachusetts General Hospital and an Assistant Professor of Psychology at Harvard Medical School.*

*The Honorable Hugh Starnes, LL.B., is a family law judge in the Twentieth Judicial Circuit in Florida.*

*Matthew Sullivan, Ph.D., is a clinical psychologist in private practice specializing in forensic child and family psychology in Palo Alto, California.*

*BeaLisa Sydlik, J.D., is Staff Counsel of Family Law for the Court Program and Services Division of the Oregon Judicial Department.*

## Notes

Authors' Note: *We wish to thank Barbara Bartlett, J.D., for her assistance on the pending Oklahoma litigation about the Parenting Coordination role.*

[1]   JANET R. JOHNSTON & VIVIENNE ROSEBY, IN THE NAME OF THE CHILD (The Free Press 1997); Joan Kelly, *Legal and Educational Interventions for Families in Residential and Contact Disputes*, 15 AUSTL. J. FAM. LL. 92 (2001).

[2]   Jack Arbuthnot, et al., *Patterns of Relitigation Following Divorce Education*, 35 FAM. & CONCILIATION CTS. REV. 269 (1997); Margie J. Geasler & Karen Blaisure, *1998 Nationwide Survey of Court-Connected Divorce Education Programs*, 37 FAM. & CONCILIATION CTS. REV. 36 (1999).

[3]   ROBERT E. EMERY, RENEGOTIATING FAMILY RELATIONSHIPS: DIVORCE, CHILD CUSTODY AND MEDIATION, (Guilford Publications 1994); DESMOND ELLIS & NOREEN STUCKLESS, MEDIATING AND NEGOTIATING MARITAL CONFLICTS. (Sage Publications 1996).

[4]   Donald B. King, *Accentuate the Positive-Eliminate the Negative*, 31 FAM. & CONCILIATION CTS. REV. 9 (1993).

[5]   E. MARK CUMMINGS & PATRICK T. DAVIES, CHILDREN AND MARITAL CONFLICT (Guilford Publications 1994); Emery, *supra* note 3; ELEANOR E. MACCOBY & ROBERT H. MNOOKIN, DIVIDING THE CHILD (University Press 1992); Joan B. Kelly, *Children's Adjustment in Conflicted Marriage and Divorce: A Review of Research*, 39 J. AM. ACAD. CHILD ADOLESC. PSYCHIATRYY 963 (2000).

[6]   S. Margaret Lee, *Special Masters in child custody case* (ASSOC. OF FAM. & CONCILIATION CTS. NEWSLETTER) 14 (1995); Johnston, *supra* note 1; Jessica Pearson, *Court Services: Meeting the Needs of Twenty-First Century Families*, 33 Family Law Quarterly 617 (1999); MITCHELL A. BARIS ET AL., WORKING WITH HIGH CONFLICT FAMILIES OF DIVORCE: A GUIDE FOR PROFESSIONALS (Aronson 2000).

[7]   Maccoby, *supra* note 5; Johnston, *supra* note 1.

[8]   The first formal conceptions of Parenting Coordination appear to have developed out of the work of Denver metro lawyers and mental health professionals who convened a high-conflict study group in 1992 and then developed a model of Parenting Coordination. Concurrently, counties in North California were developing Parenting Coordination models derived from both mediation and special master statutes in that state.

[9]   The professional may be called different things in those states implementing the parenting coordination model, for example, "Special Master" in California, "Wiseperson" in New Mexico, "Custody Commissioner" in Hawaii, and "Family Court Advisor" in Arizona. All these terms appear to describe a process that is consistent with the Parenting Coordinator role.

[10]  Gregory Firestone et al., *Parenting Coordination in Florida: Current status and future Directions* 19 THE COMMENTATOR 17 (2003).

[11]  Matthew J. Sullivan & Joan B. Kelly, *Legal and Psychological Management of Cases With an Alienated Child*, 39 FAM. CT. REV. 299 (2001).

[12]  PHILIP STAHL, COMPLEX ISSUES IN CHILD CUSTODY EVALUATIONS (Sage 1999).

[13]  Matthew J. Sullivan et al., *Parenting Coordination: The Basics and Beyond*, workshop presented at the Florida Association of Family and Conciliation Courts (AFCC) Parenting Coordination and Legislative Forum (2003).

[14]  Florida Parenting Coordination Statute, working draft of proposed parenting coordination statute prepared for consideration at the FLACC Parenting Coordination and Legislative Summit, August 2003.

[15]  S. Margaret Lee, *The Integration of Ethics and the Law in Clinical Practice*. Acting as a Special Master in High-Conflict Postdivorce Child Custody Cases (unpublished); Matthew J. Sullivan, *Ethical, Legal and Professional Practice Issues Involved in Acting as a Psychologist Parent Coordinator in Child Custody Cases*, 42 FAM. CT. REV. (forthcoming July 2004).

[16]  Terry Johnston, *Outcome Study on Special Master Cases in Santa Clara County*, (unpublished study) (1994).

[17]  Mark Vick & Robert Backerman (1996). Mediation/Arbitration: Surveys of Professionals and Clients, Paper presented at the Boulder, Colorado Interdisciplinary Committee on Child Custody.

[18]  Maccoby, *supra* note 5; Kelly, *supra* note 5.

[19]  For more information about the implementation of parenting coordination in jurisdictions across the United States. see, AFCC Task Force on Parenting Coordination, *Parenting Coordination: Implementation Issues*, 41 FAM. CT. REV. 533 (2003).

[20]  14 P. 3d 96 (2000).

[21]  IDAHO R. CIV. P. 16(1).

[22]  CAL. EVID. CODE 730. *See also*, CAL. CIV. PROC. CODE 638 and 1280.

[23]  Ruisi v. Theriot, 62 Cal. Rptr. 2d 766 (1997).

[24]  749 N.E.2d 299 (2001).

[25]  In an earlier case [Kelm v. Kelm, 68 Ohio St.3d 26, (1993)], the Supreme Court of Ohio ruled that temporary and permanent support matters could be made subject to an agreement to arbitrate. In distinguishing this holding from the 2001 *Kelm* case, *supra*, the Supreme Court reasoned "that custody and visitation have a much greater impact upon the child in *terms of both the child's daily life and his or her long-term development*" and, thus, the Court was "*less inclined than we were in Kelm I to permit arbitration to encroach upon the trial court's traditional role as parens patriae*." Cf., in the unpublished appellate decision, Beatley v. Block, 2000 WL 699653 (Ohio App. 5 Dist.), May 16, 2000, it was found that the trial court did not abdicate any judicial responsibility or unlawfully delegate its authority in appointing a parent coordinator. The court relied on the language of the order that prohibited the parenting coordinator (PC) from evaluating custody and that specified the PC's fundamental role as being "to minimize the conflict to which the children are exposed by the parties." Last, the court pointed out that the objecting party demonstrated no prejudice form the PC's appointment nor that the PC had "usurped the role of the trial court."

[26]  2003 Ohio 356, January 29, 2003 (unpublished appeal).

[27]  *Idaho Statutes*, available at: http://www3.state.id.us/cgi-bin/newidst?sctid=320070017.K (last visited on January 28, 2004).

[28]  *Minnesota Statutes, available at:* http:// www.revisor.leg.state.mn.us/stats/518/1751.html (last visited on January 28, 2004). Unlike most other PC models, the PC process in Minnesota is fully confidential and the PC may not be called to testify.

[29]  23 P.3d 395 (2001).

[30]  OR REV. STAT. § 107.425(3)(a) (2001).

[31]  FD-98-4682.

[32]  Kaiser v. Kaiser, 23 P.3d 278 (2001).

[33]  530 U.S. 57, 65 (2000).

[34]  "Motion To Retain" filed August 8, 2002, Supreme Court No. 98090, p. 1.

[35]  Once a decision has been published, it may be retrieved at the Oklahoma Supreme Court Web site, *available at* www.oscn.net.

[36]  "High conflict" includes the definition of "conditions that in the discretion of the court warrant the appointment of a parenting coordinator" OKLA. STAT. tit. 43, § 120.2 (2002).

[37]  OKLA. STAT. tit. 43, § 120.3 (2002).

[38]  AFCC Task Force, *supra* note 19.

[39]  Janet R. Johnston et al., *Therapeutic Work With Alienated Children and Their Families*, 39 FAM. CT. REV. 316 (2001).

# [15]

# Building Multidisciplinary Professional Partnerships with the Court on Behalf of High-conflict Divorcing Families and their Children: Who Needs what Kind of Help?

## Janet R. Johnston

## I. HISTORICAL BACKGROUND

During the last third of the twentieth century, the United States led many other western countries in radical legal changes that aimed to make the process of marital dissolution less acrimonious and the outcomes of divorce both gender neutral and more protective of the interests of children.[1] Throughout the United States, coincident with rapidly rising rates of divorce (to a record high of about one in two marriages)[2] between 1969 and 1985, "no fault" divorce laws replaced the previous onerous ones that required divorcing parties to establish who had violated the marital contract. Alimony and marital property rules changed dramatically around the country, ensuring a more equitable distribution of family assets between men and women. During the same period, the "tender years doctrine" dictating that the custody of young children should normally go to the mother was replaced with the "best interests of the child" standard for determining which parent should be legally and physically responsible for the care of children following divorce. Joint custody preferences or presumptions were subsequently introduced in many states.[3] During the 1980s, California led the country in these and other legal reforms, most notable of which was the introduction of custody mediation to facilitate the private resolution of disputes. During the 1990s, parenting education swept the country. This involved efforts to empower divorcing families by providing them with information on the process of divorce and the needs of their children to have frequent, continuing and conflict-free access to both parents.

Despite these radical historical changes, we are currently confronted with distressing levels of frustration, anger, alienation, and cynicism from divorcing parents and children about their experience with family courts and about the professionals who work in this field.[4] In spite of the widespread provision of mediation services, approximately one fourth to one third of divorcing couples report high degrees of hostility and discord over the daily care of their children many years after the separation.[5] Only about one tenth of all separating couples with children resort to extended litigation, court hearings, and trial.[6] However, this relatively small sub-group of the divorcing population consumes a disproportionate share of the court's precious resources, with fairly dismal outcomes using the traditional adversarial legal system.[7] Moreover, this sub-group tends to engage in protracted and repeated litigation. Outside the courts, the unremitting hostility and chaos can shadow the entire growing-up years of the children. This means that an accumulating sub-group of children are being caught up in these family situations. In fact, over the span of the past two decades in the U.S., it has been estimated that a critical mass of highly-conflicted divorcing families (with 2 million children) are passing in and out of a revolving court door.[8]

## II. SALIENT FEATURES OF HIGH-CONFLICT LITIGATING FAMILIES

The family environments of chronic custody disputes are characterized by the parents' mutual distrust, fear, anger, projection of blame onto the ex-partner, refusal to cooperate and communicate, allegations of abuse, and sabotage of each other's parenting and time with the child.[9] The extent to which parents' negative views and behaviors are realistic responses to the other parent's violent, neglectful, or substance-abusing behavior is difficult to determine. Some of the children involved clearly meet the criteria for an abused child, justifying their protection by the state. More often, when such allegations are investigated by child protective services, they are frequently dismissed by overworked staff as being either indicators of interparental spite, not able to be proven, or insufficiently serious to require state intervention. Clinical histories indicate that many of these families were dysfunctional long before the couple separated, and their children have been chronically subjected to ongoing marital conflict and the erratic, emotionally abusive care of personality-disordered and emotionally troubled parents. Studies indicate that domestic violence of varying severity is a feature of about three fourths of these families; concerns about child molestation and abuse are a feature of a substantial minority of the families (in about one tenth and three tenths, respectively).[10]

More commonly, however, the extremely negative views parents have of one another are exaggerated and emanate from one spouse's humiliation at the rejection inherent in the divorce itself. The couple's enmeshment derives from their inability to separate and realistically grieve the loss of the marriage relationship. Traumatic separations, by which a divorcing partner's sense of trust and shared reality has been precipitously betrayed and shattered, have resulted in negatively revised views of one another that are often unwittingly confirmed by others within their split social world of new partners, kin and even professionals.[11] Unable to settle their disputes with one another, these vulnerable people are then forced to enter the traditional legal system, which greatly increases their anxiety and defensiveness, and further undermines their parental competence. In the spirit of an adversarial culture, divorcing couples seek vindication through litigation by polarizing their respective positions and blaming the other parent.

In effect, the task of establishing fault in marital dissolution has not been abolished; rather, it has shifted from the divorce to the custody arena. To some extent, the battles fought over children in separating families are a reflection of custody laws that are the product of the larger societal war between men and women at this historical juncture. The problem is that children have neither a legal nor a political voice in the family battles and the larger gender wars that are fought in their name.[12] Yet they are the ones most adversely impacted.

## III. THE NEED FOR INTERDISCIPLINARY PARTNERSHIPS WITH THE COURT

The beginning of the twenty-first century finds the legal and mental health communities struggling to deepen and refine a truly revolutionary approach to helping families with separation and divorce, with the realization that it must involve a paradigm shift from an adversarial to a collaborative approach in family law. This collaborative approach suggests a fundamental redefinition of the role of family court, and it requires new multi-disciplinary partnerships between the courts and attorneys and mediators and mental health professionals, in order to arrive at viable solutions.[13] Having worked with and researched this population of embattled divorce for two decades, it is our thesis that the outcome of the divorce has very much to do with how the stormy waters of the divorce transition are navigated, and what kind of help or hindrance these vulnerable persons get from others during the process.[14] In particular, family courts, attorneys, custody evaluators, counselors, and therapists can act in ways that inadvertently contribute to family impasses; whereas, by intervening in more effective ways, these same helping professionals can play a critical role in resolving custody disputes.

This paper is intended to help summarize our collective experience in this endeavor. Specifically, it will first note how traditional professional roles and ethical constraints have contributed to rather than resolved family conflict and hurt children. Second, it will describe how moving from an adversarial to a collaborative approach in family matters requires a corresponding shift in perspectives and functions among these helping professionals and a rethinking of ethical obligations. Third, it will review the range of new dispute resolution programs, those which are alternatives to litigation, that have been emerging around the country. Specifically, the purpose is to outline the essential elements of each type of service and propose criteria as to which families need what kind of service and when.

## IV. RETHINKING THE ROLE OF FAMILY COURT IN DIVORCE MATTERS

There are a number of assumptions about the traditional role of family courts in conflicted custody matters that need to be questioned. First, family courts have primarily been used to make decisions for divorcing couples who cannot make their own. This assumes that the court has greater wisdom or some special knowledge about what is best for children. Second, family courts which make repeated decisions for some highly conflicted families have been induced to act *in loco parentis*. This assumes the court has the capacity to oversee the day-to-day care of children. Third, the custody litigation process has customarily determined which parent is the better parent, which implies that the other parent is of secondary, inferior status.[15] This assumes that it is appropriate for separating parents to be publicly scrutinized and held to a higher standard of accountability than those in non-disputing divorces and intact families.[16] Fourth, judges have been asked to pass judgment on family dilemmas that other professionals and the community-at-large have failed to resolve: the cases attorneys have failed to negotiate, or that mediators have failed to settle, and the people that counselors and therapists have failed to help. This assumes that judges are equipped to resolve the most difficult and complex of all family problems. In the face of this onerous burden, it should be no surprise that family court assignments for judges are unpopular, often avoided, and usually staffed by rotating assignments to prevent burn-out.

If we take a multi-disciplinary partnership approach, none of these functions should be primarily the court's responsibility. Rather, within the authority vested in it by law (specifically the best interests of the child), and respecting that families are entitled to the least intrusive court intervention, the new role of the family court can be one of leadership in bringing the issues, the parties and their helpers to the table to address four constructive questions that invite collaborative problem-solving:

1. How can this fractured family coordinate its resources and care for the children after the parents' separation?

2. How can we protect, reconstitute, and restore the positive parts of parent-child and family relationships wherever possible?

3. How can these parents make ongoing cooperative decisions throughout their children's growing-up years?

4. What help will these parents need from the community to raise their children?[17]

Note that this reframing of the court's primary function entails a proactive rather than a reactive stance. To accomplish the task, family court procedures will need to be revised to allow for more judicial casemanagement.[18] This can be a range of possibilities including the following: direct calendaring of cases to help ensure that one judge follows a case over time; judicial initiation of status and settlement conferences with options for telephone conferencing to expedite the decision-making process; judicial authority to require mental health and legal professionals to work collaboratively, including having disputing experts confer prior to giving their testimony; and a timely judicial review of progress whenever a succession of temporary orders is needed to settle the case.

It is essential that courts be experienced by families as supportive-rather than confusing or divisive, as is too often the case-and that provisions be made for communication between courts and consolidating actions arising in different courts. The development of unified family courts is the principal way of achieving this goal.[19] Further, to build a cadre of effective bench officers, the special expertise of family judges needs to be acknowledged by providing specialized training opportunities and incentives for career advancement within family court. These and many other reforms are necessary if the court is to provide leadership in a collaborative approach. Even so, the court, by itself, cannot provide answers to what a divorcing family needs. In partnership with the court, each of the helping professions must reorient its focus to these same primary goals.

## V. THE ROLE OF ATTORNEYS IN ESCALATING CONFLICT AND THE NEED FOR SHIFTING ROLES[20]

Traditionally, the family law attorney's role has been to initiate action from a purely partisan perspective, to strategically maneuver the presentation of evidence and evoke statutes and case law in order to win the client's case. Attorneys contribute to rather than resolve disputes when they are wedded solely to their advocacy role within an adversarial judicial system.[21] Advising the client not to talk to the other spouse, making extreme demands to increase the bargaining advantage, and filing motions that characterize the other parent in a negative light, are all typical examples. Needing to show evidence of neglect, abuse, physical violence, or emotional or mental incompetence in order to win their client's case, attorneys produce emotionally charged documents that become a public record of charges and counter-charges, citing-often out of context-the unhappy incidents and separation-engendered desperate behaviors of the emotionally vulnerable parties. The consequent public shame, guilt and fury at being so one-sidedly represented motivates the other party's compelling need to set the record straight in costly litigation. Invariably, attorneys cite their advocacy role to rationalize and justify their intractable adversarial stance. A typical hypothetical example:

> Following four years of litigation and a full custody evaluation regarding the mother's right to move away to the east coast, which clearly questioned the mother's parenting capacity compared to the father's, Mrs. K's attorney insisted on pursuing a custody trial, subjecting nine-year-old Jacob to a stressful interview with the judge. In response to the therapist's pleas on behalf of the child, the attorney answered, "I hear your concerns, but my only responsibility is to my client." He then proceeded to argue the case on a technical point, subjecting the family to six more months of costly litigation. The boy attempted to maintain a tenuous loyalty to both parents, became confused, and began to lie profusely, telling each parent what he/she wanted to hear. Of course, this justified the mother's custody suit. Fifteen years later, Jacob is still stung by the fact that his mother blamed him for the legal expenses she incurred "on his behalf" when she found out he had lied. The new collaborative approach by lawyers assumes that clients are profoundly interested in the effect of one parent's "victory" on the lives of their children, and it assumes a need for an ongoing, working relationship with the other spouse/parent. From this collaborative perspective, the family attorney's role involves counseling each client fully on their rights and responsibilities as a parent and as a co-parent, and exploring deeply the ramifications of all of their actions on the welfare of the children. Attorneys can then responsibly and ethically advocate their clients' more clearly defined and deeply explored interests.[22] When both attorneys pursue these goals in concert, creative win-win solutions are more likely to be generated.

Further, attorneys play a vital role in guarding against the dangers inherent in a collaborative approach that could become collusive. There is a potential threat for new collaborative models of alternative dispute resolution to compromise clients' civil liberties by subjecting families to unwarranted intrusiveness by outside agencies, including the vagaries and biases of an over-zealous mental health approach. Family attorneys are needed to draft creative but unambiguous stipulations and court orders with sufficient detail to, first, protect their client's civil rights, and second, to provide the kinds of external structures and constraints that allow families fragmented by ongoing conflict to proceed with some semblance of order and safety.

## VI. THE ROLE OF MENTAL HEALTH COUNSELORS IN FUELING CONFLICT AND THE NEED FOR SHIFTING ROLES

Traditionally, therapists, who see only one of the parties to the divorce conflict, can encourage uncompromising stands, reify distorted views of the other parent, write recommendations, and even testify on behalf of their adult client with little or no understanding of the child's needs, the other parent's position, or the couple and family dynamics. Furthermore, too often therapists are willing to begin treatment of a child in a custody dispute at the request of only one parent, and with no authority from the court.[23] A typical hypothetical example:

> During their turbulent separation, Mrs. P sought help from a psychiatrist who at first characterized her as "chronically depressed, suicidal, and rejecting of the child." Mrs. P soon became very dependent upon her psychiatrist. In attempts to stabilize her labile emotional states and shifting views of the world, he quickly helped her feel better by agreeing with her views that her husband was indeed "ruthless, manipulative, and possibly sociopathic." In actuality, he had never met the father. Moreover, in an attempt to help the mother with her parenting, he began treatment of the child. The father became extremely defensive and then irate about the psychiatrist's treatment of his child without his consent. He wrote belligerent letters to the psychiatrist, threatening a malpractice suit. The psychiatrist then testified against the father before the judge and reported the father's threats as evidence in his testimony. Traditionally, mental health professionals who undertake therapy with parents and children pursue their investigation into the emotional lives of their clients in isolation from the legal decision-making process. Under the rationale of client confidentiality, they work behind closed doors, too often oblivious to the fact that divorcing families are further fragmented by competing demands from professionals with access to different information, different perspectives and different agendas. This has resulted in situations, for example, where a child who refuses to visit a father is viewed by the mother's mental health consultant as having been "sexually molested" and by the father's therapist as a child who is suffering from "parent alienation syndrome." Attempting any intervention to effect a reconciliation of such a child with the father is doomed, because the parents are intractably wedded to the views of their supportive advocates, and they will wage court battles or even abduct their children with absolute moral conviction of their rectitude.[24]

Contrary to popular belief, parents in entrenched custody disputes are not characteristically aggressive, hostile, or spiteful people. Psychological testing of parents in high-conflict divorce and custody evaluations indicates that, as a group, these people are interpersonally sensitive and hypervigilant to criticism. They often lack a firm approach to solving problems, reason idiosyncratically, and tend to cognitively simplify their world.[25] This makes them especially vulnerable to conflicting views of professionals and a legal system that polarizes positions around blame and fault-finding. The worst possible scenarios occur in those high-profile cases where the parents' mental health and legal professionals squabble among themselves about the case, playing out the parental dispute in a community or court arena.

Within a collaborative paradigm such as we are suggesting, mental health counselors view it as their ethical obligation to triage and coordinate with other involved professionals in working with separating and divorced families. This approach necessitates reaching consensus about clinical goals, prognosis and intervention strategies, ensures that clients are spending their money and emotional energy in the most effective ways, and promotes healing for both the child and the family. A mental health counselor who undertakes therapy with any part of a divorcing family has the responsibility to rethink issues of confidentiality and lines of communication right from the outset (by obtaining appropriate parental permission), lest the intervention inadvertently harm rather than help. Furthermore, when differences of opinion arise, each individual professional has an ethical responsibility to initiate contact with the other professionals involved to resolve differences. If this is not possible, the intervention of choice is to call a strategy conference with all players of the disputing network, preferably before their respective positions have hardened. In these kinds of cases, the court should have the authority to bring the parties to the negotiating table. This meeting can be used to design a strategy for case management or resolution and is often the first order of business in a custody dispute that appears out of control.

## VII. HOW CUSTODY EVALUATORS CAN HELP OR HINDER THE PROCESS

Custody evaluations are a source of inordinate stress and shame for many vulnerable parents. Despite the fact that during the past decade, a number of professional organizations have developed standards of practice for custody evaluations,[26] further thought needs to be given to how they are conducted. Within a litigation-conscious arena, evaluators may become more focused upon establishing their technical expertise and protecting their own professional reputations than upon the needs of the family.[27] This can result in inappropriately exhaustive and intrusive negatively-biased assessments and reports. Among the possible negative influences of mental health professionals are written evaluations of the parents during the upheaval of the separation that explain the situation solely in terms of the individual psychopathology of the spouses. Psychodiagnostic terms, such as "paranoid," "alcoholic," "narcissistic," "sociopathic," "violent," or "battered woman's syndrome," reduce the explanation of complex marital dynamics to the psychological or moral capacities of the individual parents, clearly pathologizing and blaming one of the parties. These evaluative declarations, and many psychological tests that are used to support them, are often not clearly related to each parent's ability to care for the child.[28] Moreover, such psychodiagnostic terms have special technical meanings within the mental health professions. When used in public or in court, they become pejorative labels strategically employed to degrade or destroy the reputation of one parent and "win" custody for the other. When made known to the divorcing spouses and their legal counsels, these authoritative declarations as to the character of each parent serve to solidify already negative, polarized views, which then become "written in stone," ensuring that the dispute will continue.

An alternative conflict-reducing approach requires custody evaluators to pay more attention to prescribing how the family can resolve its impasse, the ways in which children can have access to the positive contributions of each parent, and how the children's development can be protected, rather than assessing who is and who is not emotionally disturbed, and who is and who is not "the better parent."[29]

To ensure that all parties have similar expectations and to avoid unnecessary intrusiveness and cost, it is helpful for the court to define a specific scope and purpose for the evaluation.[30] In many instances, custody evaluations can focus on particular issues (for example, which school the child should attend), and only where necessary does it need to encompass a complete family study involving psychological testing of all members, school and home visits, substance abuse assessments, and child abuse and molestation investigations.

Procedures for appointing evaluators, and for re-evaluations when a custody report is contested, need to be carefully considered so as not to subject the child and family to the inordinate stress of multiple assessments. Evaluators can serve the child most effectively if they are impartial experts appointed by the court, or by stipulation of the parties, and if they are provided with access to all family members. A multidisciplinary team of evaluators is perhaps the optimal choice here, but costs for such "team" endeavors are usually prohibitive. If the initial custody report is contested, a second evaluator appointed in the same manner should not expect to re-evaluate the family directly; rather he or she (or the multidisciplinary panel, if such is available) should review the procedures, findings, and recommendations of the first evaluator to determine whether they conform to professional standards, ethics, and scientific rigor.[31] If an update on the custody evaluation is needed, it follows that, in the interests of continuity of care and cost-effectiveness, the first evaluator should be excluded only if there is indication that standards of practice were initially violated.[32] At the very least, the first evaluator should be part of an evaluation team that undertakes the update.

Explicit prior arrangements should be made regarding the manner in which the final custody report will be disseminated and reviewed, so that the family can make good use of this information. Optimally such an arrangement should be made in writing and signed by both parties and their attorneys. Allowing each parent to hear the contents of a report from his or her attorney, in chambers, or in court, rather than in privacy with the evaluator, reinforces the win/lose mentality of the litigation, and is most likely to exacerbate the parents' sense of shame and helplessness. On the other hand, having the opportunity to review the report with its author offers a greater potential for diffusing the conflict and ensuring that the parents really hear what the report has to say about the needs of the child over the short and long term.[33]

## VIII. ALTERNATIVE PROGRAMS TO LITIGATION: WHO NEEDS WHAT KIND OF HELP AND WHEN?

If we agree that conflicted custody cases are, in part, exacerbated and entrenched by traditional adversarial proceedings and by inappropriate responses from mental health professionals, important social policy questions then arise as to what is needed in terms of a more responsive system of legal and mental health care for separating and divorced families in our courts and communities. A procedural system that has been evolving in many jurisdictions, albeit piecemeal, comprises a spectrum of services which begins with preventive measures that are minimally intrusive and designed for the broadest population of families-such as divorce orientation, parenting education, mediation, and collaborative law. Those who fail to settle through these means are referred to other, progressively more intrusive treatment interventions that wed mental health interventions to the social control mechanisms of the courts-such as therapeutic interventions, custody evaluations, ongoing co-parenting counseling, arbitration, or special masters, and various kinds of supervised visitation.[34]

This procedural organization rests on the principle that family courts should provide the least intrusive intervention into the private life of families that is sufficient for them to care for their children. While it is an improvement over a one-service-fits-all approach to divorcing families, many court staff and administrators are questioning whether the progressive steps model is the optimal solution. Do some families have to fail successively at each level of service before they get the kind of help they really need? Are there more efficient and less painful ways of matching families to the most effective kind of service? A different approach is to consider the array of services listed above as alternatives that can be made available with access governed by appropriateness for the particular family situation.

The balance of this paper briefly defines each service and proposes some criteria to determine who benefits from each kind of service, and for whom each is contraindicated. It is important to note that the proposed criteria are mostly based upon observation and deduction, and in most cases not upon systematic research. By proposing a preliminary set of guidelines for the use (and misuse) of the range of these new dispute resolution forums, we hope to stir some debate which will contribute to a more discriminating articulation of professional roles and ethics in these new models of interdisciplinary practice.

A. Divorce Orientation/Educational Programs

Separating parents embarking on divorce need easy access to preliminary information about the psychological process of divorce, legal procedures and custody options, and the general needs of children for conflict-free access to both parents. Furthermore, if they are to make informed choices, they need to know about available services in the community and to receive some guidance as to what services are likely to meet their needs. Essential information can be provided publicly through various media such as books, videos, television and brief educational classes.[35]

Evaluation of general divorce education programs is in its infancy.[36] Available data indicate high consumer satisfaction and increased knowledge and skills regardless of whether attendance is mandated or voluntary. This evidence probably translates into greater consumer good will towards the legal process and more informed choices. However, the findings are mixed as to the extent to which these brief programs promote better child and parent adjustment, or reduced conflict and litigation.[37] More thought needs to be given as to when parents in crisis are amenable to education about their children and when such information is ineffective, or will be misconstrued and used in the service of furthering parental disputes.

B. Specialized Educational Programs

There is growing awareness that one size does not fit all in approaches to parenting education. For instance, there is a need for special educational programs for never-married parents,[38] some of whom may have never lived together or established any kind of working co-parenting relationship. Many parents have new partners and extended kin who play extensive roles in the child rearing. There is also a pressing need to adapt parent educational programs to meet the needs of various ethnic groups whose language barriers and cultural mores make divorce adjustment different from mainstream North American Caucasian families and at variance with presumptions in United States laws about what kinds of custody arrangements are in the best interests of children.[39]

While divorce adjustment groups for adults have long been recognized as naturally supportive and cost-effective ways of helping, group interventions for children of divorce, where peer support helps to normalize painful and confusing experiences, have been relatively slower to develop.[40] Divorcing parents need special information about the developmental needs of children of all ages, but most especially about the needs of infants and young children. A young child's sense of security, trust, and social-emotional development can be derailed during these critical early years by chaotic and inconsistent parenting styles.[41]

High-conflict, violent, and chronically litigating families need specialized educational programs. Such programs are currently being developed in a number of jurisdictions following the recognition that, for this sub-group, generalized divorce information is both ineffective and inappropriate. In cases of domestic violence, general divorce education that encourages parental cooperation and communication may actually be dangerous for victims who are often subject to ongoing manipulation and control by the abusive partner after separation.[42] Cognitive-behavioral or skill-based approaches that teach effective communication and problem solving, and attempts to heighten parents' empathic awareness of the children's plight in conflicted custody, are the most important and effective components of these programs.[43] How to develop separate, "parallel" parenting arrangements governed by an explicit court order rather than attempting a cooperative co-parenting relationship should be taught. In addition, these classes can explain laws regarding the rights of both parents to custody and access, contempt proceedings, protection from domestic violence, management of abduction risk, criteria for child protective agencies to take action, and grounds for supervised visitation.[44]

These specialized educational programs are appropriate for families who lack general knowledge about the laws and procedures of family and dependency courts, those who are overly dependent upon litigation to make parenting decisions, and those who are deficient in communication and problem-solving skills.[45] However, providing this range of information to all divorcing families is unnecessary. Such programs are probably inappropriate or insufficient in situations requiring state intervention to protect victims: cases of serious allegations of child abuse, domestic violence, substance abuse, and mental illness. They are also questionable for those character-disordered parents who tend to use educational information to further a strategic advantage in litigation.

## C. Affordable Legal Services and Collaborative Law

There is a growing need for affordable legal consultation to help the large majority of divorcing families make the transition through separation and divorce. Large numbers of parents are now entering family courts without legal representation.[46] This raises the level of frustration and confusion for clients and court personnel alike. Moreover, it creates inefficiencies in court administration, and presents many ethical dilemmas for judges dealing with litigants who are trying to represent themselves with little or no knowledge of the law, due process, court rules, or procedures. One response to this emerging, serious problem has been the "unbundling and rebundling" of legal services in an attempt to provide specific kinds of legal counsel at affordable rates with less than full legal representation. Safeguards for clients who receive partial or limited counsel and appropriate liability protection for the professionals involved need to be clearly specified in these cases.[47]

The innovative practice of collaborative law is the most recent forum for dispute resolution as an alternative to litigation. In collaborative law, the parties and their attorneys commence the legal process of divorce by stipulating to complete, honest and open disclosure of all information, whether requested or not, and to engage in informal discussions and conferences for the purpose of reaching a settlement on all issues, with assurance that the process cannot be subverted in order to pursue traditional litigation.[48] All consultants retained by the parties (accountants, therapists, and appraisers) are likewise directed to work in a cooperative manner. While specific issues of stalemate may be resolved by a pre-appointed arbitrator, the hallmark of this process is that litigation using collaborative lawyers is not an option, nor are the work products of this process available to any other attorneys who may litigate.

Because this dispute resolution method is so new, there is little systematic information about its outcomes. Collaborative law benefits parties where there is a need to retain the advocacy role of each attorney. This protection is not always afforded in mediation, and it is especially important that it be provided where there are imbalances of power between the parties.[49] Collaborative law motivates creative "win-win" solutions, and decreases the high costs of formal fact finding, depositions, preparation of briefs, filing of motions, etc. However, these new practices demand the highest ethical standards of practice; consequently, some of the corresponding risks are lack of scrutiny and accountability when informal legal procedures are used, and the cost of starting again from scratch in court if they are unsuccessful. There are also concerns about inequities in the administration of justice by developing separate tiers or private levels of justice for people who can afford collaborative law, compared to those who use the public forum of the courts. For these reasons, in cases where there is distrust between the legal advocates, inability of the attorneys to maintain appropriate client control, or serious concerns about abuse and exploitation, the parties may be better protected in family court.

D. Mediation

Mediation is fairly widely available in the United States, both publicly and privately.[50] This forum uses a neutral third party to help parents develop custody and visitation plans (in most public settings) and both financial and child custody settlements (in the case of many private providers). Mediation is generally confidential and time-limited; it focuses on problem resolution of specific issues and does not involve psychological counseling and therapy. This kind of issue-focused mediation attains full resolution in one-half, and partial resolution in two-thirds, of all custody and access disputes that enter into court.[51] This solidly researched "success rate" of mediation supports the philosophy that most couples have the capacity to re-order their lives in a private, confidential setting, according to their personal preferences, with the relatively limited help of a mediator who focuses on specific issues.

The primary indicators for a successful outcome in mediation are parents who, with the mediator's help, demonstrate the capacity to contain their emotional distress and focus on their children's issues. Mediating parents who can behave somewhat rationally with each other and who have a history of parental cooperation tend to have more successful outcomes. Despite high levels of anger and conflict, these individuals can more easily distinguish their children's needs from their own, and tend to acknowledge, if sometimes begrudgingly, the value of the other parent in the children's lives. It is generally asserted that brief mediation of divorce disputes, especially if offered early on, is an effective preventive measure, and mediation is the intervention of choice for tailoring access schedules to fit the specific individual needs of children and families. On the other hand, mediation is considered inappropriate where there are serious concerns about abuse, violence, and mental illness. In such cases, some kind of non-confidential screening and assessment is needed with a follow-up custody evaluation, if warranted, as a prelude to a court hearing.

E. Custody Evaluation

Custody evaluations involve fact-finding by a qualified mental health professional and a written report with recommendations presented to the court. Although extremely effective in producing settlements and aiding judicial decisions (85-90% of disputing parents settle), such stipulations/court orders are twice as likely to be relitigated compared to those that are settled voluntarily.[52] Custody evaluations are also very costly, and they do not help with ongoing co-parenting problems. To date, custody evaluations have generally been the standard option when families are unable to settle through mediation and attorney negotiation. A collaborative approach, however, questions whether a custody evaluation is the optimal way of using family resources when mediation fails.

Where parents have extremely discrepant views of their child's needs, a confidential child-focused psychological assessment may suffice.[53] Often an objective assessment of the child's needs can be the basis for further mediation, counseling, or a recommended settlement. Formal custody evaluations can then be reserved for serious allegations of child abuse, neglect and molest, as well as contested claims of parental psychopathology, substance abuse, or domestic violence. If these allegations are substantiated, the court will need to impose a protective custody arrangement and a plan for monitoring it. This means that where the facts are not really in dispute, serious family or individual dysfunction need not be evaluated further, and resources can be used for treatment rather than for further investigation.

F. Therapeutic Intervention

This type of intervention (also called family "impasse-mediation") involves a combination of confidential counseling and mediation to resolve the psychological and family problems that contribute to chronic disputes or stalemates in reaching a custody settlement.[54] The intervention is undertaken by child and family therapists who are also experienced divorce mediators. They begin by taking a history of the parental disputes, identifying the family dynamics that have created the impasse, and then seeking to understand how the parental conflict is affecting the children. This information is used in brief, strategic therapeutic interventions and counseling with the family members, the goal being to develop psychologically sound child access plans and to help the parents through the emotional divorce. Unlike issue-focused mediation, the completion of a custody and access agreement is not seen as an end in itself. The attorney's role is to set up the treatment contract, translate the agreements reached into court orders, and take unresolved issues back to another dispute-resolution forum.

A series of studies have indicated that about two thirds of cases that have failed brief issue-focused mediation have been successful using these therapeutic interventions, *i.e.*, they have been settled and have stayed out of court over a two-to-four-year period.[55] Specifically, this type of intervention is useful when emotional issues intrude and disrupt regular mediation or attorney negotiations. Emotional turmoil can emanate from acute reactions to the humiliation and loss inherent in the divorce, from a recent traumatic separation experience, or when parents are so preoccupied with their own pain that they cannot respond to their children's acute distress. Family impasse intervention and mediation is also the method of choice when there is "tribal warfare" – that is, where new partners, extended kin and professionals become embroiled in the dispute. However, this forum is not appropriate for serious allegations of abuse, and it is insufficient, although helpful, for cases where there is serious parental character pathology.

G. Co-Parenting Coordination and Arbitration

Co-parenting coordination is a service for separated and divorced families who need ongoing help in coordinating parenting practices and responding flexibly to the needs of their children throughout their developmental changes, and sometimes throughout their entire growing-up years. It may be needed as a longer-term extension to therapeutic intervention, or it may be instituted after a custody evaluation in order to help families implement and monitor a parenting plan. Co-parenting counselors are generally mental health professionals who use primarily counseling and mediation techniques, but do not arbitrate. They may or may not testify in court. The use of co-parenting arbitrators (variously called special masters, wise persons, or custody commissioners), on the other hand, involves the appointment, by stipulation of the parties, of mental health or legal professional who is experienced in custody matters to manage ongoing conflict, and help parents make timely decisions for their children over the long term. Occasionally such decisions may be challenged in court, at which time the arbitrator may have to testify.[56]

There are many variations but, broadly speaking, there are two main types of co-parenting arbitrators: one who acts solely as arbitrator and is called in to settle an issue only when the parents and their other helpers cannot reach settlement; and one who acts as the parenting coordinator and mediator, and in addition has arbitration powers should the couple reach stalemate. Various arguments can been made in favor of each type, the principal one being that whereas the first (pure arbitration) avoids dual roles, the second (who uses arbitration as a last resort) is more efficient.

A detailed stipulation/court order needs to be prepared by the attorneys to address the terms of appointment, including how the co-parenting arbitrator or coordinator is to be chosen and how he or she will be terminated, domains of decision-making, methods of conflict resolution to be used, procedures for bringing an issue to him/her, permissible lines of communication with all parties (family members, children, collaterals, and other professionals), payment for services, rules for determining when decisions should be made as court orders, and procedures for challenging an arbitrated decision in court.

Following almost a decade of development of this service, co-parental arbitration has emerged as an important adjunct to family courts in a number of jurisdictions. Although preliminary outcome data indicate dramatic decreases in relitigation and moderate levels of consumer satisfaction when these kinds of arbitration are used,[57] there are no studies to date which systematically evaluate their effectiveness in other ways (*i.e.*, cost, benefit to children, decrease in disputes, improvement in co-parental and parent-child relationships). With the rapidly expanding use of this powerful and potentially intrusive intervention, there are rising concerns about ethical standards, procedural guidelines, training, and licensing requirements for this new professional practice.

It is generally believed that co-parenting arbitrators are appropriate for chronic litigants and entrenched custody conflicts emanating from serious psychopathology and personality disorders in parents who have parenting deficits. They can be used to monitor potentially abusive situations involving domestic violence and intermittent mental illness of a parent. They can also be used for children who are very young or who have special medical needs, where parents cannot communicate sufficiently to coordinate the care of the child in a timely manner.

However, appointing an arbitrator is not appropriate as a routine response for difficult, high-conflict cases where the family crisis is acute but temporary. The process should not be used where custody and access plans have not been established by the court, nor for major changes in custody or other circumstances. Nor is it appropriate for cases that need a thorough investigation of abuse claims. Most important, it not appropriate in cases where the professionals are squabbling among themselves. It is unfair to burden families with the cost and complication of yet another professional in their lives when those currently involved in the case cannot agree on its direction.

## H. Supervised Visitation and Monitored Exchange

The purpose of supervised access is to provide a protected setting for parent-child contact with a neutral third person monitoring the contact or exchange of the child between parents.[58] A court order dictates the requirements for visit supervision. This specialized service, generally staffed by trained volunteers under the direction of a professional coordinator, has grown rapidly across the United States and internationally during the past decade.[59] It is appropriately used where a victim-parent and child are at risk because of ongoing high-conflict and threat of domestic violence. This kind of protected setting is also needed for parent-child contact when the child is at high risk because of a parent's mental illness, substance abuse problems, history of emotional, physical abuse or molestation, or when there is a threat of child abduction.

Supervised access should not be a dispositional alternative when an indigent family cannot afford other types of services.[60] It is inappropriate to use supervised visitation as a replacement for an evaluation of serious allegations of abuse, or in lieu of more costly therapeutic counseling for the child or parent. Although it can be used as a short-term neutral setting for parent-child contact during a chaotic or traumatic parental separation, or while an investigation is being undertaken, it is unfair to subject a parent to supervised visitation when allegations are unfounded, in order to quiet the fears of the accusing parent. On the other hand, it is also unacceptable to use supervised visitation to ensure an abusive parent's right of access to the child when the child is chronically uncomfortable and distressed by that access.[61]

It is becoming apparent that a continuum of different kinds of affordable and specialized access services is needed in court-community partnerships in order to help parent-child relationships in high-conflict families:

- Re-connection/Re-Unification Assistance for non-custodial parents (mostly unmarried fathers who have never been involved or who have been absent for a long period) to become reacquainted with their young children in a comfortable, nurturing environment. In addition to some didactic instruction, it involves gradual introduction of the child to the parent and in-vivo demonstration of ways of relating to the child in a developmentally appropriate manner.

- Parenting and Co-parenting in Domestic Violence Families. Currently, domestic violence perpetrator and victim programs deal with the dynamics of abusive relationships in separate forums but touch little or not at all on parenting and co-parenting issues. Safe protocols for parental communication in domestic violence cases need to be developed to prevent the abusive parent from continuing to exercise control and manipulation of the victim, especially protocols that allow "parallel" rather than cooperative parenting. Children who have been damaged by witnessing family violence also need special help to deal with the residual symptoms of post-traumatic stress disorder[62] and dysfunctional adaptation to chronic trauma.[63]

- Therapeutic Supervision involves family intervention by a qualified professional counselor in cases where there has been a major violation of the child's trust in the non-custodial parent (following abuse, abandonment, or unsubstantiated molestation allegations), or where an alienated child refuses to visit the rejected parent (in part because of the custodial parent's actions). A number of experienced clinicians have expertise with therapeutic supervision, and systematic theory-based approaches are currently being developed.[64]

## IX. THE NEED FOR COORDINATION BETWEEN COMMUNITY SERVICES AND COURTS

In conclusion, and most important as we review the range of newly developed and revised services for our present-day separating and divorced families, especially those more extensive interventions designed for the high-conflict or embattled sub-group, we must be aware that with sophistication and differentiation of services that can better fit the multiple needs of these families, there is a corresponding need for coordination of these services with one another and with the court. More intransigent conflict-ridden families are likely to be more troubled by indications of domestic violence, child neglect, molestation and abuse, parental substance abuse, mental health problems, and child abduction. The family court's interventions must be closely orchestrated with interventions provided by community-based services: psychological and parenting counseling, substance abuse monitoring and treatment, batterers' treatment programs and victims' advocacy, and mental health services.

Case management protocols and time lines must be devised to coordinate, monitor and follow up on progress of the case plans that have been ordered by the family court for many of these most troubled families and high-risk children. Otherwise, our interventions run the risk of further fragmenting vulnerable families rather than helping them, permitting families to fall through the cracks between different services, or leaving families forever suspended in the never-never land of an intrusive state intervention.

*Janet R. Johnston, Ph.D., is Professor of Justice Studies at San José State University in California.*

## Notes

[1]    *See generally* ELEANOR E. MACCOBY & ROBERT H. MNOOKIN, DIVIDING THE CHILD: SOCIAL AND LEGAL DILEMMAS OF CUSTODY (1992); *see also* LENORE J. WEITZMAN, THE DIVORCE REVOLUTION: THE UNEXPECTED SOCIAL AND ECONOMIC CONSEQUENCES FOR WOMEN AND CHILDREN IN AMERICA (1985).

[2]    *See* Frank F. Furstenberg, Jr., *History and Current Status of Divorce in the United States*, 4 FUTURE OF CHILDREN 29 (1994). As a consequence of this extraordinarily high divorce rate and the unprecedented numbers of children of unwed parents, 60% of all children now spend some time in a single-head-of-household family. These children experience multiple changes in their residential living arrangements and parenting during their growing-up years. *See* Paul C. Glick, *The Role of Divorce in the Changing Family Structure: Trends and Variations, in* CHILDREN OF DIVORCE: EMPIRICAL PERSPECTIVES ON ADJUSTMENT 3 (Sharlene A. Wolchik & Paul Karoly eds., 1988). *See also* Donald J. Hernandez, *Demographic Trends and the Living Arrangements of Children, in* IMPACT OF DIVORCE, SINGLE PARENTING & STEPPARENTING ON CHILDREN 3 (E. Mavis Hetherington & Josephine D. Arasteh eds., 1988).

[3]    *See* Marsha Kline Pruett & Kathy Hoganbruen, *Joint Custody and Shared Parenting*, 7 CHILD & ADOLESCENT PSYCHIATRIC CLINICS N. AM. 273 (1998).

[4]    *See* Marsha Kline Pruett, *Children's Views of Lawyers, Judges and Family Court Counselors* (1998) (unpublished manuscript, on file with author) (paper presented at the conference "New Ways of Helping Children and Parents Through Divorce," jointly sponsored by the Judith Wallerstein Center for the Family in Transition and the University of California Extension, Santa Cruz).

[5]    *See* MACCOBY & MNOOKIN, *supra* note 1, at 137-41. *See also* JUDITH S. WALLERSTEIN & JOAN B. KELLY, SURVIVING THE BREAKUP: HOW CHILDREN AND PARENTS COPE WITH DIVORCE 206-34 (1980).

[6]    *See* MACCOBY & MNOOKIN, *supra* note 1, at 137. These data are from California, which has been in the forefront of divorce reform, and where mediation has been mandated state-wide for custody and visitation matters since 1981. *See id.*

[7]    *See generally* Mary Duryee, *Mandatory Court Mediation: Demographic Summary and Consumer Evaluation of One Court Service*, 30 FAM. & CONCILIATION CTS. REV. 260 (1992). Those who fail to settle in mediation use more than twice the hours of family court service staff. *See id.* They also presumably consume the major portion of judges' time. *See id.*

[8] *See* JANET R. JOHNSTON & VIVIENNE ROSEBY, IN THE NAME OF THE CHILD: A DEVELOPMENTAL APPROACH TO UNDERSTANDING AND HELPING CHILDREN OF CONFLICTED AND VIOLENT DIVORCE 4 (1997).

[9] Interestingly, no demographic descriptors (income, education, ethnicity) distinguish the high-conflict group from the large majority of divorcing families. *See* MACCOBY & MNOOKIN, *supra* note 1, at 237-45. Although parents of younger children and those with larger families tend to experience more conflict, no other characteristics of family composition appear to predict who will be in high conflict. *See id.* Instead, it is pervasive distrust about the other parent's ability to care for their child adequately and discrepant perspectives about parenting practices that generally typify the couples who are disputations both inside and outside the court. *See* Charlene E. Depner et al., *Building a Uniform Statistical Reporting System: A Snapshot of California Family Court Services*, 30 FAM. & CONCILIATION CTS. REV. 185 (1992).

[10] *See* Janet R. Johnston, *High-Conflict Divorce*, 4 FUTURE OF CHILDREN 165 (1994); *see also* Janet R. Johnston, *Prevention of Parent or Family Abduction of Children Through Early Identification of Risk Factors*, Stage I, Part B (1996) (unpublished manuscript, on file with author) (final report to the Office of Juvenile Justice & Delinquency Prevention, Department of Justice, Washington, D.C.).

[11] *See* JANET R. JOHNSTON & LINDA E. G. CAMPBELL, IMPASSES OF DIVORCE: THE DYNAMICS AND RESOLUTION OF FAMILY CONFLICT (1988).

[12] *See generally* MARY ANN MASON, THE CUSTODY WARS (1999).

[13] This approach is compatible with that of therapeutic jurisprudence which seeks to apply social science to examine the impact of laws on the mental and physical health of the people they affect and to propose changes in laws and procedures accordingly. *See generally* DAVID B. WEXLER, THERAPEUTIC JURISPRUDENCE: THE LAW AS A THERAPEUTIC AGENT (1990); *see also* BRUCE J. WINICK, THERAPEUTIC JURISPRUDENCE APPLIED: ESSAYS ON MENTAL HEALTH LAW (1997).

[14] *See generally* JOHNSTON & CAMPBELL, *supra* note 11; JOHNSTON & ROSEBY, *supra* note 8.

[15] *See* Robert L. McWhinney, *The "Winner-Loser Syndrome": Changing Fashions in the Determination of Child "Custody"*, 33 FAM. & CONCILIATION CTS. REV. 297 (1995).

[16] The standard for determining parental incompetence in divorcing families should be the same as that determining abuse and neglect in dependency court.

[17] *See* Leslie E. Shear, *From Competition to Complementarity: Legal Issues and Their Clinical Implications in Custody*, 7 CHILD & ADOLESCENT PSYCHIATRIC CLINICS N. AM. 311 (1998); *see also* Judith S. Wallerstein, *Tailoring the Intervention to the Child in the Separating and Divorced Family*, 29 FAM. & CONCILIATION CTS. REV. 448 (1991). This approach is also consistent with the emphasis upon developing a parenting plan, rather than deciding who is the better parent. *See* Robert Tompkins, *Parenting Plans: A Concept Whose Time Has Come*, 33 FAM. & CONCILIATION CTS. REV. 286 (1995).

[18] *See generally* Donald B. King, *Accentuate the Positive-Eliminate the Negative*, 31 FAM. & CONCILIATION CTS. REV. 9 (1993); Donald B. King, *Judicious Interventions*, 19 FAM. ADVOC. 22, 22-24 (1997); Kristena A. LaMar, *Judicially Hosted Settlement Conferences in Domestic Relations Cases*, 34 FAM. & CONCILIATION CTS. REV. 219 (1996).

[19] The numerous reform efforts around the United States and other countries to produce unified family courts are intended to produce a court system that is more rational and responsive to family problems. *See, e.g.*, Judith S. Kaye & Jonathan Lippman, *New York State Unified Court System: Family Justice Program*, 33 FAM. & CONCILIATION CTS. REV. 144 (1998).

[20] *See* Forrest S. Mosten, *Emerging Roles of the Family Lawyer: A Challenge for the Courts*, 33 FAM. & CONCILIATION CTS. REV. 213 (1995).

[21] *See generally* Janet Weinstein, *And Never the Twain Shall Meet: The Best Interests of Children and the Adversary System*, 52 U. MIAMI L. REV. 79 (1997).

[22]   *See* Nicole Pedone, *Lawyer's Duty to Discuss Alternative Dispute Resolution in the Best Interest of the Children*, 36 FAM. & CONCILIATION CTS. REV. 65 (1998).

[23]   *See* JOHNSTON & CAMPBELL, *supra* note 11, at 24-51.

[24]   *See generally* Janet R. Johnston & Linda K. Girdner, *Early Identification of Parents at Risk for Custody Violations and Prevention of Child Abductions*, 36 FAM. & CONCILIATION CTS. REV. 392 (1998).

[25]   *See* Marion F. Ehrenberg et al., *Shared Parenting Agreements After Maritial Separation: The Roles of Empathy & Narcissism*, 64 J. CONSULTING & CLINICAL PSYCHOL. 808 (1996). *See also* Carl F. Hoppe & Lynne M. Kenney, *A Rorschach Study of the Psychological Characteristics of Parents Engaged in Child Custody/Visitation Disputes* (1994) (unpublished manuscript, on file with author) (paper presented at the 102nd Annual Convention of the American Psychological Association, Los Angeles, Cal.); M. G. Walters et al., *Rorschach Findings About Parenting Capacities of Parents in Protracted Custody Disputes* (1995) (unpublished manuscript, on file with author) (paper presented at the Society for Personality Assessment, Atlanta, Ga.).

[26]   *See Ethical Principles of Psychologists & Codes of Conduct*, 47 AM. PSYCHOL. 1597 (1992). *See also Guidelines for Child Custody Evaluations in Divorce Proceedings*, 49 AM. PSYCHOL. 677 (1994); S.P. Herman et al., *Practice Parameters for Child Custody Evaluation*, 36 J. AM. ACAD. CHILD & ADOLESCENT PSYCHIATRY 57 (1997).

[27]   In fact, as forensic experts, custody evaluators are primarily servants of the court. *See generally* Jonathan W. Gould, *Scientifically Crafted Child Custody Evaluations*, 37 FAM. & CONCILIATION CTS. REV. 64 (1999).

[28]   *See* Cherry Hysjulien et al., *Child Custody Evaluations: A Review of Methods Used in Litigation and Alternative Dispute Resolution*, 32 FAM. & CONCILIATION CTS. REV. 466 (1994).

[29]   *See generally* Vivienne Roseby, *Uses of Psychological Testing in a Child-Focused Approach to Child Custody Evaluations*, 29 FAM. L.Q. 97 (1995).

[30]   *See generally* Gould, *supra* note 27.

[31]   Scientifically acceptable procedures for interviewing and protocols for investigating alleged child abuse have also been developed to guide practice. *See generally* Thea Brown et al., *Problems and Solutions in the Management of Child Abuse Allegations in Custody and Access Disputes in the Family Court*, 36 FAM. & CONCILIATION CTS. REV. 431 (1998); STEPHEN J. CECI & MAGGIE BRUCK, JEOPARDY IN THE COURTROOM: A SCIENTIFIC ANALYSIS OF CHILDREN'S TESTIMONY (1995).

[32]   *See* Philip Stahl, *Second Opinions: An Ethical and Professional Process for Reviewing Child Custody Evaluations*, 34 FAM. & CONCILIATION CTS. REV. 386, 389 (1996).

[33]   *See* Roseby, *supra* note 29, at 109.

[34]   *See* William Howe III & Maureen McKnight, *Oregon Task Force on Family Law: A New System to Resolve Family Law Conflicts*, 33 FAM. & CONCILIATION CTS. REV. 173, 173 (1995).

[35]   The vast majority of educational programs for divorcing families are from 2-4 hours duration and are probably more aptly described as divorce orientation. *See generally* Karen R. Blaisure & Margie J. Geasler, *Results of a Survey of Court-Connected Parent Education*, 34 FAM. & CONCILIATION CTS. REV. 23 (1996); Margie J. Geasler & Karen R. Blaisure, *1998 Nationwide Survey of Court-Connected Divorce Education Programs*, 37 FAM. & CONCILIATION CTS. REV. 36 (1999); Andrew Schepard, *War and P.E.A.C.E.: A Preliminary Report and a Model Statute on an Interdisciplinary Educational Program for Divorcing and Separating Parents*, 27 U. MICH. J.L. REFORM 131 (1993).

[36]   *See* Geasler & Blaisure, *supra* note 35, at 37.

[37]   *See* Jack Arbuthnot & Donald A. Gordon, *Does Mandatory Divorce Education for Parents Work?*, 34 FAM. & CONCILIATION CTS. REV. 60 (1996). *See also* JESSICA PEARSON & NANCY THOENNES, CHILD ACCESS PROJECTS: AN EVALUATION OF FOUR ACCESS DEMONSTRATION PROJECTS FUNDED BY THE FEDERAL OFFICE OF CHILD SUPPORT ENFORCEMENT (CENTER FOR POLICY RESEARCH ed., 1996); Jack Arbuthnot et al., *Patterns of Relitigation Following Divorce Education*, 35 FAM. & CONCILIATION CTS. REV. 269 (1997);

Cathleen Gray et al., *Making it Work: An Evaluation of Court-Mandated Parenting Workshops for Divorcing Families*, 35 FAM. & CONCILIATION CTS. REV. 280 (1997); Laurie Kramer & Amanda Kowal, *Long-Term Follow-Up of a Court-Based Intervention for Divorcing Parents*, 36 FAM. & CONCILIATION CTS. REV. 452 (1998).

[38]   *See* Joan L. Raisner, *Family Mediation and Never-Married Parents*, 35 FAM. & CONCILIATION CTS. REV. 90 (1997).

[39]   *See* Maria S. Schwartz, *Bringing PEACE to the Latino Community: Implementing a Parent Education Program*, 34 FAM. & CONCILIATION CTS. REV. 93 (1996). *See also* Gretchen Zegarra, *Educando a la Familia Latina: Ideas for Making Parent Education Programs Accessible to the Latino Community*, 36 FAM. & CONCILIATION CTS. REV. 281, 281 (1998).

[40]   *See* Rosemarie Bolen, *Kids' Turn: Helping Kids Cope with Divorce*, 31 FAM. & CONCILIATION CTS. REV. 249 (1993). *See also* Trecia Di Bias, *Some Programs for Children*, 34 FAM. & CONCILIATION CTS. REV. 112 (1996); Virginia Petersen & Susan B. Steinman, *Helping Children Succeed After Divorce: A Court-Mandated Educational Program for Divorcing Parents*, 32 FAM. & CONCILIATION CTS. REV. 27, 29 (1994).

[41]   *See* JOHNSTON & ROSEBY, *supra* note 8, at 77.

[42]   *See* Geri S. W. Fuhrman et al., *Parent Education's Second Generation: Integrating Violence Sensitivity*, 37 FAM. & CONCILIATION CTS. REV. 24, 24 (1999).

[43]   *See* Kevin M. Kramer et al., *Effects of Skill-Based Versus Information-Based Education Programs on Domestic Violence and Parental Communication*, 36 FAM. & CONCILIATION CTS. REV. 9 (1998).

[44]   *See* Sherrie Kibler et al., *Pre-contempt/contemnors Group Diversion Counseling Program: A Program to Address Parental Frustration of Custody and Visitation Orders*, 32 FAM. & CONCILIATION CTS. REV. 62, 63 (1994).

[45]   *See* Janet R. Johnston, *Developing and Testing Group Interventions for Families at Impasse* (1999) (unpublished manuscript, on file with author) (report to the state-wide office of Family Court Services, AOC, Judicial Council of California, San Francisco).

[46]   *See* Forrest S. Mosten, *Unbundling Legal Services*, 57 OR. B. BULL. 9, 9 (1997).

[47]   *See id.*

[48]   *See* Pauline H. Tesler, *Collaborative Law: A New Approach to Family Law ADR*, 2 CONFLICT MGMT. 12 (1996).

[49]   *See* Trina Grillo, *The Mediation Alternative: Process Dangers for Women*, 100 YALE L.J. 1545, 1545 (1991).

[50]   In California, about 20-30% of the total population of separating families file in court to resolve their disputes over the care and custody of their children and are mandated to use mediation. *See* MACCOBY & MNOOKIN, *supra* note I, at 137.

[51]   *See* Charlene E. Depner et al., *Client Evaluations of Mediation Services: The Impact of Case Characteristics & Mediation Service Models*, 32 FAM. & CONCILIATION CTS. REV. 306, 312 (1994). *See also* ROBERT E. EMERY, RENEGOTIATING FAMILY RELATIONSHIPS: DIVORCE, CHILD CUSTODY & MEDIATION (1994); MACCOBY & MNOOKIN, *supra* note 1, at 137; Charlene E. Depner et al., *Report 4: Mediated Agreements on Child Custody & Visitation: 1991 California Family Court Services Snapshot Study*, 33 FAM. & CONCILIATION CTS. REV. 87 (1995); Joan B. Kelly. *A Decade of Divorce Mediation Research: Some Answers and Questions*, 34 FAM. & CONCILIATION CTS. REV. 373 (1996).

[52]   *See* Peter Ash & Melvin Guyer, *Child Psychiatry and the Law: The Functions of Psychiatric Evaluation in Contested Custody and Visitation Cases*, 25 J. AM. ACAD. CHILD PSYCHIATRY 554 (1986). *See also* Peter Ash & Melvin Guyer, *Relitigation After Contested Custody and Visitation Evaluations*, 14 BULL. AM. ACAD. PSYCHIATRY L. 323 (1986); Barbara Hauser, *Custody in Dispute: Legal and Psychological Profiles of Contesting Families*, 24 J. AM. ACAD. OF CHILD PSYCHIATRY 575 (1985).

⁵³   *See* Forrest S. Mosten, *Confidential Mini-Evaluation*, 30 FAM. & CONCILIATION CTS. REV. 373 (1992).

⁵⁴   Families can be seen individually or in groups of 5-8 other families. Children are always included in the intervention which is usually relatively brief (25-40 hours). *See* JOHNSTON & CAMPBELL, *supra* note 11, at 198. *See also* H. McDonough et al., *For Kids' Sake: A Treatment Program for High-Conflict Separated Families (Parents' Group Manual)* (1995) (unpublished manuscript on file with the Family Court Clinic, Clarke Institute of Psychiatry, 250 College Street, Toronto, M5T1R8 Canada). This model of service has also been adapted and used within Alameda County Family Court Services. *See* Johnston, *supra* note 45.

⁵⁵   *See* JOHNSTON & CAMPBELL, *supra* note 11, at 245-55. *See also* Janet R. Johnston, *Developing Preventive Interventions for Children of Severe Family Conflict and Violence: A Comparison of Three Models* (1993) (unpublished technical report on file in the the Center for the Family in Transition, Corte Madera, Ca.); Janet R. Johnston, *Prevention of Parent or Family Abduction of Children Through Early Identification of Risk Factors* Stage II, Part B (1998) (unpublished manuscript, on file with author) (final report to the Office of Juvenile Justice & Delinquency Prevention, Department of Justice, Washington, D.C.).

⁵⁶   *See* Robert A. Zibbell, *The Mental Health Professional as Arbitrator in Post-Divorce Child-Oriented Conflict*, 33 FAM. & CONCILIATION CTS. REV. 462 (1995).

⁵⁷   *See* T. Johnston, *Summary of Research on the Decrease of Court Involvement After the Appointment of a Special Master* (1994) (unpublished manuscript, on file with author) (paper presented at the Special Masters Training Conference, Palo Alto, Cal.). *See also* M. H. Vick & R. Backerman, *Mediation/Arbitration: Surveys of Professionals & Clients* (1996) (unpublished manuscript, on file with author) (paper presented at the Boulder Interdisciplinary Committee on Child Custody, Boulder, Colo.).

⁵⁸   *See* Debra A. Clement, *A Compelling Need for Mandated Use of Supervised Visitation Programs*, 36 FAM. & CONCILIATION CTS. REV. 294, 296 (1998). *See also* Robert B. Straus & Eve Alda, *Supervised Child Access: The Evolution of a Social Service*, 32 FAM. & CONCILIATION CTS. REV. 230 (1994); Robert B. Straus et al., *Standards and Guidelines for Supervised Visitation Network Practice*, 36 FAM. & CONCILIATION CTS. REV. 108 (1998).

⁵⁹   Large scale descriptive evaluations of supervised services have been conducted in Australia, Canada, and the United States. *See* R. Abramovitch et al., *Evaluation of the Supervised Access Pilot Project* (1994) (unpublished manuscript, on file with author) (final report submitted to the Toronto, Canada, Ministry of the Attorney-General Policy Development Division). *See also* Jessica Pearson & Nancy Thoennes, *Supervised Visitation: A Portrait of Programs and Clients* (1997) (unpublished paper on file in the Center for Policy Research, 1720 Emerson St., Denver, Colo. 80218); Strategic Partners Pty. Ltd., *Contact Services in Australia: Research and Evaluation Project Year One Report* (1998) (unpublished paper on file in the Attorney-General's Department, Barton ACT 2600). Very few program evaluations are available. *See, e.g.*, Cheryl D. Lee et al., *Impact of Expedited Visitation Services: A Court Program That Enforces Access*, 33 FAM. & CONCILIATION CTS. REV. 495 (1995).

⁶⁰   Unfortunately, this may be occurring. *See* Pearson & Thoennes, *supra* note 59.

⁶¹   *See* Janet R. Johnston & Robert B. Straus, *Traumatized Children in Supervised Visitation: What Do They Need?*, 37 FAM. & CONCILIATION CTS. REV. 135, 135 (1999).

⁶²   *See* Robert S. Pynoos & Spencer Eth, *Witness to Violence: The Child Interview*, 25 J. AM. ACAD. CHILD & ADOLESCENT PSYCHIATRY 306 (1986).

⁶³   *See* VIVIENNE ROSEBY & JANET R. JOHNSTON, HIGH-CONFLICT, VIOLENT AND SEPARATING FAMILIES: A GROUP TREATMENT MANUAL FOR SCHOOL-AGE CHILDREN (1997).

⁶⁴   *See* Mary A. Duryee, *A Model for Therapeutic Supervision and a Proposal for a Family-Community Court* (1999) (unpublished manuscript, on file with author) (final report submitted to Family Court Services, County of Alameda, 1221 Oak St., Room 250, Oakland, Cal. 94612).

# F: Pro Se Litigants

# [16]

# And Justice for All – Including the Unrepresented Poor: Revisiting the Roles of Judges, Mediators and Clerks

## Russell Engler

### Introduction

UNREPRESENTED litigants are flooding the courts. In the "poor people's courts," civil cases involving at least one unrepresented litigant are far more common than cases in which both sides are represented by counsel.[1] This phenomenon is hardly surprising, given widespread reports that over eighty percent of the legal needs of the poor and working poor currently are unmet in the United States.[2] Judges, clerks, and lawyers bemoan the difficulties that unrepresented litigants cause for other participants in the legal system.[3]

An impressive variety of assistance programs, developed by bar associations, legal services offices, and the courts themselves, have sprung up in many settings in response to the "pro se crisis."[4] Individual judges and clerks worry publicly and privately about what they can and cannot do – or what they should and should not do – in handling cases involving unrepresented litigants.[5] Some lawyers and judges even express concern that unrepresented litigants are using their status to gain an unfair advantage over represented parties, who are trying to play by the rules.[6]

Missing from the discussion is a fundamental re-examination by the judiciary of the roles of judges, mediators, and clerks in cases involving unrepresented litigants. The roles of these players were developed in the context of an adversary system.[7] An underlying assumption of this system is that both sides will be represented by an attorney. The unrepresented litigant, having "chosen" to appear without a lawyer, is an aberration. Despite the vast number of unrepresented litigants, and the significant impact on the courts in which the unrepresented litigant is the norm, the roles of the players remain largely those developed for an idealized world in which all litigants are represented by lawyers.

Part I of this Article examines the traditional rules governing clerks, mediators, and judges in their interactions with unrepresented litigants. The examination reveals that the legal system has erected barriers that hinder the ability of unrepresented litigants to obtain the assistance necessary to make informed choices about their cases. The rules primarily prohibit clerks, mediators, and other court players from giving legal advice to unrepresented litigants. In theory, the prohibition is intended to protect the unrepresented litigant from receiving legal advice from someone not qualified to give such advice.[8] In practice, however, the prohibition deprives the unrepresented litigant of the opportunity to obtain legal advice throughout the course of the proceeding. She is forced to make choices at every turn without understanding either the range of options available or the pros and cons of each option.

Despite being deprived of the opportunity to make informed choices, the unrepresented litigant is deemed to be an informed, rational actor. Most cases settle, usually under pressure from the court.[9] Where the unrepresented party faces a represented one, additional settlement pressure comes from the opposing lawyer.[10] Judges routinely make, at most, a minimal inquiry before rubber-stamping the agreements and rarely undo the agreements in the face of a subsequent challenge.[11] The judges are driven by docket control, which depends on the court's ability to settle cases quickly and with minimal oversight. The need for docket control leaves judges with little incentive to expend precious judicial resources on educating and protecting unrepresented litigants. Even where cases proceed to trial, many judges are unwilling to provide more than token assistance to the unrepresented litigant.[12] Judges typically explain their reluctance to provide greater assistance as a necessary byproduct of impartiality. Some judges go further, declaring that the unrepresented litigant, having chosen to appear without counsel, must live with the consequences of her decision.[13]

These consequences are devastating for unrepresented litigants. Settlement agreements routinely involve the waiver of significant rights by unrepresented litigants.[14] Unrepresented litigants appearing before mediators suffer a similar fate, after being deemed to have made an informed choice to participate in mediation in the first place.[15] Where cases do not settle, unrepresented litigants also routinely forfeit important rights due to the absence of counsel.[16]

The forfeiture of rights flows from the barriers facing unrepresented litigants at each stage of the proceeding and each encounter with the various players in the system. As revealed in part I, the roles of the different players typically are discussed in isolation. In reality, however, the roles are inextricably intertwined. The difficulties at each stage are compounded, rather than corrected, as the case proceeds. Re-examination of the roles must therefore be part of a systemic response to the problems facing unrepresented litigants.

* * * *

## II. Revisiting the Roles of the Players in the System

Part I explored the rules and realities governing the roles of the various players in the court system in their interactions with unrepresented litigants. The discussion identified barriers that prevent various players from providing unrepresented litigants with the help they need to enable them to participate meaningfully in the legal system. This part re-examines the roles of the judges, court personnel, and other players to demonstrate how they can and should provide the necessary assistance. Because the roles must be reshaped as part of a systemic response to the problems facing unrepresented litigants, the next part begins with a discussion of underlying principles that must guide both the development of the systemic response and the reshaping of the individual roles.

## A. Revisiting the Underlying Principles

### 1. The Adversarial System

The traditional notions of who should be giving legal advice, and what it means to be impartial, were developed within the framework of the adversarial system. The adversarial system presumes that both sides will be represented by counsel, and that cases involving unrepresented litigants are the exception, rather than the rule.[166] Yet, with the dramatic increase in the numbers of unrepresented litigants, cases involving unrepresented litigants can no longer be viewed as the exception.[167] When both sides appear without counsel, the traditional configuration of the adversarial system has been altered; when one side is represented and the other is not, it has broken down.[168]

The challenge to the adversary system, however, should not lead to an abandonment of its goals. The adversarial system purports to promote fairness and justice.[169] Yet, the rules currently operate as barriers preventing unrepresented litigants from participating meaningfully in the legal system and thereby frustrate the goal of dispensing fairness and justice. Given a choice between clinging to the rules at the expense of the goal, or modifying the rules to further the goal, the rules must be modified. New rules, or new interpretations of the traditional rules, must govern scenarios that are here to stay. That the modifications may bring changes in our traditional expectations of some of the players in the system is inevitable, and should not prevent change. These changes must be designed to overcome the barriers facing unrepresented litigants and promote fairness and justice for them.

### 2. Impartiality

One important barrier is the narrow conception of impartiality that typically permeates the discussions of the various roles. The notion that a court cannot provide extensive assistance to one party without compromising its impartiality must be rejected.[170] To the contrary, a court may need to provide more help to one side than to the other to maintain the impartiality of the proceeding.[171] The absence of counsel has a dramatic effect on the outcome of the proceedings.[172] A system that routinely favors parties with lawyers over parties without, regardless of the merits of the cases, cannot be viewed as impartial.[173] As long as a court is prepared to provide extensive assistance to both parties if necessary, the court will maintain its impartiality.[174]

Cases involving a lawyer pitted against an unrepresented litigant therefore provide the greatest challenges to the impartiality of the court system.[175] Rather than refusing to provide the necessary help, the court instead may need to explain why the help is targeted to one side, and be prepared to help all parties as needed. That a given case calls for the court to provide more help to one side than the other does not merit a conclusion that the court is violating the principle of impartiality.

### 3. Voluntary Choices and Informed Consent

A second barrier is the courts' failure to measure the voluntariness of an unrepresented litigant's choices by the standards of informed consent. Unrepresented litigants routinely waive significant rights, despite having had limited, if any, opportunities for receiving independent advice. They may be acting on bad legal advice, poor explanations, or – where opposing counsel is involved – manipulation and threats. Yet, courts routinely, and swiftly, conclude that the waivers are knowing, intelligent, and voluntary.[176]

The voluntariness of an unrepresented litigant's choices must not be determined solely by whether the litigant appears to be acting by her own free will. The actions and decisions must be accepted as voluntary only if they result from informed choices. The assessment of informed choices should be analogous to the doctrine of informed consent, developed in the medical context. "True consent to what happens to one's self is the informed exercise of a choice, and that entails an opportunity to evaluate knowledgeably the options available and the risks attendant upon each."[177] The need for the rule arises from the fact that "the average patient has little or no understanding of the medical arts, and ordinarily has only his physician to whom he can look for enlightenment with which to reach an intelligent decision."[178]

Without minimizing the complexities involved in the doctrine of informed consent, or the perils of transferring doctrines from one context to another, the doctrine exposes the dangers in rubber-stamping as "knowing, intelligent and voluntary" decisions by unrepresented litigants. Just as patients have minimal knowledge of medical science, the average litigant has little or no understanding of the law. The duty to assist the litigant in making informed choices, after weighing the pros and cons of different options, rests on the lawyer.[179] Where the litigant appears unrepresented, the unrepresented litigant's decisions cannot be presumed to be informed unless someone else assumes that duty.

As in the medical context, the issue of how much information must be disclosed to ensure informed consent is an enormous one.[180] Yet, the central concept remains valid: for a decision to be informed, the litigant must have had the "opportunity to evaluate knowledgeably the options available and the risks attendant upon each."[181] The voluntariness of an unrepresented litigant's choices to settle or proceed to trial, to agree to particular terms of settlement, or to choose mediation in the first place, must be measured by the extent to which the litigant understands the risks of the alternatives, which in turn depends on the litigant's understanding of the applicable law and facts.[182] Unrepresented litigants cannot be presumed to have had the benefit of competent advice enabling them to weigh the advantages and disadvantages of the choices they are making.[183]

## 4. Legal Advice

A third barrier is the widespread use of the prohibition against giving legal advice. In redefining the roles of court personnel and those staffing assistance programs, the prohibition against the giving of legal advice by some of the actors in the system must be abandoned. The distinction between help that constitutes legal advice and help that does not provides little guidance to those on the front lines. Moreover, most assistance needed by unrepresented litigants is likely to involve what would fall within an intellectually honest definition of legal advice.[184] While guidelines should be developed for what help a particular office or program may provide in a given context, the limits should not turn on what constitutes legal advice.[185]

## 5. Voluntariness in the Choice of Appearing Without Counsel

Particularly in the "poor people's courts," a litigant's appearance without counsel must be presumed to be coerced, rather than voluntary, due to the shortage of counsel. Although some litigants who could afford counsel refrain from doing so, the notion that most litigants choose to forego legal representation is fictitious in many contexts.[186] Despite this reality, many of the rules regarding the handling of unrepresented litigants, and much of the backlash from lawyers and judges, arise in response to the behavior of notorious, overly-litigious plaintiffs.[187] Most unrepresented litigants in eviction cases and debt collection cases are defendants, as are some in family law cases.[188] Unrepresented plaintiffs in family law cases and bankruptcy cases are unlikely to be repeat players.[189] The case law that has been developed in response to actions by individual plaintiffs filing multiple proceedings is inapposite to these scenarios. The litigant who is the exception, rather than the rule, should not dictate the court's response to unrepresented litigants in general.[190]

## 6. The Importance of Context

The roles of the players are inter-connected and should be shaped by context. Yet the rules governing clerks and judges are carried over from court to court, without regard to the specific needs of a given court. Whether clerks should be encouraged and trained to provide extensive assistance should depend on whether the other players in that context are giving advice, how their roles are defined, and the needs of the unrepresented litigants in that context. Similarly, the judge's role will depend, in part, on what is happening in the clerk's office and what other assistance programs are available to the unrepresented litigants.

## B. Revisiting the Roles

### 1. The Judges

In light of the general principles outlined above, and the need to assess the individual roles from a systemic point of view, in context, it is essential to address the judge's role first. As the Illinois Court correctly observed in Oko v. Rogers,[191] "the buck stops there."[192] While the Oko court was describing the judge's role at trial, the observation applies to each aspect of the judge's role. The judge bears the "heavy responsibility" for presiding over a "fair" proceeding,[193] which includes not only what occurs at trial itself, but outcomes produced by the more common result of settlement.[194]

Because the buck stops with the judge, she must be as active as necessary to ensure that the legal system's promise of fairness and substantial justice is not frustrated by the litigant's appearance without a lawyer. Far from offending notions of impartiality, the call for judges to provide vigorous assistance to unrepresented litigants is consistent with the need for impartiality.

The judge's role at trials involving unrepresented litigants should be modeled on precedent from the small claims courts and administrative agencies. Judges should conduct trials in the manner "best suited to discover the facts and do justice in the case."[195] "In an effort to ... secure substantial justice," the court must assist the unrepresented litigant on procedure to be followed, presentation of evidence, and questions of law.[196] Further, the court may call witnesses and conduct direct or cross-examinations.[197] The court has a "basic obligation to develop a full and fair record ...."[198] Each of these duties is not only wholly consistent with the notion of impartiality,[199] but also necessary for the system to maintain its impartiality.

The need to assist the unrepresented litigant in developing a full, factual record, and to help the litigant with matters of procedure and substantive law, extends to the judge's role in settlements. Rather than pressuring the unrepresented litigant to settle the case with minimal judicial intervention, the judge must take a far more active role. The judge must help the unrepresented litigant develop the relevant facts and identify potential claims and defenses.[200] The judge must examine the papers in the case and talk to the unrepresented parties to ensure that possible claims and defenses are being articulated. Only by first assessing the merits of the case can the judge gain perspective as to what, if any, claims are being compromised or waived, whether such waivers truly are knowing, intelligent, and voluntary, and whether the judge should place the court's imprimatur on the result.[201]

The judge must identify what advice the litigant received, to correct for misinformation. Where the opposing party is represented by counsel, the judge must inquire into the substance of the negotiations with the opposing counsel, to ensure that the unrepresented litigant's decisions are not based on improper advice, manipulation, or threats.[202] As tools to aid in this inquiry, judges might ask the unrepresented litigants why they are signing the agreement and whether they think the agreement is fair. While the answers elicited may not dictate a particular result, they may assist the judge in identifying whether the decisions result from misinformation or coercion.

To the extent the judge does not oversee the negotiations and is presented with an agreement reached elsewhere, the inquiries set forth above should be undertaken by the judge prior to approving the agreement and with an eye toward rejecting agreements that do not protect the rights of the unrepresented litigant. In other cases, the judge may be involved in the negotiation that produces an agreement. Assuming the judge's involvement ensures the substantive fairness of the agreement, the judicial efforts during the negotiations would obviate the need for an extensive colloquy upon completion of the agreement.[203]

The active judicial role extends to each phase of the proceeding at which the unrepresented litigant makes decisions since the events occur under the judge's auspices. Whether a litigant decides to engage in negotiations with the opposing party, go to mediation, settle, or go to trial may be as important as the specific decisions made at trial or in settlement. These decisions, too, must be informed and knowing, and the judge must assist as necessary to ensure that they are.

Busy judges with crowded dockets, and supervising administrative judges, undoubtedly will contend that these proposals are impractical and that the court system would grind to a halt upon their implementation. Some judges, and many lawyers facing unrepresented litigants, will argue that even if it were practical for judges to take the recommended actions, doing so would compromise the impartiality of the system.[204] Where judicial intervention leads to the rejection of a proposed settlement, a further objection might be raised: that the judge is interfering with the parties' right to engage in a private contract.

Each of these objections fails to justify the continuation of limited judicial roles and the resulting harm suffered by unrepresented litigants. The concern about interference with private contract is wholly without merit. Parties are always free to engage in private contracts. If they wish, the parties could withdraw their respective claims and enter into a private contract outside the court. They do not do so because at least one party is seeking not merely a private contract, but a court order with the corresponding enforcement power. Before exercising its power, the court has not only the right, but the obligation, to ensure that the exercise of its power will further, rather than frustrate, the goal of providing justice.

The concerns about impartiality are resolved by reference to the revised understanding of the concept of impartiality.[205] As long as the court would be equally willing to help each party, as necessary, the active judicial role does not constitute partial behavior. To the contrary, the failure to accept such a role is more likely to constitute partiality, since the court's current operation, particularly where only one party appears without counsel, favors one party for reasons unrelated to the merits of the claims.

The practical concerns are the most imposing, but also the most important to overcome. In one sense, the issue may be framed as a consumer protection issue. If the courts hold out the promise of fairness and justice, but claim for practical reasons to be unable to achieve such a result, the advertising is false. It is hypocritical to claim to provide fairness to everyone through a system that is not prepared to do so for those without lawyers. An unattractive, but at least more honest solution would be to change the advertising and remove the public promise that those without lawyers will get a fair shake in court. The only acceptable solution is to overcome the practical objections.[206]

A systemic approach provides the most important clue as to how to overcome the practical problems. The judges must correct for the problems that have arisen before the cases reach them. The more that others, including court personnel, adequately assist unrepresented litigants in advance of their appearance before a judge, the easier will be the role of the judge in each case. For example, if a mediator or a judge's law clerk is involved in settlement negotiations, and intercedes as necessary to protect the interests of the unrepresented litigants, the burden on the judge will be reduced. The extent to which it is appropriate for judges in a particular context to rely on their law clerks, mediators, or other non-judicial court personnel will depend on the roles of those non-judicial actors.[207] In courts that continue to restrict the roles of court personnel, fail to provide well-funded programs offering comprehensive advice and assistance, resist the use of trained lay advocates, and refuse to appoint counsel, the judicial role will, and should be, immense. The buck stops with the judge.

## 2. The Mediators

Even without the expanded role of the judge discussed in the previous section, courts increasingly are turning to mediation in an effort to maintain docket control. The more time judges must spend with cases involving unrepresented litigants, the greater the temptation will be to utilize court-connected mediation.[208] Reports of high settlement rates and litigant satisfaction with the process will provide justification for, and added momentum to, the call for more court-connected mediation.[209] Yet, the increased use of alternative dispute resolution will cause more problems than it solves for courts in their handling of unrepresented litigants if the role of the "mediator" is not similarly revised.

As described in part I.C, the current understanding of the mediator's role, as limited by the prohibition against giving legal advice and a narrow view of impartiality, leaves unrepresented litigants vulnerable to the waiver of important rights in mediation. The danger is particularly acute where mediation involves an unrepresented litigant against a represented party. Unless safeguards are in place to ensure that the unrepresented litigant is protected during mediation, the increased use of mediation is no solution at all.

There are three general choices in response to this dilemma. One choice is to make no changes at all. Under the guise of impartiality, the court system funnels a large number of unrepresented litigants through mediation, a forum that produces systematically unfavorable results to unrepresented litigants when measured in terms of outcome.[210] Far from providing an impartial forum yielding fair results, the process routinely favors the more powerful party, particularly where one party is represented by counsel. The result is a process that is both unfair and partial.

A second choice is to maintain the current role for the mediators and leave the burden on the judges to correct resulting problems. The previous section detailed the active role the judge must play in settlement to ensure that the resulting agreement is fair and reasonable.[211] The need for such extensive judicial intervention in mediated cases is inefficient in two respects. First, one goal of court-connected mediation is to diminish the amount of judicial resources necessary. If cases "settled" by mediators nonetheless require extensive judicial resources, then the wisdom of utilizing mediation in the first place is questionable. While the judge still must provide a detailed level of oversight even where the mediator has accepted the responsibility for producing a fair agreement, the resources involved would be substantially less if the mediator has conducted the necessary inquiries during mediation. Second, if the mediators fail to consider the fairness and reasonableness of agreements, then the court presumably would need to reject an unfair agreement. At that point, the judge either must oversee additional negotiations or send the case back to mediation. The inefficient cycle continues.[212]

The third choice is to change the role of the mediator.[213] For mediation to provide a useful component for courts dealing with large numbers of unrepresented litigants, the mediators must ensure that the mediation process does not provide a forum for the represented party to gain an unfair advantage over the unrepresented party. Providing justice, rather than clearing the court's docket, must remain the primary goal of the mediation process.[214]

The mediator's role must be defined to achieve that goal. The mediator must ensure that the claims and concerns of the unrepresented party are addressed in the mediation and resulting agreements, and where one party is represented by counsel, that the agreement does not result from the advice, threats, or promises of the attorney to the unrepresented party.[215] Courts referring cases to mediators must clarify to the unrepresented litigant whether the mediation is voluntary or mandatory, and, in either case, the mediator must avoid leaving the unrepresented party with the belief that the mediation must result in an agreement.[216] The mediator must do what the previous section urged the judge to do.[217] Only in this manner can the mediator both preside over a fair and impartial process and save judicial resources.

Whether such a role is a proper or permissible one for a mediator is a matter of much dispute.[218] The role diverges from the traditional role of mediators developed in the context of mediation with represented parties.[219] Yet the traditional notions of the mediator's role fail to provide meaningful guidance for the mediator where a power imbalance exists between the parties.[220] The situation is difficult enough where the mediation involves only unrepresented litigants, and becomes most troublesome when only one party appears without counsel.[221] Mediation theory teaches that voluntariness is a cornerstone of successful mediation, both in terms of voluntary participation and voluntariness in deciding to settle on particular terms.[222] The decision to mediate cannot be truly voluntary unless consent is informed: "informed consent includes both the parties' agreement to participate in the mediation process and their acceptance of any ultimate substantive agreement."[223] The fundamental clash between the need to achieve voluntary and informed choices by disempowered and legally unsophisticated litigants without providing sufficient advice or assistance to make the choices truly informed remains a major, unresolved dilemma in the context of court-connected mediation.[224]

Something must give. One cannot cling to a classic vision of mediation while urging widespread use of mediation in settings involving unrepresented parties. Either the role of the mediator must be adapted to fit a given context, or mediation must be deemed inappropriate for certain contexts.[225] With the latter determination, the burden of adjudicating these cases may be returned to the judges, raising issues affecting judicial resources and docket control. Alternatively, someone other than a judge must be designated to facilitate settlement along the guidelines set forth above. If such a role offends the concept of "mediator," then it must be called something else. If the court is prepared to authorize existing court personnel, such as law clerks, to play the extensive and protective role in settlement, then these personnel may need to handle the cases that would have been sent to mediation. If none of the existing personnel is authorized and trained to perform the necessary role in the negotiations, then a new role must be created. Regardless of the title, the role must be performed in a manner designed to produce fair and just agreements where unrepresented litigants are involved. Otherwise, the allocation of resources is a poor one.

### 3. Court Personnel

The role of court personnel, particularly clerks, must be expanded beyond the barrier of "no legal advice."[226] Greacen's article demonstrates that the rules and practices governing clerks must be loosened for them to be able to provide effective help.[227] Another commentator goes further, urging courts to "unleash court clerks."[228] Some states have begun to recognize the need to expand the role of clerks as part of their efforts to assist unrepresented litigants.[229]

Greacen recommends that court staff keep in mind the following five principles when providing advice and information to court users:

1. Court staff have an obligation to explain court processes and procedures to litigants, the media, and other interested citizens...

2. Court staff have an obligation to inform litigants, and potential litigants, how to bring their problems before the court for resolution...

3. Court staff cannot advise litigants whether to bring their problems before the court, or what remedies to seek...

4. Court staff must always remember the absolute duty of impartiality. They must never give advice or information for the purpose of giving one party an advantage over another. They must never give advice or information to one party that they would not give to an opponent...

5. Court staff should be mindful of the basic principle that counsel may not communicate with the judge ex parte. Court staff should not let themselves be used to circumvent that principle, or fail to respect it, in acting on matters delegated to them for decision.[230]

The Greacen principles are an excellent start. The first two, which require the clerk to provide information about the processes and procedures are important guidelines; the fifth, which cautions against facilitating ex parte communications is an important safeguard as well. The fourth principle, regarding impartiality, may need to be modified to conform to the revised notion of impartiality discussed above.[231] As the first and third sentences of the fourth principle urge, court staff must indeed remain impartial and must not give information or advice to one party that they would not give to an opponent. To the extent the purpose of the second sentence of the fourth principle simply is to prohibit clerks from choosing sides and trying to help one side gain an advantage when the clerks would not provide equivalent help to the other side,[232] the sentence is redundant: the prohibition against favoring one side is included in the last sentence. The sentence may be eliminated or replaced with: "They must never favor one party over another." The sentence must not be read to prohibit clerks from providing any such assistance that might be viewed as giving one party an advantage over another. In an adversarial system, it is inevitable that much, if not all, information that helps one side could be viewed as giving one party an advantage over another. As long as the last sentence remains, and the clerks are as willing to help one side as the other, concerns about impartiality are overcome.

The third principle, prohibiting court staff from advising litigants whether to bring their problems before the court, or what remedies to seek, is troubling and ill-advised as a rule of universal application. Unrepresented litigants must have access to competent advice to help them decide whether they should bring their problems before the court, and, if so, what remedies they should seek. Without an examination of a particular context, it is not clear in the abstract who will best be situated to provide the necessary advice. In some settings, court clinics, lay advocates, and "lawyers-for-the-day" may relieve the clerks from the need to provide the assistance. If the help is non- existent or inadequate, the clerks must be trained and permitted to provide the needed assistance. Otherwise, the litigant either is deprived of the needed assistance, or the judge is required to provide it.[233]

The details of how much assistance clerks should provide must be tailored to particular courts. In some courts, compliance with procedural rules may be a major hurdle facing unrepresented litigants. In other courts, discovering and understanding possible claims and defenses may be critical. Litigants may need help completing forms, articulating their stories, or correlating their stories to cognizable claims. They may need guidance as to the importance of witnesses or documents. Nothing in the description of a clerk's job should bar this type of assistance unless a given court has provided someone else to do so.

Providing such a broad license to clerks and other court personnel may be ill-advised. The role of the clerk may feel uncomfortably close to the role of the lawyer. Clerks may not be equipped to provide the necessary advice and may give bad advice. The courts may increasingly be faced with litigants having relied to their detriment on poor advice from clerks, or on a misunderstanding of a clerk's accurate statements.

As troubling as these issues are, they do not call for blanket rules discouraging or barring clerks from providing assistance. Adding a guideline that clerks must not act as a lawyer for the unrepresented party provides little guidance for the clerks. A similar "rule" appears in the cases discussing the judge's role in interacting with unrepresented parties;[234] judges remain without appropriate guidance as to their role in such cases.[235] The provision of limited assistance by lawyers serves as a reminder that settling on a universal understanding of "the lawyer's role" is an impossible task;[236] defining the clerk's role by contrasting it to the lawyer's role is equally impossible. As with the barrier of "no legal advice," a guideline of not acting in a manner that a lawyer for the litigant might act would prove to be both unworkable and harmful to unrepresented litigants. Much of the help that lawyers often provide is precisely the help that unrepresented litigants need.

With respect to the problem of clerks not being capable of providing accurate advice, one solution is to provide sufficient numbers of appropriately trained lawyers, law students, or lay advocates to provide the needed assistance. In those contexts, limiting the clerk's role is not only acceptable, but may be advisable. Where limited assistance programs are inadequate to meet the demand, court personnel must provide the needed assistance. Training of the clerks and oversight of the advice they give is imperative. The solution to bad advice-giving should be to improve the quality of the advice, rather than eliminate the advice-giving.[237]

Where an unrepresented litigant relies on erroneous advice to her detriment, or misunderstands accurate statements by a clerk, judges should consider the reliance in determining whether to grant relief. A number of courts have found "good cause" to exist within the meaning of Federal Rule of Civil Procedure 4(j) when the failure to effect service was attributable to the advice or actions of someone in the clerk's office.[238] If an unrepresented litigant defaults based on erroneous advice from a clerk, the misunderstanding might rise to the level of excusable default, providing part of the basis for vacatur of the default.[239] Similarly, if an unrepresented litigant waives important rights in settlement due to misinformation or misunderstanding, from a clerk or otherwise, the misunderstanding might lead the court to vacate the agreement, particularly where the failure to do so would constitute a miscarriage of justice.[240]

This scenario is less troubling than it seems. As discussed in the previous section, a critical role for the judge is to identify the advice and information on which the unrepresented litigant is relying. This precaution would not only reveal any reliance on erroneous advice from clerks, but from others as well, including family friends and opposing counsel. If the judge is conducting an appropriate inquiry, before the court accepts the unrepresented litigant's choices, many of the problems can be uncovered before they cause harm. Where the problems do not arise until after the litigant has acted, such as in a situation of default, the improper advice can and should provide a basis for relief.

This discussion illustrates the inevitable connection between the role of the clerks or other court personnel and the role of the judge. The less help the nonjudicial court personnel provide, either because they refuse to do so, are prohibited from doing so, or are providing incorrect "help," the greater the burden on the judge, either in providing the help in the first place, or undoing the effects of incorrect advice. The more that clerks provide extensive, competent assistance, the less the burden on the judge.

* * * *

Part III examines particular courts involving large numbers of unrepresented litigants. The factors identified in part II.C provide the framework for analyzing the features of the different settings. The analysis reveals the need for revised roles of the judges, mediators, and clerks, the need for guidelines defining the revised roles, the need for increased assistance to the unrepresented poor, and the need to tailor changes to fit the varying contexts.

### III. Help for Unrepresented Litigants - Examples fromContext

*A. Family Court*

The numbers of unrepresented litigants in family law cases have surged nationwide, with some reports indicating that eighty percent or more of family law cases involve at least one pro se litigant.[263] The factors identified in part II.C suggest the need for a range of mechanisms for assisting unrepresented litigants. The high percentage of unrepresented litigants, combined with the huge volume of the court's cases, compels the need for a sweeping institutional response rather than an ad hoc reaction to isolated litigants; the more the numbers suggest that attorneys are becoming the exception rather than the rule, the greater the need to operate the court in a manner that reflects that reality. Early reports identified the relative lack of complexity of family law as a factor explaining the increase in numbers of unrepresented litigants;[264] where cases lack legal and factual complexity, increased information and technical assistance may be a sufficient response. At the same time, depending on factors such as the type of family law case, the assets involved, or the extent of conflict between the parties, cases may become quite complex, suggesting that assistance programs will need to have the capacity to go beyond increased information and technical assistance.[265]

The remaining factors suggest that unrepresented family law litigants often may not only need assistance, but also protection. While in many cases both sides appear without counsel, at least a third, and often more, of the cases pit an unrepresented party against a lawyer.[266] Since unrepresented litigants typically are poorer than represented ones and unrepresented litigants disproportionately are women, unrepresented women may therefore be facing their batterers in the proceeding and may be dealing with tactics such as "custody blackmail."[267] While some family law proceedings are amicable, others are quite adversarial: "matrimonial matters ... 'are unequaled in stress and emotion,'"[268] and family law lawyers have a reputation for resorting to "unfair and unscrupulous practices" in divorce litigation.[269]

The surging numbers of unrepresented litigants have caused judges and lawyers to identify pro se litigation as a major problem affecting courts that handle family law cases. The family law context has received widespread attention in bar committee reports[270] and articles[271] in an effort to respond to the problem. The proposals include: (1) a simplification of procedures, combined with utilization of court forms; (2) an increase in educational and explanatory materials, often involving self-service centers with information kiosks; (3) increased "technical" or "procedural" assistance, with some capacity to provide substantive assistance; (4) and an increase in the pool of pro bono lawyers to take cases for free or at a reduced rate.[272]

Despite their impressive breadth, the proposals fail to discuss systemically the proper roles of the key actors in the system. For example, the reports routinely discuss the important rights that unrepresented litigants forfeit during the course of their cases due to their lack of representation.[273] Yet these discussions do not arise as concerns about the impartiality of the system and the need to revise the roles of the players accordingly. Instead, impartiality is cited as a limitation on the extent to which judges can assist unrepresented litigants: providing too much help is seen as compromising the judge's position.[274] Moreover, where the judges' role is discussed, the need to ensure a fair settlement is ignored, despite the fact that most family law cases settle, with minimal judicial oversight.[275] The focus of the reports remains on the few cases that do not settle and the judges' burden in dealing with unrepresented litigants.[276]

Similar gaps appear in the discussions of clerks and mediators. Unrepresented litigants are viewed as problems, unduly burdening the clerks.[277] The reports note the difficulties in providing help without running afoul of the prohibition against giving legal advice, but do not call for the abolition of such a prohibition.[278] The discussions about mediation focus primarily on whether mediation is appropriate at all where issues of domestic violence are involved.[279] The proposals fail to confront the harm caused to unrepresented litigants in mediation conducted by a mediator who is not responsible for the substantive terms of the mediated agreements and who is barred from providing help if that help constitutes legal advice.

The support for assistance programs is increasingly accompanied by a backlash against unrepresented litigants in the form of fear that, far from being disadvantaged, unrepresented litigants use their status to gain advantage in the proceedings.[280] The backlash includes a disturbing trend calling for the adoption of rules designed to curb "pro se abuses."[281] Nowhere do the proposals talk about the need to curb attorney misconduct in cases pitting a lawyer against an unrepresented party.[282]

By failing to resolve the underlying tensions created by the application of the traditional rules to a context with a high volume of unrepresented litigants, the reports and proposals miss a crucial component of efforts to assist unrepresented litigants. Some unrepresented litigants with amicable family law cases involving less complicated legal issues, little power imbalance between the parties, and an unrepresented party on the other side may find sufficient assistance from the typical proposals. With complicated or adversarial cases involving significant power imbalances, particularly those pitting unrepresented litigants against represented ones, the limited assistance models alone are insufficient.[283]

* * * *

## Conclusion

In one sense, the "pro se problem" has been vastly understated. The flood of unrepresented litigants poses not simply a serious problem, but a fundamental challenge to many basic assumptions of our adversary system. The roles of judges, mediators, and clerks are defined in the context of an adversary system that generally assumes that both sides have lawyers. The reality of civil litigation not only in the "poor people's courts," but also in growing numbers of other courts, compels revision of our underlying assumptions.

Until and unless the courts make fundamental changes in their handling of unrepresented litigants, these litigants will continue to forfeit important legal rights due to their lack of representation. Improved information for unrepresented litigants, increased access to competent advice and assistance, and procedural reform to make the courts more accessible are important steps in helping unrepresented litigants. Yet, the effectiveness of changes such as these will be limited, if not undercut, as long as the traditional roles of the judges, clerks, and mediators remain unchanged.

As long as the rules reflect the traditional notion of impartiality, with actors limited by the traditional prohibition against giving legal advice, the actors will be unable to provide the necessary help. As long as the rules and practice further reflect a need to resolve cases, without concern for their outcomes, docket control will continue to reign supreme over fairness in courts handling cases involving the unrepresented poor. The assistance will have failed to provide the needed help.

The "pro se problem," however, is not only understated, but also misnamed. The courage to make changes necessary to help unrepresented litigants may require us to view the problem not as a pro se problem, but as a judge problem and an attorney problem. The rules of the game were crafted by judges and lawyers. Litigants not only have the right to appear without lawyers, but, in tremendous numbers of cases every day across the country, are forced to appear in court without counsel through no choice of their own. The lawyers and judges who establish the rules of the game have no right to make it impossible or difficult for unrepresented litigants to handle their own cases without forfeiting important rights for reasons unrelated to the merits of the cases.

Courts responding to the surge of unrepresented litigants likely will consider adding judges, mediators, clerks, and other court personnel as a partial response to the problem. Whether the addition of court personnel is a wise response will depend entirely on the roles of the added personnel. If the new judges will process cases without intervening in settlement and at trial as necessary to protect the unrepresented litigants, then the use of resources is a poor one. If the new mediators are not required to protect the interests of the unrepresented parties, and the clerks are limited in the help they can provide, then the decisions to add mediators or clerks are poor ones. The resources squandered on new judges, mediators, and clerks should be redirected to the provision of skilled lay advocates and lawyers, starting with cases pitting unrepresented parties against represented ones. The re-examination of the roles of the key personnel is therefore intertwined with decisions about how to allocate scarce resources in the court system.

The changes urged in this Article will not be easy to implement, will not occur without conflict, and will not occur without affecting judges, lawyers, mediators, and clerks in their daily operations. Yet, the way in which courts currently handle their caseload harms the unrepresented poor. If the courts can do no better, they should say so. If reality dictates that the true goals of the legal system, as we head to the twenty-first century, are "Justice and Fairness to the Extent Permitted by Docket Control" or "Justice and Fairness for Those with Lawyers," we should say so. But, if Justice and Fairness are goals which the unrepresented poor are equally entitled to attain, it is time to face reality and start making changes.

*Russell Engler, J.D., is Professor of Law and Director of Clinical Programs at the New England School of Law.*

## Notes

¹ See Jona Goldschmidt et al., Meeting the Challenge of Pro Se Litigation: A Report and Guidebook for Judges and Court Managers 49 (1998) [hereinafter Meeting the Challenge] ("Court managers believe that the volume of cases involving self-represented litigants has increased substantially in recent years."); infra Part III.

² See, e.g., William P. Quigley, The Unmet Civil Legal Needs of the Poor in Louisiana, 19 S.U. L. Rev. 273, 273 (1992) ("Between 85% and 92% of the low income people in Louisiana who had civil legal needs in 1991 were not represented by an attorney."); Janet Reno, Address Delivered at the Celebration of the Seventy-Fifth Anniversary of Women at Fordham Law School, 63 Fordham L. Rev. 5, 8 (1994) ("Ladies and gentlemen, at least eighty percent of the poor and the working poor in the United States do not have access to legal services." (citing Talbot D'Alemberte, Racial Injustice and American Justice, A.B.A. J., Aug. 1992, at 58, 59)). See generally Roy W. Reese & Carolyn A. Eldred, Legal Needs Among Low-Income and Moderate-Income Households: Summary of Findings from the Comprehensive Legal Needs Study 42 (1994) (finding that 71f low income people who face legal problems do not have access to the legal and judicial system).

³ See infra Parts I.A, I.D, II.B.1, II.B.3. See generally Meeting the Challenge, supra note 1, passim (discussing how self representation has increased greatly in recent years); Jona Goldschmidt, How Are Judges and Courts Coping with Pro Se Litigants?: Results from a Survey of Judges and Court Managers passim (May 1997) (unpublished manuscript, on file with the author) (considering the policy issues raised by the increase in pro se litigants).

⁴ See infra Part I.B.

⁵ See infra Parts I.A, I.D.

⁶ See infra notes 132, 134 and accompanying text.

⁷ See infra Part II.A.1.

⁸ See infra Part I.A.

⁹ See infra note 160 and accompanying text.

¹⁰ See infra Part I.B.3.

¹¹ See infra note 158 and accompanying text.

¹² See infra Part I.D.

¹³ See infra note 134 and accompanying text.

¹⁴ See infra notes 151-57 and accompanying text.

¹⁵ See infra Part I.C. As described in part I.C, court-connected mediation is mandatory in some settings. In most settings, the court-connected mediation is labeled voluntary. To many unrepresented litigants, however, pressure from the court to mediate makes the mediation feel mandatory.

¹⁶ See infra Part I.D.

¹⁶⁶ See, e.g., Model Code of Professional Responsibility EC 7-18 (1982) (stating that lawyers should not undertake to give advice to a person who is attempting to represent himself except to advise him to obtain a lawyer). The ethical rules give little direct attention to cases involving unrepresented litigants. In the Model Rules, only Rule 4.3 speaks directly to a lawyer's dealings with an unrepresented party. See Model Rules of Professional Conduct Rule 4.3 (1998). In the Model Code, only a single subsection of one disciplinary rule focuses on this scenario. See Model Code of Professional Responsibility DR 7-104(A)(2) (1982).

¹⁶⁷ In many contexts, particularly the "poor people's courts" that handle civil cases, it is the case involving two represented parties that is more likely to be the exception. See infra Part III.

¹⁶⁸ See, e.g., Sales, et al., supra note 53, at 559-60 ("Self-representation may place the litigant at a disadvantage when facing the expertise and skills of an attorney."); McLaughlin, supra note 115, at 1124 ("The effective operation of the adversary system relies on the assumption that the parties to a lawsuit

are approximately equal in their legal representation. This rough balance, however, is entirely upset when one side appears pro se." (footnotes omitted)).

[169] Embedded in the ethical rules governing lawyers and judges is the underlying goal of providing fairness and justice. See, e.g., Model Code of Judicial Conduct pmbl., at 3 (1990) ("Our legal system is based on the principle that an independent, fair and competent judiciary will interpret and apply the laws that govern us." (emphasis added)); Model Code of Professional Responsibility EC 7-19 to -39 (1982) (grouped under the title "Duty of the Lawyer to the Adversary System of Justice" (emphasis added)); id. EC 7-23 ("A tribunal that is fully informed on the applicable law is better able to make a fair and accurate determination ...." (emphasis added)); id. EC 7-24 ("In order to bring about just and informed decisions ...." (emphasis added)); id. EC 7-39 ("[P]roper functioning of the adversary system depends upon cooperation between lawyers and tribunals in utilizing procedures which will ... make their decisional processes prompt and just ...." (emphasis added)); Model Rules of Professional Conduct Rule 3.6 cmt. 1 (1984) ("It is difficult to strike a balance between protecting the right to a fair trial...." (emphasis added)); id. Rule 3.3 cmt. 15 ("The object of an ex parte proceeding is nevertheless to yield a substantially just result."). The Preamble to the ABA Canons of Professional Ethics, which preceded the Model Code of Professional Responsibility, similarly referred to "the system for establishing and dispensing Justice." Canons of Professional Ethics pmbl. (1908).

[170] For the purposes of this discussion, the word "court" applies not only to the judge but to the overall court system, including any of the individual actors in that system who must maintain impartiality.

[171] See, e.g., Ellen E. Sward, Values, Ideology, and the Evolution of the Adversary System, 64 Ind. L.J. 301, 321 n.96 (1989) ("A judge can be impartial but very active in developing the case .... Impartiality is a requirement for fair adjudication, but judicial passivity is not.").

[172] See infra Part III.

[173] Cf. Sherrilyn A. Ifill, Judging the Judges: Racial Diversity, Impartiality and Representation on State Trial Courts, 39 B.C. L. Rev. 95, 98-99 (1997) (distinguishing between structural and individual impartiality in arguing "that the Fourteenth Amendment's judicial impartiality mandate is violated by the persistent presence of an all-white bench in jurisdictions with significant minority populations" (footnote omitted)).

[174] See, e.g., Black's Law Dictionary 752 (6th ed. 1990) (listing, as the first three definitions of "impartial": "Favoring neither; disinterested; treating all alike ...."). This is not to minimize the problems created in terms of the appearance of impartiality where the court provides more help to one side than the other. Nor does it minimize the dangers that an arbiter might be moved by a "sympathetic identification" with a party that the arbiter begins to assist. See Lon L. Fuller & John D. Randall, Professional Responsibility: Report of the Joint Conference, 44 A.B.A. J. 1159, 1160-61 (1958). Given the difficulties facing unrepresented litigants in the courts, a failure to assist unrepresented litigants is a greater threat to the impartiality of the court system than the dangers flowing from the provision of assistance.

[175] See, e.g., Boston Bar Ass'n, BBA Task Force on Unrepresented Litigants Report 26 (1998) [hereinafter BBA Report] ("[T]he judges ... worry over potential unfairness to both sides in a case where one of the litigants is unrepresented."); Meeting the Challenge, supra note 1, at 52-53 (stating that judges found it difficult to maintain their impartiality where one litigant was unrepresented); Goldschmidt, supra note 3, at 13-14 ("Some judges indicate they [sic] under some agonizing moments during the course of trials where one party is represented and one is pro se .... Some of the judges' comments concerned problems arising from attorneys' actions in these situation [sic] of one party appearing pro se.").

[176] As noted, courts expect most cases to settle, provide minimal supervision to the settlement, and rarely overturn the settlement agreement. See supra notes 158-62 and accompanying text. The agreements routinely involve the waiver of significant rights by the unrepresented litigants. See id. Some commentators therefore prefer the concept of "informed waiver" to that of "informed consent."

See, e.g., Nina W. Tarr, Clients' and Students' Stories: Avoiding Exploitation and Complying with the Law to Produce Scholarship with Integrity, 5 Clinical L. Rev. 271, 298-99 (1998).

[177]  Canterbury v. Spence, 464 F.2d 772, 780 (D.C. Cir. 1972) (footnote omitted). Other formulations of the doctrine, developed in the medical context, consistently include the elements of evaluating options based on an understanding of the risks and alternatives. See, e.g., Harnish v. Children's Hosp. Med. Ctr., 439 N.E.2d 240, 242 (Mass. 1982) ("Knowing exercise of this right requires knowledge of the available options and the risks attendant on each."); Wilkinson v. Vesey, 295 A.2d 676, 685 (R.I. 1972) (describing the informed consent doctrine as standing for the proposition that "a patient's consent to a proposed course of treatment was valid only to the extent he had been informed by the physician as to what was to be done, the risk involved and the alternatives to the contemplated treatment"). For a listing of many of the landmark cases discussing informed consent, see Harnish, 439 N.E.2d at 242 n.3, 243 n.4.

[178]  Canterbury, 464 F.2d at 780 (footnote omitted).

[179]  See supra note 45 and accompanying text.

[180]  For example, the cases split over the issue of whether disclosure should be measured from the patient's point of view, see Harnish, 439 N.E.2d at 242 n.3, or in light of the standards of the medical profession, measured by the information as is customarily disclosed by physicians in similar circumstances. See id. at 243 n.4. Even when measured by the custom of the profession, the concept of putting the patient in a position to make informed choices about alternatives remains central. See, e.g., Woolley v. Henderson, 418 A.2d 1123, 1128 (Me. 1980) (explaining the general principles behind the doctrine of informed consent).

[181]  Canterbury, 464 F.2d at 780 (footnote omitted). Black's Law Dictionary defines "informed consent" as: "A person's agreement to allow something to happen ... that is based on a full disclosure of facts needed to make the decision intelligently; i.e., knowledge of risks involved, alternatives, etc." Black's Law Dictionary 779 (6th ed. 1990) (describing the concept of informed consent as the necessary disclosures so that a patient "faced with a choice of undergoing the proposed treatment, or alternative treatment, or none at all, may intelligently exercise his judgment by reasonably balancing the probable risks against the probable benefits").

[182]  The doctrine of "informed consent" already appears in the mediation literature both as a standard for measuring a litigant's decision to mediate and as a standard for measuring a decision to accept an agreement. See, e.g., Mass. Unif. R. on Dispute Resolution 9(c) (describing rules for informed consent to ADR), reprinted in 26 Mass. Law. Wkly. 2129, 2131 (1998); Henikoff & Moffitt, supra note 95, at 103 (noting that "[i]nformed consent includes both the parties' agreement to participate in the mediation process and their acceptance of any ultimate substantive agreement"); Kurtzberg & Henikoff, supra note 95, at 86-87 (describing different views of the role of informed consent in the mediation process); see also infra Part II.B.2 (describing the mediator's role). For a discussion of the concept of "informed consent" in the context of the lawyer-client relationship, see Mark Spiegel, Lawyering and Client Decisionmaking: Informed Consent and the Legal Profession, 128 U. Pa. L. Rev. 41 (1979). For recent examples of efforts to impart concepts and practices from the medical world to the legal world, see Gay Gellhorn, Law and Language: An Empirically-Based Model for the Opening Moments of Client Interviews, 4 Clinical L. Rev. 321 (1998); and Linda F. Smith, Medical Paradigms for Counseling: Giving Clients Bad News, 4 Clinical L. Rev. 391 (1998).

[183]  Rather than assuming that the unrepresented litigant has had access to help, the unrepresented litigant must be viewed at best as having received no legal advice at all. In reality, the unrepresented litigant has probably received some combination of information and misinformation, that may or may not be accurate or helpful, and that the litigant may or may not have understood. Particularly in the "poor people's courts," the litigant's appearance without counsel cannot be viewed as one of choice, but one forced on the litigant by necessity. See infra Part II.A.5.

[184]  See supra Part I.A.

[185] This point necessarily follows from the need for a broad definition of what constitutes legal advice. Moreover, it is consistent with the view that far more interactions between lawyers and unrepresented adversaries involve impermissible advice-giving than generally is recognized. See generally Engler, supra note 43, passim (examining the issues surrounding lawyers' interactions with lay adversaries). That more actors should provide more help does not imply that opposing lawyers should be unleashed on their unrepresented adversaries. The increased assistance from the court and advocates and relaxation of the prohibition against giving legal advice in that context should be combined with enforcing the limitations on the interactions with opposing counsel. The lawyer has a vested interest in influencing the unrepresented party to adopt a course of action serving the goals not of the unrepresented party, but of her client.

[186] See BBA Report, supra note 175, at 20 ("Most of the unrepresented litigants [in the Boston Housing Court] reported that they wanted an attorney but felt they could not afford one."); infra Part III.

[187] See supra notes 127-29 and accompanying text; see also Meeting the Challenge, supra note 1, at 60 (noting that pro se litigants who pursue a political agenda in court are seen as pests by judges); Robert M. Daniszewski, Coping with the Pro Se Litigant, N.H. B.J., March 1995, at 46 (discussing the trend toward pro se litigation); Paul B. Zuydhoek, Litigation Against a Pro Se Plaintiff, Litigation, Summer 1989, at 13 (discussing the difficulties of litigating against pro se plaintiffs).

[188] See infra Part III.

[189] For a description of courts handling family law and bankruptcy cases involving unrepresented litigants, see infra part III.A-B.

[190] Litigants exercising the right to self-representation should not face a bias favoring represented parties. The right to self-representation is well established. See, e.g., Faretta v. California, 422 U.S. 806, 816-32 (1975) (discussing a litigant's right to self-representation). Many observers nonetheless perceive a pattern of bias against the unrepresented litigant. See, e.g., Mosten, supra note 48, at 435 (commenting on negative perceptions of the pro se litigant); Elias, supra note 47, passim (discussing the bias in the court system against unrepresented litigants and proposing solutions).

[191] 466 N.E.2d 658 (Ill. App. Ct. 1984).

[192] Id. at 661.[FN193]. See id.

[194] Indeed, the same holds true for defaults as well. Judicial duties are not limited to ministerial acts. Compare, e.g., Fed. R. Civ. P. 55(b)(1) (discussing when a default judgment may be entered by the clerk), with Fed. R. Civ. P. 55(b)(2) (discussing when a default judgement must be entered by the clerk). Where a party fails to appear, the court still must take appropriate steps to ensure that the appearing party is entitled to any relief it is seeking against the defaulting party. The high incidence of default among debtors in debt collection cases, for example, is a poignant reminder of the need for judicial oversight even where litigants default. See, e.g., Caplovitz, supra note 158, at 221 (finding default judgement rate of three city cross-section at over ninety percent).

[195] Mass. Unif. Sm. Cl. R. 7(c).

[196] Fla. Ct. Sm. Cl. R. 7.140(e).

[197] See Ill. Sup. Ct. R. 286(b).

198 Lashley v. Secretary of Health and Human Servs., 708 F.2d 1048, 1051 (6th Cir. 1983) (quoting McConnell v. Schweiker, 655 F.2d 604, 606 (5th Cir. 1981)).

[199] See supra notes 147-50 and accompanying text.

[200] Where the opposing party is represented by counsel, the judicial inquiry could be aided by imposing a duty on the opposing counsel to "inform the tribunal of all material facts known to the lawyer which will enable the tribunal to make an informed decision, whether or not the facts are adverse [[[[,]" a requirement currently imposed by the Model Rules in ex parte proceedings. Model Rules of Professional Conduct Rule 3.3(d) (1998). Such a duty may be imposed by ethical rule or court rule. See

generally Engler, supra note 43, at 139-40, 143 (discussing the need for courts to enact rules regulating unrepresented adversaries).

[201]  See supra Part II.A.3-5.

[202]  Judicial oversight, including inquiries into the substance of the negotiations between lawyers and unrepresented parties, is one of the most important steps for the legal system to take in its effort to curb attorney misconduct in such negotiations and to protect unrepresented litigants from the misconduct. See Engler, supra note 43, at 142-47.

[203]  For a discussion of ethical issues raised by the participation of trial judges in the settlement process, see Goldschmidt & Milord, supra note 151, at 9-18. Note, however, that the discussion does not focus on cases involving unrepresented litigants or courts with a large number of unrepresented litigants.

[204]  See, e.g., Changing the Culture, supra note 58, at 27 (reporting that lawyers find it unfair when judges assisted an unrepresented opponent); Meeting the Challenge, supra note 1, at 29 ("The data collected in this study show that the most serious concern of trial judges is their perceived inability to assist a pro se litigant due to their duty to maintain impartiality."); Daniszewski, supra note 187, at 48 ("When the court deviates from its neutral course to lend assistance to otherwise overmatched pre se litigants the adversarial system itself can suffer."); Sales et al., supra note 53, at 558 ("Courts cannot be expected to assume the awkward position, not to mention the imposition, of serving as both adjudicator and counsel for the pro se litigant.").

[205]  See supra Part II.A.2.

[206]  In one survey, "[s]everal judges pointed to the need for rules permitting judges to actively assist self-represented litigants." Meeting the Challenge, supra note 1, at 59.

[207]  For a description of one judge's extensive use of law clerks as part of a "Pro Se Assistance Program" see Halberstadter, supra note 54.

[208]  As stated previously, for purposes of this Article, I am using the term "mediation" broadly enough to include all forms of court-connected ADR. See supra note 92.

[209]  See, e.g., John C. Cratsley, Mediation: A Device That Is "Here To Stay", 26 Mass. Law. Wkly. 2055, 2077 (1998) (reporting results of key findings of ADR Studies, including findings that "ADR produces high user satisfaction" and in "high settlement rates"). "When users of District Court programs --usually pro se litigants--are asked about the fairness of the mediation process, their satisfaction is overwhelming." Id. at 2055. These findings mainly relate to small claims cases, which may or may not apply to other contexts. Moreover, the perception of fairness is only one measure of fairness. See, e.g., Cecilia Albin, The Role of Fairness in Negotiation, 9 Negotiation J. 223 passim (1993) (analyzing four classes of fairness issues affecting negotiators); Bohmer & Ray, supra note 97, at 39 (same). If the unrepresented poor, routinely and without their informed consent, are waiving significant rights in court-connected mediation, high settlement rates and high litigant satisfaction should not compel a conclusion that the procedures are appropriate or fair.

[210]  See supra Part I.C.

[211]  See supra Part II.B.1.

[212]  This efficiency is illustrated by Wright v. Brockett, 571 N.Y.S.2d 660 (Sup. Ct. 1991). The Wright court declined to enforce a court mediated agreement because it was not "a provident decision by the [[[unrepresented] tenant, free of coercion ...." Id. at 665. For a discussion of the Wright decision, see Nolan-Haley, supra note 92, at 87-88.

Moreover, to ensure that litigants are making informed choices to mediate, mediators should be advising all litigants that it is not their job to ensure that agreements are fair, and that they cannot provide assistance at all. Otherwise, the unrepresented litigant might be choosing mediation based on a misunderstanding of the mediation process.

²¹³ As discussed above, the term mediation as used here is intended to cover all forms of court-connected ADR in which the unrepresented poor participate. See supra note 92. The focus must become the role played by the person conducting the settlement session, not the person's title.

²¹⁴ See, e.g., Harry T. Edwards, Alternative Dispute Resolution: Panacea or Anathema?, 99 Harv. L. Rev. 668, 671-72 (1986) (expressing concern that ADR may "result in an abandonment of our constitutional system in which the 'rule of law' is created and principally enforced by ... government"); Fischer et al., supra note 93, at 2156 ("[O]ne can infer that a primary motivation in sending [domestic disputes] ... to mediation is that it helps clear court dockets of troublesome cases ...."); Fiss, supra note 92, at 1075 (arguing that ADR "should be treated instead as a highly problematic technique for streamlining dockets"); Menkel-Meadow, supra note 92, at 13 ("As ADR becomes institutionalized within the court system, one can ask ... what are the implications for justice?").

²¹⁵ Cf. Stark, supra note 95, at 794 ("[M]ediators who undertake case evaluation ought to be obliged to provide the parties sufficient information about the law and its application to their case to enable them to make reasonably informed decisions." (citation omitted)).

²¹⁶ See id. at 794-95.

[I]ncluded within this duty [to inform] should be a responsibility to provide information fairly, objectively, and in good faith, without regard for its effect on the prospects for settlement .... Helping parties resolve their disputes and assisting in unclogging crowded court dockets are positive goals. But I am unaware of any mediator ethics code that considers them ethical goals.

Id. (citation omitted) (emphasis in original).

²¹⁷ Mediators might be assisted in this immense undertaking by development of a checklist tailored to a particular context. The checklist might include important introductory statements to clarify the role of the mediator and the mediation process. The checklist might also include inquiries to elicit information related to claims that typically arise in the context; to provide the unrepresented party with an opportunity to raise concerns other than those related to the typical claims; and to uncover improper advice, pressure, or misperceptions that might hinder the unrepresented litigants from giving informed consent or that might result in an unfair agreement.

²¹⁸ Scholars even debate whether it is proper for mediators to engage in evaluative mediation. See, e.g., Moberly, supra note 95, at 670-75 (discussing differing approaches to mediator evaluation).

²¹⁹ See supra Part II.A.1. To the extent that the impartiality requirement bars such a role, the revised notion of "impartiality" should overcome those objections for the same reason it did with the role of the judges. See supra Part II.A.2. For a suggestion that impartiality may not be essential for effective mediation, see Saadia Touval, Multilateral Negotiation: An Analytic Approach, 5 Negotiation J. 159, 167-69 (1989) (describing the effectiveness of Britain as a mediator in the dispute between China and France over Indochina at the 1954 Geneva Conference, despite the fact that Britain was not an impartial third party, but instead possessed leverage over the parties to perform an effective mediation). An exploration of that concept is beyond the scope of this Article, and unnecessary, since the revised notion of impartiality discussed in this Article should permit the mediator to maintain impartiality and protect unrepresented litigants.

²²⁰ See, e.g., Henikoff & Moffitt, supra note 95, at 89 ("For most mediators, however, questions of when and how to inform ignorant parties of the law present an unusually difficult dilemma."); Gary LaFree & Christine Rack, The Effects of Participants' Ethnicity and Gender on Monetary Outcomes in Mediated and Adjudicated Civil Cases, 30 L. & Soc'y Rev. 767, 794 (1996) ( "In the name of neutrality, mediators may fail to deal with power imbalances in negotiations.").

²²¹ See Stark, supra note 95, at 792 ("What should be done about the dangers of materially incomplete, misleading, and manipulative advice by evaluative mediators? The dangers are clearly most pronounced in cases ... in which the parties are pro se."); see also Florida Mediator Qualifications Advisory Panel, MQAP 96-003 (1997) (stating that mediators should take additional steps to ensure

fairness to unrepresented parties); Nolan-Haley, supra note 92, at 92-99 (discussing mediator's role with unrepresented parties in court).

[222] See, e.g., John D. Feerick et al., American Arbitration Assoc. et al., Model Standards of Conduct for Mediators Standard I (n.d.) ("Self-determination is the fundamental principle of mediation. It requires that the mediation process rely upon the ability of the parties to reach a voluntary, uncoerced agreement. Any party may withdraw from mediation at any time."), available in <http://www.adr.org/standard.html>; Henikoff & Moffitt, supra note 95, at 102-03 ("[T]he parties must fully understand that the process is voluntary and that they have the right to create, propose, evaluate, accept, or reject any possible solutions."); Nolan-Haley, supra note 92, at 90 ("The controlling principle of mediation is self-determination."); Stark, supra note 95, at 792 ("[A]n agreement is not truly voluntary if it is based on a factual misunderstanding (including a misunderstanding about governing law) that the mediator had an opportunity to correct but did not." (quoting James B. Boskey, The Proper Role of the Mediator: Rational Assessment, Not Pressure, 10 Negotiation J. 367, 370 (1994))).

[223] Henikoff & Moffitt, supra note 95, at 103. Kurtzberg and Henikoff illustrate the tension by discussing competing visions of the meaning of the term "informed consent." See Kurtzberg & Henikoff, supra note 95, at 86. The issue of whether the "informed consent" should be informed simply with respect to the nature of the mediation process, or with respect to the terms of any agreement, parallels the procedural versus substantive fairness debate. See supra note 97.

[224] See, e.g., Henikoff & Moffitt, supra note 95, at 102-04 (considering principles of self-determination and informed consent); Kurtzberg & Henikoff, supra note 95, at 84-87 (same); Stark, supra note 95, at 775-79 (discussing arguments and counter-arguments regarding mediator evaluation and informed consent); Nolan-Haley, supra note 92, at 79-83 (discussing the debate over the propriety of mediators giving legal assistance).

[225] Some scholars already argue that mediation is inappropriate in certain contexts--such as cases involving domestic violence--where a power imbalance exists and the mediation process may be utilized by the stronger party to further the domination of the weaker party. See, e.g., Penelope E. Bryan, Killing Us Softly: Divorce Mediation and the Politics of Power, 40 Buff. L. Rev. 441, 522 (1992) ("The insidious nature of mediation for divorcing women, though, remains hidden beneath its carefully crafted marketing rhetoric."); Trina Grillo, The Mediation Alternative: Process Dangers for Women, 100 Yale L.J. 1545, 1605-07 (1991) ("Women who have been through mandatory mediation often describe it as an experience of sexual domination, comparing mandatory mediation to rape." (citation omitted)); Henikoff & Moffitt, supra note 95, at 92-93 (criticizing mediations involving power imbalances between the sexes); Kurtzberg & Henikoff, supra note 95, at 55-60 (considering why critics find mediation to be harmful to the poor and disempowered). Similar arguments led to the exemption of unrepresented litigants from mediation in the Family Division in the Maryland Circuit Court. See, e.g., Letter from Judith Moran, Esq., Family Division Case Coordinator, Circuit Court of Baltimore City, to Sandra F. Haines, Esq. (Aug. 8, 1997) (on file with author) (critiquing the rule, labeled as Rule 9-205(b)(1)(A)).

[226] See supra Part I.A. The discussion in this section focuses on the role of clerks in the clerk's offices. A discussion of the possible role of law clerks in the settlement process is included in the discussion of the role of the judge. See supra Part II.B.1.

[227] See Greacen, supra note 24, passim. While Greacen recognizes that simplified procedures, easy-to-understand-and use forms, guidebooks, and volunteer bar efforts all are helpful, "even these efforts will not succeed unless court staff are capable of providing extensive information to litigants without lawyers, and [are] willing to do so." Id. at 12.

[228] Elias, supra note 47, at 5. Elias argues that "[c]lerks should be able to provide the same information to the self-represented as they do to lawyers and their staffs," that the boundary be pushed back as to what is considered legal advice, and that court clerks should be required "to facilitate equal access regardless of whether a party is represented by counsel." Id.; see also Goldschmidt, supra note 3, at 25 ("Assistance to the pro se litigant should also be proactively provided by court staff.").

²²⁹ See, e.g., Minn. Conference Report, supra note 40, at 14; Greacen, supra note 24, at 12 (citing The Task Force on the Future of California's Courts, Justice in the Balance 2020 (1993)). Modifying the rules regarding the unauthorized practice of law might be necessary to provide comfort to clerks providing expanded assistance. See, e.g., Meeting the Challenge, supra note 1, at 41-45 (discussing recent proposals to guide court staff).

²³⁰ Greacen, supra note 24, at 14. Graecen also develops a description of the "Sample Staff Guidelines for Providing Information." See id. at 15. For a critique of the guidelines, see Meeting the Challenge, supra note 1, at 42-43. In Michigan, a group of court managers and support staff announced a description of guidelines. See id. at 43-44.

²³¹ See supra Part II.A.2.

²³² According to Mr. Greacen, this is the reading he intended. See Letter from John M. Greacen, Director of the Administrative Office of the Courts, Supreme Court of New Mexico, to Russell Engler, Clinical Director & Professor of Law, New England School of Law 4 (July 29, 1998) (on file with the author).

²³³ As with my reservations about the fourth Greacen principle, my discomfort with the third principle may be one of semantics, rather than substance. As proponents of a "client-centered" approach to counseling might contend, even lawyers arguably should not be telling litigants whether to bring their claims to court; the lawyers should be helping clients choose by advising clients of their options and the advantages and disadvantages of the options. See generally Binder et al., supra note 45, at 258-86 (discussing the proper and desirable ways lawyers can offer advice and guidance). To the extent the third Greacen principle only prohibits the telling, it is less objectionable, but it also provides clerks with less guidance. To the extent it is intended to bar clerks in all contexts from providing the type of information that might help unrepresented litigants make informed choices, my objections remain.

²³⁴ See supra notes 123-28 and accompanying text.

²³⁵ See supra Parts I.D, II.B.1.

²³⁶ See supra Part I.B.

²³⁷ See Increasing Access to Justice, supra note 33, at 10; Meeting the Challenge, supra note 1, at 109 ("State Court Systems and Local Courts Should Train Court Staff on How to Assist Self-Represented Litigants."). Clerks may need to preface their assistance with clear disclosures about their role, including their status as non-lawyers, where appropriate, and the fact that they might be called upon to help the other side. Given the realities facing the unrepresented poor, it is hard to imagine that the disclosures will deter many litigants from accepting whatever assistance the clerks can provide. A discussion of the court's role where clerks give poor advice to a represented party is beyond the scope of this Article.

²³⁸ See Poulakis v. Amtrak, 139 F.R.D. 107 (N.D. Ill. 1991); Patterson v. Brady, 131 F.R.D. 679 (S.D. Ind. 1990) (holding that where a pro se litigant's failure to comply with service requirements was attributed in part to the clerk's office, the pro se plaintiff satisfied the good cause requirement under Fed. R. Civ. P. 4(j)), aff'd mem. sub nom. Patterson v. Rubin, 89 F.3d 838 (7th Cir. 1996); see also Patterson, 131 F.R.D. at 684 n.7 (citing cases where courts found good cause in a pro se litigant's reliance on the clerk's advice).

²³⁹ See, e.g., Fed. R. Civ. P. 60(b); Mass. R. Civ. P. 60(b).

²⁴⁰ See, e.g., supra notes 152-55 and accompanying text. Greacen refers to the consequences of misunderstood advice as an "extraneous" issue of "estoppel." Greacen, supra note 24, at 12. Greacen cites a series of cases that he contends stand for the proposition that reliance on erroneous advice from clerks does not "absolve[ ]" procedural responsibilities, constitute "excusable neglect" or permit "rel[iance] thereon for the purpose of estoppel." Id. at 12-14 (citing Brown v. Quinn, 550 N.E.2d 134, 136, 137 (Mass. 1990); Krupp v. Gulf Oil Corp., 557 N.E.2d 769, 771 (Mass. 1990); and Wyoming ex rel. Wyo. Workers' Compensation Div. v. Halstead, 795 P.2d 760, 775 (Wyo. 1990), superseded by statute as stated in Neal v. Caballo Rojo, Inc., 899 P.2d 56 (Wyo. 1995)). The cases cited by Greacen do not stand for the proposition that when an unrepresented litigant relies on incorrect advice from a clerk, such reliance

does not constitute estoppel. The two Massachusetts cases, as well as the cases cited in those two cases, do not involve unrepresented litigants. See Brown, 550 N.E.2d at 135; Krupp, 557 N.E.2d at 770-71. In the third case, which does appear to involve an unrepresented litigant, the Supreme Court of Wyoming granted relief on other grounds, "negat[ing] the need to discuss the issue of estoppel." Halstead, 795 P.2d at 762.

263  See, e.g., Changing the Culture, supra note 58, at 26 (reporting the impressions of court personnel that "in approximately 80% of cases in the [[[[Massachusetts] Probate and Family Court, at least one party is not represented by counsel"); Erin M. Moore, The Cost of Divorce: Pro Se Litigants Flood Family Law Courts, De Novo, May 1995, at 1 (reporting that 77% of all family cases in Washington State involve at least one unrepresented litigant); Sales et al., supra note 53, at 571 n.82 (noting that "in 88.2% of the divorce cases filed in Maricopa County [Arizona] in 1990, at least one of the litigants was self-represented"); McKnight, supra note 126, at 1 (revealing that 89% of the family law cases in Oregon involve at least one pro se party). The numbers have been surging at least since the 1980s. See, e.g., Rhode, supra note 77, at 214-15 (noting that the proportion of pro se filings in surveyed California counties grew from 39% to 62% of family law cases during the 1980s); Cox & Dwyer, supra note 48, at 2 (reporting that pro se filings for a sample of divorce cases in Arizona increased from 24% to 47% between 1980 and 1985); see also BBA Report, supra note 175, at 5 ("Although some growth in pro se litigation is reported in all categories of civil litigation, the most drastic and consistent increase appears to be in domestic litigation."); Meeting the Challenge, supra note 1, at 49 ("The area of law and court operations that is feeling the brunt of the increase in the volume of pro se cases is domestic relations.").

264  See, e.g., Cox & Dwyer, supra note 48, at 30 (concluding that after testing theories as to why more litigants self-represent in divorce cases than in bankruptcy cases, "[o]ur empirical findings are consistent with our hypothesis that consumers' use of self-help varies inversely with legal and factual complexity").

265  See, e.g., Sales et al., supra note 53, at 561-66 (identifying factors such as the income of the parties, the presence of any children, the amount of property, and the length of the marriage as affecting the complexity of the proceeding).

266  See, e.g., Sales et al., supra note 53, at 571 n.82 (reporting that in over 35% of the divorce cases filed in Maricopa County, Arizona, in 1990, one side was pro se, while the other was represented by an attorney); McKnight, supra note 263, at 1 (reporting that 44% of the family law filings in Oregon involved only one represented party).

267  See Jana B. Singer & William L. Reynolds, A Dissent on Joint Custody, 47 Md. L. Rev. 497, 503 (1988) (describing "custody blackmail," in which "divorcing husbands routinely and successfully use the threat of a custody fight to reduce or eliminate alimony and child support obligations"). But cf. Eleanor E. MacCoby & Robert H. Mnookin, Dividing the Child 154-59 (1992) (questioning the extent of the practice of "custody blackmail" based on a California study).

268  Jan Hoffman, New York's Chief Judge Imposes Strict Rules for Divorce Lawyers, N.Y. Times, Aug. 17, 1993, at A1 (quoting Chief Judge Judith S. Kaye of the New York Court of Appeals); see Grillo, supra note 225, at 1572 ("[F]amily conflicts ... often involve a combination of emotional and legal complaints.....").

269  See, e.g., Richard E. Crouch, The Matter of Bombers: Unfair Tactics and the Problem of Defining Unethical Behavior in Divorce Litigation, 20 Fam. L.Q. 413, 415-34 (1986) (describing unethical tactics used in divorce litigation). But cf. McEwen et al., supra note 93, at 1364-65 (describing the results of a study in Maine, including reports from lawyers that they typically try to reduce, rather than exacerbate, conflict).

270  See, e.g., District of Columbia Bar Task Force on Family Law Representation, Access to Family Law Representation in the District of Columbia: A Report of the D.C. Bar Public Service Activities

Corporation 12 (1992) (demonstrating that the majority of low income families and children in the District of Columbia are not receiving the legal assistance they need in family law matters); Changing the Culture, supra note 58, at 26 (discussing the large number of unrepresented litigants appearing in family courts); Minn. Conference Report, supra note 40, at 14 (recommending measures to address the needs of pro se litigants); Long & Lee, supra note 62, at 1-2 (discussing the pro per problem in California family law cases).

[271] See generally Millemann et al., supra note 57, passim (describing an experimental project in which law students provided legal information and advice to otherwise unrepresented parties in family law cases); Murphy, supra note 80, at 123-24 (discussing the lack of access to the courts to resolve family law disputes and recommending alternatives to adversarial proceedings); Sales et al., supra note 53, at 560 (discussing self representation as an alternative to attorney representation in divorce cases).

[272] See Responding to the Needs, supra note 25, at 12-13; Changing the Culture, supra note 58, at 29-34; Murphy, supra note 80, at 142; Yegge, supra note 74, at 10-12; Long & Lee, supra note 62, at 13-42. Some include reference to the concept of "unbundled legal services." See Responding to the Needs, supra note 25, at 37-38; Minn. Conference Report, supra note 40, at 16; Wisconsin Comm. on the Delivery of Legal Services, State Bar of Wisc., Final Report and Recommendations 29 (1996); Changing the Culture, supra note 58, at 33; Millemann et al., supra note 57, at 1188-89; Long & Lee, supra note 62, at 40-42.

[273] See, e.g., Caroline Kearney, Pedagogy in a Poor People's Court: The First Year of a Child Support Clinic, 19 N.M. L. Rev. 175, 176 (1989) ("One of the frequently cited barriers to the establishment and collection of support orders is the inability of large numbers of women to afford counsel." (citations omitted)); Golden, supra note 58, at 1 (reporting that, according to judges and other legal observers of the Massachusetts Probate and Family Courts, "[w]ithout attorneys, [unrepresented female litigants] run more risk of losing their children, paying excessive support, being pressured into an unfair settlement – or even making themselves vulnerable to batterers ...."); Yegge, supra note 74, at 10 ("Research indicates that pro se litigants frequently proceed without the benefit of critical information such as pretrial relief, allocation of insurance, pension benefits, and tax consequences."); Long & Lee, supra note 62, at 9 ("Pro pers appear to have a greater probability of experiencing an unjust result"). See generally Bryan, supra note 153, at 931 (discussing the different background conditions that women face in divorce proceedings).

[274] See Changing the Culture, supra note 58, at 29 (arguing that judges' practice of using "valuable court time to explain rules and procedures or to ask questions of witnesses in an attempt to be fair or to further discovery of critical information" may be unfair to represented adversaries "since it creates the appearance that the court favors the unrepresented party"); Cox & Dwyer, supra note 48, at 51 (noting a potential problem in divorce cases, where "courts are forced to take an active role in their cases in order to protect [unrepresented] individuals' rights, thus jeopardizing judicial impartiality"); Long & Lee, supra note 62, at 7-8.

[275] See Bohmer & Ray, supra note 97, at 40; Bryan, supra note 153, at 937; McEwen et al., supra note 93, at 1345-46; Mnookin & Kornhauser, supra note 158, at 956; Richard Neely, The Primary Caretaker Parent Rule: Child Custody and the Dynamics of Greed, 3 Yale L. & Pol'y Rev. 168, 173 n.11 (1984).

[276] See supra notes 274-76; see also Memorandum from Judith C. Nord, Staff Attorney, Minnesota Judicial Center, to All Pro Se Subcommittee Members app. G (May 2, 1997) [hereinafter Nord Memorandum] (on file with author) (recommending a protocol to be used by the court during proceedings with pro se litigants); Long & Lee, supra note 62, at 5-7 ("Pro pers demand ... more attention from judges.... [Some] judges feel that unrepresented parties place them in a compromising position.").

[277] See Daniszewski, supra note 187, at 49 ("According to one superior court clerk's informal estimate, 75 percent of the staff time at the clerk's office counter is spent dealing with inquiries by pro se litigants. Pro se litigants also consume 60 to 70 percent of staff telephone time."); Cox & Dwyer, supra

note 48, at 54 ("[T]he majority of court personnel indicated that self-help cases require more court time and resources on a per case basis than do attorney-handled cases."); Long & Lee, supra note 62, at 5.

[278] See Responding to the Needs, supra note 25, at 24-26; Changing the Culture, supra note 58, at 29 ("Significant numbers of pro se litigants seek to use court personnel as a source of legal advice."); Yegge, supra note 74, at 11 ("While court clerks may not practice law, they must not hide behind that prohibition. Clerks must be trained to give clear and correct procedural directions ...." (emphasis added)); Long & Lee, supra note 62, at 5. While observing that court staff are "appropriately reluctant to give information that could be construed as legal advice," the Minnesota Conference of Judges has proposed following the advice of John Greacen. Minn. Conference Report, supra note 40, at 14; see Nord Memorandum, supra note 276, app. F; see also supra Part II.B.3 (stating that the role of court personnel should be expanded beyond the barrier of "no legal advice").

[279] See, e.g., Committee for Gender Equality of the Mass. Supreme Jud. Ct., Achieving Equity: Recommendations for Dispute Intervention Practice in the Probate & Family Court 10-11 (1995) [hereinafter Achieving Equity] (redefining mediation as "dispute intervention" in the family setting); Mass. Gender Bias Study, supra note 49, at 23-27 (arguing that mediation, as it is currently practiced in the probate court, disadvantages women because if their generally unequal bargaining power); Grillo, supra note 225, at 1548-50 (challenging the view that mediation is preferred over the adversarial system for women in custody disputes).

[280] See, e.g., Changing the Culture, supra note 58, at 28-29 ("Pro se litigants often raise frivolous claims or legally meritorious claims in frivolous ways .... Pro se litigants are rarely penalized for failure to follow the rules."); Sales et al., supra note 53, at 558 ("An issue ... is whether judicial assistance to self-represented litigants in any way biases the outcome in their favor when the opposing parties are represented by attorneys."); Daniszewski, supra note 187, at 47 (describing one school of thought that proposes that "judges [may be] more prone to relax the enforcement of the rules when they are dealing with pro se litigants.").

[281] See Daniszewski, supra note 187, at 46; Charles P. Kindregan et al., Emerging Changes in Domestic Relations Procedure, 26 Mass. Law. Wkly. 1241, 1262 (1998).

[282] See generally Engler, supra note 43, at 122-30 (providing examples suggesting that such misconduct is commonplace). Even where ethical issues are mentioned, they are mentioned in terms of problems created for the lawyer by the unrepresented litigant, rather than as lawyer misconduct that must be curbed. See, e.g., Changing the Culture, supra note 58, at 28 ("Lawyers who represent a party against a pro se opponent are often placed in an ethical bind because the lawyer must deal directly with the unrepresented opponent."); Long & Lee, supra note 62, at 5 (noting that one party's lack of representation creates difficulties for the adversary).

[283] Even the source of the proposals underscores current limitations. The proposals come from individual lawyers and groups of lawyers, and remain as proposals. Until and unless the proposals gain the backing of court administrators, the effectiveness of the proposals will be limited. Rather than simply providing courthouse space and cooperation, court administrators need to promulgate rules redefining the proper role of the judges, lawyers, mediators and clerks consistent with the principals discussed in this Article. See supra Part II.C.

# [17]

# A Family Law Residency Program?: A Modest Proposal in Response to the Burdens Created by Self-Represented Litigants in Family Court

## Steven Berenson

## I. INTRODUCTION

Numerous recent studies confirm what insiders in our court system have known for some time: the number of self-represented litigants continues to expand. A closer look at the available data reveals that the phenomenon of increasing self-representation in litigation is primarily being driven by an increase in the number of self-represented litigants in family court. This rise in self-representation in family court has created significant burdens for judges, court administrators and staff, and for our justice system as a whole, not to mention the self-represented litigants themselves. The result is often a failure of legal justice for the parties to family law disputes. A number of possible explanations have been offered for the proliferation of self-represented litigants. Long-term societal trends, such as an increasing acceptance of divorce and non-traditional family relationships, and accompanying changes in legal doctrine, have led to an increase in the number of family law cases in general, and therefore of necessity, an increase in the number of self-represented family law litigants. However, the high cost of legal services and antipathy to lawyers are also likely contributors to the rising number of self-represented family law litigants.

A number of initiatives have been undertaken in order to address the burdens created by the increasing number self-represented family law litigants. These initiatives can generally be categorized as those which embrace self-representation, those which seek to increase the provision of legal services to self-represented litigants by non-lawyers, and those which seek to increase the availability of lawyers to self-represented litigants. Many of these initiatives have shown substantial promise in reducing the burdens associated with self-representation. However, the above-mentioned long term societal trends that have led to an increase in family law cases, as well as limits on the ability of the initiatives to completely eliminate the problems caused by the high cost of legal services and antipathy to lawyers, makes it unlikely that any of the proposed initiatives will, in themselves, eliminate all of the burdens created by the increase in self-representation. Additionally, there are professional and ethical issues that must be addressed prior to more extensive implementation of the initiatives discussed here. Thus, there is ample justification for exploring additional possible measures for addressing the burdens created by the increase in self-representation in family court.

The family law residency program proposed here is intended to be one, small-scale means of responding to the burdens created by the increase in self-representation in family law cases. The program will be loosely based on the residency programs that are the primary form of graduate medical education in America. Indeed, there is a long tradition of looking to medical education and practice for ideas to improve legal education and practice in this country. While medical education and practice in this country are certainly not without flaws, it is contended here that the medical residency model can nonetheless form the blueprint for a successful effort to provide additional legal services to many who currently go without quality legal assistance with regard to their family law cases. Rutgers law school has already implemented a type of legal residency program. However, the Rutgers program is primarily intended to provide additional, practice-oriented legal education to new law graduates. The program proposed here, by contrast, primarily focuses on the delivery of legal services to self-represented family law litigants, although providing strong practical experience to new lawyers will be a collateral benefit of the program.

This article will begin with a discussion of the research demonstrating the increase in self-represented litigants in general, and in family law cases in particular.[1] Next, it will discuss some of the burdens created by the increase in self-represented family law litigants,[2] and some possible reasons for the increase.[3] The article will then discuss some of the initiatives that have been undertaken to address the burdens imposed by self-represented family law litigants,[4] as well as some of the problems with each of these initiatives that must be addressed before the full benefits of the initiative can be realized.[5] Finally, the article will lay out, in a very general manner, the contours of the proposed family law residency program.[6]

## II. THE RISING INCIDENCE OF SELF-REPRESENTED LITIGANTS IN FAMILY COURT

There appears to be little dispute that the phenomenon of persons appearing in court without lawyers is increasing.[7] In a recent survey conducted by the American Judicature Society and the State Justice Institute (AJS/SJI),[8] 65.1% of judges surveyed indicated that the number of self-represented litigants in their courtrooms increased moderately or greatly over the past five years.[9]·By contrast, only 34% of the judges surveyed thought that the number of self-represented litigants had stayed about the same,[10] and only 1.5% thought that the number of self-represented litigants decreased.[11] With regard to court managers and administrators, 82% of those surveyed thought that the overall proportion of self-represented litigants had increased either moderately or heavily over the past five years.[12] By contrast, only 13% of the court managers surveyed thought that the percentage of self-represented litigants stayed about the same,[13] and only 2% responded that the percentage of self-represented litigants decreased over that same period.[14] Following the release of the AJS/SJI survey, a national conference was held regarding the topic of self-representation in litigation.[15] A pre-conference survey was conducted of the fifty-four state and U.S. territory teams that attended the conference.[16] Over 95% of the respondents to that survey believed that there had been an increase in self-represented litigants in their courts over the previous five years.[17]

The findings of the AJS/SJI survey and follow up conference survey are consistent with both empirical and anecdotal evidence that has been amassed in recent years regarding persons appearing in court without lawyers. Perhaps the most comprehensive study of self-represented litigants conducted to date, a 1990 study by the American Bar Association of divorce cases in domestic relations court in Maricopa County (Phoenix) Arizona, found that neither party was represented by a lawyer in 52% of the cases filed.[18] The same study found that at least one of the parties was not represented by a lawyer in more than 88% of the cases filed in 1990.[19] By contrast, previous studies conducted in that same court found that one of the parties was unrepresented in 47% of the cases in 1985, and in 24% of the cases in 1980.[20] Similarly, data from the Administrative Office of the United States Courts indicates that between 1991 and 1993, the number of litigants appearing without lawyers in the federal courts of appeals increased by 49%.[21] The AJS/SJI Report also provides anecdotal evidence from both a report by the Minnesota Conference of Chief Judges Committee on the Treatment of Litigants and Pro Se Litigation,[22] and an Iowa newspaper report,[23] indicating the widely perceived increase in the proportion of litigants appearing in court without lawyers.

A closer look at the trend of increasing appearances by self-represented litigants reveals that it is primarily being driven by persons appearing on their own behalf in domestic relations cases. In fact, the percentage of cases in which one or both of the parties appears without a lawyer is significantly higher in family law cases than in any other area of the law. For example, in a study conducted by the National Center for State Courts of case data from sixteen large urban trial courts in 1991 and 1992, 72% of all domestic relations cases involved one unrepresented party.[24] Similarly, a California Bar Report based on 1991 and 1995 data indicated that at least one party appeared without a lawyer in 67% of all domestic relations cases and in 40% of all child custody cases.[25] A review of pending family law cases in the District of Columbia Courts during one month in 1991 showed that one or both of the parties appeared without a lawyer in 53% of the cases.[26] Another report based on data from that same year from King County (Seattle) Washington concluded that about half of the family law cases involved a litigant without a lawyer.[27] A later report indicated that statewide in Washington, that figure had increased to 77% by 1995.[28] And, of course, the well known ABA study from Maricopa County focused on domestic relations cases.[29] Fifty-nine percent of the court managers surveyed in the AJS/SJI study overwhelmingly "ranked domestic relations as the area of law in which members of the public most frequently ask questions of court staff."[30] Respondents to the pre-conference survey before the 1999 National Conference on Pro Se litigation similarly stated that family law matters had seen the greatest increase in self-represented litigants.[31]

Though not nearly so high as in family court, the rates of litigants appearing without lawyers in other types of what Russell Engler refers to as "poor peoples courts,"[32] are significant as well. Though Engler does not define the term, he appears to have in mind the types of courts where low income litigants are likely to appear most frequently, including housing, bankruptcy and small claims court, in addition to family court.[33] The little empirical data that is available supports the claim that appearances by self-represented litigants are frequent in such courts, but not as frequent as they are in family court. For example, a study of cases in Chicago in 1994 found that self-represented cases accounted for 28% of the landlord-tenant caseload.[34] That same study indicated that 30% of all civil cases filed for less than $ 10,000 in 1994 were filed without an attorney.[35]

On the other hand, other types of civil cases demonstrate relatively low rates of appearances by self-represented litigants. For example, a 1995 study of forty-five urban state trial courts found that an average of only 3% of all tort cases involved a party without counsel.[36] Moreover, in federal court, a study of case data from ten federal district courts conducted by the Federal Judicial Center from 1991 through 1994 indicated that 21% of all filings were by persons without lawyers.[37] However, 63% of those filings involved prisoners.[38] Because the phenomenon of increasing appearances by self-represented litigants is primarily being driven by domestic relations cases, the focus of this paper will be on parties without lawyers in family court.

## III. THE BURDENS CREATED BY SELF-REPRESENTED LITIGANTS IN FAMILY COURT

Many of the numerous judges, court managers, lawyers, bar officials and academics who have thought seriously about the growing phenomenon of persons appearing in court without lawyers do not like to describe this trend as a problem. Rather, such persons focus on the special considerations that follow from self-represented persons' court appearances as "challenges" or even "opportunities."[39] However, it is undeniable that court appearances by persons without lawyers place burdens on court staff, administrators, judges, and our justice system itself that would not exist if all litigants were represented by lawyers. Such burdens may take the form of increases in the amount of time or other court and judicial resources needed to process cases. Or, such burdens may take the form of a perceived (or actual) sense of violation of the fundamental principle of neutral justice. Or, more likely, such burdens may simply take the form of a decreased availability of substantive justice for self-represented litigants. Each of these burdens will be explored below.

The burgeoning number of self-represented litigants, particularly in the family law area, has placed great demands on the limited time resources available to court staff. Such litigants seek additional assistance in filling out the paperwork necessary to pursue their cases. To the extent that court staff is willing to provide such assistance,[40] the time taken to provide the assistance must necessarily be taken away from the performance of other duties.[41] Often, the pressure placed on court staff to keep up with their other duties, in addition to providing special assistance to self-represented parties, can result in court personnel developing resentment towards persons who appear in court without counsel.[42]

Judges must also expend a disproportionate share of their scarce time resources in guiding self-represented litigants through the labyrinth of pretrial and trial practice. As is the case with court personnel, judges vary a great deal in the amount of leeway that they are willing to provide self-represented parties in terms of strict compliance with procedural rules, as well as in the amount of assistance that they are willing to provide self-represented parties in pre-trial and trial practice.[43] Invariably, however, as one judge stated in responding to the AJS/SJI survey, "self-represented litigants' 'lack of experience and inability to understand elementary proceedings' . . . cause the prolonging of proceedings [and] place 'a great burden on the court.'"[44] Additionally, appearances by parties without counsel tend to be more emotional than those with counsel, which also causes a greater use of judicial resources.[45] In high volume courts, and family law courts are among the highest in volume, judges feel tremendous pressures to "move" cases quickly through the system.[46] Yet their ability to do so may be greatly hampered in cases where one or both of the parties lack counsel.

Another area in which the appearance of self-represented litigants may create burdens for our justice system relates to the fundamental principle of neutral justice. Given the adversarial nature of our justice system, it is a fundamental tenet that persons other than the litigants involved in a dispute are to be evenhanded in their treatment of the parties. Neutral participants in resolving the dispute, such as court personnel and judges, are expected to provide no more assistance to one party than the other. However, to the extent that court personnel or judges are at all sympathetic to efforts by self-represented litigants to receive assistance in conducting their cases, the other party to the dispute may feel that the fundamental tenet of neutrality has been breached. On the other hand, if judges and court personnel fail to provide assistance to self-represented litigants, then the assumption that the parties are roughly equal in terms of their ability to present their cases to the neutral arbiter, which also underlies the adversary system, is not valid.[47]

Indeed, of the judges surveyed in the AJS/SJI study, most expressed that they experienced difficulty in maintaining impartiality in cases where one, but not both of the parties appeared without counsel.[48] The judges seemed to feel very uncomfortable moving from the "passive" role of "referee" of a "fight" between the litigants, to the role of a more active participant in an adversary proceeding.[49] The judges seemed to believe that assistance to the self-represented litigant might be perceived by both the other party and that party's attorney as evidence of bias.[50] Similarly, judges are rightly concerned that enforcing rules of procedure less rigidly against self-represented parties might be perceived as being unfair to the represented party.[51] On the other hand, judges are also concerned about perceptions of bias in the other direction. Judges seemed particularly concerned that sustaining proper procedural objections on the part of counsel might create the impression on the part of the self-represented party that the judge is unfairly biased in favor of the represented party or his or her attorney.[52]

In addition to concerns that providing more assistance to one of the parties to a family law case than to the other might result in a violation of the principle of neutral justice, court personnel, at least to the extent that such persons are not attorneys, must also be concerned that assistance provided to a self-represented litigant might be construed as involving the unauthorized practice of law.[53] Often, the way this restriction is formulated is that while non-lawyer court personnel can provide assistance to self-represented litigants so that such persons are able to file the necessary paperwork or take whatever other steps are required to prosecute or defend their cases, such personnel cannot give "legal advice."[54] However, virtually all would acknowledge that the line between appropriate assistance and the improper giving of legal advice is a very hazy one.[55] In order to stay on the permissible side of that line, court personnel often err on the side of caution, and offer less rather than more assistance to self-represented litigants.

Finally, and most importantly, the increase in the number of self-represented parties may result in miscarriages of substantive justice for the self-represented parties themselves. This possibility is particularly disturbing in the area of family law, given the fundamental importance of the issues involved in such cases.[56] Both court personnel and judges recognize the threat to the vindication of legal rights posed by the difficulties of navigating complex, confusing and often convoluted legal procedures without the assistance of counsel. John M. Greacen, Director of the Administrative Office of Courts for the State of New Mexico, in a very influential article that attempted to clarify the often hazy divide for court personnel between giving appropriate assistance to self-represented litigants, and impermissibly giving "legal advice," articulated five general principles that court staff should keep in mind in responding to inquiries from self-represented parties.[57] At least two of Greacen's general principles address the imperative that court staff should provide assistance to self-represented litigants to explain court processes and procedures and to help them to bring their disputes before the court for resolution.[58]

Judges also recognize the threat to substantive justice posed by the increase in self-represented parties in family law cases. Judges are aware that self-represented parties' unfamiliarity with legal procedures or the rules of evidence may result in the denial of meritorious claims on grounds that they were not properly presented. In response to the AJS/SJI survey, one judge noted the discomfort he feels when "'it appears a different legal result could (likely would) occur if the pro se party took appropriate action.'"[59] As pointed out above, judges vary a great deal in terms of their attitudes towards intervention to prevent waiver or forfeiture of important rights by self-represented litigants.

This split in perspectives is reflected in case law and commentaries regarding appropriate judicial responses to self-represented litigants. On the one hand, there is a line of authority that suggests that judges are to treat self-represented litigants no differently from represented parties, in terms of construction of pleadings, pre-trial practice, trial practice and appellate review.[60] On the other hand, many judges recognize the need to give special assistance to self-represented parties in order to provide them with access to judicial relief.[61] As one judge stated in response to a question in the AJS/SJI survey regarding his approach to pro se pleadings: "I have no particular procedure except to be extra generous in interpretations on behalf of the pro se party."[62] Some commentators have referred to these divergent approaches as the "strict" and "lenient" approaches, respectively.[63] Russell Engler contends that determination as to which of these divergent approaches will be employed will be driven more by the facts of particular cases and by judges' reactions to particular litigants, than by broader principles and consistent treatment.[64]

## IV. POSSIBLE REASONS FOR THE INCREASING NUMBER OF SELF-REPRESENTED LITIGANTS IN FAMILY COURT

A number of explanations have been offered for the increasing numbers of self-represented parties in family law cases. First, long-term trends in societal attitudes and accompanying changes in legal doctrine, which have lead to an overall increase in family law cases, have necessarily led to a corresponding increase in the number of self-represented family litigants. A second explanation for the increase in self-represented family litigants relates to the high cost of legal representation. Additionally, a third explanation for this trend relates to general antipathy to lawyers. Each of these explanations will be discussed in turn.

Beginning in the 1960s, American societal attitudes became much more tolerant of non-traditional familial arrangements, including divorce, out of wedlock births, etc.[65] Legal doctrine changed accordingly, with most states adopting forms of no-fault divorce regimes.[66] These developments led to a tremendous increase in divorce rates in America throughout the 1960s and 1970s.[67] Court dockets, naturally, reflected these developments. Though the increase in divorce rates has slowed in recent years, it is still projected that more than half of all new marriages will end in divorce.[68] Moreover, the increase in the proportion of non-custodial parents has led to increased obligations to pay child support and stepped up enforcement of child support obligations over the past two decades has also led to increasing numbers of paternity and support cases in family court.[69]

In addition to these broad societal trends, the most common explanation offered for the increasing number of self-represented litigants in family law cases is the high cost of legal representation. The AJS/SJI Report states that "the cost of litigation is perhaps the most significant factor that has directly influenced the growth of pro se litigation."[70] A recent article in the Orange County (California) Lawyer reported that "the average litigated child custody case in Orange County costs approximately $10,000 in attorneys fees, and $4,000 in forensic fees."[71] The same article reported that the average cost of a non-child custody case is running around $6,000.[72]

Certainly, fees of this magnitude would place a great strain upon the bank accounts of low and moderate income litigants. As a result, many such persons simply do without legal representation. Most of the research that has been done to date focuses more on low-income than moderate income persons. For example, a 1995 report by the American Bar Association's Commission on Nonlawyer Practice found "that as many as 70% to 80% or more of low-income persons are unable to obtain legal assistance even when they need and want it."[73] A prior study by the American Bar Association similarly found that government funded legal services and private pro bono services taken together satisfied only 20.5% of the total legal needs of those Americans whose incomes fall below 125% of the federal poverty line.[74]

\* \* \* \*

## V. RESPONSES TO THE INCREASING NUMBER OF SELF-REPRESENTED LITIGANTS IN FAMILY COURT

A number of different responses have been undertaken to address the burdens caused by the increase in self-represented litigants in family court. These responses can be placed in three general categories. The categories include responses that: 1) embrace self-representation; 2) seek to increase provision of services to litigants by non-lawyers; and 3) seek to increase the availability of services by lawyers. Some of the responses that embrace self-representation are simplification of forms and instructions for use in family law cases, increased assistance for self-represented parties by court personnel, and pro se clinics. Responses that seek to increase provision of services by non-lawyers include efforts to increase the activity of legally-trained, non-lawyer assistants such as paralegals, and mandatory court-ordered mediation of family law disputes. Efforts to increase the availability of representation by lawyers include cost reducing efforts such as unbundling or limited task representation and reduced-fee panels. Antipathy reducing efforts to increase the availability of lawyers' services include the collaborative divorce movement.

Naturally, one's disposition toward such efforts depends a great deal on the explanations one favors in terms of the reasons for the growth of self-represented litigants in family court. For example, if one believes that self-representation is being driven primarily by the cost of legal representation, then one is likely to be favorably disposed to efforts to reduce the cost of legal services. However, if one believes that the antipathy thesis is the primary cause for the increase in self-representation, then one is unlikely to support efforts to increase the availability of lawyers' services, unless such efforts are accompanied by antipathy reducing efforts. One is then more likely to favor efforts to make the courts more accessible to self-represented parties, or to increase the availability of non-lawyer legal assistance, for example.

### A. Responses That Embrace Self-Representation

Many believe, given the long term societal changes discussed above,[102] that the increase in self-represented litigants is an inevitable trend that is unlikely to be reversed anytime soon. Such persons are resigned to the need to make the court system more accessible for self-represented litigants. A number of initiatives have been undertaken in order to make self-representation in family law cases a more feasible alternative.

### 1. Simplified Court Forms and Instructions

One of the most significant steps taken toward making self-representation in family law cases more feasible has been the development of simplified forms and instructions, which give self-represented litigants a head start in preparing the paperwork necessary to pursue their family law cases. Of course, prepared forms and legal documents are not themselves a new development. Pre-printed legal forms and kits have been available through office supply stores and similar sources for many years. However, such forms were not traditionally created in a terribly "user friendly" manner, and were often utilized by attorneys as frequently as by self-represented litigants. Indeed, in the Sales et al. study, which was conducted at a time when commercially prepared forms predominated over those prepared by document preparation services and those prepared by courts,[103] a high percentage (19%) of the litigants who used commercial forms reported having difficulty in using the forms.[104]

In some cases, courts themselves have promulgated simplified forms and instructions designed to assist self-represented litigants in pursuing their cases. For example, the Supreme Court of Florida has promulgated a set of standard Family Law Forms and instructions for use in family law cases.[105] Other courts have also explored the preparation of forms to make self-representation more manageable.[106] Some courts, such as those in Denver, Colorado, have gone a step further and undertaken efforts to ensure that their forms and instructions are written in plain English that can be understood by laypersons.[107]

In addition to legal forms, courts, clerks' offices, bar organizations and a variety of other types of organizations have produced instructional materials designed to help self-represented litigants navigate their way through the court system. Such materials often take the form of brochures or pamphlets that are distributed to self-represented litigants.[108] Instructional video and audio tapes have also been produced. For example, "the Family Division of the Superior Court in Essex County, New Jersey, . . . has prepared video presentations on filing custody/visitation, child support, and domestic violence complaints."[109] Many clerk's offices and other self-help programs have started to create packets of forms and instructional materials that are assembled according to the documents that will be necessary to certain recurrent types of family law cases, including divorces, custody and child support cases, guardianships, and adoptions. For example, Central Florida Legal Services, with input from the court administrator's office, the clerk's office and family law judges and interested members of the bar from Florida's Seventh Judicial Circuit, which includes Volusia County, Florida, has put together seven different packages of forms and step-by-step instructions, adopted for local practice, to cover common types of family law cases.[110] Though some organizations offer such packets free of charge, using organization funds to finance the cost of printing the packets, most organizations charge a nominal fee for the packets to defray the cost of printing.[111] Of course, increasingly, such packets have been made available to self-represented parties over the internet.[112]

2. Increased Assistance by Court Personnel

Additionally, there has been an increase in the assistance provided by court personnel to self-represented litigants. Some of this increase in assistance has necessarily followed from the increase in the number self-represented litigants. Court personnel are simply faced on an *ad hoc* basis with an ever growing number of questions as the ever growing number of self-represented litigants file their papers in court.[113] As many court staff members wish to be as helpful as is possible to the "customers" who frequent their courts, such informal efforts have definitely increased the information available to self-represented litigants. However, even well intentioned court staff bump up against the time pressures caused by increasing requests for assistance from the public,[114] as well as the traditional prohibition against court personnel giving legal advice.[115] Therefore, court personnel have undertaken a variety of more formal and structured initiatives in an effort to provide assistance to the burgeoning population of self-represented litigants.

The range and variety of court-sponsored assistance programs is wide, but the following provide some representative examples. One model is the pro se assistance unit located within the courthouse itself. The Family Division of the Circuit Court in Ft. Lauderdale, Florida has a pro se assistance program that employs five staff attorneys to assist self-represented litigants to determine legal remedies available for specific legal problems, select proper legal forms, and understand filing requirements and court procedures.[116] A similar, smaller scale program has been set up in the Second Judicial District Court in Albuquerque, New Mexico and is staffed by a paralegal.[117] Similar types of pro se assistance programs are blossoming in courthouses throughout the country.[118]

Another model for providing assistance to self-represented litigants relies on new and emerging technologies. In addition to posting legal forms and instructions on the internet,[119] a number of jurisdictions have set up kiosks, which rely on touch screen technology to provide forms, instructions, referrals and other necessary information, to self-represented litigants in a variety of locations designed to provide easy access. Arizona and Utah have implemented such a system called QuickCourt, and have placed kiosks in locations such as clerk's offices, public libraries and community colleges.[120] Similar systems are being implemented in other jurisdictions,[121] including Missouri, which is testing a program called QuickFile, which will, among other things, allow applications for protective orders to be filed on line.[122]

Undoubtedly, the most comprehensive of these court-sponsored assistance programs are the multi-faceted Self-Help programs modeled after the renowned Self-Service Center designed by the Superior Court in Maricopa County (Phoenix) Arizona.[123] With two separate locations, one at the Superior Court in downtown Phoenix and the other at a satellite location in Mesa, the Maricopa County Self-Service Center offers court forms, instructions, and educational materials, through a variety of media including an automated telephone system, in-house computer terminals, and internet access to over 400 forms.[124] Referrals are also provided to lawyers who are willing to provide limited task representation,[125] and low cost initial consultations, as well as referrals to mediators and other relevant professionals.[126] A variety of other courts have adopted similar, if less comprehensive versions of the Maricopa model,[127] and innovations abound. For example, Ventura County California has taken its successful Self-Help Legal Access and Family Law Self-Help Centers on the road by turning a camper van into a Mobile Self-Help Center.[128]

3. Pro Se Clinics

A third response to the increasing number of self-represented litigants which embraces self-representation is the emergence of pro se clinics. As defined by Margaret Martin Barry:
Pro se clinics provide general information about the law, procedure, and practice to a group of litigants or prospective litigants who share a common category of legal issues. The idea is to provide sufficient information to allow participants to understand and access the type of

pleadings required, basic rules such as service of process, basic information that the court will require to render a decision, and a sense of the range of remedies available.[129]

Such programs may be offered through the courts themselves,[130] bar association[131] or legal services offices,[132] through law school clinical programs,[133] or through various combinations of each of these. To the extent that such programs are offered by the courts themselves, they sufficiently resemble the Self-Help Centers discussed above,[134] that they will not be discussed further here. Additionally, to the extent that pro se clinics make use of volunteer lawyers or law students practicing pursuant to state court student practice rules, such programs may offer certain types of unbundled legal services or limited task representation, which will be discussed in greater detail below.[135] Thus, the classic pro se clinic, which is the focus here, involves some sort of educational program, presented by either lawyers or non-lawyers, to a group of potential or actual self-represented litigants, designed to provide basic instruction and information necessary to the successful prosecution of certain types of legal cases.[136] Following the classroom presentation, such clinics also commonly provide access to and assistance in filling out basic legal forms, pleadings, etc.[137]

## B. Increased Involvement by Non-Lawyers

Another means of addressing the increase in self-represented litigants is the increased provision of services to self-represented litigants by non-lawyers. Of course, a number of the initiatives discussed above under the heading of programs, which embrace self-representation, rely heavily on the participation of non-lawyers. For example, many of the court-based programs rely on non-lawyer court staff to provide the bulk of the work.[138] Similarly, many pro se clinics rely on law students, paralegals or other non-lawyer personnel who are prohibited from giving legal advice pursuant to the prohibition against unauthorized practice of law.[139] However, the focus here will be on non-lawyers who assist self-represented litigants in resolving their own cases, for a fee or for profit.

## 1. Commercial Paralegal and Document Preparation Services

Commercial document preparation and paralegal services have been around for some time.[140] However, their numbers have increased along with the surge in self-representation, particularly in family court.[141] Nonetheless, the delivery of services to self-represented litigants by for profit, non-lawyer entities remains highly controversial. The traditional position of mainstream bar authorities has been one of opposition to commercial document production and paralegal services.[142] The doctrinal hook bar authorities have used in opposition to such services has been the prohibition against the unauthorized practice of law.[143] Ostensibly, the justification for the campaign against document production and paralegal services has been public protection.[144] More particularly, both competence and ethical concerns have been raised regarding the delivery of law related services by non-lawyers.[145] However, it is hard to discount the threat to the economic interests of lawyers posed by price competition by non-lawyers in reviewing the bar's efforts to prevent non-lawyer practice.[146]

Moreover, lawyers have found courts increasingly unwilling to enforce strictly prohibitions against unauthorized practice of law in regard to delivery of services by non-lawyers. For example, courts have generally found that publishers have a First Amendment right to create and sell legal forms and do-it-yourself kits,[147] and that document preparation services may help litigants in filling out such forms, provided they do not give legal advice in the process.[148] Perhaps even more importantly, bar associations, state attorneys general, and other enforcement authorities seem to have lost enthusiasm for enforcing unauthorized practice rules.[149] Perhaps this is partially in response to the unfavorable developments in legal doctrine mentioned above.[150] Additionally, public backlash against efforts to suppress non-lawyer practice may be considered too high a price to pay at a time when public opinion of lawyers continues to plummet.[151] Finally, the increase in provision of services by non-lawyers may be seen as an inevitable response to the increase in self-representation. It may be particularly easy for the elite and corporate lawyers who control bar associations to be sanguine about increases in competition by non-lawyers, when they, unlike members of lower strata of the bar, are unlikely to feel much in the way of effects from such competition.[152]

## 2. Alternative Dispute Resolution

Another manner in which persons who are not necessarily lawyers have become involved in the resolution family law disputes is through increasing use of alternative dispute resolution. In many jurisdictions, mediation in family law disputes is now mandatory.[153] Even where mediation isn't mandated, it is often highly encouraged.[154] It seems that mediation is likely to become an increasingly significant part of the manner in which family law disputes are resolved in this country.

## C. Increase the Availability of Legal Representation

In addition to responses to the increase in self-represented parties in family law cases that embrace self-representation and those that seek to increase the availability of services by non-lawyers, efforts have also been made to increase the availability of lawyers' services to self-represented litigants. Because, as discussed above, limits on the availability of legal services are generally due to reasons of cost or antipathy to lawyers, measures that have been taken to make legal representation more widely available will be discussed in terms of those categories.

## 1. Cost Reducing Measures

Included among the measures that have been considered for reducing the cost of legal services are unbundling, or limited task legal representation, reduced fee panels, and efforts to increase pro bono legal representation. Each of these approaches will be discussed below.

### a. Unbundling
As traditionally understood, "full-service" legal representation has been thought to require the lawyer to provide a wide range of services to each client. In the context of family law representation, such services have been said to include: "(1) gathering facts, (2) advising the client, (3) discovering facts of the opposing party, (4) researching the law, (5) drafting

correspondence and documents, (6) negotiating, and (7) representing the client in court."[155] Unbundling, also known as limited legal assistance, simply refers to legal representation that involves some, but not all of the services traditionally thought to be included within full-service representation.[156] A useful way to think about the provision of unbundled legal services is to envision a continuum, with full-service legal representation at one end, and general legal advice at the other.[157] All possible variations of legal representation in between the two ends of the continuum can be thought of as examples of unbundled legal services.

Of course, some of the possible variety of unbundled legal services that can be provided by family lawyers have been discussed already. To the extent that lawyers participate in either the drafting of legal forms,[158] or in pro se legal clinics,[159] they are providing a kind of limited legal assistance.[160] Other commonly discussed types of limited legal assistance include "advice only," "ghostwriting," hotlines, and limited task representation.[161] In the "advice only" context, the litigant usually approaches the lawyer with a specific question and does not seek full-service representation.[162] With "ghostwriting," the lawyer prepares pleadings, briefs or other legal documents for a self-represented litigant, who signs the documents and files them in her or his own name.[163] The lawyer does not enter an appearance in the case. A variety of telephone hotlines exist that provide either pre-recorded legal advice or a live lawyer to respond to inquiries by litigants.[164] Perhaps the best known such hotline is sponsored by the American Association of Retired Persons.[165] Increasingly, the internet is being used in a similar manner to provide either pre-packaged legal information or actual responses by lawyers to direct inquiries.[166] Finally, with limited task representation, the lawyer and litigant mutually agree that the lawyer will provide one or more, but not all, of the services associated with full-service representation.[167] For example, the lawyer might agree to provide representation to a party during a mediation session,[168] or to draft up a marital settlement agreement independently negotiated by the parties to a divorce.

Though the nomenclature of unbundling is a relatively recent development, many family lawyers will concede that they have in fact been providing unbundled legal services to clients for many years.[169] Principles of freedom of contract, as well as the profession's existing ethical principles, allow attorneys and clients to agree to terms of representation that differ from traditional full service representation, provided that full disclosure is made of the nature of such differences.[170] Yet, supporters of unbundling view increases in the practice as posing a particularly promising response to the high cost of legal representation and the increasing number of self-represented litigants in family court.[171]

### b. Reduced fee panels
Another means that has been employed by bar associations to reduce the cost of legal services is the establishment of low cost or reduced fee panels. Pursuant to such initiatives, lawyers agree to serve on panels and provide representation to clients of limited means for fees that are lower than the lawyers' normal fees for similar work.

### c. Increased Pro Bono Representation
Of course, an additional means of trying to increase the provision of legal services to self-represented litigants by reducing the cost of such services, is to increase the availability of pro

bono legal representation. Presently, Model Rule of Professional Conduct 6.1 recommends that a lawyer should aspire to provide at least fifty hours per year in pro bono legal services.[172] After soliciting public comments regarding whether the current pro bono provision should be made mandatory,[173] the American Bar Association's Ethics 2000 Commission,[174] recommended against changing the Rule from its current voluntary basis.[175]

Another alternative that has been proposed to increase the availability of free legal services to low income persons, is a kind of sales tax on the revenues of the largest law firms in the country, with the proceeds going to fund legal aid programs for poor people.[176] Such a program would free large law firms from the burdens that would be imposed by mandatory pro bono services requirements, and therefore reduce any competitive disadvantages that might accrue to firms that take their pro bono commitments seriously.[177] It would also result in a tremendous increase in the resources available to fund free legal services, over the present paltry levels of funding available.[178]

2. Antipathy Reducing Measures

In addition to measures designed to increase the availability of legal representation by reducing its cost, efforts have been made to increase the attractiveness of legal representation by reducing some of the unpleasant consequences of involving lawyers in family law cases.[179] Among the most recent and prominent of such efforts is the collaborative divorce movement. The collaborative divorce movement is based on the premise that litigation, and its adversarial nature,[180] only increases the amount of conflict present in the inherently conflict-ridden process of dissolving a marriage.[181] Therefore, both the parties to the divorce and their "collaborative lawyers,"[182] sign a participation agreement committing all the signatories to a negotiated resolution of all of the outstanding issues.[183] Moreover, pursuant to the terms of the agreement, should litigation ultimately come to pass in the event of a failure of the collaborative process, the collaborative lawyers must agree to withdraw from the representation, in favor of new litigation counsel for both parties.[184] This requirement is thought to reduce the incentives for adversarial behavior on the part of the lawyers for purposes of gaining an advantage in subsequent litigation, as well as to reduce any financial incentive the lawyers might have to sabotage negotiations in favor of the increased fees that would result from protracted litigation.

## VI. WHY ADDITIONAL MEASURES ARE LIKELY TO BE NEEDED

The above-described measures have each yielded, or have the potential to yield, significant benefits in terms of reducing the burdens created by the increase in self-representation in family law cases. However, these measures also have drawbacks that prevent any one of them, or even all of them taken together, from providing a panacea for the burdens created by the increase in self-representation. These drawbacks will be discussed in greater detail below. Taken together with the previously discussed long term societal trends that make increasing numbers of self-represented family law litigants a phenomenon that is likely to be present for the foreseeable future, these drawbacks highlight the need for additional measures to help to address the burdens created by self-representation in family court. The family law residency program proposed in the next part may offer one additional means for addressing these burdens.

## A. Simplified Court Forms and Instructions

In theory, the provision of simplified forms and instructions seems like a promising avenue to pursue to help to address the burdens created by self-represented parties in family court. Though contrary to many people's perceptions, the studies that have been done to date suggest that self-represented litigants are a fairly well educated group. The 1991 study from Maricopa County found that 88% of self-represented persons had a high school degree or above.[185] Other studies have reached similar conclusions.[186] This fact led Sales et al. to conclude that "with properly developed forms and instructions for working through the legal process, the vast majority of people who wish to self-represent are capable of doing so."[187]

Nonetheless, the task of digesting our sometimes byzantine and convoluted legal procedures into easily followed forms and instructions is perhaps more difficult than it first seems. Even in the case of the Florida Supreme Court forms, which were designed with ease of use in mind, many *lawyers* report difficulties in working with the forms, to say nothing of the experience of self-represented litigants. A tremendous amount of work needs to be done before forms and instructions that are truly accessible to laypersons will be made available in family courts throughout the county. And there are simply limits, based on statutory and constitutional requirements relating to various causes of action, on how simplified such documents can become. Additionally, there is much more to legal representation than mere document preparation. Self-represented litigants will still face difficulties in negotiating complex legal procedures, and in articulating their claims in hearings, mediation sessions, and other forums, regardless of the simplicity of related paperwork.

*Steven Berenson, J.D., LL.M., is Associate Professor of Law at Thomas Jefferson School of Law in San Diego, California.*

## Notes

[1]   *See infra* Part II.

[2]   *See infra* Part III.

[3]   *See infra* Part IV.

[4]   *See infra* Part V. Among the initiatives to be addressed are: simplified court forms and instructions; increased assistance by court personnel; pro se clinics; commercial paralegal and document preparation services; alternative dispute resolution; unbundling; reduced fee panels; increased pro bono representation; and collaborative divorce. *Id.*

[5]   *See infra* Part VI.

[6]   *See infra* Part VII.

[7]   By contrast, there appears to be little consensus regarding the term that should be used to describe such persons. Traditionally, persons appearing in court on their own behalf were referred to by the Latin terms "pro se" (which translates to "for himself" in English) or "pro per" (which is short for "in propria persona," and translates to "in one's own proper person" in English). *See* JONA GOLDSCHMIDT ET AL., MEETING THE CHALLENGE OF PRO SE LITIGATION: A REPORT AND GUIDEBOOK FOR JUDGES AND COURT MANAGERS 1 & n.1 (American Judicature Society/State Justice Institute 1998). The use of Latin terms is increasingly falling out of favor in legal discourse, and is particularly inappropriate in this context, as the use of such terms serves to reinforce the sense of alienation and

inaccessibility that persons without legal training face upon entry into the court system. Thus, a more contemporary term refers to such litigants as being "self-represented." *See, e.g., id.*; Erica L. Fox, *Alone in the Hallway: Challenges to Effective Self-Representation in Negotiation*, 1 HARV. NEGOT. L. REV.. 85 (1996). Yet Russell Engler, in his excellent recent article that advocates for making the court system more accessible to persons appearing without lawyers, takes issue with the term "self-represented." *See* Russell Engler, *And Justice for All - Including the Unrepresented Poor: Revisiting the Roles of Judges, Mediators, and Clerks*, 67 FORDHAM L. REV. 1987, 1992 n.23 (1999). Engler believes that the term self-represented connotes some degree of choice to forgo counsel and a belief in one's ability to represent oneself. *Id.* However, Engler contends that low income litigants do not make such a choice nor hold such a belief, but rather simply lack access to counsel. *Id.* at 2027. Moreover, Engler also contends that low income litigants lack the information necessary to allow them to represent themselves effectively in court. *Id.* at 1988. Therefore, Engler uses the term "unrepresented person," as it indicates the opposite of a person who is represented by counsel. *Id.* at 1992 n.23. While I agree with much of Engler's analysis in the context of low-income persons, the scope of this paper extends beyond consideration of poor litigants only. As will be discussed, *infra*, many who appear in court without lawyers must be classified as either moderate or middle income. In such circumstances, there is at least some volitional aspect to the decision to forego legal representation. Thus, throughout this paper, I will default to the *au current* term self-represented, despite qualms as to whether it accurately describes the circumstances of many of those who appear in court without lawyers.

[8]    GOLDSCHMIDT ET AL., *supra* note 7; *see also* Jona Goldschmidt, *How are Courts Handling Pro Se Litigants?*, 82 JUDICATURE 13, 14 (July-August 1998).

[9]    GOLDSCHMIDT ET AL., *supra* note 7, at 117, 177 app. I. Forty judges, or 30.1% of the total number surveyed thought that the number of *pro se* litigants "increased greatly." *Id.* Forty-six judges, or 35% of the total number surveyed, thought that the number of *pro se* litigants had increased moderately. *Id.*

[10]   *Id.*

[11]   *Id.*

[12]   *Id.* at 122 app. II. Forty-four court managers, or 45% of the total surveyed thought that the proportion of self-represented litigants "increased greatly." Thirty-eight court managers, or 39% of those surveyed, responded that the proportion of self-represented litigants "increased moderately." *Id.*

[13]   *Id.*

[14]   *Id.*

[15]   In late 1999, the American Judicature Society, with the support of the State Justice Institute, and the Open Society Institute, sponsored a national Conference on Pro Se Litigation in Scottsdale, Arizona. *See* A National Conference on Pro Se Litigation: Florida Team Report, Office of the State Courts Administrator, Florida Supreme Court (January 3, 2000) [hereinafter Florida Team Report] (unpublished manuscript, on file with author). Forty-nine states and all U.S. territories sent teams to attend the conference. *Id.* These teams were made up of judges, lawyers, court administrators, academics and even self-represented litigants. *Id.* Following the Conference, the then-Chief Justice of the Florida Supreme Court, Major B. Harding, issued an Administrative Order, creating Florida's Access to Justice Task Force, and directing the task force to: 1) hold a statewide conference on pro se litigation; 2) "[d]evelop plans to facilitate local collaborative efforts to ensure that legal services are available and affordable;" and 3) "[m]ake recommendations to the ... Court on how to build a system of services that improves access to a fair, timely, and meaningful resolution by informed family law litigants." In Re: Access to Justice Task Force, Administrative Order, Supreme Court of Florida (Jan. 7, 2000). I was privileged to attend the Florida Supreme Court's Access to Justice Task Force's Statewide Conference on Pro Se Litigation, which was held in Orlando, Florida, May 24-25, 2000. The impetus for this paper came from the thoughtful views expressed by many of the participants involved in that conference.

16    Beth Lynch Murphy, Results of a National Survey of Pro Se Assistance Programs: A Preliminary Report 1 (unpublished manuscript on file with author).

17    *Id.* at 3.

18    GOLDSCHMIDT ET AL., *supra* note 7, at 8 (citing BRUCE D. SALES ET AL., SELF-REPRESENTATION IN DIVORCE CASES (American Bar Association 1993)); *see also* Goldschmidt, *supra* note 8, at 14; Forrest S. Mosten, *Unbundling of Legal Services and the Family Lawyer*, 28 FAM. L.Q. 421, 427 (1994).

19    Mosten, *supra* note 18, at 427.

20    *Id.; see also* GOLDSCHMIDT ET AL., *supra* note 7, at 9 (citing memorandum from Steven R. Cox & Mark Dwyer, to the ABA Special Committee on the Delivery of Legal Services, *Self-Help Law and Its Many Perspectives* 21 (1987); Bruce D. Sales et al., *Is Self-Representation a Reasonable Alternative to Attorney Representation in Divorce Cases*, 37 ST. LOUIS U. L.J. 553, 594 & nn.176-77 (1993).

21    GOLDSCHMIDT ET AL., *supra* note 7, at 9 (citing *Courts of Appeals Facilitate Handling of Pro Se Cases*, THE THIRD BRANCH, July 1995, at 9); *see also* Goldschmidt, *supra* note 8, at 14.

22    The Minnesota Judges' Report notes "the increased number of pro se litigants in Minnesota." GOLDSCHMIDT ET AL., *supra* note 7, at 9 (quoting Conference of Chief Judges, Report of the Minnesota Conference of Chief Judges Committee on the Treatment of Litigants and Pro Se Representation 6 (April 1996)); *see also* Goldschmidt, *supra* note 8, at 14.

23    "[L]awsuits filed by people acting as their own attorney are increasing[.]" GOLDSCHMIDT ET AL., *supra* note 7, at 9 (quoting Frank Santiago, *Trend: Iowa Litigants Heading to Court Solo*, THE DES MOINES REGISTER, August 18, 1996, at 1).

24    GOLDSCHMIDT ET AL., *supra* note 7, at 8 (citing JOHN A. GOERDT, DIVORCE COURTS: CASE MANAGEMENT, CASE CHARACTERISTICS, AND THE PACE OF LITIGATION, IN 16 URBAN JURISDICTIONS 48 (National Center for State Courts 1992)); *see also* Goldschmidt, *supra* note 8, at 14 (citing JOHN A. GOERDT, NAT'L CTR. FOR STATE COURTS, DIVORCE COURTS: CASE MANAGEMENT, CASE CHARACTERISTICS, AND THE PACE OF LITIGATION, *in* 16 URBAN JURISDICTIONS 16 (1992).

25    GOLDSCHMIDT ET AL., *supra* note 7, at 8 (citing Long & Lee, The Pro Per Crisis in Family Law 3-4 (1995) (memorandum submitted to the state Bar of California Board Committee on Courts and Legislation)); *see also* Goldschmidt, *supra* note 8, at 14.

26    GOLDSCHMIDT AT AL., *supra* note 7, at 8 (citing District of Columbia Bar Task Force on Family Law Representation, *Access to Family Law Representation in the District of Columbia* 39 app. E (1992), *in* RESPONDING TO THE NEEDS OF THE SELF-REPRESENTED DIVORCE LITIGANT (Standing Comm. on Delivery of Legal Servs. ed., 1994) [hereinafter RESPONDING TO THE NEEDS]); *see also* Margaret Martin Barry, *Accessing Justice: Are Pro Se Clinics a Reasonable Response to the Lack of Pro Bono Legal Services and Should Law School Clinics Conduct Them?*, 67 FORDHAM L. REV. 1879, 1913 (1999); Jane C. Murphy, *Access to Legal Remedies: The Crisis in Family Law*, 8 BYU J. PUB. L. 123, 124-25 (1993).

27    GOLDSCHMIDT ET AL., *supra* note 7, at 8 (citing Report of the Domestic Relations Task Force to the Board of Governors of the Washington State Bar Association 14 (1991), *in* RESPONDING TO THE NEEDS, *supra* note 26, at 45).

28    Erin M. Moore, *The Cost of Divorce: Pro Se Litigants Flood Family Law Courts*, DE NOVO, May 1995, at 1.

29    *See supra* note 18.

30    GOLDSCHMIDT, *supra* note 7, at 49; *see also* Goldschmidt, *supra* note 8, at 20 (reporting that 59% of court managers surveyed ranked domestic relations as the area in which they received the most questions from pro se litigants and that the area of law that received the next highest number of votes in terms of frequency of questions was traffic law, at 12%).

[31] Murphy, *supra* note 26, at 3.

[32] Engler, *supra* note 7, at 2019.

[33] *Id.*

[34] GOLDSCHMIDT ET AL., *supra* note 7, at 9 (citing REPORT ON PRO SE LITIGATION (Circuit Court of Cook County Pro Se Advisory Comm. 1995)).

[35] *Id.*

[36] *Id.* at 9 (citing Smith et al., *Tort Cases in Large Counties*, Bureau of Justice Statistics-Special Report 2 (1995)).

[37] *Id.* (citing Rauma & Sutelan, *Analysis of Pro Se Case Filings in Ten U.S. District Courts Yields New Information*, Federal Judicial Center Directions 6 (1996)); *see also* Goldschmidt, *supra* note 8, at 14.

[38] GOLDSCHMIDT ET AL., *supra* note 7, at 9.

[39] *See, e.g.*, GOLDSCHMIDT ET AL., *supra* note 7 ("Meeting the Challenge of Pro Se Litigation"); Florida Team Report, *supra* note 15, at 3-4 ("Pro se's are not a 'problem' they are our customers.").

[40] *See infra* at notes 53-55 and accompanying text (discussing the court staff's willingness to provide such assistance).

[41] GOLDSCHMIDT ET AL., *supra* note 7, at 3, 49; *see also* Sales et al., *supra* note 20, at 557 & n.21 (citing Cox & Dwyer, *supra* note 20, at 54-55).

[42] *See* Engler, *supra* note 7, at 1997-98 & nn.47-48; *see also* Cox & Dwyer, *supra* note 20, at 50; Mosten, *supra* note 18, at 435.

[43] *See infra* notes 49-52 and accompanying text.

[44] GOLDSCHMIDT ET AL., *supra* note 7, at 53.

[45] *See* Goldschmidt, *supra* note 8, at 18.

[46] *See* Engler, *supra* note 7, at 2019-20. Engler argues that the pressures on judges to process cases quickly will often lead judges to place undue pressure on unrepresented parties to settle cases. *Id.* However, Engler contends that unrepresented parties lack the information necessary to make rational settlement decisions with regard to their cases. *Id.* Moreover, Engler contends that the often inappropriate role played by judges in encouraging settlement of cases involving unrepresented parties has not been adequately addressed in the cases or in the literature. *Id.* at 2028.

[47] *Id.* at 2023-24.

[48] GOLDSCHMIDT ET AL., *supra* note 7, at 52.

[49] *Id.* at 52-53.

[50] *Id.* at 53.

[51] *See* Goldschmidt, *supra* note 8, at 17.

[52] *Id.* at 17.

[53] Engler, *supra* note 7, at 1993 & n.27.

[54] *Id.* at 1993 & n.30; *see also* GOLDSCHMIDT ET AL., *supra* note 7, at 34.

[55] Engler, *supra* note 7, at 1994.

[56] *See, e.g.*, Santosky v. Kramer, 455 U.S. 745, 774 (1982) (Rehnquist, J., dissenting) (holding, despite division among the Justices in this case, that "the interest of parents in their relationship with the[ir] children is sufficiently fundamental to come within the finite class of liberty interests protected by the Fourteenth Amendment").

[57] *See* John M. Greacen, *"No Legal Advice from Court Personnel." What Does that Mean?*, JUDGES' JOURNAL, Winter 1995, at 10.

[58] *Id.* Greacen's first and second principles, stated in full, are as follows: "1) Court staff have an obligation to explain court processes and procedures to litigants, the media and other interested citizens; and 2) Court staff have an obligation to inform litigants, and potential litigants, how to bring their problems before the court for resolution." *Id.*

[59] Goldschmidt, *supra* note 8, at 17-18.

[60] *See* GOLDSCHMIDT ET AL., *supra* note 7, at 55-58; Engler, *supra* note 7, at 2013 & n.122.

[61] *See* GOLDSCHMIDT ET AL., *supra* note 7, at 55-58; Engler, *supra* note 7, at 2013-14 & n.124.

[62] GOLDSCHMIDT ET AL., *supra* note 7, at 55.

[63] Engler, *supra* note 7, at 2014; *see also* Helen B. Kim, *Legal Education for the Pro Se Litigant: A Step Toward a Meaningful Right to Be Heard*, 96 YALE L.J. 1641, 1644-46 (1987); Howard M. Rubin, *The Civil Pro Se Litigant v. The Legal System*, 20 LOY. U. CHI. L.J.J. 999, 1001-02 (1989).

[64] Engler, *supra* note 7, at 2014-15 & nn.127-34.

[65] *See* Arland Thornton, *Comparative and Historical Perspectives on Marriage, Divorce, and Family Life*, 1994 UTAH L. REV. 587, 595-96.

[66] *Id.* at 596.

[67] *Id.* at 595.

[68] *Id.*

[69] *See generally* WALTER WADLINGTON & RAYMOND C. O'BRIEN, DOMESTIC RELATIONS: CASES AND MATERIALS 417-21 (1998) (discussing developments in child support enforcement); D. KELLY WEISBERG & SUSAN FRELICH APPLETON, MODERN FAMILY LAW, CASES AND MATERIALS 763-65 (1998) (same).

[70] GOLDSCHMIDT ET AL., *supra* note 7, at 10; *see also* COMM. ON NONLAWYER PRACTICE, AMERICAN BAR ASS'N, NONLAWYER ACTIVITY IN LAW-RELATED SITUATIONS: A REPORT WITH RECOMMENDATIONS 78 (1995) [hereinafter ABA Commission on Nonlawyer Practice].

[71] Marsha Baucom, *Collaborative Divorce*, 41 ORANGE COUNTY LAW. 18, 33 (July 1999).

[72] *Id.*

[100] Nancy J. Ross, *Divorce: Does it Have to be Destructive?*, THE WOMAN'S VOICE (February-March 1999), *available at* http:// www.collaborativedivorce.com/article1.html (visited June 27, 2000).

[101] In fact, other than in the case of the most affluent clients, it seems that most family law lawyers in Broward County Florida charge a flat fee rather than hourly fees for family law cases. Though the reason for this practice may primarily be to cut down on receivables, the result is to give lawyers an incentive to resolve family law matters as quickly as is possible, rather than to drag them out.

[102] *See supra* notes 65-69 and accompanying text.

[103] Sales et al., *supra* note 20, at 568.

[104] *Id.* at 568-69.

[105] *See* Fla. Fam. L. R. P. Family Law Forms, *available at* http:// www.flcourts.org.

[106] *See, e.g.*, Rubin, *supra* note 63, at 1010.

[107] GOLDSCHMIDT ET AL., *supra* note 7, at 69.

[108] *Id.*

[109] *Id.*

[110] Robert N. Sterner, Family Court Services: Family Self Help Program, Seventh Judicial Circuit 9 (unpublished manuscript on file with author).

[111] For example, the cost of the Seventh Circuit's packets run from $13.25 for the Uncontested Modification of Family Law Final Judgments packet, to $31.80 for the Contested Modification of Family Law Final Judgments packet. *Id.*

[112] *See, e.g.*, website *supra* note 105; *see also* Engler, *supra* note 7, at 2000 & n.61.

[113] GOLDSCHMIDT ET AL., *supra* note 7, at 69.

[114] *See supra* at notes 40-42 and accompanying text.

[115] *See supra* at notes 53-54 and accompanying text; *infra* notes 195-203 and accompanying text.

[116] GOLDSCHMIDT ET AL., *supra* note 7, at 69, 86.

[117] *Id.* at 70, 98.

[118] *Id.* at 70 (discussing programs in New York City's Family Court and King County Superior Court in Seattle); *see also* Murphy, *supra* note 16, at Table 3.

[119] *See supra* note 105.

[120] GOLDSCHMIDT ET AL., *supra* note 7, at 69, 76; *see also* Engler, *supra* note 7, at 2000 & n.62.

[121] GOLDSCHMIDT ET AL., *supra* note 7, at 76 (referring to similar programs in California, Colorado, and Florida).

[122] Murphy, *supra* note 16, at 9.

[123] *See generally*, GOLDSCHMIDT ET AL., *supra* note 7, at 71; Engler, *supra* note 7, at 2000-01 & nn.63-64; Sales et al., *supra* note 20, at 595 n.178; Murphy, *supra* note 16, at 9.

[124] GOLDSCHMIDT ET AL., *supra* note 7, at 73.

[125] *See infra* notes 155-171 and accompanying text.

[126] *See* Engler, *supra* note 7, at 2001.

[127] GOLDSCHMIDT ET AL., *supra* note 7, at 71; Murphy, *supra* note 16, at 9.

[128] Superior Court of California, County of Ventura, Self-Help Programs (unpublished manuscript on file with author).

[129] Barry, *supra* note 26, at 1883.

[130] *See, e.g.*, GOLDSCHMIDT ET AL., *supra* note 7, at 70 (discussing the Family Law Pro Per Clinic in Ventura County, California).

[131] Barry, *supra* note 26, at 1901 (discussing bar association sponsorship of Maryland's Women's Law Center).

[132] *Id.* at 1894 (discussing pro se clinics set up by legal services programs in six Florida counties); *id.* at 1899 (discussing pro se clinics set up by legal services offices in Missouri); *id.* at 1902 (discussing the Maryland Legal Aid Bureau's pro se divorce clinics).

[133] *Id.* at 1920 (discussing Catholic University Law School's Pro Se Clinic); *see also* Michael Millemann et al., *Rethinking the Full-Service Legal Representation Model: A Maryland Experiment*, 30 CLEARINGHOUSE REV. 1178 (1997) (discussing the University of Maryland Law School's Pro Se Clinic).

[134] *See supra* notes 123-28 and accompanying text.

[135] *See infra* notes 155-171 and accompanying text.

[136] *See generally*, Barry, *supra* note 26, at 1895-96, 1899, 1902.

[137] *See generally, id.* at 1895-96, 1902.

[138] *See supra* note 117 and accompanying text.

[139] *See supra* notes 133, 135 and accompanying text.

[140] *See, e.g.*, Ralph C. Cavanagh & Deborah L. Rhode, *Project, The Unauthorized Practice of Law and Pro Se Divorce: An Empirical Analysis*, 86 YALE L.J. 104 (1976).

[141] *See* Deborah L. Rhode, *The Delivery of Legal Services by Non-Lawyers*, 4 GEO. J. LEGAL ETHICS 209, 213-14 (1990).

[142] *Id.* at 209-10.

[143] *See, e.g.*, Derek A. Denckla, *Non-Lawyers and the Unauthorized Practice of Law: An Overview of the Legal and Ethical Parameters*, 67 FORDHAM L. REV. 2581, 2592 (1999).

[144] *See* Hurder, *supra* note 73, at 2242; Rhode, *supra* note 141, at 209.

[145] *See* MODEL CODE OF PROF'L RESPONSIBILITY EC 3-1 (1981).

[146] Rhode, *supra* note 141, at 220; *see also* Rhode, *supra* note 94, at 712-13.

[147] *See* Denckla, *supra* note 143, at 2591 & n.68.

[148] *Id.* at 2591 & n.69.

[149] *See* Rhode, *supra* note 141, at 216.

[150] *See supra* notes 117-148 and accompanying text.

[151] Rhode, *supra* note 141, at 218-20.

[152] *See id.* at 220.

[153] CAL. FAM. CODE § 3182(a) (West 1994); Karla Fischer et al., *Procedural Justice Implications of ADR in Specialized Contexts: The Culture of Battering and the Role of Mediation in Domestic Violence Cases*, 46 S.M.U. L. REV. 2117, 2150 (1993); Craig A. McEwen et al., *Bring in the Lawyers: Challenging the Dominant Approaches to Ensuring Fairness in Divorce Mediation*, 79 MINN. L. REV. 1317, 1357 (1995).

[154] Engler, *supra* note 7, at 2007.

[155] Mosten, *supra* note 18, at 423.

[156] Mary Helen McNeal, *Having One Oar or Being Without a Boat: Reflections on the Fordham Recommendations on Limited Legal Assistance*, 67 FORDHAM L. REV. 2617, 2617 n.1 (1999).

[157] *Id.* at 2619 (discussing the work of the Working Group on Limited Legal Assistance from the 1998 Fordham Conference on the Ethical and Professional Issues in Delivering Legal Services to Low-Income Persons); *see* Green, *supra* note 7, at 1713.

[158] *See supra* notes 103-107 and accompanying text.

[159] *See supra* notes 129-137 and accompanying text.

[160] McNeal, *supra* note 156, at 2622.

[161] *Id.*

[162] *Id.*

[163] *Id.* at 2623; *see also* Engler, *supra* note 7, at 2004; John C. Rothermich, Note, *Ethical and Procedural Implications of "Ghostwriting" for Pro Se Litigants: Toward Increased Access to Civil Justice*, 67 FORDHAM L. REV. 2687 (1999).

[164] McNeal, *supra* note 156, at 2624.

[165] *See* Wayne Moore & Monica Kolasa, *AARP's Legal Services Network: Expanding Legal Services to the Middle Class*, 32 WAKE FOREST L. REV. 503, 526 (1997).

[166] *See, e.g.*, Richard Zorza, *Reconceptualizing the Relationship Between Legal Ethics and Technological Innovation in Legal Practice: From Threat to Opportunity*, 67 FORDHAM L. REV. 2659, 2663 (1999).

[167] McNeal, *supra* note 156, at 2625.

[168] *See* Mosten, *supra* note 18, at 436.

[169] McNeal, *supra* note 156, at 2617; Mosten, *supra* note 18, at 422.

[170] *See, e.g.*, MODEL RULES OF PROF'L CONDUCT R. 1.2 cmt. 4 (1999) ("The objectives or scope of services provided by a lawyer may be limited by agreement with the client or by the terms under which the lawyer's services are made available to the client."); RESTATEMENT (THIRD) OF THE LAW GOVERNING LAWYERS § 30 (Proposed Final Draft No. 1, 1996) (stating that a lawyer and client can agree to limit a duty a lawyer would otherwise owe, provided the client agrees and the limitations are reasonable).

[171] *See, e.g.*, Mosten, *supra* note 18, at 449.

[172] MODEL RULES OF PROF'L CONDUCT R. 6.1 (1998).

[173] Ethics 2000 Commission, *Memorandum Inviting Public Comment, Model Rule 6.1, at* http//: www.abanet.org/cpr/memo61.html (May 9, 2000).

[174] More formally known as the ABA's Commission on Evaluation of the Rules of Professional Conduct, the project was undertaken in 1997 to conduct the first review of the ABA's Model Rules of Professional Conduct, since their promulgation in 1983. *See* Margaret Colgate Love, *Update on Ethics 2000 Project and Summary of Recommendations to Date*, 31 SYLLABUS 19 (Winter 2000).

[175] *See* Ethics 2000 Commission Report, *Chair's Introduction and Executive Summary*, at 7-8, *at* http://www.abanet.org/cpr/e2k-intro_summary.html (Feb. 12, 2001).

[176] *See* Barry, *supra* note 26, at 1886-87.

[177] *Id.*

[178] *Id.*

[179]  *See supra* notes 99-101 and accompanying text.

[180]  *See* Engler, *supra* note 7, at 2022.

[181]  *See* Baucom, *supra* note 71.

[182]  Each party is separately represented in collaborative divorce.

[183]  For a description of the provisions of the "Collaborative Law Participation Agreement" used by the Collaborative Law Center in Cincinnati, Ohio, visit its website at http://www.collaborativelaw.com. *See also* Robert W. Rack, Jr., *Settle or Withdraw: Collaborative Lawyering Provides Incentive to Avoid Costly Litigation, available at* http:// www.collaborativelaw.com/documents/settleor.htm (visited May 22, 2000).

[184]  Rack, *supra* note 183.

[185]  Sales et al., *supra* note 20, at 563 & n.51.

[186]  *Accord* GOLDSCHMIDT ET AL., *supra* note 7, at 12-13 (citing Solomon, Analysis of Self-Service Center [Maricopa County] Exit Survey Questionnaires 2 (January 4, 1997)); Long & Lee, *supra* note 25, at 3-4; Spencer, *supra* note 85, at 1.

[187]  Sales et al., *supra* note 20, at 597.

# Part III
# The Role of Lawyers and
# Other Professionals

# A: Lawyers

# [18]

## Emerging Roles of the Family Lawyer:
## A Challenge for the Courts

### Forrest S. Mosten

*The author examines the problem of representing adverse interests of the parties in family law disputes and proposes some measures for attorneys to address this need. The role of the attorney shifts from being merely an advocate to becoming a consultant and adopting other roles, depending on the needs and wishes of the client. According to this article, the bar must become more sensitive to the needs of the public and the call for a simpler, more "user-friendly" system.*

## INTRODUCTION

Historically, family lawyers have been comfortable being the gatekeepers of legal information and the main players in a system based on the adversarial system. Lawyers are seen as having access, control, and a virtual monopoly on the processing of divorces in this country. However, the reality is that 60% of family legal needs never touch either a lawyer's office or the courts.[1] A recent study in Arizona shows that, when family matters are actually brought to court, in more than 88% of the cases only one party is represented by a lawyer and in more than 62% of cases filed both sides are unrepresented.[2]

When lawyers are used, most clients, family lawyers, and judges view the lawyer's role as that of courtroom barrister-even if settlement occurs in 90% to 95% of all family cases. Yet judges, lawyers, and clients often believe it is the adversarial vigilance of family lawyers and the hurdles of the court process that soften up the parties, forcing them to settle. Whereas full-package lawyer adversarial representation shall probably continue to be the lawyer role of choice, emerging new roles of the family lawyer are currently in successful operation in law offices throughout the world. Clients today are more active, more educated in the art of clienthood, more inquisitive, and more demanding in the quest to control the purchase and supervision of legal services. Instead of retaining a lawyer for full-service representation in which total fees often cannot be predicted accurately, today's clients may expect their lawyers to perform only part of the job for part of the total fee. Lawyers who wish to unbundle their full package of services must be willing to give up some of their customary views of maintaining control over the negotiating process, case strategy, and being on the front line in practicing their craft. Clients want more power over their own lives and to be full and active participants in solving their own problems. In short, they want to be in control and want their lawyers to be resources in helping clients translate that control into effective and satisfying results. As this changing client-lawyer relationship creates a demand for lawyers to offer nonadversarial alternatives in their law offices, court systems should also be prepared to adapt to those changes in legal service delivery (Table 1).

**Table 1**
*Emerging Roles o/the Family Lawyer*

Coach to pro se litigant
Dispute resolution manager
Consultant during mediation
Family advocate
Primary legal health provider

## EMERGING ROLE NO.1:
## THE FAMILY LAWYER AS A COACH TOTHE PRO SE LITIGANT

Historically, courts have appeared to be the private preserve of the legal profession. The legal and procedural barriers to pro se representation have been compounded by attitudes of both bench and bar alike. Pro se litigants are the unwanted prodigal children of the court system. Pro se litigants often do not speak the language, dress in appropriate costume, or prepare adequately. They are not familiar faces. They are perceived as unprepared and taking too much court time. Family lawyers and judges (often former family lawyers) too often feel that a pro se litigant symbolizes one more lawyer being cut out of a fee. These prejudices toward pro se litigants may be difficult to alter, but the drumbeat of increasing pro se representation coupled with general lawyer bashing makes it economically imperative for lawyers to understand the pro se movement and respond positively to it.

The practicing bar cannot ignore the unequivocal message that consumers in Arizona and other jurisdictions are sending to the courts and to the family law bar. The courts and the entire legal system have become more user friendly in a number of major ways:

1.       Less complex procedures in the court system, including more no-fault jurisdictions;[3]
2.       Uniform support guidelines;[4]
3.       Simplified court procedures; [5]
4.       Model pleadings and standardized forms;[6] and
5.       Greater procedural assistance both at the courthouse and in the private sector.[7]

In addition to fulfilling a need for pro se litigants, unbundled legal services may also provide a major future role for family lawyers. The 1993 American Bar Association (ABA) study indicates that court-provided written handbooks are too broad and general to give the pro se divorce litigant the necessary, detailed, and procedural information to properly protect substantive rights.[8]

It is true that the private sector is responding to this need by providing better written publications and video instructional tapes.[9] However, even though many pro se litigants have substantial educations (more than half having some college education), the 1993 study shows that pro se litigants frequently have difficulty completing the appropriate forms and filing them in court even with the use of these commercial aids.[10] The findings demonstrate that pro se litigants make less use of temporary orders,[11] obtain less spousal maintenance,[12] obtain tax advice less frequently,[13] and use alternative dispute resolution (ADR) options less.[14] These deficiencies may be the tip of the iceberg. They demonstrate the clear need for unbundled services to be provided by the family law bar as indicated by the 1994 ABA Pro Se Report:

When examining pro se activity in a specific jurisdiction, consideration should be given to the effectiveness of the various mechanisms for alerting pro se litigants about their responsibilities andIorencouraging them to get legal advice-especially concerning central issues of allocation of pensions, insurance and other employment-related assets and the income tax consequences of property and support settlement.[15]

The foundation of the coaching role is the willingness of the family lawyer to unbundle the full package of services and offer those services as determined by the client who has chosen to self-represent in the court system (Table 2).[16] As both lawyers and clients have the same traditional mindset about having the lawyer provide the full package of services and the lawyer using professional discretion and control to determine which services are necessary to solve a client's problem, unbundling the package requires a major rethinking about the lawyer-client relationship.

**Table 2**
*Coach for the pro se Litigant*

Unbundle discrete lawyer services
Educate client
Legal rights
Court procedure
Alternative dispute resolution
Parenting communication
Strategy
Client controls extent and depth of services
Coach available for full-service representation

## ASSESSMENT IN USING THE PRO SE COACH

The first step in the coaching role is to help the client assess whether a lawyer is needed at all and, if so, for which discrete tasks will the client retain the lawyer and how the relationship will be structured. This Brave New World uses a blend of education and negotiation and shared control between lawyer and client in determining the scope of the lawyer-client relationship.

Education is a two-way street. The lawyer must educate (to wit "sell") the client as to what benefits the client can derive from involving (and paying for) a lawyer's experience, knowledge, and skill on a limited basis whereas the client remains in charge of case strategy and implementation. Is the assessment conference the one and only client-lawyer meeting or will another meeting be planned now or left to client discretion? Will the client handle every aspect of self-representation (gathering facts, discovery, drafting correspondence and pleadings, negotiation, court appearances) or will some of these tasks be delegated to the lawyer/coach?

In addition to allocating services between client and lawyer, the client must be educated to decide the depth or extent of any service rendered by the lawyer/coach. For example, the client may wish to handle all court filings, discovery, negotiations, and court appearances short of trial with limited lawyer coaching but have the lawyer convert roles from coach to attorney of record at the trial itself. Conversely, a client may seek the advice and support of the coach in negotiating a settlement but may choose to self-represent or retain a different attorney for court representation. With respect to service depth, a client may want the coach to "research" the law by taking 5 minutes to look at a practice guide. On the other hand, the client may choose to pay for the lawyer to take several hours and write an exhaustive memorandum covering statutes, cases, local court rules, and law review articles.

A patient diagnosed with cancer is inexperienced in determining whether chemotherapy should be used and the nature, depth, and frequency of treatment. The patient needs the advice of a physician to make an informed patient choice. In the same way, a pro se litigant needs the advice of the lawyer/coach as to whether a coach is needed and, if so, to determine what the nature of the coaching will be. Therefore, the coach must first serve as legal counselor to help the client understand the nature of the client-coaching relationship and the cost and benefits of various options.[17]

The lawyer/coach must also be educated as to the experience and capability of the client to handle various tasks, client goals, and values given the client's time and monetary resources available. On this mutual education and assessment process, the lawyer and client collaboratively decide whether the coaching relationship should be established and the extent thereof. The lawyer serving as a client coach is certainly a far cry from the traditional paternalistic advice-giver-oriented relationship in which the client presents the problem and the lawyer directs the solution. The natural built-in conflict of interest present in the retention of professional services is somewhat ameliorated in the unbundled coaching relationship. Some client's rights advocates say that a client should have the advice of a lawyer in negotiating a contract for legal services due to the financial and role complexities in that relationship. Is the family litigator the best person to advise the client as to whether a litigator is needed and on what financial terms? If so, should the litigator about to be retained be advising clients on that business transaction? In the unbundled situation, the coach still has this financial conflict in advising whether the client needs further coaching. However, because the inherent premise in coaching is that someone other than the coach may handle legal services recommended by the coach (the client, different lawyer, or other professional) and the amount of fees to be earned by the coach is reduced drastically, the conflict of interest of the coach, although still present, is lessened greatly.

## DISCRETE TASK SERVICES PROVIDED BY THE LAWYER/COACH

If a lawyer is willing to offer discrete services, clients are generally more than willing to pay for general services such as legal counseling, help with forms, coaching for negotiations, ghost writing letters, preparing settlement documents, and reviewing proposals and drafts. In such models, clients are afforded access to a family lawyer and the opportunities to contract for discrete necessary services.[18] Some examples are as follows:

1.  The coach can assess legal strengths and weaknesses in the client's case, helping the client formulate positions for negotiations and/or court hearings.
2.  The coach can offer a psychological or negotiating profile to help the client deal with the other spouse and/or opposing counsel.[19]
3.  The coach can advise the client and offer an experienced assessment of proposed settlements or other courses of action. The coach can role play strategies and techniques in a simulated negotiation to prepare the client for actual negotiations.
4.  The coach can educate the pro se litigant about options, inside or outside the courthouse, for resolving the case without adjudication.[20]
5.  The coach can provide computer printouts on child and spousal support guidelines, develop budgets, analyze available income and perquisites, and help the client develop a realistic economic plan.
6.  The coach can refer the client to necessary ancillary professionals such as accountants, therapists, appraisers. or vocational counselors.

## EMERGING ROLE NO.2:
## FAMILY LAWYER AS DISPUTE RESOLUTION MANAGER

Just as a mindset has long prevailed that the lawyer's role is that of providing a full-service approach as a courtroom advocate, a similar mindset exists in respect to the use of courts to process disputes. Courts are often seen as the dispute resolution forum of first, rather than of last, resort. Law schools focus on the study of adversarial appellate cases that (in every single instance) resulted from an appeal of an adversarial trial. Continuing education and specialist training for judges and generally family lawyers concentrate on substantive law and the litigation process and strategy. When I took a course to qualify as a family law specialist, the respected instructor spent not more than 2 minutes on the subject of ADR in a total of 50 class hours.

Clients share the view that family lawyers are primarily advocates in a court setting. Even if they want their cases settled (to save costs if for no other reason), clients also expect a judge to decide their matter following a court hearing or trial or at least to use litigative strategy as leverage in negotiation (often on the courthouse steps). This myth of being able to "tell it to the judge"flies in the face of universal statistics that between 90% and 95% of family law matters filed in court are resolved consensually between the parties and not by a judicial officer.

If fewer than 10% of matters reach a judge's decision following a trial, clients should be retaining lawyers who are committed and trained to effectuate early, low-cost settlements. Accepting the reality of settlement, client attention should be shifted to when the case will settle and what process will be used to effectuate settlement.

## ROLE OF DISPUTE RESOLUTION MANAGER

In those situations in which the client engages a family lawyer for full-service representation, the lawyer should be a manager of dispute resolution as contrasted with being a courtroom barrister. Such dispute management includes educating the client about dispute resolution options both inside the courthouse and in the private sector, helping the client select the appropriate option(s), and effectively representing the client within that process option to obtain a settlement.

The role of dispute resolution manager (DR manager) requires the family lawyer to possess and use a different orientation and an evolved set of skills compared to courtroom advocacy. Similar to the role of client coach for pro se litigants, the full-service family lawyer continually stresses client education and client-centered decision making to ensure informed consent of the client in the process of dispute resolution as well as substantive rights and court procedures. This duty to advise clients on appropriate dispute resolution options has been the subject of activity in federal and state legislation, rules of professional responsibility, court rules, bar association policy and activity, and extensive comment within academic literature.[21] As an illustrative example, the Beverly Hills Bar Association has adopted an association-wide ADR Pledge designed to educate its members about this duty to advise clients and to initiate ADR discussions with opposing counsel and to have its members publicly declare their commitment to use alternatives to litigation. Similar pledges and ADR advice projects have been adopted by the California State Bar, S1. Louis Bar, Queensland Law Society in Australia, and Center for Public Resources in New York.

As DR manager, the family lawyer has the responsibility to guide clients through the universe (often described as "maze") of options within the courthouse itself (Table 3). As many jurisdictions mandate mediation custody disputes and/or economic issues at least once before trial (often in the form of a mandatory settlement conference), clients will generally be required to participate in one or more forms of court-mandated settlement procedures.[22] Client orientation as to the requirement for settlement participation can be contained in attorney-client consultations, court brochures, or attorney-generated informational literature prepared by the law office or bar associations, videotapes, a framed ADR Pledge on the lawyer's office wall, or in the attorney engagement letter itself. As public policy is tending to favor early ADR attempts including those conducted prior to filing a court action, this initial client orientation should occur early in the lawyer-client relationship. Many jurisdictions are requiring ADR status conferences or mandatory requirements prior to trial so that the DR manager's orientation may be in compliance with court hearing notices or pleadings requiring client participation and/or appearance in court. Given the prevalence of early ADR interventions, customary family law practice is evolving to require DR managers to employ preventive proactive ADR orientation early in the professional relationship rather than commencing a litigation course, only to later (after great financial cost and acrimony) inform the client about the inevitability of required mediation.

**Table 3**
*Family Law Alternative Dispute Resolution Options*

| Inside Courthouse | Private Sector |
| --- | --- |
| Conciliation court | Self-help |
| Custody evaluation | Informal third-party assistance |
| Mandatory mediation – | Individual divorce counseling |
| Property and support | |
| Meet and confer requirements | |
| Special masters or referees | Non-profit mediation centers |
| Mandatory settlement conference | Lawyer mediators |
| Conference in judge's chambers | Binding arbitration |
| | Med-arb and arb-med |
| | Private trials |

## OUTSIDE THE COURTHOUSE

The DR manager generally does not limit this emerging ethical obligation to required court processes. The private sector is offering accessible and affordable ADR options that can be customized to the parties and be conducted within days or weeks, with an experienced ADR neutral selected by the parties, and, if successful, can save the parties from the public scrutiny, increased stress and conflict, delay, and added cost of court proceedings. Privacy, speed, cost, and control are major components in client decision making, often more important than ensuring substantive rights or available due process. Whereas the right of judicial review and/or absolute 50-50 property split (in community property states) are important rights, a client informed of ADR options may opt for expeditious finality in return for less than an equal property division and/or a waiver of the right of appeal. The DR manager is continually helping the client assess and reassess settlement options and may guide the client in avoiding ever stepping foot in the courthouse. Even binding decisions may be obtained through arbitration of private trials. In the role of DR manager, the family lawyer uses the courthouse as a resource center to keep the case on track, to obtain referrals and appointment of third-party neutrals, as a last resort option for adjudication, and as a source for legal authority to approve settlements and enforce court orders.

## EMERGING ROLE NO.3:
## FAMILY LAWYER AS CONSULTANT DURING MEDIATION

As the DR manager helps the client decide on an appropriate settlement option, many clients still need and/or insist on maintaining the protection and advantage of attorney representation. This is particularly true when a party and/or counsel believe that an imbalance of resource and/ or negotiating power outside the mediation room might be reenacted in the mediation itself.[23]

At the early stages of ADR development, mediation was viewed primarily as a consensual tool for the two divorcing parties working alone with the mediator. In fact, a major client motivation to opt for mediation was to cut out lawyers and their resulting fees. As highly conflictual cases stayed in the adversarial court system, cases involving more amicable couples with generally modest estates were the primary earl y users of mediation. Most family lawyers generally ignored mediation as a viable option for their clients, rendered cautious warnings, or tacitly remained on the sidelines while their clients attempted to mediate.

As mediation has grown and increased in acceptance, families with large and complicated estates and/or those with highly adversarial interpersonal dynamics have also begun opting for mediation.[24] Fearful of abandoning legal rights, mediation clients also want the advice and protection of their own attorneys while still participating in the mediation process (Table 4).

**Table 4**
*Discrete Tasks of Consultant During Mediation*

Advice regarding substantive rights and legal procedures
Assessment of options to litigation
Selection of mediator
Review and/or negotiation of rules and terms of mediation
Determination of client's financial needs
Advice regarding overall objectives and negotiation strategy
Monitoring progress of mediation
Attendance at mediation sessions
Selection and monitoring of outside experts
Evaluation of estate planning needs
Review mediator progress letters
Review legal and financial documents
Limited negotiation with opposing party, opposing counsel, and mediator
Review/draft marital settlement agreement
Advice regarding tax consequences
Availability to represent client in court proceedings
Preventive planning
Legal wellness checkup
Monitor compliance with marital settlement agreement

To meet this demand, more family law specialists are choosing to serve as mediators, either full time or as an ancillary part of their practices.[25] Because the law office remains the gateway to most legal decision making, many clients are increasingly seeking the services of lawyers who are knowledgeable in and supportive of ADR goals and practices and who are skilled to represent them throughout the mediation procesS?[26]

## DISCRETE TASKS OF THE CONSULTING LAWYER IN MEDIATION

Some clients who use mediation will totally negotiate their own deals and talk with their consulting lawyers only after written settlement agreements have been prepared?[27] Others want their lawyers to be intimately involved in a number of discrete tasks such as helping identify, interview, and select the mediator; review and/or negotiate the terms of the mediation contract; advise or arrange the agenda or procedures; review the progress of each session; coordinate outside experts; negotiate with and educate the mediator; draft, review, and approve any final marital settlement agreement; and generate documents such as deeds, corporation records, and loan applications.

The consulting lawyer must be prepared to be open to a new and creative job description and to negotiate the level of service with the client. As more and more mediators are now including lawyers in the actual mediation sessions,[28] the craft of low-key participation and tactful guidance and interventions supplement aggressive courtroom advocacy as the sole effective style of legal representation.

## ECONOMIC AND PERSONAL BENEFITS TO THE LAWYER SERVING AS CONSULTANT FOR PARTY DURING MEDIATION

Another advantage of the consulting role for a lawyer is that mediation clients pay their bills.[29] If settlement is reached through consensual mediation, clients tend to have greater satisfaction.[30] Satisfied clients generally pay faster so that fewer fees are written off. Also, because bills do not skyrocket so fast and lawyer work is better understood and appreciated (the client is actually with the lawyer for much of the time billed), accounts receivables do not become so out of control.

Attorneys who sign on for the discrete task of legal consultant in mediation may also find greater personal satisfaction and congruence with their personal values than they do in the bloodletting of a courtroom. Lawyers' belief in the creative opportunities, efficiency, and cost benefits of mediation can often inspire and steady clients to persevere through the often bumpy and painful process. That inspiration and belief alone may help clients achieve satisfactory resolution.

## EMERGING ROLE NO.4:
## THE FAMILY LAWYER AS FAMILY ADVOCATE

Most judges and lawyers are aware of prevailing social science research that parental conflict is the single acute destructive variable to children of divorce. Parenting conflicts rarely are waged without polluting the other issues facing families during or after divorce. As family lawyers generally handle all issues facing a client in a single family law proceeding, custody, visitation, and other issues affecting the children often have a crossover effect on economic issues such as possession of the family residence, child support, management of children's trust funds, and award of attorney fees. Although they love their children and are concerned about issues that affect them, many clients demonstrate their primary anxiety over economic issues and select their attorneys based on whether the lawyers can get "bottom-line dollars." This is particularly true if the lawyer selected is not a family law specialist having required child custody training and experience so as to qualify before a state's licensing body. However, even many family law specialists view any dispute (child or economic) as part of the same lawsuit requiring vigorous adversarial litigation strategy and tactics.

The emerging role of the attorney as family advocate does not question the existence of such crossover of parenting and economic issues or that courtroom resolution is not sometimes appropriate. However, through exposure to research, interprofessional collaboration, and successful techniques developed by mental health professionals, modem family lawyers are enriching their representation beyond traditional adversarial jousting. A family-oriented focus need not replace being an advocate for a parent. However, a client may be better served if the family lawyer rounds out a myopic concentration on the rights of a parent client with an appreciation of the long-term welfare of the entire family system. For example, many jurisdictions use a legislative standard that gives a custody preference to a parent who encourages and implements access for the child with the other parent. A family lawyer who educates the client on the benefits to the child (and/or to the client) of providing such access to the other parent may both help the family and give the client litigation leverage should the need should arise.

Amplifying the role of DR manager, more family lawyers are explicitly defining their roles as family advocates and are announcing their commitment to long-range harmony for the family-regardless of which parent they are representing. This trend has developed, in part, because of the increased recognition of the ephemeral aspects of power[31] and the lack of client satisfaction in short-term "victories."[32] It may be more important for a parent to work toward positive adjustments of the child and to establish a working relationship with a former spouse than to press for an extra $10,000 in property settlement if receiving those dollars means causing further distress to their child leading to lower grades, problematic peer relationships, drug use, or worse.

Some parents are so self-involved and/or blinded by the habit of conflict that long-term, family-oriented trade-offs may not be appreciated. However, most parents, if educated on children's needs and family dynamics, will at least consider these ramifications (if not adopt them) in determining overall strategy to determine their own individual self-interest.

In training both lawyers and mental health clinicians in the resolution of custody disputes, Mary Lund, Angus Straghn. Lisa Harris, and I have developed a conceptual framework called the "Maelstrom of Divorce". The essence of this concept is that lawyers and therapists must use education. early intervention. and interdisciplinary collaboration to more fully address family concerns. From both the lawyer and the therapist perspectives. the essence of this approach is for the professional to serve as family advocate to help the parent understand the least adversarial options available to resolve child-related problems at the earliest available opportunity. This approach also encourages consensual discussions with the other parent and cross-disciplinary referral and collaboration to give the parent a fuller picture of information and options available.

An illustration of this family advocate role may be working with a mother currently equally sharing physical custody of two children, ages 8 and 5, who wishes to relocate to another state 2,000 miles away to be near her parents and enroll in a nearby MBA program. Under traditional family lawyer practice, after advising the mother of the legal strength of her position and the economic costs of litigation, if the mother wished to proceed, the lawyer might either file necessary court papers seeking primary custody upon relocation or, in a more enlightened approach, the lawyer might try to initiate settlement discussions with the father or his lawyer to try to achieve the mother's relocation amicably and consensually.

The role of family advocate does not necessarily alter this traditional approach; it merely enriches the quality of client decision making. After advising a client of her legal rights and procedural roadmap, the family advocate might inquire as to whether she had consulted a therapist as to the effect of relocation on the children. If such consultation had occurred, the family advocate might suggest that the lawyer and therapist collaborate and share information as to what information the client has received on child development and what emotional issues have been explored, and then jointly assess whether the client herself needs to obtain additional information before reaching a fully informed decision.[33] Once the mother has made an informed and reflective decision to seek geographical relocation of the children, the family advocate and therapist might form an ongoing collaborative team to work with her throughout the relocation process and thereafter to achieve a healing process (regardless of court outcome).

If the client had not previously consulted an expert in child development on divorcing family systems, the family advocate might educate her on the role of a therapist consultant, the benefits of the consultant, and how the two professionals could better work together for her interests by improving decision making and litigation strategy due to this interdisciplinary approach. In other contexts, most clients understand the importance of a criminal defense lawyer involving a therapist to help select and manipulate a jury. Applying that lesson to custody litigation, once clients appreciate that involving a therapist may help them obtain bottom-line goals, client resistance may be reduced. If the client decides to use a therapist consultant, the family advocate might work with the client in helping her select the appropriate professional, and the family advocate might attend the initial consultation if it were deemed appropriate and helpful. The family advocate might contribute to the agenda for the client and the therapist consultant and be available to act as the legal resource and to help redesign the client therapist consultant program as legal needs dictate. If a custody evaluation is anticipated, the family advocate could work with the therapist consultant in educating the client about this procedure including psychological testing process and obtaining and preparing collateral sources (child care providers, teachers, neighbors, etc.), and the therapist can simulate the evaluation process and use role-playing techniques to familiarize the client with the process and help address any concern she may have.

In addition to the obvious benefits of supplementing legal strategy, quite often this collaborative approach uncovers parenting deficiencies or lack of consideration of the children's needs. Regardless of the mother's ultimate decision as to relocation or whether her improved parenting would strengthen her court position, improving a client's parenting skills and her relationship with the other parent can only benefit the entire family, which includes the client.

## THE CONFIDENTIAL MINI-EVALUATION

Another role of the family advocate is to consider the needs of the entire family (which, by definition, includes one's client) in customizing family-oriented processes for settlement. One example is the confidential minievaluation[34] (CME) to facilitate resolution of custody disputes. The CME is a balancing act to give the family the input of an experienced custody evaluator without the cost, delay, adversarial posturing, and virtually binding decision of the court-appointed evaluator being imposed on the family and reported to the court. The CME can be initiated between counselor may arise out of mediation. A major advantage of the CME is that the evaluator does not render a written report that often contains negative observations and findings about both parents and the children. These written evaluation reports often have a long shelf life in family dynamics and can be indelibly woven into the family's interactions long after the immediate dispute is resolved. Instead, the CME oral findings of the expert can be used as a basis for negotiation. If resolution is not reached, either parent can still seek a formal custody evaluation or determination by the court.

Many family lawyers do not propose a CME because it is an imperfect balancing act. Being confidential and nonbinding, many lawyers consider the CME to be dangerous and misleading because of its cursory nature, at worst, and its wasting of time, at best. Often, the attorney as advocate has an inherent mistrust of the "opposition" to consensually agree to an adverse confidential recommendation by the evaluator (my therapist colleagues might call this "projection"). Given the CME's inherent shortcomings and the fact that it is a rather new and nontraditional approach, it takes courage for a family lawyer to propose this cutting-edge option. Integrating the role of family advocate, a family lawyer may be more open to the CME and other creative nontraditional alternatives due to the long-term advantages to the family of obtaining an early fair resolution based on consensual parental agreement. Employing a family advocate approach, the lawyer might stretch beyond the familiar and make efforts to educate the client about such new options[35] to be willing to risk client displeasure (caused often by mere unfamiliarity) so as to help a troubled family find an escape from long-held patterns of destructive conflict.

**Table 5**
*Preventive Legal Health Care Provider*

Symptomatic

Monitor compliance of court orders
Provide for future dispute resolution
Change documents based on marital status

Asymptomatic

Anticipate trouble
Maximize opportunities
Encourage harmonious relationships
Regular client legal checkups
Nonlitigation calendar to monitor client's life events

## EMERGING ROLE NO.5:
## FAMILY LAWYER AS PREVENTIVE LEGAL HEALTH CARE PROVIDER

In cancer treatment, chemotherapy may be preferable to radical surgery, but it does not do much for the patient's happiness, muscle tone, or pursuit of other opportunities and pleasures in life. In the same way, very few lawyers hold the belief that a settlement, even an amicable nonlitigated settlement, is the height of human experience. Research has demonstrated that mediation does not bring about long-term behavioral change in the clients. Client contact with the professionals is short term and rather superficial in psychodynamic terms.[36] The express purpose of mediation is to settle a dispute, not to promise happier and more satisfying lives for the participants (Table 5).[37]

Preventive lawyering is an approach that strives to prevent the causes of conflict in the first instance so that disputes can be avoided and dispute resolution may never be necessary. Similarly, preventive lawyering is based on the premise that the lawyer's role is to help a client recognize symptoms of legal trouble and use lawyers to maximize life's opportunities, not "win" a case or merely resolve a problem that has ripened into conflict.[38]

The underlying assumption of proactive preventive planning is that a client derives a positive benefit from an ongoing relationship with his or her attorney. By receiving updates on a client's life events[39] (not limited to disputes), the family lawyer can then assist the client to improve decision making and planning to prevent problems, reduce conflict, and increase life opportunities.

Lawyers often fear that clients might view proactive client contact as a financially motivated effort to drum up additional lawyer fees.[40] It is true that lawyers may increase their incomes due to ongoing client contact through preventive planning. Also, clients are too often accustomed to thinking of lawyers as crisis surgeons for disputes and deal breakers in regard to transactions.[41]

Clients and lawyers need education as to the value of preventive intervention. It is true that proactive preventive lawyering costs money in the short run. Yet, patients now decide whether the cost of a routine yearly physical wellness medical exam is worth the price.[42] A cost/benefit analysis is used to determine whether nonemergency medical procedures are undertaken by a patient. The same is true of a client managing preventive legal health. Unlike the crisis panic caused by disputes and attempts at resolution, preventive legal management can better control the timing and costs of legal procedures to be undertaken. The client is in total control as to whether to use the lawyer in such a preventive role and whether to take steps to solve a problem once highlighted by the lawyer.

## FROM PRO SE REPRESENTATION TO PREVENTIVE LEGAL HEALTH

Unbundling today is a growing practice method of providing legal access. Clients are beginning to understand and more carefully use limited-scope representation in crisis-driven situations; with successful pro se bundling experience, clients are gaining confidence in taking responsibility to determine the scope of legal work to meet identified legal needs. Clients are learning when, how often, and how extensively to consult lawyers. Clients are better recognizing that pro se legal access can be augmented by legal advice provided by lawyers who supplement, not dominate, the management of their cases.

This revolution in client behavior is affecting the lawyer's role. Lawyers are better learning to share control over the structure and decision making of the client-lawyer relationship. Lawyers are beginning to see new approaches that were once feared as malpractice traps[43] as opportunities in marketing and new service products. Uneducated clients concerned with fees and wanting to direct the overall case plan are being welcomed into the lawyers' offices rather than being "qualified" (rejected).[44] Lawyers are also experiencing the personal· and economic benefits that sharing decision making in a limited scope can bring to them.

Becoming accustomed to receiving symptomatic preventive advice for recognized needs during their divorce, clients are becoming more open to being reminded by their family lawyers to follow up on executory provisions or to fill lawyer prescriptions to obtain necessary ancillary services such as to draft a new will, obtain insurance protection, draft a cohabitation agreement, look at excessive alcohol consumption, or try to budget more effectively.

Lawyers are overcoming their own reluctance to suggest such preventive advice particularly as their role evolves to that of primary legal care providers. As the client's partner in ensuring legal health,[45] the lawyer is expected to advise and diagnose incipient legal trouble-not necessarily to do all the routine work. Lawyers are becoming more accustomed to probe for legal soft spots. Once diagnosed, it is becoming accepted practice for the client to decide whether to act, whether a professional is required and, if so, what type of professional should be retained. If a lawyer is needed, the client has a choice whether the diagnosing lawyer or another lawyer will do the required legal work.

The result of this role evolution is that clients are beginning to view their family lawyers as their primary family legal health care providers: helpers and family resources to be consulted to ensure legal health both when problems arise and preventively at regular intervals (e.g., each year) or on important life events.

*Forrest S. Mosten, J.D., is a mediator, trainer and family law practitioner. He teaches at the University of California at Los Angeles School of Law and in the Dispute Resolution Program at Pepperdine School of Law.*

## Notes

[1]  American Bar Association Consortium on Legal Services and the Public, Major Findings of the Comprehensive Legal Needs Study (1994), at 12 (hereinafter, ABA Legal Needs Study). Moderate-income persons reported that 61% of identified legal needs were never brought to the legal justice system; 23% were handled on the persons' own initiative, 12% were handled by nonlegal helpers, and one fourth were handled by taking no action at all. However, legal needs that found their way to the civil justice system were seen as resolved more satisfactorily than were those that did not (Ibid., at 17).

[2]  Bruce D. Sales, Connie Beck, and Richard K. Haan, Self Representation in Divorce Cases, ABA Standing Committee on the Delivery of Legal Services (January 1993), at 34 (hereinafter, Sales Report).

[3]  American Bar Association Standing Committee on Delivery of Legal Services, Responding to the Needs of the Self-Represented Divorce Litigant (1994) (hereinafter. ABA Pro Se Report). For a comprehensive discussion of findings in both the Sales Report and the ABA Pro Se Report, see Robert Yegge, "Divorce Litigants Without Lawyers," TM Judges Journal (Spring 1994).

[4]  See Sales Report, supra note 2, at 108.

[5]  Generally, ABA Pro Se Report, supra note 3.

[6]  ABA Pro Se Report, supra note 3, at 17.

[7]  Ibid., at 21.

[8]  Sales Report, supra note 2, at 37-9.

[9]  ABA Pro Se Report, supra note 3, at 11.

[10]  Sales Report, supra note 2, at 13-5.

[11]  See Sales Report, supra note 2, at 20.

[12]  Ibid., at 18.

[13]  Ibid., at 16.

[14]  Ibid.

[15]  ABA Pro Se Report, supra note 3, at 43.

[16]  See, generally, Forrest S. Mosten, "The Unbundling of Legal Services in Family Law Practice," ABA Family Law Quarterly (Fall 1994), which includes a section on legal practice and professional responsibility concerns relating to unbundling.

[17]  The California State Bar has established a Pro Se Task Force under the leadership of Peter Keene and is working with its Middle Income Committee (Marl Frank, chair) to publish a Lawyer's Guide to Being a Client Coach. The primary author is Steven Elias, senior editor at NoLo Press, 950 Parker Street, Berkeley, CA 94710, and the author of several self-help books.

[18]  For a fuller discussion of the coach's discrete services, see, generally, Forrest S. Mosten, "Unbundling Legal Services: Coaching the Pro Se Litigant," Compleat Lawyer (Winter 1995) (General Practice Section, ABA).

[19]  Helping the client understand the emotional component of divorce may be the most valuable contribution of the unbundled attorney. See Wallerstein and Blakeslee, Second Chances (New York, Ticknor & Fields: 1989), at 29-30:

Incredibly, one half of the women and one-third of the men are still intensely angry at their former spouses, despite the passage of ten years .

. . . An adult is more likely to succeed after divorce if he or she has some history of competence, some earlier reference point to serve as a reminder of earlier independence and previous successes. For all, recovery from crisis is an active process. It can be facilitated by the luck of the draw or by a chance meeting, but it involves active effort, planning, and the ability to make constructive use of new options and to move ahead.

See also Lowell Halverson and John W. Kydd, Divorce in Washington: Humanistic Approach (1990), particularly chap. I, "The Psychological Divorce: Putting the Pieces Back Together", at 1.

[20]   See Forrest S. Mosten, "Avoiding Trial in Family Law," Los Angeles Lawyer (September 1993), at 45.

[21]   For a discussion of alternatives to litigation, see Colorado Model Rule 2.1 (effective 1 January 1993), requiring lawyers to advise clients of alternatives to litigation; Edward A. Dauer and Cynthia McNeil. "New Rules of ADR; Professional Ethics Shotgun and Fish," Colorado Lawyer (September 1992); Forrest S. Mosten, "'The Duty to Explore Settlement: Beyond Garris v. Seversen," Family Law News (October 1989) (official publication of California Bar Family Law Section); Robert F. Cochran, Jr., "Legal Representation and the Next Steps Toward Client Control: Attorney Malpractice for the Failure to Allow the Client to Control Negotiation and Pursue Alternatives to Litigation," Washington '" Lee Law Review 47 (1990), at 819.

[22]   See California Senate Bill 401 (Code of Civil Procedure 1775 et seq. (effective January I, 1994), which elevates mediation as co-equal with arbitration as a judicial requirement and establishes court procedures and confidentiality requirements.

[23]   See, generally, John Haynes, "Power Balancing," in Divorce Mediation: Theory and Practice, edited by Jay Folberg and Ann Milne (1988), at 277.

[24]   In complex cases, mediation may be used as consensual case management as well as resolution of disputes. See Forrest S. Mosten, "Mediation in the Era of Direct Calendaring and Riefler," Association of Family Law Specialist Newsletter (California) (April 1994), at 5.

[25]   The ABA Family Law Section has several committees on mediation, and the ABA has recently established a separate Alternative Dispute Resolution Section. Even the prestigious American Academy of Matrimonial Lawyers is offering mediation education and training to its members, composed largely of skilled trial lawyers. The growth of private ADR firms and the proliferation of family mediation training are part of this trend.

[26]   See Jay Folberg and Allison Taylor, Mediation: A Comprehensive Guide to Resolve the Conflicts Without Litigation (1984). The authors argue for the benefits of legal review, at 247.

[27]   Mediators differ in their approaches to the Involvement of independent counsel. Some mediators actively discourage the use of independent counsel in contravention of ABA Standards for Attorney Mediators (1984). Other mediators recommend the use of counsel to review mediated agreements. Others actively encourage or require the early use of counsel to consult outside mediation services or to sit at the table and actively negotiate. See also Leonard L. Riskin and James E. Westerbrook, Dispute Resolution of Lawyers (1987), at 244:

Virtually all divorce mediators, lawyers or not, now urge both husband and wife to consult their own lawyers before, during, or after the mediation. The role of such "outside" lawyers was also unclear. Just how deeply must they delve into the basis of the Mediation Agreement. One danger, of course, is that some reviewing attorney undermine a Mediation by inappropriately imposing an adversarial perspective. But sometimes a strong adversarial impetus is just what the client needs. (cites omitted)

[28]   Forrest S. Mosten, "Role of the Consulting Attorney During Mediation Sessions," in Tips of the Experts: Family Law Symposium (Los Angeles County Bar, 1992).

[29]   Forrest S. Mosten, "Mediation and Prevention of Business Disputes," Beverly Hills Bar Journal (Summer 1993), at 105.

[30]   See Jessica Pearson, "An Evaluation of Alternatives to Court Adjudication," Justice System Journal (1982),420,439-441, cited in Riskin and Westerbrook, supra note 27, at 431:

Mediation clients also experience more user satisfaction than their adversarial counterparts. Disputants who successfully mediate generate compromise agreements that are perceived to be fair, equitable and better complied with over time.

³¹  See John Haynes, supra note 23.

³²  Creative applications can use mediation in such conflictual areas as international child abduction and family violence. On child abduction, see Forrest S. Mosten, "Mediation Makes Sense: How to Prevent an International Crisis," ABA Family Advocate (Spring 1993). On violence and abuse. see Folberg and Milne, supra note 23, at 18: "Although controversial, these programs (mediation in domestic violence and child protection) are producing high levels of satisfaction and results acceptable to prosecutors, public officials, as well as the affected parties. (cites omitted)

³³  See Lois Gold, "Lawyer and Therapist Team Mediation," in Folberg and Milne, supra note 23, at 205. See also Forrest S. Mosten and Barbara E. Biggs, "The Role of the Therapist in the Co-mediation of Divorce: An Exploration by a Lawyer-Mediator Team," Journal of Divorce 9 (Winter 1985-1986), at 27.

³⁴  See Forrest S. Mosten, "Confidential Mini Evaluation," Family and Conciliation Courts Review 30 (July 1992), at 373. originally published in Family Law News &. Review (Los Angeles Court Bar Association, 1992).

³⁵  See, generally, Lionel Margolin and Mary Lund, "Post Divorce Counseling Has a Place in Family Law," Family Law News &. Review (Los Angeles County Bar Association, 1993), at 20, in which the authors discuss the creative options of court-ordered counseling and court-ordered case management in highly conflictual custody cases.

³⁶  See Joan Kelley, Lynn Gigy, and Sheryl Hausman, "Mediation and Adversarial Divorce:

Initial Findings From a Longitudinal Study," in The Theory and Practice of Divorce Mediation, edited by Jay Folbert and Anne Milne (1988), at 465-6:

The findings of this study did not support the hypothesis that mediation is significantly more effective in reducing psychological distress and dysfunction. The mediator intervention was not powerful enough to selectively reduce major psychological distress beyond the passage of time.

³⁷  Whereas expectations concerning long-term behavioral change after mediation are muted, resolution achieved through mediation can significantly impact a participant's future life. The benefits of saved money, expeditious finality, privacy, salvaging relationships, and feeling satisfied (rather than victimized) can facilitate an improved personal life and/or limit the damage caused by the dispute compounded by the costs of resolution.

³⁸  Louis M. Brown, "The Practice of Preventive Law," Journal of American Judicial Society 35 (1951), at 45.

³⁹  Louis M. Brown, "Providing Preventive Legal Care In Prepaid Legal Service Plans: The Periodical Checkup," Preventive Law Reporter (February 1994), at 102:

A checkup may be done when certain client events take place. For example, client moves from one state to another, client changes legal status from single to married person, changes from military to civilian life, or a client is about to retire, or any time the client is considering "signing on the dotted line" with respect to any significant matter.

⁴⁰  The trend among U.S. Supreme Court cases is to support entrepreneurial- and consumer-oriented marketing of professional services. See Bates v. State Bar of Arizona, 433 U.S. 350 (1977), holding blanket bans on lawyer advertising unconstitutional, and Edenfield v. Fane, 113 S.O. 1792 (1993), permitting a Rorida certified public accountant to personally solicit clients. Also see Barbara Curren, The Legal Needs of the Public (1977) and Barlow Christianson, Lawyers for People of Moderate Means (1970). The underlying premise of both the nonlitigation calendar and the legal wellness checkup is that society benefits from the expanded use of lawyers in situations in which a client may not perceive that a problem exists (let alone believe that it requires a visit to a lawyer). This premise appears undermined by client fear that, in addition to the cost, the experience of hiring a lawyer might be unpleasant, would not help, and may even make matters worse. See ABA Legal Needs Study, supra note 1. In examining this client fear, it might be argued that the public has been demonstrating its demand for less lawyering, not more. Cynics might even suggest

that preventive lawyering is really another lawyer scheme to replace client dollars that are being lost through the pro se movement, nonlawyer alternatives, and other developments described in this article.

[41]    Lawyers want clients to know that Oliver Goldsmith was wrong when he said, "Lawyers are always more ready to get a man into troubles than to keep him out of them." See Louis M. Brown, "Open One Night a Week," Journal of American Judicial Society 35 (1951), al25.

[42]    Prenuptial and cohabitation agreements are illustrations of preventive legal services. The costs of these agreements are often high in terms of lawyer fees and stirring up latent emotional problems between a couple. However, given a recent $84 million palimony jury award, the preventive legal costs may be accepted similarly to the necessity of paying insurance premiums. See "Palimony Jury Awards $84 Million," Los Angeles Times (14 May 1994), at 1, 21. See also Jacqueline Rickard, Save Your Marriage Ahead of Time (1991).

[43]    See ABA Standing Committee on Professional Liability Lawyers Desk Guide to Mal· practice (1992), at 38.

[44]    Ibid., Malpractice Trap no. 1: "Failure to Qualify Clients."

[45]    See, generally, Thomas H. Gonser and Forrest S. Mosten, "A Case for a National Legal Health Care Strategy," Preventive Law Reporter (Summer 1993), at 32.

# [19]

# Collaborative Family Law

## Pauline Tesler

## Introduction

Since its emergence in 1990,[1] collaborative law has captured the enthusiasm and commitment of a rapidly growing segment of the family law bar across the U.S. and Canada.[2] Given its rapid expansion and the degree of support accorded it by prominent family law judges, many family law attorneys predict that by the second decade of this millennium, collaborative law may establish itself as the normative first resort for resolution of family law disputes. In the words of Hon. Donna J. Hitchens,[3]

> "I believe that my job-the job of all judicial officers in family and juvenile law-is to serve children and families, and a community in which people cannot afford to spend their whole family estate on attorneys. So I favor any system that best serves families and children, and, from everything I've seen so far, the collaborative law approach is THE best, and the least litigious. The least litigious alternative is always going to be better for families."

Because the model has as its core element an agreement that no participants, neither lawyers nor clients, will threaten or resort to court intervention during the pendency of the collaborative work, all efforts take place entirely outside the court system. For that reason, the model has proved readily adaptable across jurisdictional lines, despite sometimes significant differences in substantive and procedural laws from jurisdiction to jurisdiction. By the late 1990s, vigorous communities of collaborative practitioners had formed and begun representing family law clients in California, New Mexico, Arizona, Florida, Georgia, Pennsylvania, New York, Connecticut, Massachusetts, New Hampshire, Ohio, Illinois, Minnesota, Wisconsin, Colorado, Utah, British Columbia, Alberta, and Ontario. Today, the model has expanded to Ireland and the United Kingdom, Austria and Australia.

Collaborative Law appears to meet significant needs both among family law clients and among the lawyers who assist them through divorce. As will be discussed more fully below, clients appear to want the advantages of a contained, settlement-oriented, creative, private, respectful process without sacrificing the benefits of having a committed legal advocate at their sides. For that reason Collaborative Law appeals to clients who may hesitate to commit to a dispute resolution process facilitated solely by a neutral mediator.[4] And, while many family lawyers suffer considerable professional angst as a consequence of their awareness that family law courts are neither safe nor effective places for clients to resolve divorce-related disputes,[5] the decision by a family lawyer to become a mediator instead of a litigator in order to work in a more positive conflict resolution modality with clients requires an immense and difficult step: leaving the practice of law. Because collaborative legal practice, unlike mediation, allows family law attorneys to represent clients in the role of advocate, continuing to practice law and to be bound by all ethical mandates for lawyers, the switch from conventional lawyering to collaborative law is not a leap out of one profession into another, but rather a short step through an open door into a different approach to lawyering. As collaborative practitioners, lawyers who have become disillusioned with what they can offer clients in adversarial family law practice can embrace an identity as a member of a "helping profession" while maintaining their chosen professional identity as lawyers. Collaborative lawyers often report that the process of retooling from litigator to collaborative lawyer involves integration of personal and professional values into a coherent identity that brings a professional gratification previously absent from their work as lawyers.[6]

## Basic Elements of the Collaborative Law Model

The core element that distinguishes a collaborative law representation from "friendly negotiations" and other lawyer-facilitated efforts to settle divorce-related disputes[7] is that in collaborative law, the representation begins with the clients and lawyers signing a binding agreement (referred to as a "participation agreement" or "collaborative stipulation") that prohibits those lawyers from ever participating in contested court proceedings on behalf of those clients. With that core element, the case is a collaborative law case, and without it, no matter how cordial or cooperative the lawyers and parties may be in their behavior, attitudes and intention to reach agreement, the case is not a collaborative law case. The term "collaborative law" is not just a synonym for "nice," or "cooperative." It refers to a specifically-defined model for dispute resolution, the essential element of which is that the lawyers are disqualified contractually from ever representing those clients against one another in court proceedings.[8]

It is that unique element that gives collaborative law its considerable power to guide clients to acceptable settlements while building vigorous assistance of legal counsel into the heart of the process. Experienced collaborative practitioners who have come to this work from a background as family law litigators believe that in the face of apparent impasses in settlement negotiations, lawyers who are not contractually barred from taking the issue to court tend to decide too quickly that the issue should be taken to a third party for resolution. By temperament, lawyers tend to be impatient and result oriented.[9] Moreover, trial practice is generally the most lucrative work for lawyers. Thus, the reasoning goes, internal and external factors coincide in favor of inducing traditional litigation-matrix lawyers to abort negotiations in the face of impasse where court is an option. In collaborative practice, however, such a decision will terminate the involvement of those lawyers in the case, and for that reason, collaborative lawyers operate within a significant external incentive to remain longer at the negotiating table working with their clients to find a way through the impasse. With the contractual disqualification from going to court, the risk of failure becomes distributed to the lawyers as well as the clients. With this element, lawyers as well as clients are highly motivated by the procedural "carrots and sticks" built into the model to remain at the negotiating table in the face of apparent impasse far longer than in any other mode of lawyer-facilitated family law dispute resolution.[10] This is sometimes expressed as: collaborative practice liberates the problem solver within.

## Litigation-Matrix Divorce Dispute Resolution: the Context from which Collaborative Law Emerged

In the United States, Canada, and the European Union, roughly half of all marriages now end in divorce.[11] Over the course of the last half of the twentieth century and into the twenty-first, we have seen mainstream attitudes toward divorce move from considering it a scandalous or shameful aberration in which a "guilty party" could expect harsh treatment at the hands of the courts, to accepting it as a predictable, and statistically "normal" life passage for most people, if not in their own direct experience, then almost certainly in the experience of their extended family, friends, and colleagues. Divorced parents, remarriages, blended families, shared custody in one form or another, and all the attendant potential for parental disagreement and conflict constitute the daily life experience of a large and growing percentage of children growing up in western cultures today.

But while statistically normal, the divorce passage is far from easy for most people. It is recognized to cause emotional trauma second only to the death of a spouse, and to involve a grief and recovery process that parallels the stages of recovery from death of a loved one. Divorce requires unusual emotional resources from clients at a time when they typically are experiencing high levels of stress and lowered coping ability. Moreover, clients are expected to make financial and parenting decisions of enormous import for the future well-being of themselves and their children at a time when strong emotions often impair clear thinking. And, at a time when children need extra attention from their parents because of the dramatic life changes accompanying divorce, typically parents are distracted by the demands of the divorce and family restructuring process in ways that impair their ability to attend to the needs of children. Study after study has documented the substantial harms inflicted upon children by high conflict divorces in which parents use the courts as a battleground for seeking redress for deep emotional pain that the courts cannot possibly remedy.[12] In the face of these changes and consequent pressures, our judicial system, the cultural institution responsible for handling issues associated with the family breakdown and restructuring attendant upon divorce, has lagged behind in making the profound changes that might be expected following upon a recognition that divorce, far from being aberrant and shameful, far from being an accident or injury involving an offender and a victim, is a predictable, "normal" life passage that will be experienced by a large percentage of people embarking upon marriage.

Courts are the institution that our culture charges with conducting the official business necessary to accomplish a divorce, and lawyers are the professionals designated by default to guide divorcing couples through the significant, extended rite of passage that divorce actually represents in a human life. But courts, even with the best-intentioned judges and clerks, are poorly adapted to meet the needs of families as they break down and restructure.[13] Depending on how you look at it, courts may be seen as the arena for a ritualized form of gladiatorial combat, or a public resource for more or less orderly and predictable third party resolution of disputes, but even the most positive description of a family law court's functions would fall far short of including the kinds of comprehensive conflict resolution, financial, and psychological services that families in transition typically require.

Because courts function in an adversarial model, the necessary business of resolving divorce-related issues becomes, in the court-based paradigm, a contest between starkly opposing extremes of proposed outcome with respect to each disputed issue. The contest is orchestrated by gladiatorial attorneys whose job it is, in trial-based dispute resolution, to pare down the divorcing couple's complex emotional, financial, and material issues into readily understood black and white terms that have the appeal of simplicity in a court system that prizes efficiency and speed. For the lawyers, control over the flow of facts and argument is a vital tool in the battle to win over the decision maker. Considerable expense and effort is expended in preparing for the "main event": the trial; and while family law litigators know that settlement is the likeliest outcome for most cases they handle, it is a common saying among trial lawyers that the best way to prepare for settlement is to prepare well for trial. Information is guarded like the dwarf's treasure buried beneath the mountain; complex post-separation child-rearing dilemmas are reduced to black and white cartoons of Snow White and Hitler. Another commonplace in trial practice holds that since the judge will never award a party all the relief that he or she requests, the effective trial advocate always asks for the moon and the stars. Devastating allegations under penalty of perjury supporting requests for extreme forms of relief are filed on behalf of both parties, causing wounds that can never be repaired. This is the context in which litigation-matrix settlements are forged, often late in the process, in the shadow of trial, after irreparable damage and most of the costs of litigation have already been incurred. This is the time when litigation-matrix lawyers are expected to change roles and, after having prepared clients for a win at trial, must urge their clients to accept a far leaner settlement.[14] Most clients do in fact yield to the considerable pressure to settle that mounts as the trial date approaches; only 3% to 5% of cases in most jurisdictions actually do go to trial.

But these litigation-matrix settlements merely push clients to immediate resolution of a list of justiciable legal issues, without bringing the disputing parties to a deeper understanding and acceptance of the need for resolution or the value or appropriateness of the specific outcomes agreed to, much less incorporating true closure across the broad range of conflict that may be feeding the narrower list of specific disputes that the law permits courts to resolve. Clients typically emerge from such settlements dazed and angry, because they have read the motions and trial briefs and – unlike their lawyers – they tend to believe what they read. They expect to be awarded the moon and stars, and instead emerge from settlement negotiations with the equivalent of a lump of coal. In the words of an eminent California family law jurist, retired court of appeals Justice Donald King, "family law court is where they shoot the survivors."[15] Another experienced family law judge puts it this way: "If anyone leaves my courtroom happy, I've made a dreadful mistake."

It should come as no surprise, given the costly and conflict-engendering process that family law litigants go through on the road to settlement, that family law attorneys worry about malpractice suits and frequently find themselves in fee disputes with clients. Unhappy clients are commonplace in family law practice, where disputes above the horizon about dollars and hours with children often are the weapons with which clients fight subterranean battles that are really about who is aggressor, who is victim, who is good and who is bad.[16] Whatever the result, litigation matrix settlements and judgments rarely provide answers to those questions, and no outcome measured in dollars or hours is sufficient to salve the narcissistic wounds that often are driving the "above horizon" divorce litigation conflict. Moreover, the fees and costs incurred in family law litigation can devastate the savings of all but the wealthiest litigants.

Little wonder that family law is a field in which even the most successful practitioners experience high levels of stress and frustration. This is the context in which collaborative law emerged, the fertile ground in which it has taken such rapid root. Family law attorneys learning about the model have welcomed it as the solution to a deeply troubling problem in their daily professional lives:[17] how to provide useful, high quality, professionally appropriate legal advocacy and counsel to family law clients in a way that supports the healthy transition of a couple and a family from marriage through the normal life transition that is divorce.

Just as collaborative law seems clearly to meet a need among family law attorneys, it also appears to meet the needs of clients in a way that renders it attractive when described accurately and evenhandedly as one of a menu of dispute resolution options from which a divorcing couple can choose at the time of divorce. Family law attorneys often note that it is rare for a client to tell a divorce lawyer, "I want war! I want revenge! I want to take him to the cleaners! I want to reduce her to destitution!" While strong, primitive feelings boil and bubble close to the surface for many divorcing clients, they generally start out the divorce process by telling their lawyers, "I just want what's fair." Fair, of course, is an elastic and subjective concept that is of limited use in setting goals and strategies for divorce representation. Nonetheless, the statement, understood correctly, can be translated to mean, "I am upset and worried, but I do not want a war; I want to reach some kind of reasonable outcome, as good as I can realistically achieve for myself and my children without ending up in a costly, emotionally draining battle that nobody can really win." Many if not most family law clients at bottom aim for such an outcome, but many of them lack the emotional tools needed to get them from where they are to that kind of "good divorce."[18] Some of them are lawyer-averse, fearing that to retain a family law attorney is to guarantee costly and damaging litigation that will preclude effective co-parenting of children following the divorce. These clients, if they make use of professional advisers at all during the divorce,[19] may seek out professional mediators and perhaps even refuse to retain consulting attorneys to advise them during the mediation process. Others, worried about the potential bad behavior of the spouse, or about their own perceived weakness at the bargaining table, eschew mediation, seeking out traditional family law attorneys in order to have a strong advocate at their side during negotiations. These litigants will probably settle their issues short of trial, but have until now had no way to identify and select counsel able and willing to focus the divorce process on settlement rather than on preparing for trial.

**Collaborative Law Differs Greatly From Conventional Settlement Negotiations**

On first hearing about collaborative law, traditional family law attorneys often remark that it's nothing new, "I've been doing it for years, I just don't call it that. After all, I settle more than 90% of my cases." Family law cases do overwhelmingly settle short of a full trial on the merits, but these are settlements fashioned in the shadow of the law, with the litigation matrix shaping the representation from the first attorney-client contact. Often, family law litigators settle cases these cases virtually, if not literally, on the courthouse steps, after expenditure of enormous emotional and financial resources on pendente lite motions and discovery. The settlement may be on the eve of trial, supervised by a settlement conference judge who applies evaluative pressure on parties and counsel in the interests of lightening the court's docket.

The movement of a case from first interview to settlement in this kind of litigation-matrix settlement practice is shaped from the start by the limitations and demands inherent in court rules and legal restrictions on the family court's jurisdiction and exercise of discretion. From the start, a "litigation-matrix" attorney excludes from consideration much of what the new client considers most troubling about the divorce situation, because the court lacks the power to make effective orders about wounded feelings and the nagging annoyances that angry or vengeful spouses can inflict upon one another below the threshold of a court's power or willingness to act.

The job of the lawyer in this kind of representation is to shape and pare the facts of the client's situation into a story, a theory of the case that will enable the lawyer to "win big" on the client's behalf. To do this, the lawyer will ignore or deem irrelevant many parts of the client's story, and will emphasize or exaggerate others. From the first interview, the lawyer typically uses leading, closed-ended questions to spot issues that lie within the court's jurisdiction to resolve and develop goals, strategies, and tactics for successful outcomes. Sometimes, custody and support motions are prepared in the course of the first interview, and the client – who may be highly anxious and driven by fear, grief, or other primitive emotion – may be asked to sign inflammatory declarations under penalty of perjury then or soon afterward, for maximum tactical and strategic advantage in the litigation process. "Hurry up and wait" is the normal pace in litigation: hurry to meet arbitrary court deadlines, wait for the court calendar to have space to attend to client needs. Always, the norm of third party judicial resolution is the template that shapes development of goals, sharing of information, advocacy of positions, and pacing of resolution.

Another way to put this is that the litigation-matrix for settlement involves devoting nearly 100% of the lawyers' efforts to an event that is expected to happen less than 5% of the time, a ratio of effort to result that is matched only by the military and firefighters.[20] Client participation in the settlement process is generally minimal; the lawyers control all negotiations. Distributive bargaining is the norm, with little or no attention paid to the broader spectrum of interests that can matter greatly to divorcing clients and that could enrich settlement prospects and outcomes.[21]

In many ways, the real interests of divorcing parties get lost in the process of bringing a litigation-driven case to settlement. The focus, in these settlements, is on the immediate divorce-related financial and custody provisions of the divorce judgment. Limited or no attention is given to the interests and needs of the post-divorce restructured family, either in the sense of positive planning for healthy long term family restructuring and change, or in the sense of minimizing the destructive impacts of the divorce process itself on economic interests of family members and on possibilities for effective parenting of children after the divorce. In most U.S. jurisdictions, litigated court proceedings and files (including those of cases that ultimately settle) are open to the public and all vestiges of privacy are lost, at the same time that matters formerly decided privately by the couple are handed placed under the control of disinterested and busy professionals.

Settlements reached in a collaborative legal representation come into being in a process that differs dramatically, in nearly every important respect, from the litigation-matrix settlement process. Collaborative lawyers work from the first interview to listen deeply to the client's entire story, because only by doing so can the collaborative professionals facilitate true interest-based negotiations. Without such attention to what really matters to the client, the raw material is lacking to help clients discover common interests and goals, and to take advantage of differing perspectives on value, risk, and timing. Moreover, good collaborative practitioners begin by educating clients about the negotiating process and the divorce recovery process, and eliciting agreements about good faith bargaining and management of conflicts and strong emotions, so that clients are empowered to participate actively and effectively in direct negotiations. All substantive discussions, information-sharing, options development, and negotiations take place in face-to-face meetings with the clients at center stage, aided by their collaborative advocates. The role of the lawyer shifts from alter ego gladiator to guide for negotiations and manager of conflict. Instead of measuring success by the size of the outcome on one's own side of the table, good collaborative lawyers detach from outcome and judge their success by the degree to which both collaborative lawyers succeed in working effectively with all participants to offer the clients the best possible circumstances in which to work in a good faith, interest-based, respectful matter, at an appropriate pace, toward a mutually beneficial and acceptable outcome.

The process invites maximum client involvement and control over outcome, while maximizing privacy and creativity. The participation agreements signed at the outset commit all participants to good faith bargaining, voluntary full disclosures, interest-based bargaining, inclusion of relational and long term interests in the identification of clients' goals and strategies. The role of the lawyer is redefined in collaborative practice, as advocate for achieving the long-term enlightened interests of the client, rather than zealous advocate for goals and strategies identified by clients possessed by transient states of diminished capacity associated with the trauma of divorce. The disqualification of all professionals from participation in litigation between these clients has the effect of keeping both lawyers and clients at the negotiating table in the face of apparent impasse much longer than is typically the case in conventional settlement negotiations, where resort to the local judge to resolve impasses is a comfortable and familiar option on the dispute resolution menu that litigation attorneys carry in their mental armory. For collaborative lawyers, deciding to see what the local judge can do with an apparent impasse is identical to a decision to cease participating in the case. Unlike litigation attorneys, collaborative lawyers share the risk of failure in collaboration with their clients. Collaborative lawyers see these features of the collaborative law model as powerful aids to creative conflict resolution – as the means for liberating the effective problem solver trapped within litigating lawyers.

**Collaborative Law Resembles But Differs in Important Ways from Mediation[22]**

While collaborative law builds upon important conflict resolution skills and understandings developed in the field of mediation,[23] collaborative law differs from mediation in important ways. First and foremost, collaborative lawyers are advocates, not neutrals. They work within all professional ethics and standards of practice for lawyers and are a licensed profession. They owe a primary duty to their own clients. But, this duty is reframed not as the duty to zealously advocate for whatever fear-driven objective the client might grasp for during the course of recovering from loss of a marriage, but rather the duty to work with the client to help him or her achieve the goal nearly all clients say they want – the "good divorce", speedy, economical, respectful, individualized, and protective of children – in a process specifically tailored to help the client be able to realize that goal. This means that collaborative lawyers undertake much more than either a conventional lawyer or a mediator considers to be part of the job description: to educate clients, help them work from positions to interests, remove them from the negotiating table when they are too upset to think clearly, counsel them when they behave in self-defeating or bad faith ways, and assist them to recalibrate back to the high intentions identified at the start of the collaborative retention. Moreover, collaborative lawyers generally agree to protocols for practice whereby they will withdraw from representing a client who hides information, stonewalls, misrepresents, or otherwise misuses the collaborative process.

Where clients in mediation may occupy an uneven playing field, collaborative law builds in advocacy and legal advice into the heart of the process. Where neutral mediators may encounter great difficulty working with clients who subvert the process (whether intentionally or otherwise) while still maintaining neutrality, collaborative lawyers take on as part of their agreed job description the responsibility to work with such clients until they can return to the table willing and able to engage in effective good faith negotiations.

Finally, the structure of the collaborative legal model itself seems to offer more wattage of focused dispute resolution power than is generally available in family law mediation. Family law mediation often takes place as a three-way process, including the two divorcing spouses and one neutral mediator; lawyers for the parties, if they are involved at all, participate from their own offices, not in the mediation room. Even when consulting attorneys for the parties participate directly in the mediation, they participate not as designated conflict resolution professionals working explicitly toward settlement, but rather as conventional legal counsel who provide advice and representation in an adversarial model in which the decision to terminate mediation and take the matter to court is readily available and without built-in disincentives. Only in collaborative practice is the option-generating and negotiating process conducted by two trained legal advocates committed to consensual dispute resolution and skilled in interest-based bargaining who share a commitment to help clients stay on the high road and discover common ground for solutions. Because these advocates, who have every incentive to continue working toward settlement, meet in "real time" around a table with the clients who are expert in the facts and interests associated with the case, and everyone can hear and respond to the ideas of all the other participants in the conversation, the creative "out of the box" lateral thinking power available at the negotiating table to help clients reach agreement is considerably amplified as compared to single-neutral mediation.

## Interdisciplinary Collaborative Practice

During the early 1990's, at the same time that lawyers were developing and extending collaborative legal practice, a parallel model called collaborative divorce emerged among a certain segment of mental health professionals experienced working in the court system on the custody battles of high conflict divorcing couples. These psychologists, social workers, and counselors mediated at the courthouse, and conducted the child custody evaluations used in trials and court-annexed settlement conferences to provide recommendations and rationales about which parent was more deserving of custody of the children. These professionals came to see that their evaluation reports, though intended to serve the best interests of children, were further polarizing the already-conflicted parents and decreasing their ability to provide effective post-divorce parenting for children.

Peggy Thompson, Ph.D., a California psychologist, worked with colleagues in the early 1990's to develop an interdisciplinary team approach that would offer divorcing couples a consistent, positive, supportive, contained system for working with mental health and financial professionals on divorce-related issues. The collaborative law model, developing simultaneously and separately among family law attorneys, was the final component of an approach that now offers integrated virtual professional teams to divorcing spouses in many communities across the U.S. and Canada.[24] These teams include: two collaborative lawyers, two divorce coaches (who must be licensed mental health professionals experienced in divorce work), a child specialist, and a financial neutral. These professionals are trained in the psychodynamics of divorce and healthy family restructuring as well as effective communication skills, conflict resolution skills, and interdisciplinary collaboration.

Individuals in these professions working together on a particular case remain independent practitioners, bound by all ethical and professional mandates of their respective professional licenses or certifications. Typically, in communities where this option is available, interdisciplinary practitioners form practice groups through which they can build trust, develop protocols, and obtain training and mutual mentoring, as well as engage in public education and marketing about interdisciplinary collaborative divorce services. Clients interested in this interdisciplinary resource can select the individuals who will constitute their particular professional collaborative team from the members of the practice group.

Each client works with a trained divorce coach to learn highly focused communication, stress reduction, values clarification, assertiveness, and/or anger management skills aimed at helping the client move as effectively as possible through the collaborative divorce process. The child specialist provides balanced, non-judgmental, non-evaluative information about the children's needs and challenges during the divorce process, as an aid to developing high quality parenting plans. The financial neutral helps clients identify income, expenses, assets, and debts, efficiently marshalling necessary documentation for the collaborative lawyers to use in the legal negotiations, while at the same time helping the clients with immediate budgeting concerns, identifying key financial issues needing to be addressed by the lawyers, and assisting in the settlement process by analyzing tax issues and projecting long term financial consequences of various settlement options. Each professional bills separately at his/her own rate. Each professional has a separate fee agreement with the client. Usually, the result is to contain conflict and educate clients in ways that reduce legal fees, streamline negotiations, and provide long-lasting "value-added" professional services that do far more than simply push the clients into an agreement.

Where clients have the intention, but not the emotional or intellectual ability, to work effectively with their collaborative lawyers in legal negotiations, this interdisciplinary model can provide the additional resources needed for couple to realize their intention of having a "good divorce." For such clients, paradoxically, paying to bring in the necessary range of professional resources typically results in a divorce that costs less than it would have if they had been represented solely by collaborative lawyers, without the interdisciplinary team.[25] Interdisciplinary collaborative practice offers divorcing couples consistent, positive, integrated professional assistance, in a client-centered model aimed exclusively at helping the couple reach respectful, efficient, lasting, mutually workable solutions to divorce-related problems that will help both parents provide effective co-parenting of the children after the divorce. Like collaborative lawyers, all interdisciplinary collaborative divorce professionals sign contractual agreements with their clients that bar them from ever participating in contested court proceedings between the parties.

**Infrastructure for Collaborative Practice**

Practitioners from the three professional disciplines that are providing collaborative dispute resolution services to clients have built an umbrella organization, the International Academy of Collaborative Professionals,[26] that has been effective in sustaining a consistent vision of core elements and standards for collaborative practice throughout the English-speaking world. During the fourteen years since the first emergence of collaborative law, none of the schisms or conflicts that have fragmented the mediation movement have emerged, perhaps because collaborative practitioners cannot work effectively with their clients without basic consensus among practitioners about protocols, procedures, and values. IACP has been a force for consensus-building that continues to embrace new developments in the collaborative community.[27]

*Pauline Tessler, J.D., is a specialist in family law, practicing in the San Francisco Bay area. She is the co-founder and former president of the International Academy of Collaborative Professionals.*

## Notes

[1]     The precise date, January 1, 1990, can be pinpointed; on that day, Stuart Webb, a family law attorney in Minneapolis, decided that he would henceforth represent clients only pursuant to a binding agreement that neither he nor the lawyer for the other party would ever go to court for those clients. The sole purpose of the retention would be to help the parties reach an efficient, respectful, interest-based settlement. The originator of the collaborative law model, Webb soon realized he needed a cadre of similarly committed colleagues, and from that realization was born the Collaborative Law movement.

[2]     The International Academy of Collaborative Professionals, which includes practitioners from the fields of law, mental health, and finance, publishes a list of local, regional, and statewide practice groups in its journal, the Collaborative Review. The second issue of the Review, dated October 1999, listed 16 practice groups in six states and one Canadian province. The IACP website currently lists more than 120 practice groups in four countries, 26 states and 20 Canadian provinces. See www.collabgroups.com.

[3]     Then Presiding Judge of the Family Law Department of the San Francisco Superior Court, and now Presiding Judge of the Superior Court itself. Pauline H. Tesler, "Donna J. Hitchens: Family Law Judge for the Twenty-First Century," The Collaborative Review (formerly, Collaborative Quarterly), October 2000, Vol. 2, issue #2, pp. 1-4, at 4.

[4]     Joan B. Kelly has noted that the term mediation encompasses such a broad, diverse spectrum of dispute resolution modalities that it is difficult to make meaningful generalizations about "mediation". Joan B. Kelly, A Decade of Divorce Mediation Research, 34 Fam. & Conciliation Ct. Rev. 373-85 (1996). While different locales have differing predominant family law mediation models, it is quite common for family law mediation to involve only the two clients and the mediator, with counsel for the parties (if any) providing advice and sometimes litigation services outside the mediation process.

[5]     A vivid description of what is wrong with family law courts as family restructuring institutions is provided by judge Anne Kass, in Clinical Advice From the Bench, 7 J. Child & Adolescent Psychiatric Clinics N. Am. 247, 251-53 (1998): "(T)oo few judges and lawyers have examined their personal beliefs, attitudes, and expectations about family matters in any depth, and that leaves them vulnerable to becoming emotionally entangled in divorce and custody cases, sometimes quite unconsciously. . . . What does reach their conscious awareness is that they are extremely uncomfortable, but they haven't the skills to reflect on their discomfort through introspection. In short, family law has the propensity to diminish objectivity and blur boundaries for judges and lawyers and thus cause emotional overload." Id. Worse yet, the art of "building and maintaining appropriate boundaries is missing from legal education, so we find lawyers and judges who assume the inappropriate roles of rescuer and avenger." Communication about facts is often "tied to fault and blame," and lawyers and judges communicate in "linear and triangular patterns with little understanding that doing so causes misinterpretations, suspicion, and confusion. Id. For an in-depth analysis of lawyers' professional malaise from a psychosocial perspective see Susan Swaim Daicoff, Lawyer, Know Thyself: A psychological Analysis of Personality Strengths and Weaknesses (American Psychological Association 2004).

[6]     This and other similar observations about collaborative lawyers and collaborative practice are based on the author's work over more than a decade as a practitioner and trainer of collaborative lawyers, as well as her role as co-founder and President of the International Academy of Collaborative Lawyers and co-editor of the Collaborative Review. This work has involved teaching and mentoring thousands of collaborative lawyers and hearing first-hand their reports of the transition from litigation to collaboration. Research results are not yet available to provide empirically-based conclusions with respect to the ideas and impressions set forth in this article, but academic researchers are beginning to conduct studies focused on collaborative lawyers and clients. See e.g. Julie MacFarlane, Experiences of Collaborative Law: Preliminary Results from the Collaborative Lawyering Research Project, 1 Journal of Dispute Resolution 179 ( 2004).

[7]     Nearly all divorces and indeed nearly all litigated proceedings of every kind end not in a judgment after trial, but rather in a negotiated pretrial settlement agreement. The familiar boast of family law litigators that "I settle over 90% of my cases" is therefore likely to be true. However, as will be discussed below, such settlements typically happen in a litigation matrix in which pacing, rules, procedures, and

expectations about outcome are dictated by the practices of the local courts, and in which substantial – even irreversible – economic and emotional costs are often incurred in the lengthy preparation for trial that precedes the eventual effort to settle. Included in the data about pretrial settlements are the many agreements hammered out virtually on the eve of trial through considerable pressure from lawyers and settlement judges. Collaborative law, in contrast, takes place entirely outside the litigation matrix. No support or custody or kickout motions, no formal discovery or discovery motions, no depositions, no subpoenas, no settlement conference statements, no "fast track" or "rocket docket" timelines, impose external pacing or expectations on the process. Collaboration proceeds without reference to courts, except at the end of the process to the extent the imprimatur of the court is necessary to achieve dissolution of the marriage and incorporation of the ultimate agreement into a divorce judgment.

[8]    Some non-practitioners (including family law litigators who prefer to be able to hold onto the client and the case in the event settlement efforts fail) have expressed doubts about whether the core concept of a retention specifically limited to working toward settlement, in which the lawyers are barred from representing the clients in subsequent litigation, actually is particularly important for success in resolving conflicts. Whether or not research ultimately confirms the universal conviction of collaborative practitioners that this core element is central to the power of collaborative law in resolving family law disputes, it should be emphasized that this core element of collaborative law is definitional: that is, those practitioners who are committed to practicing collaborative law have selected the term "collaborative law" to define what they are doing. Quibbles by those who wish to do something other than this model about whether disqualification is or is not "necessary" are missing the point. From a consumer protection and malpractice protection point of view, it is important that clients understand clearly the nature of the dispute resolution options available to them as they select their preferred conflict resolution modality. Collaborative law is the term that has entered the marketplace to describe the model in which the lawyers cannot litigate but only can work toward settlement. Practitioners not wanting to enter into this kind of limited scope retention are free to offer their clients other dispute resolution modalities – described by other names – that do not require the binding agreement that the lawyers will not litigate if negotiations break down. No useful purpose would be served, however, and consumers could only be confused, if such practitioners were to call such other models by the same name – collaborative law – that is now in widespread use to describe only cases in which the lawyers cannot take the dispute to court. Collaborative practitioners and trainers across the U.S. and Canada are united in their advocacy for careful, accurate use of this terminology in the interests of clarity, consumer protection, and malpractice prevention. The International Academy of Collaborative Practitioners will adopt standards in 2004 that incorporate this definition of collaborative law. Commentators and researchers interested in comparing outcomes for clients whose lawyers use the collaborative law model, as compared to outcomes for clients whose settlements were reached in modalities that do not require an a priori agreement that the lawyers will not represent the clients in disputed proceedings in court, should be able to construct better research designs for comparing cases if this terminological and definitional clarity is respected than if it were to be blurred.

[9]    See generally Daicoff, supra note 5.

[10]    For extended discussion of how collaborative legal practice actually works, see Pauline H. Tesler, COLLABORATIVE LAW: ACHIEVING EFFECTIVE RESOLUTION IN DIVORCE WITHOUT LITIGATION (American Bar Association 2001) and Richard W. Shields, Judith P. Ryan, and Victoria L. Smith, Collaborative Family Law: Another Way to Resolve Family Disputes (2003)

[11]    See, e.g., U.S. Bureau of the Census, U.S. Gov't Printing Office, Marriage, Divorce and Remarriage in the 1990's (Current Population Reports) 5 (1992).

[12]    "Entrenched disputes often represent a response to overpowering feelings of shame and vulnerability which are evoked by the marital separation as well as by the perception that professionals are increasingly in charge of what was once the family's private life. Vulnerable parents frequently manage these feelings of shame and helplessness by projecting all incompetence and badness onto the former spouse and holding all competence and goodness for themselves. From this dynamic evolves a wish that the judge, Solomon-like, will erase the shame by publicly answering, once and for all, the

question of which parent is good and competent and which parent is bad and incompetent." Vivienne Roseby, Ph.D., Uses of Psychological Testing in a Child Focused Approach to Child Custody Evaluations, 29 Fam. L. Q. 97, 98 (1999). "(L)itigation itself is often demeaning, as litigants attempt to exaggerate each other's flaws and reopen old wounds in order to win points for themselves. Further, the process is disempowering as it forces the parties to place their fates in the hands of their attorneys and the court. In the process, the family's resources are expended and depleted with no beneficial outcomes for the child or the parents." Janet Weinstein, And Never the Twain Shall Meet: The Best Interests of Children and the Adversary System, 52 U. Miami L. Rev. 79 (1997).

¹³  See generally Daicoff, supra note 5. Courts and judges are asked to "take on and resolve family dilemmas that other professionals and the community at large have failed to resolve-cases that attorneys have failed to negotiate and mediators have failed to settle, for families that counselors and therapists have failed to help. Inexplicably, there is an assumption that judges have some special capacity to resolve the most difficult, the most complex of all family problems. Is it any wonder that family court assignments for judges are so unpopular, so often avoided, and usually staffed by rotating assignments to prevent burnout?" Janet Johnston & Vivienne Roseby, In the Name of the Child 223 (1998).

¹⁴  In California, for instance, legislative policy expressly favors settlement of family law matters, and attorneys' fee awards can be made by judges in part based on the degree to which the party and/or attorney have worked to achieve or thwart settlement.

¹⁵  Address at New Ways of Helping Children and Parents Through Divorce, conference sponsored by Judith Wallerstein Center for the Family in Transition and University of California, Santa Cruz; Quail Lodge, Carmel Valley, California (Nov. 21, 1998).

¹⁶  See, e.g., Roseby, supra note 12 at 98 ("entrenched disputes often represent a response to overpowering feelings of shame and vulnerability which are evoked by the marital separation as well as by the perception that professionals are increasingly in charge of what was once the family's private life. Vulnerable parents frequently manage these feelings of shame and helplessness by projecting all incompetence and badness onto the former spouse and holding all competence and goodness for themselves. From this dynamic evolves a wish that the judge, Solomon-like, will erase the shame by publicly answering, once and for all, the question of which parent is good and competent and which parent is bad and incompetent.")

¹⁷  The leading trainers who emerged in the collaborative law field during the early and mid 1990's concur that there is a lawyer-driven self-generating demand for training that has rendered it unnecessary to advertise collaborative law to the family law bar. Stu Webb, originator of the collaborative law concept, often refers to the rapid growth of this movement as driven by "attraction rather than promotion." Private conversation with Stu Webb, 1999. This author has been approached frequently during attorney trainings by lawyers who say with emotion that they were about to give up the practice of law, but that attending the collaborative law training was a last attempt to find a way to remain in the legal profession, and that they now see a way that they can practice family law with a sense of integrity and purpose.

¹⁸  In my trainings I refer to the "highest intentioned client," i.e., that part of the client that truly wishes for a contained, respectful, reasonable settlement of divorce issues so as to preserve resources and permit a functioning post-divorce restructured family that can parent children effectively after the divorce; and the "shadow client," i.e., that part of the client that has been deeply wounded by the loss of the marriage, and suffers transient intermittent states of diminished capacity characterized by periods of primitive emotion such as fear, rage, guilt, grief, and the like. Recovery from the trauma of divorce resembles recovery from the death of a spouse in its nature, intensity, and progression. It can take several years for a wounded client to return gradually to whatever functional state he or she enjoyed prior to the divorce trauma; recovery can be seen as spending increasingly more time in the "highest intentioned" state, and decreasing time in the "shadow" state. The degree to which the "shadow client" dominates the legal divorce process and dictates the goals, strategies, and tactics correlates directly with how likely it is that there will be a "high conflict" divorce. These concepts are discussed at greater length in Pauline H. Tesler, Collaborative Law: Achieving Effective Resolution in Divorce Without Litigation (American Bar Association, 2001)

[19]   Self-represented or "pro per" or "pro se" clients constitute a growing percentage of divorce filings in many jurisdictions, presenting delays and other significant challenges to an already-overburdened court system that cannot function smoothly with large numbers of cases lacking any knowledgeable professional working on either side of the divorce. See,e.g., Roderic Duncan, Pro Per Do-It-Yourself Divorce, Cal. Lawyer, Jan. 1998, at 44.

[20]   I am indebted to Boston collaborative lawyer Doug Reynolds for this comparison, and permission to use it.

[21]   These include material issues that may be readily negotiable even though outside the jurisdiction of the court (for instance, potential agreements about paying college education expenses for adult children, or about support of stepchildren or infirm parents, or about alimony arrangements that courts could not order, or consideration of tax issues that lie outside court jurisdiction) as well as more elusive but highly significant relational considerations that may be overlooked by distraught clients and adversarial lawyers, though if asked the clients would value them higher than achieving the marginal financial gains that may render the relational interests unattainable (for instance, the value of being able to dance at a child's wedding, or to meet over the cradle of a grandchild, or for children to be able to sustain warm relationships with extended family).

[22]   See supra note 4, for the dangers of generalizing about mediation. Notwithstanding that fact, the distinctions pointed out here between collaboration and mediation would seem to apply to virtually all the many variants of mediation described by Joan Kelly.

[23]   Standards for collaborative legal practice that will be adopted in 2004 by the International Academy of Collaborative Professionals include mediation training as one of the recommended elements of a comprehensive training program for collaborative lawyers, and identify as important many skills that are central for effective mediation, such as active listening, open-ended questioning, reframing, and the like.

[24]   See the Collaborative Review, journal of the International Academy of Collaborative Professionals, for regularly updated listings of interdisciplinary practice groups and contact persons.

[25]   In the oft-quoted words of human potential psychologist Abraham Maslow, "If the only tool that you have is a hammer, every problem you encounter will tend to resemble a nail." Lawyers are not trained in the skills required to support or contain emotionally challenged clients, but are faced with the problems such clients present during divorce on a regular basis. Doing the best they can to manage anger, grief, fear, and other "shadow" behaviors takes more skill and experience than most family lawyers have to offer, and the result is to run up legal fees with little of value to show for the expense. Lawyers may have somewhat more to offer with respect to financial issues, but typically have little patience for educating unsophisticated clients in how to manage a checkbook, or how to understand retirement plans and investments. Nor do they usually have the ability to do sophisticated tax planning, or complex projections of long term financial consequences of-for instance-keeping the family residence versus receiving liquid assets. And their services generally are billed at a higher hourly rate than mental health or financial professionals, while providing less to the clients when the problem is emotional, relational, or financial in nature rather than a legal or negotiations challenge.

[26]   IACP was founded in the mid-1990's as a 501(c)(3) tax-exempt nonprofit organization. It publishes the leading journal in the collaborative practice field, The Collaborative Review (co-edited by the author and Jennifer Jackson, J.D.). Its website, www.collabgroup.com, provides lists of practitioners and practice groups by geographic locale, and a variety of other information about collaborative publications, trainings, conferences, and other activities. IACP will adopt comprehensive standards for practitioners, trainers, and trainings in 2004.

[27]   Collaborative dispute resolution is just beginning to spread from the realm of family law into the broader field of general commercial and civil dispute resolution, and it seems likely that probate and business collaborative lawyers will be embraced within IACP. For articles addressing collaborative law in the broader legal dispute resolution community, see Pauline H. Tesler, Collaborative Law Neutrals (sic) Produce Better Resolutions, Alternatives (Journal of the cpr institute for dispute resolution), Vol. 21, No. 1, January 2003, and Douglas C. Reynolds and Doris F. Tennant, Collaborative Law: An Emerging Practice, Boston Bar Journal Vol. 45, No. 5, Nov.-Dec. 2001, pp. 1-5.

# Family Law in The Twenty-first Century:
# Note: Ethical Issues In Collaborative Lawyering

## Barbara Glesner Fines

Collaborative law practice represents the newest development in alternative dispute resolution in family law practice. At present, few mechanisms are in place to regulate or standardize collaborative practice. Indeed, even among the established collaborative law community, one can find an astounding variety of agreements that are called "collaborative law." These agreements may be between the clients and their respective attorneys, between the clients only, or between all clients and all attorneys.[1] The triggers for withdrawal from the process may range from any bad faith actions to a total breakdown of the process.

Thus, attorneys may advertise and provide representation that they call "collaborative" or "cooperative," but that process may be based on strategic, positional bargaining or may envision litigation as one possible aspect of the representation. One might suspect that these attorneys whose approach is inconsistent with emerging collaborative norms would soon become known in the family law bar.[2] Since it takes two attorneys to provide a collaborative law process, peer sanction would soon pressure these attorneys into reforming or abandoning their practice. However, market regulation will take some time, with the cost of harm to clients and confusion regarding the collaborative law process.

For the purposes of this examination of the ethical issues in collaborative law process, the collaborative law practice will be assumed to require two separate agreements: a limited scope representation agreement between each attorney and client and a separate agreement among both the attorneys and clients that commits all to engage in collaborative processes and requires both attorneys to withdraw should the collaborative process break down.

Little formal regulation of the ethical aspects of these agreements has emerged to this point. Three states have statutes expressly regulating collaborative law. California's statute merely defines the practice and notes that it is a permissible approach in family law cases.[3] North Carolina and Texas each have more detailed statutes, providing requirements for collaborative law agreements and rules governing confidentiality and evidentiary privileges for collaborative law processes.[4] The Texas statute also mandates a duty of candor in collaborative law processes.[5] More regulation is likely to emerge as the practice of collaborative law grows.[6] Currently, the National Conference of Commissioners on Uniform State Laws has created a Drafting Committee on a Collaborative Law Act.[7]

No reported cases have yet examined ethical issues in the collaborative law context. Rather, the ethical analysis of collaborative law has been provided by ethics opinions by the states and the ABA. These states, with one exception, have approved the collaborative law process in principle, while noting several cautions regarding the practice.[8]

This article catalogues some of the issues raised by these ethics opinions and regulations. The article examines competence issues in considering collaborative law practice. It then examines the limited scope representation agreement entered into between attorney and client. This agreement presents ethical challenges for communicating with the client and securing informed consent. The withdrawal terms of the agreement bear separate consideration. The article then explores the argument that these agreements require an attorney to eschew what some would consider necessary "zealous advocacy." The article examines the differing views on whether the four-way disqualification agreement presents an unethical conflict of interest for attorneys participating in these agreements and closes with an examination of the proposals for a collaborative law communications privilege.

## I. Competence and Communication

Collaborative law practice requires a sufficiently discrete set of skills as compared to the skill set required for family law litigation. Thus, one concern attorneys must address is that of competence. Attorneys should not undertake collaborative law practice without sufficient training in interest-based negotiation and other skills necessary to effectively assist their clients in collaboration.[9] Cooperative, interest-based bargaining may be sufficiently foreign to some attorneys that they may conclude that they simply lack the aptitude or attitude to be a successful collaborative law attorney. Yet, as collaborative law practice becomes more popular and more clients seek out (and attorneys advertise) collaborative law representation, market pressures may cause some attorneys to offer collaborative representation even though they lack the skills and attitudes necessary to this form of representation.

Since much of the collaborative law process builds on similar skills and perspectives as necessary to provide family law mediation, an attorney would be well advised to begin with the many training and certification programs available for family law mediators. Specialized training and peer support is available through the private associations of collaborative law attorneys.

The most fundamental skill necessary for collaborative law is that of communication. This communication begins with the client. The initial agreement between each attorney and his or her client provides that the attorney provides representation limited to collaborative negotiation and that the client consents to the attorney's withdrawal should that process break down. Is such a limitation on the scope of the representation ethically permissible? Under ABA Model Rule 1.2(c),[10] "A lawyer may limit the scope of the representation if the limitation is reasonable under the circumstances and the client gives informed consent." This rule thus requires two separate qualifications: the attorney must communicate with the client sufficiently to allow the client to make an informed choice regarding collaborative divorce and the attorney must also exercise independent professional judgment regarding the advisability of this collaborative method.

Attorneys should take great care in counseling their clients regarding the collaborative law agreement. As a matter of prudence, the client's informed consent should be in writing, but attorneys must recognize that having a client sign a representation agreement is not proof that the client has given informed consent.[11] Just as attorneys have an ethical obligation to counsel clients regarding the alternatives to litigation,[12] so attorneys should fully explain the collaborative law process and the risks and benefits of that process compared to other options. Clients should understand that, not only does the process differ from litigation or mediation, but that the outcomes and goals of the representation may differ as well. It is especially important that the client understand the costs of obtaining new representation should the collaborative process fail. Clients should understand that collaborative agreements create pressure to settle, as well as opportunities to abuse the process by refusing to settle, thus disqualifying both attorneys.

In addition to the client's informed consent, the attorney's independent assessment of the appropriateness of this process for any given client is critical to the "reasonableness" of limiting the scope of representation to negotiated settlement only. Attorneys should not only help clients to determine whether collaborative practice is appropriate for their divorce, but should exercise their independent professional judgment in screening clients for collaborative practice.[13] The risk of abuse of the process must be given careful and serious consideration. For example, just as there is an ongoing debate over the suitability of mediation in cases involving domestic violence,[14] the imbalance of power, manipulation and fear that are part of the domestic violence dynamic may make collaborative practice impossible.

Differential financial resources are also a consideration. Collaborative law, with its team of two attorneys and additional professionals as necessary to facilitate settlement, can require a significant investment. This investment is no more, perhaps, than litigation costs, but if the negotiation is unsuccessful, this investment is lost and the litigation costs remain. Where one party has limited resources, the opportunity for that client to be able to participate in a collaborative law practice may depend on modifying the rules.[15] Thus, for example, if an client is represented by a legal aid attorney in the collaborative law process and the negotiations are unsuccessful, would the entire legal aid office then be disqualified from representing the client in litigation? This would mean the client would essentially be left without counsel entirely. Emerging regulation of collaborative law processes must address these circumstances of power imbalance and determine whether the process can be modified to address these concerns.

There is a more subtle ethical concern in counseling clients that collaborative law attorneys should consider. Many family law attorneys offer collaborative law as an alternative approach to representation; others provide only collaborative law representation. For some attorneys, what has brought them to collaborative law is their own interest in preserving their career in law. It is not uncommon to hear attorneys describe their interest in collaborative law as having arisen because they were "burned out" or couldn't stand the adversarial process any longer.[16] In other words, some attorneys practice collaborative law for themselves as much as for their clients. While these attorneys may reject traditional representation in family law litigation, they must nonetheless respect the value of these approaches for some clients.

Traditional litigators must recognize that there are some situations and some clients for which litigation is an inappropriate and ineffective method of dispute resolution and so counsel their client. A longstanding criticism of family law litigation is that some attorneys unnecessarily increase the adversarial nature of the dispute, causing increased expense and conflict. A similar, though perhaps more subtle, problem can arise in collaborative law. If attorneys practicing collaborative law allow their own personal distaste for litigation to cloud their judgment regarding the suitability of collaborative law for their clients, they may be "selling" a dispute resolution approach to their clients.[17] This would not result in a client's informed consent to a reasonable limitation on the scope of representation. Thus, the New Jersey Supreme Court Advisory Committee's Ethics Opinion concludes:

> Given the harsh outcome in the event of such failure [to reach agreement], we believe that such representation and putative withdrawal is not "reasonable" if the lawyer, based on her knowledge and experience and after being fully informed about the existing relationship between the parties, believes that there is a significant possibility that an impasse will result or the collaborative process otherwise will fail.[18]

## II.  Required and Prohibited Withdrawal in Collaborative Law Agreements

A second lens through which to view these limited representation agreements is that of ethical withdrawal. Here again, there are a wide variety of models of collaborative law practice. While nearly all collaborative lawyers insist that the requirement that both attorneys withdraw if the process is unsuccessful, there is a group of attorneys who practice "cooperative" law in which they use the interest-based, cooperative methods of collaborative law but, failing to reach settlement, they then proceed to represent their clients in litigation.[19] For purposes of this analysis, the mandatory withdrawal will be treated as an essential aspect of collaborative law.

The attorney-client retention agreements provide a client's advance consent to the lawyer's withdrawal under certain conditions. These might include bad faith tactics by the client, withdrawal by the opposing attorney or client from the collaborative law process, or a breakdown in the negotiation process. Would an attorney's withdrawal be required in the absence of  this agreement? State ethics rules governing withdrawal generally follow the pattern of Model Rule 1.16. Under that rule, withdrawal is only mandatory if the client fires the attorney, the attorney is violating the rules of professional conduct, or the attorney becomes unable to practice.[20]

Permissive withdrawal is permitted only under limited circumstances. One such circumstance is whenever there would be no material adverse effect to the client. Clearly, this basis for permissive withdrawal would not apply in a collaborative law agreement since withdrawal does work a significant detriment to the client - indeed, it is the very threat of this withdrawal that provides the "engine" that encourages continued negotiation. Other justifications for permissive withdrawal include circumstances in which a client insists on pursuing an objective that the lawyer considers repugnant or imprudent (here, the client insists on adversarial or uncooperative negotiation), or when the client fails to fulfill an obligation to the lawyer after being given reasonable warning (here the client fails to fulfill the obligation to engage in collaborative processes).[21] Under this analysis, the attorney's withdrawal upon the breakdown of the collaborative process would be permissible, especially given the client's advance agreement to that outcome. Of course, there is a difference between the attorney being permitted to withdraw by the rules and being required to withdraw because of the agreement with the client, but to the extent the client is always able to fire the attorney, it seems well within the client's authority to require an attorney to withdraw.

## III. Zealous Advocacy and the Collaborative Agreement

A third aspect of this limited representation is the agreement that the attorney and client will cooperate in negotiating a settlement. This required cooperation includes an agreement that the parties voluntarily disclose all material facts, correct one another's misunderstandings and errors, and work to generate mutually agreeable solutions. However, isn't agreeing to these requirements inconsistent with the attorney's duty to zealously represent a client? The concern reflects a view that ethical rules require something beyond competent and diligent representation. However, in the Model Rules of Professional Conduct, as adopted by the majority of states, "zealousness" has been relegated to a comment to the requirement of diligence.[22] While that comment notes that "A lawyer must also act with commitment and dedication to the interests of the client and with zeal in advocacy upon the client's behalf," the comment takes care to qualify that statement by noting that:

> A lawyer is not bound, however, to press for every advantage that might be realized for a client. For example, a lawyer may have authority to exercise professional discretion in determining the means by which a matter should be pursued. See Rule 1.2. The lawyer's duty to act with reasonable diligence does not require the use of offensive tactics or preclude the treating of all persons involved in the legal process with courtesy and respect.[23]

Moreover, in the family law context, many norms of cooperation are already built into the rules of procedure. Discovery rules in most family courts ordinarily include standard, broad required disclosures from both sides. Mandatory mediation, parenting plans, and other devices designed to encourage cooperative resolution are a common component of many family courts. There is little to suggest that cooperative disclosure is unethical or that a commitment to a cooperative attitude would result in representation that lacks competence or diligence.

## IV. Conflicts of Interest and Four-way Agreements

While collaborative law could conceivably proceed with each client entering into a limited scope representation agreement and no express agreement across the table, the more common description of the collaborative law process provide that both attorneys and clients agree to a cooperative ethic and to withdrawal in the event of breakdown of the process. It is this aspect of the collaborative law process that has caused the most ethical concerns. In the Colorado ethics opinion finding collaborative law unethical, it was the four-way agreement with a mandatory withdrawal provision that the Colorado ethics opinion found to constitute a conflict of interest and an impermissible restraint on and attorney's independent professional judgment.[24] Ethics opinions from other states and that of the ABA Committee on Professional Judgment have concluded that these agreements need not constitute a conflict of interest.[25]

The concern that four-way agreements violate conflicts rules rests in the notion that the attorney, by becoming contractually obligated to an opposing client and his or her attorney, has created a situation in which the attorney's representation "may be materially limited by the lawyer's responsibilities to ... a third person."[26] By disqualifying himself from adversarial representation, the collaborative attorney has, according to the Colorado ethics opinion, materially interfered with his "independent professional judgment in considering alternatives" or has "foreclosed courses of action that reasonably should be pursued on behalf of the client."[27] The Colorado opinion found particularly troubling that the power to force a withdrawal lies in the hands of an opponent.

> It is also noteworthy that disqualification from future litigation is not contingent upon any good faith erosion of the collaborative process. If the process does not result in an agreement between the parties, regardless of the good or bad faith participation of any party to the process, the Four Way Agreement requires the Collaborative Law practitioner to withdraw. The process is particularly susceptible to abuse in this respect.

The ABA's ethics opinion, on the other hand, found no inherent conflict of interest in this four-way agreement because the clients involved had already agreed with their attorneys to the attorney's withdrawal.[28] Nonetheless, just as attorneys should carefully consider whether to counsel their clients to consent to a limited scope representation agreement, so too attorneys should carefully assess the reasonableness of counseling their clients to enter into a four-way agreement. Attorneys should consider whether the opposing attorney and client are able to enter into the collaborative law process fairly and with minimal risk of failure of the process. An attorney should ordinarily advise against entering into a collaborative process if the attorney is aware that the bargaining across the table is likely to be colored by "puffery"[29]"strategic positioning" and other attitudes toward the process that, while permitted by the rules of professional conduct, are nonetheless destructive of the overall collaborative process. Likewise, where the power balance or emotional stability of the parties is such that a collaborative process is unlikely to be fair or stable, collaborative agreements would be unreasonable.

## V. Confidentiality and Collaborative Processes

A final issue incident to the collaborative law process is the protection of confidentiality. Just as with mediation, if information exchanged under the agreement of collaboration could later be used in court as evidence, one might create incentives for tactical abuse of the collaborative law process. Thus, the drafters of the Uniform Collaborative Law Act have suggested that states create a privilege for collaborative law communications similar to that provided for mediation statements.[30] The privilege would belong the parties but would also allow nonparty participants in the process to refuse to disclose and prevent others from disclosing his or her communications in the collaborative law process. Like other communications privileges, the protection provided by this provision would extent only to collaborative law communications and not to information otherwise discoverable or admissible. Thus, the ability to use collaborative law processes as a tactical tool for adversarial discovery still exists for the parties, though the mandatory withdrawal provision is designed to protect against an attorney's strategic abuse of collaborative processes. Under the proposed uniform act, the privilege can be waived only if all parties to the process agree to waive the privilege. Nor does the act allow waiver through conduct as would occur with the attorney-client privilege.

The scope of the exceptions to be built into this privilege and the right of parties to opt-out of the privilege are important and controversial matters to be decided by legislatures in drafting privilege statutes for collaborative law processes. However, the legislatures can benefit from the experience of courts in applying mediation privileges in crafting these exceptions.[31] In any case, clear and enforceable rules for confidentiality in these processes is critical to their integrity.

In conclusion, in the absence of more defined regulations of collaborative law practice, attorneys wishing to represent their clients in this process will need to be extremely diligent in their evaluation of their clients, the opposing attorneys and parties, and of their own skills and motivations in order to provide ethical representation. Attorneys must insure clear communication and carefully drafted agreements. Collaborative law practice presents an exciting variation on the growth of consensual, cooperative dispute resolution processes in the family law field. If attorneys participating in the process continue to maintain a careful scrutiny of their ethical obligations in the practice, the public will be well-served by having available this option.

*Barbara Glesner Fines, JD, LLM, is the Ruby Hulen Professor at the University of Missouri-Kansas City School of Law.*

## Notes

[1]    See generally Scott R. Peppet, The Ethics of Collaborative Law, J. Disp. Resol. Forthcoming, Available at SSRN: http://ssrn.com/abstract=1097315 (describing a variety of collaborative law agreements and the variety of contractual/hortatory language contained in these).

²   See, e.g., Julie Macfarlane, Experiences of Collaborative Law: Preliminary Results from the Collaborative Lawyering Research Project, *2004 J. Disp. Resol. 179, 196* (noting the assumption of this market form of monitoring).

³   *Cal Fam. Code § 2013* (West 2007) permits (but provides no substantive regulation of) a "Collaborative law process" in specified family law matters. The statute defines collaborative law as a "process in which the parties and any professionals engaged by the parties to assist them agree in writing to use their best efforts and to make a good faith attempt to resolve disputes... on an agreed basis without resorting to adversary judicial intervention." Likewise, the North Carolina statute identifies the four-way agreement and withdrawal provision as essential to the process. See *N.C. Gen. Stat. § 50-72* (2006)("A collaborative law agreement must be in writing, signed by all the parties to the agreement and their attorneys, and must include provisions for the withdrawal of all attorneys involved in the collaborative law procedure if the collaborative law procedure does not result in settlement of the dispute.").

⁴   *N.C. Gen. Stat. § 50-70* to 50-79 (2006); *Tex. Fam. Code Ann. §§6.603* & 153.0072 (Vernon 2005).

⁵   *Tex. Fam. Code Ann. § 6.603(c)* ("A collaborative law agreement must include provisions for:
(1) full and candid exchange of information between the parties and their attorneys as necessary to make a proper evaluation of the case").

⁶   For a discussion of the wisdom and necessity of discrete regulation of collaborative law, see generally, John Lande, Principles for Policymaking About Collaborative Law and Other ADR Processes, *22 Ohio St. J. Disp. Resol. 620 (2007)*.

⁷   Uniform Collaborative Law Act, Discussion Draft (October 2007) at http://www.law.upenn.edu/bll/archives/ulc/ucla/oct2007draft.htm (last visited April 9, 2008).

⁸   See e.g., ABA Comm. on Ethics and Prof'l Responsibility, Formal Op. 07447 (Aug. 9, 2007); Kentucky Bar Ass'n Op. E-425 (June 2005), "Participation in the 'Collaborative Law' Process," available at http://www.kybar.org/documents/ethics opinions/kba e-425.pdf; New Jersey Adv. Comm. on Prof'l Eth. Op. 699 (Dec. 12, 2005), "Collaborative Law," available at http://lawlibrary. rutgers. edu/ethicsdecisions/acpe/acp699 1.html; North Carolina State Bar Ass'n 2002 Formal Eth. Op. 1 (Apr. 19, 2002), "Participation in Collaborative Resolution Process Requiring Lawyer to Agree to Limit Future Court Representation," available at http://www.ncbar.com/ethics/ethics.asp?page=2&from=4/2002&to=4/2002; Pennsylvania Bar Ass'n Comm. on Legal Eth. & Prof'l Resp. Inf. Op. 2004-24 (May 11, 2004), available at http://www.collaborativelaw.us/articles/Ethics Opinion Penn CL 2004.pdf.

⁹   See Gay M. Cox, et al., The Case for Collaborative Law, *11 Tex. Wesleyan L. Rev. 45, 47 (2004)* (describing the several hundred members of the Collaborative Law Institute in Texas (CLI-TX) and its training and marketing plans).

¹⁰   The American Bar Association Model Rules of Professional Conduct have been adopted in some form by nearly every state in the United States.

¹¹   See Model Rule 1.4(b), which requires that a lawyer "explain a matter to the extent reasonably necessary to permit the client to make informed decisions regarding the representation" and Model Rule 1.0(e) which defines "Informed consent" as "the agreement by a person to a proposed course of conduct after the lawyer has communicated adequate information and explanation about the material risks of and reasonably available alternatives to the proposed course of conduct." *Model Rules of Prof'l Conduct R. 1.4(b)*, 1.0(e).

¹²   Colorado and Hawaii each expressly provide that an attorney must advise clients regarding alternatives to litigation. Other authorities have suggested that Rule 2.1 necessarily incorporates such a duty. See Michigan Informal Ethics Op. RI-262 (1996); Pennsylvania Ethics Op. 90-125 (1990). See generally Monica L. Warmbrod, Comment, Could an Attorney Face Disciplinary Action or Even Legal Malpractice Liability for Failure to Inform Clients of Alternative Dispute Resolution? *27 Cumb. L. Rev. 791, 812 (1997)*(suggesting duty to discuss mediation inferred under Rule 2.1),

[13] "Ensuring that participation in the Collaborative Law Process is voluntary is often challenging in the context of divorce and family law disputes. Parties involved in such disputes are often in emotional turmoil, suffer from depression or other mental illness or engage in substance abuse. See Carla B. Garrity & Mitchell A. Baris, Caught in the Middle: Protecting the Children of High-Conflict Divorce 45 (Lexington Books, 1994). Sometimes they are victims or perpetrators of family violence. See Eleanor E. Maccoby & Robert H. Mnookin, Dividing the Child: Social and Legal Dilemmas of Custody 287 (Harvard University Press, 1992)." Uniform Collaborative Law Act, Section 3, comment, Discussion Draft, October 2007 http://www.law.upenn.edu/bll/archives/ulc/ucla/oct2007draft.htm.

[14] See Mary Kay Kisthardt, The Use of Mediation and Arbitration for Resolving Family Conflicts: What Lawyers Think About Them, *14 J. Am. Acad. Matrim. Law. 353, 374 (1997)*; Nancy Ver Steegh, Yes, No and Maybe: Informed Decision Making About Divorce Mediation in the Presence of Domestic Violence, *9 Wm. & Mary J. Women & L. 145 (2003)*.

[15] Regarding relative cost estimates of collaborative law and litigation, see William H. Schwab, Collaborative Lawyering: A Closer Look at an Emerging Practice, *4 Pepp. Disp. Resol. L.J. 351, 356 (2004)*.

[16] See Christopher M. Fairman, A Proposed Model Rule for Collaborative Law, 21 Ohio St. J. on Disp. Resol. 73, 73 (2005); Stuart Webb, Collaborative Law: An Alternative for Attorneys Suffering from "Family Law Burnout," Matrim. Strategist 7 (July 2000).

[17] One commentator has suggested that "The danger is that a lawyer committed to the collaborative law process may lack the capacity, even unconsciously, to provide a client with a fair representation of the risks and benefits of utilizing such a process." See Larry Spain, Collaborative Law: A Critical Reflection on Whether a Collaborative Orientation Can Be Ethically Incorporated into the Practice of Law, *56 Baylor L. Rev. 141, 161 (2004)*.

[18] New Jersey Supreme Court, Advisory Committee on Professional Ethics, Op. 699, Collaborative Law, *182 N.J.L.J. 1055* (Dec. 12, 2005). See also 2002 N.C. Eth. Op. 1, *2002 WL 2029469* (N.C. St. Bar) ( *RPC 1.2(c)* permits a lawyer, if the client consents after consultation, to ask a client to agree, in advance, that the lawyer limits representation the collaborative family law process and will withdraw from representation prior to court proceedings).

[19] John Lande & Gregg Herman, Fitting the Forum to the Family Fuss: Choosing Mediation, Collaborative Law, or Cooperative Law for Negotiating Divorce Cases, *42 Family Ct. Rev. 280, 282 (2004)*.

[20] Rule 1.16(a) provides: "Except as stated in paragraph (c), a lawyer shall not represent a client or, where representation has commenced, shall withdraw from the representation of a client if: (1) the representation will result in violation of the rules of professional conduct or other law; (2) the lawyer's physical or mental condition materially impairs the lawyer's ability to represent the client; or (3) the lawyer is discharged." Model *Rules of Prof'l Conduct, R. 1.16(a)*.

[21] *Model Rules of Prof'l Conduct, R. 1.16(b)*.

[22] *Model Rules of Prof'l Conduct, R. 1.3* Diligence, Comment 1

[23] Id.

[24] Colorado Ethics Op. 115: Ethical Considerations in the Collaborative and Cooperative Law Contexts, Feb. 24, 2007.

[25] See supra note 8.

[26] Colorado Op. 115, supra note 24.

[27] Id.

[28] ABA Comm. on Ethics and Prof'l Responsibility, Formal Op. 07447 (Aug. 9, 2007).

[29] ABA Comm. on Ethics and Prof'l Responsibility, Formal Op. 06-439 (Apr. 12, 2006) ("the ethical principles governing lawyer truthfulness do not permit a distinction to be drawn between the caucused mediation context and other negotiation settings. The Model Rules do not require a higher standard of truthfulness in any particular negotiation contexts. Except for Rule 3.3, which is applicable

only to statements before a "tribunal," the ethical prohibitions against lawyer misrepresentations apply equally in all environments.").

[30]  Uniform Collaborative Law Act, supra note 8.

[31]  Kelly Browe Olson, Lessons Learned from a Child Protection Mediation Program: If at First You Succeed and then You Don't ..., *41 Fam. Ct. Rev. 480 (2003);* Ellen E. Deason, Secrecy and Transparency in Dispute Resolution: The Need for Trust as a Justification for Confidentiality in Mediation: A Cross-Disciplinary Approach, *54 Kan. L. Rev. 1387 (2006).*

# B: What Role for the Child's Voice?

# [21]

# What's Wrong with Children's Rights

## Martin Guggenheim

The "best interests of the child" standard is popular not merely because of its gender neutrality, but because it purportedly puts the children's interests above those of adults. Adults ultimately settled on this standard as the end game of a major struggle among themselves. By itself, this strongly suggests that the standard was not designed with children in mind. That hardly gets to the bottom of it. There is less connection between the best interests standard and a child-centeredness policy than even this history suggests.

The best interests standard comes into play in an extremely limited context. Parents continue to have the power to avoid a best interests inquiry by agreeing between themselves what their post-divorce family will look like. In particular, parents are free to separate from each other without getting divorced and make any custody arrangement they wish. So long as their agreement does not endanger a child, no court has any power to question the agreement. This is true even when virtually no one who would be in a position to review the agreement would conclude that it serves the child's interests.

This is so in large measure because of the principle of parental rights described in Chapter 2. Parents are free to raise their children as they see fit, so long as they do not abuse or neglect them. Upon a breakup of the family unit, parents are entitled to agree between themselves who the primary caretaker will be. When parents agree how to raise their children, the state may not intervene. Even when they disagree, parents are arguing about issues in which the state has virtually no interest.

Parents are also free to choose the mechanism by which their disagreement will be resolved. As a result, parents (when they agree) remain in charge of their case at almost every step of their divorce until the court issues its order.[43] Just as parents may avoid the court initially by making whatever agreement about their children they wish (providing, of course, the agreement does not contemplate abuse), in many states they may also settle their disagreement at any time during the litigation if they so choose.[44]

Although, technically, courts have the residual power to disapprove divorce-related agreements, private settlements are routinely approved by courts in uncontested divorces. Even in the rare instance that a court rejects a settlement and imposes a child custody arrangement that neither parent wants, parents who agree among themselves need not enforce the order once they are out of court. In this basic sense, private ordering of the family remains the rule for intact families as well as for families that separate.

But perhaps the strongest proof that custody disputes are really about parental rights is how judges view them. It is a commonplace that judges agonize over child custody cases and consider these cases among the most difficult on their docket. In 2002, for example, one state supreme court justice had occasion to write in a child custody decision, "if one were to poll the judges of this state as to what type of case is the most difficult to decide, a substantial portion, if not all of them, would respond that it is in the area of child custody."[45] The Supreme Court of Alaska expressed the identical sentiment, calling "child custody determinations. . . among the most difficult in the law." One can pick up almost any book containing court decisions and find trial judges telling the reader how they "agonized in making this most difficult decision." A senior law professor recently wrote that "every judge" he ever interviewed "said that a child custody decision is the single most difficult" one they had to make.[46]

Think for a moment what it means to be judging a difficult case. By definition, it would be one in which the judge cannot easily choose between the competing parties. "Easy" cases are those in which it is clear that one parent is inadequate or the other outstanding. So what are judges really telling us when they describe custody cases as agonizing? In an overwhelming percentage of child custody cases, judges are unable to determine to whom custody should be awarded.

If these cases were really about children, judges would experience very few cases as difficult and even fewer as truly agonizing. If these cases were about children and their best interests, judges would hardly agonize simply because they are unable to conclude that one parent was superior to the other. This would mean (if these cases were really about children) that the judge could not make a mistake. Cases in which judges cannot go wrong hardly make the list of the year's most troubling legal decisions.

Let's consider the opposite situation. Judges would have no reason to designate as difficult those cases in which it was clear that a child's best interests would be served by awarding custody to one of the parents. Judges have little difficulty entering orders when there is abundant evidence that no real alternative exists.

The *only* conditions under which a judge could feel agonized-if these cases were really about children-is when the judge believes neither parent is an adequate resource for the child, but the law gives the court no choice but to choose between two bad options. Fortunately, those cases are few. It is plain from reading judges' speeches and decisions that these extreme situations are not the only ones that give them difficulty, however.

Rather, judges are referring to cases in which both parents are obviously good enough to deserve to win, but one of them must be designated the loser. We can certainly sympathize with judges who have to make what often amounts to an arbitrary choice, realizing the real world costs to the losing party.

In a world in which the judge's purpose is to issue an order watching out exclusively for children, the troubling quality of arbitrariness would be nonexistent. In such a world, the judge would understand from the beginning that the child will be sent to live (at least primarily) with one of the competing parties. The judge would further know that his or her job is to enter an order that does not harm (ideally that best serves) the child. If, after hearing the evidence, the judge is comfortable concluding that the child will be (reasonably) well served by living with either parent, the judge should be content that in either case the child will be well served.

It may be that some of the discomfort judges experience is based on their sense that no matter what they do, children are suffering a loss. Regardless of how well a judge decides (and regardless of the fact that often both parents would be good caretakers), the child may be hurt by the parents' separation and sometimes by the poor handling of their separation. Judges, like friends of divorcing couples, may well find it difficult to see children hurt in such ways; and judges, like friends, may often feel helpless to prevent it. Not only do custody cases tend to bring out the worst in adults, but those harmed are far more sympathetic than the victims found in other sorts of cases. It is certainly unpleasant to see how badly people can treat their former life partners and to see their inability to put their children's interests over a desire to hurt the other parent.

Having said this, much of the judges' discomfort stems not from their concern for the children; it has to do with their concern for the parents. Parents demand (one might even say *need*) the opportunity to prove they have the right to be with their child, not that their child has the right to be with them. What bothers the judges is having to accept that their order will gravely hurt the losing parent. Anyone even remotely familiar with child custody litigation appreciates the emotional baggage they carry for the contesting adults.

These adults are fighting for the most important thing in their world. In the words of Lee Teitlebaum, "If there is one thing about which virtually everyone interested in divorce and custody would agree, it is that this process involves, and perhaps creates, the most deeply antagonistic relations suffered by humans in modern society."[47] Because of this, I do not mean to mock the sentiments of the judges who find these cases so difficult. They *are* difficult. But they are difficult because they are about adults fighting over something very precious to them. As Jon Elster explains, "the knowledge that the decision will have momentous importance for the parties directly involved and the recognition that it may not be possible to have a rational preference for one parent over the other. . . conspire to create a psychological tension in decision makers that many will be unable to tolerate."[48]

It is against this backdrop that we are able to appraise the true significance of the best interests standard. We have seen how the standard represents a compromise in an ongoing fight between adults. The compromise works at many levels for adults. It provides useful cover for those uncomfortable with the possibility that their actions are harmful to their own children. It also allows judges and legislators to feel they are doing their part to advance children's well-being.

All the while, another set of adults gains by this, too. These are the professionals who service the multi-billion dollar custody and visitation industry. They are lawyers both for parents and, as we shall see, for children. They are also psychologists, psychiatrists, and other forensic experts who are hired to interview, investigate, provide written reports and recommendations, and testify in court proceedings. And they are mediators, lay counselors, and others who become involved with parents fighting over custody.

It should also be easy to see how transparent the whole business is and that these rules were not designed principally with the children in mind. The best interests standard solves various conflicts adults have with each other and allows adults to feel noble in their fight for children because they, along with the judge and other court personnel (if not their ex-spouse), are only pursuing the case in order to do what is best for their child.

Yet, a remarkable thing has happened along the way. A significant number of adults who ought to know better have taken far too seriously the importance of furthering a child's best interests through the complete investigation and resolution of custody disputes. Indeed, it is astonishing to observe how much the best interests and child-centered rhetoric is taken seriously by countless children's advocates. Thus, it is typical to read, as one highly influential family law scholar has written, that in custody and visitation cases, "The parents' interests are to be ignored" because "all states expect courts to make the children's interests the sole focus of their attention."[49] This child-centered focus is touted both as a major change of emphasis and a wonderful new form of children's rights.

If this were all there is to it, perhaps this would be merely a problem of self-delusion. But what is most disturbing is the degree to which the best interests standard does not serve children. So much is said in praise of the standard that the pervasive problems it causes too commonly are ignored. Among these problems is that, paradoxically, by relying on such an indeterminate standard, parents are encouraged to litigate their dispute with their ex-partner. Since the best interests standard can be used to support virtually any result, parties cannot be certain who is most likely to win a contested custody dispute. As a result, in the years since the best interests standard has replaced the tender years presumption, custody cases have become exponentially more disputatious in many jurisdictions.

Unsurprisingly, child custody disputes were relatively rare when the parties knew that mothers would win custody almost every time. Fathers had little incentive to bother contesting the custody arrangement. In many jurisdictions today, by contrast, these disputes are among the ugliest and most expensive of all lawsuits. What purpose do they serve? The reasons given by mental health professionals include the notion that "The fight for a child may serve profound psychological needs in a parent, including the warding off of severe depression and other forms of pathological organization."[50] As a direct consequence of the ubiquity of the best interests standard, parents are encouraged to roll the dice and contest a custody case in court. Fathers may be said to be better off under the child's best interest standard, but it is considerably more difficult to make the case that children are.

But the child-centered rhetoric has contributed to even worse problems for children. Not only are there more contested cases, the cases are costlier and take longer to resolve. When the question before the court is what is best for children, judges tend to insist that all of the parties (including the children) be subject to a battery of tests, interviews, and evaluations by psychologists, psychiatrists, or trained court personnel. These cases cost much more than they did twenty years ago because of the proliferation of professionals.

## Lawyers for Children

Perhaps the least necessary member of this new group of costly professionals is the lawyer for the child. The children's rights movement had its greatest victory in 1967 when the Supreme Court ruled that juveniles accused of being delinquent have a constitutional right to court-assigned counsel. In *In re Gault's* wake, many writers have reasoned that the Constitution requires counsel for children in other types of legal proceedings as well. Indeed, some have even suggested that children have a constitutional right to counsel in all divorce-related custody cases.[51]

Every jurisdiction in the United States currently permits the judge to appoint a representative for the child in a custody proceeding. Moreover, lawyers are being used to represent children in divorcerelated proceedings in ever-increasing numbers throughout the country. This is happening even though vast numbers of Americans are underrepresented in legal proceedings affecting their interests in other areas ranging from landlord-tenant disputes to child welfare. Today, in some jurisdictions, it is commonplace for middle-class and wealthy parents to walk into a courtroom and realize that their children are being represented by someone who is legally antagonistic to them.

Leading the call for children's lawyers in custody proceedings are children's rights advocates. Many of these stress that children have the moral right and ought to have the legal right to be heard about their own future. They commonly seek to ensure that the child's "voice" be included in the proceeding and that the child's viewpoint be advocated. Some even seek to ensure that the child's preference be a major (perhaps even dispositive) determinant in the ultimate custody decision.

Katherine Federle, for example, insists that among children's basic rights is the right to "empowerment."[52] Barbara Woodhouse also wants children's voices to be prominently considered in all custody cases and believes that the independent representation of children is essential to further children's rights. These advocates even rely on international law to support their position. Thus, the United Nations Convention on the Rights of the Child, originally promulgated in 1989, requires that "In all judicial or administrative proceedings affecting a child that is capable of forming his own views, an opportunity shall be provided for the views of the child to be heard, either directly or indirectly, through a representative, as a party to the proceedings."[53] Woodhouse condemns the United States' failure to ratify the Convention (the only country in the world to have failed to do so), in part because it has slowed efforts to ensure that children everywhere are represented in custody proceedings.[54]

Children's rights advocates greatly exaggerate the legal significance of a contested custody dispute. These advocates criticize a system that forces children to live with one of their parents even when they would prefer to live with the other (or when the other would better serve them). They ignore the obvious truth that children are forced to live with a parent whenever the parents mutually agree on which adult gets custody. After all, why make such a fuss to ensure that children's best interests are being served after a divorce? As we have seen, there is no requirement to ensure that children's best interests are being served *before* divorce. Children are forced to live with adults whose parenting skills are limited or even inadequate so long as the parenting remains above a minimum standard of fitness.

Forcing children to live with one of two fit parents without determining which parent is more fit (assuming for these purposes this is even possible to do) is not significantly different from forcing children to live with parents without making a preliminary determination of their fitness as parents. Why is it that we are so comfortable eschewing this inquiry before divorce, and yet so manifestly uncomfortable with the prospect of a court saying to divorcing parents that the court is neither capable of nor interested in determining which parent is better for the child?

We (properly) subordinate the interests of children when they are being raised by their parents before divorce (or when the adults are not contesting the terms of a divorce). Yet, some would allow the excuse of parents' disagreeing with each other to become the justification for placing the child's interests above their parents. If it *is* sensible to insist that children's interests come before their parents after a divorce one would expect a greater movement to try to put children's interests ahead of parents all of the time.

Such a goal, of course, is an unachievable fantasy. We are not at risk of this happening both because adults do not want it to happen and because we could not accomplish it even if we had the will. We can ensure that a judge's opinion about what is best for a child controls, but we cannot be confident that the judge's opinion is on the mark or superior to the parents. Recalling the real reason we ended up with the best interests standard, we need to clarify more precisely what it means.

The children's best interests is simply the method for resolving the dispute; it is a means for deciding the case, not a manifesto for children. Children have no say in whether their parents decide to terminate their relationship. Parents are free to end their relationship with each other without requiring them to take into account the impact of their decision on their children.[55] Even when the adults decide to end their relationship, only if parents cannot agree between themselves and go to court to settle their dispute do they delegate their legal decisionmaking power over their children to the state.

Yet advocates of separate counsel in custody proceedings argue that, even though the court is making the same decision that the parents could have made themselves without participation by the child and even though it is making that decision at the request of the parents, the child now has a right to be heard through counsel in the proceeding. The child's right to participate in the decisionmaking process and to have his or her preferences and interests consulted is triggered by whether the parents have been able to reach their own decision concerning custody.

It is far from clear that giving children a significant voice in these disputes is a good thing. In the ordinary adult client-lawyer relationship, the client is the principal and the lawyer serves as his or her agent. Clients set the objectives of the case and the lawyer's most important task is to seek to secure the objective set by the client. Lawyers, as counselors, also are expected to perform the important role of helping a client clarify the objectives that best serve the client's interests. In performing that counseling role, however, lawyers are expected to help clients find their own answers. The central purpose of the representation is to advance the client's autonomy.

For many reasons, we should not want children's lawyers in custody proceedings performing this role, despite the call for the child's "empowerment" by some children's advocates. For one thing, such a role would be inconsistent with the basis upon which the case itself is to be decided. Judges are expected to learn a child's preferences in order to factor them in when making the ultimate custody determination. But no state wants the child's preferences to become too significant a factor in the outcome. This is, in part, to prevent children from becoming too entangled in the case (and suffer from the cajoling and influencing that would surely take place if their parents knew the child's preferences mattered too much). It is also because we do not believe that children have the maturity or experience to make the best decision for themselves.

Custody proceedings are emotionally difficult, often involving a mixture of feelings of rejection, guilt, pain, and anger. Placing children at the center of the dispute by informing them that their preference as to custody is the primary or even a central factor in deciding custody may make them feel the need to choose-and thereby reject-one parent over the other.[56] Protecting children from being forced to choose where to live may, in the long run, best serve the interests of most children. When the child's preference will be accorded prominence by the child's lawyer, there is a danger that one or both parents will be encouraged to attempt to influence the child. When this occurs, children become pawns of a different order. It rarely will serve children's best interests to have parents actively trying to persuade children to tell their lawyers that they want to live with one parent rather than the other.[57]

Apart from giving children a "voice," children's rights advocates insist that children be represented separately because "without separate legal representation, the child's interests are left to the inadequate protection of parents and the court."[58] This reasoning stresses the potentially adverse effects of divorce on the child and the right of children, consistent with the basic meaning of the best interests standard, to focus the proceedings and its outcome exclusively on what is truly best for the child. This effort at isolating children's interests, however, ignores the complicated calculus involved in separating the interests of children from their parents. The few existing studies of children of divorce make clear the interdependency of children's interests and their parents'. Judith Wallerstein and others consistently show that unless one takes seriously the desires of the custodial parent, the child will likely lose. An unhappy parent frequently results in an unhappy child.[59]

If there are to be lawyers for children, there must be a clear definition of the lawyer's role. Remarkably, current law fails to provide any meaningful guidelines concerning the role of these lawyers. After lawyers were representing children in custody cases in Connecticut for more than twenty years, the best the Connecticut Supreme Court could muster when asked to clarify what is expected of these lawyers was "The legislature has not delineated, nor has this court yet been presented with the opportunity to delineate, the obligations and limitations of the role of counsel for a minor child. We recognize that representing a child creates practical problems for an attorney and that this important issue, at some point, needs to be addressed."[60] Connecticut is hardly alone in its unwillingness to clarify this role. Virtually no state has done so.

It would be inconceivable for the legal profession to call for lawyers for adults without having first identified the purpose and role of the lawyer. Much is revealed when a system sets loose a cadre of lawyers to represent children in the name of advancing children's rights without bothering to clarify the lawyer's role. It suggests that adults are primarily concerned with appearing to advance the interests of children (by providing them with representation). This ought not be confused with ensuring that children actually are well served in the process.

This complete lack of clarity of the role of lawyers for children means that lawyers are free to allow their child clients to set the objectives of the case to the extent the lawyers choose to do so. But it also means that lawyers for children in these proceedings are not required to seek the outcome the child would prefer. Although there are strong reasons to be wary of lawyers for children taking their marching orders from their clients in contested custody proceedings, there are even stronger reasons to oppose lawyers deciding for themselves what outcome best serves their clients' interests.

For most of my career, I have been a critic of the assumed value of providing counsel for children in custody proceedings. Time and again I have seen lawyers choosing for themselves what outcome to argue for on behalf of their child clients and gaining the advantage in the case for no other reason than that they became the recognized voice for the children's interests. Even when the judge knows full well that the position the children's lawyer is taking is really nothing more than the product of the lawyer's personal views, judges give considerable weight to that lawyer's position.[61] It seems that because the lawyer *chose* the position (as opposed to arguing for it because that is what the client wanted), the judge thinks it deserves greater consideration. A lawyer's life experiences, values, and biases surely influence the opinion he or she is advancing; regrettably, these biases are ignored by the courts.

Consider the case of a custody dispute in which the mother, a lesbian, wants to live with her lover and have custody of her two children, a six-year-old boy and a four-year-old girl. The court assigns an attorney to represent the children. The attorney meets with all parties, including his young clients, and is impressed by the children's father, who appears to be a fine, able, and concerned parent. The attorney concludes that custody should be awarded to the father and vigorously presses for this result in negotiations with the attorneys for each of the parents and in chambers with the judge; at trial, he critically cross-examines the mother while supportively cross-examining the father.

Now assume that a different attorney had been assigned to represent the same children. This attorney similarly meets with all parties, including the children. Impressed with the mother, she concludes that the children will be served best by having them remain in their mother's custody. The attorney vigorously presses for this result in negotiations with the attorneys for the individual parents, in chambers with the judge, and at trial in supportive cross-examination of the mother. Moreover, the attorney presents an expert witness of his own, allegedly "for the children," who testifies that exposing young children to homosexuality has no bearing whatsoever upon their sexual preferences.

It is highly probable that the outcome of this imagined case will depend on which position the child's attorney adopts. The judge may be impressed by the number of advocates supporting each parent's cause (two against one) or may believe that the particular outcome sought by the children's attorney is what the children themselves desire. Or the judge, viewing the attorney as the children's spokesperson, may simply defer to his or her "informed" judgment about what is best for the children.

For these reasons, the appointment of a lawyer for children in custody proceedings who is free to decide what position to advocate injects an unacceptable element of arbitrariness into the outcome.Which party wins in such cases will depend less on the factual and legal arguments made to the court than on the position taken by the child's lawyer. Furthermore, the more difficult a case is, the more probable it is that different lawyers would disagree on which result to seek. In the closest cases, the judge will be least certain of the best outcome and more likely to be tempted to rely on the children's lawyer's judgment. For every lawyer who would advocate a particular result in a close case, there will be a different lawyer who would urge the opposite outcome. In the end, it will be the child's attorney, and not the judge, who decides the case.

I have been involved in countless cases in which young children were represented by counsel. The one constant through these cases is the crucial need for the parent's attorney to win the support of the child's attorney to maximize the chances for success. This does not mean the child's lawyer's view always controls. But it is vitally important because it often can be devastating to a party's hopes for success if the child's lawyer proves to be a foe.

Children's advocates sometimes seek counsel for children in custody disputes to protect them from the travails of the litigation process itself. This is a laudable but ironic goal. It is certainly sensible to worry about the choices parents and their lawyers make when cases become deeply contentious. Anyone who has seen just how ugly contested divorces can become certainly understands that parents may lose their ability to think rationally about what is best for their children in the midst of battle.

For this reason, it is hardly irrational to favor providing children with legal representation to constrain the worst of the free-floating adversary system currently employed.[62] Lawyers performing this role should seek to speed up the proceedings and to ensure that the child is kept out of them to the greatest extent possible. This laudable purpose of protecting children in divorce cases is, however, more than a bit ironic. It is because of the best interests standard that children are being made ever more the focus of contested custody cases. Now, because of this focus, we find the need to provide children with special protective devices, such as their own lawyers, to protect them from the harm of bitterly contested cases. There is a simpler way to accomplish this. If we insisted that children be kept out of these cases in the first place, there would be no need for creating additional procedures to protect them.

It is useful to wonder why this is the only country in the world that even takes seriously the importance of providing three lawyers in a custody dispute. Perhaps it is because we have allowed adults to run wild in their efforts to win against their former partner. In a different culture-one in which there would be less need in the first place to speak in terms of children's rights-adults would never have reached the point where they would imagine they have the right to seek sole custody of a child born to two people. It would be inconceivable to atomize rights in this way and make us into individuals with rights separate from the intimate associations we have formed. In other cultures, certain commitments made would have lasting implications. Such a culture would be far less likely to have developed anything resembling the sophisticated notion of children's rights that has dominated American society over the past generation.

This hardly proves which culture honors children more. A society that truly cherishes children needs no prodding to do so. Nor is such a society likely to bother developing claims for children's rights.

*Martin Guggenheim, J.D., is the Fiorello LaGuardia Professor of Clinical Law at New York University School of Law.*

## Notes

[43]    Although some courts have rules that authorize judges to review and set aside agreements they regard as unacceptable, in the overwhelming majority of cases such supervention is unthinkable. But see *McClain v. McClain,* 716 P.2d 381, 385 (Alaska 1986) (parents' agreement is not binding on the court, and court must independently determine what arrangement is in the best interests of the child); *In re Marriage of Fesolowitz,* 852 P.2d 658, 662 (Mont. 1993) (court is not bound by parents' agreement and has power to order a custody arrangement in accordance with the best interests of the child).

[44]    Some commentators have suggested limitations on divorce during children's minority. See, e.g., Judith T. Younger, "Marital Regimes: A Story of Compromise and Demoralization, Together with Criticism and Suggestions for Reform," *Cornell Law Review* 67 (1981): 45, 90; Debra Friedman, *Towards a Structure of Indifference, The Social Origins of Maternal Custody* (Berlin: Aldine de Gruyter, 1995), pp. 133-135.

[45]    *Meldron v. Novotny,* 640 N. W.2d 460, 466 (N. D. 2002). Even more remarkably, one of the "KeyCites" used by Weslaw to aid in speedy legal research actually begins by announcing "Because

child custody issues are some of the most difficult and agonizing decisions a trial judge must make. . ." West KeyCite 76D.

⁴⁶    Roger M. Baron, "Child Custody Determinations in South Dakota: How South Dakota Courts Decide Child Custody Cases," *South Dakota Law Review* 40 (1995): 411. See *Matter of O'Shea v. Brennan,* 387 N.Y.S.2d 212, 216 (N.Y. App. Div. 1976). *Horton v. Horton,* 519 P.2d 11312, 1132 (Alaska 1974).

⁴⁷    Lee E. Teitlebaum, "Divorce, Custody, Gender and the Limits of Law: On Dividing the Child," *Michigan Law Review* 92: 1808, 1816.

⁴⁸    Jon Elster, *Solomonic Judgements: Studies in the Limitations of Rationality* (New York: Cambridge University Press, 1989), p. 124.

⁴⁹    David Chambers, "Rethinking the Substantive Rules for Custody Disputes in Divorce," *Michigan Law Review* 83 (1984): 477, 499.

⁵⁰ Judith S. Wallerstein and Joan B. Kelly, "Children and Divorce: A Review," *Social Work* 24 (1979): 468.

⁵¹    Catherine J. Ross, "From Vulnerability to Voice: Appointing Counsel for Children in Civil Litigation," *Fordham Law Review* 64 (1996): 1571; Howard A. Davidson, "The Child's Right to Be Heard and Represented in Judicial Proceedings," *Pepperdine Law Review* 18 (1991): 255.

⁵²    See, e.g., Katherine Hunt Federle, "Looking Ahead: An Empowerment Perspective on the Rights of Children," *Temple Law Review* 68 (1995): 1585, 1594-1596. See also Randy Frances Kandel, "Just Ask the Kid! Towards a Rule of Children's Choice in Custody Determinations," *University of Miami Law Review* 49 (1994): 299, 347.

⁵³    Art. 3(2),281. L. M. 1448 (Nov. 20,1989).

⁵⁴    Barbara Bennett Woodhouse, "Talking About Children's Rights in Judicial Custody and Visitation Decision-Making," *Family Law Quarterly* 36 (2002): 105.

⁵⁵    See Younger, "Marital Regimes," p. 90.

⁵⁶    Emery, *"Marriage, Divorce,"* pp. 132-133. "If being caught in the middle of the parents' conflict is one of the greatest sources of distress for children then soliciting their opinion as to who is their preferred custodian is hardly a solution. The articulation of a preference can be tantamount to asking children to choose between their parents."

⁵⁷    See, e.g., Kim J. Landsman and Martha L. Minow, Note, "Lawyering for the Child: Principles of Representation in Custody and Visitation Disputes Arising from Divorce," *Yale Law Journal* 87 (1978): 1126, 1165.

⁵⁸    Landsman and Minow, "Lawyering," pp. 1133-1134.

⁵⁹    Judith S. Wallerstein and Sandra Blakeslee, *Second Chances,* p. 238; Judith S. Wallerstein and Tony J. Tanke, "To Move or Not to Move: Psychological and Legal Considerations in the Relocation of Children
    Following Divorce," *Family Law Quarterly* 30 (1996): 305, 312.

⁶⁰    *Knock v. Knock,* 621 A.2d 267, 276 (Conn. 1993).

⁶¹    Landsman and Minow, "Lawyering."

⁶²    See, e.g., Shannan L. Wilber, "Independent Counsel for Children," *Family Law Quarterly* 27 (1993): 349, 362; Linda D. Elrod, "Reforming the System to Protect Children in High Conflict Custody Cases," *William Mitchell Law Review* 28 (2001): 495. Most children's rights advocates, however, particularly those interested in empowering children, would not be satisfied by limiting the children's lawyer's role to protecting children.

# Children's Participation in the Family Justice System –

# Translating Principles into Practice

## Nigel Lowe and Mervyn Murch

### INTRODUCTION

This paper examines the increasingly important issue of children's participation in the family justice system, focusing on two key questions.[1] First, what are the value positions underlying the concept of children's participation? Secondly, how might the concept be translated into practice? In considering these issues particular reference will be made to two recent Cardiff Studies, one concerned with adoption[2] and the other with divorce.[3]

New focus on children's participation in the legal process

Historically, the great shift in English law governing parent and child was the move from the position where children were of no concern at all to one where their welfare was regarded as the court's paramount concern. This fascinating development has been well charted and needs no further elaboration here.[4] Notwithstanding the entrenchment of the welfare principle,[5] traditionally, under English law, children's futures have been decided upon the views of adults, that is, of parents and professionals. In other words, the welfare principle itself is adult-centred and paternalistic.[6] Even so, what we have been witnessing over the last decade or so is an equally significant cultural shift in which children are no longer simply seen as passive victims of family breakdown, but increasingly as participants and actors in the family justice process. In consequence, in various family proceedings it is incumbent upon the courts to ascertain and to take duly into account children's own wishes and views.

Internationally, impetus for this new focus has been given by Article 12 of the UN Convention on the Rights of the Child 1989, under which:

'States Parties shall assure to the child who is capable of forming his or her own views the right to express those views freely in all matters affecting the child, the views of the child being given due weight in accordance with the age and maturity of the child ... The child shall in particular be provided the opportunity to be heard in any judicial and administrative proceedings affecting the child, either directly, or through a representative or appropriate body, in a manner consistent with procedural rules of national law.'

In Europe, the European Convention on the Exercise of Children's Rights 1996[7] aims to supplement the UN Convention, inter alia, by providing procedural mechanisms by which the voice of the child can be heard in legal proceedings concerning them. In particular, Article 3 provides that a child 'considered by internal law as having sufficient understanding' shall, in the case of judicial proceedings affecting him, be granted and entitled to request the following rights:

(a) to receive all relevant information;
(b) to be consulted and express his or her views;
(c) to be informed of the possible consequences of compliance with these views and the possible consequences of any decision.

While Article 4 further provides for children to have the right:[8]

'to apply, in person or through other persons or bodies, for a special representative in proceedings before a judicial authority affecting the child where internal law precludes the holders of parental responsibilities from representing the child as a result of a conflict of interest with the latter.'

Another international instrument of importance is the European Convention for the Protection of Human Rights and Fundamental Freedoms 1950 (the Convention), which, as a result of the Human Rights Act 1998, became internally binding in English courts from 2 October 2000. Of particular interest in this context is Article 6, which provides, inter alia, that: 'in the determination of his civil rights and obligations ... everyone is entitled to a fair and public hearing within a reasonable time by an independent and impartial tribunal established by law' (emphasis added). As Fortin has observed: 'on the face of it, Article 6 delivers a great deal. It guarantees the right of access to a court or tribunal, and, once there, the right of a fair hearing. It might, therefore, provide the means for challenging the law relating to children and their families'.[9] Notwithstanding the hitherto restrictive interpretation of this Article, Fortin nevertheless suggests that Article 6 could be thought to vest a right in a child to have separate legal representation in proceedings brought by or concerning him. Lyon has gone further by suggesting that the way in which children are currently treated in private family proceedings is in breach of Article 6 when read in conjunction with Article 14 (which prohibits discrimination on any ground), which she contends could be wide enough to include a child's or young person's age.[10]

Another issue highlighted by the implementation of the Human Rights Act 1998 is the compatibility of the paramountcy principle with Article 8.[11] Although the judicial view is that it is compatible,[12] it has been argued by Herring[13] and others[14] that, insofar as the courts apply a purely individualistic approach, based solely on weighing the child's interests, they are acting in breach of the Convention because too little attention is paid to parents' rights. Herring suggests that the courts should instead apply what he calls a 'relationship-based welfare approach' and 'to move away from conceiving the problem as a clash between children and parents and in terms of weighing two conflicting interests and towards seeing it rather as deciding what is a proper parent-child relationship'. While it remains to be seen whether the courts will apply this somewhat sophisticated approach, there seems little doubt that they will have to give more attention to the parents' position than they have done in the past. Nevertheless, whatever attention is paid to parents' interests, the child's welfare must remain the court's paramount consideration and, consequently, it seems clear that the international obligation to listen to the child can in no way be diminished by the implementation of the Human Rights Act 1998.

The place of the child in English domestic proceedings

Substantively, English domestic law, arguably cautiously, complies with the essential requirements of Article 12 of the UN Convention.

THE POSITION IN ADOPTION PROCEEDINGS

So far as adoption law is concerned, it has, perhaps surprisingly, always been incumbent upon the court to give due consideration to the wishes of the children concerned, having regard to their age and understanding.[15] Currently, section 6 of the Adoption Act 1976 obliges both a court and an adoption agency, when 'reaching any decision relating to the adoption of a child', to 'so far as practicable ascertain the wishes and feelings of the child regarding the decision and give due consideration to them, having regard to his age and understanding'. On the other hand, children are only made parties to adoption proceedings where they are in the High Court[16] and, consequently, it is only at that level that they are separately represented.[17] Moreover, unlike Scottish law,[18] English law makes no provision for requiring even older children's agreement to their adoption.[19]

THE POSITION IN PRIVATE LAW PROCEEDINGS OTHER THAN ADOPTION

So far as private law proceedings concerning children other than adoption are concerned, it was only under the Children Act 1989 that the courts became formally obliged to consider the child's wishes and feelings, although in practice this had long been the position.[20]

The Children Act 1989 obligation derives from the opening part of the so-called 'statutory checklist', namely section 1(3)(a), under which the court must have regard to 'the ascertainable wishes and feelings of the child concerned (considered in the light of his age and understanding)'.

However, the obligation to apply the checklist in private law proceedings only arises in contested applications.[21] In other words, even where private law orders are sought under the Children Act 1989,[22] if the adults are agreed there is no obligation to consult these children. Indeed, one of the reasons for limiting the application of the checklist to contested cases was to protect family autonomy. This non-interventionist standpoint is particularly evident in divorce proceedings. Before the Children Act 1989, section 41 of the Matrimonial Causes

Act 1973 required the divorce court to be satisfied that the proposed arrangements for the welfare of any child of the family were 'satisfactory'; or 'the best that can be devised in the circumstances'; or that 'it is impracticable for the party or parties appearing before the court to make any such arrangements'. The Children Act 1989,[23] however, amended section 41 so as to require the courts instead merely to 'consider ... whether it should exercise any of its powers under the Children Act 1989 with respect to [any children of the family]' (emphasis added), and only in exceptional cases delay the granting of the divorce decree. In so doing, the legislation has, in the words of Douglas et al shifted the focus of the court's attention 'away from having to be satisfied that the divorce may proceed in the interests of the children, to finding some exceptional reason why the divorce should not go ahead. The assumption which lies behind this approach is that parents may be trusted, in most cases, to plan what is best for their children's futures, and that, where they are in agreement on this, it is unnecessary and potentially damaging for the state, in the guise of the court, to intervene'.[24]

Since the implementation of the Children Act 1989, Parliament has had cause to rethink the wisdom of this non-interventionist strategy and, indeed, during the passage of the Family Law Bill 1996, concern was expressed about insufficient attention being paid to children's interests in the divorce process.[25] Reflecting this concern, the Family Law Act 1996 would have strengthened the emphasis on the children's welfare, first by setting out in section 1 the basic principles to which the court should have regard, namely, the need to bring to an end an irretrievably broken down marriage:

(i) with the minimum distress to the parties and the children affected;
(ii) with questions dealt with in a manner designed to promote as good a continuing relationship between the parties and any children affected as is possible in the circumstances.

Secondly, it was intended to replace section 41 of the Matrimonial Causes Act 1973 with section 11 of the 1996 Act. This, whilst not changing the fundamental standpoint established by the Children Act 1989, was to have obliged a divorce court, when deciding whether it should exercise its powers under the Children Act 1989: (a) to treat the child's welfare as the paramount consideration; and (b) to have particular regard to a checklist of factors including 'the wishes and feelings of the child considered in the light of his age and understanding and the circumstances in which those wishes were expressed'. Commenting on this provision, the Lord Chancellor, Lord Irvine of Lairg, said it:[26]

'is fully in tune with the new and increasing contemporary awareness that a child is a person in his or her own right ... the divorce process must now have regard to the interests and views of the children. They will now have a right to be consulted about the proposals which parents are making for the future in which they have a vital interest.'

## THE EFFECT OF ABANDONING PART II OF THE FAMILY LAW ACT 1996

Despite the obvious importance of these provisions, the Government announced, in January 2001, that, in the light of disappointing findings from the research at Newcastle University into the proposed scheme for information sessions for divorcing parents, the whole of Part II of the 1996 Act would not be implemented and, indeed, in due course, would be repealed.[27]

Even where their views and wishes and feelings have to be taken into account, children are not normally made parties to the proceedings, although there is power to do so in proceedings before the High Court and county court,[28] but not the magistrates' court. The normal process through which the court will learn of the child's views is through a court welfare report,[29] although a judge does have power to interview a child in private.[30] The current practice is to use this power sparingly.[31]

The use of the welfare officer[32] means, of course, the involvement of yet another adult in the judicial process. Moreover, valuable though the system undoubtedly is, it is to be noted that the welfare officer's function is to provide an independent report on the family's circumstances for the court. It is not to represent the child.[33]

THE POSITION IN PUBLIC LAW PROCEEDINGS

In contrast to private law proceedings, the child's voice is much better served in public law proceedings. First, it is incumbent on the court to have regard to the child's ascertainable wishes and feelings in all proceedings (ie whether or not contested) under Part IV of the Children Act 1989.[34] Secondly, under section 41 of the Children Act 1989, courts are required in public law proceedings[35] to appoint a guardian ad litem[36] for the child 'unless satisfied that it is not necessary to do so in order to safeguard his interests'. Furthermore, unlike welfare officers, guardians represent children in the proceedings and are, therefore, parties to them. They also have the power to instruct legal representation for the child.[37] Notwithstanding his party status, the child does not have a right to attend the hearing[38] and, indeed, there is a general feeling that it is commonly not in a child's interest to do so.[39]

CHILDREN'S ABILITY TO BRING THEIR OWN PROCEEDINGS

One innovation of the Children Act 1989 was to make clear provision for children to bring their own proceedings.[40] The scheme is that children wishing to seek a section 8 order must first obtain leave of the court. It is established that leave must be sought in the High Court,[41] and before it can be given, the court must be satisfied that the child has sufficient age and understanding.[42] Where the child is of sufficient understanding, then the normal rule of having to bring proceedings through a next friend does not apply,[43] and, instead, the child may instruct a solicitor in his own right. In practice, very little use is made of this provision because it takes an extremely confident, knowledgeable, resourceful and determined child or young person to commence such proceedings.

REFORM

Not withstanding non-implementation of Part II of the 1996 Act, certain parts of the current system are set to change. In particular, the Government has decided to amalgamate the court welfare service with the guardian ad litem service by establishing a new Children and Family

Court Advisory and Support Service (CAFCASS) under the Criminal Justice and Court Services Act 2000, which came into force on 1 April 2001.

TRANSLATING PRINCIPLES INTO PRACTICE

It is one thing to accept that children's voices should be listened to when legal and administrative authorities are taking decisions about them, but quite another to get beyond the rhetoric of legislative aspiration, so as genuinely to enable children to have a greater say in the processes which shape their futures. There is, in fact, a growing body of research[44] to suggest that most practitioners in the family justice system – court welfare officers, guardians ad litem, solicitors and judges etc – lack the necessary skills and understanding for effective, direct face-to-face work with children.

These studies highlight three areas of concern:

(1) Historically, in our culture children are not used to being listened to. For example, as Schofield and Thoburn have commented: 'Children in our society are not accustomed to having their views taken into account in their everyday lives at home or at school. We do not live in a culture which supports participation by children'.[45]

(2) Many adults seem to have difficulties in listening to children. A number of reasons have been advanced for this. For example, Neale has commented: 'Adults view children as essentially other. They are seen as less important and they are dependent and less powerful. Language is a tool used communally or on the basis of shared understandings. Adults interpret what children say. Welfare professionals do so on the basis of their understanding of what is in the child's best interest'[46] Smith postulates that adults fear they will upset children by talking about difficult experiences, such as separation and divorce.[47] Hunt and Lawson, comment that many professionals are aware of their lack of training and experience in talking to and listening to children.[48] Even more challengingly, Day Sclater and Piper assert that adults protect themselves from their own vulnerabilities by projecting them (unconsciously) on to the children. They suggest that, in order to keep that anxiety contained, adults rationalise that it is vital not to listen to children's own constructions of their needs, but instead to act as if they know children's best interests better than they do.[49] Finally, Murch et al believe that many adults (including welfare professionals, solicitors and judges) confuse 'participation' with decision-making. They are reluctant even to speak to or to listen to children, because they see this as inappropriately asking the child to decide.[50]

(3) Children can have disturbing experiences when talking to professionals. In this respect, the Joseph Rowntree Research Review makes five important and troubling points:[51]
(a) Children were generally reluctant to talk to outsiders about family issues as this was seen as disloyal and liable to lead to an escalation of problems.
(b) Professionals were seen as having been interventionist, rather than supportive.
(c) The discussions that children had with professionals often felt like interrogations.
(d) Adults were frequently experienced as judgmental and intrusive in their approach.
(e) Discussions were often not treated as confidential.

Neale and Smart concluded their study thus: 'Professionals may be perceived as inflexible, intrusive, condescending, deceitful, untrustworthy, disrespectful and reinforcing in a myriad of ways their superiority to the child'.[52]

We would add that children, in certain respects, inhabit different cultural worlds from adults. Moreover, they can be baffled by the language of adults, especially by professional jargon. Equally, adults are often unfamiliar with children's language codes which, in any event, can differ from age group to age group. In the family justice system there are emerging practice debates on how to develop the communication skills required by children's representatives and about whether, and if so how, judges should see and listen to children when taking decisions about them. The prevailing practice in England and Wales, as we have seen, is that they should not, in part because with the adversarial culture it is not possible to promise children that what they say to the judge will be treated in confidence.[53] But in this respect, as Lyon has pointed out, judges are not in a substantially different position from court welfare officers or guardians ad litem.[54]

Ascertaining the wishes and feelings of the child – do differences of principle lead to differences in practice?

One of the possible reasons why the Government has abandoned Part II of the Family Law Act 1996 is that there are divergent views about the assumptions underlying provisions relating to children. For example, in much socio-legal writing, the theoretical debate is assumed to revolve around the potentially conflicting paradigms - a welfare best interests approach on the one hand and a rights approach on the other.[55]

THE TRADITIONAL 'BEST INTERESTS' APPROACH

Piper takes the view that both the Children Act 1989 and the Family Law Act 1996 (which she anticipated being fully implemented) provide a framework which means that children's views are ascertained:[56]

> 'as part of a process in which adults decide what is best for the child and within the context of divorce try to protect the child from a particular set of perceived risks of harm. These risks, predicated on the influential image of the child as a vulnerable victim of divorce whose present happiness and future stability is deemed to depend upon harmonious joint parenting, can be removed only by the encouragement of parental decision making and control.'

Such a view places section 11 of the Family Law Act 1996 firmly within a traditional, paternalistic, child-saving model, and is consistent with much of the research material concerning practitioners' approach to children, which was reported in the Cardiff study of section 41 of the Matrimonial Causes Act 1973, carried out for the Lord Chancellor's Department.[57] In our opinion, one unfortunate consequence of this approach is that most children of divorcing parents are badly informed about the processes involved and are left feeling excluded from and unrecognised by the system.

## CHILDREN'S 'RIGHTS' APPROACH

The 'rights of the child' approach is sometimes referred to as being constructed on a liberationist position.[58] This takes the view that children should have similar basic rights to adults, that the distinction between childhood and adulthood is arbitrary[59] and that to apply the traditional best interests approach is to label children as objects of welfare rather than as young citizens who are the subject of rights.[60] This young citizen approach was endorsed by Giddens in his 1999 Reith lectures on the family, in which he advanced the view that modern western family life is increasingly based on a participant democratic approach in which parents consult children when taking important decisions about them.

In addition to these two contrasting approaches, which have largely dominated social-legal discourse on the subject of children, there are signs that two more distinct approaches are emerging from the theoretical worlds of the sociology of childhood and the behavioural sciences. The former views children as social actors in their own terms; the latter adopts the community mental health approach.

## THE CHILD AS SOCIAL ACTOR

This third approach, which is assuming increasing significance in the developing social research literature of modern childhood,[61] sets out to understand children's experiences 'in their own terms' and to take their words at face value as the primary source of knowledge about their experience.[62] This approach, endorsed incidentally by the Scottish Law Commission,[63] is concerned, as Butler and Williamson point out, with 'hearing the voice of the child, untrammelled by professional discretion or interpretation'.[64] It could, therefore, be argued that, if a court is to understand children's perceptions in their own terms and to appreciate what the experience of divorce and family change means to them, a similar approach should be applied. Yet, as Roche points out, to move from the current position, in which the words of the child are 'filtered through the lens of concern of mediators and other welfare professionals, operating the current family justice system', to one in which the child's concerns are considered in their own terms, will involve a major cultural shift in family law practice.[65] Even so, Roche is an optimist. His plea is that we 'need to be able to hear the unfamiliar and the law could provide one framework in which many voices of childhood can be heard on matters that move and concern them'.

## THE COMMUNITY MENTAL HEALTH APPROACH

This approach starts from the position that the practices and procedures of the family justice system (as other state social care and educational systems) impact on children's lives, whether or not their wishes and feelings are ascertained. This is acknowledged, for example, in section 1(2) of the Children Act 1989, which states that delay is normally to be regarded as detrimental to the child. The underlying thinking behind this principle is that a young person's sense of time is different from that of an adult, and that delay in reaching decisions about a child's future care can add to stress and anxiety, particularly if the child experiences a threat, actual or imagined, of separation from those with whom he is attached. In this sense, therefore, avoidable delay can be described, to use a medical metaphor, as iatrogenic (ie system-induced harm). But the converse is also true: practice and procedures can be designed and operated positively to promote a child's well-being, to buffer the impact of stressful events and even to increase a child's capacity to cope with stressful, critical situations. In adoption, both the recent review by the Prime Minister's Performance and Innovation Unit[66] and the White Paper[67] have highlighted the serious problem of delay, particularly for children who are to be adopted out of care. One of the intractable weaknesses of our current child care system and the slow moving nature of court proceedings is that, following their removal from often dangerous and neglectful families, children can be placed in a series of short-term foster-homes before permanent adoptive homes can be found for them. The stress involved in moving from one placement to another and the adverse effects on a child's behaviour, concentration levels, educational attainment and, above all, capacity to form secure attachments, may well be cumulative.[68] Of seminal importance in this approach is the work of Rutter,[69] Hetherington, Cox and Cox,[70] and Caplan and Caplan.[71] Such an approach would justify, for example, giving children reliable information about the processes of divorce, enabling them not to feel excluded if they wish to participate in certain aspects of proceedings themselves, and providing them with support, if they need it, at critical times in the divorce process.[72] Moreover, it seems to us that any support which reduces child suffering at the time is justification in itself. It is notable that this approach is less paternalistic than the conventional child-saving welfare approach and can be used to make a supporting behavioural science case for both the children's rights and the child as social actor approaches, which are outlined above.

Variable competence in children: how can the family justice system respond?
The four approaches outlined above in practice represent a spectrum of opinion. As Hendrick observes: 'there are many gradations of perspectives amongst scholars and activists'.[73] The issue of assessing a child's competence to participate is central to the whole debate. As Lord Scarman observed in the Gillick case:

'The underlying principle of the law ... is that parental rights yield to the child's right to make his own decisions when he reaches a sufficient understanding and intelligence to be capable of making up his own mind on the matter requiring decision.'[74]

In practice, the crucial questions that follow from this are: first, how do courts assess when a child has reached sufficient understanding and intelligence; and, secondly, what best is the way to facilitate the child's capacity to participate in proceedings to the extent that they might wish to and to express their wishes and feelings? Although, in general, developmentally their social competence and capacity to understand increases as they get older, children vary widely. Some children as young as five can have a command of language as good as others of 10 years of age or more. Some are emotionally resilient and others very vulnerable. Some are extrovertedly confident, others introvertedly inhibited and shy. Some children have learning difficulties and are unable to read, for example, information leaflets, and can be easily confused by articulate practitioners who lack responsive skills to communicate appropriately. The challenge, therefore, is for the family justice system to develop both practices and procedures to enable children to participate to the extent that they might wish and to find practitioners equipped with the necessary skills for direct face-to-face work with children – listening to them and seeking to understand their, at times, unexpected and unfamiliar messages. Marshall rightly argues that:

> 'those charged with assessing the child's maturity ... should be mature themselves and trained in child development and in communication with children and young people, including particular groups such as adolescents and those with special needs who present difficulties with some adults.'[75]

\*   \*   \*   \*

CONCLUSIONS

*The overarching messages of the Cardiff studies*

The overarching message of the Adopted Children Speaking study is that the adults involved in the adoption process need to be sensitive to children's individual needs, particularly by involving them and keeping them informed in a way which takes account of their age, understanding and sense of time. The support offered needs to be underpinned by good adult-child and child-adult communication; but the responsibility for establishing the effective communication lies with the adults.

But such a message would not have been out of place in the KIDs study. Equally, one of the points to emerge from KIDs is that many of the children's concerns are not being picked up and responded to, which is no less true of the adoption study.

Both adoption and divorce of their parents represent critical, initial life-changing events for the children. A number of children are confused and have poor information about the process (be it adoption or divorce) and about what to expect. That, in turn, contributes to their understandable anxiety, stress and sense of isolation, which consequently makes the process of adjustment more difficult. In the case of children of divorcing parents, the children's confusion and lack of information can result from one or both of the parents finding it difficult to talk to their children, although as often as not the parents themselves may be confused or uncertain about the future. Moreover, since most divorces and related children's issues are uncontested, the professionals involved in the process (solicitors, welfare officers, mediators, judges, etc) hardly ever see them and because there are no other obvious sources of support and information, children are frequently left to find their own ways of coping.

In contrast to children of divorcing parents, children involved in the adoption process will have been seen by a number of professionals, yet all too frequently they too are left uninformed about the legal process and sometimes bewildered and confused as to what is happening. In this, they share the experience of many adopters, who are also left uninformed about the adoption process.[86] Indeed, the message from the adoption study is that while professionals work hard for children, they do not necessarily work with children. Certain obvious things need to be addressed, for example the ignorance and fear about the court. Here, there is a crying need to develop ways and means to explain the court process and to familiarise children with the courtroom and judge before any hearing. Practitioners also need to remember not to talk about the children in their hearing unless they address them directly. Children, just like adults, need to be fully informed as to what is going on. It is unacceptable to make children wait many months for an adoptive placement without even attempting to inform them as to what is happening.

Being able to communicate with children and being sensitive to their needs are the absolute minimum requirements of putting into practice legal obligations to ascertain and have regard to children's wishes and feelings. It is evident from these two studies that there is a long way to go even for professionals, let alone parents, to achieve this.

*Towards a new conception of support services for children in the family justice system*

The challenge facing those responsible for developing the family justice system is how to take on board the important messages from the growing body of recent empirical studies, including the Cardiff research summarised in this paper, which has sought to ascertain how children themselves view the practice and processes of the family justice system and child protection services. Ironically, whilst the abandonment of Part II of the Family Law Act 1996 is, in many respects, to be regretted, it at least gives more time to consider how best to translate the findings of research into practice.

THE NEED FOR CULTURAL AND ORGANISATIONAL CHANGE

As Piper points out, at a rhetorical level – that of professional and political aspiration – a great deal of emphasis is given to the child's rights and to hearing the voice of the child, but is still largely framed in a traditional child-saving paternalistic approach.[87] There remains 'an undercurrent of non-engagement with children which must be brought to the surface before there can be any real hope that more than a very small minority of children feel that they have been heard'. Fundamentally, therefore, what is required is nothing less than a major shift in the culture of family law practice, namely to take much more seriously children's rights to information and participation in decisions which directly affect them.[88] The movement towards this is, of course, well underway throughout the developed western industrialised world, reinforced as it is by the UN Convention on the Rights of the Child 1989 and, although this has still to be ratified by the UK, the European Convention on the Exercise of Children's Rights 1996.

Yet some idea of the ambivalent way in which the Government is approaching this issue can be seen by comparing the proposals for reforming adoption with those for divorce law. Thus, in the context of adoption, the White Paper, issued in December 2000, states:

'Children have a right to have their views listened to, recorded and acted upon, subject to their age and understanding, in the process of planning and making decisions about their future.'[89]

Whilst the subsequent draft National Adoption Standards, issued for consultation, reinforces this approach by adding that:

'Where the views of the child are not acted upon, the reasons for not doing so will be explained to the child and properly recorded.'[90]

In contrast, in the so-called 'private' realm of divorce, by abandoning Part II of the Family Law Act 1996, the Government has shied away from those provisions which would have made it obligatory to ascertain the wishes and feelings of the children. For the time being, at least until it becomes clear whether these provisions can be salvaged and incorporated in any subsequent divorce legislation, English family law will, therefore, manifest an ambivalent approach to the participation of children, involving them in the adoption process, but, whilst not overtly keeping them out, by no means being so ready to include them in the divorce process, even where their interests are directly involved.

Of course, it could be argued that one reason for the abandonment of section 11 of the Family Law Act 1996 was that the Government saw clearly that, as far as support services for the Family Justice System are concerned, there would be little point in introducing its provisions in private family law if the court welfare service had little experience of direct work with children.[91] The study by Hunt and Lawson showed clearly that the needs of children and families in private law cannot always be adequately met under current arrangements; improvements in the standard of court welfare practice depended on developing certain skills, 'particularly working with children and understanding child care and child protection'; and there was a widespread perception that the court welfare service would not be able to develop in these respects until the organisational link with the Probation Service (predominantly an adult-focused community crime treatment service) was severed.[92] As previously mentioned, that major policy step has now been taken with the decision to create the new Children and Family Court Advisory and Support Service (CAFCASS), which became operational on 1 April 2001.[93]

THE NEED FOR SPECIALIST TRAINING

Nevertheless, organisational change will not necessarily in itself enable practitioners to acquire the necessary skills and understanding to communicate better with children in ways that are acceptable to, and supportive of, them. Professional and post-professional education and training will have to change too. This is in order to equip staff of the new service to take on more appropriate roles to support children and families, to listen properly to children, to meet their information needs when their lives are undergoing major change, and to enable them to participate more effectively in the family justice process.[94]

Currently, arrangements for this type of training in the family justice system are woefully deficient. The problem is the more bizarre because judges commonly assume, mistakenly, that court welfare officers and guardians ad litem, as trained social workers, have the necessary skills and understanding. It may well be the case that, in comparison to court welfare officers, guardians ad litem, who are usually selected for their experience of local authority child care work, have much more experience of direct work with children. However, this does not necessarily mean that they have received special training in this area of work. As The Prime Minister's Review of Adoption points out:

> 'Professional social work training has become ever more generic meaning that social workers entering children and families work have limited specialist skill and are likely to have received little training on fostering and adoption issues.'[95]

In practice, experience counts for a good deal. Some professionals pick up the necessary skills on the job by trial and error. A small exploratory study by Masson and Oakley on the representation of children by guardians ad litem and solicitors in public law proceedings found that most guardians were skilled at establishing a rapport with children, but often felt constrained by the limited time they had.[96] With respect to children's' solicitors the study observed:[97]

> 'Solicitors representing children receive little training about how to relate to children, yet children involved in care proceedings are often the most vulnerable of all children. Many solicitors learn to relate to children by experience but some solicitors in the study indicated they had little confidence in their ability to speak to children.'[98]

## ONE WAY FORWARD?

All the available evidence, therefore, suggests that, in England and Wales, the professional educational task of learning the art and skills of communicating successfully with children, as far as family justice practitioners are concerned, has barely begun. This is, in part, because the necessary educational provision at both professional and post-professional level does not as yet exist. As the Rowntree report observes:[99]

> 'Professionals very often do not have the skills to help children to talk ... there is at present no training course teaching the skills needed by people working in this way with children.'

Now that the President of the Family Division has established an interdisciplinary committee with a special education and training sub-committee, the opportunity exists to review all the core competencies of family justice practitioners, including their skill levels in working with children (ie judges, solicitors, barristers and staff of the new CAFCASS) and the available educational provision for post-professional development.[100] It is to be hoped that the development of the special skills and understanding needed to work with children to enable them to participate more appropriately in proceedings, will be high on the agenda of this sub-committee and that the Government will acknowledge the issue and provide appropriate funding for the necessary training. If this were to happen, then some of the research experience about the best ways of approaching children and listening to their views, which research teams, including those at Cardiff, have developed and which have been explained in this article, may have wider application.

*Nigel Lowe, LL.B., is Deputy Head of School and Professor of Law at Cardiff Law School in Wales, UK*

*Mervyn Murch is Professor of Law at Cardiff Law School in Wales, UK.*

## Notes

[1]    It should be noted that the questions of whether children should participate and how to weigh children's views when they conflict with those of parents and other adults will not be discussed, since these have been considered extensively elsewhere, see, for example, C. Piper, 'Ascertaining the wishes and feelings of the child' [1997] Fam Law 796; C. Piper, 'The wishes and feelings of the child' and J. Roche, 'Children and Divorce: A Private Affair', in S. Day Sclater and C. Piper (eds), Undercurrents of Divorce (Ashgate Publishing Ltd, 1999), at pp 55-98.

[2]    C. Thomas and V. Beckford with N. Lowe and M. Murch, Adopted Children Speaking (British Agencies for Adoption and Fostering, 1999).

[3]    'Children's Perspectives and Experience of the Divorce Process' (co-directed by Professors I. Butler, G. Douglas, F. L. Fincham and M. Murch). This project, known by its acronym 'KIDs' (KIDs in Divorce), was completed in June 2000. The first report was submitted to the Economic and Social Research Council (ESRC) and published in December 2000 as Children 5-16: A Research Briefing No 21. See further n 61, below. See also G. Douglas et al, 'Children's Perspectives and Experience of the Divorce Process' [2001] Fam Law 373.

[4]    See, for example, J. Hall, 'The Waning of Parental Rights' [1972] CLJ 248; S. Maidment, Child Custody and Divorce (Croom Helm, 1984), chapter 4; N. Lowe, 'The Legal Position of Parents and Children in English Law' [1994] Singapore Journal of Legal Studies 332; and N. Lowe and G. Douglas, Bromley's Family Law (Butterworths Law, 9th edn, 1998), at p 300 et seq, and the authorities there cited.

[5]    In particular, by the House of Lords' decision in J v C [1970] AC 668 and, to a lesser extent, Re KD (A Minor) (Ward: Termination of Access) [1988] AC 806. But note the much earlier decision in Ward v Laverty [1925] AC 101. For an extensive analysis of these and other House of Lords' decisions on the development and application of the welfare principle, see N. Lowe, 'The House of Lords and the Welfare Principle', in C. Bridge (ed), Family Law Towards the Millennium - Essays for P. M. Bromley (Butterworths, 1997), at p 125 et seq. But see further below for discussion of whether the paramountcy principle is human rights compliant.

[6]    As S. Maidment, op cit, n 4, at p 149, commented in 1984: 'the welfare principle, ostensibly child-centred, has also been and probably always will be a code for decisions based on religious, moral, social and perhaps now social science-based beliefs about child rearing', but she adds that: 'these decisions were in the past and are for the present made by adults for adults about adults. When a court makes a custody decision it may attempt to heed the child's needs, but it is essentially making a decision as to which available adult ... is to care for the child'.

[7]    This Convention came into force on 1 July 2000, following ratification by Greece, Poland and Slovenia.

[8]    This is subject to Art 9, which empowers the judicial authority to appoint a special representative for children (irrespective of their capacity or understanding) in cases of a conflict of interest between a child and the holders of parental responsibility. See further the Explanatory Report on the Convention published in 1997 by the Council of Europe.

[9]    J. Fortin, 'The HRA's impact on litigation involving children and their families' [1999] CFLQ 237, at p 244.

[10]   See C. Lyon, 'Children's Participation in Private Law Proceedings', in M. Thorpe and E. Clarke (eds), No Fault or Flaw: The Future of the Family Law Act 1996 (Family Law, 2000), at p 70. Query whether this argument would be accepted, since the courts might well say that there are good reasons for differentiating between children and adults in the matter of participating in legal proceedings, with the former needing more protection from, for example, the rigours of cross-examination, than the latter.

[11]   It should be pointed out that, long before the Human Rights Act 1998 was ever enacted, the House of Lords had ruled in Re KD (A Minor) (Ward: Termination of Access) [1988] AC 806 that the paramountcy of the child's welfare was compatible with the European Convention for the Protection of Human Rights and Fundamental Freedoms 1950.

¹²    See Re L (Contact: Domestic Violence); Re V (Contact: Domestic Violence); Re M (Contact: Domestic Violence); Re H (Contact: Domestic Violence) [2000] 2 FLR 334, at p 346, in which Dame Elizabeth Butler-Sloss P observed that the European Court of Human Rights has long accepted that: 'where there was a serious conflict between the interests of a child and one of its parents which could only be resolved to the disadvantage of one of them, the interests of the child had to prevail under Art 8(2)'. For this she relied upon, inter alia, Johansen v Norway (1996) 23 EHRR 33. See also Payne v Payne [2001] EWCA Civ 166, [2001] 1 FLR 1052, at [38], per Thorpe LJ.

¹³    In 'The Human Rights Act and the welfare principle in family law - conflicting or complementary?' [1999] CFLQ 223.

¹⁴    See, for example, H. Reece, 'The Paramountcy Principle: Consensus or Construct?' (1996) 49 Current Legal Problems 267 and A. Vine, 'Is the Paramountcy Principle Compatible with Article 8?' [2000] Fam Law 826.

¹⁵    See the Adoption of Children Act 1926, s 3(b). This was subsequently re-enacted in the Adoption Acts of 1950, s 5(1)(b) and 1958, s 7(2).

¹⁶    See the Adoption Rules 1984 (SI 1984/265), r 15(2).

¹⁷    Under English law, adoption applications may be made to a magistrates' court, county court or the High Court. In practice, most are made in the county court. There is also provision allowing proceedings to be transferred from one court level to another. For details, see op cit, n 4, at p 665.

¹⁸    Originally provided for by s 2(3) of the Adoption of Children (Scotland) Act 1930, it is currently required by s 6(2) of the Adoption (Scotland) Act 1978.

¹⁹    Under the 'proposed' Adoption Bill 1996, clause 41(7), it would not have been possible to make an adoption order in relation to a child aged 12 or over unless the court was satisfied that the child consented or was incapable of giving such consent. Interestingly, however, no such provision was contained in the Adoption and Children Bill 2001, introduced on 15 March 2001.

²⁰    As Butler-Sloss LJ said in the pre-Children Act decision, Re P (A Minor) (Education) [1992] 1 FLR 316, at p 321: 'The courts over the last few years, have become increasingly aware of the importance of listening to the views of older children and taking into account what children say, not necessarily agreeing with what they want nor, indeed, doing what they want, but paying proper respect to older children who are of an age and maturity to make their minds up as to what they think is best for them'.

²¹    Children Act 1989, s 1(4)(a).

²²    Viz under s 8, namely, residence, contact, specific issue or prohibited steps orders.

²³    Schedule 12, para 31. As S. Cretney has commented in 'Defining the Limits of State Intervention', in D. Freestone (ed), Children and the Law (Hull University Press, 1988), at p 61, it was with 'an astonishing stroke of tactical boldness' that this crucial change was contained in a schedule entitled 'Minor Amendments'.

²⁴    G. Douglas, M. Murch, L. Scanlan and A. Perry, 'Safeguarding Children's Welfare in Non-Contentious Divorce: Towards a New Conception of Legal Process?' (2000) 63 Modern Law Review 177, at pp 183-184. As the authors point out, contrary to the Law Commission's recommendation, under r 2.39 of the Family Proceedings Rules 1991 (SI 1991/1247) this scrutiny is not carried out until after the district judge has determined that the petition is made out.

²⁵    The Lord Chancellor's Department is currently reviewing the working of the Children Act 1989.

²⁶    Hansard, HL Deb, vol 573, col 1076, June 1996.

²⁷    See the Lord Chancellor's announcement on 16 January 2001: HL Official Report, col WA 126. For discussion of the many issues and implications of non-implementation, see M. Thorpe and E. Clarke (eds), op cit, n 10.

²⁸    Under the Family Proceedings Rules 1991, r 9.5: see, for example, Re A (Contact: Separate Representation) [2001] 1 FLR 715. J. Fortin, op cit, n 9, has commented that it is 'questionable whether the existing system denying legal representation to mature children in private law disputes over their upbringing can continue without challenge under the European Convention on Human Rights'. Normally,

where a child is made a party to proceedings the court will appoint the Official Solicitor (subject to his consent) or some other proper person to represent the child: Family Proceedings Rules 1991, r 9.5. However, if the child is of sufficient understanding he may defend proceedings without a next friend: r 9.2A, discussed further below.

29    The power to order a report is through s 7 of the Children Act 1989.

30    See N. Lowe and G. Douglas, op cit, n 4, at p 462.

31    For critical analysis of current judicial practice, see C. Lyon, op cit, n 10, at pp 67-79.

32    Court welfare officers are qualified probation workers. Following the establishment of the new Children and Family Court Advisory and Support Service (CAFCASS) under the Criminal Justice and Court Service Act 2000, court welfare officers will henceforth be known as child and family reporters.

33    For further discussion of the role of the welfare officer under English Law, see N. Lowe and G. Douglas, op cit, n 4, at p 455 et seq.

34    Section 1(3)(a) and (4)(b).

35    Technically, the power arises in 'specified proceedings', which includes care and supervision proceedings, emergency proceedings brought by a local authority, contact in care proceedings and those concerned with discharge from care applications.

36    A guardian ad litem is an individual qualified in social work. For a detailed discussion of this service see N. Lowe and G. Douglas, op cit, n 4, at p 552 et seq. Under the new Family Proceedings (Amendment) Rules 2001 (SI 2001/821) relating to the establishment of CAFCASS, guardians ad litem will henceforth be termed children's guardians. See op cit, n 32 and n 93 below.

37    See, for example, Re S (A Minor) (Guardian Ad Litem/Welfare Officer) [1993] 1 FLR 110, at pp 114-115, per Butler-Sloss LJ.

38    Under the Family Proceedings Rules 1991, r 4.16(2) and the Family Proceedings Courts (Children Act 1989) Rules 1991 (SI 1991/1395), r 16 (2) and (7), the court has a discretion to hear the case in the child's absence if it considers it in the interest of the child.

39    See, for example, Re C (A Minor) (Care: Child's Wishes) [1993] 1 FLR 832, in which it was held that guardians ad litem should think carefully about the arrangements for children who are to be present in court. J. Fortin, op cit, n 9, questions whether this reluctance to allow children to attend care proceedings is consistent with Art 6 of the European Convention for the Protection of Human Rights and Fundamental Freedoms 1950.

40    Before the Act, wardship offered a limited means by which children could initiate legal proceedings, see N. Lowe and R. White, Wards of Court (Barry Rose, 2nd edn, 1986), at paras 3-4.

41    Practice Direction (Applications by Children: Leave) [1993] 1 All ER 820.

42    Viz under s 10(8) of the 1989 Act. As established by the leading decision, Re S (A Minor) (Independent Representation) [1993] 2 FLR 437, there is no hard and fast rule in determining whether a child is of sufficient age and understanding. As Sir Thomas Bingham MR put it: 'Different children have differing levels of understanding at the same age. And understanding is not absolute. It has to be assessed relatively to the issues in the proceedings'. His Lordship added, however, the following caveat: 'Where any sound judgment in these issues calls for insight and imagination which only maturity and experience can bring, both the court and the solicitor will be slow to conclude that the child's understanding is sufficient'.

43    Family Proceedings Rules 1991, r 9.2A, for the application of which, see Re T (A Minor) (Child: Representation) [1994] Fam 49.

44    Much of which is summarised by A. O'Quigley, Listening to children's views and representing their best interests - a summary of current research (Joseph Rowntree Foundation, 1999), at pp 35-36. Note also C. Sawyer's work, particularly on solicitors' ability in assessing children's competence. See, for example, 'The competence of children to participate in family proceedings' [1995] CFLQ 180 and the study for the Calouste Gulbenkian Foundation by C. Lyon, E. Surrey and J. Timms Effective Support Services for Children and Young People when Parental Relationships Break Down (Liverpool University Press, 1998).

[45]   G. Schofield and J. Thoburn, Child Protection: the voice of the child in decision making (Institute for Public Policy Research, 1996), at p 62. Note also the comment by A. L. James and A. James, 'Pump up the Volume' (1999) 6(2) Listening to Children in Separation and Divorce in Childhood 206: 'Ours is a culture that does not particularly like children. The adage that "children should be seen and not heard" has an authentically English ring about it'.

[46]   B. Neale, 'Dialogues with children in participation and choice in family decision making' (unpublished paper, 1999).

[47]   N. Smith, 'All Change' (Spring 1999) UK Youth, at p 12.

[48]   J. Hunt and J. Lawson, Crossing the boundaries - the views of practitioners of Family Court Welfare and Guardian ad Litem work on the proposal to create a unified court welfare service (National Council for Family Proceedings, 1999), at p 38 .

[49]   S. Day Sclater and C. Piper, op cit, n 1, at p 8.

[50]   M. Murch, G. Douglas, L. Scanlan, A. Perry, C. Lisles, K. Bader, M. Borkowski, 'Safeguarding children's welfare in uncontentious divorce; a study of section 41 of the Matrimonial Causes Act 1973', Research Series No 7/99 (Lord Chancellor's Department, 1999), at pp 178-185.

[51]   Op cit, n 44. This report draws upon studies by B. Neale and C. Smart, 'Agents or Dependents? Struggling to listen to children in Family Law and Family Research', Working Paper No 3 (Centre for Research on Family, Kinship and Childhood, Leeds University, 1999); and L. Trinder, 'Competing Constructions of Childhood: Children's rights and children's wishes in divorce' (1999) 19 JSWFL 291.

[52]   Ibid, at p 33.

[53]   See B v B (Interviews and Listing Arrangements) [1994] 2 FLR 489, at p 496, per Wall J, sitting in the Court of Appeal.

[54]   C. Lyon et al, op cit, n 44, at p 74.

[55]   For fuller discussion of the interaction of these two approaches, see J. Roche and C. Piper in Undercurrents of Divorce, op cit, n 1; H. Hendrick, Children, Childhood and English Society (Cambridge University Press, 1880-1990), at pp 97-99; and K. Marshall, Children's Rights in the Balance: The participation - protection debate (The Stationery Office, 1997).

[56]   Op cit, n 1, at p 88.

[57]   Op cit, n 50, at p 42.

[58]   See J. Roche, op cit, n 1, at p 56.

[59]   See D. Archard, Children, Rights and Childhood (Routledge, 1993).

[60]   See K. Marshall, op cit, n 55. Marshall's small interdisciplinary study of how children's participation was viewed by various practitioners concluded: 'if children are truly to be regarded as human beings and citizens in their own right, the professionals who provide the framework within which the system operates must become accustomed to considering children of all ages as consumers and clients'.

[61]   See, for example, many of the studies in the recent ESRC research programme: Children 5-16: growing into the twenty-first century. Its 22 different projects have a common theme, looking at children as social actors. Its findings about children's experience of and response to contemporary society have wide-ranging implications for policy and practice. Other studies within this programme (1996-2000) include D. P. Alderson and S. Arnold, Children's Rights in Schools (London Institute of Education); M. Cadappa, I. Egharerba, M. Grenier and P. Moss, Extraordinary Childhoods: Social Roles and Social Networks of Refugee Children (Thomas Coram Research Unit); A. James, C. Jenks and P. Christiensen, Changing Times: Children's Understanding and Perception of the Social Organisation of Time (Hull University and Goldsmith College); C. Smart, B. Neale and A. Wade, New Childhoods: Children and Co-Parenting after Divorce (University of Leeds); G. M. Valentine, S. I. Holloway and N. Bingham, Cyberkids, Children's Social Networks, Virtual Communities, and Online Spaces (Sheffield University and Loughborough University).

[62]   See, for example, L. Marrow and M. Richards, 'The Ethics of Social Research with Children' (1996) 10 Children and Society 90, at pp 90-105.

[63]    The Scottish Law Commission Report on Family Law (SLC, 1992) explores the meaning of terms such as 'wishes and feelings', 'maturity' and the general concepts of competence, at paras 260-264, and took the view that a child's own view ought to be taken into account and not just as an aspect of welfare.

[64]    I. Butler and H. Williamson, Children Speak: Children, Trauma and Social Work (Longman, 1994).

[65]    Op cit, n 1, at p 71.

[66]    The Prime Minister's Review of Adoption (Performance and Innovation Unit, 2000).

[67]    Department of Health, Adoption: A New Approach (2000) Cm 5017, at p 15.

[68]    See H. Rudolf Schaffer, Making Decisions about Children: psychological questions and answers (Blackwells, 1999), at p 231. Schaffer, a leading developmental child psychologist, observes: 'Isolated crises need not lead to later disorder. Specific stresses are only of long-term significance if they are the first link in a chain of unfortunate events ... It is the totality of experience as it impinges on the child throughout the formative years, rather than a specific event, that accounts for the end result'.

[69]    M. Rutter, 'Resilience in the face of adversity: protective factors and resistance to psychiatric disorder' (1985) 606 British Journal of Psychiatry 47.

[70]    E. M. Hetherington, M. Cox and R. Cox, 'Long term effects of divorce and remarriage on children' (1995) 245 Journal of the American Academy of Child Psychiatry 518.

[71]    C. Caplan and R. Caplan, 'Primary Prevention of Psycho-Social Disorders in Children of Divorce': lecture given to the 5th World Conference on Innovations in Psychiatry, Central Hall, Westminster (Jerusalem: Institute for the Study of Psychological Stress, 1995).

[72]    G. Douglas, M. Murch and A. Perry, 'Supporting children when parents separate - a neglected family justice or mental health issue?' [1996] CFLQ 121 and G. Douglas, M. Murch, L. Scanlan and A. Perry, 'Safeguarding children's welfare in non-contentious divorce: towards a new conception of the legal process' (2000) 63 Modern Law Review 177, at pp 177-196.

[73]    Op cit, n 55, at p 77.

[74]    Gillick v West Norfolk and Wisbech Area Health Authority [1986] AC 112, at p 186D.

[75]    K. Marshall, op cit, n 55.


[86]    See generally, N. Lowe and M. Murch et al, op cit, n 76, who recommend (see pp 434-436) that adopters should be treated as working in partnership with the adoption agency and with whom there should be an adoption agreement through which applicants would be fully informed about the process.

[87]    C. Piper, op cit, n 1.

[88]    K. Marshall, op cit, n 56, at p 103. In offering a possible framework for children's participation, based on what she refers to as a 'child-centred system', she asserts that 'a child's right to participate should not be qualified by considerations of the child's interests. Adults cannot deny children the possibility of participation on the ground that involvement in existing decision-making processes would be damaging to a child. It is the task of adults to devise a system which facilitates appropriate participation of children'.

[89]    Op cit, n 67, at para 5.16.

[90]    Department of Health, Draft National Adoption Standards for England, Scotland and Wales (The Stationery Office, 2000), at p 4, para 3. See also n 93, below.

[91]    Similar research-based concerns are expressed by C. Piper, op cit, n 1, at pp 87-88.

[92]    Op cit, n 48, at p 104.

[93]    Note that the Adoption White Paper, op cit, n 67, at para 8.19, indicates the Government's intention to develop national standards for this new service. It will also be noted that following amendments introduced by the Family Proceedings Courts (Children Act 1989) (Amendment) Rules 2001 (SI 2001/818), r 4.IIB requires the children and family court reporter, inter alia, to notify the child of the contents of his report as he considers appropriate to the child's age and understanding.

[94]   The Adoption White Paper, op cit n 67, at para 8.20 also acknowledges that the creation of CAFCASS presents an opportunity to develop more specific training and development for its officers.

[95]   Op cit, n 66, at p 16. Note also the comment by P. Marsh and J. Triseliotis, Ready to Practice?: Social workers and probation officers - their training and their first year of work (Avebury, 1996), at p 183: 'in spite of the fact that the majority of children entering local authority care or who are placed on supervision are now adolescents and young people, there were almost no references to courses targeting the skills and knowledge required to work with this age group and their families'.

[96]   J. Masson and A. Oakley, Out of Hearing: Representing Children in Care Proceedings (Wiley, 1999). This was based on an interview sample of 20 children and young people (six girls and 14 boys) aged 9-16 years.

[97]   Ibid, at p 71. See also findings by C. Sawyer, op cit, n 44.

[98]   Op cit, n 96, at pp 74-75. See also C. Piper, 'Norms and Negotiation in Mediation and Divorce', in M. D. A. Freeman (ed), Divorce: where next? (Dartmouth, 1996) for a review of research on divorce solicitors generally.

[99]   Op cit, n 85, at pp 50-52.

[100]   The Education and Training Sub Committee (ETSC) advises the President's Interdisciplinary Committee on: (a) the continuing need for interdisciplinary education and training within and across the family justice system; (b) the opportunities to develop and deliver such education and training; (c) the potential for financial underpinning for such education and training; and (d) the ways in which relevant organisations, professional bodies and government departments might best be involved to support the strategic aims of the ETSC.

# [23]

## Representing Children:
## The Ongoing Search for Clear and Workable Standards

### Barbara Ann Atwood

In a dependency proceeding, a lawyer is appointed to represent a five-year-old child in foster care. The nature of the lawyer's role is not spelled out in the order of appointment. Over a period of months, the lawyer establishes a relationship of trust and confidence with the child, and the child comes to expect the lawyer to advocate for his wishes – to be returned to his mother. At the same time, the lawyer fears that such a result might expose the child to significant harm because of the mother's past alcohol abuse and her volatile relationship with a boyfriend. The child has told the lawyer of several experiences indicating that the mother has been intoxicated when caring for her son. In a quandary as to her obligations as legal counsel for this young child, the lawyer finds little guidance in law.[1]

In the scenario described above, should the lawyer represent her client's wishes as if the client were an adult? Would the lawyer be justified in advocating against the client's desires? Conversely, should the lawyer simply present the court with evidence of the boy's circumstances without taking a position on the ultimate outcome? Should the lawyer disclose any information she has received from the child? Little in the way of consensus exists among child advocates as to these questions. The role of children's representatives in legal proceedings has been the topic of widespread debate across the United States[2] and within the international community.[3] While many courts and commentators agree that children should have a "voice" in proceedings affecting their interests, the meaning of the child's voice is fraught with ambiguity. The lack of clear guidance for children's representatives, in turn, can produce frustration among child advocates[4] and poor representation for children.[5]

Disagreements focus on such fundamental questions as whether a child is entitled to a representative under any circumstance and, if so, whether that representative should be an attorney, a guardian ad litem, or some combination of the two. When an attorney is appointed for a child, no clear consensus exists as to the standards governing that attorney's representation.[6] In particular, courts have questioned whether children's attorneys have the same ethical duties to pursue their clients' wishes and to maintain client confidentiality that ordinarily inhere in the lawyer-client relationship.[7] The chameleon designation of "guardian ad litem" has given rise to rampant confusion.[8] Moreover, when an attorney functions both as a lawyer and a guardian ad litem, disagreements abound as to the ethical obligations of that hybrid role.[9]

Children's representatives appear in a variety of settings, including child custody disputes, abuse and neglect proceedings, contested adoptions, civil commitment, procedures for obtaining judicial consent for abortion, and, of course, juvenile delinquency cases. This article will describe the most prominent approaches to child representation within the United States, with a focus on the legal representation of children in abuse and neglect proceedings and private custody disputes. To illustrate the range of approaches currently in place across the United States, Part I highlights differences in the laws of several states regarding children's attorneys and guardians ad litem. In some states, legislatures have codified guidelines for children's representatives in an effort to bring clarity and predictability to this area of the law. In other states, courts have announced principles governing lawyers and guardians ad litem on an ad hoc basis. The various approaches, while often contrasting markedly one from another, generally reflect policy choices about what best protects children. Part II analyzes a few of the key ethical issues that can arise in the course of a lawyer's representation of a child client. Ethical tensions have driven many of the proposals regarding children's attorneys, and courts have resolved these tensions differently. Part III summarizes the competing proposals governing children's representatives that have emerged within the United States, with particular attention to the American Academy of Matrimonial Lawyers' ("AAML") guidelines for lawyers representing children in custody disputes and the contrasting American Bar Association ("ABA") proposed standards of practice for children's attorneys.

Throughout this analysis, I offer reflections on the relative merits of the competing models of children's representatives, emphasizing the points of agreement as well as the points of contention. The passion with which children's advocates defend their positions has convinced me that universal consensus is unlikely to be achieved soon. On the other hand, the very existence of the debate can be seen as a positive development. As we move into the twenty-first century, I find hope and promise in the fact that child advocates, professional associations, legislatures, and courts are engaged in a conversation about how best to speak for our most vulnerable population.

## I. Current Approaches to Representation of Children

## A. The Appointment of a Representative – Mandatory or Discretionary

Although the Supreme Court held that children have a due process right to counsel at the adjudication phase of juvenile delinquency proceedings in In re Gault,[10] the Court has not recognized a comparable right to counsel for children in other civil contexts. Nevertheless, the trend across the United States does seem to be toward greater recognition of the value of legal counsel for children in a variety of settings. Because children's fundamental interests are at stake in child welfare cases, child advocates have long argued that every child involved in an abuse or neglect proceeding should be represented by counsel,[11] and a few state courts have endorsed the right to counsel in that context as a matter of due process.[12] Moreover, a federal district court recently held that foster children have a constitutional right to counsel as a matter of state constitutional law in dependency cases and termination of parental rights proceedings. In Kenny A. ex rel. Winn v. Perdue,[13] a Georgia federal court recognized that the children had profound liberty interests in their own safety, health, and well-being as well as interests in maintaining the integrity of the family unit and a relationship with their birth parents. An erroneous decision to terminate parental rights would unnecessarily destroy the child's family relationships, while an erroneous decision not to terminate might subject the child to the risk of abuse or extended impermanency. In light of the strength of the child's interests and the serious risk of error, the court concluded that "only the appointment of counsel can effectively mitigate the risk of significant errors in deprivation and TPR proceedings."[14] The court pointed out that neither citizen review panels nor court-appointed special advocates could engage in adequate investigation to effectively represent the child.[15] The potential fiscal burden of appointment of counsel, in the court's view, was far outweighed by the state's parens patriae obligation to protect the child and the child's fundamental interests.

The Kenny court's holding, while based on state constitutional law, rests on the importance of the children's interests at stake in child protective proceedings and the effectiveness of lawyers in helping courts avoid error. Moreover, Kenny did not rely on any unique features of Georgia's state constitution in analyzing the due process claim but instead employed the familiar due process framework from Matthews v. Eldridge.[16] Thus, the case is an important recent precedent for those who have argued that children have a right to counsel in child welfare cases as a matter of federal constitutional law.

Constitutional entitlement aside, children have statutory rights to representation under federal and state law in defined circumstances. The federal Child Abuse Prevention and Treatment Act ("CAPTA") requires the appointment of a "guardian ad litem" for every child involved in an abuse or neglect case as a condition of receiving federal CAPTA funding.[17] According to CAPTA, a guardian ad litem, who has received training appropriate to the role, and who may be an attorney or a court appointed special advocate who has received training appropriate to that role (or both), shall be appointed to represent the child . . . (I) to obtain first-hand, a clear understanding of the situation and needs of the child; and (II) to make recommendations to the court concerning the best interests of the child.[18]

Thus, while the statute does not specify the nature of the representative, it does provide that the guardian may be "an attorney or a court appointed special advocate"[19] charged with representing the best interests of the child. In response to CAPTA, almost all states now require some form of child representation in abuse and neglect proceedings,[20] but the role of the representative varies widely. In a few states, the federal CAPTA requirement may be deemed satisfied through the highly economical court appointed special advocate ("CASA") program.[21] Although CASAs are often a valuable source of information about the child, exclusive reliance on a lay volunteer in child protection proceedings would seem inadequate. CASAs generally do not possess specialized expertise in the social sciences or mental health fields and thus may not have the requisite professional expertise to competently evaluate a proposed placement for a child. Moreover, CASAs generally are not appointed as attorneys and therefore may be ineffective in bringing relevant evidence to the attention of the court and in protecting the child's legal rights.[22] Thus, a court's exclusive reliance on a CASA would give short shrift to advocacy of the child's wishes.[23]

Although CAPTA explicitly permits the guardian to be a lawyer, the statutory reference to the duty "to make recommendations to the court concerning the best interests of the child" is a function ordinarily associated with non-lawyers. As a result, many states routinely appoint lawyers as guardians ad litem, without careful delineation of the distinctions between the ethical responsibilities of a lawyer as a zealous advocate for the client's position and the professional obligations of the guardian ad litem as a best interests witness for the court.[24] In some states, however, statutory provisions identify situations in which the lawyer should function in the role of legal counsel for the child.[25]

Wholly apart from CAPTA, some states have independently required appointment of legal counsel for children in proceedings to terminate parental rights. In Ohio, for example, the courts have reasoned that the child's status as a party to such proceedings under Ohio statutory law requires that he or she be represented by counsel.[26] Moreover, although a guardian ad litem who is a lawyer may in some situations function as legal counsel in the Ohio scheme, a separate lawyer must be appointed if the guardian ad litem recommends a position that is contrary to the child's expressed wishes.[27] At the same time, the Ohio courts have recognized that counsel's role may vary, depending on the maturity of the child and other circumstances of the case.[28] Wisconsin takes a somewhat different approach by statute, tying the right to legal counsel to the child's age: under Wisconsin law, a child twelve years old or older must be provided an attorney in abuse and neglect proceedings, while a child under the age of twelve is entitled to a guardian ad litem.[29] At the same time, every guardian ad litem in Wisconsin is required to be a lawyer.[30]

Outside the context of abuse and neglect and termination of parental rights, state law varies widely on the question of children's representatives. A few states require the appointment of representatives for children in select proceedings, such as contested paternity determinations,[31] contested adoptions,[32] and civil commitment proceedings.[33] In contrast, in the context of custody disputes – arguably the category of proceedings most likely to impact children today – most states grant full discretion to courts in deciding whether to appoint a representative for the child.[34] The Uniform Marriage and Divorce Act has served as a model in this area, providing that courts may appoint "an attorney to represent the interests of a child" with respect to support, custody, and visitation.[35] In contrast, about ten states require the appointment of a representative for a child in custody actions under certain circumstances, such as where there are allegations of abuse.[36] In Minnesota, for example, a guardian ad litem is mandatory if there are allegations of abuse or neglect that are not being litigated in another court.[37] Placing more emphasis on the child's right of autonomy, Oregon requires the appointment of an attorney if the child requests it.[38] In Wisconsin, on the other hand, a guardian ad litem for the child is viewed as mandatory in all contested custody disputes.[39]

In sum, both federal and state law impact the appointment of children's representatives, and the rules vary across the United States. Because of CAPTA, almost every state guarantees that children involved in abuse and neglect proceedings will have a representative, although the nature of that representative ranges from a legal advocate to a lay guardian or CASA. In court proceedings not governed by CAPTA, wide variation exists but the majority approach is for states to leave the question of children's representatives to the discretion of the family court judges.

B. The Representative's Role

Just as no uniformity exists with respect to the discretionary or mandatory appointment of representatives for children, a similar lack of uniformity surfaces with respect to the professional role of children's representatives. Although people often view children's representatives as occupying two competing camps,[40] the representative's professional roles might be better framed as falling on a continuum, with the lay guardian ad litem committed to protecting the child's interests at one end of the spectrum, the zealous attorney committed to advocating the child's wishes at the opposite end, and various hybrid models falling at different points in between. Those who endorse the guardian ad litem model of children's representation emphasize the unique vulnerability of children and their need for adults to protect them and to make decisions for them concerning their welfare. Most fundamentally, those who are responsible for deciding a child's future placement want the assurance that they will be informed of potential harms to the child. If a child's lawyer is committed only to advocating the child's expressed wishes, a judge may worry that the lawyer's presentation is incomplete or deliberately slanted to achieve the child's goal. As Judge Debra Lehrmann asks,

> Does the child's interest in directing the actions of counsel outweigh the child's interest in being assured that all evidence bearing on his or her welfare is presented to the court? . . . . Do we truly have the best interests of children at heart or are we caught up in an image of ourselves that precludes acknowledgment of the need for a protective approach to family law?[41]

Others point to the risk for children of too much autonomy. Robert Emery, for example, worries that placing undue emphasis on a child's wishes may shift decision-making responsibility from the adults to the child for emotionally charged issues like child custody. "Rights and responsibilities," he explains, "go hand-in-hand, and many of our well-intentioned efforts to increase children's rights have, unfortunately, burdened children with adult responsibilities."[42] Similarly, many commentators have recognized that children may suffer loyalty conflicts if they are forced to articulate a preference in custody disputes.[43]

In contrast, those who endorse a child's attorney model emphasize the child's basic right to have his or her wishes presented by a zealous advocate.[44] Proponents emphasize the child client's autonomy and the value to the child and to the court of the child's participation in the proceedings.[45] Under this approach, the child's dignity interests are served when the child has a representative committed to advocating the child's preferences. Professor Katherine Hunt Federle has argued that children have a basic right to "empowerment" and that children's lawyers should enable their clients to make choices and to participate in the legal system.[46] In her view, children involved in child welfare proceedings would benefit if the courts were to emphasize their status as "powerful, rights-bearing individuals" rather than focusing on their vulnerabilities and dependence. She also maintains that the child-directed lawyer can ensure that other adults in the proceeding take the child's view seriously.[47] Others have insisted that even young children should be deemed competent to make legal choices. Professor Randy Kandel, for instance, argues that children as young as seven or eight years of age have the requisite cognitive and emotional maturity to choose their custodians.[48] In addition, children may benefit emotionally from knowing that their views were considered by the decision maker, even if the ultimate result is not in line with their preferences.[49] Of course, a child's attorney who is determined to represent the client's wishes may face an inherent tension if the child's position appears to the attorney to be contrary to the child's best interests. Moreover, a child's attorney must decide what action to take when the child cannot or will not direct the attorney as to a particular issue. These ethical dilemmas and alternative resolutions are addressed in Part II.

Although wide variations in the role of children's representatives exist, some broad generalizations are possible. In the abuse and neglect context, due in part to the federal mandate of CAPTA,[50] children's representatives are more likely to be appointed as guardians ad litem, or lawyers functioning as guardians ad litem, than as children's attorneys.[51] As such, the child's representative generally is appointed to assist the court in determining a resolution that will be in the child's best interests and is not bound by the child's wishes. Indeed, while many states require the guardian to report the child's expressed wishes to the court,[52] some do not explicitly impose such a duty on the guardian.[53] Moreover, the role of the guardian ad litem varies from state to state. While courts often refer to the guardian ad litem as "the arm of the court,"[54] the guardian's role may encompass acting as expert witness or mediator as well as investigator and court advisor.[55] In states where the duties of guardians ad litem are spelled out by statute or court rule, they often include investigation of the case, interviews with parties and others knowledgeable about the child, review of relevant records, participation in court proceedings and settlement discussions, and reporting of findings and recommendations to the court.[56]

In the context of child custody disputes, the statutory law of most states authorizes courts to appoint an attorney or a guardian ad litem for the child.[57] Regardless of label, the representative's role generally is to assist the court in protecting the child's best interests rather than to advocate the child's wishes.[58] A statute's terminology can give rise to confusion about the appropriate professional role for the representative, especially if the appointed representative is a lawyer.[59] Section 310 of the Uniform Marriage and Divorce Act ("UMDA"), for example, provides for the discretionary appointment of "an attorney to represent the interests of a minor or dependent child," and the Comment explains that "[t]he attorney is not a guardian ad litem for the child, but an advocate whose role is to represent the child's interests."[60] Although some commentators have read this to mean "expressed interests,"[61] the choice of the term "interests" seems ambiguous. The drafters of the UMDA knew to use "child's wishes" when that was their intent.[62] Moreover, by stating that the attorney is not a guardian ad litem, the drafters could have been clarifying that the representative was supposed to function as a lawyer rather than as a witness. Thus, appointments that simply incorporate the language of the UMDA could certainly give rise to confusion. In any event, to the extent that state law requires the attorney for the child to represent the child's best interests, the attorney is functioning in an unusual capacity – one, however, that several proposed standards of practice have endorsed.[63] The expectation is that the lawyer will advocate for the child's interests in court, whether or not those interests coincide with the child's expressed wishes. A few states have tried to address the potential conflict when the child's preferences conflict with the attorney's perception of the child's interests.[64] Most states, however, have simply left the potential conflict for resolution by the representative on a case-by-case basis.

The widespread use of guardians ad litem in custody disputes has come under sharp attack in recent years.[65] Critics argue that courts give too much weight to recommendations by guardians ad litem and that reliance on the recommendations amounts to an abdication of judicial responsibility.[66] Also, serious due process concerns are present when guardians' reports and recommendations have been considered by courts without an opportunity for cross examination by the parties.[67] Moreover, the common use of the hybrid attorney/guardian ad litem model has been questioned, with many critics emphasizing that lawyers lack the professional expertise to offer opinions and recommendations on a child's best interests.[68] Similarly, commentators worry that the absence of clear standards for guardians ad litem permits them to act on the basis of subjective, unconstrained bias.[69] Although views about the utility of guardians ad litem differ, the overwhelming consensus among commentators and courts is that clearer guidelines are needed.[70]

* * * *

IV. Conclusion

Defining appropriate standards for children's representatives poses difficult questions of policy and ethical responsibility, and the answers that have been provided in court decisions, statutes, and model standards vary markedly. Nevertheless, the proverbial "laboratory" of experimentation provided by the fifty states is always a valuable resource. Some closing thoughts on the relative merits of existing and proposed approaches may be helpful.

First, context matters. The nature of the legal proceeding in which the child is involved and the child's legal rights within that proceeding should inform a court's decision whether to appoint a representative for the child. The appointment of representatives for children in private custody disputes, for example, properly remains a discretionary matter under the law of most states and under the standards proposed by both the AAML and the ABA. In contrast, the mandatory appointment of legal counsel for every child involved in abuse and neglect proceedings is an ideal, partially driven by CAPTA,[166] that is gradually becoming the norm across the nation. The profound impact that a child protective proceeding may have on the life of a child warrants the appointment of legal counsel, at public expense, to ensure informed and sensitive decision-making.

Second, children are vulnerable yet deserving of respect, and the value to the child of having a lawyer advocate his or her wishes should not be underestimated. In the introductory fact pattern, the lawyer for the child finally chose to follow her five-year-old client's directions but also asked the court to appoint a guardian ad litem without revealing the nature of her concerns to the court. The lawyer's strong sense that she should not betray the trust of her vulnerable, traumatized client persuaded her to advocate for his expressed objective. Although most people would consider a five-year-old much too young to direct representation, the lawyer had developed a "thickly textured understanding"[167] of that particular child's world and felt obligated to champion the child's viewpoint. At the same time, the lawyer took precautionary measures to protect the child. In this manner, the lawyer tried to ensure that the judge would consider the child's strong desire to return home, as well as facts weighing against a return, in the ultimate disposition. In contrast, under an age-based presumption such as that recommended by the AAML and others,[168] the lawyer would be unlikely to advocate for the child's wishes. Instead, she would be relegated to the role of investigator and monitor. Even in that constrained mode, however, the lawyer might work against the child's stated objectives by shading the introduction of evidence to block the child's return. From the child's perspective, a lawyer's failure to advocate his views might be one more betrayal by the adult world, one more insult to dignity. Although the AAML's age-linked presumption would lend certainty and predictability to the representative's role, it would likely exclude many children who are capable of directing at least some aspect of their representation. Moreover, even where a client-directed model is inappropriate, guidelines ought to require the child's representative – whether a best interests lawyer or a guardian ad litem – to communicate the child's views to the court unless the child objects. Otherwise, the voice of the person whose welfare is most at stake is effectively silenced.

Third, even very young children who cannot direct a lawyer in any sense still deserve a legal advocate under certain circumstances. Decision-makers look to children's representatives for guidance, and it seems both unrealistic and misguided to bar lawyers for young children from advocating a particular resolution for their clients. Moreover, the development of objective criteria to guide the determination of a child's best interests can help reduce the risk of unconstrained discretion (on the part of both best interests lawyers and guardians ad litem).

Fourth, the widespread use of the hybrid attorney/guardian ad litem model is inherently problematic. The range of responses to the ethical tensions within that hybrid role shows that there is no easy resolution. Instead, the better approach seems to be a separation of the function of attorney from that of guardian ad litem – a position that has been endorsed by a few states and by both the AAML and the ABA. On the other hand, if the attorney/guardian ad litem is retained as an essential (or economically efficient) means of serving children's interests, then rules of professional conduct need to be developed to govern the conduct of such representatives in their attorney capacity.

Child advocacy is a growing field of law and is receiving more attention today than ever before.[169] Across the nation, a consensus exists that children deserve better quality representation, whether by attorneys, guardians ad litem, or the dual attorney/guardian ad litem model. State legislatures, courts, and bar associations could bring much needed clarity to this area by adopting standards of practice. At this point in time they have a number of different models from which to choose, each resting on legitimate policy choices. While many heartfelt disagreements exist among law reformers, there is no doubt that the law governing children's representatives is being "reformed." Children can only benefit from the ongoing efforts to improve the performance of those who speak for them.

*Barbara Ann Atwood, J.D., is the Mary Anne Richey Professor of Law at the University of Arizona James E. Rogers College of Law.*

## Notes

[1]    This illustration is based on the author's supervision of a dependency proceeding in the Spring Term of 2005 at the Pima County Juvenile Court, Tucson, Arizona, handled by students with the Child Advocacy Clinic at the University of Arizona James E. Rogers College of Law.

[2]    Some of the more prominent contributions to the literature governing the responsibilities of children's lawyers include Ann M. Haralambie, The Child's Attorney (1993) (proposing that a child's attorney should advocate the child's wishes unless they are potentially harmful to the child, but suggesting that the attorney can minimize ethical dilemmas by paying more attention to counseling of child); Jean Koh Peters, Representing Children in Child Protective Proceedings: Ethical and Practical Dimensions (2d ed. 2001) (recommending that attorneys should develop a sensitive, contextual relationship with child clients over time and interpret children's wishes through the lens of the children's individualized circumstances); Emily Buss, Confronting Developmental Barriers to the Empowerment of Child Clients, 84 Cornell L. Rev. 895 (1999) (examining children's limited cognitive and emotional capacity to direct counsel); Donald N. Duquette, Legal Representation for Children in Protection Proceedings: Two Distinct Lawyer Roles Are Required, 34 Fam. L.Q. 441 (2000) (arguing that no single role will fit the needs of all children and proposing that children's evolving capacities require separate standards for a client-directed attorney and a best interests guardian ad litem); Katherine Hunt Federle, The Ethics of Empowerment: Rethinking the Role of Lawyers in Interviewing and Counseling the Child Client, 64 Fordham L. Rev. 1655 (1996) (suggesting that a lawyer can empower a child client by greater advocacy of the child's wishes); Martin Guggenheim, A Paradigm for Determining the Role of Counsel for Children, 64 Fordham L. Rev. 1399 (1996) (advocating that a lawyer for a young child should focus on enforcing the child's legal rights rather than on carrying out the child's expressed objectives); Sarah H. Ramsey, Representation of the Child in Protection Proceedings: The Determination of Decision-making Capacity, 17 Fam. L.Q. 287, 316 (1983) (recommending representation of a child's expressed wishes when the child is "capable of making a considered decision").

[3]    The United Nations Convention on the Rights of the Child (CRC) provides that children are entitled to participate, directly or through a representative, in judicial or administrative proceedings affecting their interests. See Article 12 of the Convention on the Rights of the Child, G.A. Res. 44/25, U.N. GAOR, 44th Sess., at art. 1, U.N. doc. A/Res/44/25 (1989), available at 28 I.L.M. 1448 (1989). In light of the child's right of participation, courts and scholars from other nations have explored the role of children's counsel in a variety of contexts. See, e.g., Cynthia Price Cohen, The Developing Jurisprudence of the Rights of the Child, 6 St. Thomas L. Rev. 1, 63 (1993) (discussing efforts in European Union to give children greater roles in divorce proceedings as a mandate of CRC); Hon. Claire L'Heureux-Dube, A Response to Remarks by Dr. Judith Wallerstein on the Long-Term Impact of Divorce on Children, 36 Fam. & Conciliation Cts. Rev. 384 (1998) (reporting on efforts in Canada to enhance children's voices in family law cases under CRC); Nicholas Bala, Child Representation in Alberta: Role & Responsibilities of Counsel for the Child, Legal Education Society of Alberta, Child Representation Training, Edmonton, April 1-3, 2005 (manuscript on file with author)(assessing professional role of children's counsel under law of Alberta).

⁴    See Sharon S. England & Robert E. Shepherd, "I Know the Child is My Client, but Who Am I?" 64 Fordham L. Rev. 1917 (1996); Martin Guggenheim, Reconsidering the Need for Counsel for Children in Custody, Visitation and Child Protection Proceedings, 29 Loy. U. Chi. L.J. 299 (1998); Randi Mandelbaum, Revisiting the Question of Whether Young Children in Child Protection Proceedings Should be Represented by Lawyers, 32 Loy. U. Chi. L.J. 1 (2000).

⁵    See Andrew I. Schepard, Children, Courts, and Custody, 140-43 (2004) (describing the need for clearer standards for guardians ad litem and lawyers for children).

⁶    See Haralambie, supra note 2, at 2 ("No uniformity exists with respect to what it means to be appointed to represent a child.").

⁷    See, e.g., Leary v. Leary, 627 A.2d 30 (Md. Ct. Spec. App. 1993) (describing differing roles for children's attorneys). See generally Linda Elrod, Counsel for the Child: The Time Is Now, 26 Fam. L.Q. 53 (1992).

⁸    See, e.g., Jacobsen v. Thomas, 100 P.3d 106 (Mont. 2004) (holding that guardians ad litem for children ordinarily may testify and be cross-examined and should not function as attorneys unless explicitly directed to do so in the order of appointment). See generally Richard Ducote, Guardians Ad Litem in Private Custody Litigation: The Case for Abolition, 3 Loy. J. Pub. Int. L.106 (2002).

⁹    See, e.g., Clark v. Alexander, 953 P.2d 145 (Wyo. 1998) (determining that an attorney/guardian ad litem is bound by a child's best interests rather than a child's preferences and may disclose confidential client communications to the court).

¹⁰    387 U.S. 1 (1967) (children are "persons" within meaning of the Fourteenth Amendment and are entitled to counsel in proceedings where their liberty interests are at stake).

¹¹    See generally American Bar Association, Proposed Standards of Practice for Lawyers who Represent Children in Abuse and Neglect Cases, 29 Fam. L.Q. 375, 375-76 (1995) (explaining the historical support for appointment of attorneys for children in abuse and neglect proceedings); Jacob E. Smiles, A Child's Due Process Right to Legal Counsel in Abuse and Neglect Proceedings, 37 Fam. L. Q. 485, 486-87 (2003) (arguing that children have a due process right to counsel in child welfare cases).

¹²    See, e.g., In re Jamie TT, 599 N.Y.S. 2d 892 (N.Y. App. Div. 1993) (holding that a child is entitled to effective legal representation as matter of due process in child abuse proceeding); contra In re D.B. and D.S., 385 So.2d 83 (Fla. 1980) (deciding that a child does not have a constitutional right to counsel in abuse and neglect proceedings).

¹³    356 F. Supp. 2d 1353 (N.D. Ga. 2005).

¹⁴    Id. at 1361.

¹⁵    According to the court, "[j]udges, unlike child advocate attorneys, cannot conduct their own investigations and are entirely dependent on others to provide them information about the child's circumstances.... CASAs are also volunteers who do not provide legal representation to a child." Id.

¹⁶    424 U.S. 319, 335 (1976) (stating that due process analysis requires consideration of the private interest that will be affected by official action, the risk of erroneous deprivation of such interest and the probable value of additional procedures, and the government's interest).

¹⁷    See 42 U.S.C. § 5106a(b) (2) (A) (xiii) (2000).

¹⁸    Id. (emphasis added).

¹⁹    The court appointed special advocate, or CASA, is a lay volunteer whose duties generally include investigation of a child's circumstances and making recommendations to the court based on the child's best interests. The National CASA Association was formed in 1984, and today CASA programs exist in almost every state. See Michael S. Piraino, Lay Representation of Abused and Neglected Children: Variations on Court Appointed Special Advocate Programs and Their Relationship to Quality Advocacy, 1 J. Center Child. & Cts 63 (1999) (describing the history and success of CASA programs). Federal law authorizes the U.S. Department of Justice, Office of Juvenile Justice and Delinquency Prevention, to enter into cooperative agreements with the National CASA Association to expand CASA

programs throughout the nation. See 42 U.S.C. § 13013 (2000) (authorizing grants for qualifying CASA programs).

[20] See Howard Davidson, Child Protection Policy and Practice at Century's End, 33 Fam. L.Q. 765, 768-69 (1999). Indiana is alone among the states in not mandating the appointment of a guardian ad litem in all abuse and neglect cases. See Ind. Code §31-34-10-3 (2004) (permitting but not requiring the appointment of a guardian ad litem or court appointed special advocate for many categories of abuse and neglect proceedings).

[21] See, e.g., N.H. Rev. Stat. Ann. § 169-C:10(I) (2004) (court shall appoint a guardian ad litem or a court-appointed special advocate guardian ad litem); Ohio Rev. Code Ann. § 151.281(J) (1) (West 2004) (court shall appoint a qualified volunteer as guardian ad litem when one is available and the appointment is appropriate).

[22] See Bridget Kearns, Comment, A Warm Heart but a Cool Head: Why a Dual GAL System Best Protects Families Involved in Abused and Neglected Proceedings, 2002 Wis. L. Rev. 699 (suggesting that a volunteer advocate acting without counsel lacks legal expertise to adequately protect a child's legal rights).

[23] See generally Katherine Hunt Federle, Children's Rights and the Need for Protection, 34 Fam. L.Q. 421, 436-40 (2000)(arguing that legal advocacy of a child's views would empower the child).

[24] See, e.g., Ala. Code § 12-15-1 (2004) (guardian ad litem must be licensed attorney appointed by court); N.Y. Fam. Ct. Act § 242 (2004) (law guardian must be attorney). See Federle, supra note 23, at 424-34.

[25] See, e.g., Wash. Rev. Code Ann. § 13.34.100(6) (West 2004) (the court may appoint counsel for children age twelve or older at the child's request); N.C. Gen. Stat. § 7A-586(a) (2004) (if a non-attorney is appointed as guardian ad litem, the court shall appoint a lawyer for the child).

[26] In re Williams, 805 N.E.2d 1110 (Ohio 2004).

[27] The court noted that there may be a "fundamental conflict" between the guardian ad litem's duty to recommend whatever the GAL determines to be in the child's best interests and the duty of a lawyer to advocate the client's wishes. Id. at 1114.

[28] Id.

[29] See Wis. Stat. Ann. § 48.23 (2004).

[30] See Wis. Stat. Ann. § 48.235 (2004) (the guardian ad litem shall be an attorney whose duty is to advocate for the child's best interests).

[31] See, e.g., Iowa Code Ann. § 598.21 (2004) (requiring appointment of a guardian ad litem in a contested paternity action); Kan. Stat. Ann. § 38-1125 (2003) (requiring appointment of a guardian ad litem for the child in a paternity action if the interests of the child and the petitioner differ); Me. Rev. Stat. Ann. tit. 18-A,§ 9-201(f) (2004) (requiring appointment of an attorney for the child in paternity action); Mont. Code Ann. § 40-6-110 (2004) (requiring appointment of a guardian or guardian ad litem for the child in a paternity action); Unif. Parentage Act § 612 (2000) (requiring appointment of an "attorney ad litem" if the child is a party or the child's interests are not adequately represented).

[32] See, e.g., Miss. Code Ann. § 93-17-8 (West 2004) (requiring appointment of an attorney as a guardian ad litem for the child in a contested adoption); Okla. St. Ann. § 7505-1.2 (2004) (requiring appointment of an attorney for the child in a contested adoption and a guardian ad litem if requested); S. Car. Code § 20-7-1732 (requiring appointment of a guardian ad litem for the child in an adoption proceeding); Unif. Adoption Act § 3-201 (1994) (requiring appointment of a guardian ad litem in a contested adoption).

[33] See, e.g., Ariz. Rev. Stat. § 8-221 (2004) (requiring appointment of an attorney for the child in a commitment proceeding unless the right is waived); Fla. Stat. Ann. § 39.407(5) (2004) (requiring appointment of a guardian ad litem for the child in a proceeding for residential mental health treatment).

³⁴   According to a recent ABA survey, thirty-nine states leave appointment of representatives for children to the complete discretion of the court. See ABA Child Custody Pro Bono Project, Appointment Laws in Divorce Cases (Aug. 2003), reprinted at Linda D. Elrod, Raising the Bar for Lawyers Who Represent Children: ABA Standards of Practice for Custody Cases, 37 Fam. L. Q. 105, 126-29 (2003) (Appendix)[hereinafter "ABA Survey".

³⁵   Unif. Marriage & Divorce Act § 310, 9A U.L.A. 13 (1998).

³⁶   See ABA Survey, supra note 34.

³⁷   See Minn. Stat. Ann. § 518.165 (2004).

³⁸   See Or. Rev. Stat. § 107.425(6) (2004).

³⁹   See Wis. Stat. Ann. § 767.045 (2005). In Lofthus v. Lofthus, 678 N.W.2d 393 (Wis. Ct. App. 2004), the court held that appointment of a guardian ad litem for the children was required in a proceeding to modify physical custody.

⁴⁰   See Emily Buss, "You're My What?" The Problem of Children's Misperceptions of Their Lawyers' Roles, 64 Fordham L. Rev. 1699, 1699 (1996) (describing competing models as "best interests" and "expressed interests"); Marvin Ventrell, Legal Representation of Children in Dependency Court: Toward a Better Model–The ABA (NACC Revised) Standards of Practice (1999) (reporting that attorney/guardian ad litem and traditional attorney are the models that have dominated representation of children).

⁴¹   Debra H. Lehrmann, Who Are We Protecting? 63 Tex. B.J. 122, 126 (2000).

⁴²   Robert E. Emery, Hearing Children's Voices: Listening-and Deciding-Is an Adult Responsibility, 45 Ariz. L. Rev. 621, 622 (2003).

⁴³   See, e.g., Martin Guggenheim, What's Wrong with Children's Rights 162 (2005); Florence W. Kaslow & Lita Linzer Schwartz, The Dynamics of Divorce: A Life Cycle Perspective 162 (1987); Richard Wolman & Keith Taylor, Psychological Effects of Custody Disputes on Children, 9 Behav. Sci. & L. 399, 407 (1991).

⁴⁴   An article by Professor Martin Guggenheim has been identified as starting a "paradigm shift" toward the view that children capable of directing a lawyer should have counsel committed to pursuing the child's legal objectives. See Peters, supra note 2, at 47-48, citing Martin Guggenheim, The Right to Be Represented But Not Heard: Reflections on Legal Representation for Children, 59 N.Y.U. L. Rev. 76 (1984) [hereinafter Guggenheim, The Right to Be Represented But Not Heard] (suggesting that children over age of seven should be deemed responsible for directing their attorneys and that younger children should be deemed incapable). Guggenheim, it should be noted, has revised his thinking in this area to more carefully tie the attorney's role to the substantive rights that children have in particular substantive areas. See Guggenheim, Paradigm for Determining Role of Counsel, supra note 2, at 1420-21.

⁴⁵   See Federle, supra note 2, at 1680.

⁴⁶   Id. at 1695-96.

⁴⁷   Federle, supra note 23, at 439-40 (suggesting that empowering children to participate in proceedings affecting their relationships with their parents might lead to more accurate and just determinations).

⁴⁸   Randy Frances Kandel, Just Ask the Kid! Towards a Rule of Children's Choice in Custody Determinations, 49 U. Miami L. Rev. 299 (1994).

⁴⁹   I have explored this topic elsewhere. See Barbara Ann Atwood, The Child's Voice in Custody Litigation: An Empirical Survey and Suggestions for Reform, 45 Ariz. L. Rev. 629, 660-62 (2003) (describing intangible "dignity value" and mental health benefits of children's participation in custody disputes). Similarly, the Pew Commission on Children in Foster Care has recommended that foster children have an informed voice in decisions that are made about their lives. See The Pew Commission on Children in Foster Care, Fostering the Future: Safety, Permanence and Well-being for Children in Foster Care (May 18, 2004), available at http://pewfostercare.org.

⁵⁰   See notes 17-25 supra and accompanying text.

<sup></sup>[51]    See Federle, supra note 23, at 424-26 (noting that at least forty-one states mandate or permit the appointment of a guardian ad litem in abuse and neglect proceedings).

[52]    See, e.g., Me. Rev. Stat. Ann, tit. 22, § 4005(1) (E) (West 2004) (guardian ad litem must make child's expressed wishes known to court); 42 Pa.. Consol. Stat. Ann. § 6311(b) (9) (2004) (guardian ad litem must advise court of child's wishes; conflict between guardian's recommendation and child's wishes shall not be considered conflict of interest). See Federle, supra note 23, at 427-28.

[53]    See, e.g., R.I. Gen. Laws § 40-11-14 (2004) (requiring court to appoint "a guardian ad litem and/or a court-appointed special advocate" without specifying duties).

[54]    See, e.g., Clark v. Alexander, 953 P.2d 145, 152 (Wyo. 1998) (stating that the traditional role of a guardian ad litem is to serve as an "arm of court"); Collins v. Tabet, 806 P.2d 40 (N.M. 1991) (holding that a guardian ad litem functioning as an "arm of the court" is entitled to absolute quasi-judicial immunity).

[55]    Copyright (c) 2005 American Academy of Matrimonial Lawyers; Barbara Ann Atwood See Raven C Lidman & Betsy R. Hollingsworth, The Guardian Ad Litem in Child Custody Cases: The Contours of Our Legal System Stretched Beyond Recognition, 6 Geo. Mason L. Rev. 255 (1998).

[56]    See, e.g., Minn. Stat. § 518.165 (2004) (enumerating a broad range of duties for guardians ad litem in custody cases); Ariz. Rev. Stat. § 8-522 (2003) (listing duties of "special advocates" in dependency actions).

[57]    See ABA Survey, supra note 34.

[58]    Id.

[59]    Id. See also Richard Ducote, Guardians Ad Litem in Private Custody Litigation: The Case for Abolition, 3 Loy. J. Pub. Int. L. 106, 109 (2002) (reporting that in most states guardians ad litem fill the role of children's legal representatives in custody cases).

[60]    Unif. Marriage. & Divorce Act § 310 (emphasis added).

[61]    See Haralambie, supra note 2, at 2-3 (stating that an attorney may assume an appointment under the UMDA is to represent a child's expressed interests).

[62]    See Unif. Marriage & Divorce Act § 402(2).

[63]    See infra notes 146-58 and accompanying text.

[64]    See infra notes 86-96 and accompanying text.

[65]    See, e.g., Ducote, supra note 59; Raven C Lidman & Betsy R. Hollingsworth, The Guardian Ad Litem in Child Custody Cases: The Contours of Our Legal System Stretched Beyond Recognition, 6 Geo. Mason L. Rev. 255 (1998) (arguing that the confusing term "guardian ad litem" should be discarded altogether and recommending that courts designate representatives by role, such as investigator, mediator, or expert witness).

[66]    See Comment to Standard 3.2, AAML Standards for Attorneys and Guardians ad Litem in Custody or Visitation Proceedings (1995) (stating that the standard prohibiting guardians ad litem from making recommendation on contested issues "avoids the serious danger of abdication of judicial responsibility").

[67]    A number of state courts have upheld due process challenges based on trial judges' reliance on reports or recommendations by guardians ad litem. See, e.g., Ex parte R.D.N., ___So.2d ___, 2005 WL 503568 (Ala. 2005) (holding that a father's due process rights were violated when the trial court adopted a guardian ad litem's ex parte custody recommendation); In re Marriage of De Bates, 819 N.E.2d 714 (Ill. 2004) (holding that a mother's due process rights were violated when she was not permitted to cross-examine the child's representative but finding the error was harmless); Pirayesh v. Pirayesh, 596 S.E.2d 505 (S.C. App. 2004) (reversing a custody order based on a guardian ad litem's biased and incomplete investigation).

[68]    See Ducote, supra note 59.

[69]    See Lidman & Hollingsworth, supra note 65.

[70]   See, e.g., In re Tayquon H., 821 A.2d 796 (Conn. App. Ct. 2003) (decrying the lack of standards and attempting to differentiate between the roles of guardian ad litem and attorney for child). Several states have recently promulgated guardian ad litem guidelines, and the ABA Family Law Section has formed a committee to draw up proposed standards of practice for guardians ad litem in private custody disputes. See Margaret Graham Tebo, The Most Vulnerable Clients: Attorneys Must Deal With Special Issues When Kids Come Into Contact With the Courts, 89 A.B.A. J. 48, 51-52 (2003).

[166]   See notes 17-24 supra and accompanying text.

[167]   See Peters, supra note 2, at 50.

[168]   The AAML Custody Standards do not apply to abuse and neglect proceedings, but the use of the child's age as a proxy for capacity can be found in the statutory law of a few states in the abuse and neglect context. See, e.g., Wash. Rev. Code. Ann. § 13.34 (West 2004) (child twelve years of age or older may request legal counsel rather than guardian ad litem); Wis. Stat. Ann. § 48.23 (2004) (child twelve years of age or older entitled to legal counsel while younger child entitled to attorney/guardian ad litem).

[169]   See generally Marvin Ventrell, The Practice of Law for Children, 66 Mont. L. Rev. 1 (2005) (describing children's law as emerging legal specialty, with marked increase in professional organizations, development of standards of practice, and law school curricular offerings).

# C: Mental Health Professionals and Interdisciplinary Collaboration

# [24]

# Making a Place at the Table: Reconceptualizing the Role of the Custody Evaluator in Child Custody Disputes

## Mary Kay Kisthardt and Barbara Glesner Fines

*This response to Timothy Tippins and Jeffrey Wittmann's article "Empirical and Ethical Problems with Custody Recommendations: A Call for Clinical Humility and Judicial Vigilance" builds upon the authors' conclusions that custody evaluations cannot and should not be a substitute for the socio-legal judgment of the best interests of the child. Recognizing that clinical humility and judicial vigilance may not be sufficient to restrain the misuse of psychological evaluation, we offer for consideration three structural changes that would provide for a more appropriate use of the skills and talents custody evaluators bring to legal decisions. We suggest using custody evaluators in the less adversarial setting of preparing parenting plans, revising the procedures by which custody evaluations are elicited in litigation, and adopting the approximation standard for child custody determinations.*

Tippins and Wittmann provide much food for thought about why we have come to the present situation and what we can do about it. In the first instance, they make a very persuasive case for the exclusion of forensic psychological assessments on the ultimate questions presented in disputed child custody cases. Their conclusions appear to be based on two general theories: first, there is simply no reliable scientific basis for making such determinations, and second, the best interest standard currently used by the courts is not a psychological construct but rather a legal and socio-moral one. As to the first point, they make a compelling case for the lack of empirical research sufficient to make these judgments and we are not prepared to dispute those findings. Rather, as lawyers and law professors, it is the second basis for their conclusion that raises more interesting questions.

To describe the "best interest standard" as both a legal and socio-moral concept foreshadows the reason why it has proved to be so difficult to apply. Unlike more determinative standards, the "best interest standard" invites the most subjective of analyses. It might be suggested that judges are in no better position to determine the best interest of the child than are psychologists.

Their unease in doing so has, no doubt, led to the excessive reliance on psychological assessments reported by the authors. The authors exhort custody evaluators to be restrained in their testimony while encouraging judges to take greater care in evaluating the admissibility of this testimony. While important short-term considerations, these cautions are unlikely to significantly improve the use of mental health professionals in crafting custody decisions. Moreover, the adversarial pressure on attorneys, particularly in high-conflict divorces, is one for which there exists few checks. While the rules of professional conduct have substituted standards of competence and diligence for the older duty of zealous representation, the adversary system remains structurally designed for opposition, not cooperation. Attorneys have a duty to "present the client's case with persuasive force."[1] In doing so, attorneys are unlikely to be able to effectively evaluate when an expert has moved from Level II testimony to Level III testimony because they have every incentive, and even a duty, to move the expert in a direction that will provide the most persuasive testimony possible. Courts as well, hoping to have an objective grounding that will provide efficient disposition of their ever-growing family law dockets, have little incentive to police the boundaries of expert testimony. If custody evaluators increasingly pull their punches by significantly hedging their observations and refusing to provide opinions on the ultimate question in custody disputes, attorneys and judges alike may conclude that they have little value in the adversarial contest.

Rather than writing off the entire profession, which brings important and useful knowledge and skills to the custody determination, the legal system must find better ways to use those skills and talents. For that to happen, we believe more substantial structural changes are necessary. We suggest three such changes: using custody evaluators in the less adversarial setting of preparing parenting plans, revising the procedures by which custody evaluations are elicited in litigation, and adopting the approximation standard for child custody determinations.

One way to better use the special expertise of child custody evaluators would be to bring these professionals in at a much earlier stage, before the parties have polarized their positions and the evaluator is viewed as choosing sides. Currently, when custody evaluators are used, the rate of relitigation of the resulting stipulations or orders is dramatically high.[2] With the trend toward requiring the use of parenting plans in all child custody cases comes the opportunity to engage child custody evaluation experts to assist in crafting these plans. A parenting plan is a detailed description of the manner in which parents intend to continue caring for their children after divorce. The development of these plans benefits children by requiring their parents to focus on the specific needs of the children and to anticipate and address expected changes in their lives. Hopefully this forethought, as well as an agreement on how to resolve disputes that arise, will reduce future conflict that is so detrimental to children's well-being. Making these plans mandatory requires parents to sit down and think very specifically about what the child's life is going to look like after divorce. It does not permit parents to simply and very generally portray the other parent as inadequate thereby placing themselves in the primary parenting position.

In this context, it would seem that psychologists might play a very valuable role. To begin with, we know that children's reaction to change and separation from a parent is based not just on individual differences but also on their developmental stage. Psychologists have much to offer parents in terms of suggestions related to developmental processes. Furthermore, by the very nature of its subject matter, a parenting plan will have to respond to change. Again, alerting parents of the need to be flexible as their children age would be most useful in avoiding future conflicts.

Additionally, interviewing the child in order to ascertain his/her individual differences would allow a psychologist to work in the best interest of that child by assisting the parents themselves in making good decisions. Rather than being put in a position of having to assist (in a very direct way, if the authors are correct) a judge who relies so heavily on the report because of a lack of knowledge of the child or the family, the psychologist would be in the position of assisting the appropriate decision makers, the parents who are in a superior position to judge what is in their child's best interest. Obviously, all the cautions the authors provide regarding restraint in providing opinions on ultimate plans apply here as well. However, this is made easier by the absence of the adversarial pressure that may come later should the parties fail to reach an agreement.

When adversarial litigation does result, there are structural reforms that the legal system might consider to improve the ability of lawyers and judges to understand the limits of custody evaluations. There is an informational disconnect between lawyers and psychologists about the work they do and the limits of their "science." Mental health professionals are often surprised to learn that there is not a definitive answer to the question of "what is the law in this situation?," in much the same way that lawyers will be surprised to learn that a psychologist is not qualified to make a recommendation on what child custody plan would be best for a child. The authors' recommendation that there be a better effort made in cross-disciplinary understanding is a welcome one indeed.

Judges and lawyers might better understand the limits of science if they heard from more than one custody evaluator. Many commentators suggest that, to reduce cost and acrimony, courts should appoint custody evaluators, who can then provide "objective and neutral" testimony.[3] However, the authors provide many examples of how evaluator testimony may be less than objective – even without the weight of adversarial bias. It may be that the practice of each side engaging a custody evaluator may result in greater, rather than less, objectivity as the differences in their observational standpoints and theoretical orientations may then be disclosed. The federal courts of Australia have adopted a number of innovations in using multiple experts, including pretrial conferencing between experts to prepare a joint report and the so-called "hot tub rule" for testimony. Seeking to provide expert testimony in dialogue between the professionals rather than in adversarial testimony, experts are called as a panel, rather than individually, and are allowed to ask one another questions, rather than routing all their testimony through the attorneys.[4]

Obviously, increasing the number of custody evaluators or bringing them in at an earlier stage may increase the cost of custody determinations. More fundamental structural reforms may be required before the skills and knowledge of mental health professionals can effectively and ethically guide the custody decision. The difficulties identified by the authors and the obvious reluctance of both sets of professionals to make these decisions should lead us to a closer examination of the broader issues: questioning the advisability of the "best interest" standard as the overriding criteria for making these decisions and determining an appropriate role for mental health professionals to play. Criticisms of the best interest standard are long-standing[5] and will no doubt be renewed by the authors recommendations. In response to these criticisms several alternatives have been proposed including a change in the standard courts should use and the creation of parenting plans in all child custody cases. If the appropriate use of psychologists could enhance either of these alternatives, they are likely to be viewed more favorably.

For making child custody determinations in contested cases, the American Law Institute has proposed that the proportion of custodial responsibility allocated each parent should approximate the proportion of caretaking functions each parent exercised prior to the separation. This standard, known as the "approximation" standard, is designed to reduce litigation by making the outcome of child custody cases more predictable. Several concerns raised by the authors may be addressed by the adoption of this standard.

First, who are the families for whom child custody evaluations are currently being ordered? A vast majority of child custody cases are settled by the parents, often with the assistance of their lawyers. Cases that proceed to the point of needing a third party decision maker are generally disputes between fairly contentious parents.[6] This is not to say that there are not many meritorious reasons why a parent would need to resort to litigation, but for many families the dispute is between fairly equally "good" parents or fairly equal "not so good" parents who are for whatever reason intent on continuing the fight. For these families the use of the "best interest" standard provides a fertile battleground. Proponents of the approximation standard suggest that replacing the best interest standard with one that makes the outcome more predictable will reduce the opportunity for legally sanctioned combat.

Another rationale presented for the standard is that it removes much of the speculation about future conduct as a basis for making a decision. This aspect is particularly attractive to those who argue that the adversarial system is not particularly well adapted to that task. Most legal decisions are made by determining what has occurred in the past and assigning the appropriate consequence to it. Predicting future human behavior is far more difficult than assessing what happened in the past. Furthermore, proponents of the approximation standard argue that, with respect to parenting, past behavior is predictive of future parent-child interactions, citing the Mnookin and Maccoby study which showed that over time, parents tend to revert to their predivorce parenting patterns.[7]

As proposed, the standard does have exceptions and this is perhaps where the psychologist might be most helpful. The most relevant exception refers to a situation in which the presumptive allocation would harm the child because of a strong disparity in the quality of the emotional attachment between each parent and the child, or in each parent's demonstrated ability or availability to meet the child's needs. It would seem that the psychologists are on much firmer ground here in evaluating not the future but the *demonstrated* ability of the parent to meet the child's needs. This assessment could be done at a Level I or II, thereby meeting our concerns. Furthermore, an additional exception permits accommodation of a firm and reasonable preference of a child who has reached a specific age. It would seem that psychologists could also be of assistance in this regard. Interviewing children is not generally a highly developed skill for lawyers or judges.

The custody decision is one of the most fundamental decisions courts are called upon to make. The need and desire to inform (or even shift) that decision through the expertise of mental health professionals is understandable and perhaps even unavoidable. We provide a great service in identifying the risks inherent in involving mental health professionals in that decision beyond the boundaries of their expertise and ability. The challenge for law is to find appropriate, helpful, and efficient methods to reduce family conflict and help parents craft appropriate custody arrangements. All professionals and policy makers involved in these decisions must give much more careful consideration to the appropriate stage at which mental health professionals can contribute, the optimum procedural structure for their participation, and the standards for decision making that can be best informed by their expertise.

*Mary Kay Kisthardt, J.D., LL.M., is Professor of Law at the University of Missouri-Kansas City School of Law.*

*Barbara Glesner Fines, J.D., LL.M, is the Ruby M. Hulen Professor of Law at the University of Missouri-Kansas City School of Law.*

**Notes**

[1]   MODEL RULES OF PROF'L CONDUCT R. 3.3 cmt. 2 (2002).

[2]   Janet R. Johnston, *Building Multidisciplinary Professional Partnerships with the Court on Behalf of High-Conflict Divorcing Families and Their Children: Who Needs What Kind of Help?*, 22 U. ARK. LITTLE ROCK L. REV. 453, 472-73 (2000).

[3]   Linda D. Elrod, *Reforming the System to Protect Children in High Conflict Custody Cases*, 28 WM. MITCHELL L. REV. 495 (2001).

[4]   Justice Garry Downes AM, *Concurrent Expert Evidence in the Administrative Appeals Tribunal: The New South Wales Experience*, Paper presented at the Australasian Conference of Planning and Environment Courts and Tribunals in Hobart February 27, 2004, *available at* http:// www.aat.gov. au/CorporatePublications/speeches/downes/concurrent.htm (last visited September 28, 2004).

[5]   Robert H. Mnookin, *Child-Custody Adjudication: Judicial Functions in the Face of Indeterminacy*, 39 L. & CONTEMP. PROBS. 226, 251-52 (1975).

[6]   Elrod, *supra* note 5.

[7]   Robert H. Mnookin & Eleanor Maccoby, *Facing the Dilemmas of Child Custody*, 10 VA. J. SOC. POL'Y & L. 54 (2002).

# [25]

# Commentary on Tippins and Wittmann's "Empirical and Ethical Problems with Custody Recommendations: A Call for Clinical Humility and Judicial Vigilance"

## Joan B. Kelly and Janet R. Johnston

*Although in substantial agreement with Tippins and Wittmann's analysis, their call for a moratorium on the practice of custody evaluators making recommendations to the court does not solve the many problems that they have raised, and may have unintended consequences which place families at even greater risk. This commentary reflects our agreement with some of the authors' major points of contention, focuses on several points of disagreement, and suggests alternative remedies for the shortcomings and ethical problems described in child custody evaluations.*

Tippins and Wittmann (this issue) have written a thoughtful, well-researched, and provocative article that merits response. We fully agree with them that the custody evaluation and related judicial decision has the potential to change the entire course of children's lives, including the extent and meaningfulness of their parent-child relationships, emotional and social adjustment, school functioning, and economic well-being. While their article focuses on psychologists as custody evaluators, in many family courts mediators, counselors, and guardians ad litem provide judges with opinions and recommendations as to custody and access, sometimes after spending only one to two hours with the parents. Tippins and Wittmann's concern and caution are warranted, and should serve as a clarion call to the entire family law field involved in custody and access determinations.

The authors' four-level conceptual model for stratifying data and clinical inferences provides a helpful framework for mental health and legal professionals to examine the evaluation process, whether or not one agrees with their conclusions. Custody evaluators without sufficient scientific training are unaware of the serious limitations of the data they collect, the validity of the testing instruments they use, or the rigor needed to make inferences and draw conclusions from this information. Instead, the authors contend, such custody evaluators are more likely to make inferences and recommendations from unsubstantiated theory, personal values and experiences, and cultural and personal biases. Our own observations and reviews of evaluations over several decades lead us to the same conclusion. Common examples include unexamined strong beliefs in the primacy of mothers (or essentiality of fathers) regardless of the circumstances, biased perception of their clients derived from their own negative marital and divorce experiences, or a conviction that joint physical custody benefits (or harms) all children.

Too few custody evaluators are well acquainted with, and make use of, the existing body of empirical literature on divorce, parenting, child development, and children's emotional and social adjustment for purposes of formulating questions to guide the collection of data, and for making inferences and recommendations. Too often simplistic research, replete with outdated findings and formulations is used in the area of divorce and attachment theory and its effects on children's adjustment; overgeneralizations from empirical data are also especially common. Parental conflict, for example, is often treated as an undifferentiated variable without awareness of the different effects on children; the intensity and content of conflict; whether conflict is expressed in avoidance, angry words, hostility, or physical violence; whether parents protect or expose their children to their differences and unresolved disputes, and whether buffers exist that ameliorate the potentially negative effects of high conflict.

In their discussion of Level III inferences arising from Level I and II observations, Tippins and Wittmann are correct to infer that too many evaluators state as "facts" certain conclusions without disclosing that some of these issues or conclusions are the focus of considerable disagreement if not raging controversy in the field, or that these "facts" are not supported by well-designed, replicated, empirical research. A common example is the position that if overt alienating behaviors are identified in one parent when a child resists visitation, custody should be shifted to the other parent. The controversy in the field regarding overnight visits for very young children is another example. Without reference to any empirical data that supported his or any other viewpoint, one evaluator stated, "This five-year-old child will be irreparably damaged were she to spend even one overnight away from her mother."

The immediate and obvious implication of Tippins and Wittmann's valid concerns is that more stringent ethical, professional, and scientific standards of practice should be required of custody evaluators with respect to drawing clinical inferences. This surely requires higher standards for initial training and certification to perform custody evaluations, as well as ongoing professional development to update the evaluators' knowledge base in social science and law at regular intervals. It is striking that the AFCC Standards of Practice for Child Custody Evaluations (1994) do not mention knowledge of relevant research as an important aspect of the process, nor does it raise issues of reliability or validity. Hopefully, this will be remedied in a revision of the standards currently being prepared by the AFCC Task Force.

The contribution of evaluators involves collecting Level I data and these behavioral observations are especially valuable when guided by key concepts and variables abstracted from relevant research. For example: "With respect to this child's ability to separate from one parent and transition to the other, it was noted that at each of the four interviews the child clung to her mother and resisted entering the room where her father was waiting." Level II data – conclusions about the psychology of the parent, child, and family – can be made, provided that the custody evaluator can support these clinical inferences by citing relevant research studies from the literature within the custody report. For example "According to criteria developed by Main, Kaplan, and Cassidy (1985), this six-year-old child has an ambivalent attachment to her mother (marked by clinging dependency and intermittent hostility) and a disorganized attachment to her father (marked by a mix of fear, avoidance and passive compliance)."

## POINTS OF DISAGREEMENT

Tippins and Wittmann take the position that few statements can be made at Level III that are within the requisite ethical and scientific parameters. By this they mean, conclusions based on Level I and II data relevant to custody and access questions, such as a particular child's functioning and needs, or the fit between a child's needs and parental abilities. They concede that clinicians can be useful to the court at Level III when they summarize important psychological risks or advantages regarding certain parenting plans, but only if they provide "clearly articulated qualifications, cautionary statements to the court, and references to the limitations of the evaluation methods used" (Tippins & Wittmann, this volume).

In support of their argument, the authors cite the absence of predictive validity for such constructs as parent-child fit, different parenting plans, and future child outcomes. They also cite the fact that empirical research related to Level III conclusions is quite limited. We take issue with this latter point, and suggest that, provided the appropriate precautions are taken with respect to Level III summaries and conclusions, the authors are more conservative than they need to be. There is far more empirical research describing specific factors associated with risk and resiliency in children following divorce than the authors appear to indicate. While it is true that most empirical research was designed to assess the various impacts of separation and divorce on children's adjustment, rather than test predictive statements about custody or access plans, the results of three decades of increasingly sophisticated research has provided a more complex understanding of variables associated with risk and resilience following divorce to guide the well-informed evaluator.

Well-designed empirical studies point to the negative impact of parental depression, anxiety, mental illness, and personality disorders on child adjustment during marriage and after divorce. Diminished parenting following separation and the importance of postdivorce parenting characterized by warmth, emotional support, adequate monitoring, authoritative discipline, and age-appropriate expectations have been widely reported. Risk and protective factors associated with attachment processes, loss of relationships, long-term parent-child relationships, academic functioning, school drop-out, and higher education have been described. Access frequency, shared physical custody, quality of father-child relationships, father-child closeness in relation to different access patterns, children's resistance to visitation, children's views of their access patterns concurrently and retrospectively, and more recently, overnight visits for young children, all in relation to children's adjustment, have received substantial research attention. Multiple dimensions of the effects of high conflict and parent violence on child adjustment, and protective buffers against conflict have been reported, as have the various impacts of remarriage and re-partnering. Articles and books reviewing the empirical literature on children and divorce contain descriptions of and citations to such relevant variables and studies (Amato, 2000; Barber, 2002; Emery, 1999; Hetherington, 1999; Hetherington & Kelly, 2002; Kelly, 2000; Kelly & Emery, 2003; Maccoby & Mnookin, 1992; Pruett, Williams, Insabella, & Little, 2003; Waxler, Duggal, & Gruber, 2002), and evaluators should search out updates regarding newer empirical research on such controversial variables as overnight visits for young children (Pruett, Ebling, & Insabella, 2004), child alienation (Johnston, 2003; Johnston & Kelly, 2004), and shared physical custody and conflict (Bausermann, 2002; Lee, 2002). Research reviews of various clinical, mediation, and arbitration interventions can inform the evaluator as to the effectiveness of the services they suggest (Johnston, 2000; Kelly, 2002, 2004; Pruett & Johnston, 2004).

Hence, we suggest that to the extent that available research can be cited that includes studies of variables pertaining to child custody and access, circumscribed inferences at Level III might be drawn. Following our example of the six-year-old child who had difficulty transitioning between parents, the evaluator could state:

> Research studies show that hostility and unresolved parental conflict undermines parenting capacities and negatively impacts the child (Cummings & Davies, 1994; Krishnakamur & Beuhler, 2000; Tschann, Johnston, Kline, & Wallerstein, 1989), and that following divorce, expressing anger in the presence of or through the child is associated with children's depression and anxiety (Buchanan, Maccoby, & Dornbusch, 1991; Hetherington, 1999). In this family, the father's expressed anger toward the mother, in the presence of the child appears to contribute to the mother's distress and emotional unavailability to the child as well as the child's fear of him. Without remedying this family dynamic, shared physical custody arrangements that require parents to communicate will probably be detrimental to this child.     In more complex cases, the custody evaluator must draw upon a number of different studies and weigh the beneficial buffers that are present (like a good parent-child relationship) with the risks that are posed (like ongoing parental conflict and parental psychopathology) together with the resiliency of the child (age, temperament, etc.) in order to support Level III conclusions regarding beneficial access patterns. Thus, for example, if the evaluator observes a close, supportive relationship between a father and his nine-year-old son, but also notes a high level of interparental conflict, the following could be stated:
>
> Traditional access of every other weekend is experienced as insufficient time and distressful for most children and is likely to erode the child's relationship with the nonresidential parent over the long term (Kelly & Emery, 2003). In contrast, more frequent access between children and fathers when the relationship is positive is associated with better behavioral adjustment and academic performance in children (Amato & Gilbreth, 1999), especially when fathers are more involved in children's school activities and projects and provide authoritative discipline and emotional support (Amato, 2000; Menning, 2002; Nord, Brimhall, & West, 1997; Simons, 1996). Studies point to the benefits of substantial time with both parents even in the presence of parental conflict provided that parent-child relationships are positive, with diminishing benefits of shared residential arrangements in the presence of very high and sustained conflict (Bausermann, 2002; Lee, 2002). In this family, the warmth and support in both parent-child relationships appears to buffer this bright and adaptive boy against the potential negative effects of his parents' conflict (Emery, 1999; Kelly, 2000). This is a fairly recent separation and the parents have no significant psychopathology. It is therefore unlikely that these parents will be among the 8-15% of parents who continue in high conflict several years after divorce (King & Heard, 1999).     Such references to the research can form the basis for the evaluator's comments at Level III that "the customary jurisdictional guideline of four days per

month would be depriving and unsatisfactory for this particular child, and has the potential to cause more negative adjustment problems."

Tippins and Wittmann have taken a strong position – based on the American Psychological Association Ethical Principles of Psychologists and Code of Conduct (2003) – that it is unethical for evaluators to make recommendations to the court (Level IV inferences) because of the limitations of the data collected, and the lack of empirical knowledge that links data to specific parenting plans and outcomes for children. Moreover, they back up this position by a legal objection, arguing that recommendations to court amount to the custody evaluator usurping the role of the judge as trier of fact.

In cases where trained and experienced evaluators have collected data systematically, used valid and reliable testing instruments, and linked their Level I and II observations and data to Level III conclusions, citing empirical research to support these conclusions, then we believe it is ethical to make recommendations as to custody and access that provide the trier of fact with some options for parenting plans that might benefit this particular child. The contribution at Level IV could involve the custody evaluator offering a series of alternative hypotheses, predictions about the future functioning of the child under different custody and access scenarios, also backed by research findings. To return to our example of the six-year-old girl, the evaluator could state:

According to Maccoby and Mnookin (1992) and Hetherington (1999), it is rather unlikely that highly conflicted parents will develop a cooperative co-parenting relationship within the next few years. Hence, primary residence with one parent and a specific, clearly structured access plan with a neutral place of exchange is likely to be more supportive of this child's security. Alternatively, if parents, especially the father, successfully complete psycho-educational parenting counseling, then a more shared parenting arrangement might be warranted (Arbuthnot, Kramer, & Gordon, 1997). More definitive recommendations at Level IV might be made in the case of the nine-year-old boy described above: "While no research exists to support one specific parenting plan, the research cited suggests this child would most likely benefit from liberal access to the father during some part of each week, including a stable pattern of school days and weekend time." Requiring the custody evaluator to document knowledge claims and to present clinical inferences and hypotheses that are conditional would ensure more accountability. It would also allow appropriate challenge from competing facts, theories, and research findings.

While we have indicated our agreement with many of the arguments made by Tippins and Wittmann, we disagree with the authors' call to place a moratorium on making recommendations because the alternatives are dismal, even destructive, and may cause even more harm to families and parent-child relationships. We do not agree that judges should be left to make the final decision without any input from custody evaluators or others about what is considered to be "in the best interests of the child." In the face of this vague legal mandate, judges are even less qualified in training and experience than are mental health professionals to address this question without undue influence of their personal biases.

In the absence of recommendations by custody evaluators who have considered each child and family situation in great depth, judges and legal advocates will probably rely more and more on prescriptive guidelines (like primary residence with one parent and every-other-weekend with the other). It is even more likely that judges' decisions will be governed by presumptions that will increasingly be cast into statutes by political and professional interest groups with access to the state legislatures (like the American Law Institute's approximation rule, or a primary parenting presumption advocated by women's lobbyists, or joint parenting presumptions touted by fathers' rights groups). These prescriptive rules and presumptions are not research based and they do not consider the individual needs of children and variations in parent-child relationships. Rather, they are simplistic answers, a one-size-fits-all substitute for the vexing question of what is in the best interests of each child.

A promising alternative is the development of parenting plans that could provide judges (and parents) with a range of possible alternative dispositions on custody and access. Such model parenting plans would be based on the empirical literature to date, and offer choices for the court that address the needs of different kinds of family situations and developmentally appropriate options for different age groups. Some states (like Arizona) have piloted this approach, using an interdisciplinary task force, with promising results (Arizona Supreme Court, 2001). It is indeed true that custody arrangements are based on a mix of tradition, law, science, untested theory, and prevailing cultural values about child rearing. For this reason, local task forces of community members made up of interested citizens, and mental health and legal professionals, could participate in the development and updating of these parenting plan models for the use of judicial and parental decision making.

## THE OVERUSE OF CUSTODY EVALUATIONS

Acknowledging the serious deficits in custody evaluations, particularly the flimsy grounds (ethically, empirically, and legally) for making recommendations on the ultimate issue, leads one to question the appropriateness of this tool for developing clarity and dispute resolution for many cases in family court. Clearly, evaluations can be more solidly grounded when they are investigating serious allegations of physical abuse, sexual abuse, and neglect of the child as well as mental illness, substance abuse, and domestic violence on the part of parents. In these domains, community standards and values are more clearly defined and the empirical research literature is more extensive and robust in its findings of what is *not* in children's best interests.

In the absence of such serious concerns about family abuse and neglect, mental illness, or substance abuse, too often custody evaluations must focus on who is and who is not more emotionally healthy and "the better parent." Personality testing is undertaken with no solid basis for concluding how the findings might impact parenting (Brodzinsky, 1993; Roseby, 1995; Tippins & Wittmann, this volume). Particularly in those cases where angry, hurt, but "good enough" parents are contesting custody or the allocation of time sharing, there is generally no basis in psychology or law for choosing between parents. Evaluators split hairs to make a case for one parent or the other, and the evaluator's personal values and cultural biases are likely to be more prominent in this decision making. This may also be the case when both parents have demonstrated significant character or psychological problems and parenting deficits, and it is impossible to argue for a preference between parents without relying on subjective reactions and biases.

In this quest, custody evaluations may have inadvertently produced de facto double standards, where those held up for parents in family courts are far more stringent than those faced by parents in dependency courts. The result is that custody evaluators are now producing exhaustive, intrusive, negatively biased assessments, psychological testing, and written reports in which separating parents are scrutinized and held to a higher standard of accountability than those in nondisputing divorces and intact families. This seems unfair, unnecessarily stressful for already vulnerable families, and may even constitute grounds for claiming violation of parents' civil rights. It is in the search for the elusive "better or best parent" that personal values and cultural beliefs are likely to infiltrate and contaminate what is supposed to be a scientifically defensible investigative process and report.

## ALTERNATIVE REMEDIES

A better policy would be for forensic custody evaluations to be reserved for serious allegations of child abuse, neglect, and molestation, as well as contested claims of parental psychopathology, substance abuse, or domestic violence, where standards for parental behavior in family court would be more on a par with those in dependency court. Where parents have extremely discrepant views of their child's needs, difficulty making decisions together in a timely manner, and co-parenting disagreements that do not rise to the level of abuse allegations, the use of extended interventions such as confidential child-inclusive mediation and therapeutic mediation (Kelly, 2002; Pruett & Johnston, 2004; Sanchez & Kibler Sanchez, 2004).

*Joan B. Kelly, Ph.D., is a clinical psychologist, researcher, teacher and consultant. She was a Founder and Executive Director of the Northern California Mediation Center from 1981-1999.*

*Janet R. Johnston, Ph.D., is Professor of Justice Studies at San José State University in California.*

## REFERENCES

Amato, P. (2000). The consequences of divorce for adults and children. *Journal of Marriage and Family*, *62*, 1269-1287.

Amato, P., & Gilbreth, J. (1999). Nonresident fathers and children's well-being: A meta-analysis. *Journal of Marriage and the Family*, *61*, 557-573.

Arbuthnot, J., Kramer, K. M., & Gordon, D. A. (1997). Patterns of relitigation following divorce education. *Family & Conciliation Courts Review*, *35*, 269-279.

Arizona Supreme Court. (2001). *Model parenting time plans for parent/child access*. Phoenix, AZ: Administrative Office of the Courts, Family Law Unit. Retrieved November 8, 2004, from www.supreme.state.az.us.

Association of Family & Conciliation Courts. (1994). Model standards of practice for child custody evaluations. In P. Bushard & D. Howard (Eds.), *Resource guide for custody evaluators*. Retrieved November 8, 2004, from www.afccnet.org/pdfs/Child_Model_Standards.pdf.

Barber, B. K. (Ed.). (2002). *Intrusive parenting: How psychological control affects children and adolescents*. Washington, DC: American Psychological Association.

Bausermann, R. (2002). Child adjustment in joint-custody versus sole-custody arrangements: A meta-analytic review. *Journal of Family Psychology, 16*, 91-102.

Bow, J. M., & Quinnell, F. A. (2002). A critical review of child custody evaluation reports. *Family Court Review, 40*(2), 164-176.

Brodzinsky, D. M. (1993). On the use and misuse of psychological tests in child custody evaluations. *Professional Psychology: Research and Practice, 24*, 213-219.

Buchanan, C., Maccoby, E., & Dornbusch, S. (1991). Caught between parents: Adolescents' experience in divorced homes. *Child Development, 62*(5), 1008-1029.

Cummings, E., & Davies, P. (1994). *Children and marital conflict: The impact of family dispute and resolution*. New York: Guilford Press.

Emery, R. E. (1999). *Marriage, divorce, and children's adjustment* (2nd ed.). Thousand Oaks, CA: Sage.

Hetherington, E. M. (1999). Should we stay together for the sake of the children? In E. M. Hetherington (Ed.), *Coping with divorce, single parenting, and remarriage* (pp. 93-116). Mahwah, NJ: Erlbaum.

Hetherington, E. M., & Kelly, J. (2002). *For better or for worse: Divorce reconsidered*. New York: W. W. Norton & Co.

Johnston, J. R. (2000). Building multidisciplinary professional partnerships with the court on behalf of high-conflict divorcing families and their children: Who needs what kind of help? *University of Arkansas at Little Rock Law Review, 22*, 453-479.

Johnston, J. R. (2003). Parental alignments and rejection: An empirical study of alienation in children of divorce. *Journal of the American Academy of Psychiatry & Law, 31*(2), 158-170.

Johnston, J. R., & Kelly, J. B. (2004). Rejoinder to Gardner's "Commentary on Kelly and Johnston's 'The alienated child: A reformulation of parental alienation syndrome'." *Family Court Review, 42*(4), 622-628.

Kelly, J. B. (2000). Children's adjustment in conflicted marriage and divorce: A decade review of research. *Journal of Child and Adolescent Psychiatry, 39*, 963-973.

Kelly, J. B. (2002). Psychological and legal interventions for parents and children in custody and access disputes: Current research and practice. *Virginia Journal of Social Policy and Law, 10*, 129-163.

Kelly, J. B. (2004). Family mediation research: Is there empirical support for the field? *Conflict Resolution Quarterly, 22*(1/2), 3-35.

Kelly, J. B., & Emery, R. E. (2003). Children's adjustment following divorce: Risk and resilience perspectives. *Family Relations, 52*, 352-362.

King, V., & Heard, H. E. (1999). Nonresident father visitation, parental conflict, and mother's satisfaction: What's best for child well-being? *Journal of Marriage and Family, 61*, 385-396.

Krishnakamur, A., & Buehler, C. (2000). Interparental conflict and parenting behaviors: A meta-analytic review. *Family Relations, 49*, 25-44.

Lee, M-Y. (2002). A model of children's postdivorce behavioral adjustment in maternal and dual-residence arrangements. *Journal of Family Issues, 23*, 672-697.

Maccoby, E., & Mnookin, R. (1992). *Dividing the child*. Cambridge, MA: Harvard University Press.

Main, M., Kaplan, N., & Cassidy, J. (1985). Security in infancy, childhood, and adulthood: A move to the level of representation. In I. Bretherton & E. Waters (Eds.), *Growing points of attachment theory and research. Monograph of the Society for Research on Child Development* (Vol. 50(1/2); pp. 66-104). San Francisco: Jossey-Bass.

Menning, C. L. (2002). Absent parents are more than money: The joint effects of activities and financial support on youths' educational attainment. *Journal of Family Issues, 23*, 648-671.

Nord, C. W., Brimhall, D., & West, J. (1997). *Fathers involvement in their children's schools* (NCES 98-091). Washington, DC: National Center for Education Statistics.

Pruett, M. K., & Johnston, J. R. (2004). Therapeutic mediation with high conflict parents: Effective models and strategies. In J. Folberg, A. Milne, & P. Salem (Eds.), *Divorce and family mediation: Models, techniques, and applications* (pp. 92-111). New York: Guilford Press.

Pruett, M. K., Ebling, R., & Insabella, G. (2004). Critical aspects of parenting plans for young children. *Family Court Review, 42*(1), 39-59.

Pruett, M. K., Williams, T. Y., Insabella, G., & Little, T. D. (2003). Family and legal indicators of child adjustment to divorce among families with young children. *Journal of Family Psychology, 17*, 169-180.

Roseby, V. (1995). Uses of psychological testing in a child-focused approach to child custody evaluations. *Family Law Quarterly, 29*, 97-110.

Sanchez, E. A., & Kibler-Sanchez, S. (2004). Empowering children in mediation. *Family Court Review, 42*(3), 554-575.

Simons, R. L. (Ed.). (1996). *Understanding differences between divorced and intact families: Stress, interaction, and child outcome*. Thousand Oaks, CA: Sage.

Tippins, T. M., & Wittmann, J. P. (2005). Empirical and ethical problems with custody recommendations: A call for clinical humility and judicial vigilance. *Family Court Review, 43*, 193-222.

Tschann, J., Johnston, J., Kline, M., & Wallerstein, J. S. (1989). Family process and children's functioning during divorce. *Journal of Marriage and Family, 51*, 431-444.

Waxler, Z. W., Duggal, S., & Gruber, R. (2002). Parenting and psychopathology. In M. H. Borstein (Ed.), *Handbook of parenting* (Vol. 4; pp. 295-327). Mahwah, NJ: Erlbaum.

# Part IV
# Preventive and
# Supportive Strategies

# Between Private Ordering and Public Fiat:
# A New Paradigm for Family Law Decision-making

## Howard Fink and June Carbone

**Summary**

This article concerns the pervasive problems American family law now faces given the cascading advances in reproductive science, the changing concepts and the definitions of a family, and the changing roles of women in the family and in the world of work. There is the almost universal recognition that the devices that the law provides for settling family disputes are themselves proving unsatisfactory, costly and often unfair. We think that the heart of the problem is the uncertainty caused by relying on after-the-fact litigation to solve problems that could have been anticipated when the relationship was entered. We find that this failure is common to such subjects as the ownership of frozen embryos, prenuptial property agreements and surrogate motherhood agreements.

We find that the central problems are a lack of understanding of the ramifications that those entering a contractual family relationship can face in the future, unequal bargaining power on the part of those entering a relationship, and the possibility that a future court will find that the contractual relationship is legally invalid. The latter determination is itself often influenced by the attitude of the judge toward the social acceptability of the relationship. The judge's prejudices may play an unstated part in deciding whether the contractual relationship is itself valid. And when this happens, it is often too late to repair the situation.

Our thesis is that most, if not all, matters that can be litigated later can be anticipated earlier. Often the parties themselves are incapable of articulating these pitfalls and their attitude at the beginning of the relationship does not put them in a frame of mind to think critically and to imagine future trouble. Or the inequality of their social status or bargaining power makes them diffident about raising possible failure in the relationship.

Our proposal draws from the ante-mortem probate model that has been adopted in several states and that allows a testator to seek a binding determination that his or her will meets the state requirements for drawing a valid will and that he or she is of sound mind and free of undue influence while the testator is alive and able to rectify any mistakes that have been made.

We propose using three procedural devices, each of which has precedent in other contexts, to assist the parties at the outset of the process to understand what they are getting into, to avoid one-sided pressure, and to secure a determination at the outset that will be assuredly legally binding in the future. The three devices are declaratory judgments, mediation, and judicial or administrative approval. Each of these devices has a long history. What we propose is that states adopt a regime, using courts or administrative agencies, to secure a legally binding contract, judgment or administrative order at the outset, created with full counseling of the parties to the agreement by an agent of the government, looking objectively at the validity of the proposed agreement and explaining to the parties, in the drafting stage, how they might anticipate future scenarios. At the end of the process, a judgment or administrative order would be entered that would seal the agreement and protect it from a future court declaring it to be invalid knowledge of the weaker or less affluent parties to the prospective agreement; to assure that if a mistake has been made that it can be corrected before the parties have changed their behavior in reliance upon the agreement; and to prevent a future court from acting upon a covert or unconscious dislike of one or more the parties or dislike of the kind of agreement that has been entered into to invalidate the agreement when it is too late to start over.

Family law is in a period of pervasive uncertainty. The changing technology of assisted reproduction has called into question the definition of the most basic of family relationships – the meaning of motherhood. At the same time, legal changes in the relationship between marriage, biology and paternity have led to rapidly changing definitions of fatherhood that vary from state to state and year to year. Changing expectations in marriage have increased interest in ante-nuptial and even post-nuptial agreements that specify the parties' understandings and attempt to govern their affairs in the event of dissolution. Life and technology are changing so quickly that traditional family law methods are insufficient to fulfill the desire of partners for certainty in their relationships – whether they seek recognition of unconventional parenthood, decision-making power over fertilized eggs, a pre-divorce determination of property rights, surrogate birth motherhood, or legal regulation of an unmarried partnership.

## I. Introduction

Legal uncertainty has already inspired innovative procedures in some states, such as pre-birth declarations of non-biological parenthood[1] and pre-divorce determinations of the validity of post-nuptial agreements,[2] that have begun to remake the nature of family law jurisprudence. These innovations create a dilemma. On the one hand, they offer the potential of making the legal system more responsive to the needs of modern families and more proactive in its impact on family life. On the other hand, the more the party with greater bargaining power is able to control the outcome, the more likely the procedure will be invoked and the less likely it is to be given deference in later proceedings. We believe that the time is ripe for systematic consideration of these procedures in order to realize the promise for greater certainty that the devices hold while insuring protection for the weaker parties in these relationships. We advocate that states consider a mix of already existing procedures, such as declaratory judgments, judicial approval of settlements, mediation, and administrative action to remake the possibilities for family certainty.[3]

Consideration of these procedures will involve an examination of the role of private bargaining in family governance. In other fields, contracts have filled in at least some of the gaps created by changing technology and new legislation, but even in fields, such as intellectual property, that are governed by arms-length commercial transactions, disagreement exists on the appropriate ambit of contract.[4] Within family law, contract alone could never fill the need for innovation. Intended parents, however complete their agreement, cannot determine the status of children without the imprimatur of the state.[5] Even premarital agreements limited to the financial relationship between the adults vary in enforceability from state to state and from year to year, with different jurisdictions disagreeing in their interpretation of the language of supposedly uniform acts.[6]

This article examines the extent to which a new procedural regime that combines declaratory judgments, court-sponsored mediation, and judicial approval can constrain the uncertainty. The new regime would permit parties embarking on marriage or parenthood to test the validity of their understandings before the relationships become final. Fiancees, rather than accept marriage as either a fixed status or a contract of uncertain legality, could select from a menu of administratively prescribed form contracts or seek judicial validation of a premarital agreement.[7] Prospective parents employing novel reproductive techniques could secure a pre-birth identification of the parents whose names should appear on the birth certificate.[8] The objective would be to realize the unfulfilled promise of family courts to provide a supportive environment for family decision-making, and to do so in a way that respects private ordering while limiting the results of unequal bargaining power and providing a measure of protection for children.

We believe that the new, more proactive family law regime we are proposing will permit more effective family planning. First, declaratory judgments will allow the courts to resolve disputes before they become intractable. Parties contemplating marriage or parenthood are more promising prospects for amicable agreements than those facing divorce or separation. They are more amenable to counseling and mediation and more ready to work cooperatively to iron out any difficulties that arise.[9] Moreover, if the parties acquire new information that changes their perspectives or if the court disappoints their expectations about the legal validity of their proposals, they can plan more rationally for the consequences before the event than afterwards.

Second, counseling, and where appropriate mediation, gives those who are contemplating an agreement a neutral setting and a sounding board – one who might ask the difficult questions for which the parties' inexperience does not prepare them or that reticence does not permit them to raise themselves. Premarital agreements and fertility contracts often occur in settings in which those making the proposals present the draft as a take it or leave it document. Participation in court-structured counseling or mediation would counter that impression, and encourage a more equal exchange of views.[10]

Third, judicial or administrative approval provides a mechanism to consider the broader effects of the proposal. Judicial approval of class action settlements, as provided in Rule 23(e), takes into account the interests of the members of a class even though they have been "adequately" represented by named plaintiffs under the standards of Rule 23(a);[11] so, too, judicial approval here could safeguard the interests of children, weaker parties or the public, even if the parties agreed on an issue.

In calling for a separate system of family courts, judicial reformers have attempted to create a setting, not always successfully, that allows for something more than either a hands off attitude toward privately negotiated results or the winner take all adversarial proceedings that characterize most litigation.[12] We believe that combining the procedures we have identified will allow family courts to realize the potential for an alternative set of procedures that build, rather than detract from, family harmony. We emphasize the need for flexibility to accommodate the different state constitutional approaches to the separation of powers.[13] At the same time, we recognize that the lack of an adversary model may make it difficult to lock in final determinations that will withstand later judicial scrutiny.[14] We explore the alternatives in an effort to promote an appropriate balance between flexibility, fairness, and finality.[15]

This article will provide a systematic examination of the procedures necessary to combine contractual bargaining with mediation and family court or administrative approval. It will begin with consideration of the debate over the role of contract in family law and the precedent provided by ante-mortem probate. It will conclude that neither private bargaining nor publically mandated status arrangements can fully govern modern family arrangements on their own, and that the three procedures we have identified, which have never been used in tandem, offer an innovative way to use the law to shape the beginning, rather than the end, of intimate relationships.

The second section will examine the implications for premarital agreements. "Good lawyering practices," that is, the suggestions the best lawyers give their clients, emphasize greater fairness as the most effective way to secure greater certainty in the enforceability of premarital agreements. This section explores how new procedures might systematically prompt such tradeoffs. It concludes that pre-marital judicial review might offer greater certainty in a setting with more scrutiny, but might also strengthen the hand of the more powerful or sophisticated.

To balance these concerns, this section considers combining declaratory judgments with greater guidance, either through provision of presumptively valid form clauses or agreements or through a court-sponsored process that combines counseling, mediation, and judicial approval.

The third section will develop the procedures necessary to permit pre-birth declarations of parentage. While the issues underlying premarital agreements are the subject of centuries old discussion, parentage issues are framed to a greater degree by changing reproductive technology and the tensions between parental plans and state policy. These procedures will therefore be designed to test changing law as much, if not more, than to encourage private bargaining fairness. Nonetheless, a measure of certainty for the children who are the subject of these agreements is even more critical than certainty for newlyweds.

Finally, the article will consider application of the procedures to fertility clinic contracts and the disposition of frozen pre-embryos. Recent judicial decisions have changed the landscape of fertility clinic arrangements from a judicial call to contract to a public policy retrenchment with mandated outcomes. This section will examine the degree to which new family court procedures can be used to keep open a middle ground that preserves the possibility of private bargains undertaken with greater procedural safeguards and greater substantive attention to public policy concerns.

The article will conclude that any family matter that can be litigated after a dispute arises is likely to be amenable to pre-dispute determinations that offer a foundation for faster, cheaper, and more amicable resolutions. We believe that the procedures we are proposing are the missing piece of the efforts to make family courts a constructive part of family life.

## I. The Limits of Contract in Family Law

Our legal system places great weight on assuring that contracts will be enforced as written.[16] Private agreements allow the parties to specify the terms of their interaction with a degree of detail statutory law could never supply; they also allow parties to negotiate around the uncertainty created by new developments, changing mores, or conflicting legal interpretations.[17] Yet, from the earliest days of the Anglo-American legal system, private agreements have never been sacrosanct. The courts – and particularly the equity courts – have found ways to review private transactions, enjoining the enforcement of contracts procured by fraud, striking inordinate penalties, reforming or rescinding unconscionable agreements, dissolving partnerships, and altering child custody agreements that do not advance the children's best interests.[18] These judicial interventions in private ordering may protect the weak and the unrepresented and promote the larger interests of justice,[19] but they also disrupt the parties' expectations. And sometimes they inject, consciously or unconsciously, the judge's prejudices about the worthiness of the parties to an otherwise valid contract or bequest.[20]

This dilemma of justice versus certainty plays out in every issue of contract enforcement. While the law courts have made the intention of the parties the talisman of commercial contracts, the equity courts have long intervened to police contracting capacity, duress and unconscionability.[21] Within the family, contracts have been suspect altogether. The courts have repeatedly ruled that family members lacked the intent to establish legally binding arrangements,[22] that the services performed could not constitute adequate consideration when rendered by a wife to her husband or a child to his or her parent,[23] or that intervention in ongoing family matters was beyond the competence of the courts.[24] Nonetheless, family contracts have, for almost as long, served to fill in the gaps in changing or uncertain family orders. In many times and places, marriage was by definition a contract with express terms carefully negotiated by the bride and groom's families.[25] Michael Grossberg describes the increasing use of contract during the nineteenth century – often in the form of family trusts – as a way station between status-based marital ideals.[26] Over the last thirty years, contract has again emerged as way to restructure marriage to account for the changing status of women and the failure of the law to keep up with more varied and less traditional intimate relationships.[27] Greater use of family contracting, however, has never eliminated the tension between the need for judicial supervision and the interference with predictability such after-the-fact supervision brings.

These tensions are limited neither to family law nor to traditional contracts. Will contests pose many of the same dilemmas. From the early days of the ecclesiastical courts, Anglo-American jurisprudence recognized testators' rights to leave their property to anyone they chose, subject only to certain formal requirements[28] and spousal share provisions.[29] Nonetheless, the ecclesiastical courts, and later their successors, the probate courts, permitted will contests against the executor alleging that the testator was not of sound mind or was subject to duress or undue influence at the time the will was signed.[30] These contests, while necessary to protect the elderly and the infirm from unscrupulous associates, often substituted the court's view of appropriate bequests for the testators', disguising the value judgment with a retroactive determination of testamentary capacity.[31] The "natural objects of the testators' bounty," i.e., spouses, children, and sometimes distant relatives, frequently win such contests at the expense of lovers, pets, charitable institutions – and the testators' intent.[32]

To give testators greater security, several states enacted ante-mortem probate procedures during the 1970s.[33] These statutes allow a testator to bring a declaratory judgment action against his or her intestate successors and those named as beneficiaries in the will in order to determine the will's validity while the testator is alive.[34] The testator can obtain a ruling that the will has been signed and witnessed by the requisite number of persons and that the testator is of sound mind and free from undue influence.[35] This procedure is designed for the rare case of an unusual bequest or an elderly and infirm testator that might foster a will contest after the testator has left the scene.[36] And it has been upheld against attempts to reopen the judgment affirming a will after the testator's death.[37]

Ante-mortem probate involves a proactive use of judicial power that builds on the concept of declaratory judgments. The initiating party is a testator who fears his or her will may be challenged after the testator's death.[38] The testator joins the parties who may seek to challenge the will after his or her death and forces them to state their objections, if they are to be raised at all, during his or her lifetime.[39] The court ruling addresses the potential grounds for invalidating the will, whether the individual defendants raise these issues or not.[40] The result is a final judgment that forecloses will contests that would ordinarily not arise until after the testator's death.

The first efforts to bring ante-mortem probate actions were dismissed in the 1880's on due process grounds.[41] After the Supreme Court upheld the constitutionality of the federal declaratory judgment statute, however, the courts became more willing to hear prospective disputes, so long as the action presented something more than a request for an advisory opinion.[42] The three states to adopt the ante-mortem procedure did so through statutory enactments specifically authorizing the process.[43] The Ohio courts upheld the statute in the few cases that challenged its constitutionality.[44]

Extending declaratory judgments to premarital agreements and parenthood declarations would be similar in principle to ante-mortem probate. The moving party would be required to name potentially adverse, interested parties.[45] The defendants would be required to raise any grounds they had to oppose the requested relief or they would be barred from doing so later. The court could be specifically required to review the primary indicia of validity (e.g., voluntariness, disclosure, unconscionability in the premarital agreement context; the children's interests or the requirements of state law in the parenthood declaration), and then issue a declaratory order resolving the matter. The use of declaratory judgments in these contexts has ample precedent. The courts have resolved disputes about the interpretation or validity of premarital agreements during on-going marriages for almost a century.[46] Most states also have parenthood procedures that provide for identifying non-marital parents, whether or not the parties are in agreement.

Nonetheless, states vary in the degree to which they might be willing to authorize their courts to settle prospective disputes.[47] Some states take an expansive view of the power of their courts, and no change is necessary to permit to these courts to consider the validity of family agreements.[48] Other states take a narrow view of the role of courts (and a correspondingly strong view of separation of powers).[49] They limit courts to settling disputes between adverse parties that are not future or hypothetical but present and real, where one party threatens to act coercively toward another.[50] These states might be uncomfortable committing the initial role in determining or approving the validity of family arrangements to the judiciary.[51] Actions that did not involve adverse conduct on the part of one party against another might be seen as a request for an advisory opinion.[52]

In states that narrowly limit the power of the courts, administrative agencies, such as the bureaus that issue marriage licenses or the mediation, counseling and conciliation services that address divorce and dependency might be revamped to provide an initial determination of validity, subject to judicial review.[53] A party who wished to challenge the administrative determination would have to do so within the time periods provided.[54] If the time period elapsed without review, the administrative determination would become presumably final.[55] Thus, if a state provided a procedure for determining the validity of a prenuptial agreement or the ownership of fertilized ova, the rights created by such a procedure should be as fixed as those created by a declaratory judgment.[56]

The challenge for a state that wishes to adapt these procedures is to determine whether new legislation is necessary. Some states, including those which have otherwise articulated a narrow view of judicial authority, have found the declaratory judgment legislation sufficient to authorize judicial review of post-nuptial agreements or parenthood determinations.[57] In the ante-mortem probate context, legislation helped secure acceptance of the constitutionality of the procedures.[58] Other states might prefer an administrative procedure, either to insure its constitutional validity or to provide a less formal and less expensive process.[59] The states nonetheless face a tradeoff: administrative procedures are less likely to be held to violate the separation of powers requirement, but they may be also less likely to be treated as final judgments entitled to full faith and credit in other jurisdictions.[60] The larger issue then becomes not the identity of the forum, but the nature of the proceeding. Declaratory judgments, without anything more, are likely to rubber-stamp the agreement of the parties.[61] Premarital agreements already work to the advantage of the stronger, wealthier or more sophisticated party to the agreement; declaratory judgments in a proceeding in which no one questions the agreement the parties present to the court is likely to enhance the effect.[62] And the procedures we propose would be implemented at the time of greatest family harmony when there is the least rancor – and thus the least real adversity – in considering the options available.

Family courts in the divorce context counter this potential inequality of bargaining power by providing for divorce education and counseling, mandatory mediation in custody disputes, judicial consideration of children's interests, and other measures that shape divorce resolutions.[63] Ante-mortem probate critics[64] have similarly questioned the statute's 'contest model,'[65] and argued that it should be coupled with arbitration,[66] mediation,[67] or the use of a conservator[68] in order to preserve family harmony.[69] Pre-event procedures could benefit from these suggestions. Parties who initiate the judicial approval process[70] could be given information on the rights they are relinquishing, and referred to counseling or mediation. Alternatively, the parties could be provided with presumptively valid form agreements that address the most common subjects of premarital bargaining.[71] The goal should be to encourage family harmony, and the expression of all of the parties' desires and interests.[72]

Finally, judicial approval is necessary for the protection of unrepresented interests, particularly where children are involved. In class actions, the court reviewing a proposed settlement must independently assess the proposal to insure that it protects the interests of all class members, not just those actively involved in the litigation.[73] A declaratory judgment procedure without this type of judicial approval might still examine a premarital agreement for unconscionability or duress.[74] Where children's interests are at issue, however, the court has a stronger obligation to consider the agreement's impact on the children's best interests.[75]

These three mechanisms – declaratory or administrative procedures, mandatory counseling and mediation, and approval coupled with the opportunity for judicial review – have the potential to transform the judicial role in family decision-making. In earlier eras, marriage served as formal marker of legal status that determined parties' rights and obligations.[76] Married couples engaged in a public ceremony that marked the transition from one stage of life to another, and signaled acceptance of the terms of a well-defined relationship. Children were either born within a marriage or were "illegitimate" and of legally uncertain parentage.[77] With the growing importance of individually negotiated understandings about both partnership and parenthood, we have lost the ability to cement understandings within a widely agreed upon social context. Couples have become more likely to cohabit without marriage, and marriage has become more like cohabitation – with an almost endless array of possible understandings about the nature of the relationship.[78]

The procedures we propose provide a way to facilitate long term agreements that can provide a foundation for family relationships as broadly defined as society now allows. For those states with a strong family court tradition, these procedures will enhance the courts' ability to play a constructive role in family life. In those states with a more restrictive conception of the judicial role,[79] administrative agencies, subject to judicial review for errors of law or abuses of discretion,[80] can provide a comparable model. In both systems, family law can be remade to combine the flexibility of contract with the certainty and fairness that represents the best of the family law ideal.

## II. A Premarital Process for Validating Nuptial Agreements

Premarital agreements offer the opportunity for the most straightforward application of these proposed procedures. First, the parallels to ante-mortem probate are the most direct – ante-nuptial agreements involve intent-based arrangements subject to after-the-fact challenges. Second, premarital bargaining illustrates in classic ways the tension between the desire for certainty and the need for judicial intervention to further the interests of justice. Finally, the law addressing the validity of premarital agreements reflects a recently heightened degree of uncertainty and popularity, with the use of premarital agreements tripling between 1978 and 1988, along with concerns about their fairness – legitimate concerns that we believe can be fully addressed only by rethinking of the negotiation process.[81]

### A. The Uncertain State of Premarital Bargains

Premarital agreements are of both ancient origin and historically suspect. Marriage is often thought of as a contract in the sense that it is a voluntary arrangement between two people who choose to accept its obligations and responsibilities.[82] The controversial part is the extent to which the couple can vary the terms of their relationship by prior agreement. Historically, the contractual nature of marriage probably reached its height during the periods in which the two families negotiated an agreement that detailed how many cows the bride's family was to provide as dowry, the groom's contributions to the bride's well-being, and who got to keep what if the marriage failed.[83] By the time marriage changed from an arranged affair to an expression of love between two people who chose their mates with or without the approval of their respective families, such financial contracting had fallen into disrepute.[84] Marriage became a state-dictated status with little ability to vary its terms.

Until the mid-1970s, most American courts held that premarital agreements and other contracts made 'in contemplation of divorce' were unenforceable as against public policy. Brian Bix reports that the courts "reasoned that the agreements were void either (1) because they purported to alter the state-imposed terms of the status of marriage, which were not subject to individual alteration, or (2) because they tended to encourage divorce."[85] Kate Silbaugh explains that some courts interpreted any agreement contemplating divorce as condoning it, and therefore encouraging it.[86] The only premarital agreements that won greater acceptance were those addressing death. They most commonly involved second marriages with a new spouse who agreed not to invoke the state's elective share provisions or to contest a will that left an estate to widow or widower's adult children.[87]

The seventies, however, witnessed a shift from wholesale opposition to agreements providing for divorce to cautious acceptance of at least the financial part of such arrangements.[88] Several factors triggered the shift: the changing status of women and the corresponding conviction that women could look out for their own interests, dissatisfaction with traditional marriage and a growing desire to explore alternative models, and the rising divorce rate.[89] Feminists, particularly inspired by Lenore Weitzman's 1981 book The Marriage Contract, argued that women could wrest marriage from its patriarchal underpinnings by crafting agreements that better reflected their preferences.[90] The Uniform Premarital Agreement Act was promulgated in 1983 and, by 1996, twenty-eight states had adopted it. While the drafters insisted that the act reflected existing law, they interpreted that law to reflect the move toward greater recognition of premarital agreements.[91]

Despite greater acceptance, the validity of prenuptial agreements has remained far from certain. First, the states continue to vary in the standards they apply to determine the enforceability of prenuptial pacts.[92] Second, states that require substantive review of the fairness of such agreements engage in a determination that is intrinsically amorphous and case specific.[93] Third, even the states that confine their review to procedural considerations are often influenced by the agreement's perceived fairness in ways that undermine the consistency and predictability of their decisions.[94] Finally, topics remain – fault-based considerations, custody and child support – that cannot be resolved by private bargain alone.[95] All of these factors are compounded by the tendency to change the standards of review over time, and to judge both the procedural and substantive fairness of the agreement from the perspective of a divorce that may occur decades after the agreement was signed.

The states have split most fundamentally in deciding whether premarital agreements should be subject to the same deference and limited review as ordinary business contracts or subject to more exacting standards for enforceability. Simeone v. Simeone,[96] a favorite of casebook authors, is one of the most deferential of the modern decisions.[97] In that case, the Pennsylvania Supreme Court decided that state courts would no longer "inquire into whether the terms of the premarital agreement were fair or whether the parties had informed understandings of the rights they were surrendering. These contracts would offer only the same defenses available for conventional contract agreements, e.g., duress, unconscionability, and misrepresentation."[98]

*        *        *        *

## B. Private Marital Ordering and Its Critics

We believe that some measure of skepticism toward the enforceability of such privately negotiated pacts is appropriate and inevitable. Judith Younger, a frequent commentator on the state of marital agreement law, argues that they are intrinsically different from other contracts:

> The first difference is the subject matter. These agreements typically deal with one of, or a combination of, three things: property and support rights during and after marriage; the personal rights and obligations of the spouses during marriage; or the education, care and rearing of children who may later be born to the marrying couple. These subjects are of greater interest to the state than the subjects of ordinary commercial contract; the state wishes to protect the welfare of the couple and their children during and after marriage, and to preserve the privacy of the family relationship
> . . . .

The second difference is the relationship of the parties to each other. It is a confidential relationship involving parties who are usually not evenly matched in bargaining power. The possibility, therefore, that one party may overreach the other is greater than in the case of ordinary contracts.

The third difference is the fact that antenuptial agreements are to be performed in the future, in the context of a relationship which the parties have not yet begun and which may continue for many years after the agreement it executed and before it is enforced. The possibility that later events may make it unwise, unfair, or otherwise undesirable to enforce such agreements is greater than in the case of ordinary contracts.[123]

There is another difference as well, which Kate Silbaugh laid out in a recent article. Marriage often involves an exchange of monetary and non-monetary benefits; yet only the monetary half of the exchange tends to be enforceable in premarital agreements.[124] The most classic marital exchange is the one of support for domestic services. As Lloyd Cohen recognizes, however, these contributions, even if equal, are not necessarily symmetrical.[125] The traditional wife's greatest contribution comes relatively early in the relationship with her participation in childbirth and childrearing. The husband's earning power will not peak until later in his life, and his ability to secure an attractive alternative mate will increase with his income. [126] A prenuptial pact that eliminated support might increase his temptation to trade in his wife for a younger model at a time when he has realized the major expected benefits from the marriage but she has not.[127] Marital agreements tend not to write penalties for adultery or desertion into their financial provisions, and it is not clear that such penalties would be enforceable if they did.[128] A commercial contract with such asymmetrical contributions would almost certainly take either the timing of the breach or the identity of the breaching party into account, but the elimination of fault considerations from the financial determinations at divorce makes that impossible.[129] A commercial contract might also provide restitution for the uncompensated services performed, but family law refrains from recognizing the market value of domestic chores.[130] The critical exchange of promises in traditional marriage was the commitment to remain married until "death do us part;" making the monetary part of an agreement enforceable without recognition that a major part of the consideration for the agreement is the promise to stay married increases the risk of unfairness.[131]

For less traditional couples, the relationship between monetary and non-monetary contributions changes, but never disappears entirely. An idealistic couple committed to an egalitarian relationship might, for example, agree to keep their property separate and their financial lives independent in the belief that they will continue to contribute equally to the family's domestic needs. They both work, they both like to cook, and they are delighted to have found a partner who shares the same interests. Marriage, however, may bring uncontemplated triplets, a promotion that involves a long distance commute, physical illness or disability. If he quits his job to care for the triplets, or she no longer fixes gourmet meals because of her travel, the expectations on which the agreement were premised may be frustrated. While it is possible to express these expectations in contractual terms, not many couples do, and even if they did, the less tangible parts of their understandings--her commitment to seek income enhancing promotions, his willingness to arrange daycare, her production of gourmet meals – would be impossible to enforce.[132] Judith Younger is right; marital bargains are not exactly like commercial contracts for reasons that will always interfere with the predictability of their enforcement.[133] What few scholars before Silbaugh have recognized is that premarital agreements may be uniquely subject to claims of unfairness, not just because of inequality of bargaining power, but because so many of the assumed terms on which the agreement may be based (the exchange of promises to remain married, the commitment to an egalitarian division of marital responsibilities) may not be on the table of legal enforceability.

Kate Silbaugh finds the exchange between the monetary and non-monetary aspects of marriage so intrinsic to the exchange, and so systematically skewed to deny recognition of women's non-monetary contributions, that she would forbid premarital contracting altogether. [134] Her position runs against the tide of recent legal developments, and three major considerations counsel against it. The first is that, even if Silbaugh's argument contains a devastatingly accurate description of the flaws of marital bargaining, it is not a description of all bargains. The least objectionable premarital agreements, for example, are those like the Greenwalds', which involve an exchange between older couples, eager to preserve property from a first marriage for the children of that marriage. Silbaugh's objection is simply inapplicable in those cases.[135] Secondly, denying the enforceability of such agreements may persuade those with the most bargaining power not to marry, and one-sided contracts about property rights are easier to enforce outside of marriage than within.[136] Third, the absolute bar, unless it speeds decline in marriage across the board, may forestall more considered premarital planning between committed couples. At least part of the problem with antenuptial planning is the couple's failure to accurately anticipate predictable events. The expectation that the relationship will remain the same over twenty years is inevitably shortsighted, that couples will equally share childrearing responsibilities unrealistic, that a given marriage will beat the odds on divorce about half right.[137] The current process is flawed in large part because only part of the marital exchange is the subject of discussion; it is also flawed because we are in a period of changing expectations about marriage, and engaged couples may not fully realize the extent to which their expectations diverge.[138] We believe that rather than despair over the prospects for fair premarital agreements, the process itself should be the subject of reexamination.

## C. Good Lawyering and Better Bargains

Good lawyers, who do what they can to draft enforceable agreements, do at least three things that mitigate the impact of a potentially one-sided agreements. First, they refuse to handle cases that involve a surprise draft presented on the eve of the wedding. (Indeed, the lawyers who have advised author Carbone's family law classes refuse to draft agreements if the wedding date has been set).[139] Second, they make some provision for shared property over the course of the marriage and, in appropriate cases, support that limits the substantive objections to a proposed agreement.[140] Finally, the lawyers make sure that the other party is either represented by counsel or has a reasonable understanding of the consequences of the agreement.[141] Nonetheless, not all couples are represented by "good" lawyers, and many potentially good lawyers refuse to draft antenuptial pacts for fear of exposure to malpractice claims.[142]

We believe that, in creating an alternative process, it is important to encourage these good lawyering practices and to create incentives for contracting parties to engage in the procedure.

We would therefore start by offering engaged couples a way to trade greater premarital review for greater certainty with respect to the enforceability of the resulting agreement. The declaratory judgment process described above or its administrative equivalent offers that possibility.[143] A couple who seek to enter an antenuptial arrangement could seek a declaratory judgment, or equivalent administrative proceeding as the state chooses, of the agreement's validity before the wedding occurs. Or they could seek the validation of a financial agreement even after the marriage took place.[144] The court would apply the existing standards in that state for determining the enforceability of such agreements. Depending on state law, a judgment upholding the agreement would either be conclusive or would limit the grounds on which a party could challenge the agreement in the future.[145]

In all jurisdictions, the judgment should be conclusive on the voluntariness of the agreement and its fairness at the time it is formed.[146] The court could review the negotiations that led to the agreement, and the parties' understanding of their pact. As with antemortem probate, it is easier to create a record with the interested parties before the court earlier than it is to recreate the facts many years after the event.[147] The court's conclusion with respect to the absence of duress, undue influence, fraud, misrepresentation, and anything else that would interfere with the voluntary nature of the transaction should be final.[14]

For this type of procedural determination to be effective, it is important that the parties comply with the state requirements for disclosure. The best existing agreements attach an appendix listing the parties' assets and their estimated valuation.[149] Some states require this type of detailed disclosure; others permit a knowing waiver of full disclosure.[150] The UPAA provides that agreements may be enforceable notwithstanding the absence of either disclosure or waiver where the information is publically available.[151] A declaratory judgment of validity should depend on the parties' demonstration that the state requirements have been met. If they have, and if no evidence is later produced that would show a fraud on the courts, the determinations of voluntariness and disclosure should be final.[152]

Judicial approval of the substance of the agreement is another matter. The finality of the substantive review may depend on the jurisdiction. The UPAA provides that an agreement will be enforceable unless inter alia it is "unconscionable when it was executed."[153] Other states require consideration of whether the agreement is unconscionable or unfair at divorce, expressly acknowledging the limits of foreseeability.[154] Under the UPAA, the unconscionability determination should be a binding one since the court will be ruling on the substantive aspects of the agreement at the time of its execution. In the jurisdictions that permit consideration of changed circumstances, on the other hand, a court will never be able to render a final decision in advance on fairness at divorce. Nevertheless, in such states, a court can consider whether an agreement makes adequate provision for otherwise unanticipated illness, diminished earning capacity due to domestic contributions, or other events. To the extent that the court makes an express finding, for example, that an agreement makes adequate provision for support in the event of disability and that the dollar amount takes into account the possibility of future inflation, it should be very difficult to challenge the agreement on that issue twenty years later.[155]

In all jurisdictions, moreover, the court reviewing the agreement should be able to determine whether agreement is void as against public policy. Most jurisdictions identify topics they deem inappropriate subjects of marital bargaining. Accordingly, waivers of child support, for example, are almost always void because the parents cannot waive the child's rights.[156] The UPAA prohibits waivers of spousal support that might have the effect of leaving a spouse a public charge.[157] Review of proposed agreements to determine their compliance with public policy is usually straightforward, and the effect of a judgment that there is no conflict with public policy should be final, entitled to full faith and credit.[158]

In those states in which the initial reviewing body would be an administrative agency, it is generally held that an unreviewed administrative order resembling a judicial order has the same res judicata effect as a judicial determination.[159] Accordingly, unless one of the parties seeks judicial review, which is usually conducted on a clearly-erroneous basis, administrative orders resembling a court proceeding should enjoy the same degree of finality as a court-issued declaratory judgment.[16]

A declaratory judgment procedure of this type, paralleling the ante-mortem procedure, could be brought in most jurisdictions under existing law in order to reduce the risk that a premarital agreement will later be held invalid.[161] Moreover, such actions are likely to promote better lawyering practices in that a) they would be difficult to spring on the eve of wedding and still secure a judgment, b) the prospect of outside review is likely to serve as a deterrent to the more one-sided and ill-considered agreements, and c) judicial review is likely to encourage inclusion of sound boilerplate provisions, such as adequate consideration of possible disability.[162] Nonetheless, the most likely outcome of such a procedure is a judicial rubberstamp of an uncontested proposal, perpetuating, in harder to challenge form, existing inequities in bargaining power.[163]

Two additional procedures would mitigate against these potential inequities: greater review of substance and/or greater emphasis on process. The single easiest way to review the substance of agreements is to provide pre-approved form agreements that address a variety of common marital issues. Covenant marriages are an excellent example. They give prospective couples a choice of marital terms, with the new terms prescribed by statute.[164] Barbara Stark, in a recent article on "post-modern marriage," has suggested that the concept be extended to a variety of arrangements, with the legislature or an administrative agency setting forth a menu of presumptively valid terms.[165] Couples who seek marriage licenses could be handed a booklet, and perhaps access to a counselor, who would help them choose among the form agreements to govern their relationship.[166] The result would be a relatively simple, inexpensive and fair[167] expansion of the role of choice in marital bargaining.

For those who nonetheless insist on custom-tailored agreements, greater procedural protections could take the place of pre-approved agreements in providing protection for the more vulnerable. Counseling or mediation, for example, might serve as a prerequisite for access to declaratory approval. Individual counseling or a mandatory educational session could encourage the parties to consider a laundry list of issues that should be a staple of marital planning, with mediation-like procedures for those who have a difficult time reaching agreement.[168]

After such a session, the court would still need to review the substance of the agreement, and the degree of protection the procedure provides will still ultimately depend on the decision-makers' willingness to engage in more than a pro forma review. A declaratory judgment or equivalent administrative proceeding in a Simeone jurisdiction need involve no more than a determination that the agreement is free from procedural irregularities and is not unconscionable at the time of execution.[169] In a jurisdiction that, like Wisconsin, requires consideration of substantive fairness, the risk remains that the courts will rubberstamp uncontested bargains.[170] To counter these possibilities and make consideration of both parties' interests more than a perfunctory recital, we would require that the court specifically review and make formal findings with respect to a statutorily specified list of criteria. The UPAA already identifies suitable subjects for prenuptial bargains, including waivers of support, and limited identification of agreements that would violate public policy.[171] We favor requiring judicial findings on a combination of these topics, with special emphasis on the subjects Silbaugh identified that tend to involve monetary and non-monetary exchanges.[172] Ideally, the court or administrative body would have to declare that the parties fully understood the terms of their agreement, and its likely consequences before approving a departure from the default terms governing marriage.

Any procedure that strengthens the validity of prenuptial agreements is likely to work to the benefit of those who hold greater power before marriage. While we therefore acknowledge that the risks associated with our procedure are real, we nonetheless believe that it is worth having for three reasons. First, a declaratory judgment accompanied by counseling or mediation and judicial or administrative approval is more likely to encourage explicit consideration of the tradeoffs in premarital bargaining than the one-sided process characteristic of existing agreements. Second, we are willing to trade greater predictability for the roulette-like decisionmaking that randomly invalidates current agreements. Third, we believe that judicial review of the substance of the bargaining process will eliminate the worst inequities, if only because of the greater care that tends to come with third party involvement.

While we would ideally like to see these procedures used together with greater provision for a variety of pre-approved form agreements, the procedures have merit even without legislative reconsideration of the substantive basis for enforceability. Some authors (most notably Jeff Stake) have been so committed to private ordering in an era of family diversity that they have proposed mandatory premarital agreements.[173] Others like Kate Silbaugh are so opposed that they would ban all such attempts.[174] Louisiana has already enacted a covenant marriage statute that provides for counseling as a precondition for parties who wish to elect fault-based dissolution procedures.[175] Martha Ertman has suggested using premarital bargaining and security agreements to change the gender balance in marriage.[176] What no state has attempted is the combination of private ordering with civic education and judicial approval suggested here. Marriage, whether conceived as a religious, civil or private institution, marks a right of passage. Preparation for assumption of its responsibilities has sometimes been a formal part of religious training, sometimes an informal matter of family upbringing, and other times a conscious part of civic understandings.[177] If more of the content of intimate relationships is to be left to private bargaining, procedures that encourage a full exchange of views, and comprehensive consideration of the parties' interests are needed.[178] If the excesses of private bargaining are to be constrained, then procedures that help shape fairer exchanges from the outset offer more promise than a haphazard system of after the fact review.[179] Parties seeking either a marriage license or legal advice about premarital agreements could be routinely referred to the new procedures.[180] Family courts could become to a much greater degree than they have been in the past institutions that provide a stronger foundation for family harmony.

## III. A Pre-birth Process for Determining Parenthood

If marriage is a rite of passage that encourages couples to think through, and formalize the relationship between them, then parenthood involves an even more fundamental change in status and in the nature of the family relationships. Much of the historical force behind the emphasis on marriage has been the effort to reinforce the unity of sex, reproduction and child-rearing.[181] In most societies, marriage is accordingly synonymous with preparation for parenthood, and the institution governs the legal relationships between parents and children. In our society, however, sex, reproduction, and child-rearing are growing increasingly independent of marriage, and of each other, and the marriage contract – express or implied – can no longer be viewed as the exclusive basis for governing relationships to children.[182] Even more than with pre-marital agreements, therefore, pre-birth (and perhaps even pre-conception) determinations of parenthood[183] offer the possibility of resolving the uncertainty that has arisen from the divergence of law and practice.

Changing reproductive practices – from egg donation to surrogacy to the growing percentage of unmarried parents – combine legal and factual uncertainty in the determination of parentage.[184] In a simpler time, the mother of a child, legally and biologically, was the woman giving birth.[185] Only with the advent of in vitro fertilization has the possibility arisen that the woman who carries a child to term may not be her genetic relative.[186] Genetic fatherhood has historically been harder to determine, but marriage served as the preferred route for a man to secure parental status and a role in the child's life.[187]

Social and technological innovations are challenging the older paradigm that tied parental status to marriage and maternity without diminishing children's need for certainty in securing their relationship to the people who will act as their parents, or making functional parents' attachment to their children any less intense.[188] The law has eliminated most of the distinctions that depended on marriage[189] at a time of greater uncertainty in the father's social role.[190] For women, innovations in assisted reproduction for the first time separate genetic and gestational motherhood. A child may now be born with six possible parents: a genetic mother and father who contribute an egg and a sperm to conception in a petri dish, a gestational mother, who is genetically unrelated to the embryo implanted in her womb, and her husband, and two intended parents who may have no biological connection to the child.[191] For men, the separation of genetic parentage and childbirth is a given that has generated centuries of legal solutions; for women, it is an unprecedented development.

* * * *

## B. Declaratory Judgments and Parenthood

While premarital review of the validity of prenuptial agreements is rare,[231] pre-birth declarations of parenthood have ample precedent. Given the exponential increases in the non-marital birth rate, and the state interest in establishing paternity for child support purposes, most states have statutes expressly providing the establishment of parenthood.[232] Allowing judicial actions to be filed before rather than after the birth involves no procedural innovation.[233] The critical event – conception – has already occurred. The purpose of the proceeding is to resolve the potential parents' legal status on the basis of a fixed set of facts. Where the parties disagree, as they often do when a mother brings a paternity action against a putative father, there is an adversary relationship between the parties, and parenthood declarations fit easily within the scope of existing declaratory judgment statutes.[234] In practice, however, the most common issues – viz., those addressing biological paternity – do not lend themselves to early resolution because of the practicalities of assembling the evidence.[235]

If, on the other hand, parentage is a legal matter, with no dispute as to the underlying facts, but some uncertainty in the law, then a pre-birth judicial declaration may be an effective way to quell uncertainty, particularly in cases employing novel reproductive techniques. In these cases, adversity may be more of an issue. If two parents ask a court to recognize their parenthood, they are unlikely to be in disagreement with each other. Nonetheless, these cases present at least as strong and probably a stronger case for adversity as the premarital agreement declarations. First, with parenthood, other parties may be involved. In pre-birth cases, the parties may seek to insure that their names are shown on the birth certificate, and they may seek to join the hospital or appropriate state officials in the case to insure recognition of the result. Moreover, in a number of states, a guardian ad litem may be appointed to represent the child.[236] Second, determinations are more immediate (and thus less of an advisory opinion) than the premarital agreement cases. Parents may face almost daily issues that may begin while the child is in utero with respect to who can act for the child, authorize medical treatment, consent to release from the hospital, etc.[237] Married couples may never divorce or otherwise dispute the terms of a premarital agreement. Would-be parents will necessarily act differently in dealing with third parties if the legality of their parenthood is not recognized. Thus, a declaration that resolves the issue of which names should appear on a birth certificate would appear to present a strong case for the propriety of declaratory judgments even in states that strictly adhere to separation of powers doctrine.[238]

The most common present usage of these techniques builds on Buzzanca. In Litowitz v. Litowitz.[239] for example, an infertile couple arranged for the conception of a child with a donated egg, and the husband's sperm. A surrogate genetically unrelated to the child gave birth. During the pregnancy, the Litowitzes secured a California court order declaring them to be Micah's legal parents.[240] Had they not done so, David Litowitz would still be the genetic and intended father of the child, with his legal status secure.[241] Becky Litowitz, the intended mother with no biological connection to the child, might have found her legal status in doubt, even after years of acting as the only mother in Micah's life.[242] The pre-birth declaration settled the issue of parentage and rendered resort to adoption unnecessary.

The more frequent use of this procedure, at least in California, involves gay and lesbian couples, for whom adoption may be painful or unavailable. One of the first cases involved lesbian partners who sought a declaration that they were both mothers of an unborn child in accordance with the Uniform Parentage Act, as it had been interpreted in the Calvert case.[243] One woman donated her ova for in vitro fertilization by an unknown sperm donor. Doctors then implanted the fertilized eggs into the second woman, who became pregnant. The two women sought a declaration during the course of the pregnancy that they were both mothers of the child and the court issued such a order in March 1999, decreeing that the "as yet unborn child . . . is judged to be the natural child of both [the egg donor and the birth mother]" and further providing that "a birth certificate shall issue showing both [the egg donor and the birth mother] as the minor's parents."[244] In May, 1999, after the birth of the child, San Francisco Family Court Judge Donna J. Hutchins issued a statement of decision that affirmed the decree of parental relationship that had been issued in March.[245]

This proceeding expeditiously resolved a question of first impression. The case involved the first time (of which we have been able to find a legal record) in which an egg contributed by one woman was carried to term by a second woman, with the intent that both would share legal motherhood. The Calvert case had used intent as a tie-breaker in a case where two women (the ovum donor and the gestational mother) had biological connections to a child.[246] In this case, the women's shared intent was that they both have the legal status of motherhood, and the court agreed.

Since then, the same procedure has been used to determine parenthood in cases where only one of the partners has a biological tie to the child. In Southfox v. Southfox, for example, the Superior Court of San Diego County issued a "Uniform Parentage Act Judgment" holding that two lesbian partners were the parents of a child genetically related to one of them.[247] Relying on Buzzanca and Calvert,[248] the court reasoned that: "the preconception intent of the intended parent is dispositive in the establishment of parental rights because intentions that are voluntarily chosen, deliberate, express and bargained for ought presumptively to determine legal parenthood."[249]

The Southfox case, like the Litowitz case, did not fit squarely into the appellate precedents. In both Southfox and Litowitz, one of the intended parents bore a genetic relationship to the child while the other did not. In both cases, a strong, but not conclusive, argument existed that the intended parents were the legal parents of the child. The two cases and nonetheless differed in that Southfox involved a married, heterosexual couple while Litowitz involved a lesbian partnership.

The difference matters for two reasons. First, under existing law, the husband of a birth mother is presumed to be the father of the child and given important preferences, even if he turns out to have no genetic connection to the child.[250] Equal protection considerations would suggest that the wife of a legal father be accorded the same parental status. Gay and lesbian partners are given no such recognition or preference in most states, and equal protection considerations are unlikely to apply.[251] Indeed, as the Dunkin case illustrates, unmarried partners, whether gay or not, have no parental standing in many states, even if they have an express agreement with the legal parent, and have legally functioned as a parent since the child's birth.[252]

Second, second-parent adoptions by lesbian partners pose more challenges than adoptions by married heterosexual couples. Some states prevent gays and lesbians from adopting altogether;[253] a larger number refuse to recognize the possibility of two same-sex parents; almost all states require a home life inquiry that may reflect disapproval of gay or lesbian intimacy.[254] It is much easier to imagine a caseworker disapproving of Treesa Southfox, or conducting the inquiry in a distasteful and intrusive way, than in the case of Becky Litowitz.[255]

This means that gays and lesbians and other controversial couples are more likely to use pre-birth declarations – and to create new law in the process.

## C. The Use of Pre-Event Declarations: Separating Procedure from Substance

Marsha Garrison has written a controversial article that maintains that technological innovations in conception should not be the vehicle for creating new law.[256] She argues that parental status should be based on "current family policy and widely shared public values instead of the circumstances of a child's conception."[257] She thus favors, for example, statutes that prevent single women from terminating a sperm donor's parental rights on the ground that the law otherwise promotes two-parent families, and that it remains current family policy to do so.[258] She maintains that since the law promotes two-parent care when the child results from non-marital intercourse, it is anomalous to provide for a different result solely because the conception takes place through use of artificial insemination.[259]

Our procedure, while it does not necessarily draw distinctions on the basis of the technology used to achieve conception, might well produce results that will vary with the timing of the action. As the Southfox case demonstrates, gay and lesbian couples have had more success winning recognition of their parenting partnerships pre-birth than post-dissolution. The reasons have something to do with the procedure itself. Pre-birth, the couple presents a united front. No opposing interests exist.[260] The sperm donor has agreed to terminate parental rights. The child's interests presumably lie with recognition of both of the partners who plan to act as parents,[261] and the couple can choose to file in a jurisdiction or before a judge supportive of gay and lesbian relationships.

Post-dissolution cases, in contrast, involve warring parties. The cases typically arise when the biological parent terminates the relationship, and refuses to permit her former partner continued access to the child. Existing custody law is often an all or nothing affair that depends on parental status. If the non-biological partner is recognized as a parent, her standing to seek custody may be equal to the biological parent's, and she is entitled to at least visitation absent a strong showing that it would be detrimental to the child.[262] If, on the other hand, the court refuses to recognize the non-biological partner's parental status, it may then be compelled in many states to dismiss the custody or visitation action for lack of standing, avoiding what may be a difficult and painful evidentiary hearing.[263] Pre-birth cases are more likely to change the law in part because they present the most attractive scenarios for the result the initiating parties desire. Recognizing the parenting status of committed partners is psychologically and practically easier than recreating the terms of a splintered agreement that may have occurred years earlier.

In considering the merits of the parentage procedure, it is important to separate the substantive disputes about the wisdom of parental status from issues about the timing of the procedure. Recognition of unmarried partnerships generally, and same-sex relationships in particular, remains controversial.[264] Marriage has historically rested on the unity of sex, reproduction, and child-rearing,[265] and while the role of marriage in policing permissible and impermissible sexual relationships has atrophied, public policy continues to promote childrearing within two-parent heterosexual families.[266] The continued strength of this policy rests to some degree on the evidence that two-parent families produce better outcomes for children, and that married parents make a commitment to each other that unmarried parents do not, and that this commitment benefits their children.[267]

The state, Carl Schneider concludes, has an important interest in "channeling" behavior in appropriate directions.[268] At the same time, some of the opposition to unmarried parents rests on prejudice and homophobia. Gay and lesbian couples, who are committed to each and who plan to raise children whether or not the state recognizes the validity of their relationship, cannot marry, and in many states cannot jointly adopt.[269] Pre-birth declarations often serve, for better or ill, as an end-run around restrictive statutes and hostile precedents. Is this an appropriate use of the procedure?

We believe that the question of whether these issues should be resolved by case-by-case decisionmaking rather than legislative action is a different one from the timing of pre- or post-conflict resolution. If a particular issue, e.g., donor responsibility in cases of artificial insemination, is better resolved through broad-based legislative action, then the courts should continue to adhere to existing precedent whether the issue arises pre-conception or post-birth.

If, on the other hand, the courts are likely to resolve the issue (whether or not they create new law in the process) on a case-by-case basis, then we believe that there is value to resolving parentage at birth, laying the legal foundation for recognition of the adults who will play an important part in the child's life. The fact that pre-birth declarations have sometimes been used to decide issues of first impression does not necessarily mean that the process itself requires the creation of new law. Indeed, what it suggests is that existing law is, at very least, subject to greater uncertainty than the relevant precedents might indicate, and these procedures offer a way to resolve that uncertainty sooner rather than later. The procedure itself is not novel, and its advisability is not dependent on the outcome of particular cases, but rather the advantages of an earlier, rather than later, determination of parenthood.[270]

If pre-birth declarations are already established to a greater degree than pre-marital determinations of the validity of prenuptial agreements, what then of our other proposals for counseling and mediation? Counseling and mediation are intrinsically of less utility if negotiation is not a possibility. In the ante-nuptial context, fully informed parties might choose to negotiate a different agreement. Parenthood, in contrast, is an all or nothing status. Pre-birth agreements between two legal parents to provide for or limit custody and visitation rights are unenforceable.[271] While counseling could insure that a biological or legal parent welcoming the participation of another parent understood the consequences, such information should be provided in the context of existing procedures.[272]

The harder issue is whether this process should be combined with adoption procedures designed to safeguard the interests of the child. The new Uniform Parentage Act uses gestation to draw a clear distinction between intended mothers who give birth, and will be regarded as legal parents whether or not they bear a genetic relationship to the child,[273] and those who use a gestational surrogate, who must confirm their maternity through an adoption-like procedure whether or not the child is genetically theirs.[274] The Act promotes certainty by adopting a bright- line test of maternity,[275] and requiring judicial proceedings to establish the maternity of any woman who does not give birth.

Marsha Garrison would draw a different line. She objects to using gestation, as opposed to the genetic relationship, as an appropriate dividing line because of gender equality concerns. She argues that:

> This conclusion is buttressed by the fact that use of gestation as the determinant of motherhood would introduce a gender-specific element into parentage law. Just as this seems undesirable in the case of AID and IVF, it also seems undesirable here. Indeed, one can make an argument that the Equal Protection Clause mandates a similar approach to maternity and paternity determinations; the fact that a gestation-based approach to maternity relies on traditional stereotypes of female nurturance only lends weight to this argument.[276]

Instead, Garrison would distinguish between donated pre-embryos, and children conceived from eggs or sperm from their intended parents. Where the intended parents plan to raise a child conceived through the use of donated eggs and sperm, Garrison would require an adoption procedure irrespective of who gives birth.[277] Such a procedure would involve, at a minimum, the donors' agreement to sever parental ties, and then perhaps a home study to determine the intended parents' suitability, and judicial approval of the adoption.[278] Where, instead, the child is genetically related to either the intended father or mother, Garrison would recognize the intended parents as the legal parents without adoption.[279] Her approach would thus differ markedly from the new version of the UPA.

Both the new UPA and Garrison's proposals are controversial and we take no position on the their wisdom. Instead, we would note that the ability to incorporate counseling, mediation and adoption procedures is at least partially dependent on the timing of the hearing. Pre-birth, post-conception declarations of parenthood are best suited for resolving legal uncertainty about an existing state of affairs.[280] The child is already in utero; if neither intended parent is a legal parent, and the home-study finds them to be unsuitable, the child may literally have no parents. Such determinations, and the more extended inquiry they involve, are best conducted before conception, and we will address the possibility of such procedures in the next section. The purpose of post-conception declarations is far more limited. Such declarations have been most commonly used (and we believed that they are best suited) for establishing parental status,[281] and determining whether the unmarried partner of a legal partner can obtain formal recognition. In most of these cases, the child's household does not depend on the outcome of the suit; rather early resolution of the legal status of each of the adults who plan to be a part of the child's life can provide a firmer foundation for family planning. The pre-birth, post-conception declaration is the equivalent of marriage rather than of adoption.[282] It validates the legal status of the adults who plan to play a parental role in the child's life.

*   *   *   *

*Howard Fink. LL.B, is Professor Emeritus of Law at the Ohio State University, Michael E. Moritz College of Law.*

*June Carbone, J.D., is the Edward A. Smith/Missouri Chair of Law, the Constitution and Society at the University of Missouri-Kansas City School of Law.*

*We would like to thank Brian Bix, Peg Brinig, Naomi Cahn, Leslie Harris, Sanford Katz, Kate Silbaugh, Jack Sampson, Elizabeth Scott, Gary Spitko and Richard Storrow for their advice and assistance on earlier drafts of this article, and Rosa Tsongtaatarii and Kara Koerner for their research assistance. June Carbone would also like to thank the Santa Clara Center for Science and Technology for its research support.*

## Notes

[1]     See infra note 48 and accompanying text.

[2]     See infra note 47 and accompanying text.

[3]     See infra discussion Part I.

[4]     See, e.g., William W. Fisher III, *Property and Contract on the Internet,* 73 Chi.-Kent L. Rev. 1203, 1203 (1998) (contract outpacing intellectual property in creating rights and understandings on the internet).

[5]     Marriage, of course, creates a presumption of parenthood for children born within it, but even the marital presumption is not absolute, and it is of little help to those who cannot marry, do not wish to marry, or cannot bear children without the assistance of a surrogate. See generally Weisberg and "Appleton, Modern Family Law: Cases and Materials 521-34 (1998). But see E. Gary Spitko, *Reclaiming the "Creatures of the State": Contracting for Child Custody Decision Making in the Best Interest of the Family,* 57 Washington and Lee L. Rev. 1139, 1180 (2000) (arguing that courts should recognize agreements to arbitrate custody disputes in the interest of family harmony).

[6]     See infra note 192 and accompanying text.

[7]     Subject, of course, to the justiciability requirements of the jurisdiction. See infra note 165 and accompanying text.

[8]     See infra p. 107.

[9]     Indeed, family law reform has emphasized the role of mediation in the less promising setting of custody disputes. See *Cal. Fam. Code 3181* (West 1998) (mandating mediation in custody disputes). See also Jane W. Ellis, *Plans, Protections, and Professional Intervention: Innovations in Divorce Custody Reform and the Role of Legal Professionals,* 24 U. Mich. J.L. Ref. 65 (1992) (examining the role of mediation in efforts to reform divorce); Louise Everett Graham, *Implementing Custody Mediation in Family Court: Some Comments on the Jefferson County Family Court Experience,* 81 Ky. L.J. 1107, 1107 (1993) (examining the integration of mediation into the resolution of custody disputes); see Holly

A. Streeter-Schaefer, *A Look at Court Mandated Civil Mediation,* 49 Drake L. Rev. 367, 372-80 (2001) (discussing various states' approaches to mediation).

[10]   The precise nature of the process would depend on the setting and could be court initiated or administratively prescribed. See discussion infra. Forrest S. Mosten, *Mediation and the Process of Family Law Reform,* 37 Fam. & Concil. Cts. Rev. 429, 429 (1999) (advocating mediation as an alternative to settling family law disputes); Cf. Trina Grillo, The *Mediation Alternative: Process Dangers for Women,* 100 Yale L.J. 1545, 1547 (1991) (warning of the dangers of mediation in a setting that emphasizes substantive objectives that favor the stronger party).

[11]   See 5 James Wm. Moore et al., Moore's Federal Practice § 23.80(3d ed. 1999). The section discusses issues with regard to the discretionary character of independent approval of a settlement, and standards of appellate review of this discretion.

[12]   See, e.g., Hon. William J. O'Neil and Hon. Barry C. Schneider, *Recommendations of the Committee to Study Family Issues in the Arizona Superior Court: A Family Court System* 37 Fam. & Concil. Cts. Rev. 179, 180 (1999) (proposing a family court system to meet the unique needs of settling family disputes); Jay Folberg, Family Courts: Assessing the Trade-Offs, 37 Fam. & Concil. Cts. Rev. 448 (1999) (reviewing history of family court proposals and arguments for and against a separate family law approach); Mosten, supra note 10 at 445; Peter Salem, *Education for Divorcing Parents: A New Direction For Family Courts,* 23 Hofstra L. Rev. 837, 838-40 (1995) (reviewing history of family court sponsored divorce education).

[13]   For example, California requires mediation in family law disputes. See *Cal. Fam. Code 3181* (West 1998). See also Ellis, supra note 9 at 68 (examining the role of mediation in efforts to reform divorce); Louise Everett Graham, *Implementing Custody Mediation in Family Court: Some Comments on the Jefferson County Family Court Experience,* 81 Ky. L.J. 1107, 1107-31 (1993) (examining the integration of mediation into the resolution of custody disputes); Holly A. Streeter-Schaefer, *A Look at Court Mandated Civil Mediation,* 49 Drake L. Rev. 367, 372-80 (2001).

[14]   See infra discussion Part I.

[15]   See infra discussion Part I.

[16]   This does not mean, however, that contracts will be specifically enforced, as opposed to damages awarded for breach. See E. Yorio, Contract Enforcement: Specific Performance and Injunctions 101-26 (1989) (surveying contract remedies, and concluding that the distinctions between law and equity allow the court to balance competing interests); A. Mitchell Polinsky, An Introduction To Law and Economics 31-38, 59-65 (2d ed. 1989) (evaluating expectancy damages in light of three economic objectives: efficient breach, efficient reliance, and efficient risk allocation); Cooter & Eisenberg, *Damages for Breach of Contract,* 73 Calif. L. Rev. 1434, 1459-77 (1985) (defending the expectancy measure, to the extent that it is the remedy the parties would have bargained for under ideal conditions).

[17]   See, e.g., Fisher, note 4, supra at 1203 arguing that contract is a more effective way to deal with e-commerce than property.

[18]   See J.H. Baker, An Introduction to English legal history 112-33 (3rd ed. 1990). See also Emily L. Sherwin, *Law and Equity in Contact Enforcment,* 50 Md. L. Rev. 253, 253-54 (1991) (arguing that to be enforced in equity, as opposed to law, contracts must be substantively "fair.").

[19]   See Sherwin, *id. at 255-56* (approving judicial refusal to enforce unfair bargain that would have deprived unsophisticated elderly couple of their home).

[20]   See, e.g., Willy E. Rice, *Judicial Bias, The Insurance Industry and Consumer Protection: An Empirical Analysis of State Supreme Courts' Bad-Faith, Breach-of-contract, Breach-of-Covenant-of-Good-Faith and Excess-Judgment Decisions, 1900-1991,* 41 Cath. U.L. Rev. 325, 382 (1992) (concluding that courts engaged in unconscious bias in insurance industry decision-making). See also *In re Marriage of Bonds,* 83 Cal. Rptr. 2d 783, 788 (Ct. App. 1999), reversed on different grounds in 99 Cal. Rptr. 2d 252 (Ct. App. 2000) ("Judicial review of these agreements, undertaken in the difficult circumstances of marital dissolution and under greatly changed circumstances, sometimes results in judges' enforcing

or voiding such contracts based on their personal assessments of the prudence of the parties who made them. Such results are too often dependent upon a particular judge's value judgments rather than upon uniform rules of law").

21    17 James Wm. Moore et al., Moore's Federal Practice '120 App.02 (3d ed. 1999) (historical background of the growth of the common law and equity).

22    *Balfour v. Balfour,* 2 K.B. 571, 575 (C.A. 1919) (refusing to enforce husband's promise to provide a specified amount of support to the wife on the ground that the parties did not intend their exchange of promises to be attended by legal consequences in spite of the express written promise, and the exchange of consideration.).

23    *Borelli v. Brusseau,* 16 Cal. Rptr. 2d. 16, 20 (Ct. App. 1993) (refusing to enforce husband's promise to leave certain property to his wife in exchange for her promise to care for him at home because spouses have a mutual duty to care for each other, and therefore there was no consideration).

24    *McGuire v. McGuire, 59 N.W.2d 336, 339B42 (Neb. 1953)* (refusing to intervene in on-going marriage to require husband to support wife).

25    See Leah Guggenheimer, *A Modest Proposal: The Feminomics of Drafting Premarital Agreements,* 12 Women's Rts. L. Rep. 147, 147-48 (1996). See also Lawrence Stone, The Family, Sex and Marriage: In England 1500-1800 37-38 (abridged ed.) (1979) (discussing the family strategy to marriage).

26    Michael Grossberg, Governing the Hearth: Law and the Family in Nineteenth Century America 23B24 (1985) (The importance of contract swelled and then receded over the course of the nineteenth century as a new marital regime took hold).

27    See, e.g. Lenore Weitzman, The Marriage Contract XIX (1981); Marjorie M. Schultz, *Contractual Ordering of Marriage: A New Model for State Policy,* 70 Cal. L. Rev. 204, 208-09 (1982).

28    See Ronald Chester, *Less Law, but More Justice? Jury Trials and Mediation as Means of Resolving Will Contests,* 37 Duq. L. Rev. 173 (1999).

29    See Peter N. Swisher, Anthony Miller, Jana B. Singer, Family Law: Cases, Materials and Problems § 2.03[C] at 121-22 (2nd ed. 1998).

30    J.H. Baker, supra note 18, at 435.

31    See E. Gary Spitko, *Gone But Not Conforming: Protecting the Abhorrent Testator from Majoritarian Cultural Norms Through Minority-Culture Arbitration,* 49 Case W. Res. 275, 277 (1999) (arbitration as a solution); Susan N. Gary, *Mediation and the Elderly: Using Mediation to Resolve Probate Disputes Over Guardianship and Inheritance,* 32 Wake Forest L. Rev. 397, 398 (1997) (mediation as a solution); Ray D. Madoff, *Unmasking Undue Influence,* 81 Minn. L. Rev. 571, 574 (1997); Joseph W. DeFuria, Jr., *Testamentary Gifts Resulting from Meretricious Relationships: Undue Influence or Natural Beneficence?,* 64 Notre Dame L. Rev. 200, 200-07 (1989); Dawn Allison, *Note: the Importance of Estate Planning Within the Gay and Lesbian Community,* 23 Marshall L. Rev. 445, 446 (1998); Veena K. Murthy, Note: *Undue Influence and Gender Stereotypes: Legal Doctrine or Indoctrination?,* 4 Cardozo Women's L.J. 105, 105-06 (1997).

32    Spitko, supra note 31. See also Madoff, 81 Minn. L. Rev. 572-74.

33    See supra notes 6-8.

34    These statutes have withstood a constitutional challenge that the courts lacked authority to issue such declaratory judgments because of the lack of a case or controversy in the one case to raise the issue. See Aloysius A. Leopold & Gerry W. Beyer, *Ante-Mortem Probate: A Viable Model,* 43 Ark. L. Rev. 131, 133 (1990); Spitko, supra note 31, at 294-98.

35    Howard Fink, *Ante-Mortem Probate Revisited: Can an Idea Have a Life After Death?,* 37 Ohio State L.J. 264, 266 (1976).

36    In fact, the most frequent use of the Ohio statute has been to determine the testamentary capacity of testators executing wills through court-appointed guardians, where the guardian rather than the testator is often the moving force behind the procedure, and the potential heirs may or may not be

inclined to contest the result. Dara Greene, *Note and Comment: Ante-Mortem Probate: A Mediation Model*, 14 Ohio St. J. on Disp. Res. 663, 677 n.102 (1999).

[37]   *Horst v. First National Bank in Massillon*, No. CA-8057, 1990 Ohio App. LEXIS 2691, at *5-7 (5th Dist. Ct. App.).

[38]   Fink, supra note 35, at 274-75.

[39]   See Fink, supra at 276.

[40]   The testator is required to establish the prerequisites for the will's validity, such as testamentary capacity and the requisite witnesses, even if the other parties to the action do not deny their existence. See Fink, note 35, supra at 276.

[41]   See *Lloyd v. Wayne Circuit Judge,* 23 N.W. 28, 28 (Mich. 1885) (invalidating antemortem probate statute because it did not provide wife and other interested parties notice or a right to be heard).

[42]   *Aetna Life Insurance Co. v. Haworth,* 300 U.S. 227, 240-41 (1937) "'controversy' in this sense must be one that is appropriate for judicial determination.... A justiciable controversy is thus distinguished from a difference or dispute of a hypothetical or abstract character; from one that is academic or moot.... The controversy must be definite and concrete, touching the legal relations of parties having adverse legal interests.... It must be a real and substantial controversy admitting of specific relief through a decree of a conclusive character, as distinguished from an opinion advising what the law would be upon a hypothetical state of facts.... Where there is such a concrete case admitting of an immediate and definitive determination of the legal rights of the parties in an adversary proceeding upon the facts alleged, the judicial function may be appropriately exercised although the adjudication of the rights of the litigants may not require the award of process or the payment of damages.... An as it is not essential to the exercise of the judicial power that an injunction be sought, allegations that irreparable injury is threatened are not required."

[43]   See note 6-8, supra.

[44]   See *Cooper v. Woodward,* No. CA-1724, 1983 WL 6566 at *1-2 (Ohio Ct. App.) (the court decided that there was a valid controversy, and that no evidence had been introduced to rebut the presumed constitutionality of the statute); Horst, 1990 Ohio App. LEXIS No. CA-8057 at *5-6 (5th Dist. Ct.).

[45]   In the premarital context, the prospective spouses are ordinarily the only interested parties. In the context of a parentage declaration, there may be a guardian et litem representing the child, or a hospital or other offical responsible for overseeing the issuance of the birth certificate. See, e.g., *Baby Doe v. John and Mary Doe,* 421 S.E. 2d 913, 916 (1992) (guardian et litem, who contested assertions in complaint, contributed to determination of adversity).

[46]   For the history of the use of declaratory judgments in the premarital agreement context, see *Trossman v. Trossman,* 165 N.E.2d 368, 370 (Ill. 1960) ("'[The declaratory judgment]...is designed to afford security and relief against uncertainty with a view to avoiding litigation, rather than in aid of it, and to settle and fix rights before there has been an irrevocable change of position of the parties in disregard of their respective claims of right, and thus promote peace, quiet and justice, with the end always constantly in view that one of the chief purposes is to declare rights rather than to execute them.'").

[47]   See, e.g., Harold H. Bruff, Symposium on the Texas Constitution: *Separation of Powers Under the Texas Constitution,* 68 Tex. L. Rev. 1337, 1337 (1990) (excellent discussion of the general subject and the relationship between administrative agencies and courts in Texas and why Texas has historically confined the power of its courts in the post-Reconstruction era); John V. Orth, *"Forever Separate and Distinct": Separation of Powers in North Carolina,* 62 N.C.L. Rev. 1, 10-11 (1983). Reported decisions using declaratory judgments to test the validity of premarital agreements are rare. See Kosik v. George, 452 P.2d 560, 564 (Ore. 1969) (exercising jurisdiction over declaratory judgment action brought by daughter of decedent against her father's widow and executor of his estate seeking determination of validity of premarital agreement); *Trossman,* 165 N.E.2d at 324, finding justiciable declaratory judgment

action to determine validity of a premarital agreement during an on-going marriage). But see *Miller v. Miller*, 151 So. 2d 869, 871 (Fla. Dist. App. 1963) (holding no justiciable controversy when widow tried to use declaratory judgment action to contest validity of a premarital agreement because widow had not yet complied with statutory procedure necessary to assert a claim to the assets in the estate.) The courts have also used declaratory judgment actions to address the validity of postnuptial agreements. See, e.g., *Bavido v. Weixel*, 459 So. 2d 701, 702 (La. Ct. App. 1984) (declaring property agreement invalid); *Eaton v. Eaton*, 366 A.2d 121, 122 (Md. Ct. Spec. App. 1976) (declaring property agreement invalid); *Wolfe v. Wolfe*, 491 A.2d 281, 282 (Pa. Super. Ct. 1985) (declaring postnuptial agreement to be valid in the context of a divorce action). In all of these cases, however, the parties had conflicting views as to the validity of the agreement.

[48]   See *Orth*, 62 N.C.L. at 11-15. In the family law context, a number of states have been routinely using the type of declarations we advocate without directly addressing the issue of justiciability. See, e.g., *Calvert v. Johnson*, 851 P.2d 776, cert. denied, 510 U.S. 874 (1993). Other states have refused to issue the declarations on substantive grounds without specifically considering the procedural propriety of a pre-birth declaration. See, e.g., *A.H.W. v. G. H. B.*, 772 A.2d 948, 949 (N.J. 2000) (New Jersey court found that a pre-birth order declaring the egg and sperm donors to be the unborn child's parents would violate public policy, but did not consider the propriety of a declaratory judgment to that effect). Cf. *R.R. vs. M.H.*, 689 N.E.2d 790, 797 (Mass. 1998) (Massachusetts law permitted trial court to certify issues for appeal that resulted in a declaration finding surrogacy agreements to be unenforceable in spite of trial court settlement by the parties).

[49]   See, e.g., Bruff, 68 Tex. L. Rev. at 1340 *and* Orth, 62 N.C.L. at 11-15, discussing the particularly narrow view adopted in the South.

[50]   Although these states have upheld the constitutionality of declaratory judgment acts, they still require consideration of justiciability, adversity and subject matter jurisdiction. See, e.g., *Trossman, supra* note 47, 165 N.E.2d 368, 374B75 (In actions for declaratory judgments, "just as in equitable actions to quiet title or quia timet, no wrong need be proved but merely the existence of a claim or record which disturbs the title, peace, or freedom of the plaintiff, so any claims, assertions, challenges, records, or adverse interests, which, by casting doubt, insecurity, and uncertainty upon the plaintiff's rights or status, damage his pecuniary or material interests, establish a condition of justiciability.") (Citations omitted).

[51]   It is difficult to predict how these states are likely to rule with any certainty. State courts have generally upheld declaratory judgment statutes from constitutional challenges however strict the state approach to separation of powers. See cases cited in note 57, infra. The ante-mortem statutes have also been upheld in the one case to involve a direct attack. See supra, note 44.

[52]   See, e.g., *Board of Supervisors of Fairfax County v. Allman*, 211 S.E.2d 48, 55 (Va. 1975) ("The court's action is at odds with the decisions of this court and with the holdings of a majority of other jurisdictions. The ultimate classification of lands under zoning ordinances involves the exercise of the legislative power and under the doctrine of separation of powers this field shall not be invaded by the courts. The courts may not rezone property to specific categories upon a finding of the invalidity of a zoning ordinance. It is not the province of courts to zone or rezone, thereby substituting their judgment for that of the legislative body. This was our holding in Boggs v. Board of Supervisors, Supra, where we said: 'Lastly, plaintiffs ask this court to rezone their land to permit the construction of a four-story office building and concomitant commercial facilities. "Zoning is properly a legislative function. Under the evidence presented, this court will not substitute its judgment for that of the Board in determining the proper rezoning classification for plaintiffs' land." 211 Va. at 492, 178 S.E.2d at 511.'"). See also discussion in note 57, infra.

Even the states with the narrowest view of judicial authority, however, have declaratory judgment procedures. And their courts get into disputes that might come close to the borders of separation of powers. See e.g., *Carr v. Union Church of Hopewell*, 186 Va. 411. 42 S.E.2d 840 (1947) (battle over church funds; ecclesiastical matters not outside jurisdiction of trial court if there is an actual dispute over money); *Krebs v. Keating*, 42 Va. Cir. 248; 1997 Va. Cir. LEXIS 122 (1997) (declaratory judgment as to ownership of church property); *Makar Production Co. v. Anderson*, 1999 WL 1260015 (1999) (interpretation of rights under continuing petroleum extraction lease); *Imperial Tobacco Group Ltd. V. Peoples Bank and Trust Co. Of Rocky Mount, North Carolina*, 7 N.C. App. 202, 171 S.E.2d 807 (1970) (rights in deceased husband's pension fund by widow who was separated but not divorced from deceased); *State of North Carolina ex rel. James L. Martin as Governor of the State of North Carolina and As a Citizen of North Carolina v. Melott*, 320 N.C. 518, 359 S.E.2d 783 (1987) (action by Governor for declaratory judgment that statute granting authority to the Chief Justice of the state supreme court to appoint the director of the Office of Administrative Hearings violated the separation of powers doctrine of the state constitution).

[53] See the discussion at Bruff, Symposium on the Texas Constitution *Under the Texas Constitution*, 68 Tex. L. Rev. 1337, 1344 ("Finally, statutes define the scope of judicial review of agency action to provide a meaningful checkon an agency's fidelity to law.").

[54] Virtually all agency action is subject to judicial review under the state constitution or state versions of the administrative procedure act. See, e.g., Paul R. Verkuil, *Cross-currents in Anglo-American Administrative Law*, 27 Wm. & Mary L. Rev. 685 (1986); Sandra Day O'Connor, *Reflections on Preclusion of Judicial Review in England and the Unites States*, 27 Wm. & Mary L. Rev. 685 (1986); Claudia Tobler, Note, The *Standard of Judicial Review of Administrative Agencies in the U.S. and EU: Accountability and Reasonable Agency Action*, 22 B.C. Intl. & Comp. L. Rev. 213 (1999): Rebecca L. Donnellan, Student Work, The *Exhaustion Doctrine Should Not Be a Doctrine with Exceptions*, 103 W. Va. L. Rev. 361 (2001); Julie Ann Sebastion, Rosalyn Kaplan, William A Price, Stephen J. Rotello, James M. Reilly, and Matthew W. Beaudet, *Survey of Illinois Law: Administrative Law*, 24 S. Ill. U. L.J. 661 (1999) (good survey of one state's experience, including allowance of review by common law writs when administrative procedure act did not apply).

[55] The U.S. Supreme Court has held that an unreviewed administrative determination is entitled to the same full faith and credit in federal court as it would have had in the state in which it was rendered, unless Congress chooses otherwise with regard to a federal right asserted in a state administrative proceeding. *University of Tennessee v. Elliott*, 478 U.S. 788 (1986). The Constitution mandates that the states give full faith and credit to judgments from sister states. *28 U.S.C. § 1738* extends the same principle between federal and state courts, but since this principle is not a Constitutional mandate, Congress can change the requirement through legislation.

Consent judgments are generally entitled to the same full faith and credit as litigated judgments. See Katherine C. Pearson, *Common Law Preclusion, Full Faith and Credit, and Consent Judgments: The Analytical Challenge*, 48 Cath. U. L. Rev. 419 (1999) (commenting, however, on Baker v. General Motors Corp., 118 U.S. 657 (1998), in which the Court refused to preclude a party who settled an injury claim with G.M., promising not to testify, from being compelled to testify in another action).

Administrative determinations pose more of a challenge. An administrative determination can range from the issuance of a marriage license or birth certificate to an adversary proceeding that produces a judgment from a quasi-judicial body. The more the administrative determination resembles a judicial proceeding, the more likely an unappealed administrative order is to be entitled to full faith and credit. See David A. Brown, Note, *Collateral Estoppel Effects of Administrative Agency Determinations: Where Should Federal Courts Draw the Line?*, 73 Cornell L. Rev. 817, 819-20, 830 (1988) ( "Courts currently apply a flexible standard in determining whether to grant an agency determination collateral estoppel effect. The standard involves several elements. An agency must act in a "judicial capacity," adjudicate in a trial-like manner, and follow precedents that provide the litigant his "full and fair opportunity" to participate in the adjudicatory process. Only then will courts grant collateral estoppel effect to the agency's determinations.") See also Heather Rutland, *Civil Rights are Civil Rights are Civil Rights: The Inapplicability of Preclusion to Unreviewed State Administrative Decisions*, 20 Journal of the

National Association of Administrative Law Judges, 1999; Richard L. Revesz, *Specialized Courts and the Administrative Lawmaking System,* 138 U. Pa. L. Rev. 1111 (1990).

Nonetheless, the courts' willingness to give full faith and credit to another jurisdiction's unappealed administrative decision can vary with the nature of the proceeding. See *Thomas v. Washington Gas Light Co.,* 448 U.S. 261 (1980) (Although recognizing the general rule that administrative proceedings that resemble court proceedings must be given full faith and credit, the court nonetheless allowed a District of Columbia court to add to a workmen's compensation award that a sister state had awarded plaintiff in an unappealed state administrative determination. The Court was sharply divided and there was no majority opinion.) In Elliot, supra the Court, applying the full faith and credit statute, held that while a federal court must give an unappealed state administrative determination that a person was not unconstitutionally fired from the University of Tennessee preclusive effect in a Section 1983 action, the state ruling did not preclude a Title VII action in the same case because Congress has provided that Title VII actions are not barred by state actions. See also *Astoria Fed. Sav. & Loan Assn. v. Solimino,* 501 U.S. 104 (1991).

Accordingly, a declaratory judgment action, if it can meet the state's requirements for adversity, is more certain to be given full faith and credit in other states than an administrative determination. An administrative determination that is appealed and upheld by the courts is more likely to be given full faith and credit than an unappealed determination. An unappealed determination that resembles an adversary proceeding will be given more weight than a ministerial act such as the issuance of a birth certificate. See William L. Reynolds, The *Iron Law of Full Faith and Credit,* 53 Md. L. Rev. 412, 412 (1994) (arguing that the requirement to give full faith and credit to a sister state's final judgment "is so clear and strong that it might be called the "Iron Law" of Full Faith and Credit").

[56]     Moreover, if the judgment were reviewed, there would be a judicial determination. If unreviewed, the right would become fixed after the time for appeal had run, if state law so provided. See *Brosterhous v. State Bar,* 906 P.2d 1242 (1995) (A final decision in an administrative adjudication may be given res judicata or collateral estoppel effect in a subsequent judicial proceeding if the issues were identical in the administrative proceeding. It may do so if the agency was acting in a judicial capacity and resolved disputed issues of fact which the parties had adequate opportunity to litigate).

It might be argued that a state determination where both parties agree on the result, such as the ownership of fertilized ova, is not a litigation and therefore not entitled to full faith and credit in sister states or res judicata and collateral estoppel at home. But many rights are created by state law that are not the result of adjudication. A marriage is created by state law and is generally entitled to recognition in other states (absent conflict with a strong public policy of the state) and certainly recognition in the state in which it was rendered. A driver's license is a right created by state law that is recognized in sister states although it is not created by adjudication. See note 55, supra.

[57]     State declaratory judgment acts may be sufficient grants of authority in themselves. See, e.g., *Tex. Civ. Prac. & Rem. Code Ann. § 37.004,* which provides that: "A person interested under a deed, will, written contract, or other writings constituting a written contract ... may have determined any questions of construction or validity arising under the instrument, ... contract," etc. See similar language in the Uniform Declaratory Judgment Act, 12A U.L.A. 3 (1996).

Most states also have statutes that deal with parenthood, and other family law matters. In *Smith v. Brown,* 718 N.E. 2d 844 (1999), the court implicitly upheld a lower court determination of parenthood pursuant to the state's paternity procedures, even though the parties were in agreement, and the case arguably presented no case and controversy. The Smith case involved a surrogacy agreement in which the sperm and egg donors asked the court to rule that they were the parents of the child. The gestational surrogate (who was also the egg donor's sister) and her husband admitted all of the allegations in the complaint. Id. at 1005. The parties then moved for the entry of an agreed on judgment prior to the child's birth. The judge denied the motion on the grounds that, lacking a dispute, the Probate and Family Court lacked authority to enter the proposed judgment under the statutory provision addressing births to married couples. Id. The complaint was amended (with the judge's approval) to use the framework of G. L. c. 209C, the statute governing the status of non-marital children, to secure the parenthood declaration. The court then entered a judgment agreeable to the parties, and no appeal was taken. Id. The judge, however, reserved and reported the case with questions of law that went beyond the issues addressed in the parenthood judgment. The Massachusetts Supreme Court found the certification of the hypothetical questions inappropriate, in part because there was a final judgment in the case that had not been appealed. The parenthood determination was nonetheless left intact. In California, the courts have heard similar cases during the pregnancy, delaying issuance of the final order until after birth. See discussion infra. In *A.H.W. v. G. H. B.,* 772 A.2d 948 (2000), the New Jersey court exercised jurisdiction in a declaratory judgment action in which the parties were in agreement, but found that a pre-birth order declaring the egg and sperm donors to be the unborn child's parents would violate the public policy of the state giving birth mothers 72 hours after birth to contest a surrender of parental rights. *Id. at 954.* In Virginia, the court in *Baby Doe v. John and Mary Doe,* 421 S.E. 2d 913 (1992) also found that it had jurisdiction to determine maternity and paternity in a pre-birth surrogacy case under the state's parentage procedures, but it based its conclusion that an "actual controversy" existed the fact that the guardian ad litem appointed to represent the unborn child had filed an answer contesting denying material allegations in the complaint. *Id. at 916.*

[58]   See notes 44 and 57, supra.

[59]   Indeed, the Louisiana covenant marriage statute already employs such procedures, with provision for counseling, and the selection of form agreements as a way to alter the default rules that govern marriage. See discussion at note 55, supra. For a discussion of mediation, see notes 9, 10, and 12, supra.

[60]   They may, however, be less faster, and less expensive. See more extended discussion at note 55, supra, and accompanying text.

[61]   See Pearson, supra note 55, at 420 ("In reality, [consent] judgments are often little more than the parties' contracts, rubber-stamped by the court.) This, of course, is one reason why such lawsuits may be held to lack adversity. See, e.g., *Baby Doe v. John and Mary Doe, 421 S.E. 2d 913 (1992)* (finding adversity only because the guardian ad litem appointed to represent the child contested the allegations in the complaint).

[62]   See Leah Guggenheimer, A Modest Proposal: The Feminomics of Drafting Premarital Agreements, 12 Women's Rights Law Reporter 147 (1996) (practice guides advise lawyers to incorporate provisions that favor the higher earning or wealthier spouse); Katharine B. Silbaugh, *Marriage Contracts and the Family Economy,* 93 Nw. U.L. Rev. 65, 72 (1998) (premarital agreements systematically favor the higher earning or wealthier spouse because they fail to take the intangible contributions to marriage into account).

[63]   See notes 9, 10 and 12, supra, on the role of mediation in family law decision-making. For a discussion of the educational efforts in family law disputes, see Peter Salem, *Education for Divorcing Parents: A New Direction for Family Courts,* 23 Hofstra L. Rev. 837, 840-42 (1995); Karen R. Blaisure and Margie J. Geasler, *The Divorce Education Interventional Model,* 38, Fam. & Concil. Cts. Rev. 501, 506B11 (2000); Nancy Thoennes and Jessica Pearson, Survey, *Parent Education in the Domestic Relations Court: A Multisite Assessment,* 37 Fam. & Concil. Cts. Rev. 195, 195B98 (1999).

[64]   The proposal has sparked debate since its initial advocacy in 1976, with new articles appearing as recently as 1999. See John H. Langbein, *Living Probate: The Conservatorship Model,* 77 Mich. L. Rev. 63 (1978); Gregory S. Alexander & Albert M. Pearson, *Alternative Models of Ante-Mortem Probate and Procedural Due Process Limitations on Successions,* 78 Mich. L. Rev. 89 (1979); Mary Louise Fellows, The Case Against Living Probate, 78 Mich. L. Rev. 1066 (1980); Timothy R. Donovan, *Comment, The Ante-Mortem Alternative to Probate Legislation in Ohio,* 9 Capitol U. L. Rev. 717 (1980); Aloysius A. Leopold & Gerry W. Beyer, *Ante-Mortem Probate: A Viable Model,* 43 Ark. L. Rev. 131 (1990); Gerry W. Beyer, Pre-Mortem Probate, Prob. & Prop., July/Aug. 1993; Tracy Costello-Norris, Is *Ante-Mortem*

*Probate a Viable Solution to the Problems Associated with Post-Mortem Procedures?,* 9 Conn. Prob. L.J. 327 (1995); Dara Greene, Note & Comment, *Antemortem Probate: A Mediation Model,* 14 Ohio State J. On Disp. Resol. 663 (1999); Spitko, supra note 31.

65    John H. Langbein, Gregory S. Alexander, Albert M. Pearson, Mary Louise Fellows, Dara Greene, supra note 64.

66    E. Gary Spitko, note 31, supra, at 294-98. Spitko suggested binding arbitration on the issue of testamentary capacity, despite the fact that such arbitration is not that different from the contest model. Arbitration, however, would permit the parties to select a decision-maker compatible with their perspectives, facilitating family dispute resolution with some hope of encouraging harmony. Id.

67    Greene, supra note 64, 679-86.

68    See Langbein, supra note 64, at 77.

69    John H. Langbein, Gregory S. Alexander, Albert M. Pearson, Mary Louise Fellows, Dara Greene, supra note 64 . Other writers, however, have supported the idea in its original form. See Aloysius A. Leopold and Gary W. Beyer, supra note 64.

70    Indeed, in the premarital contexts, all couples who apply for marriage licenses could be given information about the ability to specify the terms that will govern their marriage. See Jeffrey Evans Stake and Michael Grossberg, *Roundtable: Opportunities for and Limitations of Private Ordering in Family Law,* 73 Ind. L.J. 535 (1998); Eric Rasmusen and Jeffrey Evans Stake, *Lifting the Veil of Ignorance: Personalizing the Marriage Contract,* 73 Ind. L.J. 453 (1998); Jeffery Evans Stake, *Paternalism in the Law of Marriage,* 74 Ind. L.J. 801 (1999); Peter N. Swisher, Anthony Miller, Jana B. Singer, Family Law: Cases Materials and Problems '13.01 (2nd ed. 1998).

71    See discussion infra.

72    Working through the consequences of these procedures is complex, however, and the premarital and parenthood contexts are sufficiently different from each other that we will address them separately below. Nonetheless, we would note some caution at the outset. First, care must be given to managing "mediation" between parties in agreement at the time they initiate the procedure. If the mediator remains true to the neutral role ordinarily identified with mediation and rubberstamps the prearranged agreement, then mediation becomes a wasteful formality in this context. If, on the other hand, the mediator steps beyond that role and takes actions likely to disrupt the agreement, it reduces both the likelihood of marriage, and the likelihood that procedure will be used in future. Mosten argues that the ideal mediating role is to provide at least a minimum level of counseling to insure that the parties understand the consequences of their agreement and the alternatives. See Mosten, supra note 10, at 430-31 on the advantages of mediation in a family court setting, and more generally, supra notes 9, 10, and 12 on family law mediation. Second, there will almost inevitably be a tradeoff between the resources devoted to the procedure and its effectiveness. If the courts simply provide for declaratory judgments and nothing more, the procedure is most likely to be used by the most sophisticated, well funded parties for their own benefit. Only if family courts fund some degree of counseling or mediation is the process likely to protect the interests of weaker parties. See Guggenheimer, supra note 62, and Silbaugh, supra note 62, on the inequality in bargaining power in the premarital context. Third, the process may develop a life of its own. Right now, for example, many family practitioners are reluctant to draft premarital agreements because of malpractice concerns. Use of the procedures we are proposing may become the norm, not to protect the interests of the client, but to insulate lawyers from malpractice. Indeed, we can imagine the party benefitting from a premarital agreement later invalidated by the courts winning a claim that it was malpractice for his attorney not to have sought a declaratory judgment before the marriage. Without careful implementation, these practices will simply serve to enhance the already strong bargaining power of the wealthier or more sophisticated parties.

73    See James Williams Moore, et al., 5 Moore's Federal Practice § 23.82. "A class action settlement, like an agreement resolving any other legal claim, is a private contract negotiated between the parties. Nevertheless, Rule 23(e) requires the court to intrude on that private consensual agreement to ensure

that the agreement is not the product of fraud or collusion and that, taken as a whole, it is fair, adequate, and reasonable to all concerned." Id. Thus Rule 23(e) requires the court to approve a settlement of a class action even though it has been freely negotiated by the attorneys for the representatives of the class and the attorneys for the defendants. Indeed the Supreme Court has approved of class actions brought solely to approve a settlement. See *Amchem Products, Inc. v. Windsor,* 521 U.S. 591 (1997). In § 23.85, Moore's states: "Although Rule 23(e) is silent respecting the standard by which a proposed class action settlement is to be evaluated, the universally applied standard is whether the settlement is fundamentally fair, adequate, and reasonable. Some courts also require that settlements be consistent with the public interest. Finally, the court must determine that the terms of the settlement do not violate any applicable federal law."

[74] The precise standard will depend on how the state decides to shape the proceeding. If the courts were simply to employ a declaratory judgment procedure to judge the validity of a premarital agreement under existing law, for example, the standard of review would depend on the jurisdictions' approach to premarital agreements, and most states would not consider the fairness issues required by Rule 23 (as opposed to unconscionability). See discussion supra at 73. A jurisdiction permitting a final determination of validity before marriage, however, could insist on a fairness review as a prerequisite for the finality of the determination. Such a requirement might be particularly appropriate in those jurisdictions that now determine unconscionability at the time of the divorce, rather than the time of the agreement. See discussion infra. Another possibility is that the state might limit final approval to certain state specified form agreements. Covenant marriage in Louisiana, for example, allows couples to choose between two forms of marriage, rather than to draft custom designed premarital agreement. See infra note 95. The Louisiana precedent could be extended to a larger number of form agreements, permitting, for example, different arrangement for defining separate versus marital property.

[75] Indeed, representing children's interests completely might require appointment of a guardian ad litem. Nonetheless, we believe that such appointments will be limited. The traditional premarital agreement does not involve children. For the other contexts, see infra note 76.

[76] See June Carbone, From Partners to Parents: The Second Revolution in Family Law 129 (2000). See also Grossberg, supra note 26, at 23; Sir William Blackstone, 1 Commentaries on the Laws of England 447 (Thomas M. Cooley, ed., 3rd ed., 1884); Allison A. Marston, *Planning for Love: The Politics of Prenuptial Agreements,* 49 Stan. L. Rev. 887, 904-06 (1997).

[77] See Lynne Marie Kohm, *Marriage and the Intact Family: The Significance of Michael H. v. Gerald D.,* 22 Whittier L. Rev. 327 (2000) (examining the historical importance of legitimacy, and its continuing relevance for the status of children).

[78] For a discussion of the changing nature of cohabitation, see Carol Smart, Symposium, *Stories of Family Life: Cohabitation, Marriage and Social Change,* 17 Can. J. Fam. L. 20, (2000); Winifred Holland, Symposium, Intimate Relationships in the New Millennium: The Assimilation of Marriage and Cohabitation?, 17 Can. J. Fam. L. 114, (2000); J. Thomas Oldham, *Jerry Hall v. Mick Jagger Regarding U.S. Regulation of Heterosexual Cohabitants Or, I Can't Get No Satisfaction,* 76 Notre Dame L. Rev. 1409 (2001).

[79] See supra notes 47 to 49, and accompanying text.

[80] See supra notes 51 to 53 and accompanying text.

[81] For statistics, see Leah Guggenheimer, supra note 62, at 151. The agreements addressing intimate partnerships run the gamut from purely financial arrangement to efforts to specify the most intimate of partners' understandings. Although only financial agreements are likely to be enforceable, we leave open the possibility that other forms of agreement may become be subject to these procedures. Couples contemplating marriage, for example, should know from the outset that their efforts to specify custody arrangements in the event of divorce will not find later courts. See Weitzman, supra note 27, advocating such agreements and discussion infra of the tradeoff between the financial and non-financial considerations underlying marital bargaining.

[82]    The Philosophy of Law: An Encyclopedia, vol. ii (ed. Christopher Gray), Marriage Contract, 535-37 (1999).

[83]    See, e.g., Lawrence Stone, The Family, Sex and Marriage: In England 1500-1800, 70-71 (abridged ed.) (1979).

[84]    Id.

[85]    Brian Bix, *Bargaining in the Shadow of Love: The Enforcement of Premarital Agreements and How We Think about Marriage*, 40 Wm. and Mary L. Rev. 145, 150 (1998) (citations omitted).

[86]    Silbaugh, supra note 62, at 72. Brian Bix has pointed out that the courts in these cases treated a waiver of rights as creating an incentive to divorce in that it made divorce cheaper than it would be otherwise be for at least one of the parties. See, e.g., *Cartright v. Cartright*, 43 Eng. Rep. 385 (L.J. Ch. 1853). For a recent case employing such reasoning, see *In re Marriage of Noghrey*, 215 Cal. Rptr. 153 (Cal Ct. App. 1985) (invalidating dowry like pre-marital agreement that conveyed a substantial portion of the husband's property to the wife at divorce, in spite of the fact that the divorce occurred only months after the wedding).

[87]    Silbaugh, id., at 72.

[88]    As Kate Silbaugh notes, the property provisions of premarital agreements are the most likely to be enforced, while the nonfinancial provisions are the least likely to enjoy judicial favor, with spousal support somewhere in between. Id. at 77-79. See also Sanford N. Katz, *Propter Honoris Respectum: Marriage as Partnership,* 73 Notre Dame L. Rev. 1251 (1998) (tracing the changes in attitude with respect to the parties ability to address not just their financial affairs, but the more intangible terms of their relationship).

[89]    Weisberg and Appleton, supra note 5, at 147. Brian Bix suggests that these changes occurred at the same time as the palimony cases were winning greater acceptance, making marriage with a premarital agreement a better deal for the wealthy than living together without one. (E-mail from Brian Bix, March, 18, 2001, on file with author.)

[90]    Lenore Weitzman, The Marriage Contract (1981).

[91]    Silbaugh, supra note 62, 75-76 (noting, in particular, the split among states over whether to judge the agreement at the time of enforcement or at the time of contracting, and whether to consider substantive fairness or only unconscionability).

[92]    Id. at 72. See also Barbara Ann Atwood, *Ten Years Later: Lingering Concerns about the Uniform Premarital Agreement Act,* 19 J. Legis. 127, 136 (1993); Shukhman, infra note 41. Compare, e.g., *In re Estate of Lutz,* 563 N.W. 2d 90, 97, 98 (1990*)* (lack of legal advice to a prospective spouse is a significant factor in weighing the voluntariness of a premarital agreement) with *Penhollow v. Penhollow,* 649 A.2d 1016, 1022 (R.I. 1994) (lack of independent counsel does not render premarital agreement unenforceable.) Indeed, the court of appeal in Bonds commented that: "Despite adoption of the Uniform Premarital Agreement Act (UPAA) by many states, uniform standards regarding enforcement have yet to be universally realized. Accordingly, analyses of the enforceability of premarital contracts by the courts have, thus far, continued to be ad hoc, often inconsistent, and sometimes contradictory." 71 Cal. App. 4th at 293-94.

[93]    Id., at 65.

[94]    See, e.g., the different approaches of the Supreme Court and the Court of Appeal in the Bonds case, supra note 20. Sanford Katz observes that "so long as a disappointed spouse can be successful in avoiding an agreement that was entered into at the time of marriage, many years before the divorce, in an atmosphere of complete openness, there is very little point in having such agreements except to force a discussion of certain matters that would ordinarily not be raised, or to serve as some kind of memorandum of understanding." Katz, supra note 88, at 1261-62.

[95]    Indeed, the inspiration for the covenant marriage legislation adopted in Louisiana was authorization of a broader array of topics for marital bargaining as a way of using private agreement to achieve substantive law reform. See Elizabeth S. Scott, *Rational Decionmaking about Marriage and*

*Divorce,* 76 Va. L. Rev. 9 (1990) (discussing the importance of precommitment strategies); Katherine Shaw Spaht, *Louisiana's Covenant Marriage: Social Analysis and Legal Implications,* 59 La. L. Rev. 63, (1998); Lynne Marie Kohm, *A Comparative Survey of Covenant Marriage Proposals in the United States,* 12 Regent U.L. Rev. 31, (1999 /2000) (noting that common features include premarital and pre-divorce counseling and a clear statement of intent); Katherine Shaw Spaht, *What's Become of Louisiana Covenant Marriage Through the Eyes of Social Scientists,* 47 Loy. L. Rev. 709 (2001) (finding that state clerks do not necessarily make mandated information available).

[96]   581 A.2d 162, 163 (Pa. 1990).

[97]   The Bonds case, supra note 20, decided in California in 2000, and reversed prospectively by the legislature may be an even greater embracement of freedom to bargain.

[98]   Bix, supra note 85, at 156-67.

[123]   Judith T. Younger, *Perspectives an Antenuptial Agreements: An Update,* 8 Am. Acad. Matrim. Law, 1, 3-4 (1992) (internal footnotes omitted).

[124]   Silbaugh, supra note 62, at 78-79.

[125]   Lloyd Cohen, Marriage, *Divorce and Quasi-Rents; Or, "I Gave Him the Best Years of My Life,"* J. Leg. Studies 267 (1987) (women make greater contributions to marriage earlier in the relationship and are thus disadvantaged by divorce law that fails to take their greater contributions into account).

[126]   Cohen, id. at 285 (men's income increases over time while the value of housekeeping does not) and 285B86 (men value physical appearance, fertility and other qualities linked to youth more than women do).

[127]   See Cohen, id. at 287-89.

[128]   Cf. *Sanders v. Sanders,* 288 S.W. 2d 473, 478-79 (Tenn. 1956) (premarital agreement between parties who had married and divorced several times that provided financial penalties for filing for divorce held void as against public policy). But see Theodore F. Haas, The *Rationality and Enforceability of Contractual Restrictions on Divorce,* 66 N.C. L. Rev. 879 (1988) (arguing that contractual restrictions on divorce should be enforceable).

[129]   Sanders, id. See also Cohen, supra note 125, at 287-89 (comparing marriage and commercial contracts).

[130]   But cf. *Dunkin v. Boskey, 98 Cal. Rptr.2d 44, 60-61 (2000)* (allowing damages for unjust enrichment).

[131]   While Silbaugh, supra note 62, emphasizes the unfairness for women, the failure to recognize non-monetary issues also affects men. Women initiate two-thirds of all divorces, the majority without what historically would have been recognized as fault, or breach of the marriage contract. For men, the biggest non-financial loss in these cases is the ability to control access and custody to their children. See Carbone, The *Futility of Coherence: The ALI's Principles of the Law,* 4 J.L. & Fam. Stud. 43 (2002).

[132]   Silbaugh, *supra, at note 62, nn. 45-49* and accompanying text.

[133]   See Younger supra at note 123 at 3-4. This argument is nonetheless distinct from Younger's third point about the passage of time. Many long term contracts will not be enforced until years after their execution, and this does not in itself mean that they become unenforceable when the intervening events make them seem unfair. Rather, what is special about the family exchange is that it may involve an agreement in which half of the bargain is enforceable and the other half isn=t. A traditional breadwinner/ breadmaker couple partook in a relationship in which they promised to remain married. No fault eliminated that part of the bargain, while leaving the financial provisions untouched. The unfairness is not the substantive result of unequal financial footing, but the willingness to enforce one part of the bargain without acknowledging the true consideration for the exchange (in this case the promise to remain married). See Cohen, supra note 125, at 285-87, on the asymmetry of marital contributions. See also Margaret F. Brinig and June Carbone, The *Reliance Interest in Marriage and Divorce,* 62 Tulane

L. Rev. 855 (1988) (arguing that the expectation interest in marriage cannot be protected without some recognition of which party breached the agreement).

To the extent that the issue is the passage of time, however, existing premarital agreements already make some provision for "escalator clauses," which increase support with the length of the marriage, or "sunset" provisions that retire certain clauses after a specified number of years. See Bix, supra note 85, at 179-80.

[134]  Silbaugh, supra note 62, at 122-42.

[135]  Silbaugh notes that the majority of premarital agreements are designed to govern death rather than divorce, and they are intended to circumvent elective share laws so that the children from a first marriage (when the property is more likely to have been accumulated) rather than the spouse of a second marriage receives the bulk of the decedent's estate. Id. at 72-73. Silbaugh nonetheless objects to premarital agreements even in these cases because of the possibility (as in *Borelli*, supra note 23) that the second spouse will provide extraordinary (and otherwise uncompensated) care for the other. We believe that the procedure we have provided for below provides a way around this conundrum by making it easier for spouses to create enforceable bargains during the marriage. The caring spouse in *Borelli*, for example, could have sought a judicial ruling on the validity of the agreement, and if unhappy with the result, could have insisted on transfer of the disputed property into escrow.

[136]  Compare *Marvin v. Marvin*, 557 P. 2d 106, 110 (Cal. 1975) (overturning lower court ruling that contract between unmarried couple exchanging financial support for services was meretricious) with Borelli, supra note 23 (refusing to enforce property agreement between married couple for lack of consideration). Silbaugh argues that the effect is symmetrical. That is, those with concerns about their extraordinary wealth may not marry if the agreements are barred, but those otherwise prepared to make extraordinary non-monetary contributions may not marry if the agreements are permitted. Supra, note 62, at 141-42. But while the first group may not marry, the second group may simply become less likely to make extra-ordinary contributions.

[137]  Current statistics show that about one in two marriages end in divorce. Carbone, supra note 76, at 87.

[138]  Lynn Baker, *Promulgating the Marriage Contract*, 23 U. Mich. J.L. Reform 217, 229-33 (1990).

[139]  See, e.g., William Cantwell, *Premarital Contracting: Why And When*, 8 Am. Acad. Matrim. Law 45, 56-57 (1992) (The agreement should be executed long before the wedding to prevent invalidation for duress; the weaker party should be counseled, and given full disclosure, and the disclosure should be documented in writing, to prove that the weaker party waived any rights to greater disclosure.) See also new legislation in note 38, supra, mandating such procedures.

[140]  Skoloff, et al, Drafting Prenuptial Agreements V-65, V-71-75 (1994); Joseph Zwack, Premarital Agreements: When, Why, And How To Write Them 44-45 (1987); Linda S. Gross & Peter M. Walzer, Premarital Agreements, California Marital Settlement and Other Family Law Agreements §§ 17.22-17.34 at 293-301 (2d. ed. 1997).

[141]  Gross and Walzer, id. at § 17.11, § 17.47. Alex Shukhman, 20 Loy. L.A. Ent. L.J. 457, n.243 (2000) ("The American Law Institute ('ALI ')-American Bar Association Continuing Legal Education practice guide advises if one party has an attorney and that attorney does not insist on the other party having independent legal counsel, the attorney is probably committing malpractice.") See also Lewis Becker, Premarital Agreements: An Overview, in Premarital And Marital Contracting 14 (1993) (discussing role of counsel in validity of premarital agreements). See also *Fletcher v. Fletcher*, 628 N.E. 2d 1343, 1348 (Ohio 1994) (where there is less than equitable distribution, a 'meaningful opportunity to consult with counsel' is mandatory for the disadvantaged party).

[142]  Katz, supra note 88, at 1262-63 ("At the present time, because of the uncertainty of the enforcement of antenuptial agreements as written, even with procedural safeguards in place (for example,

representation by counsel), some lawyers refuse to draft them for fear of malpractice actions brought by their clients after their antenuptial agreements have been made ineffective.")

[143] For a description of the distinction between an administrative procedure and a judicial one, see notes 47-57 supra, and accompanying text. Two considerations should affect the choice between the two. First, in some jurisdictions, judicial review of the validity of a premarital judgment before the marriage may not meet the case and controversy requirement of the state constitution. See notes 47, 49, 50 and 52, supra. Second, some states may want to encourage premarital bargaining as a routine part of the marriage process. They might do so by informing every couple of their ability to enter a premarital contract, and by providing form agreements authorized by the legislature. For a proposal that would make such bargaining a mandatory part of the marriage process, see Jeffrey Evans Stake, *Mandatory Planning for Divorce,* 45 Vand. L. Rev. 397, 429-30 (1992). The simpler, and less expensive the process, the more likely it is to be used. But compare Spaht, supra note 95, observing that marriage license clerks have not fully complied with covenant marriage legislation mandating education and counseling, partly explaining the low rate (5%) of usage.

[144] See *Bonds,* supra note 20, 24 Cal. at 27-30 (comparing standards for premarital and postnuptial agreements in California); *In re Marriage of Richardson,* 606 N.E.2d 56 (Ill. 1992) (postnuptial agreement void because of fraudulent representation and duress); *Wolfe v. Wolfe,* 491 A.2d 281 (Penn. 1984) (postnuptial agreements presumed to be valid and binding).

[145] States that view conscionability at the time of enforcement, for example, might limit the grounds on which a premarital agreement could later be challenged. See Silbaugh, supra note 62, at 74-76, on the split among the states on whether to view unconscionability at the time of contracting or the time of enforcement. Of course, the most common forms of changed circumstances are predictable, and can be provided for in advance. If a premarital determination, for example, considers whether the parties have provided for illness, disability, or unemployability, then it should be harder to challenge the provision later if one of the events occurs.

[146] The determination of voluntariness with respect to a premarital agreement is essentially the same as the antemortem probate determination that a testator had testamentary capacity and was free from undue influence. See Fink, supra note 35, at 276. If the state relies on an administrative proceeding, the proceeding is less likely to be entitled to full faith and credit. The state should allow, however, for appeal of the administrative ruling to the courts. An unappealed determination, where state law provides for judicial review, should be entitled to full faith and credit on the same terms as any other final ruling. See notes 54B56, supra.

[147] See Greene, supra note 36, at 664-65 (determining testator's intent, in particular, is more easily done while the testator is alive). See also Spitko, supra note 31, at 283, n.32, documenting abuses in the probate process, particularly with respect to undue influence and testamentary capacity, and listing considerations a court should address in determining voluntariness of a transaction.

[148] Absent, of course, extrinsic evidence that permits the overturning of other kinds of judgments. See Fed. R. Civ. Pro. 60(b), discussed at James Williams Moore et al., Moore's Federal Practice §§ 60.01-60.03. An Ohio appellate court affirmed the refusal of a trial court to reopen a judgment that had applied ante-mortem probate to a will. See note 44, supra.

This leads to the question of whether such agreements would be recognized by other states. In general full faith and credit is required to be given to laws and judgments of sister states by the full faith and credit clause of the Constitution. But states have sometimes refused to apply full faith and credit to transactions or laws that violate their "strong public policy." Thus, a state might refuse to enforce a surrogate-mother contract if surrogate contracts were banned in that state. Professor Larry Kramer effectively argues that such exceptions to an explicit duty to enforce the laws of sister states in United States Constitution are themselves unconstitutional. See Larry Kramer, *Same-Sex Marriage, Conflict of Laws, and the Unconstitutional Public Policy Exception,* 106 Yale L.J. 1965 (1997). But the subject is unsettled. See Friederich K. Jeunger, Choice of Law and Multistate Justice (1993); Thomas

M. Keane, Note, *Aloha, Marriage? Constitutional and Choice of Law Arguments for Recognition of Same-Sex Marriages,* 47 Stan. L. Rev. 499 (1995); Deborah M. Henson, *Will Same-Sex Marriages Be Recognized in Sister States?:Full Faith and Credit and Due Process Limitations on States' Choice of Law Regarding the Status and Incidents of Homosexual Marriages Following Hawaii's Baehr v. Lewin,* 32 U. Louisville J. Fam. L. 551 (1993-1994); Candice L. Sage, Note, *Sister-State Recognition of Valid Same-Sex Marriages; Baehr v. LewinCHow Will it Play in Peoria?,* 28 Ind. L. Rev. 115 (1994); Joseph W. Hovermill, *A Conflict of Laws and Morals: The Choice of Law Implications of Hawaii's Recognition of Same-Sex,* 53 Md. L. Rev. 450 (1994).

With respect to the issue of duress or voluntariness, it is difficult to believe that a ruling in one state will violate the strong public policy of another state. The issue is more likely to arise if the substantive standard for review varies. If, for example, a state finds that waivers of spousal support violate the strong public policy of the state, then that state might not recognize a judgment from another state upholding the validity of a premarital agreement that waived support.

[149]  See Gross and Walzer, supra note 140, § 17.20.

[150]  Compare *Ortel v. Gettig,* 116 A.2d 145, 153 (Md. 1955*)* (finding that confidential relationship arises between parties engaged to be married, requiring full and truthful disclosure of wealth) and *In re Estate of Benker,* 331 N.W.2d 193, 196 (Mich. 1982) (duty of full disclosure required) with Uniform Premarital Agreement Act, (infra note 151) permitting waiver of disclosure. See generally, James O. Pearson, Jr., Annotation, *Failure to Disclose Extent or Value of Property Owned as Ground for Avoiding Premarital Contract,* 3 A.L.R.5th 394 (1992).

[151]  *Uniform Premarital Agreement Act Sec. 6(a)(2)(iii),* 9B U.L.A. 369 (1987).

[152]  Judicial approval of the substance of the agreement, however, is a separate matter. A court could withhold approval of a procedurally valid agreement if the agreement is found to be unconscionable at the time that it is signed or otherwise fails to meet the requisite standard established in the jurisdiction. See Silbaugh, supra note 62, at 74-76. Moreover, if a court found an agreement to be conscionable at the time of the marriage, and the enforcing jurisdiction determined conscionability at the time of the divorce, the initial judgment would not be binding (though it might be influential) because it would have addressed a different issue.

[153]  §6(a)(2)(iii), 9B U.L.A. 369 (1987).

[154]  See, e.g., Melvin Eisenberg, The *Limits of Cognition and the Limits of Contract,* 47 Stan. L. Rev. 211, 254 (1995) (arguing that the limits of foreseeability provide a strong argument for considering fairness at divorce). For states that reserve the right to review the substance of an agreement for its fairness at the end of a marriage in light of the changes that have occurred since the beginning of the marriage, see *Scherer v. Scherer,* 292 S.E.2d 662, 666 (Ga. 1982)*; Lewis v. Lewis,* 748 P.2d 1362, 1366-67 (Haw. 1988) (fairness of alimony provision judged at the time of divorce, while property provision judged at time of inception of marriage); *Osborne v. Osborne,* 428 N.E.2d 810, 816 (Mass. 1981); *McKee-Johnson v. Johnson,* 444 N.W.2d 259, 267 (Minn. 1989); *Gross v. Gross,* 464 N.E.2d 500, 509 (Ohio 1984)*; Button,* 388 N.W.2d at 551-52. *In re Dechant,* 867 P.2d 193, 195 (Colo. Ct. App. 1993) and *Kolflat v. Kolflat,* 636 So.2d 87, 90 (Fla. Dist. Ct. App. 1994, and discussion in Silbaugh, supra note 62, at 75B76.

[155]  Under existing law, Pennsylvania courts start with presumption that premarital agreements are valid. Wolfe, 341 Pa Super. at 317-18. Of course any determination of validity may be challenged by proof of fraud or duress, if the court had no way to determine the fraud or duress at the time of the judgment. See *Richardson,* 237 Ill. App. 3d at 1078-84.

[156]  *Uniform Premarital Agreement Act § 3(b),* 9B U.L.A. 369 (1987).

[157]  Id. at 6(b).

[158]  For an exploration of how the California courts might address the issue of the waiver of spousal support in the absence of a per se rule, see Charlotte K. Goldberg, *'If It Ain't Broke, Don't Fix it':* *Premarital Agreements and Spousal Support Waivers in California,* 33 Loy. L.A. L. Rev. 1245 (2000).

The trial court or administrative agency's initial approval of the agreement could be overturned by an appellate court if it were found to be wholly unsupported by the facts and a breach of discretion. If the time for appeal passed and the judgment became final, however, the judgment should be final not only in the home jurisdiction, but in every other jurisdiction that does not have a tougher public policy standard. See notes 54B56, supra, and accompanying text.

[159] See *University of Tennessee v. Elliott*, 478 U.S. 788 (1986) and note 55, supra.

[160] The parties, however, are unlikely to appeal an uncontested order upholding the validity of a premarital agreement, particularly if counsel advises them that it is unnecessary to the order's finality. See University of Tennessee v. Elliott, id.

[161] See note 47, supra.

[162] Gross & Walzer, supra note 140, § 17.51, at 319B26.

[163] It is also possible that some "good lawyers," who would otherwise draft more reasonable premarital agreements for their clients, might feel free to push to the limit of what the other spouse will accept, secure in the knowledge that the judge will either approve the document or permit its reformation, insulating the lawyer from malpractice woes in either event. See Pearson, supra note 55, at 470, on the tendency to rubberstamp uncontested agreements.

[164] *La. Rev. Stat. Ann. § 9:272(A)* (West 2000). For a detailed discussion of the qualifications of the counselor and the content of the counseling, see Spaht, supra note 95, Social Analysis and Legal Implications, at 84B90. See also Katherine Shaw Spaht, *What's Become of Louisiana Covenant Marriage Through the Eyes of Social Scientists,* 47 Loy. L. Rev. 709, 726 (2001) (finding that state clerks do not necessarily make mandated information available).

[165] See, e.g., Barbara Stark, *Marriage Proposals: From One-Size-Fits-All to Postmodern Marriage Law,* 89 Calif. L. Rev. 1479 (2001) (proposing that couples be allowed to choose from a variety of types of marriage the one that best fits their relationship).

[166] Indeed, Jeff Stake has suggested a regime of mandatory premarital bargaining that would require couples to specify the terms of their marriage as a condition for getting a marriage license. Our proposal could require that they elect from a menu of approved terms. See Stake supra note 70 and 143.

[167] The fairness of the result would obviously depend on the choice of alternatives. Legislatures could, however, limit certain options, e.g., authorizing a complete waiver of community property or spousal support only to couples entering marriage with independent means of support.

[168] See Gary J. Friedman & Steven C. Neustadter, Mediation: California Marital Settlement and Other Family Law Agreements § 2, 2.9 (2d ed. 2001). Neither mediation nor counseling, however, are panaceas. Beginning with Trina Grillo's critique of California's mandatory child custody mediation, an extensive literature has developed that warns of the "process dangers" for women of entering mediation with either a stronger party or a presumption in favor of agreement. These concerns are particularly valid here in that a) premarital agreements overwhelmingly seek to secure greater protection for the stronger (or at least wealthier) party in a relationship, and b) the default marriage rules (and therefore the benefits of not reaching an agreement) are likely to favor the weaker party. See Grillo, supra note 10, at 1549-50, 1597-1600. See also Penelope E. Bryan, *Killing Us Softly: Divorce Mediation and the Politics of Power,* 40 Buff. L. Rev. 441, 441 (1992) (cautioning against use of mediation where a serious power imbalance may exist); Sara Cobb & Janet Rifkin, *Practice and Paradox: Deconstructing Neutrality in Mediation,* 16 L. & Soc. Inquiry 35, 60 (1991) (contending that mediation is essentially 'a highly political process' in which mediators and the process contribute to the oppression of one party's story); Martha A. Fineman, The Illusion of Equality: The Rhetoric and Reality of Divorce Reform 144-46 (1991) (asserting that the bias of divorce mediation toward shared custody harms women); John O. Calmore, *Close Encounters of the Racial Kind: Pedagogical Reflections and Seminar Conversations,* 31 U.S.F.L. Rev. 903 (1997). But see Mary A. Duryee, *Mandatory Mediation: Myth and Reality,* 30 Fam. & Conciliation Cts. Rev. 507, 509-10 (1992) (suggesting that Grillo's critique is inconsistent with empirical evidence); Joshua Rosenberg, In *Defense of Mediation,* 33 Ariz. L. Rev. 467, 467-68 (1991)

(arguing that Grillo has exaggerated the potential dangers of mediation and that mandatory mediation is generally helpful both to women and men).

[169] See Simeone, supra note 96, holding that premarital agreements must not be unconscionable at the time that they are signed.

[170] Spouses may also form binding contracts, and our procedure could easily address post-nuptial as well as ante-nuptial pacts, but the substantive standard for review may be different. See L. A. Bradshaw, Annotation, *Waiver of Right to Widow's Allowance by Postnuptial Agreement,* 9 A.L.R.3d 955 (2001). See also use of declaratory judgment process to address validity of postnuptial pacts in note 47, supra.

Each jurisdiction also needs to address the availability of these procedures for unmarried couples. Such procedures would be attractive to couples who cannot marry since they provide a measure of legal recognition for their relationships. Existing law, however, now makes it relatively easy to enforce financial contracts between unmarried couples. See, e.g., *Marvin v. Marvin,* 557 P.2d 106 (Cal. 1976). Conversely, the courts may find it harder to review the enforceability of an ordinary contract (as opposed to a premarital agreement) even in jurisdictions with relatively few limits on declaratory judgments, and legislatures may be less likely to approve new procedures expressly designed to aid unmarried couples. For a survey of the enforceability of such agreements, see Katherine C. Gordon, Note, The *Necessity and Enforcement of Cohabitation Agreements: When Strings Will Attach and How to Prevent Them: A State Survey,* 37 Brandeis L.J. 245 (1998/1999).

[171] *Uniform Premarital Agreement Act § 3(b)*, 9B U.L.A. 369 (1987).

[172] Silbaugh, supra note 62, at 121B26. For example, we would favor addressing whether the agreement adequately recognizes domestic contributions particularly over a long term marriage or in the presence of small children, changes in earnings and the allocation of responsibility over the course of the marriage, voluntary and involuntary unemployment, and other events that affect the substantive fairness of an agreement.

[173] See supra notes 70 and 143.

[174] Silbaugh, supra note 62, at 67.

[175] *La. Rev. Stat. Ann. § 9:272(A)* (West 2000). For a detailed discussion of the qualifications of the counselor and the content of the counseling, see Spaht, supra note 95, Social Analysis and Legal Implications, at 84B90. See also Katherine Shaw Spaht, *What's Become of Louisiana Covenant Marriage Through the Eyes of Social Scientists,* 47 Loy. L. Rev. 709 (2001) (finding that state clerks do not necessarily make mandated information available).

[176] Martha Ertman, *Commercializing Marriage: A Proposal for Valuing Women's Work Through Premarital Security Agreements,* 77 Tex. L. Rev. 17 (1998) (using security agreements to protect women's domestic contributions).

[177] See, e.g., William A. Galston, Liberal Purposes: Goods, Virtues, and Diversity in the Liberal State 284 (1991) (arguing that liberalism requires the nurturance of liberal values, including the family settings that best inculcate liberal virtues).

[178] Indeed, only a new legally authorized process could permit substantial family law innovation such as consideration of fault or provision for third parties such as children. See supra notes 95 and 128.

[179] Although we acknowledge that the greater the safeguards, the less the likelihood of use. See supra note 73.

[180] These procedures could dovetail with Stake's call for mandatory premarital agreements. See supra notes 70 and 143. All parties seeking a marriage license could be required to complete a joint form, specifying the terms of their relationship. The licensing office could provide them with a pamphlet explaining their rights under existing law, and the most popular alternatives. The parties could then choose the combination of rights and responsibilities that best fits them. See supra Spaht, Social Scientists, note 95 (describing covenant marriage in similar terms). Such a process might appeal to a variety of would-be marriage reformers. Feminists who argue that women are shortchanged by existing

law would have the opportunity to encourage better bargain. See, e.g., Weitzman, supra note 27. The conventional wisdom has long held that women's bargaining power is greatest at the beginning of a relationship, see Cohen, supra note 125, at 285-87, and polls show that newlyweds believe that the law provides greater protection for women than it actually does. See Baker, supra note 138. If couples were told what the law actually provides and given an opportunity to provide greater protections for the dependent party at the beginning of a marriage, they might elect to do so. See Ertman, supra note 176. Those who favor a return to more traditional family values could also use this as an opportunity to encourage couples to embrace a more conventional set of provisions in their premarital agreements. Covenant marriage, after all, which combines counseling with an opportunity to reintroduce fault-based considerations into marital dissolutions, is an effort to use private bargaining to remake public values. See Scott, supra note 95, on precommitment strategies, and other sources in note 95 generally. A full exploration of the substance of these proposals is beyond the scope of this article. Nonetheless, we wish to emphasize that private bargaining can take a range of forms, with or without public supervision, and that the purpose of this discussion is to demonstrate how the innovative use of family law procedures can contribute to the process. See also Stark, supra note 165.

[181] See generally Carbone, supra note 76 (arguing that the law has shifted from the relationship between intimate partners to the relationship between parents and children as the primary focus of family obligation).

[182] Carbone, id. at 49, noting, for example, that one third of American births are pre-marital, one of two marriages end in divorce, and 60% of American children will spend some of their childhood in a single parent family.

[183] We are using the term "parenthood" here rather than "paternity" as the more gender neutral term.

[184] The most fundamental change has come with in vitro fertilization, i.e., the fertilization of an egg by a sperm outside the body, and the possibility that a woman giving birth is not the child's mother. The Uniform Status of Assisted Reproduction Act, 9B U.L.A. 155 (Supp. 1994) defines "donor" to mean Aan individual who produces egg or sperm for assisted conception" in circumstances where the donor intends to sever any legal relationship as the child's parent. "Surrogacy" can refer to "traditional" or "simple" surrogacy in which a woman is artificially inseminated, with the sperm of a man to whom she is not married, with the intention that she will sever her parental rights at birth. See note 248, infra. "Gestational" surrogacy, on the other, refers to a woman's decision to carry a child to term to whom she is not genetically related, with the intention that she will sever her rights at birth. See note 248, infra.

[185] See *Johnson v. Calvert,* 851 P.2d 776 (Cal. 1993), cert. denied, *510 U.S. 874 (1993).*

[186] See note 184, supra, on the importance of in vitro fertilization.

[187] See *Michael H. v. Gerald D.,* 491 U.S. 110, reh'g denied, *492 U.S. 937 (1989).*

[188] See David L. Chambers, *Rethinking the Substantive Rules for Custody Disputes in Divorce,* 83 Mich. L. Rev. 477 (1984) (summarizing the implications of the child development literature, and emphasizing the importance of attachment for children); Eleanor Willemsen and Kristen Marcel, *Attachment 101 for Attorneys: Implications for Infant Placement Decisions,* 36 Santa Clara L. Rev. 439, 468-69 (1996) (discussing importance of at least one secure caregiver, and possibility of multiple attachments).

[189] For a summary of these developments, see Carbone, supra note 76, at 164B79.

[190] See June Carbone, The *Missing Piece of the Custody Puzzle:Creating a New Model of Premarital Partnership,* 39 Santa Clara L. Rev. 1091 (1999).

[191] See, e.g., *Buzzanca v. Buzzanca,* 72 Cal. Rptr. 2d 280 (1998). For an effort at reconciling the definitions of motherhood, see Jonathan B. Pitt, Note, *Fragmenting Procreation,*108 Yale L.J. 1893 (1999).

[231]   See Trossman, supra note 46.

[232]   See Weisberg & Appleton, supra note 5, 512-15. In order to remain eligible for federal welfare benefits, all states must provide for civil paternity actions, and voluntary paternity declarations. Id. at 515. See also W. Craig Williams, Note: *The Paradox of Paternity Establishment: As Rights Go Up, Rates Go Down,* 8 U. Fla. J. Law. & Pub. Pol'y 261, 264 (1997) (70% of paternity proceedings are brought by the state to secure child support payments).

[233]   See, e.g., *Johnson v. Calvert,* supra note 185, *Smith v. Brown,* supra note 57, *Baby Doe v. John and Mary Doe,* supra note 57 (California, Massachusetts and Virginia actions all filed before child's birth). The newly proposed Uniform Parentage Act 93 U.L.A. 299 (2000) would explicitly permit a proceeding to determine parentage to "be commenced before the birth of the child, but may not be concluded until after the birth of the child." Section 611. It would authorize the following actions may be taken before birth: (1) service of process; (2) discovery; and (3) except as prohibited by Section 502, collection of specimens for genetic testing. The official comments recognize that "establishing a parental relationship as quickly as possible may be in the best interest of a child." While the comments do not explain why the parentage declaration cannot be issued pre-birth, the section appears to contemplate a paternity proceeding in which blood or genetic testing that can only be secured post-birth may be the most important factor in the determination. See, e.g., the comment to section 601 that refer to proceedings to establish "paternity."

[234]   See, e.g., *In re Adoption of A.N.S.,* 741 N.E.2d 780 (Ind. App. 2001) (acknowledging statutory requirement that putative father file paternity action within thirty days of notice that mother intended to place unborn child for adoption, but holding that paternity ruling was not properly appealed); *S.B. v. D.H.,* 736 So. 2d 766 (Fla. Dist. Ct. App. 1999) (the initial 'legal father' of any child of a married woman must be the husband unless a paternity action is resolved prior to the child's birth).

[235]   For a comparison of blood testing with the more recently available DNA tests, see *Comment: Who is my Daddy? Using DNA To Help Resolve Post-Death Paternity Cases,* 8 Alb. L.J. Sci. & Tech. 151 (1997).

[236]   Danny R. Veilleux, J.D., Annotation: *Necessity or Propriety of Appointment of Independent Guardian For Child Who is Subject of Paternity Proceedings,* 70 A.L.R.4th 1033 (West 2001). The annotation observes that A [s]tipulations regarding paternity, even those accepted by a child's guardian ad litem, may be disapproved if not substantiated by sufficient evidence. Thus, it has been held that a child's guardian ad litem and her attorneys were without power to enter into, and the court was without power to approve, a stipulation which rested the determination of an unborn child's paternity solely upon the unverified report of two physicians. See, e.g., *Berry v Chaplin,* 169 P.2d 442 (Cal. Dist. Ct. App. 1946). But see *Cal. Fam. Code § 7632* (West 2000), which expressly provides that consent between an alleged father and the mother of the children does not bar a paternity action under California law.

[237]   On parental authority generally, see Weisberg & Appleton, supra note 5, at 951-62, 998-1007.

[238]   See supra note 47.

[239]   10 P.3d 1086 (Wash. Ct. App. 2000).

[240]   *Id.* at 1089. The order does not appear to be reported. The case commenting on the order's existence involved a later dispute between the parents over the fate of the remaining frozen pre-embryos.

[241]   The surrogate's husband, if she is married, might be presumed to the husband of the child. However, under California law, the presumption is rebuttable by blood tests taken within two year of the child's birth. Cal. Family Code 7541(b) (1994).

[242]   The uncertainty proceeded in part from the fact that this case is not exactly like the existing precedents. Unlike *Buzzanca,* supra note 215, the father in this case bore a genetic relationship to the child, and therefore it could not be said that the child had no legal parents. Nonetheless, unlike Moschetta, supra note 210, where the court recognized the surrogate mother and the intended father/sperm donor as parents, the egg donor and the gestational mother had both severed their maternal rights. The pre-birth

declaration could be reconciled with the earlier cases, but it was sufficiently distinct to present a case of first impression.

243 See *In Re McAllister & Subak*, No. FL032006 (Cal. Super., San Fran. Co., May 24, 1999) (unpublished opinion), discussed in California Superior Court Grants Legal Parent Status to Lesbian Couple Prior to Child's Birth, Lesbian/Gay Law Notes (LeGaL Found. of the Lesbian & Gay Law Ass'n of Greater N.Y.), Summer 1999, at 110. See also Audra Elizabeth Laabs, *Lesbian Art*, 19 Law & Ineq. J. 65, 73, n.61 (2001) (discussing McAllister).

244 Order on file with author.

245 Copies of the documents from this unreported case are on file with the author.

246 See supra notes 199-209, and accompanying text.

247 *Southfox v. Southfox*, Findings of Fact and Conclusions of Law, Case No. D453867 Superior Court of the State of California for the County of San Diego, Family Division (Alan B. Clements, J.) (January 19, 2000).

248 Buzzanca, supra note 215, *Johnson v. Calvert*, supra note 199. See also *People v. Sorenson*, 68 Cal. 2d 280 (1968) (finding that husband who consents to his wife's insemination with another man's sperm is father of child).

249 Southfox, supra note 247, at 4.

250 See, e.g., Michael H., supra note 187; Carbone, supra note 190. In addition, step-parents, even if they are not recognized as parents, find it easier to adopt or to compel visitation than unmarried non-parents. See, e.g., *Colo. Rev. Stat. § 19-4-107(1)(e)(11) (1978)*; *La. Rev. Stat. Ann. § 9:422.1 (West Supp. 1984)*; *Mich. Comp. Laws Ann. § 710.51(6) (West Supp. 1984-85)* (all making it easier for step-parents to adopt). See also Harris, Teitelbaum & Weisbrod, Family Law 1155 (1996) (most courts find a way to permit visitation in step-parent cases).

251 See generally Laabs, supra note 243 (summarizing disadvantages lesbians face when using assisted reproduction). California has recently passed legislation, however, allowing unmarried domestic partners to adopt on the same terms as step-parents.

252 See, e.g., *Kathleen C. v. Lisa W.*, 84 Cal. Rptr. 2d 48, 51 (Ct. App. 1999) (former partner did not have standing to sue for custody or visitation under the UPA because she could not show that the natural mother was unfit); *Nancy S. v. Michele G.*, 279 Cal. Rptr. 212, 216-17 (Ct. App. 1991) (holding that because partner was not the natural mother, had not adopted the children, and was not legally married to her former partner, she could not establish a legally cognizable parent-child relationship); *Kazmierazak v. Query*, 736 So. 2d 106, 108-10 (Fla. Dist. Ct. App. 1999) (non-UPA state holding that it is necessary to show that custody with biological parent would be detrimental to the child in order to grant custody to non-biological parent); *Alison D. v. Virginia M.*, 572 N.E.2d 27, 29 (N.Y. 1991) (non-UPA court holding that the word 'parent' in the statute granting standing to sue for visitation foreclosed any claim by biological mother's former partner).

253 See *Fla. Stat. Ann. § 63.042(3)* (West 1997), ('No person eligible to adopt under this statute may adopt if that person is a homosexual. '). See also *Conn. Gen. Stat. Ann. § 45a-726a* (West 2000) (authorizing adoption agencies to discriminate against homosexuals when placing children in adoptive or foster homes); H.R.J. Res. 35, 1998 Alabama Laws Act 98-439 (H.R.J. 35) (issuing a joint resolution stating the state legislature's intent to prohibit adoption by homosexuals). See, in particular, *Lofton v. Kearney*, 157 F. Supp.2d 1372 (S.D. Fl. 2001) (upholding constitutionality of Florida statute as rationally related to legitimate state interest).

254 Maxwell S. Peltz, *Second-Parent Adoption: Overcoming Barriers to Lesbian Family Rights*, 3 Mich. J. Gender & Law 175, n.9 (1995) (no state statute explicitly permits second parent adoption). For cases ruling against such adoptions, primarily on the ground that the birth mother or father's rights must first be terminated, see *In re Adoption of T.K.J. and K.A.K.*, 931 P.2d 488 (Colo.Ct. App. 1996); *In re Adoption of Baby Z*, 724 A.2d 1035, (Conn. 1999); *In re Angel Lace M.*, 516 N.W.2d 678 (Wis. 1994). For a full account, see Nancy G. Maxwell, Astrid A.M. Mattijssen, and Charlene Smith, *Legal*

*Protection for All the Children: Dutch-United States Comparison of Lesbian and Gay Parent Adoptions,* 17 Ariz. J. Int'l & Comp. Law 309 (2000); . Devjani Mishra, The *Road to Concord: Resolving the Conflict of Law over Adoption by Gays and Lesbians,* 30 Colum. J.L. & Soc. Probs. 91, 92-93 (1996) (describing exercise of discretion by social service agencies to block gay and lesbian adoptions).

255 But see *Litowitz v. Litowitz,* 48 P.3d 261, 265 (Wash. 2002) (alleging that Mrs. Litowitz was engaged in drug use, and had tried to hire a third party to kill her husband). See also Marsha Garrison, *Law Making for Baby Making: An Interpretative Approach to the Determination of Legal Parenthood,* 113 Harv. L. Rev. 835, 918 (2000) (in most states step-child adoption is subject to different rules than unrelated-child adoptions.)

256 See generally id.

257 Id. at 920.

258 Id. at 903.

259 See generally id. Garrison does not fully address the argument, however, that the contexts are different. Artificial insemination necessarily involves intentional parenthood, and an express relinquishment of the sperm donor's rights. Most "natural," unmarried conceptions do not. See Akeloff, Yellin & Katz, *An Analysis of Out-of-Wedlock Childrearing in the United States,* 111 Q. J. Economics 277 (1996).

260 Adversity may nonetheless exist. First, a hospital or state official may refuse to recognize parentage. Second, a guardian ad litem may be appointed to represent the child. Third, as with other legal actions, the failure of the parties to disagree may not necessarily in itself defeat adversity. See supra note 57. Finally, many states do not insist on a strict separation of powers approach. California, for example, expressly provides that consent between an alleged father and the mother of the children does not bar a paternity action under California law. *Cal. Fam. Code § 7632* (West 2000). See also supra note 236 and accompanying text.

261 The issue in these cases is whether the child's interests lie more with decision-making entrusted to a single caretaker, or continuing contact with the two parties with whom the child bonded early in life. In the cases of lesbian partners who brought the child into the world with the understanding that they would both act as parents, the legal status of the relationship is unlikely to affect the parents' parenting arrangement, and the strength of the bond between the child and the second parent. So the real issue is likely to rest on the importance of continued contact with the second parent when the relationship dissolves versus the security of the custodial parent in making decisions on the child's behalf.

In the heterosexual context, the issue has been resolved in favor of continuing contact between both parents. See supra Carbone, note 190. Part of the reason, however, has been the importance of the father's financial contribution to the child's well-being. An earlier generation of family law scholars, however, embraced the security of the custodial parent as more central to children's well-being. See J. Goldstein, A. Solnit & A. Freud, Beyond the Best Interests of the Child (1973). See also Martha Fineman, The Neutered Mother, the Sexual Family, and other Twentieth Century Tragedies (1995).

262 By "equal standing," we mean equal standing to make a showing that the best interest of the child lies with the non-biological parent receiving custody. In contrast, step-parents who have not formally adopted the child have more limited rights vis-a-vis the biological parent. See, e.g., *Cal. Fam. Code § 3040 (1994),* creating a custody presumption in favor of both parents jointly or either parent, in accordance with §§ 3011 and 3020 (favoring continuing contact with both parents). See also § 3102, permitting stepparent visitation.

263 See authorities cited in note 252, supra. But see notes 222 and 228, supra, noting authorities from other states adopting a more liberal approach.

264 See supra Carbone, note 76, at 133B43.

265 Id. at 136.

266 Garrison, supra note 255, at 907.

[267] For a discussion of the literature on this point in the context of the Hawaii same-sex marriage litigation, see Carbone, supra note 76, at 111-19. See also Carlos A. Ball & Janice Farrell Pea, *Warring With Wardle: Morality, Social Science, and Gay and Lesbian Parents,* 1998 U. Ill. L. Rev. 253 (1998); Policy Statements, Coparent or Second Parent Adoption by Same-Sex Parents, 339-40 (Feb. 2002) American Academy of Pediatrics available at http:// www.aap.org/policy/020008.html, last visited 11/13/02.

[268] Carl E. Schneider, The *Channelling Function in Family Law,* 20 Hofstra L. Rev. 495 (1992).

[269] The recently adopted Vermont Civil Unions Law (2001) is an exception. 18 Verm. Stat. Anna. § 1201, et seq. See supra notes 253 and 254.

[270] Indeed, a number of states impose strict time limits on parenthood determinations. See, e.g., authorities cited in note 234, supra.

[271] See supra note 5.

[272] To the extent that counseling exists under current procedures, it is provided by the parties' counsel. The primary issue, however, tends to be the fight to win recognition of same sex relationships rather than the pros and cons of shared parenthood. In the heterosexual context, the importance of two parents and the legal relationships that result from marriage tend to be a given. Recognition of lesbian parenthood tends to involve ideological issue about whether the relationships be accorded the same legal status making individualized counseling difficult and complex.

[273] Section 201(a) defines mothers as those who give birth, or are determined to be mothers through a legal proceeding or through Section 8. Section 8 contemplates an adoption like hearing in those cases where egg donors, who do not themselves give birth, wish to be recognized as the child's legal parents.

[274] See Uniform Parentage Act § 8 (2000). Whether the act will in fact be interpreted to hold that intended mothers who contribute an egg to a gestational surrogate are strangers to the child absent an adoption like proceeding remains to be seen, however. The new act clearly provides that a father who provides sperm and does not otherwise relinquish parental rights is ordinarily the father, and that the act is to be interpreted in gender neutral ways. It nevertheless treats relies on the unique experience of pregnancy to distinguish mother and fathers participating in assisted reproduction.

[275] In practice, whether the outcomes will be so predictable is less certain. Section 8 of the Act, which addresses gestational agreements, is meant to be independent of the rest of the act so that states that find the subject too hot to handle can simply delete that portion of the Act.

[276] Garrison, supra note 255, at 913B14. See *Soos v. Superior Court,* 897 P.2d 1356, 1360 (Ariz. Ct. App. 1994) (holding that the Equal Protection Clause requires genetic determination of maternity in a case of gestational surrogacy).

[277] Garrison, supra note 255, at 917-20.

[278] Id. at 919-20.

[279] Id. at 913-14.

[280] Moreover, most jurisdictions authorize paternity actions, so no new law will be necessary absent a strict interpretation of separation of powers doctrine. In that case, authorization of an administrative proceeding may be necessary. See supra notes 69 to 75, and accompanying text.

[281] Parentage declarations, like adoptions, should be res judicata on the determination of parenthood. Even if the underlying statute is later repealed or declared invalid, if the time for appeal has expired in a particular case, the ruling in the individual case should still be res judicata for those parties. See *E.I.B. v. J.R.B.,* N.J. Super. 99, 611 A.2d 662 (1992) (action brought under later-repealed New Jersey statute, which had not allowed children to institute paternity actions, was res judicata in action brought by child subsequent to new statute's adoption since the matter had been fully litigated by child's grandparent). Entry of a paternity judgment in a non-adversarial proceeding by a settlement does not change the res judicata effect. See Moore v. Moore, No. C-910846 (Ohio App. LEXIS 6576) (1st Dist. Ct.) (stressing the importance of leaving paternity determinations undisturbed). See also *Federated Department Stores, Inc. v. Moitie,* 452 U.S. 394 (1981) (unappealed decision by one party is res judicata where other parties

successfully appealed and had anti-trust statute later held to be applicable to similarly situated plaintiffs). Only if there is fraud (e.g., misrepresentations about biological parenthood) might the judgment be subject to challenge. Id. at 402.

[282] This raises the further question of whether the failure to seek a parenthood determination at the child's birth precludes later recognition. Since the states differ in their approach to the substantive grounds for legal parenthood, with some recognizing parenthood by estoppel, a uniform approach to this issue is unlikely. Nonetheless, given the importance of parenthood, it would be appropriate to require that parties seeking recognition of parenthood on the basis of something other than biological connection, marriage or adoption, secure a judgment establishing their parental status within a short period after the child's birth. Statutes providing very short time periods for declarations of paternity have passed constitutional muster in similar circumstances. See, e.g., procedures referred to in note 281, supra. But see *Clark v. Jeter,* 486 U.S. 456 (1988) (invalidating six year statute of limitation, where it precluded child from securing recognition as father's heir). See Harris, Teitelbrod & Weisbrod, supra note 250, at 1123, observing that the right involved in Jeter was the child's, not the parents.Cal. Fam. Codes" 9000-9005 have recently been amended to extend stepparent adoption procedures to the registered domestic partners. This raises the policy question of whether domestic partners should be required to go through the adoption process, which does not require a homestudy for stepparents, or whether those involved in arranging for the child's conception and birth should be recognized as parents without an adoption proceeding. Either way, we believe that use of the judicial process to confirm the result is appropriate, and that in appropriate cases, the action should be available before the child's birth.

# [27]

# Parental Conflict Prevention Programs and the Unified Family Court: A Public Health Perspective

Andrew Schepard

## I. The Challenge Facing Family Courts

Twenty-first century family courts need better ways to help divorcing and separating parents minimize the impact of conflict on their children. Social attitudes towards marriage, divorce, and separation have changed radically in the last half-century. What were once comparatively rare, fault-based events discouraged by convention are today predictable stages in the lifecycle of an American child. Family court caseloads arising from divorce and separation spiral ever upward with no stopping point in sight. Evidence continues to accumulate that a child's future welfare depends on her parents' ability to help her navigate the experience without lasting scars caused by parental bickering and instability.

Traditionally, family courts take the view that their responsibility is to decide specific disputes between parents after an adversary hearing. Evidence continues to accumulate, however, that this traditional adversarial approach to divorce and separation drives parents further apart, rather than encouraging them to work together for the benefit of their child. Overall, adversary procedure usually does children more harm than good.

The family court must reinvent its role to serve children of divorce and separation. In addition to thinking about divorcing and separating families as presenting cases to be decided, courts should think of them as having symptoms of a disease made worse by continuing parental conflict. The progression of the disease can be prevented and its effects mitigated through measures familiar to the public health community-preventive education programs carefully structured to match the level of family conflict.

The thesis of this article is that every unified family court should develop a prevention plan to help parents reduce conflict arising out of divorce and separation. A coherent prevention strategy should become a fundamental criteria for distinguishing high-quality family courts from those that do not serve their publics as well. Models of useful programs already exist and can be incorporated into a court's prevention plan. Judges, legislators, lawyers, mental health professionals, and child advocates should insist that they are.

Section Two of this article describes the problems facing courts, parents, and children resulting from divorce and separation in terms of a public health rather than a caseload model. Then, this article details the epidemic-like crisis facing family courts because of increased caseloads and troubled parents and children. The fourth section describes already existing preventive education programs that family courts can draw on and briefly summarizes the available research on their effectiveness. The fifth section describes the comprehensive prevention approach designed by Oregon's interdisciplinary Task Force on Family Law. Finally, this article discusses how a unified family court can incorporate a prevention strategy into its mission.

## II. A Public Health Parable

Imagine that you are the Commissioner of Public Health of your state. Over the last decade, the mental health clinics of your major hospitals have reported a huge increase in the number of parents and children who exhibit a constellation of symptoms of emotional distress. These patients account for about 25 percent of your total patient population and the total number of patients in this population has increased 70 percent since 1984.

These parents and children present symptoms that share common themes of emotional distress and decreased capacity to function effectively. A majority of the parents experience mood swings and anger easily. Some exhibit paranoid tendencies and feel abandoned by former friends and neighbors. Sometimes, the parents are violent toward each other, violence witnessed by their frightened children. Many of the parents are depressed and abuse drugs or alcohol. Some parents are unable to provide their children with consistent nurturing, support, and guidance. Many parents are not able to perform as effectively at work as they did before the symptoms began.

Many of the children are also depressed, frightened or anxious. Some constantly worry about their parents. Some are unable to function at school. Some, particularly the older ones, engage in high risk behavior like premature sexual activity, or drug and alcohol abuse. In some cases, their academic achievement takes a precipitous drop.

In many instances, the parents battle endlessly about finances for the children. Because of the parents' problems, there is less money around to finance the children's regular activities which raises the children's stress and anxiety levels.

While all of the patients who present themselves at the hospitals have some degree of emotional upset, the majority of adults and children seem to recover their equilibrium over a period of time and function relatively normally, albeit with painful memories. About one-fourth to one-third of the adults, however, need intensive intervention and supervision over a lengthy period of time to achieve the level of personal competence that they exhibited before the onset of their symptoms. Moreover, about 10 percent to 15 percent of the total parent and child population never recover. The parents in this category still take their anger out on each other and their children. They continually express verbal or physical aggression towards the other parent. Their children never recover a sense of optimism about life and its possibilities, engage in high risk behavior, and are at significantly higher risk of psychosocial problems than others in their age group.

The parents and children with these symptoms are overwhelming your mental health facilities. The treatments that are available at the hospital for them are very labor intensive, cost thousands of dollars, and require extensive commitments of time and energy from doctors and patients alike. In a significant number of cases, the treatment is likely to take several years with no guarantee of success. Indeed, in some cases, treatment seems to make symptoms worse, not better.

The delivery system for the necessary mental health services is tenuously financed and there are increasing signs that the patients who come into contact with it are very dissatisfied with its performance. There are simply not enough personnel to cope with the patient increase. There is no realistic prospect that your anti-tax increase legislature and governor will provide the necessary funding for the personnel necessary to cope with the avalanche of patients.

*    *    *    *

## IV. Public Health Theory and Family Conflict Prevention Programs

Overall, the situation facing courts overseeing disputes arising out of separation and divorce is roughly like the public health crisis facing the Commissioner of Public Health with which we began:

- Parents and children suffer serious emotional distress because of conflict resulting from family reorganization;
- Many of those affected recover, but a significant portion do not and they require a dispro-portionate share of scarce judicial resources for the care and management of their chronic litigation;
- An increasing number of parents handle their and their children's problems arising out of divorce and separation without legal advice because of lack of funds or lack of belief legal advice will help them;
- There are too many cases for the judicial system to handle;
- There is no realistic prospect that the necessary resources will be made available to the judicial system to cope with the projected caseload increase; and
- Parental conflict management through the adversarial process is likely to take a long time, and increase conflict rather than reduce it, to the children's detriment.

Analogizing family conflict resulting from divorce and separation to a disease allows prevention of family conflict to be discussed in terms of a "public health" concept. The medical community has adapted this concept as a measure of its effectiveness in coping with disease. A standard textbook defines public health as "the organization and application of public resources to prevent dependency which would otherwise result from disease or injury"[26] and states that " prevention is the purpose of public health."[27]

Public education is a primary public health prevention tool. Over the years, the medical community has increasingly incorporated preventive education programs into its strategies for reducing the spread of such diseases as skin cancer, heart disease, drug abuse, low birth weight, rubella, and infectious diseases with positive results.[28] For example, pre-natal care for mothers reduces low-birth weight babies, which in turn reduces infant mortality and developmental disabilities. Expectant mothers who receive comprehensive preventive education which emphasizes specific behaviors that reduce the risk of low birth weight babies (e.g., reducing or eliminating alcohol and tobacco use and eating appropriately) are less likely to deliver low-birth weight babies than those who do not.[29] Education which combines information with essential emotional and social skills also shows promise in helping prevent the incidence of teen pregnancy and suicide.[30] Because of their usefulness in promoting well-being and efficient use of medical resources, the organized medical community generally advocates strongly for the expansion of preventive public health programs.

*A. Primary, Secondary, and Tertiary Prevention Programs*

Public health theory postulates that education can take place at "any point along the spectrum from the prevention of disease or injury to the prevention of impairment, disability or dependency."[31] It distinguishes between different types of prevention, depending on the stage of a disease which a patient is experiencing.

Primary prevention programs seek to prevent the disease or injury itself (e.g., school education programs that seek to reduce smoking or immunization programs). Secondary prevention efforts seek to block the progression of an injury or disease from an impairment to a disability (e.g., early detection of high blood pressure can reduce the probability of a heart attack or stroke through changes in diet and exercise patterns). Tertiary prevention blocks or retards the progression of a disability to a state of dependency (e.g., prompt medical care and rehabilitation can limit the damage that a stroke or heart attack does to a patient).

Preventive education programs for family conflict management can be classified along similar lines if the filing of an action in court by one of the parents is analogized to a symptom of a disease-parental conflict which cannot be resolved without court intervention. This analogy is not, of course, perfect and must be made with great caution. Parents file actions in court for many reasons. Some are not in conflict at all, having reached an agreement between themselves. Nonconflicted parents file an action in court largely for ministerial purposes, such as securing an uncontested divorce decree. Other parents, such as victims of domestic violence, file a complaint in court because they need protection from violence that only the legal system can provide.[32] Nonetheless, many parents file an action with the court because they are unable to resolve their conflict about their children themselves and need court intervention. The filing of the action is the first time the court becomes aware of the parents' dispute and is thus a logical point around which to focus classification of family court involvement in prevention programs for parental conflict.

Primary prevention programs operate before filing and seek to reduce conflict by educating children or parents in conflict management techniques and emotional literacy. These programs may be organized by schools or community agencies with active support from the courts.

Secondary prevention programs are, in contrast, organized under the auspices of the court system. Parents and children participate in them after filing, but before perpetual relitigation (the chronic and dependent stage of family conflict) sets in. Most of the growth of prevention programs in family courts around the country, to date, has been secondary prevention in the form of court-affiliated education programs for parents and children.[33]

Tertiary prevention programs aim to reduce the dependency of chronic relitigants on the adversarial process to manage their family life. Some court-affiliated prevention programs have been designed to focus specifically on this population which, while comparatively small in numbers, takes up a disproportionate share of judicial resources.

### B. Program Descriptions and Evaluations

This section provides examples of primary, secondary, and tertiary programs designed to reduce or eliminate parental conflict arising from separation and divorce. The programs chosen are among those that the author is familiar with from personal knowledge.[34] Many others share similar aims. The descriptions are brief. They summarize the program's philosophy, structure, and important administrative elements. Footnote references for each program identify where to obtain more information about it.

Following the program descriptions, this section summarizes what is known about the effectiveness of primary, secondary, and tertiary prevention programs. Readers should be aware, however, that research on the efficacy of prevention programs aimed at reducing conflict around family reorganization is in its infancy. There is no single study which summarizes all available data or compares and contrasts different kinds of programs or different stages of intervention. Evaluating intervention programs presents substantial methodological challenges.[35] Nonetheless, there are promising suggestions in existing research, briefly summarized here, that prevention programs can make a difference in reducing family conflict.

### C. Primary Prevention: Preparation for Marriage

Parents who are motivated to and skilled in resolving disputes with each other are less likely to need court intervention. School-based primary prevention programs aim at instilling those motivations and skills before young people get married. These programs aim at preventing: (1) weak marital commitments by helping future parents understand their obligations to each other, and (2) poor communication and conflict resolution skills between marital partners.

## 1. PARTNERS

An example of a primary prevention program is PARTNERS, an interdisciplinary educational program on family law and communication skills for high school students created by the Family Law Section of the American Bar Association.[36] PARTNERS offers teenagers information about the legal obligations created by marriage and parenthood. It also teaches communication and conflict management skills that can keep marriages together. The PARTNERS curriculum has been enthusiastically received in numerous high schools throughout the United States.

The model curriculum lasts ten weeks, divided into five units. Each PARTNERS unit consists of a fifty-minute videotape-based lesson combined with classroom activities and one activity-based classroom hour the following week. The PARTNERS videotape dramatizes a young married couple with a baby going through typical marital difficulties. A family lawyer presents basic family law concepts; a communications expert from the PAIRS FOUNDATION (an organization devoted to helping develop positive communication methods between couples) analyzes and seeks to improve their communications.[37]

## 2. EVALUATION OF PRIMARY PREVENTION

A significant amount of evaluation research has focused on primary prevention programs in school systems. Daniel Goldman, in his landmark book *Emotional Intelligence*,[38] concludes that the available data suggests that primary prevention programs for children are a valuable long-term investment in the capacity of children to control and manage conflict of all kinds. He reports on comprehensive research over a five-year period designed to identify the characteristics of effective prevention programs for children and youth.[39] The researchers distilled the active ingredients of successful programs and the key skills that should be covered no matter what specific problem the prevention program is designed to prevent:

The emotional skills include self-awareness; identifying, expressing and managing feelings, impulse control and delayed gratification and handling stress and anxiety. A key ability in impulse control is knowing the difference between feelings and actions, and learning to make better emotional decisions by first controlling the impulse to act, then identifying alternative actions and their consequences before acting. Many competencies are interpersonal: reading social and emotional cues, listening, being able to resist negative influences, taking others perspectives, and understanding what behavior is acceptable in a situation.[40]

Goldman then goes on to describe a number of school programs that teach children these skills. Their evaluation provides grounds for cautious optimism that primary prevention can improve students' future emotional competencies:

> The data suggest that although such courses do not change anyone overnight, as children advance through the curriculum from grade to grade, there are discernable improvements in the tone of a school and the outlook-and level of emotional competence-of the boys and girls who take them.

[T]he courses seem to help children better fulfill their roles in life, becoming better friends, students, sons and daughters-and in the future are more likely to be better husbands and wives, workers and bosses, parents and citizens. While not every boy and girl will acquire these skills with equal sureness, to the degree they do we are all the better for it.[41]

## D. Secondary Prevention: After a Case is Filed in Court

### 1. MARICOPA COUNTY (PHOENIX) ARIZONA: INFORMATION RESOURCES FOR PRO SE LITIGANTS

As previously discussed, courts can no longer assume that parents are represented by counsel. The Maricopa County courts have developed a comprehensive program of information for pro se litigants to make their experience in court more "user friendly."[42] Mechanisms used include:

- Court staff facilitators to help pro se litigants;
- Telephone audiotapes explaining court procedures and offering tips on self-representation;
- Automated information kiosks with court forms and schedules; and
- A seminar program called "Litigants Without Lawyers."

### 2. COURT AFFILIATED EDUCATION FOR PARENTS AND CHILDREN

In addition, like many other jurisdictions, Maricopa County requires that parents attend a court-mandated educational program before their divorce.[43] Arizona (along with Connecticut, Utah, and Iowa[44]) mandate that all divorcing and separating parents attend a court-affiliated education program. Legislation in at least eleven other states authorizes courts to implement parent education programs.[45] In many other states, court rules implement parent education programs without legislation.[46] Courts in more than forty states now offer separated and divorcing parents, and in some cases their children, the opportunity to attend educational programs to help them with the difficult life transitions they face when their family reorganizes. Two recent national surveys conducted by the Association of Family and Conciliation Courts (AFCC) and researchers at Western Michigan University combined to identify programs in more than 541 counties, 80 percent of which were created since 1990.[47] The United States Commission on Child and Family Welfare just commended this trend and recommended all states create such programs.[48]

These court-affiliated programs are, in effect, secondary public health prevention programs.[49] They offer parents a valuable commodity-information, perspective, and skills on how to help their children at a time when the parents themselves are in the throes of stress and conflict. Education programs help parents recognize that others have been in similar situations and coped effectively. They also help participants begin to understand the emotional, social and legal complexities of divorce and separation.

Some jurisdictions take secondary preventive education a step further and mandate educational programs for the children of divorcing or separating parents. While some schools offer programs to support children of divorce and separation, many do not. Court programs for children are a promising approach to fill a very important gap in needed services.

There is no typical parent education program. They are presented in a wide variety of formats including lecture, interactive role play, group discussion, demonstration, and video. Presenters include lawyers, judges, psychiatrists, psychologists, educators, and others. Programs vary in length from thirty minutes to twelve hours; the most popular length is four to six hours over two or three sessions. Classes may have as few as ten participants or as many as 150. In some jurisdictions parents do not attend the same session; in others, they are expected to attend together. Most states offer spouses the option of attending separately. Some programs include information on the legal process, while others focus solely on emotional issues for parents and children. The courthouse is the meeting place for some programs, while other programs meet in community centers, universities or houses of worship.

While content varies, the core of most programs is the same. Generally, court-mandated educational programs emphasize that parents should solve problems rather than find fault with each other. AFCC's recent survey found that the most intensively covered topic is the benefits of parental cooperation versus the costs of parental conflict.[50]

Several basic distinctions help to frame the role of these secondary prevention programs. The first is between them and programs of alternative dispute resolution such as mandatory child custody mediation.[51] Both types of programs are aimed at managing family conflict, are created under the auspices or with the cooperation of the court system, and the court system compels participation by family members. The goal of preventive programs, however, is education. Education, in turn, aims at preventing court intervention in the lives of the family by promoting better communication and conflict reduction skills and to promote better parent-child relationships. The aim of mediation programs, in contrast, is to facilitate the resolution of a particular dispute or develop a parenting plan for particular children. The distinction is, in other words, between providing parents with generally applicable information and skills (education) and trying to develop an agreement to resolve their specific dispute through third party intervention (mediation). Education can, and often is, usefully combined with mediation, but the two are conceptually distinct.

Preventive education programs can also be distinguished on the basis of who is providing the educational services. All of the programs described below are court-mandated, meaning that parents are compelled to attend by court order. A court-mandated program, however, can be either court-affiliated or court-based or some combination thereof. A court-affiliated program is organized by private service providers, usually a nonprofit agency. A court-based program, in contrast, is organized by court employees.

a. P.E.A.C.E. (Parent Education and Custody Effectiveness)

P.E.A.C.E. is a court-affiliated educational program for parents with a particularly strong legal content offered in a number of judicial districts throughout New York State.[52] P.E.A.C.E. educates parents about three topics related to divorce and separation: the legal process, typical adult reactions, and, most importantly, the child's experience and how parents can make it better.

Founded by attorneys, P.E.A.C.E. is a joint project of the Hofstra University School of Law and the Hofstra University School of Education's Graduate Programs in Marriage & Family Counseling. P.E.A.C.E. is co-sponsored by the Interdisciplinary Forum on Mental Health and Family Law, an umbrella organization of leading mental health and family law groups in New York. P.E.A.C.E.'s development has been guided by the advice and support of a Statewide Interdisciplinary Advisory Committee. Local programs are organized by volunteer Local Advisory Committees of judges, court administrators, lawyers, and mental health professionals.

Local programs have significant flexibility which results in the P.E.A.C.E. curriculum being presented in a variety of formats. In Nassau County, for example, P.E.A.C.E. is presented in three two-hour sessions over a three-week period. In contrast, Erie County (Buffalo) presents its P.E.A.C.E. program in a five-hour Saturday session.

Most P.E.A.C.E. pilot programs combine large group presentations with small group discussions following a standard curriculum. Some, however, use a small group format throughout.

b. Parents Apart

Parents Apart, in Massachusetts, is a five-hour, court-affiliated program offered at seven sites designed to be taught by mental health professionals with expertise in children's issues related to divorce. It is a collaborative effort between the University of Massachusetts Medical Center Department of Psychiatry and Family Services of Central Massachusetts.[53]

Parents Apart takes a different approach from most parent education programs which emphasize the importance of parental cooperation and teach "cooperative" parenting strategies. Instead, Parents Apart suggests that post-divorce parenting relationships can progress from "parallel" to "cooperative" parenting. In parallel parenting, each parent assumes total responsibility for the children during the time they are in his or her care without expectation of flexibility from the other parent. Like many programs, Parents Apart teaches that the parental relationship must be good for the children and manageable for the adults. While communication, flexibility and respectful behavior are an ideal, Parents Apart points out that high interpersonal conflict may result from efforts to communicate by parents who are simply not ready to cooperate.

Therefore, Parents Apart recommends parallel parenting for those unable to cooperate successfully. While Parents Apart acknowledges that parallel parenting may not be an ideal for children, the program considers it far superior to exposing children to ongoing parental conflict and a useful bridge as parents adjust to separation and divorce.

c. Kid's Turn

Also founded by attorneys, Kid's Turn is a child-oriented court-affiliated educational program for San Francisco Bay Area families in the process of reorganization.[54] It focuses on children ages four to fourteen and is offered at four different sites. Parents are charged a sliding scale fee for participation. The course is taught by professionals with backgrounds in education or psychology.

The focus of Kid's Turn's six, ninety-minute educational workshops spread over a six-week period is to teach the children skills that help them cope with the changes in their family that occur when parents divorce or separate. The workshops incorporate age-appropriate games and activities to help children learn most effectively. Children learn (1) to identify and communicate their feelings about their parents' separation or divorce; (2) ways to talk about these changes with other children and adults at home and at school; (3) some basic concepts about the legal process of divorce and child custody decision-making; and (4) problem-solving methods for dealing with conflict-laden situations that children of divorce frequently encounter.

Kid's Turn also provides information to parents to help them help their children adjust to family reorganization and implement what they learn in the classroom.

d. Families in Transition

Families in Transition (FIT) is a court mandated and affiliated divorce adjustment program in Jefferson County (Louisville), Kentucky.[55] It is one of the few programs to mandate that both parents and children (ages eight to sixteen) attend. FIT is six hours long and is offered in weekly two-hour sessions over a three week period. One parent and the child(ren) attend concurrent but separate sessions while the other parent attends the program at a separate time. A "parents together" program is available if both parents independently select this option.

The FIT curriculum has five major objectives: (1) to increase children's competence by teaching specific skills to identify divorce-related feelings in the self and others; (2) reduce feelings of isolation and misperception about divorce; (3) increase children's awareness of how divorce affects their parents; (4) increase awareness of appropriate ways children respond to anger; and (5) develop parental competence by teaching skills to handle life adjustment issues, children's divorce-related concerns, the parental relationship, and the parent-child relationship. Children's programs are primarily activity-based while parent programs use open discussion, role-play, and small group exercises.

FIT enjoys the strong support of Jefferson County Family Court judges, the Family Law Section of the Louisville Bar Association, and the University of Louisville, all of whom have representatives on the FIT Advisory Board.

## 3. EVALUATION OF SECONDARY PREVENTION

Available research on court-affiliated secondary prevention programs provides grounds for optimism that parents can learn to help their children cope with the difficulties that result from separation and divorce. It tentatively supports several important propositions for courts organizing prevention programs:

- Most parents do not willingly attend prevention programs and will only do so if compelled by the court;
- Most importantly, parents who are compelled to attend report an overwhelmingly positive feeling that they learn important new information, skills, and attitudes that will help their children adjust to divorce and separation;
- Many parents who attend report a greater degree of cooperation with the other parent and greater willingness to accept helping services;

By overwhelming numbers, parents who attend court-affiliated educational programs feel that such programs should be required for all divorcing and separating parents;

- Relitigation and conflict rates for parents who attend court affiliated programs seem to be lower than comparable rates for those who do not; and
- Parents should attend prevention programs as soon as possible after a complaint is filed with the court;
- The judges who refer parents to court mandated educational programs overwhelmingly believe that parents have benefitted from the referral.

Several thousand parents in different areas of New York State, for example, have participated in P.E.A.C.E. since the pilot programs funded by a State Justice Institute grant began in 1993.[56] Those closely monitored pilot programs have resulted in much valuable experience about the reactions of parents to court-affiliated education programs.

Parent evaluations of participation in court-mandated educational programs must be put in the context of mandated participation. Every attempt to organize a purely voluntary P.E.A.C.E. program which parents can choose to attend or not has resulted in negligible attendance. Many parents, apparently, do not recognize their own emotional turmoil and want to blame the problems the family is experiencing solely on the other parent.

Most parents attend P.E.A.C.E. only because they are "strongly encouraged" to do so by individual judges supportive of the program, encouragement parents interpret as an order to attend. After such judicial referrals, parental attendance increases sharply.

Many parents initially resent being "required" to attend P.E.A.C.E. by the court's referral. Nonetheless, on confidential post-program evaluation sheets designed by an independent evaluator:

- Eighty percent of a mostly initially unwilling parent audience felt that the courts should require all divorcing and separating parents to attend P.E.A.C.E. as a condition of getting a divorce, results identical to the reactions of parents compelled to attend parent education programs elsewhere,[57]

- Eighty percent of participating parents said that participation in P.E.A.C.E. increased their knowledge about families, divorce, and separation; and
- Over 95 percent said that they would use what they learned at the program.

More subjective statements on P.E.A.C.E. evaluation forms indicate that divorcing and separating parents deeply appreciate the premise of parent education programs once they are exposed to them-that even though their relationship is ending, they are still responsible parents going through a difficult transition who want to do what is best for their children. Similar statements indicate that participants have a more favorable view of the court system because of the program. Many also seem to be more willing to accept helping services for themselves and their children than they were before participation in P.E.A.C.E.

Evidence from small control group studies of other mandated programs also suggests that they improve the attitudes of parents and the emotional climate for children. Six months after participation in such a program, parents self-reported that they became more aware of their children's needs. They also reported greater tolerance for the parenting role of the other parent.[58] A recent control group evaluation study of two Florida programs concluded: "Parents with greater divorce knowledge experienced better communication, decreased conflict, and decreased violence. Parents who were better skilled in what to say and do exposed their children to less conflict."[59]

Relitigation rates may also be reduced by mandated education programs. A recent study tracked two demographically similar groups of parents for two years following a divorce. One group attended a mandatory court-affiliated divorce education program while the other did not. At the time of the follow-up assessment, the parents who did not attend class returned to court more than twice as often as those who did.[60]

The optimism generated by these tentative findings is reinforced by the general finding of psychological research that anger at moderate levels can be controlled by interventions which challenge the thoughts that trigger the surges of anger. Essentially, court-mandated educational programs provide a parent with information that mitigates anger at the other spouse for the sake of the children. Research suggests that such mitigating information can be very helpful in anger management, although timing is very important to the effectiveness of the intervention. The earlier in the anger cycle that the mitigating information is introduced, the more likely it is to reduce anger provoked actions.[61] Intervention through provision of mitigating information is nowhere near as effective if anger is long-term and the hormones generated by anger come to dominate a person's emotional life. This finding strongly suggests that parents should attend educational programs as soon as possible after a complaint is filed with the court.

The judiciary also recognizes the value of parent education programs. A national provider of curricula for court-affiliated educational services conducted a survey of judges who referred parents to its programs over a six month period and concluded:

Nearly 80% of the judges [who responded] believed that the [parent education] seminar contributes to a quicker resolution of custody arrangements. On the issue of relitigation, 79% of respondents believed the seminar lessened court action regarding the child, while 73% believed it lessened court action generally. In regard to the benefits of the seminar, 96% believe it lessens the negative effects on children and fully 98% believed it benefits the families who participate.[62]

## E. Tertiary Prevention for High Conflict Families and Chronic Litigants

Tertiary prevention programs serve a chronically litigious and conflicted parent population. Because of the nature of the participants, tertiary prevention programs are necessarily more labor intensive than programs for less conflicted parents. The aim of tertiary programs is to teach the parents how to live without litigation through better conflict management skills and to help the children cope until the parents do.

## 1. GROUP MEDIATION MODEL OF FAMILY COURT SERVICES OF ALAMEDA COUNTY

Alameda County California Family Court Services, for example, has designed a court-based program specifically addressed to parents and children endlessly enmeshed in custody and visitation disputes.[63] The goal of the program is to reduce relitigation and continuous conflict by encouraging compliance with court orders and parenting plans. It also aims to provide peer support for children caught in the middle of their parents' disputes.

While called a mediation model, many elements of the Alameda program are also educational in function, emphasizing insight and skill building for parents. The Alameda program is, however, far more intensive than the typical secondary prevention program, and the number of participants is much lower.

Screening for program participation is conducted by court employees; families are eligible to participate if two attempts at mediation fail and there is evidence that the children are suffering. About one-half the participating parents agree to attend the program voluntarily while the other half are court-ordered to attend.

Eight families participate together in the group intervention in ninety-minute sessions over an eight-week period. Sessions are led by mixed gender group counselors. Parents are separated for some of the sessions and separate sessions are held for their children at the same time. For the first four sessions, parents are expected to describe their children, identify their own contribution to the impasse, consider how the children are affected by the parents' battles, and set personal goals for the last four sessions. The fifth session is a joint one for parents and children with counselors. The final three sessions are for parental conflict management skill building within the group framework.

## 2. CONTEMNORS

Los Angeles County Family Court Services has developed a PRE-CONTEMPT/ CONTEMNORS Group Diversion Program designed to deal with the problems of parents who have high levels of conflict, are chronically in violation of custody and visitation court orders, and seek frequent court intervention. While also more labor intensive than the typical secondary prevention program, CONTEMNORS serves more parents than the Alameda County program. It does not, however, include children in the educational process.

CONTEMNORS was created because of the lack of enforcement remedies for noncustodial parents denied access to their children. As the program creators note: "The program model is designed similarly to diversion programs created to address driving under the influence and drug abuse defendants."[64]

Referrals to CONTEMNORS are made by judges, and the court orders parents to attend. "Many come unwillingly and resentfully, others with more grace and interest. Some are ordered back a second time or required to write a class paper on what they learned. The size of the group varies widely, depending on the number of referrals (twenty-five to seventy-five at any one time)."[65]

CONTEMNORS' goal is to provide parents with information about the effects of their behavior on their children and its legal consequences. It also seeks to improve parents' communication and conflict resolution skills. The program consists of six sessions, each with a different educational theme. During the first five sessions, parents practice conflict-resolution skills on nondivorce-related conflicts. In the last session, the parents focus on common custody and visitation disputes.

## 3. EVALUATION OF TERTIARY PREVENTION PROGRAMS

Research on tertiary prevention programs for chronic family conflict is even less developed than research on primary and secondary programs. Few such programs exist and even fewer have been studied by careful researchers.

Professor Janet Johnston has, however, undertaken an evaluation of the Alameda County program which suggests that even chronic litigants can benefit from carefully structured educational interventions. When compared to a control group of similarly litigious parents nine months later, Professor Johnston reports "strong and consistent statistical findings that both men and women who received the group mediation model were substantially more cooperative, expressed less disagreement with each other, and were more likely to resolve the disputed custody issues with their ex-partner.... Furthermore, domestic violence between parents diminished to a negligible amount."[66] She further reports a substantial drop in new client-initiated filings in the group intervention families. Professor Johnston does, however, note the comparatively high expense of the program (although she does not compare its cost to those of further litigation between the parents) and that her study is a small preliminary sample of a developing model from which global conclusions are unjustified.

## V. A Comprehensive Family Conflict Management System: Oregon's Task Force on Family Law

The prevention programs just described were implemented by individual courts working with strong community resources. More comprehensive prevention planning can also occur at the state level. Oregon, for example, has taken great strides toward integrating primary, secondary, and tertiary prevention programs into a coherent pre-and post-conflict prevention program. Working in tandem with the Future of the Courts Committee, the Oregon Legislature established a bipartisan interdisciplinary Task Force on Family Law that developed a guiding vision for a comprehensive family conflict management system.[67]

The Oregon Task Force translated its vision statement . . . into a proposed comprehensive family conflict management program. Although the Task Force did not use public health terminology in describing the proposed system, its emphasis is on primary, secondary and tertiary conflict prevention programs . . . .

## VI. Incorporating Prevention into the Mission of the Unified Family Court

The overall picture that emerges from review of existing prevention programs and the emerging evaluation data, while certainly not definitive, suggests that families and court dockets both have much to gain from integrated preventive programs. Every unified family court should develop a coherent prevention strategy to reduce conflict resulting from divorce and separation for two reasons: self-preservation and potentially better outcomes for parents and children. The investment in prevention, however, must be long-term and not be viewed as a "quick fix" for rising family court caseloads. Over time prevention should pay off in improved parental conflict management attitudes and skills and less damaged and alienated parents and children.

*Andrew Schepard, J.D., is Director of the Center for Children, Families and the Law and Professor of Law at Hofstra University School of Law in Hempstead, New York.*

## Notes

[26]  GEORGE PICKETT & JOHN J. HANLON, PUBLIC HEALTH: ADMINISTRATION AND PRACTICE 6 (9th ed. 1990) [hereinafter PICKETT & HANLON].

[27]  *Id.* at 81.

[28]  *See, e.g.,* Stewart I. Donaldson et al., *Drug Abuse Prevention Programming,* 39 AM. BEHAV. SCI.. 868 (1996) (drug abuse); Caroline Thorton & Daniel J. Piacquadio, *Promoting Sun Awareness: Evaluation of an Educational Children's Book,* 98 PEDIATRICS 52 (1996) (skin cancer); Marianne Haenlein Alciati & Karen Glanz, *Using Data to Plan Public Health Programs: Experience from State Cancer Prevention and Control Programs,* 111 PUB. HEALTH REP. 165 (1996) (cancer).

[29]  Marjorie R. Sable & Allen A. Herman, *The Relationship Between Prenatal Health Behavioral Advice and Low Birth Weight,* 112 PUB. HEALTH REP. 332 (1997).

[30]  GOLDMAN, *supra* note 22, at 256-60, 301-02.

[31]   The discussion and illustrative graph are adopted from PICKETT & HANLON, *supra* note 26, at 83.

[32]   A detailed discussion of the use of prevention programs in cases involving family violence is beyond the scope of this article. *See War and P.E.A.C.E., supra* note 24, at 170-71 for a discussion of how court mandated educational programs can respond to the problems of domestic violence and child abuse. *See also* Deborah A. Daro, *Prevention of Child Sexual Abuse, in Sexual Abuse of Children,* 4 THE FUTURE OF CHILDREN 198 (Center for the Future of Children of the Packard Foundation ed. 1994), for a useful summary of child sexual abuse prevention programs.

[33]   *See War and P.E.A.C.E., supra* note 24, at 186-88.

[34]   The Association of Family and Conciliation Courts published a *Directory of Parent Education Programs* in 1997 containing program names, addresses and basic organizational information. The *Directory* is available from AFCC at 329 W. Wilson Street, Madison, Wisconsin 53703.

[35]   *See* Sanford L. Braver et al., *Methodological Considerations in Evaluating Family Court Programs: A Primer Using Divorced Parent Education Programs as a Case Example,* 35 FAM. & CONCILIATION CTS. REV. 9 (1997), for a discussion of the complexities of creating a meaningful program evaluation.

[36]   *See* AMERICAN BAR ASSOCIATION SECTION OF FAMILY LAW, PARTNERS FOR STUDENTS: CURRICULUM MANUAL FOR TEACHERS (1996). I worked closely with Lynne Gold-Bikin, then Chair of the Family Law Section, in developing the PARTNERS curriculum. Additional information about PARTNERS can be obtained from the website of Family Law Section of the American Bar Association which can be accessed at <http://www.abanet.org/family/partners/curriculum.html>.

[37]   Some states are considering requiring preventive education before a couple is issued a marriage license, proposals which are controversial among researchers. For background and discussion consult the package of materials assembled at AABT Couples Special Interest Group, *Should Premarital Counseling Be Legally Mandated?* (visited Nov. 9, 1997) <http:// www.psy.sunysb.edu/aabt/mandated. htm>. Besides effectiveness issues, there are also constitutional questions (e.g., the relationship between religiously sponsored marriage preparation courses which are a requirement for marriage by clergy of particular faiths and secular requirements) and philosophical and practical concerns which are beyond the scope of this article.

[38]   GOLDMAN, *supra* note 22

[39]   *Id.* at 257. To be sure, there are many ineffective prevention programs as well. Goldman reports:

> Educational programs to prevent one or another specific problem such as drug use and violence have proliferated wildly in the last decade or so, creating a mini-industry within the educational marketplace. But many of them-including many of the most slickly marketed and widely used-have proven to be ineffective. A few, to the chagrin of educators, even seemed to increase the likelihood of the problems they were meant to head off ....

*Id.* at 257. The key to the future of effective primary prevention is continuing research and development.

[40]   *Id.* at 259.

[41]   *Id.* at 283, 285.

[42]   The discussion which follows is adopted from FORREST S. MOSTEN, THE COMPLETE GUIDE TO MEDIATION 376-80 (1997) [hereinafter MOSTEN, MEDIATION]. More information about the Maricopa County program can be obtained from the Conciliation Services of the Superior Court of the State of Arizona, Maricopa County, 201 West Jefferson Street, Third Floor, Phoenix, Arizona 85003-2205.

[43]   ARIZ. REV. STAT. § 25-352 (1996).

[44]   *See* Eileen Biondi, *Legal Implementation of Parent Education Programs for Divorcing and Separating Parents,* 34 FAM. & CONCILIATION CTS. REV. 82 (1996).

[45]   *Id.* at 84, IOWA CODE § 598.19A (1997) (requiring course within forty-five days of service of notice of petition or application for modification of a custody or visitation order).

[46]   Biondi, *supra* note 44, at 87.

[47]   Karen R. Blaisure & Margie J. Geasler, *Results of a Survey of Court-Connected Parent Education Programs in U.S. Counties,* 34 FAM. & CONCILIATION CTS. REV. 23 (1996); Sanford Braver et al., *The Content of Divorce Education Programs: Results of a Survey,* 34 FAM. & CONCILIATION CTS. REV. 41 (1996).

[48]   UNITED STATES COMMISSION ON CHILD AND FAMILY WELFARE, *supra* note 5, at 32-33.

[49]   The description of court-affiliated educational programs which follows is adopted from Andrew Schepard et al., *The Push for Parent Education,* 19 FAM. ADVOC. 53 (1997).

[50]   Braver et al., *supra* note 47, at 51.

[51]   See *War and P.E.A.C.E., supra* note 24, at 186-88.

[52]   *See generally id.* More information about P.E.A.C.E. can be obtained from The P.E.A.C.E. Project, Hofstra University School of Law, 121 Hofstra University, Hempstead, New York 11550-1090.

[53]   More information about Parents Apart can be obtained from Geri Fuhrmann, University of Massachusetts Medical Center, Department of Psychiatry, 55 Lake Avenue North, Worcester, Massachusetts 01655.

[54]   More information about Kid's Turn can be obtained from Kid's Turn, 1242 Market Street, 4th Floor, San Francisco, California 94102.

[55]   More information about Families in Transition can be obtained from Families in Transition, c/o Family Court Administrator, Hall of Justice, 600 West Jefferson, 2nd Floor, Louisville, Kentucky 40202.

[56]   A fuller description of P.E.A.C.E., and its pilot programs and evaluation results can be found in *War and P.E.A.C.E., supra* note 24.

[57]   Jack Arbuthnot & Donald A. Gordon, *Does Mandatory Divorce Education for Parents Work? A Six Month Outcome Evaluation,* 34 FAM. & CONCILIATION CTS. REV. 60, 79 (1996) (summarizing study of Ohio program).

[58]   Cathleen Grey et al., *Making It Work: An Evaluation of Court-Mandated Parenting Workshops for Divorcing Families,* 35 FAM. & CONCILIATION CTS. REV. 280 (1997) (evaluation of Montgomery County, Maryland program); Arbuthnot & Gordon, *supra* note 57 (evaluation of Athens County, Ohio program).

[59]   Kevin M. Kramer et al., *Effects of Skills-Based Versus Information-Based Divorce Education Programs on Domestic Violence and Parental Communication,* 36 FAM. & CONCILIATION CTS. REV. 7, 23 (1998).

[60]   Jack Arbuthnot et al., *Patterns of Relitigation Following Divorce Education,* 35 FAM. & CONCILIATION CTS. REV. 269 (1997).

[61]   GOLDMAN, *supra* note 22, at 62.

[62]   Robert L. Fisher, *The Impact of an Educational Seminar for Divorcing Parents: Results From a National Survey of Judges,* in AFCC CONGRESS PROCEEDINGS, *supra* note 15, at 65 (246 of the 625 judges in the survey sample responded to the survey instrument).

[63]   The description of the Alameda County program that follows is adapted from Johnston, *supra* note 15, at 10-11. More information about the program can be obtained from Larry Lehner, Alameda County Superior Court, 1221 Oak Street, # 260, Oakland, California 94612.

[64]   Sherrie Kibler et al., *PRE-CONTEMPT/CONTEMNORS Group Diversion Counseling Program,* 32 FAM. & CONCILIATION CTS. REV. 62-63 (1994). More information about CONTEMNORS can be obtained from the Family Mediation and Conciliation Court Services of the Los Angeles Superior Court, 111 North Hill Street, Los Angeles, California 90012. The Division of Family Court Services of

the Fourth Judicial District of the Circuit Court of Oregon in Portland operates a similar program called Parents Beyond Conflict. More information about that Program can be obtained from them at Room 350, Multnomah County Courthouse, 1021 S.W. 4th Avenue, Portland, Oregon 97204-1154.

[65]   JANET R. JOHNSTON & VIVIENNE ROSEBY, IN THE NAME OF THE CHILD: A DEVELOPMENTAL APPROACH TO UNDERSTANDING AND HELPING CHILDREN OF CONFLICTED AND VIOLENT DIVORCE 228-29 (1997).

[66]   Johnston, *supra* note 15, at 12. Professor Johnston is also presently undertaking an evaluation of Los Angeles County's CONTEMNORS Program. *See* JOHNSTON & ROSEBY, *supra* note 65, at 229.

[67]   *See* William Howe III & Maureen McNight, *Oregon Task Force on Family Law: A New System to Resolve Family Law Conflicts,* 33 FAM. & CONCILIATION CTS. REV. 173 (1995).

# [28]

# Keeping in Contact:
# The Role of Family Relationship Centres
# in Australia

## Patrick Parkinson

### Introduction

In the first few years of the twenty-first century, debates about family law reform in both Britain and Australia have centred around the issues that are of greatest importance to non-resident parents, mostly fathers. This has indeed been the decade of the non-resident parent. Issues concerning post-separation parenting,[1] contact enforcement[2] and child support[3] have dominated the political agenda. Pressure groups are active in the political arena, in particular, groups representing fathers[4] and those promoting shared parenting.[5] In both countries, there has been discussion about whether there should be a starting point or legal presumption that parents should share in the care of children for equal amounts of time.[6]

While there are many parallels between the debates about post-separation parenting in the two countries, there can be little doubt that Australia is currently embarking on a more ambitious path in terms of family law reform. Indeed, it is the most radical reform of family law since no-fault divorce was introduced by the Family Law Act in 1975. The government announced in the 2005 budget that $397 million of new funds over four years were to be dedicated to the task of family law reform.[7] However, not one cent of this is being spent on courts or legal aid funding for litigated solutions to parenting disputes. Nor is reform of the laws governing parenting after separation a particularly significant aspect of the reform process. The major focus is on the resolution of parenting disputes outside of the court system, together with reforms of court processes to make them less adversarial and more appropriate for the resolution of parenting disputes in a manner that does not cause further alienation between the parents.

Central to the government's proposed reforms is the creation of a network of Family Relationship Centres all over the country, announced by the Prime Minister in July 2004.[8] Sixty-five such centres are to be established in total. The plan is to create 15 centres in 2006, 25 more by the end of 2007 and the remaining 25 by the end of 2008. The locations have already been announced and the organisations selected to run the first 15 centres.[9] In addition, there will be a significant expansion of other services for families experiencing separation. This includes enhanced funding for existing mediation services, an expansion of the network of supervised contact centres and a growth in services for families where there are problems in achieving compliance with court orders.[10]

The purpose of this article is to explain how the proposal for Family Relationship Centres emerged as the centrepiece of the government's response to the Parliamentary Inquiry and what the functions of these Family Relationship Centres (FRCs) are intended to be.

*What are Family Relationship Centres?*

The idea of Family Relationship Centres is a new one, however, it is more evolutionary than revolutionary. The proposed FRCs build upon more than 25 years of experience of having a court-based counselling service in the Family Court of Australia, 30 years of federally funded relationship counselling programs and, in recent years, the development of a range of community-based mediation services to assist separated parents.

FRCs will be established in major population centres and regions. The provision of 65 such centres across the country equates to approximately one centre for every 300,000 people in the population. The centres will be funded by the government and will operate in accordance with guidelines set by the government. However, they will actually be run by non-government organisations with experience in counselling and mediation, selected on a tender basis, and staffed by professional counsellors and mediators.[11] Many of these organisations have developed great experience in the relationships counselling area, are already funded by the Federal Government and meet quality assurance standards. Although actually run by different service providers in different localities, the FRCs will have a common identity and badging to the public.

The proposed FRCs will have many roles.[12] First and foremost, they are an early intervention initiative to help parents work out post-separation parenting arrangements in the aftermath of separation, managing the very difficult transition from parenting together to parenting apart. They will provide an educational, support and counselling role to parents going through separation, with the goal of helping parents to understand and focus upon children's needs, providing them with initial information about such matters as child support and welfare benefits, and negotiating workable agreements about parenting after separation. They will also be available to help resolve ongoing conflicts and difficulties as circumstances change. They will not only be a resource for parents but for grandparents as well.

The FRCs will not only have a role in helping parents after separation. They will also play a role in strengthening intact relationships by offering an accessible source for information and referral on marriage and parenting issues, providing a gateway to other government and non-government services to support families. These services are to receive increased funding as well.[13]

The development of FRCs, taken together with a significant expansion of other mediation and counselling services for families, represents an important strategy for supporting families, especially those going through the turmoil of separation. The government's announcement amounts to a major new investment in the health of family relationships in Australia.

## Context: Concern about Fatherless Families

The proposal for the establishment of FRCs cannot be understood without reference to a prime motivating factor for reform – the problem of the disappearance of fathers from their children's lives in the aftermath of separation and divorce.

In one study of a nationally representative sample of separated parents,[14] interviewed in 2001, it was found that 36% of children had not seen their non-resident father in the last 12 months.[15] A further 17% had day-only contact. Three-quarters of the non-resident fathers indicated dissatisfaction with the amount of contact they had. Fifty seven per cent of fathers indicated that they had nowhere near enough time with their children and a further 18% said they did not have quite enough time with their children.[16] Other studies have also demonstrated a great deal of unhappiness with levels of father-child contact and a desire by fathers for much greater involvement in post-separation parenting.[17]

The issue of non-resident fathers' contact with children was also a matter of great concern to members of parliament, who had constant complaints from constituents about family law matters. In the light of this and given the pressure for change from fathers' groups, the Prime Minister indicated in June 2003 that he wanted a Parliamentary Committee to explore the option of introducing a rebuttable presumption of 'joint custody'.[18] He expressed concern that many boys growing up in single parent families lack male role models both at home and in school until their teenage years.[19] What was meant by joint custody, in this context, was a rebuttable presumption that children would spend equal time with each parent.

## Report of the Parliamentary Inquiry in 2003

The Family and Community Affairs Committee of the House of Representatives was asked to examine whether there should be a presumption that children would spend equal time with each parent and, if so, in what circumstances such a presumption could be rebutted. It was also asked to consider grandparents' rights to contact and whether changes should be made to the formula for calculating child support liabilities.[20]

The Committee reported at the end of 2003 after one of the largest and most intensive public inquiries ever conducted by a parliamentary committee.[21] It received more than 1,700 submissions and took evidence all over the country. The issues also generated a great deal of discussion in the media.

Despite the difficulty of the issues involved, the Committee's report was bipartisan and unanimous. On the issue of 'joint custody', it did not recommend a presumption in favour of equal time. Instead, it recommended in favour of equal parental responsibility.[22] The

Committee's proposals on this were accepted by the government and are now contained in legislation.[23] It made a range of other recommendations in response to its terms of reference, including the establishment of a Taskforce to conduct a thorough review of the child support formula in the light of the available evidence concerning the costs of raising children.[24]

The Committee also proposed radical changes to the family law system in Australia.[25] Most publicity was given to a recommendation that the government should establish a multi-disciplinary Families Tribunal, which, it was expected, would deal with most disputes between parents that require an adjudication. In the Committee's view, lawyers should not normally be allowed to appear before the Tribunal. It would thus have a different character from litigation in the Family Court or Federal Magistrates Court on parenting disputes. The Committee also proposed shopfront centres where people could go to get help after separation and which would endeavour to resolve cases without the need for a tribunal hearing.

*Debate about a Tribunal*

There was potential merit in the concept of a tribunal. If the tribunal could have been made sufficiently user-friendly that lawyers were not needed, it would have allowed disputes to be resolved without the enormous expense associated with running hearings involving lawyers on both sides. A multi-disciplinary tribunal could also have taken advantage of the expertise of child psychologists and other appropriate professionals as decision-makers rather than just as expert witnesses.

Nonetheless, there were also many drawbacks to a Tribunal. One issue was constitutional. Although the Committee had received oral advice from a senior constitutional expert within the government that the tribunal could make enforceable orders,[26] the matter was not at all beyond doubt. Even if it could make enforceable orders in most cases, the constitutional advice made it clear that where it would be necessary to make an order for sole parental responsibility to one parent, for example in cases involving proven violence or child abuse, then such an order could only be made by a court established under Chapter III of the Federal Constitution. Thus many of the most difficult and hotly contested cases would still need to be dealt with by the courts. As a consequence, the establishment of the families tribunal would need to be additional to the existing infrastructure of courts.

There was also the obvious question whether a tribunal would end up making decisions that were substantially different from those made by the courts. If not, then the anger experienced by disappointed litigants would be no different than in relation to orders made by the Family Court or Federal Magistrates Court.

There were also issues raised about the particular model of a tribunal proposed by the Committee. In particular, the idea of a tribunal in which lawyers would not normally be permitted to appear was one that caused concern. It was pointed out that some people feel much more comfortable with an advocate, rather than having to negotiate a tribunal hearing without anyone to speak on their behalf. There might be advantages overall in a lawyer-free tribunal, but there would be disadvantages also.

An initiative of the Family Court also influenced the debate. At the end of March 2004, a pilot project commenced in Sydney, New South Wales, known as the Children's Cases Program.[27] This pilot program relies upon the informed consent of the parties. They agree to waive most of the rules of evidence and to accept a process that involves the judge in trying to resolve the dispute and to determine which evidence will need to be adduced if the matter proceeds to a hearing. The Children's Cases Program utilises many of the features which might be seen as desirable in a tribunal, such as introductory questionnaires to gain much of the basic information about the case, an investigatory rather than adversarial process and simplification of the rules for providing evidence to the decision-maker. The argument was made that if this pilot project was successful, then the argument for establishing a tribunal would not be as strong as it might be otherwise.

The differences of view about the tribunal were reflected within the government. While the proposal had its advocates within Cabinet, the Prime Minister made it clear that he had misgivings about the idea. Other members of Cabinet were also unpersuaded about the proposal. After some considerable debate in Cabinet, it became clear that it was unlikely to reach an agreement to implement the recommendation for a tribunal. At the same time, given the level of support for the tribunal from the Committee and the backbench, there was a reluctance to do nothing by way of a response to the Committee's recommendations.

*Need for a Third Way*

The idea of FRCs emerged as a compromise proposal.[28] While FRCs may seem to be a quite different concept from the idea of a tribunal, it was put forward as another way of achieving the same objectives that the Committee sought to advance, building on another of its key recommendations, that there should be a shop-front service to help people reach agreement on parenting arrangements in the aftermath of separation. FRCs respond to three central objectives of the Committee, first, to try to assist more non-resident parents (and particularly fathers) to remain involved in their children's lives, secondly, to reduce the reliance upon lawyers in resolving post-separation conflicts and, thirdly, to reduce the debilitating effect of conflict on children.

Certainly, the strategy for reducing the reliance on lawyers is a different one from that proposed by the Committee. While the establishment of a tribunal would have involved more resources being made available for adjudication, the development of the FRCs will involve substantial new resources going into education and dispute resolution to seek to avoid the need for adjudication. A tribunal, as envisaged by the Committee, would have removed lawyers from representing parents in the hearing of a dispute, but lawyers would still have been allowed to advise and assist parents up to the door of the hearing room. The FRCs seek to offer a different pathway for people to sort out parenting arrangements after separation. That pathway will make it easier for people to access advice, information about post-separation parenting and free mediation without going to a lawyer or having to file legal proceedings.

One of the aims of the FRCs is, therefore, to achieve a long-term cultural change in the pathways people take to resolve disputes about parenting arrangements after separation. The need for cultural change is because, at present, lawyers are understood to be the professionals to whom one must turn in the event of such conflicts.[29] When people experience acute and serious illness or suffer a significant injury, they know they can go to the emergency room of their local hospital. If they are unemployed, they know they have the option of going to an employment centre to help them find suitable employment. If they fall victim to a crime, they know they can go to the police. These are all publicly funded services available to people at a time of need. Currently, if they are in dispute about parenting arrangements after separation, most people know only that they can go to a lawyer.

The goal, then, is to change the cultural understanding that if there is a disagreement about the structuring of post-separation parenting arrangements, then one or both parents need legal advice in the first instance. The philosophy is that post-separation parenting should not be seen in the first place as a legal issue. It may become a legal issue, particularly if both parents want to be the primary caregivers of the children and have a realistic case for an order in their favour. There may also be legal dimensions to agreements about post-separation parenting. For example, there may be impacts on the calculation of child support and the manner in which the agreement is formalised may matter if removal from the jurisdiction is a possibility. However, when parents are having difficulty agreeing on the post-separation parenting arrangements, they have a relationship problem, not necessarily a legal one. If no other solution can be found, it may need to go to an adjudication by someone who can make a binding decision; but it should not be seen as a legal issue from the beginning.

The strategy of developing a cultural alternative to lawyers as a first port of call in the event of relationship breakdown may be contrasted with the development of the Family Advice and Information Networks (FAInS) in England and Wales, established by the Legal Services Commission. These use family lawyers as the reference point for referral to other services.[30] While this could be done in Australia, there would have been no support on either side of politics for expanding the funding of lawyers. That was evident from the unanimous, bipartisan support of the Parliamentary Committee for solutions that excluded lawyers.

Nonetheless, the establishment of Family Relationship Centres was not motivated by antipathy for lawyers, although that was part of the political context in which the proposal was made. Rather, the impetus for the development of the FRCs was a realisation that people need a range of services other than legal advice in the aftermath of separation and that while family lawyers are often an excellent source of advice and assistance on the non-legal, as well as the legal needs, of separating parents, much of the advice and assistance that they provide does not require legal training. Furthermore, while lawyers can and do play an important role in resolving disputes, the provision of free mediation in highly visible and accessible community centres could play a valuable part in enabling the development of workable parenting arrangements without the need for lawyers, except to the extent that advice is needed to formalise the arrangements. Private lawyers are expensive for people on relatively low incomes who cannot access legal aid or community legal centres. A substantial proportion of separated parents, both mothers and fathers, are on very low incomes. Separation in itself, is often a time of great financial stress for one or both parents. The FRCs will offer a free public service that aims to meet a variety of needs and not only those needs for which lawyers are particularly qualified. One of the aims of the FRCs is to greatly expand access to the information, advice and assistance that people need in the aftermath of separation and which is currently available only to those who consult lawyers.

*Importance of an Early Intervention Strategy*

Family Relationship Centres offer an early intervention strategy to assist parents going through separation at a time when most of them have not embarked down an adversarial path and have not begun legal proceedings.

One of the most common problems experienced by people in the aftermath of separation is where to find appropriate help, advice and support. The first few weeks and months after separation are a particularly important period. The House of Representatives' Committee recognised this in its recommendation for a shopfront centre where people could get help. So too did the Family Law Pathways Advisory Group, a committee set up to examine the family law system which reported in 2001.[31] As the Family Law Pathways Advisory Group wrote:[32]

> It is always difficult when families split up. Parents, children and other family members have to grapple with complex practical, legal and emotional issues; everyone has to adjust to change and loss. Helpful and relevant information and support often aren't easily available and services are hard to find, sometimes leading to ill-informed choices and unexpected outcomes. Stress and grief can make it hard to reach sensible decisions and some families experience a lot of conflict. The children of families in conflict suffer the most.

This need is also recognised by the British Government in its White Paper on parental separation.[33] It indicated that it would work in partnership with existing information and advice providers such as Parentline Plus, Sure Start and Relate, to improve the existing provision of information, advice and help.[34] It would also take steps to improve access to legal advice by piloting a telephone helpline.[35]

However, as noted above, it is becoming more widely realised that people going through separation usually do not just have problems about the parenting arrangements and legal issues arising from the separation. As British research has demonstrated,[36] they may need to have advice on a range of issues, such as benefit entitlements, debt management and housing needs. Divorce and separation is also traumatic for many people emotionally, and some may need appropriate advice and support in relation to depression and suicidal ideation.

There are numerous services in Australia available to assist people going through separation, as there are in Britain. Most are already supported through the Family Relationships Services Program (FRSP) of the Commonwealth Government. An evaluation of the FRSP conducted in the second half of 2003 and commissioned by the government found a very high level of client satisfaction indeed.[37] However, one of the biggest problems identified in the evaluation was a lack of awareness of the services. When told by the researchers about these services, most non-users of these services indicated that they wished they had known about them.[38] There is no equivalent in Australia to the Citizens Advice Bureaux in Britain where people can find out about services relevant to them.

A core aim of the FRCs is to fulfil this need for a readily available and easily accessible source of advice and assistance. In order to be effective as a first port of call in the public mind, the public needs to be aware of the services that the Centres can offer. For this reason, the government has emphasised that the Centres will be 'highly visible'.[39] This requires that they are located in the main business district of the localities in which they are established, just like other major federal government services. One of the problems with the existing non-government mediation services is that their facilities are often some distance from the major shopping and business thoroughfares of the local population.

The accessibility of the FRCs, their national organisation and promotion by government through an education campaign,[40] are all significant factors in marking this out as a major new national initiative. They will provide an initial point of information, advice and assistance, from which referrals can be made to the range of existing community-based services as appropriate.[41] FRCs will, therefore, act both as the emergency room and the triage unit for family breakdown. An FRC will not be able to resolve all the needs of those coming to it, but by dealing with some of those needs and identifying what further help parents need to deal with the issues arising from separation, people will be informed about and directed to government and non-government services appropriate to their situation.

The FRC in a given locality, whichever organisation runs it, will need to work closely with other relationship counselling and mediation organisations in the area. One way of understanding its role is to see it as a trustee acting on behalf of all those organisations. It will refer people to the range of organisations as needed, publicise the programs and courses of those organisations, and act as a focal point for co-operation in service delivery in the locality.

*Roles of Family Relationship Centres*

The FRCs will have five major roles:

(1) Information, advice and referral to services which can strengthen relationships.

(2) The provision of seminars, individual advice and free mediation when parents separate.

(3) Assistance in resolving ongoing disputes about post-separation parenting arrangements.

(4) Assistance to grandparents.

(5) Help in resolving child support issues.

*Role in supporting intact relationships*

While the primary role of the FRCs will be in helping parents and grandparents deal with issues of post-separation parenting, the centres will also have a role in supporting people entering into relationships or experiencing problems within intact relationships. While this aspect of the centres' work will not be resource-intensive, it is integral to the vision for these centres.

Given the obvious economic costs of broken relationships, not least for the health system, and other costs in terms of people's sense of life satisfaction, it is an appropriate investment of resources to increase the visibility and availability of services to help people in their family relationships and parenting. Perhaps at one time, churches and other faith communities offered such support. However, their reach has greatly diminished over the last 50 years. New, population-wide services are needed to complement them.

One of the major tasks of FRCs initially will be to develop a positive identity within local communities as one of the places where people can get information and resources to support them in their family life. The centres are not merely divorce centres, but there is likely to be considerable demand for their services from parents who have separated. One of the challenges of implementation, therefore, will be to ensure that the demand from those parents who are living apart will not so overwhelm the centres that they miss some of their potential for a supportive and preventive role in strengthening family life and in helping people whose relationships are beginning to experience significant difficulties.

It will be up to each individual centre how it fulfils its mission at the level of detail. The government's information paper suggests that outreach strategies could include the use of local radio, mail outs, stalls at community events, school visits, presentations to meetings of local organisations and providing kits or video/DVD-based presentations.[42]

The centres will also assist people whose relationships are in difficulties, mainly by referral to relationship counselling organisations and other sources of help, such as drug and alcohol or gambling addiction services and financial counselling organisations. They could also offer assistance to parents having problems in relation to their parenting role, providing referral, for example, to family support services and parent-adolescent mediation services. Promoting services to assist people whose relationships are in difficulties will also be an important aspect of the community outreach of these centres.

It is envisaged also that the centres will provide a location in which different non-government funded organisations could present an evening seminar on relationship and parenting issues which could then act as a conduit to other programs run by those agencies in their own premises.

*Role in supporting parents following separation*

The centres will have a major role in the education, support and counselling of parents going through separation. The goals of these interventions are to:[43]

- help identify parents' needs;

- provide relevant information on post-separation parenting;

- help parents access relevant services; and

- help to negotiate workable agreements about parenting after separation.

*Information sessions on parenting after separation*

The centres will run group information sessions for parents experiencing separation. Parenting after separation seminars, required by courts, are an established feature of the landscape in the USA.[44]

The information sessions are likely to cover such issues as: the way people deal with separation emotionally; the need to separate the parents' conflicts from issues about the children; the value of a parenting plan; what helps children get through the divorce process; what harms them; how parenting arrangements need to take account of the needs of children at different developmental stages; options for structuring post-separation parenting arrangements; shared parenting, and when shared parenting is contra-indicated; the importance of children's participation in decision-making about arrangements; sources of help to deal with domestic violence and child protection issues; and comparing mediation and litigation as options for dealing with disputes about the children.

The experience in Britain with pilot information meetings indicates that the overwhelming majority of attendees (90%) were glad to have gone to such a meeting.[45] In particular, the British experience suggests that information about children's needs and interests may be of considerable assistance to parents going through separation. The majority of parents involved in the pilot meetings reported feeling better informed about how divorce affects children and other such topics.[46]

*Providing initial advice on sources of assistance – personal interview*

Parents inquiring at the FRC will also be given the option of having an individual session with an adviser to receive initial, basic advice about options and sources of help for dealing with the problems arising out of separation. In the British pilot, the highest levels of satisfaction were recorded for individual sessions.[47]

The variety of government agencies and non-government services which may be relevant to a person going through separation can be very confusing for the uninitiated. The kinds of issues which might be covered include: information about relationship counselling; about mediation; initial advice about how to apply for income support payments if needed; initial advice on applying for child support or seeking departure from an administrative assessment; how to get an interpreter to help if the person has language difficulties; and referral to sources of support for people with personal safety concerns. Of course, the relevant agencies would remain the most appropriate source of detailed advice on such matters as child support or welfare benefits.

An important role of the initial personal interview will be to help people access the services and agencies they need. It is important that this service be a personal one. It would be a lot cheaper to provide free booklets from an information stand or to put all the relevant information people want to know in a 'frequently asked questions' section on a website, but this is not what people need at times of great difficulty in their lives. They need individual attention and a personal, listening ear, to begin to move forward in addressing their difficulties. Some people will need assistance in making links with the other service. The government information paper indicates that, with the consent of the client, the interviewer could make an appointment for them, introduce the client to the other service by a three way phone call or provide the other service with the client's contact details.[48]

The kind of person who would be recruited to this role need not be an expert on the variety of different government benefits and services. Nor need he or she be a professional counsellor. The goal of the interview is to provide people with quite basic information and advice about relevant services, options and pathways, not to provide personal counselling about the relationship and the problems of separation. Nonetheless, advisers involved in this work will need to be able to keep confidences and to respond empathetically to people at a time of crisis.

*Negotiating a parenting plan*

The FRCs will also provide parents with initial assistance in trying to develop a parenting plan. This may or may not be in the immediate aftermath of separation. It is not uncommonly the case that parents who have separated have informal and unstructured contact arrangements with the non-resident parent. Even if they have structured arrangements, they often reach them without the need for anyone else's assistance. However, such arrangements may subsequently break down because of conflicts between the parents about other issues or because one sees the need for more structure and consistency in the contact arrangements than the other is willing to have.

The provision of some free mediation is a very important feature of the FRCs and central to the goal of achieving cultural change concerning the negotiation of post-separation parenting arrangements. There is already a lot of mediation experience in Australia and it has a workforce that is generally highly qualified and skilled in this area. Since 1976, when the Family Court of Australia was established, alternative dispute resolution has been an integral part of the family law system. The Family Court was given its own Counselling Service and this conducted free conciliation conferences in cases involving disputes about children. It is now known as the Mediation Service. In recent years, the Court's services have been augmented by a range of community organisations who offer mediation in relation to parenting disputes. The development of FRCs is thus evolutionary, not revolutionary, and builds upon an existing and well-tried service capacity.

The FRCs take this service provision one step further, by making free mediation available in a centre which has a high level of visibility in the community and which operates as a hub in the system of services available to parents after separation. There is ample evidence from the history of counselling in Australia and the experience of other jurisdictions,[49] that the earlier parents can be involved in negotiating a compromise to their disputes, the more likely it is that the dispute will be resolved.

There are, of course, numerous issues involved in providing mediation, notably the need to screen for domestic violence and to address other situations where mediation is inappropriate. The FRCs offer a new context for mediation, but do not need to 'reinvent the wheel' in terms of when and how mediation is offered.

The government has indicated that parents will be able to receive up to three hours' free mediation through the FRCs. This does not include the initial meetings between the mediator and each parent to assess suitability for mediation and to discuss the process.[50] Three hours is not a great deal of time, but it is hoped that at the very least, short-term parenting arrangements can be put in place that allow both parents to remain involved in caring for the children and that these will then form the basis of more enduring arrangements. One option is that parties in high conflict could be offered sample parenting plans appropriate to their situation, with the advice just to try one out for a few weeks or months, while continuing to try to negotiate a longer-term set of arrangements. This is a strategy also being promoted by the British Government.[51]

It remains to be decided how best to ensure continuity in terms of mediation personnel if agreement is not possible in the limited time available or if the parents want to go on from the initial mediation to do further work on reaching agreement for the future. As the government information paper notes:[52]

> At the end of the three hours, clients may decide to continue at the Centre, subject to a fees policy and the Centre's capacity to provide the service, or accept a referral to an alternative service. The Centre should aim to avoid if possible the need for families to have to re-commence a dispute resolution process and form a new relationship with a different practitioner.

One possibility is that mediators from a variety of organisations could be rostered to conduct mediation at the centres and could then offer to continue working with the parents through their usual organisation. The final model for service delivery will be up to the successful tenderer in each locality, depending on what will work best for that area.

While it is expected that many parents will be content to have their agreements enshrined in a parenting plan, people will be given information about the differences between a parenting plan and consent orders, and referred to lawyers if they want to formalise their agreements by way of a court order. While there is no need for lawyers in the centres (for the centres are not trying to replicate or replace legal services), it is anticipated that the centres will endeavour to work closely with Legal Aid and private family lawyers, making referrals as needed. The FRCs have been warmly welcomed by leaders of the legal profession and the courts, and it is expected that once the centres become an established part of the family law landscape, a very constructive relationship will develop between them, and others involved in the family law system.

*Assisting in resolving ongoing disputes about post-separation parenting arrangements*

The FRCs will also play a role in resolving disputes after initial post-separation parenting arrangements have been put in place. Parenting plans and court orders reflect the circumstances of the family at a particular moment in time. As the circumstances of either parent or the children changes, so arrangements that were once workable need to be changed also. Clients will be entitled to free mediation up to a maximum of three times in any two-year period. However, the centre may decline to provide further assistance if it believes that such assistance is unlikely to be successful in resolving the dispute.[53]

The FRCs will have a particular role to play in the resolution of disputes about alleged contraventions.[54] Experience in the courts has shown that at least some contravention disputes are problems which arise from contact orders, frequently made by consent, which are either unworkable or which have become unworkable as circumstances have changed. The FRCs offer an option to triage these cases and to work out which cases can be resolved by negotiating variations in arrangements or by allowing parents to resolve their disputes by agreement, before going down the road of filing a contravention application.

*Assistance for grandparents*

It is anticipated that grandparents will also be able to use these centres to deal with problems in maintaining a satisfactory relationship with their grandchildren. As the government's announcement explained:

> Grandparents play an essential role in children's lives but can feel cut off and helpless when families separate ... Grandparents already have the right to apply for a residence or contact order under the Family Law Act but often are not aware of their rights or simply want to have a role in their grandchildren's lives without taking the matter to court ... Through a community education campaign, grandparents will be encouraged to use the Family Relationship Centres, dispute resolution services and the new national advice line to obtain information and assistance.

Grandparents, in particular, are little assisted by being provided with formal rights to make court applications. Ultimately, their contact with grandchildren depends on the relationship with the parent of the children who is the primary caregiver. Litigating is understandably not something that the great majority of grandparents want to do because of its impact upon the relationship with that parent.

*Help in resolving child support issues*

The FRCs have an important role in providing initial information and advice to people who have little understanding of the range of services available to them to assist them in the transition to post-separation parenting. One such issue is child support. It is not envisaged, of course, that FRCs will provide detailed information on this in the parenting seminars, or detailed advice in a personal interview. They may nonetheless play an important role in explaining in basic terms what child support is, how to apply for it, how assessments can be varied as income changes and other such matters, so that people going through separation have a better understanding of the Child Support Scheme.

In August 2004, the government established a Ministerial Taskforce on Child Support to review aspects of the scheme. One of its terms of reference was to consider the role of FRCs in helping people deal with child support issues. The Taskforce, which reported in May 2005, saw an important role for the FRCs,[55] and its recommendations have been accepted by the government. It proposed that the information sessions and other educational programs of the FRCs should explain in outline about the Child Support Scheme, the basis on which child support obligations have been calculated and the way in which regular contact and shared care are dealt with in the formula. The government's information paper states that it is expected that centres will host information sessions by the Child Support Agency.[56]

The Taskforce also recommended that child support issues and other financial issues be among the topics for discussion and negotiation in the mediation sessions conducted under the auspices of the FRCs, as these are often matters that get in the way of reaching agreement about parenting issues.

The Taskforce considered that a better understanding of the Scheme and, in particular, its flexibility and responsiveness to many individual circumstances, may reduce the level of frustration expressed to members of parliament about child support. One way in which that information may be conveyed is for Child Support Agency staff to conduct workshops at the FRC or to have rostered sessions to provide information and advice to individuals. Other agencies might also provide information and advice sessions on the premises.[57]

*Family Relationship Centres as Gateways*

The FRC is not a one-stop shop. It is a gateway. Certainly, FRCs will provide all that many people need in making the difficult adjustment to separation as parents. Many such people will receive the information they need to work out their own parenting plan, or will benefit sufficiently from the availability of free mediation.

However, it is unrealistic to think that any one service can provide all that people need. For some people, the issue will be timing. There will be those who simply are not ready, early on in the separation, to reach a long-term agreement about post-separation parenting because they are still working through the emotional response to the other parent's decision to leave. There will be other people who feel the need to 'have their day in court' and will not be ready to settle arrangements until they realise that litigation may not be in their best interests or the interests of the children. There will be others still who need to go to court because there are serious issues about domestic violence or child abuse.

In these kinds of cases, the FRCs may do no more than to help the parties on the road towards an agreement, or will give them a much better understanding of what they need to do to resolve the issues. It is to be hoped that many, once they have begun to negotiate parenting arrangements with the help of the FRC, will see the value in continuing down this path rather than litigating. The FRC, by giving parents an experience of what mediation is and informing parents of other available counselling and mediation services with which they can continue, will act as a gateway to these other services.

There will also be those who, after attending a post-separation parenting seminar, or attempting mediation, may want to attempt reconciliation with the assistance of relationship counselling services; others who will join a program for perpetrators of domestic violence or for gambling addiction, if either of these have been a major reason for the separation; others still who will want to access other kinds of services, for example, support programs for separated fathers. The FRCs are thus about much more than organising post-separation parenting.

It will not in any sense be a failure of the FRCs if, for some people, the next step in the process is to consult a lawyer or to file a court application. That will be necessary in many cases and it is appropriate that people should feel free to seek advice from any professional they choose to consult and to seek court orders if they choose to do so. The FRCs will be a success if they assist people who do not need to make court applications to resolve their disputes in a different way, while assisting people who need protective orders or for whom court-ordered residence and contact orders are a necessary security, to be more informed about the available options and to resolve at least some issues without the need for litigation.

*Before Going to Court*

There will be a requirement that people should have attempted to resolve parenting issues before filing legal proceedings.[58] It will not be in any sense compulsory to attend a FRC as a precondition to filing a court application. People will still be able to choose to take their problems directly to a family lawyer who would refer them on to a dispute resolution service, or to go directly to a mediation service of their choice.

However, the carrot to attend such a service initially is that it will be a free service. The 'stick' is contained in the draft legislation. This provides that a court must not hear an application for a parenting order unless the applicant files a certificate stating either that the applicant has attended family dispute resolution with the other party or parties, before applying for a parenting order or that the applicant's failure to do so was due to the refusal, or the failure, of the other party or parties to the proceedings to attend.[59] There are exceptions, including where the court is satisfied that there are reasonable grounds to believe that there has been abuse of the child by one of the parties to the proceedings or family violence.[60]

No specific consequences will follow from a failure to comply with the requirements. However, it can be expected that the courts will police this provision by examining the application soon after it is filed and will reject applications that neither comply with the certificate requirement and nor are accepted as falling within one of the exceptions.

*Conclusion*

FRCs are a significant new initiative. They form a critical part of a sustantial reform agenda that also includes changes to the law of post-separation parenting,[61] significant legislative changes to the processes for hearing children's cases,[62] based upon the Children's Cases Program[63] and reform of the Child Support Scheme.[64]

The development of the FRCs represents a major investment in family life and, in particular, in promoting better arrangements for children with less conflict than at present. The centres should also have many benefits for the courts in removing much of their lower-conflict workload. Many cases that now settle at the case assessment conference or in court-ordered mediation, may well settle without the need for filing. The centres may also impact upon the volume of the courts' high conflict workload to the extent that this early intervention strategy is successful in helping parents avoid adversarial conflicts.

The success of the centres will nonetheless depend upon a great deal of cooperation and goodwill among professionals working in the family law system. In Australia at least, family law professionals and the courts have a long history of such successful cooperation. Their success will also depend on adequate levels of resourcing, a consistent national approach, and a national education campaign. The central place these centres have been given by the Prime Minister as a strategy for helping separated parents and strengthening intact relationships, indicates the priority which will be attached to their funding and development.

*Patrick Parkinson, M.A., LL.M., is a specialist in family law and Professor of Law at the University of Sidney Law School in Australia.*

## Notes

[1]    In England and Wales, see eg Green Paper, Parental Separation: Children's Needs and Parents' Responsibilities, Cm 6273 (TSO, 2004); White Paper, Parental Separation: Children's Needs and Parents' Responsibilities: Next Steps, Cm 6452 (TSO, 2005). In Australia, see Family Law Amendment (Shared Parental Responsibility) Act 2006.

[2]    In England and Wales, see, eg Advisory Board on Family Law, Children Act Sub-Committee, Making Contact Work: A Report to the Lord Chancellor on the Facilitation of Arrangements for Contact Between Children and Their Non-Residential Parents and the Enforcement of Court Orders for Contact (DCA, 2002); White Paper, ibid; Children and Adoption Bill 2005. In Australia, see Family Law Council, Child Contact Orders: Enforcement and Penalties (1998); H. Rhoades, 'Contact Enforcement and Parenting Programmes - Policy Aims in Confusion?' [2004] CFLQ 1.

[3]    In Britain, see R. Collier, ''Coming Together?': Post-heterosexuality, Masculine Crisis and the New Men's Movement' (1996) 4 Fem Leg Stud 3. In England and Wales, see the Child Support, Pensions and Social Security Act 2000. In Australia, see Ministerial Taskforce on Child Support, In the Best Interests of Children: Reforming the Child Support Scheme (2005), available at http:/ /www.facs.gov.au.

[4]    In Australia, see M. Kaye and J. Tolmie, 'Fathers' Rights Groups in Australia' (1998) 12 AJFL 19; M. Kaye and J. Tolmie, 'Discoursing Dads: The Rhetorical Devices of Fathers' Rights Groups' (1998) 22 MULR 162. The term 'father's rights groups' is an externally imposed label. Such groups would not generally characterise themselves as being motivated by a concern for their own rights. They

present their concerns as being about the best interests of children. The names of some of the groups also reflect a commitment to shared parenting.

⁵    In Britain, the lead organisation is the Equal Parenting Council, see: http://www.equalparenting. org. In Australia it is the Shared Parenting Council of Australia, see: http://www.spca.org.au.

⁶    In Britain, this movement has been given particular impetus by the advocacy of Sir Bob Geldof: B. Geldof, 'The Real Love that Dare Not Speak its Name' in A. Bainham, B. Lindley, M. Richards and E. Trinder (eds), Children and Their Families: Contact, Rights and Welfare (Hart Publishing, 2003). See also A. Buchanan and J. Hunt, 'Disputed Contact Cases in the Courts', in the same volume, at pp 371 and 380. 20% of respondents to the government's Green Paper supported a legal 'presumption of equal contact': White Paper, Parental Separation: Children's Needs and Parents' Responsibilities: Next Steps, Cm 6452 (TSO, 2005), at para 11. In Australia, see House of Representatives Standing Committee on Family and Community Affairs, Every Picture Tells a Story: Report of the Inquiry into child custody arrangements in the event of family separation (Parliament of Australia, 2003).

⁷    Australian Government, A New Family Law System: Government Response to Every Picture Tells a Story (2005), at pp 1-2.

⁸    Prime Minister John Howard, announcement 29 July 2004, 'Reforms to the Family Law System', at http://www.pm.gov.au/news/media_releases/media_Release1030.html.

⁹    Details are available at http://www.ag.gov.au/family. The government released a paper on the implementation of the FRCs in September 2005: 'Family Relationship Centres - Information Paper', available on this website.

¹⁰   Australian Government, A New Family Law System: Government Response to Every Picture Tells a Story (2005).

¹¹   Commonwealth of Australia, Framework Statement On Reforms to the Family Law System (29 July 2004), at www.pm.gov.au/news/media_releases/media_Release1030.html.

¹²   The government released a Discussion Paper in November 2004 that outlines the proposals: A New Approach To The Family Law System: Implementation of Reforms. It is available at http://www. ag.gov.au/agd/WWW/familylawhome.nsf.

¹³   Australian Government, A New Family Law System: Government Response to Every Picture Tells a Story (2005).

¹⁴   P. Parkinson and B. Smyth, 'Satisfaction and Dissatisfaction with Father-Child Contact Arrangements in Australia' [2004] CFLQ 289. The data came from the Household Income and Labour Dynamics in Australia survey (HILDA). Interviews were conducted with 13,969 members of 7,682 households. For comparable British data, see A. Blackwell and F. Dawe, Non-Resident Parental Contact (Department of Constitutional Affairs, 2003) available at http://www.dfes.gov.uk/childcontactsurvey (14% of non-resident parents reported that they never see their children, whereas 28% of resident parents said that the non-resident parent never sees the child).

¹⁵   The methodology required respondents to focus on the youngest natural or adopted child, and averages the responses of both mothers and fathers. The figure of 36% is exactly the same as that reached by the Australian Bureau of Statistics (ABS) in 1997: Family Characteristics Survey 1997, Cat No 4442.0 AGPS (Canberra, 1998). A further analysis of Australian Bureau of Statistics interviews in 2003, again, based only on resident parents' reports, found that 26% of children saw their child less than once per year, or not at all: B. Smyth, 'Time to Rethink Time? The Experience of Time with Children after Divorce' (2005) 71 Family Matters 4. The ABS surveys are based on resident parents' reports only and report on contact patterns for all the children.

¹⁶   P. Parkinson and B. Smyth, 'Satisfaction and Dissatisfaction with Father-Child Contact Arrangements in Australia' [2004] CFLQ 289. It is not only fathers who want more time with their children. Mothers also want to see more contact between the children and their fathers. In this study, although the majority of resident mothers expressed satisfaction with the contact arrangements, 25% reported that they thought there was nowhere near enough father-child contact taking place and a further

15% said there was not quite enough contact. Only 5% thought that there was too much contact. The greatest levels of satisfaction for both mothers and fathers were with shared parenting arrangements.

[17]   In one study, 41% of fathers contacted in a random telephone survey of divorced parents in 1997 indicated that they were dissatisfied with the residence arrangements for the children. Two-thirds of this group said that they wanted to be the primary residence parent, the remaining third wanted to have equal time with their children. On average this was about five years after the divorce. The study also indicated a very high level of dissatisfaction with levels of contact: B. Smyth, G. Sheehan and B. Fehlberg, 'Patterns of Parenting After Divorce: A Pre-Reform Act Benchmark Study' (2001) 15 AJFL 114.

[18]   The government utilised the traditional language of 'custody' despite the removal of the language of custody by the Family Law Reform Act 1995. This Act adopted reforms on similar lines to the Children Act 1989 in England and Wales with the terms 'custody' and 'access' being replaced by 'residence' and 'contact', and the rhetoric of 'parental responsibility' driving out notions of parental rights. See J. Dewar, 'The Family Law Reform Act 1995 (Cth) and the Children Act 1989 (UK) Compared - Twins or Distant Cousins?' (1996) 10 AJFL 18. Further reform to the language of parenting orders has occurred in the Family Law Amendment (Shared Parental Responsibility) Act 2006.

[19]   Reported in The Australian, 18 June 2003, at p 3.

[20]   For a commentary on the issues raised by the terms of reference see P. Parkinson, 'Custody Battle' (2003) 18 About The House 16.

[21]   House of Representatives Standing Committee on Family and Community Affairs, Every Picture Tells a Story: Report of the Inquiry into child custody arrangements in the event of family separation (Parliament of Australia, 2003).

[22]   The Committee wrote: 'the goal for the majority of families should be one of equality of care and responsibility along with substantially shared parenting time', ibid, at p 30. The Committee gave a number of reasons for considering that there should not be a presumption in favour of equal time for each parent (at p 31):

'Two aspects of an equal time template have been highlighted. First, there are dangers in a one size fits all approach to the diversity of family situations and the changing needs of children. Secondly, there are many practical hurdles for the majority of families to have to overcome if they are to equally share residence of children. Many have pointed to the increased risk of exposure of children to ongoing conflicted parental relationships and the instability that constant changing would create for children. Family friendly workplaces are rare, as are the financial resources necessary to support two comparable households. Some parents lack the necessary child caring capabilities. Distance between households creates problems for transport and for schooling. Second families can also bring complications. Indigenous families' approach to parenting does not fit with the expectations of equal time.

Some have talked about the factors that support successful equal sharing, such as cooperative relationships, geographical proximity, prior sharing of parental care, good communication, agreement about matters relevant to the child's day to day care, parental commitment to the arrangement and to a focus on the child's interests. The more these characteristics exist, the more likely a shared arrangement will be workable and positive for the child.'

[23]   Family Law Amendment (Shared Parental Responsibility) Act 2006.

[24]   The Taskforce, chaired by the author, reported in May 2005. Ministerial Taskforce on Child Support, In the Best Interests of Children: Reforming the Child Support Scheme (2005), available at http://www.facs.gov.au. The Government announced its acceptance of the Report's recommendations, subject to minor adjustments, in February 2006.

[25]   House of Representatives Standing Committee on Family and Community Affairs, Every Picture Tells a Story: Report of the Inquiry into child custody arrangements in the event of family separation (Parliament of Australia, 2003), chapter 4.

[26]   Ibid, ns 71 and 91.

[27] D. Sandor, 'A More Future-Focused Approach to Children's Hearings in the Family Court' (2004) 18 AJFL 5.

[28] The author was consulted by the Prime Minister's Office at a time when it was clear that Cabinet was unlikely to agree on the establishment of a families tribunal. The proposal for Family Relationship Centres was set out in a paper which the author wrote following these discussions, entitled 'Parenting After Separation: New Pathways to Dispute Resolution' (April 2004). This paper formed the basis for the plans then developed by the government and announced in July 2004.

[29] In one major British study, 81% of people experiencing family or relationship difficulties chose to visit a solicitor: H. Genn et al, Paths to Justice: What People Do and Think About Going to Law (Hart Publishing, 1999).

[30] J. Walker, 'FAInS - A New Approach for Family Lawyers?' [2004] Fam Law 436.

[31] The Family Law Pathways Advisory Group was established to advise the government on how best to ensure that people choose the most appropriate pathway in reorganising parenting arrangements in the event of family separation. Family Law Pathways Advisory Group, Out of the Maze: Pathways to the Future for Families Experiencing Separation (Commonwealth of Australia, 2001).

[32] Family Law Pathways Advisory Group, ibid, executive summary (ES1).

[33] White Paper, Parental Separation: Children's Needs and Parents' Responsibilities: Next Steps, Cm 6452 (TSO, 2005).

[34] Ibid, at paras 25 and 28.

[35] Ibid, at paras 36-41.

[36] G. Douglas and R. Moorhead, 'Providing Advice for Lone Parents: From Parent to Citizen' [2005] CFLQ 55.

[37] The FRSP Review report released in February 2004 reported:

- 94% of users find services funded under the Program beneficial with the benefits including more effective family relationships, improved parenting skills and better approaches to dealing with conflict.
- Up to 70% of counselling clients are in intact relationships and are seeking counselling services to address relationship issues. Around 70% of these clients are still in their relationship 6 months after counselling.
- Men make up around 47% of FRSP clients and in particular are seeking extra support around parenting skills.
- Agreement is reached in around 70% of mediations and users find these services cheaper and less stressful than going to court.

Colmar Brunton Social Research, Family Relationships Services Program: Client Input Consultancy (Commonwealth of Australia, 2004), see http:/ /www.facs.gov.au/internet/facsinternet.nsf/VIA/frsp_ review/

ile/frsp_client_input_consultancy_062004.pdf.

[38] Colmar Brunton Social Research, ibid.

[39] 'Family Relationship Centres - Information Paper' (September 2005), at p 2, available at: http:/ /www.ag.gov.au/family.

[40] Commonwealth of Australia, Framework Statement On Reforms to the Family Law System (29 July 2004), at www.pm.gov.au/news/media_releases/media_Release1030.html.

[41] Family Relationship Centres - Information Paper' (September 2005), at p 3, available at: http:/ /www.ag.gov.au/family.

[42] Family Relationship Centres - Information Paper' (September 2005), at p 3, available at: http:/ /www.ag.gov.au/family.

[43] Family Relationship Centres - Information Paper' (September 2005), at p 4, available at: http:/ /www.ag.gov.au/family.

[44] See eg http:/ /www.puttingkidsfirst.org/; http:/ /www.parentschildrenanddivorce.com/.

45    J. Walker et al, Information Meetings and Associated Provisions Within the Family Law Act 1996: Final Evaluation Report (Lord Chancellor's Department, 2001), 'Key Findings from the Research', at p 2. While saving marriages was an important focus of the information meetings in the British pilot study, it is not likely that information meetings in the FRCs will have such a focus. Supporting relationships in intact families, and helping relationships that are in trouble, is certainly an important objective for the FRCs, but it will be achieved through other strategies, including seminars conducted on the premises of the centres, information provision through such means as booklets and videos or DVDs, and through referral to other agencies.

46    M. Richards and C. Stark, 'Children, Parenting and Information Meetings' [2000] Fam Law 484. See also G. Mayes, G. Wilson, R. MacDonald and J. Gillies, 'Evaluation of an Information Programme for Divorced or Separated Parents' [2003] CFLQ 85 (voluntary programme in Scotland); J. Hunt with C. Roberts, Intervening in Litigated Contact: Ideas from Other Jurisdictions, Family Policy Briefing 4 (Department of Social Policy and Social Work, 2005), at pp 2-5.

47    J. Walker et al, Information Meetings and Associated Provisions Within the Family Law Act 1996: Final Evaluation Report (Lord Chancellor's Department, 2001).

48    'Family Relationship Centres - Information Paper' (September 2005), at p 4, available at: http://www.ag.gov.au/family.

49    See eg J. Zuberbuhler, 'Early Intervention Mediation: The Use of Court-Ordered Mediation in the Initial Stages of Divorce Litigation to Resolve Parenting Issues' (2001) 39 Family Court Review 203.

50    'Family Relationship Centres - Information Paper' (September 2005), available at: http://www.ag.gov.au/family.

51    White Paper, Parental Separation: Children's Needs and Parents' Responsibilities: Next Steps, Cm 6452 (TSO, 2005). See further Department of Education and Skills, Putting Children First: A Guide for Separating Parents, Consultation Draft available at http://www.dfes.gov.uk/consultations/ (January 2005).

52    'Family Relationship Centres - Information Paper' (September 2005), at p 9, available at: http://www.ag.gov.au/family.

53    'Family Relationship Centres - Information Paper' (September 2005), available at: http://www.ag.gov.au/family.

54    Commonwealth of Australia, Framework Statement On Reforms to the Family Law System (29 July 2004), at www.pm.gov.au/news/media_releases/media_Release1030.html.

55    Ministerial Taskforce on Child Support, In the Best Interests of Children: Reforming the Child Support Scheme (2005), available at http://www.facs.gov.au.

56    'Family Relationship Centres - Information Paper' (September 2005), at p 3, available at: http://www.ag.gov.au/family.

57    Recommendation 19.5 of the Taskforce report (Ministerial Taskforce on Child Support, In the Best Interests of Children: Reforming the Child Support Scheme (2005)) states: 'Organisations selected to run Family Relationship Centres should be encouraged to invite the Child Support Agency, Centrelink, Legal Aid and community legal centres to conduct regular advice and information sessions on the premises of the Centre'.

58    Commonwealth of Australia, Framework Statement On Reforms to the Family Law System (29 July 2004), at www.pm.gov.au/news/media_releases/media_Release1030.html.

59    Family Law Amendment (Shared Parental Responsibility) Act 2006, introducing new subsections s 60I(7) and (8).

60    Ibid, introducing new subsection 60I(9).

61    Family Law Amendment (Shared Parental Responsibility) Act 2006.

62    Ibid, Sch 3.

63    D. Sandor, 'A More Future-Focused Approach to Children's Hearings in the Family Court' (2004) 18 AJFL 5.

64    Government response to Ministerial Taskforce report announced in February 2006.

# Name Index

Abel, Richard 256
Abrahamson, Shirley 105, 107
Addams, Jane 132
Alpert-Gillis, L. 152
Amato, P. 472
Arbuthnot, Jack 473
Atwood, Barbara Ann xviii, 447–60

Baar, Carl 76, 78
Babb, Barbara A. xv, xvi, 19–31,
Barber, B.K. 472
Barbieri, Raye 88, 89, 90, 93, 96, 97
Barry, Margaret Martin 354
Bartholet, Elizabeth 33
Bausermann, R. 472
Beck, C.J.A. 150
Benjamin, M. 149
Berenson, Steven xix, xxii, 345–66
Berman, Greg xiv, xvi, 73–82
Bernstein, Nina 122
Bickerdike, A.J. 155
Bix, Brian xvii
Blackmond, Brianna 130
Blades, John 175
Bodtker, A. 149, 150
Bohm, P. 149
Boldt, Richard xxii
Brandeis, Justice 123
Braver, S.L. 147
Brett, Jeanne 7
Brimhall, D. 472
Brodzinsky, D.M. 474
Brown, Scott 91, 93
Bryan, Penelope 159, 161, 173–75 *passim*
Buehler, C. 472
Bush, Robert A.B. 165
Butler, I. 434

Campbell, Linda E.G. 208, 209
Cannata, K.V. 148
Caplan, C. 435
Caplan, R. 435
Carbone, June xvii, 481–524

Carbonneau, Thomas E. 174
Cassidy, J. 471
Chandler, David B. xiv, 175
Chase, Deborah xxi
Coates, Christine xvii, xxi, 277–95
Cobb, Sara 166
Cohen, Lloyd 491
Constantino, Cathy 7
Coogler, O.J. 173
Cox, M. 435
Cox, R. 435
Cummings, E. 472

Davies, P. 472
Denckla, Derek 78, 79
Depner, C.E. 148
Deutsch, Robin 277–95
DiFonzo, J. Herbie 58
Dion, M. Robin xvii
Dornbusch, S. 472
Douglas, G. 430
Duggal, S. 472
Duryee, M.A. 150

Ebling, R. 472
Elias, Sian xviii
Ellis, Desmond 207
Ellis, Elizabeth 209
Elster, John 417
Emery, Robert E. xiii, xiv, xxv, 143–58, 451, 472
Engler, Russell xxii, xxiv, 319–44, 347, 348, 350
Erickson, Stephen K. 209
Ertman, Martha 495

Federle, Katherine 419, 451
Feinblatt, John xiv, xvi, 73–82
Fineman, Martha 174
Fink, Howard xvii, 481–524
Firestone, Gregory xiii–xiv, 3–17
Folberg, Jay 161, 168, 209
Forehand, R. 145
Fortas, Justice 110
Fortin, J. 428

Freud, Anna  59–60 *passim*

Gage, Michael  86
Garrison, Marsha  499, 501 *passim*
Geraghty, Anne H.  xx, xxii, 119–39
Giddens, A.  434
Gigy, L.  150
Gilbreth, J.  472
Giovannuci, M.  xiv
Girdner, Linda  209
Glendon, Mary Ann  39, 110
Glesner Fines, Barbara xv, xxi, 403–11, 463–7
Goldberg, Stephen  7
Goldkamp, John  79, 80
Goldman, Daniel  530
Goldstein, Joseph  59–60 *passim*
Goodmark, Leigh  208
Gordon, D.A.  473
Gray, Pauline  91, 92, 94
Greacen, John M.  328, 350
Gregory Firestone  3–17
Grillo, T.  150, 159, 161, 168, 171, 174, 175
Grossberg, Michael  485
Grover, Tara  xiv, 143–58
Gruber, R.  472
Guggenheim, Martin  xviii, 415–25

Hardcastle, Gerald  xx
Harris, Lisa  380
Hart, Barbara  208
Haynes, John  161
Heard, H.E.  472
Hetherington, E.M.  435, 472
Hitchens, Donna J.  389
Hoffman, Morris B.  76
Horlick, Lisa  93, 94
Hunt, J.  432, 438
Huntington, Clare  xiii–xiv, xxi, 33–50, 215–35
Hutchins, Donna J.  498

Insabella, G.  472
Irvine of Lairg, Lord  430
Irving, H.H.  149

Johnson, Monica Kirkpatrick  xvii
Johnston, Janet R.  xvi, xxi, 208, 209, 297–312, 469–75, 538
Jones, T.S.  149, 150

Kandel, Randy Frances  452

Kaplan, N.  471
Kaye, Judith S.  74, 84, 85
Kelly, Joan B.  xxi, 147–50 *passim*, 469–75
Kibler-Sanchez, S.  475
Kimmelman, Ray  84, 96
King, Donald  392
King, V.  472
Kisthardt, Mary Kay  xxi, xxiv, 463–67
Kitzmann, K.M.  149–51 *passim*
Kline, M.  472
Kluger, Judy Harris  78
Kornhauser, Lewis  163, 170
Kramer, K.M.  473
Krishnakamur, A.  472
Kuhn, Jeffrey A.  xvi, 110

Laumann-Billings, L.  145
Lawson, J.  432, 438
Leberman, Cindy  110
Lee, M.-Y.  472
Lehrmann, Debra H.  451
Lerner, J.  165
Lindsey, Duncan  40, 224
Lindsey, Judge  132
Little, T.D.  472
Littlefield, I.  155
Lowe, Nigel  xviii, 427–45
Lund, Mary  380
Lyon, C.  428, 433

McCarthy, P.  149
Maccoby, Eleanor  145, 146, 466, 472, 473
McCrory, John  168
MacDonald, G.  149
McEwen, Craig  xxiii, 159–204
McIntosh, J.  155
Mcknight, Marilyn S.  209
Maiman, Richard  159–204
Main, M.  471
Manzie, Sam  112–13
Marshall, John  78
Marshall, K.  436
Martin, Brad  89, 93
Masson, J.  439
Matthews, S.G.  147, 149 *passim*
Menkel-Meadow, Carrie  xx, 215
Menning, C.L.  472
Merchant, Christina  7
Merkel-Holguin, Lisa xiv
Miller, Jonathan  166

Milne, Anne 209
Mlyniec, Wallace J. xix, xxii, 119–39
Mnookin, Robert 145, 146, 163, 170, 215, 466, 472, 473
Mosten, Forrest S. xv, 371–85
Murch, Mervyn xviii, 427–45
Murphy, Jane C. xxv

Neale, B. 432, 433
Nedelsky, Jennifer 39, 224
Nicholson, Alastair xviii
Nord, C.W. 472

Oakley, A. 439

Parkinson, Patrick xv, xviii, 543–62
Pearson, Jessica 147, 149, 168
Pedro-Carroll, J. 152
Piper, C. 432, 433, 437
Pound, Roscoe 78
Pruett, M.K. 472, 475
Pryor, J. 144

Rand, Sheldon 92, 96
Richardson, Edwinna 89–90, 92, 94, 98
Richter, Ron 86, 97, 98
Rifkin, Janet 166
Robbennolt, Jennifer K. xvii
Roberts, Dorothy E. 33
Roche, J. 434
Rodgers, B. 144
Rogers, Nancy 159–204
Roseby, V. 474
Rosenberg, Joshua 161, 173–75 *passim*
Ross, Catherine J. xv, xx, xxii, 103–18
Rowe, Mary 8
Rutter, M. 435

Sack, Emily 88
Sagarin, B.J. 147
Salem, Peter xv
Sales, B.D. 150, 352, 359
Sanchez, E.A. 475
Sander, Frank 62
Santeramo, Jordan xxi
Sbarra, David xiv, 143–58
Scarman, Lord 435
Schepard, Andrew xv, xvi, xvii, 55–69, 525–42
Schneider, Carl 500
Schofield, G. 432

Sclater, S. Day 432
Seltzer, J.A. 151
Silbaugh, Kate xvii, 489, 491–92 *passim*, 495
Simon, M.B. 148
Simons, R.L. 472
Sinden, Amy xxi, xxii, xxv, 237–74
Singer, Jana xxii
Smart, C. 433
Smith Michael 79
Smith, Melanie 147
Smith, N. 432
Solnit, Albert J. 59–60 *passim*
Sosa-Lintner, Gloria 84, 85, 89–96 *passim*
Stake, Jeff 495
Stark, Barbara 494
Starnes, Hugh 277–95
Straghn, Angus 380
Stuckless, Noreen 207
Sullivan, Matthew 277–95
Sydlik, BeaLisa 277–95

Teitlebaum, Lee 417
Tesler, Pauline xiv–xv, 389–402
Thoburn, J. 432
Thoennes, Nancy 147, 149
Thompson, Peggy 397
Timms, N. 149
Tippins, Timothy M. xxi, 463, 469–75
Tschann, J. 472

Ury, William 7

Ver Steegh, Nancy xxiv, 205–14

Walker, J 149
Wallerstein, Judith S. 145, 422, 472
Waxler, Z.W. 472
Weinstein, Janet xiii–xiv, 3–17
West, J. 472
West, J. 472
West, S.G 147
Wexler, David B. xvi
Whittmann, Jeffery xxi
Williams, T.Y. 472
Williamson, H. 434
Winick, Bruce J. xvi, xxii
Wittman, Jeffrey P. 463, 469–75
Wolchik, S.A. 152
Wolf, Robert xiv, 83–99
Woodhouse, Barbara 419

Woods, Laurie  163
Wroblewski, Michael  95
Wyer, M.M.  144, 147, 149, 150
Wyman, Rosemarie  86

Younger, Judith  490, 491

Zuberbuhler, J.  148